A. A. Heggestad

Financial Institutions

Financial Institutions

Donald P. Jacobs, Ph.D.
Professor of Finance

Loring C. Farwell, Ph.D.
Professor of Finance

Edwin H. Neave, Ph.D.
Associate Professor of Finance

All of Northwestern University

Fifth Edition

1972
RICHARD D. IRWIN, INC.
HOMEWOOD, ILLINOIS   60430
IRWIN-DORSEY LIMITED, GEORGETOWN, ONTARIO

Fifth Edition

First Printing, January, 1972
Second Printing, August, 1972

Library of Congress Catalog Card No. 73–158044
Printed in the United States of America

Preface

Financial Institutions is designed to be used in a first course in finance. Its purpose is to give the student an understanding of the operations of financial institutions and of the interrelationships between their operations and economic activity. The discussion assumes no prior knowledge of finance, of accounting, or of economic theory; nonetheless, a number of sophisticated issues in these areas are discussed in a nontechnical manner. Thus the volume is useful both as an introduction to finance and as a reference work for professionals in financial institutions.

The text attempts to provide the reader with both an appreciation of the overall patterns of money and credit flows within our economy, and an appreciation of the operations of financial institutions that are the central transactors in the credit flows. Thus the text discusses the importance of financial institutions as their operations affect the savings-tangible investment process, and hence the functioning of the economy, and discusses in detail the operations of the different types of institutions which perform credit warehousing functions.

The text's examination of money and credit flows is divided into six major sections which deal respectively with the money and capital markets from the suppliers' (savers') side, with the markets for business and consumer loans from the demanders' (borrowers') side, with governmental taxing and spending activities, and with international finance. In each section an attempt is made to combine economic analysis with a description of the operations of financial institutions, so that the reader is provided not only with a picture of what the institutions are, but of how and why they operate in the manner they do.

The original design of this volume was to blend an institutional description of finance and financial institutions with analysis of the economic implications of their activities. In the 25-year period since the first edition was written, American financial institutions have greatly changed and, more importantly, our understanding of the implications of their activities has substantively improved. Changes in institutional operations and the economic implications of these changes have been incorporated in previous editions as they appeared. This latest edition appears at a time of great flux in our nation's financial institutions. Interest rates have recently risen to historical peaks; existing institutions are altering their modes of operations with great rapidity, and a number of new types of institutions have developed. These important developments in financial institutions and their ramifications in the economy are discussed in the current edition, so that the present work gives a comprehensive and current picture of institutional operations and their economic effects. An attempt has been made to show how this represents adaptation to a changing environment. Thus it has been felt appropriate to retain historical discussions when these contribute to an understanding of the present situation.

This text has had the benefit of contributions from a number of men who have competence in the study of finance. In its beginning, these included Charles M. Bliss (Harris Trust and Savings Bank, Chicago), Francis J. Calkins (Marquette University, Madison, Wisconsin), Paul L. Howell, Norman Strunk (United States Savings and Loan League, Chicago), and Kenneth R. Wells (Northern Trust Co., Chicago). There were many others who contributed by using—and criticizing—the text or by acting as editorial consultants.

Special words of recognition go to Erwin W. Boehmler and Roland I. Robinson, both of whom made fundamental contributions in earlier editions. Erwin Boehmler edited the first edition, providing the significant force for the book's original development. Roland Robinson edited the third edition. Both will recognize their own ideas and, indeed, their own writing in this edition, but, regrettably, neither worked directly on it. Sidney Jones contributed to the past edition and parts of his effort are evident in this edition.

The work of bringing the present edition into line with current developments has been done by Donald P. Jacobs, Loring C. Farwell, and Edwin H. Neave, all of the Finance Department, Graduate School of Management, Northwestern University. We accept responsibility for the errors and difficulties which students may find in this text without for a moment relinquishing our respect for those who have contributed to the book in the past.

December, 1971
Donald P. Jacobs
Loring C. Farwell
Edwin H. Neave

Contents

PART I. INTRODUCTION

Money. Basic financial functions: *Exchange. Channeling saving into investment.* Financial management in a free economic society: *Monetary management. Management of productive resources. Management of personal finances. Public financial management. International finance. How financial markets reconcile managerial acts of individual economic units.* What are financial institutions? *Monetary financial institutions. Savings institutions. Market institutions for finance. Insurance and pension intermediaries as financial institutions. International financial institutions. Form of organization of financial institutions.* Evolutionary changes in financial institutions: *Regulatory and economic environment. Changing technology.* The study of finance.

PART II. MONEY AND MONETARY INSTITUTIONS

Money and economic development. Functions of money in developed economies: *Medium of exchange. Store of value. Unit of account.*

Money and its substitutes: *Media of exchange. Alternate stores of value.* Money and its supply in the United States: *The dollar's standard of value. The gold standard, 1900–1933. Gold Reserve Act, 1934. Paper money in the United States since 1934. Demand deposits. Money supply: stocks and flows.* The demand for money. Changes in the value of money: *Causes of changes in the purchasing power of money. Index numbers: measuring money's purchasing power. Effects of changing purchasing power.*

Governors. Federal Reserve banks. Federal Open Market Committee. The Federal Advisory Council. Informal groups in the system. Interrelationships within the system. The public-private blend in organization. Principles of Federal Reserve banking: *The significance of reserves in modern banking. Federal Reserve notes.* Federal Reserve monetary controls: *Federal Reserve rediscounting operations. Federal Reserve open market operations. Control of member bank reserve requirements. Applying monetary controls. Coordinating the instruments of monetary control.* Monetary functions of the Treasury: *Treasury currency. Treasury cash balance. Treasury debt management.* Federal Reserve direct credit controls: *Stock market margin control. Control of consumer credit. Control of interest paid on time deposits.* Federal Reserve financial services: *Clearing and collecting checks. Currency supply and redemption. Issuing and retiring federal government securities. Fiscal agency for other government bureaus. Wire transfers of funds.*

PART III.   CAPITAL MARKET INTERMEDIARY INSTITUTIONS

practices. Trends in stock ownership: *Broadened public ownership. Ownership of institutional investors.*

Introduction: *General characteristics of thrift institution deposits. Flows of funds to deposit-type thrift institutions.* Savings and loan associations: *Development of the savings and loan industry. Status of the savings and loan industry. Asset and investment structure. Regulation and safety.* Mutual savings banks: *Development of mutual savings banking. Status and growth of the industry. Asset and investment structure. Regulation and safety of savings banks.* Savings departments of commercial banks: *Development of commercial bank savings accounts. Growth of commercial bank deposits. Effects of the rising total of savings deposits.* Credit unions. U.S. savings bonds.

Life insurance: *Types of life insurance contracts. Other types of policies.* Annuities: *Variable annuities.* Life insurance investment policies: *The insurance dollar: income and disbursements. Distribution of assets. Investment principles of life insurance companies. Regulation of the insurance industry.* Fire, property, casualty, and other forms of insurance. Investment policies of fire, property, and casualty insurers.

Investment companies: *Origin of the investment company. Development of investment companies in the United States. Fixed trusts. Renewed interest in investment companies. Closed-end and open-end investment companies. Investment company legislation. Summary and evaluation. Kindred plans.* Investment counsel: *Origin of investment counseling. Operation. Organization. Performance. Regulation. Other supervisory agencies. Ancillary service.*

Concept of trusteeship. Trust business. Trust institutions. History of the trust business in the United States. Trust companies versus trust departments. Extent of the trust business. Classification of trust services. Services rendered to individuals. Common trust fund. Trust provisions. Prudent man rule and legal lists. Corporate versus the individual trustee. Compensation of the trustee.

Types of pension and retirement plans: *Insured pensions. Trusteed or self-administered funds. Special governmental retirement plans.*

Old Age, Survivors, and Disability Insurance (social security or OASDI). Terms for accumulation and distribution of pension funds: *Contributions and payments. Funding. Vesting. Variable annuities.* Investment policies. Economic effects of pension funds: *Effects of pensions on saving. Influence of pensions on capital flow. Effect of pensions on number of persons in labor force. Pension-fund accumulation and interest rates.*

PART IV. BUSINESS FINANCE

expansion needs. Long-term sources of funds. Government agencies. Development corporations. Small business investment corporations (SBICs).

PART V. CONSUMER FINANCE

Nature of consumer credit. Who uses consumer credit? Classification of consumer credit. Consumer credit transactions and their terms: *Installment sale credit. The installment loan. The noninstallment loan. The noninstallment sale credit.* Institutions that advance consumer credit: *Sales finance operations. Commercial banks. Small loan companies. Industrial banks and industrial loan companies. Credit unions.* The pro and con of consumer credit: *Economic stability and consumer credit. Regulation W.* Supplement: computation of consumer credit interest rates and charges.

Credit principles and practices: *Appraisal. Legal documents. Adaptation of loan to borrower's capacity. Residential loans.* Extent of urban real estate financing. Private sources of real estate credit: *Savings and loan associations. Commercial banks. Mutual savings banks. Life insurance companies. The mortgage correspondent system. Individuals.* Federal agencies: *Department of Housing and Urban Development. Federal Housing Administration. Federal National Mortgage Association. Government National Mortgage Association. Veterans Administration guaranty and loan programs. Federal Reserve Board Regulation.* Present problems and outlooks.

PART VI. PUBLIC FINANCE AND PUBLIC POLICY

Federal government expenditures: *National security. Health, education, and welfare expenditures. Commerce, transportation, and housing expenditures. Agriculture and natural resources. General government. How extensive should government services be?* Government revenues: *Types of taxes. Who pays the taxes? Who should pay the taxes? How large should the total tax bill be?* Government debt and its effects: *Growth of the public debt. Effects of an existing public debt.* Financial markets and the federal government's budget: *Effects of federal government borrowing and refunding. Control and management of federal finance. Managing the federal trust funds.*

List of exhibits

List of tables

PART **I**

INTRODUCTION

CHAPTER 1

The role of finance

Money and finance have been matters of concern for thoughtful citizens in all modern societies. Money and finance serve fundamental purposes. A monetary system succeeds, or fails, as that system serves to make the attainment of the objectives of society possible. In this century our monetary system has been subjected three times to serious, intensive study by public commissions seeking to ascertain whether the American system was indeed serving public ends as well as it might. The last of these commissions to complete its investigations, the Commission on Money and Credit, began its report of findings in 1961 as follows:

Our monetary, credit, and fiscal policies and the instruments and institutions through which they operate must be so designed that they can make an essential contribution in the decades ahead to the improvement of our standards of living through simultaneously achieving low levels of unemployment, an adequate rate of economic growth, and reasonable price stability. And the more successful we are in achieving these goals, the better able we will be to achieve our most fundamental goals: to enhance the freedom and dignity of our citizens, indeed of men everywhere, and to ensure the survival of our country and its system of government.[1]

It is with this sense of concern for an understanding of the monetary system that we approach the discussion of money, credit, and financial

---

[1] Commission on Money and Credit, *Money and Credit: Their Influence on Jobs, Prices, and Growth* (Englewood Cliffs, N.J.: Prentice-Hall, Inc., 1961).

institutions in the following pages. It should be noted that as this volume is written another public commission, the Commission on Financial Structure and Regulation, has been appointed by the president to suggest regulatory changes which will improve the operations and performance of financial institutions in the United States. Thus, this volume stresses the continuing modifications in structure which develop in response to changing economic, regulatory, and technological environments and improved understanding of their implications.

Money

At some stage or other in his life almost every thoughtful person has said: "I don't care for money; all I want is a good life. I want to read good books, enjoy my friends, educate my children decently, and maybe travel a bit." This sort of thing is said by businessmen as well as college professors. Said with a bit different emphasis, it can be found in the polemics of today's radicals. Perhaps never spoken at all but only thought and in very simple terms, this is the goal of decent people everywhere.

This view is, of course, wholly sensible. In itself money has very little final value. But to leave the subject of money at this point would be to perpetrate a serious error of logic. This statement confuses the instruments for achieving a satisfying life with our final values. A printing press by itself has relatively little final value, but it is wholly necessary in the production of a book. Leading a good life and enjoying one's friends almost certainly means living with a middle-class set of consumption standards—the comforts of home, of an adequate diet, and of shelter and clothing—and the enjoyment of the amenities we tend to take for granted. As for sending children to college, most of you who are reading these words probably have been told quite eloquently by your own parents how costly that process has become. As for travel—

In point of fact, money—and the financial arrangements that go with a money system—are extraordinarily important instruments in achieving the final cultural and personal values we all prize. The many ways in which money and finance contribute to these final ends are almost self-evident. Not quite so self-evident but just as important are the functions of the institutions of finance and money that lie back of this system. The first task of this text will therefore be to examine the basic functions of money.

Basic financial functions

An effort to divide a field such as finance into functional areas is difficult and can be done in a number of ways. The two-way classification used in this introductory section simply divides finance into its current or day-to-day functions and those that relate to saving and capital trans-actions.

Exchange

Our modern economic system would not be possible without an extensive and detailed division of labor. While the total range of economic products has been widened, most people are performing more and more specialized roles in the production process; in other words, the productive process has been increasingly divided. Division of labor invariably means that there must be extensive exchanges of final goods and services. Only by such exchanges can each consumer enjoy a wide range of goods and services. Each worker produces, by himself, only a single service or one small part of a good. Exchange in a very primitive economy would be accomplished by barter, but barter is not a very practical system even in the simplest economics. Money is almost always required as soon as an economy advances beyond a very elemental stage. A basic function of finance, therefore, is to facilitate the exchange of goods and services through the use of money.

Exchanges, however, are not always effected by money. In a modern economic system, buying and selling often involves a very extensive and complex set of credit arrangements. Some of this credit is at the consumer level, but an equally detailed and important network of credit lies back of each stage of productive economic activity. Without these credit arrangements, the whole system of exchanges would collapse almost immediately. One might go even further and point out that the system of buying and selling required by the modern division of labor necessarily involves the maintenance of inventories of goods and of capital assets at many different levels in the economy. These accumulations of wealth require financing and represent still another functional responsibility of finance.

Volume of money exchanges. Although we know a great many facts about our economy, it is surprising that existing figures cannot give us a very precise notion of the magnitude of money transactions in our economy. We do know that annual income per person in the United States now averages well over $4,500. Income per family unit is more than $9,500. Net national income is more than $750 billion. A much larger volume of money payments is made, however, in generating this sizable national income.

We know that the check payments going through banks in 233 standard metropolitan statistical areas now amount to almost $10 trillion annually. When allowance is made for check payments in other, smaller centers and also for payments made by currency, we estimate that gross money payments in our system exceed $11 trillion a year. This means that, for each dollar of net national income, expenditures of $14 or $15 are made.

In order to make this huge volume of money payments, individuals and businesses carry sizable cash balances. Checking accounts in banks total more than $150 billion, and there are more than $45 billion outstanding in the form of currency. Thus each dollar of money held turns over more than 50 times a year. Both individuals and businesses also hold other financial instruments of varying degrees of liquidity to supplement their basic cash balances.

Channeling savings into investment

The second great service performed by finance and financial institutions is that of channeling savings into real investment. The real wealth of a nation is its supply of buildings, homes, and machines, and even intangible items, such as education and personal development. In order to accumulate wealth, an economy must save. The commonest form of saving is that done by individuals who consume less than their total income. Saving is also done by other than individuals—for example, business and government.

The savings accumulated by individuals or by businesses or by government would do no good if not converted into real wealth; indeed, saving would not have taken place unless there had been some creation of real wealth. In modern economic society those who promote the creation of various forms of real wealth may not themselves do the saving which pays for, or *finances*, the investment they promote. Indeed, this is the usual case. The promoters who develop new businesses or build homes for sale normally do not themselves have adequate savings to finance the process. Frequently, governments can build schools or university buildings only if they borrow. Business concerns that build new plants or buy new equipment must often get the funds to pay for these expenditures elsewhere in the economy. There is, thus, within our financial system a constant flow of savings from those who originate them through the channels that distribute them to final users. This distribution is one of the central and principal functions of our financial mechanism. This theme will recur constantly throughout the text.

Although the channeling of savings into investment is one of the most profoundly important of our economic functions, we do not have precise figures for measuring the relative importance of this operation. We do know that the gross savings of all sectors of the economy are currently more than $200 billion annually. However, a large portion of this amount represents the consumption of capital by depreciation or obsolescence; net savings are more nearly $75 billion a year.

Savings measured in this way, however, do not necessarily equate with the volume of financial instruments created. In a recent active year net new financial instruments of approximately $110 billion were created.[2] The total of such instruments in the United States is now probably more than $2 trillion at current market values. It is not possible to arrive at a precise figure, however, because an important component of this total is the value of common stocks, which tends to fluctuate widely in the markets.

Financial management in a free economic society

The various acts of exchanging goods and services for money or of spending money for goods and services, together with the various steps that channel savings into investment, can be considered acts of financial management. When financial management is defined in terms as broad as this, it becomes almost equivalent to general economic management. The way in which finances are managed has a great deal to do with the effectiveness and character of our economic system. One of the major propositions supported by many economists is that in an economic system like ours the efforts of individuals to maximize their money income or financial wealth have the ultimate effect of maximizing the real economic product and benefits of the entire system. Optimum performance flows from the discipline of markets, including the discipline of financial markets.

While the United States has been unable to achieve complete economic freedom of the individual, we have approached about as closely to that ideal as is probably practicable in the real world. The individual, not the state, is the focus of our system, and most of the important economic decisions are made individually. This means that finances are managed at many different places and at various levels in the economy. Thus we shall find that our study of financial institutions and of financial practices requires looking at the customs and traditions observed in various sectors of the economy. We shall also have to inquire into the way in which all these differing individual policies are reconciled by the economic system.

One of the principal virtues of a free economic system is that it is flexible and can adapt to current needs. When an economic system like the one we live in is faced with a compelling political necessity such as war, quite a bit of economic freedom may be temporarily sacrificed. The financial and economic management of the system is bent toward its primary goal: winning the war. At other times the role of government may be reduced in accordance with the changed conditions in the economy. The overwhelming advantage of freedom, however, is that it brings out the most creative aspects of the individual and maximizes his productivity.

---

[2] See "Flow of Funds," *Federal Reserve Bulletin*, February, 1970, p. A70.

Indeed, freedom is itself a condition of well-being. This means, however, that we need institutional arrangements by which the freedom of the individual can be reconciled with the economic use of our total resources.

In the sections that follow, the areas of individual financial management will be reviewed against this combined background of individual freedom and governmental control.

Monetary management

The money system is usually considered a governmental function and is generally managed by a governmental institution, such as the central bank (the Federal Reserve System in the United States), or some department of the central government, like the Treasury Department. The monetary system includes parts of the private economy, primarily the commercial banking system; but most elements of discretionary management are reserved for public control.

Management of productive resources

Most factors of economic production are controlled in the private sphere and are managed by businesses operated for private profit. Some businesses are giant corporations; others are relatively small enterprises. A few businesses are operated by government in the United States, but fewer than in most other countries. Business financial management comprehends the problems of raising capital for business ventures and the management of the funds of going enterprises. While most managerial actions are taken at the level of the individual business, there are, nevertheless, some public restraints on such management. For example, businesses must observe regulatory standards of disclosure in raising capital from the public.

Management of personal finances

By all odds, the largest sums and the most important elements of economic activity are involved in the area of personal economic or financial management. The income received by individuals is either saved or spent. Sometimes it is spent before being earned through the medium of either intermediate or long-term consumer credit. On the other hand, net positive saving by individuals gives rise to our most important source of net new social capital. This area of financial management is under the control of individuals and represents a vast diversity of both preferences and taste. A very large number of financial institutions serve the primary purpose of supplementing the financial knowledge of individuals. The need for the performance of this function is one of the most important reasons for the proliferation of financial institutions in an affluent society.

Public financial management

Public finance is the finance of governments in the performance of their functions. The finance of the federal government now accounts for almost one seventh of the income of the United States. State and local government finance, which accounts for approximately the same fraction of national income, has been growing more rapidly than federal expenditures. Policies followed in public financial management are not usually aimed at maximizing profit or income for government. Other goals determined by the social, economic, and defense needs of the nation are the primary purpose of public finance.

International finance

Each nation has financial relations with other nations, and many businesses have financial relationships across national boundaries. The management of financial relationships with other nations, at either governmental or business levels, involves special problems that are usually considered under the term *international finance*. These managerial problems may be thought of as coming at a variety of levels. Businesses operate across national boundaries primarily in order to find external markets or to find external sources of raw materials. Governmental financial relationships with other nations, however, may involve no effort at maximization of income but rather may be for more political purposes. International financial relationships may be managed by governments for the purpose of strengthening their allies or of increasing the number of nations friendly to them or of solidifying their economic position in case of disaster such as war.

How financial markets reconcile managerial acts of individual economic units

So far, this description of financial management has pictured each sector of the economy going its respective way without any interconnection between sectors. There are, in fact, a great many connections between sectors, of which financial markets supply some of the most important.

Members of most sectors are borrowers of funds at different times in their lives. Individuals borrow to buy homes or automobiles; businesses borrow for capital expenditures; governments frequently are borrowers for many other purposes as well as for capital expenditures. There is even some borrowing by nations in foreign capital markets. Although there are great formal differences in the way in which these various sectors borrow, their demands are competitive in the long run.

The way in which the various sectors supply funds to the money or capital markets through saving is likewise linked. Most savings supplied to the market come from individuals, since businesses quite frequently employ a large part of the savings they generate. However, businesses do supply funds to the markets from time to time. Governments may also be suppliers of funds, usually in the form of debt repayment. All these suppliers of funds are in competition with one another, so that the influences of both demand and supply pervade the entire range of borrowing and lending arrangements.

The specific way in which these crosscurrents of influence penetrate from sector to sector is reflected primarily in the level and structure of interest rates. Not all borrowers have to pay the same rates in the money and capital markets. Likewise it is true that some savers are able to secure better returns from investment than others. In the end, however, the interest rates paid by borrowers and received by savers are very much interrelated and tend to move in a parallel fashion. Just as the price system can be said to allocate the resources of raw materials and of labor and of land, the interest rate, as a price, can be said to allocate capital as a factor of production. Financial markets link together the separate sectors of financial management.

What are financial institutions?

The word *institution* has two different meanings, both of which will have to be used at various places in this text. One's first inclination is to think of a financial institution as a legal organization, probably housed in a brick and mortar structure, with a fairly clearly definable economic purpose. Such institutions do exist and will be a large part of our survey. It would be less than adequate, however, if we did not start out by explaining that some of our most important financial institutions are nothing more nor less than habits or customs that have come to influence and sometimes control our economic behavior. Some of these habits and customs have been with us so long that they have acquired standing in the common law; others are still more formally ensconced in statute law.

Widespread payment by checks rather than by currency, for example, is a financial institution of great importance in the United States and a number of other advanced commercial nations. This practice is much less common in primitive economies, though it seems to be spreading. The negotiability of such checks accumulated precedents embodied in the common law, but in many jurisdictions the older common-law standards have been replaced by very explicit statutes.

Much the same sort of thing could be said about a great many other debtor-creditor relationships. These relationships started out with relatively simple foundations. They depended on some degree of social stability and moral honesty. In time, however, they became more formalized and surrounded by rather more complex legal arrangements. Financial agencies often developed in the same way: they started out as relatively simple and informal organizations but came to be more formalized and governed by much more explicit legal arrangements. In this text we shall deal with financial institutions at all these levels.

Financial institutions of the more formal sort are sometimes referred to as intermediary institutions: indeed, the title of this text could well have been *Financial Intermediaries*. An institution may be considered to be a financial intermediary if it has financial or monetary relationships on each side of its balance sheet. Ordinary industrial corporations have some financial assets, but the focus tends to be on their buildings, machines, and inventories and the other things with which they do business (real assets). The liability and owners' equity sides of their balance sheets, of course, are basically financial in character. The asset side of the balance sheets of financial intermediaries, however, consists mostly of financial claims and only incidentally includes holdings of either buildings or machines or other so-called real assets that are relatively small. In other words, a very simple test of whether or not an institution is a financial institution is whether its balance sheet assets are largely financial in nature. When it has mainly financial relationships on the asset as well as on the liability or owners' equity side of its balance sheet, an institution can be considered an intermediary.

There are many kinds of financial institutions. This book describes more than 60 such institutions in one way or another. Only relatively small differences distinguish some types of financial institutions from similar types; in other cases there are very sizable differences among types of institutions. At this stage, however, we shall undertake to classify financial institutions only in broad terms.

Monetary financial institutions

The monetary financial institutions are basically those that either directly or indirectly supply a recognized form of money. In the United States we use coins, paper currency, and demand deposits in commercial banks as *money*. A monetary financial institution is one that supplies some one of these forms of money or controls its supply. Those institutions having demand deposit liabilities—the commercial banks—are the most important of our monetary financial institutions. Of very great importance in terms of control, though of somewhat less importance in terms of dollar magnitudes, is the Federal Reserve System, which directly supplies a large part of the currency used by the public but indirectly influences the volume of commercial-bank, demand-deposit liabilities. To a much smaller extent the Treasury Department is also a monetary financial institution.

Savings institutions

A very large number of savings institutions specialize in collecting the savings of those who accumulate funds in modest amounts, or who have limited self-confidence in the field of direct financial investment, and invest these funds in one form or another. A wide range of such institutions operates in the United States: the savings departments of commercial banks, mutual savings banks, savings and loan associations, credit unions, the Treasury Department's own system of savings bonds, and, finally, the various types of investment companies. Most savings institutions, except possibly the last listed above, attempt to appeal to quite broad groups within the population. The ways in which these institutions actually invest their assets, however, vary considerably, depending on the basic purposes for which they were organized.

Market institutions for finance

Another broad category of financial institutions includes those that provide markets for various classes of financial obligations. Many of the most important financial markets have no formal identity; they are simply the informal, though probably conventional, circumstances in which financial bargaining and transactions take place. Such markets have no set physical location: they are in business offices, in lawyers' offices, in banking offices, or possibly even out in open fields. There are, however, some rather more formal kinds of financial markets. The most conspicuous type of such market institution would be exemplified by the New York Stock Exchange. There are also more than a dozen other organized securities exchanges. These securities exchanges handle bonds as well as common stocks, but they tend to specialize in the latter class of obligations. In addition to the organized exchanges, informal over-the-counter markets service a very wide range of securities, including those of the federal government, those of state and local governments, corporate bonds, and some stocks, as well as most foreign securities. The merchandising of newly issued securities is handled by investment bankers, who perform an underwriting, as well as a marketing, function.

These principal financial markets collect around them a number of other related financial services: for example, brokers and dealers and other specialists such as those who find or place security credit.

Insurance and pension intermediaries as financial institutions

The principle of insurance is basically that of converting risk into a cost. In its simplest form this could be done without much accumulation of financial assets, but in practice it is found to function better if working reserves are held. Insurance institutions have, in fact, come to be large holders of financial assets and extraordinarily important investors. In some ways this considerable degree of insurance prepayment, particularly in the case of life insurance, would make it logical to treat insurance institutions as savings institutions. Still another specialized type of institution that makes use of the insurance principle but is possibly even more clearly a savings institution is the pension plan or pension trust.

International financial institutions

International finance is usually a sideline for basically domestic financial institutions such as commercial banks, but a few specialized international financial institutions, most of them intergovernmental agencies, may be found. The leading examples are the International Monetary Fund, the International Bank for Reconstruction and Development, and the Bank for International Settlements. A few private international financial institutions have been organized primarily for trading or capital-movement purposes.

Form of organization of financial institutions

Although most of the financial institutions enumerated so far are private in nature and are organized as corporations, partnerships, or proprietorships, a considerable number of them are not formally considered profit-making institutions. Mutual savings banks, most savings and loan associations, and large portions of the insurance industry, for example, are organized according to the so-called mutual principle. A mutual institution is one in which no stockholder group exists apart from the customers of the institution. This use of the mutual form of organization has grown up in a variety of ways, and its presence gives rise to some quite interesting special problems.

Some financial institutions have been organized by government. For example, social security could be considered a governmental kind of retirement system. National life insurance for war veterans and a great many agricultural and mortgage credit institutions such as the Federal

National Mortgage Association are further illustrative of governmental sponsorship.

Evolutionary changes in financial institutions

Finance is not a static subject. During the last several decades there have been many important changes in the character of financial institutions. It is worthwhile to take a preliminary look at some of the changing environmental factors that have contributed to these changes.

Regulatory and economic environment

Most financial institutions operate within a net of regulatory constraints that were for the most part imposed during the early years of the great depression of the 1930s. In the intervening years some individual regulations have been rescinded and others added but, by and large, the framework has remained intact. The major thrust of regulatory prohibitions on the operations of financial institutions has been to restrict the operations of each type of institution either in the types of businesses they can engage in or in the geographic area in which they can operate. In large measure the regulations were adopted as a consequence of the experiences of failures and problems encountered by financial institutions during the depression of the 1930s.

In the 1950s and 1960s, the American economy grew very rapidly. Inflation, rather than depression and unemployment, was the major problem facing the economy. Thus the regulations and mode of operations of financial institutions that were appropriate during the 1930s were largely outmoded and too confining for the conditions which existed in the 1960s. As a consequence, during the decade of the 1960s the pace of change in the operational modes of the various financial institutions greatly accelerated. These changes have substantially altered the relative size and competitive position of the various financial institutions and considerably broadened the potential avenues of financing for businesses and consumers. Even with the changes that have occurred in the operations of the financial institutions which will be discussed at length in this book, there is great concern that the existing regulatory framework does not allow financial institutions to properly adapt to the changing needs for financing of the various segments of the economy.

Changing technology

Technological advance has been a major factor in the growth of the American economy since the beginning of the Republic and the pace of technological change continues to accelerate.

Many of the changes that have occurred in the operations of financial institutions have been facilitated by new technological developments. The operation of financial institutions now requires the transmission of large volumes of information. The development of computers and other communication and information retrieval and storage devices has permitted financial institutions to efficiently deal with these increasing volumes of information. Thus, to some extent technology has allowed financial institutions to broaden their operations within a relatively stable regulatory environment. Moreover, there is good reason to believe that improved technology in information handling will induce further rapid change in the operations of financial institutions in the next decade.

The study of finance

The study of any subject involves an ancient pedagogical problem: Where should the student start, and how should he break into the ring of the known and the unknown? Should he start with forms of organization or should he start with a consideration of the functional operations of the system? Should a well-known and familiar subject be approached differently from one that is completely foreign and unknown?

Most people have some knowledge of finance. But, oddly enough, this knowledge can be almost as much a hindrance as a help. Many people disclaim any knowledge of such fields as investment banking or foreign exchange; yet these are relatively easy subjects. On the other hand, most people assume they know something about money. The subject of money, however, is honeycombed with subtleties and difficulties that have been debated by monetary theorists for many years with only moderate success in reaching agreement. The quantity theory of money seemed a self-evident truth to scholastic philosophers; yet it is still being debated by contemporary monetary economists.

The authors of this text have chosen to combine functional analysis with institutional description. The six main parts of the book deal with the principal functional areas of finance: money and monetary institutions, intermediary financial institutions, business finance, personal finance, government finance, and international finance. Within each of these broad areas the leading institutions are reviewed and their workings examined, with a view at all stages to the functional or economic purpose served by these financial arrangements.

This text is organized along the following lines. The seven chapters that follow this introduction are devoted to money and monetary institutions. The primary purpose of these chapters is to show how money is used in a modern economic system. These chapters also show how money is supplied and how the supply is controlled. This section introduces and describes some of our most fundamental financial institutions and deals with several basic financial functions.

Chapters 9–15 deal with a number of capital market intermediary financial institutions. The word *intermediary* used in this connection refers to institutions that lie between the ultimate economic entities. The best illustration of an intermediary financial institution is a thrift or savings institution. On the one hand, these institutions serve savers by paying them for the use of their funds, and on the other hand, they serve borrowers by making funds available to them at an acceptable price and on suitable terms. Modern intermediary financial institutions have evolved interesting and subtle arrangements for channeling savings into the form of loanable funds.

Chapters 16–19 are devoted to the special problems of business finance. The economic system of the United States is built on the faith that the free actions of individuals will become organized voluntarily into units that make private economic activity possible and efficient. Business is perhaps the leading means for organizing private economic activity, and the financing of business is therefore very vital in making this system work.

The fourth major section of this text, Part V, deals with the problems of consumer finance. It is devoted to an examination of the institutions which provide consumers with most of their borrowed funds.

Part VI treats governmental activities in the field of money and finance. These problems are so diverse that it is perhaps better to allow them to be introduced by that section itself when it is reached than to speak inadequately and obscurely of the problem at this point.

Finally, problems of international finance are discussed in Part VII. International financial institutions and their relationships in both the private and governmental areas are considered. Over the last several decades, international trade and international finance have grown rapidly, greatly increasing the importance of the institutions and arrangements for lending funds raised in one country to borrowers who will put the funds to work in another.

Questions and problems

1. When monetary systems are destroyed by war or revolution, informally invented ones almost always spring up in their place. Why does the use of money persist in the face of war and disaster?
2. Even socialist economies find it necessary to have a money system. Why?
3. What is the special role of financial markets in a free economy?
4. Why can the management of finances also be considered the management of final economic resources?

5. Why is it not exactly proper to speak of international financial management?
6. What very general role do interest rates play in our financial system?
7. Is General Motors a financial institution? Is General Motors Acceptance Corporation a financial institution? What is the essential difference?
8. Name a number of financial institutions that can be found within your home city.
9. Why are insurance companies considered financial institutions?

Bibliography

The principal work summarizing quantitatively the network of financial institutions is R. W. Goldsmith's *Financial Intermediaries in the United States since 1900* (New York: National Bureau of Economic Research and Princeton University Press, 1958). This author's three-volume *Study of Saving* (same publishers, 1955 and 1956) also contains a wealth of factual detail. The third volume suggests a number of analytical approaches to various aspects of finance.

Carl Madden's *The Money Side of the Street* (New York: Federal Reserve Bank of New York, 1959) is primarily a survey of money-market institutions, but discloses interesting details of many other financial institutions.

The series of monographs in the *Foundations of Finance* series published by Prentice-Hall, Inc. (Englewood Cliffs, N.J.) under the editorship of Ezra Solomon provides both excellence in discussion and wide coverage of topics a student of finance may wish to consider further.

PART II

MONEY AND MONETARY INSTITUTIONS

The purpose of this part is to introduce the reader to a modern economic system's uses of money and to the processes by which the supply of money can be altered. The discussion is a descriptive one which attempts to provide a picture of the institutions most important to very short-term financial markets, called the money markets, and to indicate the manner in which these institutions and markets are interrelated. This first chapter of this part, Chapter 2, discusses money and its functions in a modern economy. Chapters 3, 4, and 5 describe and analyze the role of commercial banks in this system. Banks are important money market institutions, they are the largest and most important capital market intermediary in the economy, and they also play a unique role in affecting the economy's money supply through their credit-creating activities. Chapter 3 traces the origin and development of commercial banks. Chapter 4 discusses bank sources and uses of funds in greater detail, and Chapter 5 covers bank credit, bank earnings, and credit expansion. Chapter 6 then discusses banking structure and supervision and Chapter 7 the roles the Federal Reserve System and the Treasury play in affecting the money supply. The eighth chapter, which concludes the section, discusses the money markets and the operations of money market financial institutions.

CHAPTER 2

Money and its functions

Widespread use of money and credit is to be found in all developed economies. Primitive economies, on the other hand, effect most transactions by means of barter. This is not a coincidence—economists agree that an important measure of an economy's development is the sophistication of its monetary and financial systems.

Money and economic development

There are several reasons why economic development is intimately related with the extent to which money and credit are used. First, when it is easy to carry out financial transactions, firms and individuals can specialize their activities (thereby gaining the advantages of specialization) and they can quite easily exchange the goods and services they produce for those produced by others. Second, money and credit facilitate the capital formation process so necessary to economic development. Economic units having incomes in excess of their spending plans can save these funds; through the use of money and financial institutions, the savings can be collected and re-lent to finance the construction of new plants and equipment, or of new homes and apartment buildings. Money and credit also assist individuals to make installment purchases, thereby smoothing out their expenditure patterns to a greater degree than would be possible if money and credit did not exist.

The importance of money and credit in developed economics can further be stressed by considering some of the characteristics of economies in which transactions are carried out by barter. When Americans lived on the frontier, they were required to be almost entirely self-sufficient. If he captured no game, a frontiersman could well go hungry. If he were lucky and captured more than he could eat, the frontiersman might trade game for other types of supplies—providing he could find someone willing to trade. One difficulty with barter, then as now, is that if a trade is to be completed, each of the two parties must have goods the other wants. As the economists put it, barter requires a double coincidence of demand. A second difficulty with barter is that capital to develop business is difficult to obtain. Instead of being able to borrow the savings of many others, say in order to set up a trading post, the would-be trader would have to find a wealthy patron or accumulate furs on his own until he had enough to trade them for an initial amount of supplies.

In early stages of economic development, men resolved the problem of double coincidence by adopting some commodity, readily and widely acceptable in exchange for goods and services, as a medium of exchange. The commodity used varied with the culture and with the location, whether on the water or inland, whether in tropical or temperate climates. This medium of exchange was generally some object prized in the community either as an ornament or because it was useful as a tool, food, or clothing. Thus a wide variety of objects could be and actually were used as money. In addition to gold and silver, the list included:

Grain	Beads	Ivories
Spices	Brick tea	Human hair
Rock salt	Animal claws	Shark teeth
Furs	Banana seeds	Plumage
Shells	Fishhooks	Stone disks

and many others.

The problem of facilitating the savings-investment process, however, is not so easily solved in primitive economies. Commodity monies were sometimes perishable and certainly difficult to keep safely, and as mentioned above, credit was difficult to arrange. These problems were made no easier by the absence of established prices. The range of prices that sometimes did exist was wide because in bargaining transactions the actual amount of a good exchanged for another depended a great deal on the circumstances of the two traders.

Functions of money in developed economies

The preceding discussion contained hints of the functions of money in developed economies. These functions are usually referred to in terms of money's role as a medium of exchange, as a store of value, and as a unit of account. We now consider each of these functions.

Medium of exchange

When economists talk about money as a medium of exchange they mean that money is the common commodity in terms of which most trades are carried out. As the American frontier developed, furs frequently functioned as a medium of exchange—the homesteader might trade grain for furs and later exchange the furs for whiskey, clothing, or other commodities. In developed economies, the role of money as a medium of exchange is so widespread that we hardly notice it—few persons other than economists think of selling their labor for dollars when they go to work or of selling their dollars for stereo records on their way home from the office. A great advantage of having an acceptable medium of exchange is that it facilitates specialization, as we have already mentioned.

Store of value

Money facilitates economic development not only because it is a medium of exchange but also because it is a store of value. If a firm or individual earns more than is spent during a given period of time, the difference can conveniently be saved, either as cash on hand or in the form of bank deposits. When the savings are drawn down at a later date, the money will still (in the absence of inflationary price level changes) have its purchasing power.

Similarly, a firm that wants to command the resources it needs to build a factory depends upon the existence of money. For during the period of construction, no output is produced. Yet the people who sell their labor and material to the firm want to be compensated for their services. If only bartering were feasible, it would be almost impossible to construct a building or project of any size. In a money economy, however, a firm can borrow funds from the financial institutions in which savers place their money. These funds can then be used to pay the workers, and the construction of large projects is no longer financially infeasible.

Unit of account

Money is also the unit of account in which the books of a nation are kept. In the United States, we keep our books in dollars; in France, the unit of account is the franc, and so forth. Because money is so universally used, prices are more readily established and become better known in exchange rather than in barter economies. In addition, it is difficult to overstress the importance money has in a modern society's record keeping. Commonplace transactions can be quite complicated: for example, when an automobile is purchased, some money may be paid at the time of purchase and the rest may be paid over the next three years. Moreover, an interest charge may be levied on the amount of funds that are borrowed. Imagine trying to carry out this transaction in an economy without money! Finally, when money is used as a unit of account we can learn much more about an economy than we could otherwise know— plow horses and objets d'art can be measured in terms of each other through the use of money values.

In short, money is a medium of exchange, a store of value, and a unit of account. No modern society can function effectively without it. It is no surprise then that the economic development of a country closely mirrors the degree of sophistication of its monetary and financial systems.

Moreover, the significance of money is not limited to our markets and the distribution of our savings. Many political problems of national interest have monetary connotations. Not only do we live in a money and credit economy, but our economic prosperity is tied closely to the manner in which our monetary system is administered. For example, if anything occurs to affect the normal flow of money from consumers to producers and back again to consumers, the entire economy is affected. The volume of goods produced, the number of workers employed, the size of wage payments, and the rate of saving may all be changed, and an inflation or deflation be generated. An analytical discussion of how money can bring about these effects appears later in this text; the purpose of this chapter is primarily to describe the manner in which money is employed in our economy.

Money and its substitutes

Although the evolution of the transactions and payment mechanism from bartering began with the advent of currency and coin, a number of substitutes or near monies soon emerged.

Media of exchange

Let us provisionally define money as anything that serves as a medium of exchange. Then, the currency and coin that all of us carry about in our pockets is clearly money. The amount of currency and coin outstanding in the United States in mid-1969 was $51 billion. Of this, $36 billion was in coin and small bills; the remaining $16 billion was in large denomination currency. However, currency and coin are not the most important media of exchange in America today. Rather, the demand deposits of commercial banks, or what are commonly called checking accounts, are roughly three times as important in dollar value as currency and coin. In June 1969, the demand deposits that individuals, corporations, and government units could draw upon to pay for the goods and services they purchased was in excess of $154 billion.

While currency and coin are used for many transactions, there are a growing number of transactions in which payment by check is preferred. Currency is usually employed where there is no need to keep a record of the transaction, where the item is highly perishable, where the seller does not know the buyer, and where the size of the transaction is relatively small. For example, most people pay cash when they buy lunch or a magazine at the corner newsstand. As the transaction becomes larger, the product more durable, and the need for a record of the transaction emerges, a check may be the preferred instrument. A check can be made out for any specific amount; buyers using checks therefore do not have to carry large sums of cash with them and expose themselves to the risk of robbery when they purchase a high-cost item. Moreover, the canceled check is recognized as a proof of payment. If a question arises at a later date about where or when the product was purchased, it can be answered by data on the check.

But currency and checks are not the only media of exchange that we now have. In recent years, an increasing number of individuals have begun to buy merchandise through the use of credit cards. When this happens, a third party, the company that issues the credit card, becomes involved in the transaction. Thus, if Mr. A buys a meal at a restaurant and pays for the meal with a credit card, the restaurant owner will receive payment from the credit card company, not from Mr. A. The credit card company will then bill Mr. A for the meal and receive payment from him.

The advantage of the credit card to Mr. A is that he now has a record of even his small purchases. Moreover, merchants recognize that there is little risk of loss associated with credit card transactions. As a consequence, a restaurant may accept it as a means of payment in preference to Mr. A's personal check. Finally, if Mr. A is temporarily short of funds, the credit card is a convenient way to borrow money. In this instance the issuer of the card advances the loan to Mr. A.

One effect of credit cards is to increase the number of dollars that flow through the system to effect a final payment. Had Mr. A in our example not used the credit card, only one transaction would have occurred; he would have paid the restaurant. When the credit card is used, two transactions arise: the company pays the restaurant and Mr. A pays the company. If the meal cost Mr. A $6, the face value of the two transactions will be approximately $12.

If all of the credit transactions in the economy are now aggregated, i.e., if we look at the entire economy as a unit, it is clear that the use of credit leads to an increase in the dollar volume of transactions that arise. Moreover, if the amount of currency, coin, and demand deposits remains constant, the rise of credit sales will lead to an increase in the turnover rate of demand deposits and currency. Statistics prepared by the Board of Governors of the Federal Reserve System indicate that the deposits in banks in major metropolitan centers now turn over about 70 times a year. Phrased differently, the average length of stay of a dollar deposited in anyone's account is about 5 days as compared to a stay of 14 days (turnover of 25 times a year) in 1950.

Alternate stores of value

Credit cards, then, have begun to substitute for money as a medium of exchange at the retail level. At the same time, other instruments have arisen as substitutes for money as a store of value. Time deposits at a commercial bank or a savings and loan association are such substitutes for money. These instruments are close substitutes because they perform the store of value function as well as money and they can be converted into a medium of exchange at virtually no cost. Moreover, they have the advantage that financial institutions are permitted to pay interest for these types of deposit, while they are not permitted to pay interest on deposits left in checking accounts.

A government bond is another substitute for money, but it is not as good a one as the time deposit. Like the time deposit, these instruments provide a return to their owner and cannot be spent directly. They can also be converted into a medium of exchange at a negligible cost. Government bonds, however, are different from time deposits in that government bonds (other than savings bonds) fluctuate in price as interest rates change. At maturity, the bond will be paid at its full face value, but if the owner wants to sell the bond at some point of time before maturity, he may sustain a loss. In this sense, bonds are riskier than time deposits and therefore must yield a higher return in order to induce investors to buy them.

There are still other substitutes for money when it is considered to be a store of value. For example, an investor can purchase common stock. The transaction costs that are required to convert this asset into a medium of exchange are, however, no longer nominal—they average about 1% of the purchase price—and like government bonds, stocks fluctuate in price. Unlike bonds, stocks have no maturity value. Thus the investor is uncertain as to the actual amount of money he will receive when he sells the securities, no matter when he should elect to carry out the sale.

The list of substitutes for money as a store of value could be extended further yet. Such a listing would only continue to show that there can be an honest difference of opinion over how to define money. For as both a medium of exchange and a store of value, currency and coin have close substitutes. Each of these substitutes has both advantages and disadvantages relative to currency and coin. Therefore, rather than fixing a hard and fast definition of money at this point, the practice will be followed throughout this text of letting the problem that is under consideration dictate the definition that will be used. At times, money will be defined as currency and coin plus demand deposits; at other times, as currency, coin, demand, and time deposits; and at still other times, other liquid assets may be included in the definition.

Money and its supply in the United States

The monetary system of our nation consists of all the instruments of payment which perform the functions of money. However, for purposes of the present discussion, we shall restrict our definition of the money supply to include currency, coin, and the demand deposit liabilities of commercial banks; because money in this section is regarded as a medium of exchange. The section describes money in terms of the way our unit of account (the dollar) is defined, how paper currency and coin are issued through the central bank, and the meaning of demand deposits at commercial banks. The discussions of these topics include brief histories that explain how present arrangements came into being.

The dollar's standard of value

The value of the U.S. dollar is legally defined in terms of gold. While gold does not have special intrinsic virtues absent from all other commodities, several of its properties do enhance its general acceptability as a means of payment between nations. These are chiefly that it is not perishable, its quantity and rates of production are limited, and it has traditionally been regarded as precious by most men and most nations. One of the chief difficulties with paper currency as a substitute for gold is that paper money is too easy for governments to print, and therefore the purchasing power of paper currency is not so stable as that of gold.

Other nations have also made gold the basis of their financial systems, and gold functions as a medium of international exchange. So long as a nation manages its affairs in such a way that its unit of account's buying power remains about the same as the buying power of its legal equivalent in terms of gold, most international transactions can now be settled with the use of paper currencies. Nonetheless, gold remains a key element of the system because people and nations alike believe its buying power to be at least as stable as that of any currency and will resort to its use when the buying power of a currency is expected to change.

All nations' units of account and monetary standards are not defined in terms of a commodity such as gold or silver. Since World War I, many countries have been unable or unwilling to tie their systems rigidly to gold and therefore have adopted some form of administered paper standard. Under such a plan the word *standard* has lost its traditional meaning because circulating forms of currency are not related to, or convertible into, a valuable and generally acceptable commodity. If a small gold reserve is held, a link between paper forms of money and gold may remain and extend a stabilizing influence upon the volume of currency and the general level of prices. On the other hand, if no metallic base is present, the system exists only on the basis of governmental decree or fiat, and the value of money is regulated by monetary authorities. Regulated paper issues are usually made legal tender for all government and private obligations, and legislative restrictions are placed upon the amount that may be issued. Because other forms of money (of a commodity type) are not available, fiat issues are generally acceptable and function satisfactorily as' media of exchange as long as the volume of currency issued bears a reasonably stable relationship to the volume of trade to be financed.

The gold standard, 1900–1933

From 1900 to 1933 the United States was on a gold standard, with the dollar defined as 23.22 grams of pure gold. This meant that the mint price of gold was fixed at $20.67 an ounce and that the U.S. Treasury would purchase, or sell, unlimited amounts of the metal to any individual or nation at that price. Gold coins were made legal tender for all government and private debts; paper money and subsidiary coins were convertible into gold; and no restrictions were placed upon the use and movement of gold coin or bullion.

The depressed levels of economic activity that developed in widely scattered areas of the world in 1929–33 and the resulting competitive devaluation of currency practices followed by many nations brought almost universal abandonment of the gold standard. In the United States in 1933, all banks were closed by federal and state orders; the Treasury ceased all gold payments and the redemption of gold certificates; gold hoarding was prohibited, and all persons were required to surrender gold coin and bullion and gold certificates in exchange for other kinds of money. The gold standard was replaced by a gold exchange standard.

Gold Reserve Act, 1934

The Gold Reserve Act of January 30, 1934, and a presidential proclamation issued the day following established the gold exchange standard now in effect in the United States. These measures provide that the dollar consist of 13.71 grains of pure gold but prohibit the issuance of gold coin or paper notes fully backed by gold. No hoarding or transporting of the metal is permitted except under treasury license. All the money used as media of exchange—silver dollars, subsidiary silver and minor coin, and all forms of government and central bank notes—is full legal tender for public and private debts. No money is redeemable in gold except under treasury regulation designed to effect international payments. Gold is released for use in domestic industry and the arts only under license from the Treasury. The Treasury will purchase unlimited quantities of gold from foreign and domestic producers at $35 an ounce, less handling charges.

Despite the restrictions on gold and the fact that paper money may not be freely converted into gold for domestic uses, the monetary system is not a *fiat* standard in the usual sense of the term. The gold stock acts as a partial reserve for Federal Reserve notes and deposits and may be used to preserve the value of the dollar in foreign-exchange markets. However, the legal requirement that gold be held as a reserve against currency issues has been rescinded. As of December 31, 1969, the United States held about $12 billion worth of gold as reserves against its currency and coin issues of $46 billion.

Paper money in the United States since 1934

The paper currency issued by the federal government and the Federal Reserve banking system is an important part of the U.S. money supply.

Federal Reserve notes. The most important type of paper currency in use in the United States today consists of Federal Reserve notes. The volume outstanding on July 31, 1970, was $51 billion, an amount approximately seven times as great as all other forms of paper and coins together. In 1930 total paper currency and coins (including gold) amounted to only $4.2 billion, and of this the Federal Reserve notes constituted only one third. More will be said of the method of issue and and the unique features of Federal Reserve notes in Chapter 7. It should be noted here, however, that of all the forms of government or bank issues in our system the Federal Reserve note has proved most adaptable to the needs of commerce, industry, and agriculture. The volume of Federal Reserve notes and other forms of money in circulation is shown in Table 2–1.

Treasury currency. The monetary system of the United States is unnecessarily cluttered by most of the paper issues included in treasury currency. Many of the items in this category are relics of former days and, it is hoped, will gradually be reduced in volume or eliminated by the action of some future Congress. We could hardly dispense with coins, but the paper forms of treasury currency are unnecessary.

In spite of the fact that they are redundant, certain items of treasury currency retain the interest of monetary historians. For example, U.S.

notes first issued in 1862, in the administration of President Lincoln, are the famous "greenbacks." They were irredeemable, noninterest bearing notes that had no specific backing but circulated because they were legal tender for all private debts.

Another interesting issue was placed in circulation by commercial banks organized under the charter-granting privileges of the National Bank Act of 1863. The notes were not legal tender until 1933 but were a significant part of our currency system for many years. In the mid-1930s, national banks lost the power of issue, and the Treasury took over the obligation of their redemption. Those outstanding are now legal tender for all public and private debts but are gradually being retired.

TABLE 2–1

Kinds of U.S. currency outstanding and in circulation (*on basis of compilation by U.S. Treasury, in millions of dollars.*)

Kind of currency	Total outstanding* July 31, 1970
Gold	11,367
Gold certificates	11,045
Federal Reserve notes	51,120
Treasury currency—(coin $6.4 billion)	7,011

* Outside Treasury and Federal Reserve banks. Includes any paper currency held outside continental limits of the United States and currency held by commercial banks.

Source: Adapted from table in *Federal Reserve Bulletin*, August 1970, p. A16.

Treasury coin. An important form of treasury currency is subsidiary coin. Coins have been used for centuries and they continue today to be a very necessary medium for retail transactions in small amounts.

Coins are normally a form of credit money in that the value of the metallic content is less on the market than the face value of the coin in trade. The credit element is useful since it reduces the cost of maintaining a circulating medium and insures that the coins will not be melted down for sale as metal if the market price of the metal rises moderately. Table 2–1 shows that approximately $6.4 billion in coin was outstanding as of July 31, 1970.

In an attempt to retard the drain of silver from the monetary system and to overcome a coin shortage which developed in the early 1960's, Congress passed an act in 1965 that reduced the amount of silver in coins[1] issued. Any coin minted under the authority of this act is composed of three layers of metal. The two outer layers, which are of identical com-

---

[1] P.L. 89–81, 89th Congress, S. 2080, July 23, 1965.

position, are bonded to an inner layer. New dimes and quarters contain no silver but are a composite faced with an alloy of 75% copper and 25% nickel bonded to a core of copper. The new half-dollar is also a composite coin with its overall silver content reduced to 40% from the former 90%.

These measures have postponed the serious problems accompanying a dwindling stock of silver but provide no permanent solution.

Demand deposits

The largest element in the money supply of the United States is the demand deposits that result from the operations of the commercial banking system. First, bank deposit obligations can be exchanged for cash. Second, and more important, banks can create deposit money. For example, if banks grant loans to customers for $10 billion, the proceeds of which are credited to the borrowers' checking accounts, the banks have created $10 billion of money that did not exist before. The banks have traded debt claims with their borrowing customers, accepting promissory notes that are not money and creating checking deposits. Checks drawn against these deposits have a high degree of acceptability and perform a money function in paying for goods, securities, and services. Banks may also purchase corporation or government debt obligations in the form of notes or bonds in exchange for deposit claims on themselves. In America today most demand deposits are created by bank purchases of debt claims of others, and since there is usually no offsetting decrease of coin or paper money in circulation, the banks make a net addition to the money supply.

On December 31, 1969, adjusted demand deposits of all insured commercial banks (excluding interbank balances) aggregated more than $154 billion. That amount is more than three times the supply of currency in use in the United States today.

In spite of the broad use of checking accounts by the public, many misconceptions about their nature exist. Deposits obviously are not stores of coin and paper currency held in trust by banks for their customers; their volume greatly exceeds the amount of coin and paper money in the system. Deposits are liabilities or contractual obligations arising out of the receipt of some consideration from banks' customers. The individual desiring to spend or invest draws on his account. He may exchange his check at the drawee bank for coin or paper money, he may purchase a cashier's check, he may draw a check in favor of another depositor of his bank, or he may make the check payable either to the depositing customer of another bank or to someone who has no deposit. Although the liquid reserve in the drawee commercial bank is only a small fraction of its demand deposits, if the drawee honors all checks at their face value and maintains their convertibility into currency, checks become an acceptable means of payment and, as stated above, checking deposits constitute part of the money supply.

Money supply: stocks and flows

On concluding this discussion of the money supply, we must make a distinction between money supply and money flows. The supply is a *stock* or quantity of money in existence at a specific point in time. It may be increased or decreased from time to time by monetary and banking authorities. Money *flow* is the rate at which the stock is being used in transactions. Money flow is frequently discussed in terms of a concept called velocity—the rate at which the stock is expended. For example, if transactions in an economy amount to $1 billion per year, and if the money stock is $100 million, the annual velocity of circulation is said to be 10. The velocity of money depends upon decisions of owners of the stock as to how long money will be held before it is spent.

Money flows are usually expressed as annual rates but are subject to wide variations from the average as the economy passes through seasonal and cyclical swings. Managers of business concerns consider the size of money flows as much more significant than money stock in making their decisions relative to pricing, volume of output, and size of labor force. Although the stock of money is a major determinant of money flow, it is not correct to assume that money supply and velocity are mechanically related in some constant fashion. If that were true, control of stock would make possible closer control of total flow than is in fact possible.

Accurate determination of the velocity of the coin and currency items of the money supply is an impossible task that no one attempts. On the other hand, the average velocity of demand deposits is easily computed by dividing yearly bank debits by annual average deposit balances. The annual rate of demand-deposit turnover for 1969 was 145.7 in New York City, 69.6 in six other large cities, and 40.8 in 226 other reporting centers.

The demand for money

The concept of the velocity of money introduces to us the unceasing movement of the stock of money. For purposes of analyzing the movement of funds through our economic system, economists have classified the flows into several streams. Classification is an aid in measuring the size, the rate, and the direction of flow. Flows in a free economy may be thought of as movements of funds brought about by the concerted actions of individuals or institutions with definite uses in mind. So considered, all flows are the results of demands for funds, whether it be for use by householders, business firms, government, financial institutions, or foreign nations. (Although some movements leave the supply of money unchanged, others give rise to changes in supply that may either retard or accelerate the rate and size of flow. These are topics in macroeconomics which receive attention in Chapters 22 and 24.)

Economic theorists consider the quantity of money demanded to be the stock of money (measured in terms of purchasing power) that members of an economy desire to hold. This quantity demanded depends on a relationship between desired stocks of money and economic variables such as wealth and expected interest rates; the relationship itself is known as the demand for money function. The sizes of balances actually held may from time to time diverge from amounts desired; when this occurs they are brought back into correspondence with desired holdings by changing the rate of expenditure. For example, if holdings appear greater than circumstances warrant, the balance is reduced by an increase in spending or in the payment of debts. If balances are less than the desired amount, they will be built up by a decreased rate of expenditure.

Economic units desire to hold money balances for a variety of reasons, and it is useful to discuss these reasons separately even though the unit's money holdings may not actually be separated into portions earmarked for these different purposes. Money holdings may be desired as a means of making future payments, as a store of value representing generalized purchasing power, or as an alternative to owning securities or other investments having uncertain returns or for which future price movements are anticipated.

One important reason for either a household or a business firm maintaining a money balance results from inability to accurately estimate money flows. If a company or a household could be sure that cash inflow in the next year would more than cover cash outlay, it could afford to reduce its cash holdings. However, even if total outlay were balanced by total cash receipts in the period assumed, the inflow might be so irregular that the economic unit would be unable to take cash discounts as a reward for prompt payment on its purchases. A money balance would bridge the gap between outflow and inflow and save the discount. The same type of benefit would be present if a crisis occurred after a period of prosperous activity. The company or household with an adequate money balance may be able to continue operating through the period of recession and reduced receipts. In addition, the balance may permit its owner to take opportunities to purchase inventories at sale prices.

Money holdings are maintained at some cost to the owner. The costs include the sacrifice of income which could be earned if the balance were used in purchasing an earning asset, or the reduction in interest cost which could be effected if debt were retired. In determining the amount of money to hold, the owner attempts to strike a balance between the costs and the benefits of maintaining the balance, although circumstances are always at work to alter the desired amount. For example, declines in the prices of inventories and supplies, in the wage bill, or in taxes might justify a reduction in the money balance without endangering the solvency of a business. A rise in interest rates might act to draw money out of the balance for investment in financial markets; the threat of an inflation might dictate a policy of rapid inventory acquisition requiring depletion of the balance. On the other hand, the expectation of a decline in business activity, with the possibility of declining receipts, might lead an individual or a firm to demand a greater amount of money to meet anticipated future payments.

The amount of money held by an economic unit is also affected by motives other than those of being able conveniently to effect transactions. One of the advantages of money, an advantage not possessed by physical goods, securities, or evidence of ownership, is that it is liquid. Hence, in emergencies money can be used as a means of payment without delay, cost, or inconvenience. The distinction between money held for reasons of conveniently effecting ordinary transactions (transactions motive) and money held for reasons of making payments in emergencies (precautionary motive) is one intended primarily for analytical purposes. In households or firms, the money held for these two conceptually distinct reasons is not usually earmarked for these purposes.

Money may also be demanded instead of securities because securities' returns are uncertain (another form of the precautionary motive), or because price changes in the securities are anticipated (speculative motive). An economic unit with excess money holdings may continue to hold the excess if a decline in the price of securities to be bought is expected. By the same token, money demand may be less than some average amount if the unit expects shortly to realize cash from security sales. This type of money holding is in a modern economy likely to be quite small and of short duration; interest-bearing time deposits or Treasury bills are generally purchased by economic units having surplus money not intended for immediate investment in longer term securities.

Changes in the value of money

We have seen that in a modern economy the analysis of demand and supply can be applied to money in much the same manner (so far!) as it can be applied to other commodities (as already noted, the interrelations between money supply and demand and economic activity are to be discussed later in this text). It is, however, important to bear in mind that the analysis even at this point is predicated on the purchasing power money commands; that is, economic analysis does not claim that "a dollar is a dollar is a dollar," but rather that "today's dollar may not have the same buying power it had a year ago."

Causes of changes in the purchasing power of money

Economists argue extensively over what occurs if the amount of money supplied differs from the amount that economic units desire to hold. For the sake of categorizing the two positions (few economists adhere strictly to either caricature) the debate might be put as follows. Suppose an increase in the number of dollars representing the money supply occurs, but that for the moment the purchasing power demand for money is unchanged. One of the things that could happen is for everyone to recognize that the number of dollars has changed, but that the economy's supply of available goods and services is unchanged. Then everyone would simply pay more dollars for the same amount of goods, realizing that "today's dollar is not worth what yesterday's was." In other words, an extreme representation of one side of the argument is that increases in the money supply bring about increases only in price levels.

The other caricature holds essentially that increases in the money supply are not recognized immediately as causing changes in purchasing power and that economic units find themselves with more purchasing power than they wish to hold. To get rid of the excess, they spend; the spending creates (in the absence of full employment) additional income through mechanisms discussed in later chapters. Thus this view argues that increases in the money supply bring about income changes (which may in turn change the amount of money demanded, but that is another matter) but not price level changes, at least if the economy is underemployed.

It is very likely not incorrect to say that money supply changes lead to both price and income level changes; what makes the debate so interesting is that economic policy is vitally concerned with questions such as "how much change of each type?" The effects of economic policy on the lives of us all are pervasive and sometimes profound, so that the questions represent a good deal more than idle speculation. They are also difficult to answer except in such extreme cases as manyfold increases in the money supply which are well known to cause large price level changes.

Changes in the purchasing power of money may come about for other reasons as well, reasons relating to demand shifts in one or more markets for goods and services, to increases in production costs in one or more sectors, and to general downward rigidities of prices in modern economies such as our own. A somewhat more detailed examination of these causes of inflation is conducted in later chapters: our present purpose is to recognize that changes in the value of money occur, to provide a means of measuring these changes, and to examine the financial effects such changes bring about.

Index numbers: measuring money's purchasing power

For the purpose of measuring changes in the general level of prices, statistical devices known as index numbers have been developed. Essentially, the method used in constructing an index number is to obtain the average price of each commodity included in the index over some period of time known as the base period. Thenceforth, as changes occur, the new prices are expressed as percentages above or below the price prevailing in the base period.

Because the average annual price of such dissimilar items as a ton of coal, a drum of oil, and a bushel of wheat cannot in themselves be averaged to obtain the average general level of prices, the average price of each commodity during the base period is set up as 100%. Changes in individual prices in subsequent periods are stated as percentages of the base period price and are called *price relatives*. These price relatives are

TABLE 2–2

Commodity price changes (*wholesale*)

Commodity	Average annual price		Ratio of price in current year to price in base year
	Base year	Current year	
Wheat (per bushel)	$ 1.06	$ 1.80	170.00
Pig iron (per gross ton)	22.18	24.39	110.00
Rubber—crude (per pound)	0.75	0.47	62.66
Beef (per pound)	0.17	0.25	147.06
Average price relative	—	—	122.43

averaged and compared with the average of the base period. Deviations in the average of price relatives in subsequent periods then show as percentage changes above or below the 100% taken as the base.

A purely hypothetical case (see Table 2–2) will serve to clarify this description.

The right-hand column of Table 2–2 contains the price relatives which show the current price as a percentage of the price of the base year. Thus, if wheat is being considered, the 170 indicates a rise of 70% in the price of wheat in the period from the base year to the current year. These price relatives are averaged to obtain the index number 122.43, which indicates that the general level of prices has increased 22.43% since the base year. It is evident that, if prices have risen, the amount of money required to purchase a given list of goods has also increased; the value of each unit of money has therefore declined.

If we wish to compute the degree to which the purchasing power of money fell, as the general price level increased to 122.43, we may say that it has fallen reciprocally, and use the following formula:

$$\frac{\text{Base-year price level}}{\text{Price level of current year}} = \frac{\text{Value of money in current year}}{\text{Value of money in base year}}.$$

The base-year price level is always 100; the purchasing power of money in the base year is also 100. Our index (122.43) has provided the price level of the current year. By substitution, we obtain the purchasing power for the current year as follows:

$$\frac{100.00}{122.43} = \frac{x}{100.00}$$
$$22.43x = 10,000.00$$
$$x = 81.53$$

Thus the purchasing power of money fell 18.47% (100.00 − 81.53), while the price level rose 22.43%. It must be recognized that there is no comprehensive measure of the price level. Therefore, no more than rough significance can be attached to these computations. They are shown here only to illustrate a crude device for measuring the ·changing value of money.

It is not the function of this text to consider the problems of selecting the type of average to be used in an index or the method of weighting the commodities included, i.e., determining the economic significance of each item and the other technical aspects related to the construction of index numbers. It must be noted, however, that there are several different types of indexes and that each has definite merits and also certain shortcomings. Some indexes deal exclusively with prices at wholesale, others at retail; some include only raw-material prices, others the prices of raw material, semifinished goods, and finished products. Cost-of-living index numbers that include the costs of services and rents as well as commodity prices are usually considered more satisfactory than commodity index numbers for showing changes in the value of the consumer's dollar. Some comments on the fact that indexes do not adequately reflect changes in commodities' quality are given in Chapter 24.

Although index numbers may be presented in the form of tables, variations in the general price level can be more fully appreciated when the data are plotted in chart form. Exhibit 2–1 illustrates the monthly average of wholesale prices in the United States from 1915 to 1969. The chart is based on the index of the U.S. Bureau of Labor Statistics, commonly referred to as the "BLS Wholesale Commodity Price Index." Exhibit 2–2, showing what is probably the most widely used price index in our economy, one also prepared by the Bureau of Labor Statistics, is a chart of consumers' prices, 1915 to 1969.

EXHIBIT 2–1

**Wholesale prices in the United States, 1915–69
annual average (1957–59 = 100)**

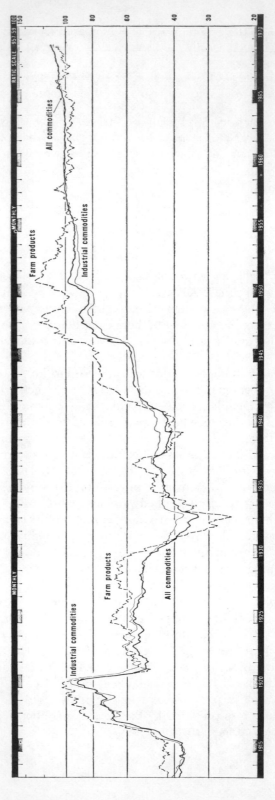

Source: Board of Governors, Federal Reserve System.

EXHIBIT 2-2

**Consumer prices in the United States, 1915–69
annual average (1957–59 = 100)**

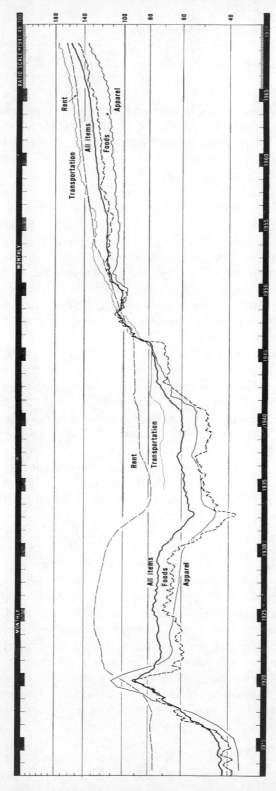

Source: Board of Governors, Federal Reserve System.

Effects of changing purchasing power

The significance of price changes, or changes in the purchasing power of money, is due primarily to two factors. One is that the prices of different items do not all change at the same time, or in the same direction, or to the same degree. The second factor—and it is closely related to the first—is that individual, business, and industrial incomes do not automatically and quickly adjust themselves to changed expense requirements, and vice versa. The result may be serious hardship for certain groups as the general price level fluctuates. In periods of declining prices, creditors gain at the expense of debtors because the fixed number of dollars received in interest or repayment have more purchasing power than when the debt was contracted; but during price inflation, debtors can repay funds more easily and gain at the expense of creditors.

If we assume that all prices, including commodities, interest, wages, and rent, stood at 100 in 1945 but moved upward to 200 in 1969, it is apparent that the purchasing power position of those people who depend entirely on current income unaffected by long-term contracts would be but slightly affected. Incomes would double, but costs would keep pace, and the net effect would be nil.

Actually, however, the relationships existing within the price structure would be very likely to change in the years under consideration. The price paid for labor (wages) may advance more rapidly than wholesale prices, although not always as rapidly as retail prices. Further, those people receiving an income in the form of rent or interest have the amount of income stated in long-term contracts which usually permit no adjustment in the rate. Insurance companies receive premium payments and pay benefit claims based on expenditures and income of past years. The current premium income and benefit liabilities are on a contract basis not subject to adjustment to present conditions. Users of public utility services pay a rate per unit of product which is adjusted as the expenses of operating utilities fluctuate, but only after considerable delay. The return on common stocks of utility companies would therefore be likely to fall as expenses rise and find reflection in lower prices of the securities.

Business profits in general, however, would be likely to react in just the opposite way, although the amount of dividends paid to shareholders seldom keeps pace with expanding profits. There would be no change in interest payments to holders of bonds or long-term notes. In short, the welfare of different groups in society would be affected differently by a rise in the general price level because the increased income and increased expenses are not immediately distributed equitably to wage earners, to owners of land and capital, and to the management of industry.

For a specific illustration of the effect of changes in the purchasing power of money, let us assume that in 1933, when the consumers' price index shown in Exhibit 2–2 was at 60, a businessman retired on a pension paying him $100 a month. As time passed, note that his living expenses in the form of food, rent, and apparel (as represented in the index)rose until, in 1951, he was spending almost $200 for items that cost only $100 when he retired. If his pension were his only source of income, the standard of living of the pensioner would be seriously undermined by the decreased purchasing power of his monthly income.

A decline in the price level may work an equally unjust fate upon an agriculturist who goes heavily into debt at the top of a price cycle for his crop, for the purchase of capital improvements or more land. The expenditure is justified only if the price of products available for sale remains high. If prices decline, the resulting income may be too small to permit the buyer to meet principal payments on his debt or even to make interest payments on the obligation. This type of situation was faced by farmers who borrowed money to purchase land and equipment when prices were at their high in 1918–20. In the ensuing collapse of agricultural prices in 1921 (see Exhibit 2–1) and the resumption of their downward movement from 1928 to 1932, thousands of farmers were forced into bankruptcy.

The possibility that sudden or long-continued reductions in the value of money may wipe out accumulated savings, business profits, and even the very business venture itself is a positive deterrent to the expansion of a private enterprise economy.

It is sometimes contended that merit is attached to a relatively high, rather than to a low, price level. Actually, no price level is sacred in itself. If it is high, other factors will tend slowly to adjust themselves upward to it; if it is low, adjustment will be downward to it. The significant aspect of any price level is the degree to which changes in it are anticipated and allowed for in economic decisions. Regardless of its position, the expected price level is the basis for a multitude of contracts involving payment and receipt of money in the future. Any marked departure from expected levels results in a disturbance to the entire economic structure and in a "violation" of the contracts made at the former level.

Questions and problems

1. Our text implies that present-day markets would utterly collapse if dependent upon barter. Explain.
2. In what respects are gold and silver superior to cattle, diamonds, and tobacco as media of exchange and standards of value?
3. Describe the monetary structure of the United States. What function or functions are performed by the standard of value?
4. How would an individual or a business firm determine its demand for money?

5. Why is the annual flow of money of more significance to a business-man than the stock of money?

6. Demonstrate that an increase in the velocity of the use of money has the same effect upon the price level as an expanded supply of money.

7. Describe the course of the average of farm prices in recent years and account for their movement as compared to the average of all whole-sale prices.

8. Why does the dispersion of prices within the general price structure create economic problems?

Bibliography

Many intermediate texts on money and banking and on monetary theory are available; a list is given at the end of Chapter 5. Important advanced works are listed below.

A scholarly defense of the quantity theory of money in its strict form is presented in the work by I. Fisher, *The Purchasing Power of Money* (rev. ed.; New York: Macmillan Co., 1920).

A classic book in the field of monetary theory is the work by John Maynard Keynes, *The General Theory of Employment, Interest and Money* (New York: Harcourt, Brace & Co., Inc., 1936).

Much of the research in the modern quantity theory of money is due to Milton Friedman and his associates at the University of Chicago. See, for ex-ample, M. Friedman, *The Optimum Quantity of Money and Other Essays* (Chicago: Aldine Publishing Company, 1969).

For neo-Keynesian views of monetary theory, see J. R. Hicks, *Critical Essays in Monetary Theory* (Clarendon Press, 1967), and Harry G. Johnson, *Essays in Monetary Economics* (Cambridge, Mass.: Harvard University Press, 1967).

CHAPTER 3

Commercial banking: origin and development; present-day operations

In Chapter 1 it was pointed out that our system of production depends upon the accumulation of adequate supplies of funds to finance the acquisition of tangible investments. We saw that a great number and variety of financial institutions perform functions in funneling funds from savers to borrowers, who use the funds either for temporary purposes or as permanent capital.

This chapter briefly traces the origin and development of commercial banking, and then describes, through the use of balance sheets, the operations of present-day commercial banks. This is the first of three chapters describing and analyzing the role of banks in our economic system.

The development of commercial banking

Commercial banking in the United States has evolved into its present form through a long series of developments. The early banks in the United States were patterned on existing banks abroad, but through time a unique banking system evolved to suit the specific requirements of this nation. This section traces the development of banking from its origins through the major evolutionary changes that have occurred. It is aimed at providing insights into the long-run trend of changes, and thus at developing an understanding of the present-day operations of the banking system which are dissussed in the following two chapters.

Origin of banking

Although the exact origin of banking is hidden in antiquity, there is evidence to show that the practices of safekeeping and savings banking flourished in the temples of Babylon as early as 2000 B.C. Clay tablets discovered in the ruins of Babylonia indicate that credit instruments in the form of promises and orders to pay gold and silver coins were used in the ninth century B.C., much as promissory notes and bank checks are used today. Loans made on the security of real estate mortgages were recorded as early as the sixth century B.C.

For several centuries before the development of private banking, the priests of the Greek temples carried on a thriving business. Operations were at first confined to the safekeeping of valuables in the sacred vaults but were later expanded to include lending. Even after the rise of private banking enterprise, the priests continued to receive a large volume of savings and to conduct lending operations. Private bankers, however, became more than mere money changers; they loaned their own accumulated profits in addition to some of the precious metal deposited with them for safekeeping.

Many practices common to present-day banking flourished in the Roman Empire at the zenith of its power. Bankers accepted deposits, purchased drafts drawn on banks and on traders in foreign and domestic cities, made commercial loans, bought and sold mortgages, and issued letters of credit. Deposits in the banks were classified on the basis of their maturity dates, and interest was paid on time accounts.

The art of banking fell with the empire, reappearing only with the Renaissance, when trade and commerce began to flourish in Venice and Florence. A public bank established in Venice (1587) became a pattern for public banks established in Amsterdam (1609) and Hamburg (1618) and ultimately influenced the growth of banking in England.

Rise of goldsmith banking in England

Prior to 1640, British merchants and tradesmen made deposits for safekeeping in the Tower of London; but in that year King Charles I seized £130,000 for his own uses. These funds were finally restored to their rightful owners, but in the meantime merchants had begun placing their money and bullion in the vaults of local goldsmiths, who were not only artisans in precious metals but also money changers.

Although the owners of precious metals, jewels, and other items of wealth originally made deposits to obtain safety for their valuables, they soon recognized an additional advantage—the convenience of making payment by transferring the goldsmith's receipt or by writing a draft on their deposit ordering the smith to transfer a designated portion of the account to the bearer of the order. Later, instead of giving a personalized receipt for money or bullion received, the goldsmith issued a formal promissory note which served as a medium of exchange upon endorsement. When notes payable to bearer, requiring no endorsement, were issued by the smith, the prototype of the modern bank note was created. Thus ownership of deposited wealth was transferred from hand to hand, and exchanges of goods and settlements of debt were effected while the valuable assets remained as a reserve in the vaults of the goldsmith.

The convenience of the new method of payment, coupled with confidence in the integrity of the goldsmith, served to hold demands for coin and paper money to a volume much smaller than the funds on deposit. It was practicable, therefore, for the goldsmith to use some of the deposited gold in his own craft or to lend his notes to others. When first introduced, the lending operations were not publicized. Rather, they were carried on in strictest secrecy. Depositors at that time expected to obtain later the identical object or items of wealth left with the goldsmith and would have considered his loan of their property a breach of trust. In making a loan the smith obtained a promise from the borrower to repay the funds in kind on demand or at the end of a short, definitely determinable period. The borrower agreed to repay not only the full amount borrowed but an amount in addition to compensate the smith as lender and risk taker.

At this point in his evolving business the goldsmith became a commercial banker in the modern sense. By lending sometimes gold and sometimes bearer notes payable in cash on demand, the smith had created obligations in excess of his liquid assets. He had, therefore, taken possession of the promissory note of a borrower and created a net addition to the volume of purchasing power in the form of an acceptable medium of exchange.[1] The risks incurred required the smith to invest his own funds in the banking operation, to borrow from others, and to take the chances of going bankrupt. The fee paid by each borrower included some compensation for assuming these risks. The community as a whole was served by the increase in the amount of money made available by the lending process.

---

[1] The exchange of bank notes or deposit credit for the promissory notes of borrowers is known as *monetization of debt*. Notes are evidence of the borrowers' indebtedness to the bank. By exchanging these notes for its own promise to pay or by establishing a deposit account permitting the borrower to draw checks on it, the bank has increased the volume of money available for general use as a circulating medium. Monetization of government debt occurs in similar fashion when obligations of the public treasury are left with banks in exchange for creation of government deposits.

Banking development in the United States

Pre-revolutionary banks in America operated under charters granted by British or colonial authority. They were few in number and confined their operations largely to lending their own note issues. Deposit banking was slow to develop in pioneer regions, where people were poor and transportation and communication were difficult.

After the revolutionary war and the release of American colonies from British law, the need for a satisfactory means of payment became increasingly apparent, and banks were chartered under authority of state governments in Philadelphia, Boston, New York, and Baltimore in the years between 1781 and 1791.

Congress authorized the establishment of two federal institutions that operated with 20-year charters: the First Bank of the United States, from 1791 to 1811, and the Second Bank of the United States, from 1816 to 1836. Although both these banks maintained branches in various sections of the country, neither was a central bank in the sense that the term was applied to the Bank of England at that time or to the Federal Reserve banks in our country today. The two banks of the United States did not have a monopoly on the issuance of bank notes; neither of them held liquid assets as reserves for commercial banks; nor was it possible for individual banks to acquire funds from them for use in emergencies.

State banking in America spread rapidly after 1811. Many of the new institutions were the fly-by-night type or wildcat banks opened by unscrupulous promoters who flooded the country with worthless paper money backed by few or no assets of value. On the other hand, there were notable exceptions—banks that were founded on sound principles that later became integral parts of commercial banking law and practices. Among these was the Suffolk Bank of Boston (1819), which, by the use of an ingenious collection system, forced neighboring banks to redeem their notes in specie at face value. Another was the safety fund plan applied to certain banks organized in New York after 1829. Banks chartered under this statute contributed to a state-administered fund that was used to pay creditors (i.e., noteholders and depositors) of banks that failed. This was the earliest American forerunner of the plan of deposit insurance now in effect in this country under the administration of the Federal Deposit Insurance Corporation. A third outstanding attempt to attain higher standards of banking practice and greater safety for holders of bank notes was found in the free-banking plan adopted by New York in 1838. Provisions were made to grant charters to newly incorporated banks through a state board rather than by special action of the state legislature. The latter practice had resulted in graft and bribery that permitted unprincipled promoters to start banks that fleeced the general public. The free-banking law also made it necessary for a bank to deposit high-grade bonds with a state banking official in an amount equal to the total note issue of the bank. In the event of bank failure, the state official sold the bonds and distributed cash to reimburse the noteholders. Both aspects of this law were incorporated into national banking law in 1863.

In 1842 the state legislature of Louisiana enacted a sweeping reform of its banking law and included a requirement that each bank should maintain a cash reserve equal to one third of all its liabilities to the public. The other two thirds of its liabilities were to be represented on the asset side of the balance sheet by short-term commercial paper having maturities of 90 days or less. The specie-reserve principle of this act also became part of federal law in 1863.

Federal chartering of banks was reintroduced during the Civil War by passage of the National Bank Act (1863). This act, as amended, is still in effect. In contrast to its actions in connection with the First and Second Banks of the United States, the government, under the new legislation, did not subscribe to shares of stock or occupy a position as administrator of local bank operations. Although individual banks receive a charter and operate under the administration of a federal bureau (Office of the Comptroller of the Currency), national banks are privately owned institutions. They operate in all states of the Union alongside similar banks chartered and administered under laws and rulings formulated by state governments.

In 1913 the Federal Reserve System was established. This is the American version of a central bank. Unlike most foreign central banks, consisting of a parent and several branches, the Federal Reserve System is composed of 12 regional banks that have a measure of local autonomy under the general oversight of one Board of Governors. The 12 regional banks and their branches are owned by commercial bank members, including all national banks and those state banks that wish to belong to the system. Federal Reserve banks now have a monopoly on bank note issue and act as fiscal agents for the federal government. They hold liquid reserves for their member banks, act as agents in the clearing and collecting of checks drawn on commercial banks, provide funds for members by lending to them or purchasing assets from them, and have regulatory power with respect to extension of credit to business by member banks. (Chapter 7 is devoted to a detailed discussion of the Federal Reserve System.)

Commercial banking functions

The processes of present-day commercial banking that distinguish it from other types of banking are all illustrated in the operations of the 17th-century goldsmith. These include the acceptance of deposits for safekeeping and convenience in making payments by check; the granting of loans or advances of funds to meet the needs of individuals or business firms; and in this process the creation of net additions to the effective supply of money. Although a savings institution may accept deposits and make loans, the right to transfer funds through depositors' checks is held only by commercial banks.

"Department store" banking

Large metropolitan banks perform additional services that fit naturally into the operations of institutions dealing with the purchase and sale of credit instruments, the transfer of funds by check, and the administration of savings and trust funds. An examination of Exhibit 3–1, adapted from an early post–World War II advertisement of the Continental Illinois

EXHIBIT 3–1

Banking services

	Commercial Department	
Accepts deposits of coin, currency, checks, and other bankable items received over the counter or by mail		Grants lines of commercial credit
Cashes and certifies checks		Makes secured and unsecured loans
Collects checks payable at other Chicago banks		Maintains comprehensive credit and financial information
Collects—by messenger—drafts, notes, and other obligations payable in Chicago and suburbs	Performs all the duties of "correspondent" for banks—giving specialized deposit, safekeeping, credit, and other services	Buys and sells, for customers, securities of the United States Government and its instrumentalities, and securities of States, counties, cities, and other municipal bodies
Collects—through correspondent and Federal Reserve banks—checks, drafts, notes, coupons, bonds, and other securities payable anywhere outside the Chicago area	Arranges for the collection of money due on contracts, mortgages, warrants, and other obligations	Purchases commercial paper for customers
Issues cashier's checks and bank drafts		Places customers' orders, with brokers, for the purchase and sale of securities
Maintains records of all customer transactions and submits advices and statements covering the transactions	Maintains special facilities for accepting and supplying coin and currency	Acts as cashier for brokers
		Transfers funds by mail and telegraph anywhere in the United States
Arranges for the shipment, transfer of ownership, and exchange of denomination of securities, also for delivery of securities against payment, and a variety of other such services		

	Trust Department	
Acts as executor, or co-executor, of estates—seeing to the probate of the wills and the collection, conservation, and distribution of the assets		Performs—for corporations—all duties as trustee under indentures controlling bonds, notes, debentures, and equipment trust certificates
Performs all the services of trustee under will, managing and distributing the assets in accordance with the provisions of the will		Pays—as agent—maturing bonds and coupons for corporations and for governmental units and agencies
Acts as administrator, under court appointment—collecting, managing, and distributing the assets of estates		Performs—as transfer agent for corporations—all work incident to the transfer of stock from one owner to another
Serves as conservator of estates of incompetent persons and as guardian of estates of minors, managing the assets until distributed		Provides—as registrar—an independent control over the amount of corporate stock issued and transferred
Relieves individual administrators, executors, conservators, and guardians of detailed work, by providing various depositary arrangements		Relieves corporations of the work involved in paying dividends, by acting as dividend disbursing agent
Acts as trustee under agreements entered into by individuals for specific purposes—managing and distributing the assets in accordance with the trust agreements		Acts as depositary for securities in corporate reorganizations
Performs the duties of insurance trustee—under a special form of trust under agreement—when the proceeds of insurance policies comprise all or part of the assets of a trust		Relieves banks, corporations, associations, societies, and institutions of the details of caring for their securities, by acting as depositary for safekeeping or as agent, with or without investment assistance
Relieves individuals of the details of caring for their securities, by acting as depositary for safekeeping or as agent, with or without investment assistance		Serves corporations and other organizations as escrow agent, by holding property or documents in accordance with the terms of the escrow agreement
Serves individuals as escrow agent, by holding property or documents in accordance with the terms of the escrow agreement		Acts—for corporations—as trustee under agreements covering retirement and profit-sharing systems and other arrangements

National Bank and Trust Company of Chicago, clearly indicates that big city banks have long been a veritable department store of banking services. In the 1950s and 1960s, the range of services offered has continuously expanded, and this trend is expected to continue and accelerate. In recent years a large proportion of new services offered have been oriented around, and utilize, the computer capability of large banks. The following section of this chapter and the next two chapters are devoted primarily to operations of the commercial department and to the interrelationships of the departments that create of each bank a system. Later chapters will present more detailed views of other functions, such as savings and trust services.

The remainder of this chapter is designed to familiarize students with

EXHIBIT 3–1 (continued)

Banking services

the balance sheet of a commercial bank and in this way to develop the concepts of commercial banking from their basic beginnings.

Present-day operations: the bank balance sheet

The balance sheet of any banking corporation is a summary statement of the assets or resources of the bank and the claims of creditors against those assets.

In any solvent organization the assets are larger than the claims, and the difference is the amount owned by the stockholders. The difference is called net worth or owners' equity; the individual items make up the capital account considered in Chapter 4. Accountants place the assets and their value in a column at the left of the statement; opposite that list they show the bank's liabilities to its creditors. To the sum of this list of claims the accountant adds the owners' equity. Since the assets must equal the value of liabilities and owners' equity, the report is called a balance sheet. It is a statement of the condition of the bank on the date it is drawn up. Our purpose in this chapter is to show how several transactions affect the balance sheet of a commercial bank.[2]

Banking transactions

Sale of capital stock. The first transaction reflected on the balance sheet is the sale of capital stock at a premium, i.e., at a price above its par value. From this sale the bank acquires an asset in the form of cash in exchange for stock certificates indicating the ownership interest in the corporation by its shareholders. The premium is noted in bank records and will later appear in the published report as a paid-in surplus or capital surplus. Thus, if we assume distribution of 2,000 shares of stock of $100 par value sold at a premium of 20%, the balance sheet will show:

Assets		Liabilities	
Cash	$240,000	Common stock	$200,000
		Paid-in surplus	40,000

Increases and decreases in the value of assets and liabilities will from this point forward be indicated by plus (+) and minus (−) signs, respectively, placed to the left of the item that is affected. No attempt will be made at this time to cumulate the effect of individual transactions. That is, we are not at this point interested in building a statement on the foundation laid in the first transaction.

---

[2] Readers having no experience with bookkeeping or accounting will find Supplement A at the end of this chapter helpful in understanding the material presented in the pages that follow.

Purchase of stock in Federal Reserve bank. If the new institution is chartered as a national bank or is a state bank belonging to the Federal Reserve System, it must invest an amount equal to 3% of its capital and surplus in the purchase of Federal Reserve bank stock. On the basis of the data of the previous transaction the following changes would be noted:

+Federal Reserve bank stock	$7,200
−Cash	7,200

Purchase of bank building. The bank must acquire fixed assets by either purchase or lease. The dollar value of this entry is of little consequence to us; but, assuming $40,000 in cash is used to purchase a bank building and equipment, the statement change is:

+Building and equipment	$40,000
−Cash	40,000

Checks and collections. When the bank is ready to open its doors to the public, it will actively solicit new business. Local shareholders will immediately transfer deposits from other banks into their own institution. Other local individuals will open accounts by depositing their salary checks, and business firms will bring in daily receipts of checks and cash. Of the checks deposited, some will be drawn on banks outside the city and others on local institutions. For purposes of illustration they will all be shown as *items for collection.* It is assumed that a total of $540,000 is placed in checking accounts as demand deposits and $60,000 in savings or time deposits. These transactions are recorded as follows:

+Items for collection	$600,000	+Demand deposits	$540,000
		+Time deposits	60,000

Cash deposited. The bank will also receive cash deposits, especially from local tradesmen who receive coins and paper money in the operations of their retail stores. If cash deposits of $80,000 are received and credited to checking accounts, the following change occurs in the bank statement:

+Cash	$80,000	+Demand deposits	$80,000

Check collections and due from Federal Reserve. The *items in process of collection* are checks drawn on other banks; they are in the process of collection because the institution in which they are deposited sends them forward for collection from the drawee banks. As shown below, there are several routes by which they may be collected or cleared; but at this point it is assumed that all collections are made through the Federal Reserve System with instructions that the proceeds shall be left on deposit at the Federal Reserve bank of the district:

—Items in process of collection	$600,000
+Due from Federal Reserve bank	600,000

Commercial banks having membership in the Federal Reserve System are required to keep a reserve equal to a specified percentage against time and demand deposits. The reserve may be partially in vault cash but is maintained chiefly as a deposit in the district Federal Reserve bank.

Assuming that the legal minimum-reserve requirements were $16\frac{1}{2}\%$ of demand deposits and 4% for time or savings deposits, this bank would be forced to maintain a primary reserve of at least $104,700; of this, $2,400 would be reserve against time deposits and $102,300 against demand deposits. The bank at this point has $272,800 in cash and $600,000 on deposit at the Federal Reserve bank (resulting from the collection of checks); it has substantially more than the required minimum reserve. The amount of its liquid assets in excess of its legal requirement is called *excess* reserves.

Due from banks. For convenience in operations, most banks maintain deposit balances with a few big banks in large cities—their *city correspondents*. In Chapter 6 we shall consider the origin of the correspondent relationship and the part it plays in banking. For the moment, we shall simply assume that our bank establishes such an account by transferring $100,000 from its Federal Reserve balance to a *due from other banks* account:

—Due from Federal Reserve bank	$100,000
+Due from other banks	100,000

Transactions—credit operations

Loans to customers. Assume that a local merchant now wishes to purchase more inventory than he can buy with his cash resources or more than he can acquire on open account from his trade creditors. He may approach the new bank—to which he has already transferred his deposit account—and request a six-month loan of $20,000. When the loan officer of the bank has satisfied himself that the merchant can be expected to repay the loan at maturity with interest, the borrower will be asked to make out a promissory note to the bank, and the advance of funds will be made. Ordinarily, borrowed funds are not paid out immediately in the form of currency or other cash; rather, the borrower's demand deposit account is increased, and the borrower then writes checks against his account as funds are needed. The bank has acquired an earning asset by receiving the written promise of the merchant to pay the face value of the note, with interest, six months hence. This transaction is recorded and is reflected in the balance sheet of the bank in this form:

+Loans and discounts	$20,000	+Demand deposits	$20,000

Loan repaid. Six months later the merchant will repay his note at the bank by drawing a check for $20,600 on his deposit account in favor of the bank. The $20,000 is to repay the principal of the loan, and $600 is for interest at 6% for six months. In return the borrower receives his canceled promissory note to file in his own records. The bank has earned $600, which will be shown on its balance sheet as an addition to the stockholders' ownership interest. The transaction requires the following entries to maintain a balance in the bank statement:

−Loans and discounts	$20,000	−Demand deposits	$20,600
		+Undivided profits	600

Interest received on loans and investments is usually shown on published bank statements, after it has been earned, as *undivided profits*—that is, profits the disposition of which has not yet been decided upon. It may later be paid out as a cash dividend or retained and placed in an earned surplus account.

Loans on a discount basis. It will be noted that a bank does not make use of the term *notes receivable* when it obtains a promissory note from a borrower. Its loans are, for purposes of these illustrative transactions, however, assumed always to be made only upon receipt of such instruments.

Banks may lend on an interest or on a discount basis. The term *discount* when used in this sense means an advance to a borrower in which the interest charge is deducted at the time the transaction originates rather than when the note falls due. For example, if in transaction under loans to customers, above, the bank has discounted the note of the merchant, the entry on the original date (assuming that the discount rate is 6%) would have been:

+Loans and discounts	$20,000	+Demand deposits	$19,400
		+Interest collected but	
		unearned	600

Although the bank collected interest on the date the advance was granted to the borrower, the interest was not yet earned, and the undivided profit account was not built up at once. Periodically, a part of this interest is considered earned and is transferred to undivided profit. At the date of maturity of the loan, the $600 discount will all have been transferred from interest collected but unearned to undivided profits.

In this instance the borrower has the use of only $19,400 for six months; yet he pays $600 for its use. The actual rate of interest is somewhat higher than the nominal rate of 6% [($600 ÷ $19,400) × 2 = 6.18%].

Purchase of government bonds. Detailed statements of condition usually list as bank investments the bonds of the U.S. government, agencies of the United States, states, and municipalities. When the investment asset is purchased, the bank may use cash or pay for it from a deposit held in the Federal Reserve bank or a correspondent bank. Assuming that the first alternative is used in buying bonds worth $40,000, the statement change is:

+U.S. securities	$40,000		
−Cash	$40,000		

If a bank pays for bonds by writing a check or draft on its balance in a Federal Reserve bank, the transaction will be recorded as follows:

+U.S. securities	$40,000		
−Due from Federal Reserve bank	$40,000		

When interest is received on bonds owned by the bank, cash and earned surplus or undivided profit are increased:

+Cash	$1,000	+Undivided profits	$1,000

Miscellaneous transactions

Letters of credit. The foreign department of a commercial bank assists in the movement of merchandise between nations by substituting its credit for that of a merchant whose financial position is not known in foreign circles. This is accomplished when a bank issues a commercial letter of credit and accepts drafts drawn against itself under the terms stated in the letter. The transaction shows up on both sides of the published report of the bank. An asset item called "customer's liability account, letters of credit and acceptances" appears on the statement; the same amount is shown as a liability, "letters of credit and acceptances outstanding." The usual pattern for the transaction is as follows:

An American importer wanting to obtain foreign goods several weeks or months before paying for them may ask his bank to forward to the foreign exporter a commercial letter of credit authorizing the foreign shipper to draw a time draft on the American bank. The bank agrees to pay drafts drawn under circumstances clearly set forth in the letter. On the date of shipment the exporter will draw a time draft on the American bank, attaching the ocean bill of lading, consular invoice, insurance policy, and other documents necessary to get the cargo out of his nation and into a U.S. port. The draft will then be discounted or purchased by a bank in the exporter's country. The exporter has disposed of his goods and been paid. The foreign bank will then forward the time draft and attached documents to the American bank for acceptance and ultimate payment. Actual presentation for acceptance of the draft may be made by an American correspondent of the foreign bank. The American importer, on his part, has agreed to reimburse the local bank before the latter is required to pay the holder of the draft at maturity. By accepting the draft, the American bank has promised to meet the obligation and will insist that its domestic customer live up to his bargain by paying the bank on or before the date of maturity of the instrument. The transaction is reflected by the following entries on the published statement:

+Customer's liability for letters of credit and acceptances $18,000	+Letters of credit and acceptances outstanding $18,000

If the American importer's hopes are realized, he will have sold the foreign product in the time intervening between receipt of shipment and date of maturity of the draft. The bank, by permitting substitution of its well-known name, as drawee on the draft, for the name of its relatively unknown customer, has assisted in financing a short-term, self-liquidating commercial transaction. For its services the bank will collect from the local merchant a service charge of possibly one fourth of 1% of the face amount of the authorization in the letter of credit. If the item on the left side of the statement (customers' liability) shows a somewhat lower amount than the corresponding item on the right side (letters of credit, etc.), it is because some customers may have taken up their obligations at the bank a day or two ahead of the date on which the acceptances were paid by the bank.

Payment of outside checks. When a depositor draws checks against his commercial account and forwards them to payees outside his immediate locality, the local bank loses funds when the checks are presented to it for payment. Checks are usually routed back to the drawee bank through the district Federal Reserve bank. Since the Reserve bank acts as a depository for commercial banks, it is a simple bookkeeping operation for it to collect the funds to pay checks by reducing the drawee bank's balance and transferring funds to the credit of payee banks in its own or other Federal Reserve districts. The transaction will be shown on the drawee bank's balance sheet as a reduction in demand deposits and a corresponding decrease in the asset item *due from Federal Reserve bank*. If $130,000 in checks is drawn and sent back for collection, the changes are recorded in this manner:

—Due from Federal Reserve bank	$130,000	—Demand deposits	$130,000

Borrowing by the bank. Commercial banks are sometimes forced to borrow. They may get advances that will permit them to grant more loans, or they may borrow to replenish dwindling reserves. The source of their funds may be other commercial banks or the district Federal Reserve bank. In either case, the funds will probably be used to increase the borrowing bank's deposit in the Federal Reserve bank and will be offset in the bank's statement by an increase in notes payable or rediscounts. A $50,000 transaction of this nature would change the statement as shown below:

+Due from Federal Reserve bank	$50,000	+Bills payable and rediscounts	$50,000

Minor services. The list of operations noted in connection with department store banking is evidence that many other transactions might be examined and their effect upon the balance sheet explained. Among these would be certifying a personal check by either drawer or payee to assure the recipient that funds available for encashment are on deposit in the drawee bank; issuing a cashier's check by a bank officer in exchange for a check drawn by an individual on his own balance; and crediting a depositor's account for interest received on bonds when the bank has forwarded the coupon to the issuer for collection. These and other transactions are commonplace practices of commercial banks but are subordinate to the more significant functions of accepting deposits and making loans and investments.

Capital account. After a period of successful operation the income received in the form of service charges on deposits, fees, and interest on loans and investments is carried from temporary accounts into *undivided profits* or *retained earnings* and shown on the balance sheet. These items are part of the bank's capital account; they represent the ownership interest of holders of bank shares. During periods when bank earnings are regular and adequate in size, the board of directors of the bank votes a cash dividend. After being voted but before being paid, dividends declared appear as a liability on the statement under the caption *dividend declared*. An entirely different type of account is set up as a *reserve for taxes,* which represents funds needed later to discharge the property and income tax obligations of the banking corporation.

Now that the reader has an understanding of the usual items contained in the statement of condition or balance sheet of a commercial bank, he may wish to examine the accompanying statement (see Exhibit 3–2, pp. 58–59) of a large metropolitan institution, the Northern Trust Company of Chicago.

Supplement A

The accounting equation

Although the nature of the operations of any business may be explained in words common to all forms of descriptive writing, a more effective approach utilizes the specialized terms of the accountant. Accounting provides a record of business transactions in financial terms. It makes use of a careful and systematic recording of all assets and liabilities and of the changes that take place in the volume and value of each.

Large business units require a complex system of record keeping and accounting; but no less significant is the simple set of books, or even the vest-pocket notes, kept by almost every individual, whether business proprietor or merely an employee.

Each of us has the ever-recurring desire to know just where we stand financially. We make a list of our assets, including items of value we now possess plus whatever is owed to us by others. But from total value thus obtained we deduct the sum of our debts to others. The resulting figure shows our net worth or the excess value of assets over liabilities.

To illustrate: Assume that a grade-school boy asks his father: "Daddy, just what are we worth?" The parent may begin to make a list of valuable items, at the top of which he places *residence* valued at $30,000 but with only $20,000 paid, the balance due on a mortgage note. Then he lists *household goods,* all clear of debt, $5,400. Next the new *automobile,* cost $4,100 but with six monthly installments of $120 each remaining to be paid. The father lists his *deposit* in the local bank, $380; an *insurance* policy having a cash surrender value of $1,950; 25 shares of *corporate stock* quoted at $54 per share, and some *government saving bonds* now worth $2,840. He estimates personal property in the form of family clothing, watches, jewelry, silverware, canned and frozen foods, and a few miscellaneous items as worth $1,400. A business acquaintance owes him $100. But he owes the public service company, the drugstore, two department stores, and a local hardware dealer a total of $170.

For convenience the assets are grouped together, and their total value is recorded. Liabilities or debts are grouped separately, and their value is summarized. The resulting two columns appear in the form shown in Table 3–1. It is apparent that the real worth of this family is the difference between $47,520 and $10,890, or $36,630.

An accountant, or a bookkeeper, would insert an item called *Owners' equity*, $36,630, below the accounts payable figure on the liability side of the statement, so that the two sides of the account would equalize. Such a report of assets and liabilities would then be called a balance sheet.

EXHIBIT 3–2

The Northern Trust Company* (*statement of condition, December 31, 1969*)

Assets

CASH AND DUE FROM BANKS . . . .$ 399,996,842 This represents cash held in our vaults, on deposit as our reserve at the Federal Reserve bank, or due to us from corres- pondent banks and checks in the process of being collected.	
U.S. GOVERNMENT SECURITIES[†] . . . . . 213,548,068 This amount is invested in obligations of the U.S. Government, such as bonds, notes, certificates and treasury bills.	
OTHER BONDS AND SECURITIES . . . . . . 199,625,714 This amount is invested in state, municipal and other high-grade bonds.	
LOANS AND DISCOUNTS[‡] . . . . 1,167,062,680 This is the amount loaned to customers.	
DIRECT LEASE FINANCING. . . . . 8,896,272 Equipment purchased by the bank and leased to customers.	
BANK PREMISES AND EQUIPMENT . . . . . 39,974,733 This represents the book value of real estate, the main bank building used in carrying on our business and equipment	
CUSTOMERS' ACCEPTANCE LIABILITY . . . 1,488,282 This is our customers' liability for drafts accepted, the payment of which is guaranteed by the bank.	
OTHER ASSETS. . . . . 19,114,267 This represents miscellaneous items, not appropriately classified above.	
TOTAL. 2,049,706,858	

* Member Federal Deposit Insurance Corporation.

† U.S. government obligations and other securities carried at $128,970,073 are pledged to secure public and trust deposits and for other purposes as required or permitted by law.

‡ Reserves for possible losses are maintained in the amount of $23,117,824.

Financial institutions

The fundamental balance sheet equation is: *Assets = Liabilities + Owners' equity* or *proprietorship*. It shows the equality of balance between property and rights to property and the claims of creditors against the property. It may be stated in the account form shown in Table 3–1 or in report form in which liabilities are subtracted from assets to give the residual owners' equity. Any item may be transposed,

EXHIBIT 3–2 *(continued)*

Liabilities

DEPOSITS: Demand . . . . 802,828,638 Savings . . . . 448,005,956 Other Time . . . . . . 185,238,360 Foreign Offices 305,374,719	$ 1,741,447,673
PURCHASED FUNDS . . . . Represents short-term utilization of funds not classified as deposits.	127,125,000
LIABILITIES OR ACCEPTANCES . . . . Represents the bank's liability on its guaranty of the payment of foreign or domestic drafts drawn on behalf of our customers.	1,488,282
ACCRUED TAXES AND OTHER EXPENSES . . This is the amount set aside for accrued taxes, interest, and other expenses.	30,622,933
OTHER LIABILITIES . . . . This amount represents miscellaneous items not classified above.	6,484,802
DIVIDEND DECLARED . . . . Represents dividend declared but not yet paid to stockholders.	1,300,000
CAPITAL STOCK . . . . The bank is owned by 3,223 stockholders, who hold the 2 million shares of its common stock with a par value of $20 per share.	40,000,000
SURPLUS . . . . This is the amount allocated by the directors as a surplus fund, originating in part from contributions by stockholders and in part by transfers from Undivided Profits or Reserves.	60,000,000
UNDIVIDED PROFITS . . . . This amount represents accumulated earn- ings belonging to the stockholders but not yet distributed as dividends or transferred to surplus or reserves.	22,797,791
RESERVE FOR CONTINGENCIES . . . . This amount is a part of the equity capital of the bank and has been set aside to cover extraordinary contingencies.	18,440,377
TOTAL	2,049,706,858

as in any algebraic equation; for example, *Assets − Liabilities = Owners' equity.*

The reader will recognize that a balance sheet presents the condition of a business as of a given moment in its history. But the condition of the institution changes from moment to moment as business is carried on. The first summary soon will not reflect the current condition, and a second summary statement will be required to give a true picture of the new position. The second summary could be obtained in the same manner as the first—by listing and evaluating all possessions, debts, and the owner's claims. This is a costly process in practice, and not too satisfactory in theory. A better way to keep a reasonable record of the changing condition of the firm is to record transactions as they occur.

TABLE 3-1

Assets		Liabilities	
Residence	$30,000	Mortgage note payable	$10,000
Household goods	5,400	Due on car	720
Automobile	4,100	Accounts payable (total)	170
Bank deposit	380	Total Liabilities	$10,890
Insurance policy	1,950	Owners' equity	$36,630
Corporation stock	1,350		
Savings bonds	2,840		
Personal property	1,400		
Notes receivable	100		
Total Assets	$47,520	Total	$47,520

Each individual or business firm must select a method, or establish a system, for recording transactions. The details of the method selected are of no significance here, but we do wish to demonstrate a simple and convenient method to show how each transaction finds reflection in balance sheet changes. In an arithmetic illustration, the data growing out of each transaction are shown on what is called an accounting T-form. The T-account represents the business concern's assets and liabilities.

Value of things owned (*Assets*)	Value of things owed (*Liabilities*) Net ownership interest (Owners' equity)

The possessions of the firm are recorded on the left side of the T account, and the debts and owners' claim are recorded at the right. In a commercial bank the principal classes of items for which values will be found are indicated below:

	(Owns)	**Bank**	(Owes)	
Cash on hand	$1,000	Deposits		$5,200
Loans	2,000	Owners' claim or net worth		1,325
Investments	3,000			
Building	500			
Miscellaneous	25			
	$6,525			$6,525

As daily operations are performed, the values recorded above change. Some transactions have no effect on the totals because they represent an exchange of one asset for another or of one liability for another (transactions 1 and 2, below, are of this type). In other cases, the aggregate figures are increased or reduced. Additions are indicated with a plus sign (+) and substractions by a minus sign (−). Examples follow:

1. The bank spends cash to acquire equipment such as filing cases:

+Equipment	
−Cash	

2. A depositor purchases stock in the bank and pays for it by writing a check on the bank. The depositor reduces his claim as a creditor and transfers it into a claim of ownership.

	+Capital
	−Deposits

3. A customer brings currency to the bank for deposit.

+Cash	+Deposits

4. Stockholders are paid a cash dividend out of earnings that have accumulated in the bank. This reduces the amount of claims of owners against the bank.

−Cash	− Owners' claim

Since the two sides of the balance sheet must be equal, it can be observed that only four general types of transaction occur. They balance out in the manner shown in Table 3–2.

TABLE 3–2

Assets	*Liabilities and owners' equity*
Plus	Plus
Minus	Minus
Net plus or minus	Net plus or minus

By keeping an accurate record of daily transactions as they occur, it becomes a relatively simple matter to add or subtract values from the proper accounts to arrive at a current statement of assets, liabilities, and net worth.

Questions and problems

1. What information may be found in a bank statement that shows the quality of the assets? What supplementary information would be welcomed by a bank's depositors?

2. Does a "solvent" bank necessarily need to be a "liquid" bank? Explain.

3. Do you believe potential bank organizers should be required to show a need for an additional banking facility to be given a charter to start a new bank?

4. Under what conditions may bank earnings increase in the face of an increase in the rate of interest paid on time and savings deposits?

5. Compute the effective rate of interest paid by a borrower who has his $1,000 six-month note discounted at 5% by a bank that forces him to maintain an average deposit balance of 20% of the face value of his note.

6. If a bank sells a $1,000 government bond that it had purchased at par for $120 less than par, how is the transaction recorded on T accounts?

7. How would a bank statement be changed if a commercial bank rediscounted customers' notes at a Reserve bank and took the proceeds in Federal Reserve notes? (Disregard discount cost.)

8. What has your local banker to say about the advantages and disadvantages of operating under a state charter rather than a national charter?

9. Explain this statement: "From the point of view of an individual bank, an increase in deposits supports an expansion of loans and investments. From the standpoint of the country as a whole, bank deposits expand primarily because loans and investments expand."

10. Does the fact that a bank has an excess of reserves necessarily mean that its loans will increase?

Bibliography

(Bibliography at end of Chapter 5.)

CHAPTER 4

Sources and uses of commercial bank funds

Chapter 3 provided a discussion of the origin and development of commercial banking, and through the use of a balance sheet approach, introduced the reader to the present-day type of operations in which commercial banks engage. The present chapter extends the discussion of operations by considering bank sources and uses of funds in greater detail.

Sources of commercial bank funds

Funds available for the use of a bank in performing its lending and investing functions are acquired from three sources: from depositors and other creditors, from the sales of capital stock and notes, and from retention of earnings.

Deposits

Banks accept deposits from individuals or business concerns that deposit their receipts periodically. These may be left partly for safekeeping and partly for the convenience of writing checks to make purchases or settle debts.

In addition, however, a bank may *create* deposits by granting loans to borrowers, who leave the proceeds of the loan as a deposit in the bank. The original or *primary* deposit of currency or checks drawn on other banks, plus the bank's capital, provide a basis on which the bank may grant loans and create *derivative* deposits.

Both the primary and the derivative deposits are subject to immediate withdrawal and, as checked out, cause the credit of the drawee bank to circulate in an endless round as it performs its functions of making payments and settling debts. It is estimated that over 90% of total money transactions were settled by checks drawn against the $178 billion of individuals, partnerships, and corporate demand deposits held by insured commercial banks in the year 1969. Thus deposits lie at the center of both the operation of the individual commercial bank and the functioning of the monetary and banking system as a whole.

Once the process of lending is started and deposits are created, it becomes impossible to distinguish primary from derivative deposits. All deposits are then considered a source of funds to the bank. The unadjusted total of insured commercial bank demand deposits as of December 31, 1969, was $240 billion. If time and savings deposits (not subject to withdrawal by checks to a third party) are included, gross deposits were $437 billion.

Definition and classification of deposits. Deposits held in commercial banks may be classified on any of several bases, depending on the purpose to be served by the classification. The primary purpose of classification is to break the aggregate figure into useful components. Perhaps the deposit figure for the nation as a whole, or for a group of banks of similar size or location, may be of great significance for the student of banking and monetary theory, but a breakdown of the deposits of an individual bank is of significance to those who manage that bank's operations. In any event, the two bases of classification commonly used are (1) term to maturity and (2) type of depositor. The former separates deposits into those payable at once (demand deposits) and those whose withdrawal may be delayed (time deposits). A breakdown by type of depositor merely indicates ownership of the deposits; that is, individual, business, bank, or government.

Demand deposits. Defined by the Board of Governors of the Federal Reserve System as deposits payable in less than 30 days from the date of the withdrawal notice, demand deposits are, in practice, payable on demand when requested in person at the bank or by the issuance of a request for payment with a check. This official definition is important, however, because of the federal prohibition of the payment of interest on demand deposits. Because of the inability of banks to make interest payments for these deposits, bank customers have little incentive to increase their holdings of demand deposits. Thus banks have had to turn to alternative sources to attract funds. In the 11-year period from the end of 1958 to the end of 1969, demand deposits of all insured commercial banks increased only about 65% from $151 billion to $240 billion, substantially slower than the approximately 110% growth of total assets of all insured banks during the same period.

Condition reports which banks are required to submit to the federal bank supervisory authorities subdivide demand deposit accounts on the basis of ownership. This breakdown shows demand deposits of individuals, partnerships, and corporations; certified and officers' checks, letters of credit, traveler's checks, and so on; U.S. government; state and political subdivisions; domestic interbank; and foreign government, central banks, and foreign banks.

The largest category, and the one most closely related to business activity, is individual and business deposits. At year-end 1969, these deposits totaled $178 billion. As would be expected, a time series of the total of this account has a cyclical pattern that fluctuates around the trend line representing the growth of the banking system as a whole. For example, demand deposits of individuals, partnerships, and corporations approximated $85 billion in 1947 and $111 billion in 1956. During the recession of 1958, this class of deposits was reduced to $102 billion. The cyclical decline was substantial, but the general trend was upward. Growth of the banking system and an increased liquidity of the economy brought the 1969 total above $178 billion.

The amount of demand deposits in the personal and business subdivision ranges normally from 70% to 80% of all demand deposits. This is true of country banks as well as of banks in metropolitan areas. In the former, the relative absence of deposits in other classifications, such as foreign governments and central banks, domestic interbank and governmental deposits, as well as certified checks, keeps the percentage of personal and business deposits on a par with large city banks, where industrial and commercial deposits are highly concentrated.

The second largest subdivision is that of domestic interbank demand deposits. At the end of 1969, there were $25.9 billion in such accounts. These balances are highly concentrated in large city banks and are an integral part of the American plan of correspondent banking. This concentration results from the need of outlying banks to maintain large deposit accounts in banks located in money market centers in order to clear checks and to pay for services the large banks provide.

The third largest category of demand deposits is that of state governments and political subdivisions. On December 31, 1969, state and other political units were credited with over $17.6 billion of demand deposits in commercial banks. Thus deposits of state and local tax units were approximately 10% as large as personal and business deposits.

The fourth largest category at year-end 1969, which accounted for $11.5 billion in deposits, was certified and officers' checks, letters of credit, and traveler's checks. These accounts arise because of the need to have checks of unquestioned credit standing available to make payment.

U.S. government deposits were the fifth category by size with $5 billion in deposits. The dollar volume of federal government deposits in the banking system was, therefore, less then 30% as large as the state and other political subdivision accounts. The size of federal deposits is, however, much more volatile than deposits of states and political subdivisions because federal deposit balances are closely tied to the issuance and retirement of government obligations, tax collections, and government expenditures. For example, in the six months between December 29, 1962, and June 29, 1963, federal government demand deposits in all commercial banks increased from $6.8 billion to $11 billion but by December 20, 1963, had declined to less than $7 billion. On June 30, 1964, they totaled $10.2 billion and declined to $6.5 billion by December 31, 1964.

The smallest of the six categories enumerated is deposits of foreign governments, central banks, and foreign banks. These depositors had balances of $3.4 billion at the end of 1969, and it is interesting to note that more than two thirds of these deposits were held by foreign banks. The deposits of foreign banks are held largely in the money-market center banks in Chicago and New York, for reasons similar to those that account for the concentrated holdings of domestic and interbank deposits. Foreign government and central bank deposits are also held at the Federal Reserve.

Since demand deposits constitute a heterogeneous series, including such diverse elements as deposits of individuals, business firms, governmental units, and banks, it is easily seen that the aggregate may be of little significance to bank managers. It is unsafe to assume that growth in one subdivision always occurs at the expense of another. Two or more types, or even all forms of deposits, may increase or decrease together, but individual rates of change may vary.

Bank officers carefully analyze deposit movement with regard to size and timing because the bank must remain sufficiently liquid to meet demand obligations. Deposit accounts that move rapidly with little or no warning place a greater burden on bank management in maintaining solvency than do stable deposits.

The velocity of demand deposits, or the number of times during a given period that the average deposit dollar is used, may be an indicator of the condition of business. Turnover of deposits reflects the rate of the owners' spending, whether the owner be an individual, a business concern, or a governmental unit. As velocity increases, business activity and commodity prices tend to rise. This movement may release other expansive forces in the economy and may act as a barometer, or at least a rough indicator of the change in general business conditions. Conversely, a decline in the rate of deposit turnover acts as a depressing influence on business activity and prices.

Time and savings deposits. Time and savings deposits, as the name suggests, are liabilities that commercial banks are not legally required to pay on demand. Of the $197 billion of such deposits held at the end of 1969, individuals, partnerships, and corporations held $176.2 billion; governments, virtually all state and local governments, held $13.5 billion; foreign governments and banks held $6.7 billion; and domestic banks held less than a half billion. Of course the major motive for holding deposits in this form is the interest that banks pay for such deposits. The maximum payment that banks can make, however, is determined by the Federal Reserve through its Regulation Q.

Regulation Q distinguishes three categories of time and savings deposits; first, funds which are placed with the bank for a period, and withdrawal is at the discretion of the depositor. Banks may require a 30-day notice of withdrawal before relinquishing such funds, but ordinarily they waive their legal right and pay out such deposits on demand. A withdrawal is permitted the owner when he presents himself with his passbook at the bank or mails the passbook to the bank and receives funds through the mail. The depositor cannot transfer these funds by writing a check. At the present time (1970), $4\frac{1}{2}\%$ per annum is the maximum rate banks are permitted to pay on such deposits.

A second class is termed multiple-maturity deposits. This includes funds the depositor agrees to leave in the bank for some period longer than 90 days. On such deposits, the bank can presently pay up to a maximum of 5% for up to one-year maturity, $5\frac{1}{2}\%$ for maturities longer than one year but less than two years, and $5\frac{3}{4}\%$ for maturities longer than two years.

A third class combines size of deposits and a fixed maturity date. The purpose of this distinction is to allow banks to compete for funds which could easily be invested in other money market securities. Thus, at the time this is written, banks are not limited for deposits over $100,000 if the maturity date is less than 90 days in the future; they are permitted to pay up to $6\frac{3}{4}\%$ for maturities between 90 and 179 days, 7% for such funds left on deposit 180 days to a year, and $7\frac{1}{2}\%$ for funds left longer than a year.

The latter two categories of deposits are usually evidenced by a certificate with a maturity date rather than by the traditional savings passbook, and for the larger denominations of such deposits, a secondary market has developed. Thus, if a depositor desires to liquidate his deposit, he is able to sell his certificate just as he could an investment in treasury bills or commercial paper.

The development of a secondary market for large-size certificates of deposit in the late 1950s substantially increased the ability of commercial banks, especially large money-market banks, to attract this type of deposit. Outstanding certificates grew from just over $1 billion at the end of 1960 to $6.2 billion by December 1962.[1] In December 1968, such deposits reached a peak of $24.3 billion. But in 1969, as interest rates on other money-market instruments rose above the $6\frac{1}{4}\%$ ceiling then current under Regulation Q, these instruments became noncompetitive and outstanding amounts began a rapid decline. Banks that had relied on sales of certificates for funds found themselves in the awkward position of having to redeem these deposits during a period of very heavy loan demand. More will be said of this development in a later chapter.

Borrowings

Funds for bank operations may be borrowed from other commercial banks or from the Federal Reserve. There is a tradition that banks should be lenders rather than borrowers; hence, such borrowings made by banks are usually of short duration. But sometimes forces beyond the control of commercial banks produce deficiencies in required reserves, or an expansion in business brings demands for loans which cannot be met without short-term additions to operating funds.

To cover a temporary deficiency in reserves, banks can borrow either in the federal funds market or directly from the Federal Reserve. If they are not members of the Federal Reserve, they can borrow from their correspondent bank. To meet longer term needs to finance cyclical operations of commerce and industry, banks normally sell investment securities. In recent years they have issued unsecured notes for sale in the open markets or purchased funds in the Eurodollar market. Details of these transactions will be discussed in subsequent chapters.

Capital funds

Capital funds are the contribution made by the owners through the purchase of shares of the bank and the reinvestment of earnings in the institution. They may properly be regarded as the most basic source of funds whose principal function is to provide a buffer of safety to depositors and other creditors. An indication that capital stock is considered the basic and permanent source of a bank's operating funds is found in state and federal laws providing that any impairment of capital funds shall be stated in terms of (a percentage of) capital stock and surplus. These funds serve not only to absorb losses from shrinking value of assets in

---

[1] "Negotiable Time Certificates of Deposit," *Federal Reserve Bulletin*, April 1963, p. 458.

times of depression but also to augment the confidence of depositors and act as a basis for extension of credit in good times.

Capital stock. The initial capital for commercial bank operations is acquired by the sale of capital stock. Federal and state laws stipulate the minimum amount of stock required of a newly organized bank. For example, banks chartered under federal statutes may organize with capital stock of only $50,000 if 6,000 or fewer inhabitants reside in the town or area to be served by the bank. In towns having between 6,000 and 50,000 residents, the minimum capital is $100,000; in cities with a population of over 50,000, capital of at least $200,000 is required. Many states require the same minimum amounts, although a few permit banks to organize in rural areas with a capital subscription of no more than $25,000.[2] Many states also follow the National Bank Act in requiring that stock be sold at a 20% premium above par. The premium provides funds for absorbing some of the initial costs of organization and also creates a feeling of confidence in the strength of the new institution.

As a bank grows, it may attract new capital by the sale of additional shares of stock, or an increase in capital stock may result from the declaration of a stock dividend. The latter is merely a transfer of earned surplus into the stock account. Such a dividend is a bookkeeping transaction that has no effect on the bank's assets or the earning power of the institution. The transfer of surplus into stock may, however, permit a bank to lend greater amounts to a single borrower.

Normally, capital stock is one of the most permanent and fixed items in a bank's statement. Changes in the amount of capital stock require the consent of banking authorities and an affirmative vote of a large majority of shareholders. Growth in capital funds is therefore most noticeable in an expansion of the volume of earnings retained in other capital accounts.

Prior to the severe banking crisis of 1933, banks issued only common stock. But in the emergency then existing, federal and state laws were modified to permit—even to require—the sale of preferred shares, capital notes, or debentures. These were sold principally to the Reconstruction Finance Corporation and saved hundreds of banks whose capital had been impaired. The preferential shares or debentures were retired rapidly as bank earning power was restored after the crisis.

In 1962, the Comptroller of the Currency issued a ruling permitting national banks to issue convertible and nonconvertible capital debentures. At the end of 1969, commercial banks had almost $2 billion of such securities outstanding.[3]

---

[2] As a matter of practice, bank supervisory authorities place great emphasis upon a strong capital position and oftentimes insist on a minimum subscription of stock far above the legal minimum.

[3] Federal Deposit Insurance Corporation, *Annual Report* (1969), p. 266.

Surplus

As noted above, the law under which a bank operates may force the creation of a surplus through the sale of stock at a premium, i.e., at a price above par value. It may also limit dividends until surplus is equal to capital stock. However, most mature banks have built surplus far above these minimal amounts. An example is that of the Northern Trust Company, whose statement appears in Chapter 3 (Exhibit 3-2).

Data published by the Federal Deposit Insurance Corporation (FDIC) show that 13,462 insured commercial banks had equity or owners' capital of $37.6 billion as of December 31, 1969. Of this total, $10.5 billion was classified as common stock, $0.1 billion as preferred stock, and $17.5 billion as surplus. The remaining $9.5 billion consisted of undivided profits and reserves. Thus, capital stock amounted to only 74% of surplus and less than 34% of all capital funds.[4]

Undivided profits and capital account reserves

It is typical accounting practice for banks to establish a transitory capital account into which net profits of each accounting period are credited. In contrast to the common stock and surplus accounts, which may remain at a fixed level for years, the undivided profits account varies widely from period to period. It grows as earnings are realized; it shrinks when cash dividends are declared, when portions are transferred to surplus, when asset values are written down, and when expenses are incurred in the issuance of new stock. On December 31, 1969, the undivided profits account of all insured banks was $8.4 billion or approximately 20% of all capital funds and 47% of surplus.

Capital account net worth reserves are so small as a percentage of capital funds that they often are not reported separately on published bank statements. If they do appear, however, they are usually under the caption *reserve for contingencies*. These reserves represent a portion of surplus that has not been designated for use in any specific manner; they are set up in a flexible account, whose size will be adjusted as unusual or unexpected expenses are incurred. The report of all insured commercial banks in December 1969 shows $1.1 billion in such reserve accounts; this was approximately 3% of all capital funds.

Valuation reserves. A form of capital funds seldom carried on a bank balance sheet under the title of capital account is *valuation reserves.* Following a ruling in 1947 by the Bureau of Internal Revenue, banks be-

---

[4] Federal Deposit Insurance Corporation, *Annual Report* (1969). The FDIC was established at the time of the banking crisis of 1933 to provide insurance against loss for bank depositors. It publishes quarterly reports of the condition of insured banks. Its operations will be discussed in Chapter 6.

came free from federal income taxation on that portion of earnings that is transferred to a valuation reserve. This type of reserve is set up as a deduction from gross loans; its purpose is to cover anticipated losses on loans that are expected to become uncollectible. The reserve may appear on official statements of the bank as deductions from gross loans or may be shown in a footnote to the statement.

On December 31, 1969, valuation reserves of all insured commercial banks amounted to approximately $5.9 billion, or 14% of the amount commonly classified as owners' capital; they amounted to 2.1% of gross loans outstanding. Valuation reserves are also established to meet possible losses on securities owned by banks. These reserves totaled $184 million at the end of 1969.

Total owners' capital in insured commercial banks as reported by the FDIC at the end of 1969 was slightly greater than 7% of bank assets. This means that for every dollar controlled by commercial banks only 7 cents was contributed by stockholders through stock purchase and retention of earnings.

Uses of bank funds

Although commercial banks are service institutions that are chartered only if they are expected to fulfill the financial needs of their communities, the individual institution is organized to provide an income to its shareholders. This income is derived principally from interest received on investments, on direct loans to business concerns, and on profits from security transactions. If every available penny were put to work, profits would be maximized; but we must remember that many depositors have left funds with the bank on a temporary basis and without notice may either request cash or order the bank to transfer cash to some one else by check. Also, one of the most important activities of banks is to make loans to their customers. Banks must, therefore, be prepared to meet such loan demands. If all its resources were invested, a bank would be unable to meet these demands for cash. Hence it must have some cash or ready access to cash.

Loans and investments

A major class of bank assets is that portion of total resources representing credit advanced for personal or business uses in the form of loans. Although such advances are usually made to the depositing customers of a bank, a few loans are made to business corporations through purchase of short-term commercial paper (promissory notes) in the open market.

Earning assets not included in the secondary reserve are often termed the *investment account*. As would be supposed, they consist mainly of long-term bonds of the federal or local governments, railroads, public utilities, industrial companies, and some long-term loans made to finance real estate transactions. Federal Reserve bank stock owned by members of the Federal Reserve System is also included, for it must be held as long as the bank retains membership in the system.

Primary reserves

A reserve of cash or its equivalent is regarded by the bank as insurance of its liquidity. Moreover, banking statutes of state and federal governments require the maintenance of minimum reserves against deposits. These reserves are nonearning assets held either in the form of cash in a bank's own vault or as deposits in other banks. Banks that belong to the Federal Reserve System maintain their reserves chiefly as deposit balances in the Federal Reserve; nonmember banks hold the bulk of their reserves as deposits in other commercial banks known as correspondents.

Several factors influence a bank to increase or decrease the proportion of deposits maintained as a liquid reserve. For example, if demand deposits are converted into time or savings accounts, demand obligations will decline, and a smaller liquid reserve will be needed. If time deposits or savings accounts are converted to demand deposits, the reverse is true. If a larger number of its customers have seasonal needs for cash, the bank must increase its reserves shortly before these demands occur. If the institution has a few large depositors whose accounts vary erratically, the bank will be forced to maintain larger reserves than if it has many depositors whose deposits and withdrawals offset each other or whose withdrawals can be quite accurately anticipated. Two other factors are significant. One is the liquidity of the bank's loans and investments, that is, the ease or rapidity with which its earning assets can be converted into cash or reserve balances in other banks. If a large portion of noncash assets can be converted speedily with little or no shrinkage in value, the bank can safely maintain a relatively small liquid reserve. The other factor relates to the organization of the banking system. If there is a central bank in which commercial bank reserves are mobilized, the central bank may advance funds to needy members by making direct loans or rediscounting commercial paper presented by the members. If a central bank performs a clearing and collection service, as described in Chapter 6, such a service enables commercial banks to operate with lower reserves than would otherwise be possible.

From time to time it is noted that reserves tend to rise or fall proportionately for the system as a whole. This is not a result of localized or isolated bank policy. It is due to widespread developments, such as a general increase or decrease in lending activity, changes in the confidence of depositors in the banking system, or perhaps changes in rulings or statutes governing bank policy and operation. Examples of these variations are not difficult to find: On December 31, 1935, cash and reserves of insured commercial banks were 27% of total bank assets; in 1940 they were 37%; in 1950 they had fallen to 21.4%; and on December 31, 1961, they were 19%.[5]

Some degree of conscious control over reserves is maintained by the local bank management. The foregoing paragraphs have indicated that an increase in reserves will result from the sale of assets and from borrowing or rediscounting at a central bank. In addition, a commercial bank may request customers to pay up their loans at once and in this way add to its reserves. But there are times, as we shall see later, when a commercial bank's control over its reserve position is considerably reduced by the actions of central banks and the Treasury.

Reserve provisions, 1917–68. In the years between 1913 and 1936, the Federal Reserve Act required that legal minimum reserves against time and demand deposits of member banks should be held as deposits in Federal Reserve banks. For purposes of computing reserves, member banks were classified as central reserve city banks, reserve city banks, and country banks. Central reserve city banks included only large banks in New York and Chicago and required reserves were 13% of net demand deposits. About 50 cities were classified as reserve cities with the banks in these cities being required to hold a reserve of 10%. All banks not otherwise classified were country banks, whose reserve requirement was 7%. The reserve required on time deposits was 3% for banks of all classes. These percentages became fixed in 1917, soon after the entrance of the United States in World War I.

In the critical years of the early 1930s the Board of Governors of the Federal Reserve System was given power to adjust required reserve percentages within a range from their then existing level to double that amount. This power remains today as a permanent device for controlling member bank reserves. Changes in requirements may be applied to one or both classes of deposits at the same time but must be uniform for all banks within a class.

In 1959, provisions were made for the elimination of the central reserve city classification and for the use of vault cash as part of legally required reserves. The latter provision became effective on November 24, 1960, and the former on July 28, 1962. On the two categories of banks that now remain, reserve requirements may be varied, at the discretion of the Board of Governors, between 10% and 22% for demand deposits of reserve city banks and from 7% to 14% for country banks. On time deposits the statutory range for all banks is from 3% to 10%. On December

---

[5] Federal Deposit Insurance Corporation, *Annual Report*, 1935, 1940, 1950, 1960, and 1969.

31, 1969, there were 182 banks in the reserve city classification; the remaining 5,796 were country banks.

As of December 31, 1969, the required level of reserves was 16½% on demand deposits on reserve city banks, 12% for country banks, and 3% on all time deposits regardless of where located.

In the Federal Reserve System's experience, changes in reserve percentages have been used in meeting bank reserve situations that the system believed had more than temporary significance. For example, in the 1930s the system increased reserve requirements to absorb what it considered to be an unnecessarily large volume of excess reserves that it believed posed a threat of inflation. In the early post-World War II years, percentages were increased to the legal limits in order to absorb member bank reserves that the Federal Reserve had supplied by supporting prices of government securities. The reduction of reserves on time deposits— from 5% to 4%—in October 1962 was the only change made in eight years in the reserves against time deposits. This reduction was apparently made in an effort to keep short-term interest rates from falling and to provide funds for seasonal holiday needs.[6] The economic significance of these actions is discussed in Chapter 24 below).

Reserve requirements of nonmember state banks are subject to state regulations. In the main, state provisions are similar to those of the Federal Reserve System, except that in addition to vault cash some specified amount of government securities and deposit balances in other commercial banks may be legal reserves.

Secondary reserves

Banks often depend less on their primary reserves than on secondary reserves in meeting unexpected deposit withdrawals. Secondary reserves are earning assets that yield an income to the bank in the form of interest payments; but the real reason for their presence in a bank's portfolio is that they may readily be liquidated with little or no shrinkage in value. They are a second line of defense behind primary or liquid reserves for quick conversion into cash to meet unexpected demands for funds by depositors. Items found here include U.S. treasury bills, which may be sold in the open market or to Federal Reserve banks; other treasury obligations that fall due within three years; commercial paper; bankers' acceptances or bills of exchange; open-market loans payable by borrowers on demand or call; and items that can be used as security for a loan from a Federal Reserve bank or may be rediscounted at a Reserve bank. It is evident, also, that all securities or loans fall into this category as they approach maturity and are about to be paid.

---

[6] Board of Governors of the Federal Reserve System, *The Federal Reserve System—Purposes and Functions* (5th ed; 1963), pp. 54–55.

Banks have not yet developed, and may never develop, any definite tradition about the proper amount of secondary reserves to hold. Requirements vary with the region: seasonal fluctuations are of differing magnitudes, the composition of bank customers varies, and accessibility to sources of funds differs. Yet bank managements are cognizant of the forces that produce variations in the demand for funds in their own regions, and more particularly in their own bank, and approach the problem of making adjustments in realistic fashion. The reader of a bank's financial statement, however, is unable to determine the amount held in the secondary reserve of a bank because he lacks knowledge of the maturity dates or the marketability of the individual items composing the bank's earning assets.

Other assets

The few items not included among reserves and earning assets are of minor significance. Chief among them are the bank premises, furniture and fixtures, and miscellaneous operating assets. These are necessary requisites of bank operation and would be liquidated only if the institutions were to dissolve.

Table 4–1, which covers all insured commercial banks on December

TABLE 4–1

Summary of assets and liabilities of operating insured commercial banks, December 31, 1969

Assets, liability, or capital account item	Amounts (in millions)	Percentages of total assets
Assets (uses)		
Cash, balances with other banks, and cash collection items	$ 89,335	16.8
Securities	135,097	25.5
Loans and discounts, gross	286,752	54.0
Bank premises, etc., and other real estate	8,070	1.5
Miscellaneous assets	11,461	2.2
Total Assets	$530,715	100.0
Liabilities (sources)		
Deposits		
Demand	$240,131	45.2
Time	196,859	37.1
Miscellaneous liabilities	47,967	9.0
Reserve on loans and securities	6,179	7.5
Capital accounts	39,576	1.2
Total Liabilities and Capital Accounts	$530,715	100.0

Note: Details do not add to totals because of rounding.
Source of data: Federal Deposit Insurance Corporation, *Annual Report* (1969), p. 264–66.

31, 1969, summarizes the major sources and uses of commercial bank funds discussed in this chapter.

The rate of interest earned on loans and on securities held in the investment account is in most periods higher than the rate on secondary reserves. This is due to a number of factors. First, assets included in the secondary reserves category do not involve high costs in their purchase or sale. Moreover, these asset holdings entail only a minimum amount of risk of loss due to changes in interest rates or default. Loans must be negotiated and monitored and are thus costly to administer, whereas, long-

EXHIBIT 4–1

Percentage composition of assets of insured commercial banks (*as of December 31*)

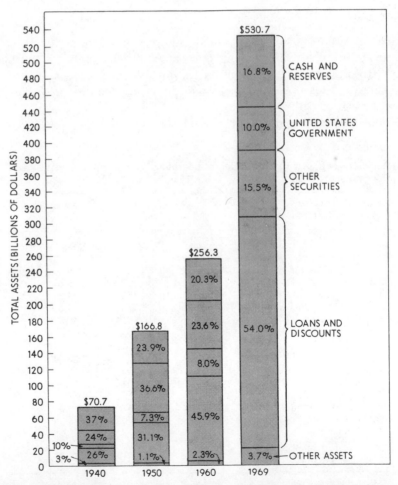

Source: Federal Deposit Insurance Corporation, *Annual Report* (1940), pp. 144–45; *Annual Report* (1950), pp. 236–37; *Annual Report* (1960), pp. 146–47; *Annual Report* (1969), pp. 264–66.

Financial institutions

or medium-term bonds or investments contain large elements of risk due to possible interest rate fluctuations and because of longer maturities' higher potential defaults.

Percentage relationships change with variations in business conditions, regulations by banking authorities, and decisions of bank managements. An indication of such changes, as well as growth in the total value of the assets of insured commercial banks, in selected years is shown in Exhibit 4–1.

Questions and problems

1. What are the essential differences between savings banking, investment banking, and commercial banking?
2. How may a large bank be departmentalized? Point out the main functions of each department.
3. List the principal sources of bank funds and discuss each.
4. Many nonbanking concerns finance themselves by the sale of long-term debt obligations. Why do commercial banks seldom do this?
5. Is there any reserve in a nonfinancial business that compares with the net asset reserve of banks?
6. Differentiate the primary and secondary reserves of commercial banks. Discuss the components and functions of each.
7. How does the Board of Governors of the Federal Reserve System explain the difference between gross demand deposits and adjusted demand deposits? What is the significance of the distinction?
8. What change in the ratio of loans to investments would you expect to occur as the economy moves from prosperity into depression? Why?

Bibliography

(Bibliography at end of Chapter 5.)

Commercial bank credit, bank earnings, and credit expansion

The fundamental processes of commercial banking are too significant in our economy to be dismissed by an examination of bank balance sheets and statistical data of the banking system. Published reports referred to in previous pages convey some idea of the nature of the operations and the relative importance of each in quantitative terms. The true characteristics of commercial banking are not, however, shown by the mechanics of operation. A knowledge of essentials comes from a study of the nature and interrelationship of bank loans, investments, and deposits. For that reason we devote this chapter to the amplification of these topics. Our discussion—perhaps at the risk of some repetition—will shed more light on the financial relationship of banks to the entire business and economic structure.

Commercial bank loans

A close relationship exists between the depositing and the lending functions of banks. Through lending and investing operations, banks put to work funds entrusted to their care. By making short-term advances, they enable borrowers to acquire funds for temporary use in business undertakings. By purchasing securities or making loans with longer term maturity, banks supply funds that enable borrowers to gain control over assets that have years of productive life.

Many kinds of wealth owned by individuals and business units are not in liquid form and obviously do not pass currently from hand to hand as money. Yet these assets may often be used as security for a bank loan that provides purchasing power in the form of deposit credit.

Economies in the use of wealth are not the only advantages growing out of the lending process. The bank distributes its advances in a discriminating manner among its customers by directing funds into the hands of producers best able to use them. In this way, credit definitely fosters the effective use of productive equipment and the maximum expansion in the supply of consumer goods.

Through the banking system, purchasing power is shifted from one user to another as a sort of revolving fund. Many loans are made to help business concerns meet temporary and seasonal demands for funds. As one such loan matures and is paid off, the bank diverts the proceeds to a borrower in a different line of business whose peak loan requirements lag seasonally behind those of the prior borrower. If it were not possible for enterprises to borrow to cover irregular seasonal needs, their permanent investment would necessarily be larger, or the seasonal volume of business would have to be less. As integration of banks' operations and interbank relationships are fostered within the banking system, the shift of funds from business to business and from one geographical area to another is made with a minimum of disturbance to the capital markets and to the activities of producers.

Credit analysis

Loans and discounts are made by lending officers or by a loan committee to whom that function is delegated by the bank's directorate. Before making a loan, however, the bank tries to obtain assurance that it will be repaid. This ordinarily means that the financial standing, worth, and character of the prospective borrower will be investigated.

In small banks, credit analysis may be the function of an individual, perhaps the president or cashier. In large metropolitan institutions, however, a credit department is usually entrusted with the job. Regardless of whether analysis is conducted by a large or a small bank, the methods used are similiar, and the type of information sought is fairly well standardized.

All forms for use in credit analysis are similar in nature. If the applicant wishes a business loan, he must submit a balance sheet of assets and liabilities, an income statement, and some form of cash flow projection. He is asked to provide a wide range of information on his activities, such as any contracts or commitments outstanding; the amount of insurance carried on merchandise inventory, on machinery and fixtures, and on buildings; the amount of credit insurance on notes receivable; use and occupancy insurance; and life insurance.

From this information and from that received from mercantile agencies such as Dun & Bradstreet, local credit bureaus, trade journals, and other banks, and from personal interviews with representatives of the applicant, the credit department attempts to determine the ability of the debtor to pay, based on a consideration of reputation, business competence, assests employed, and possible collateral that might be pledged.

All information gathered from the sources mentioned is placed on file in the credit department. If the applicant is granted a loan, he is required to keep the file up to date by reporting changes in assets, liabilities, sales volume, income and expenses, profits, and other information that might affect his ability to repay the loan.

The line of credit

Many commercial banks do a substantial part of their lending to business borrowers who have prearranged lines of credit. The line is generally an understanding between the borrower and the bank as to the maximum amount of credit that the bank will provide the borrower at any one time. The arrangement is seldom considered a binding contract, and the line may be canceled by the bank as the result of an adverse change in the borrower's position. After the line is established, the borrower may obtain credit to the maximum amount without further negotiation when he needs a loan. At such a time the borrower merely forwards his promissory note to the bank and receives a credit of equal amount in his deposit account.

Limitations governing the size of a credit line may arise from the credit standing of the debtor, from general business and credit conditions, and from legal restrictions on the amount and type of loans the bank is permitted to grant to one customer.

Virtually all banks making advances under a line of credit limit the duration of the agreement to one year or less. Some banks review the position of the debtor each time an application for credit is received, but the prevailing practice is to examine the condition of the applicant's business once a year and to require information on significant changes in the interim.

Periodic repayment of loans made under a line are usually required, and some banks insist that the borrower make an annual "clean up" and get completely out of debt for one or more months each year. This last requirement is imposed to assure the bank that the short-term loans which it extends are not substitutes for long-term capital requirements of its business customers.

Minimum balance requirements

A further common requirement of many lending arrangements is maintenance of a minimum deposit balance by the borrower. This may be enforced only while the loan is actually on the books of the bank, or as is more often the case, it may be an average deposit required for the duration of the lending agreement. The compensatory balance can be viewed as payment to the bank for maintaining lending capacity which the borrower can use when and if it is needed.

The requirement of deposit balances raises the effective yield to banks on loans. The increased rate of return to the bank may be illustrated in this fashion: Assume that a borrower has a line fixing his maximum at $100,000 and that he wishes to make full use of the line for six months. If the interest rate is 6% a year, the credit will cost the borrower $3,000 for the half year. If the bank requires a 20% compensatory deposit balance during the loan period, however, the borrower will be paying $3,000 for the use of only $80,000. The effective rate of interest would in fact be 7.5%. Moreover, if the balance is required during the life of the agreement and the borrower does not use the line for the entire period, the effective cost to the borrower is even higher.

The practice of requiring deposit balances is not quite as unfair to the debtor as it appears, for banks not uncommonly charge a lower rate of interest on loans to depositing customers. Indeed, the level of interest charged on a loan is often related to the level of deposits maintained. Furthermore, in the example given, it was assumed that the borrower had to borrow the funds for the deposit balance. In reality many businesses desire to maintain deposit balances in excess of the requirements on loan agreements and thus suffer no additional costs due to compensating balance requirements. Moreover, as mentioned above, the implied guarantee of a loan when requested by a business imposes costs on the bank in the form of a need to maintain additional low-yielding liquid assets in the secondary reserve portion of the balance sheet to assure the availabiliy of reserves when a loan is requested.

The policy of requiring minimum balances to be maintained is determined by individual bank management and varies considerably from bank to bank. In general, compensating balances are applied more commonly to finance companies and commercial-industrial customers than to agricultural and consumer borrowers. They are required more widely by banks in urban centers than by smaller institutions in rural areas and are more rigidly enforced on finance companies than on other types of borrowers.

In an early survey, the required deposit as a percentage of the loan, or the credit line, was found to be between 11% and 20% for four fifths of the banks and between 16% and 20% for approximately one third. There was no marked relationship between the size of the bank and the minimum-balance requirements.[1] Variations in the size of the balances required tend to be related to the competitive position of the individual bank, its desire to attract reserves, and its desire to increase the effective yield of the loan made to the customer.

Classes of loans

Traditionally, commercial banks were supposed to extend only self-liquidating loans to give temporary assistance to commercial borrowers. This tradition, even in the early years of commercial banking, was probably more of an ideal than a reality. Surely today in the United States many loans are not short term, not commercial, and not self-liquidating. The wide variety of loans may be classified for purposes of discussion on the basis of (1) purpose, (2) security, and (3) maturity. Published loan reports of federal and state banking authorities are sometimes confusing because the bases of classification are not uniform and at times appear to overlap.

The classification of loans by insured banks reporting to the Federal Deposit Insurance Corporation at the end of 1969 is shown in Table 5–1. The loans listed are classified primarily on the basis of purpose or the type of business in which proceeds of the loans are to be put to work. For example, 37% are for commercial and industrial uses; 24%, in the real estate market; 22%, for individual personal expenditures; and 5%, for purchasing and holding securities. Together, these four classes of loans comprise $252 billion of the total $287 billion or 88% of the gross loans of the 13,464 insured commercial banks. Some of these loans are secured; some are to be repaid in a lump sum and others in installments. Nothing definite about the maturity of any loan is indicated.

Secured loans. In an attempt to gain protection against losses that may arise from failure of borrowers to repay loans, banks often insist, when advances are made, that title to specific assets be left in their possession. The collateral pledged may consist of stocks and bonds; merchandise or inventory covered by warehouse receipts, trust receipts, or bills of lading; mortgages on real estate or personal property; discounted notes receivable or assigned accounts receivable; life insurance; or other assets. When collateral is left with the bank, it is frequently accompanied by a power of attorney authorizing the bank to obtain title to

---

[1] Board of Governors of the Federal Reserve System, *Federal Reserve Bulletin,* June 1956, pp. 573–79.

TABLE 5–1

Loans and discounts of operating insured commercial banks, December 31, 1969 (*amounts in thousands of dollars*)

Loans and discounts—total	286,751,602
Real estate loans—total	70,325,953
Secured by farmland	3,992,931
Secured by residential properties:	
Secured by 1- to 4-family residential properties:	
Insured by Federal Housing Administration	7,262,023
Guaranteed by Veterans Administration	2,596,261
Not insured or guaranteed by FHA or VA	31,210,921
Secured by multifamily (5 or more) properties:	
Insured by Federal Housing Administration	562,501
Not insured by FHA	2,647,857
Secured by other properties	22,053,459
Loans to domestic commercial and foreign banks	2,425,147
Loans to other financial institutions	14,938,963
Loans to brokers and dealers in securities	5,646,962
Other loans for purchasing or carrying securities	3,994,818
Loans to farmers (excluding loans on real estate)	10,323,657
Commercial and industrial loans (including open market paper)	108,393,788
Other loans to individuals—total	63,355,683
Passenger automobile installment loans	22,706,108
Credit cards and related plans:	
Retail (charge account) credit card plans	2,639,497
Check credit and revolving credit plans	1,082,791
Other retail consumer installment loans	6,269,924
Residential repair and modernization installment loans	3,654,863
Other installment loans for personal expenditures	9,936,340
Single-payment loans for personal expenditures	17,066,160
All other loans (including overdrafts)	7,346,631

Source: Federal Deposit Insurance Company, *Annual Report* (1969), p. 264.

the security and to liquidate it if that is necessary to protect the bank against loss.

The most recent survey of the assets accepted as security by commercial banks was made on October 16, 1957. The proportion of secured loans to total loans was 66.9% by number and 50.3% by dollar volume. This survey indicated that 18.8% of secured loans were backed by "plant and other real estate" and 81.2% by "other forms of security."[2]

In an earlier survey, a more elaborate breakdown of types of security was developed, see Table 5–2.

In addition to the safeguard for loans provided by the types of security mentioned above, commercial banks have received protection

---

[2] In this chapter a substantial amount of descriptive material about the operations of commercial banks dates back to 1955 and 1957. These data were provided by two special surveys of bank loans in those years. Unfortunately, no such surveys were conducted in the 1960s and so these important data cannot be updated to describe any changes that may have occurred.

in recent years through guaranty provisions of federal laws. For example, the Federal Housing Administration (FHA) has, since 1934, guaranteed commercial banks and other lending agencies against loss of loans made to private borrowers for the acquisition and improvement of residential property which they have insured. The Commodity Credit Corporation guarantees loans to farmers under the federal crop support program. Other instances of federal guaranty are loans granted for the purpose of producing munitions of war; loans under the GI Bill of Rights to eligible veterans for use in acquiring homes, farm equipment,

TABLE 5–2

Secured loans of commercial banks (1955)

Type of security	Percent of total secured loans
Endorsed and co-maker	17.5
Assigned claims, contracts, etc.	17.9
Inventories	9.2
Equipment	14.0
Plant and other real estate	22.9
U.S. government securities	1.2
Other bonds	1.1
Stocks	6.4
Life insurance	2.8
Other security	7.0
Total	100.0

Source: *Federal Reserve Bulletin*, September 1959, pp. 1114–19, and Table 3, p. 1119.

or assets required to set the borrower up in business; and loans to college students.

Term loans. Notable among the exceptions to credit advances of short maturity traditionally made by commercial banks are *term loans,* granted for periods running from 1 to 10 or more years.

The development of these loans to finance intermediate and long-term capital needs of business have been one of the most significant banking developments of recent years. Prior to 1940, term loans were novel, but as early as 1946, almost three fourths of all member banks, large and small alike, had term loans outstanding; today practically all banks are making them.

In 1957 two major industry groups accounted for nearly 40% of the term loans outstanding. Transportation, communication, and other public utility companies had term loans equal to 68% of all their bank borrowing, while petroleum, coal, chemical, and rubber companies' term loans were 73.7% of all the advances they had received from commercial banks. The high ratios of term loans to total bank loans reflects the large proportion of borrowers' assets in heavy investment having relatively long service life. A contrasting position was exhibited, both in absolute amount and relative to their total bank loans, by commodity dealers and finance companies, which have few fixed assets.

In general, except for the two groups of business firms mentioned above, the ratio of term loans to total bank borrowing decreased as the size of the borrower increased. For example, in 1955 the ratio was 41% for firms with less than $50,000 of assets and 24% for firms in the $1–$5 million group. Above the $5 million class the ratio grew until it became almost 49% in the $25 million to $100 million group. These large firms accounted for a substantial proportion of the amounts loaned, but about 40% of the number of advances were made to firms with assets of $5 million or less.[3]

Term loans are said to be "tailor-made," in that details of the agreement are fixed only after a careful analysis has been made of the borrowers' financial needs and his ability to repay. Their most common feature is that they run for a year or more and contain a serial plan of installment repayment under a schedule that is arranged when the analysis of anticipated income and expenses has been completed. Small loans are commonly secured by the equipment or facilities acquired by the borrower when he spends the proceeds of the loan. Large loans are frequently unsecured.

The 1957 survey indicated that about 60% of the volume and 90% of the number of term loans were secured by collateral or backed by some form of repayment guarantee. During a period of monetary restraint, such as from 1955 to 1957, there is a tendency for banks to require increased security of long-term borrowers. This phenomenon has continued to be observed in such later periods of monetary restriction as 1966 and 1968–70.

Effective interest rates on installment loans vary widely from one loan to another. Interest may be computed by applying a stated rate either to the original amount of the loan or to the unpaid balance outstanding. If the latter method is used, the charge declines as the loan is repaid. When based on the original amount, the charge does not decline, even though the unpaid balance is reduced. The effect is to impose a much higher rate than is stated on the face of the note. In 1957 less than one tenth of the dollar value of term loans outstanding had interest calculated on the original amount of the loan. To these borrowers in 1957 the average rate of interest was 8.7%, and to borrowers paying on the amount outstanding the average rate was 4.6%. Banks justify the high rate to borrowers paying on the original amount of the loan because this type of advance is usually small and requires a

---

[3] "Member Bank Term Lending to Business, 1955–57," *Federal Reserve Bulletin*, April 1959, pp. 332–33.

higher percentage of income on the principal to cover the fixed expense of making the loan and current administrative costs.

Often banks are asked to make term loans that are in excess of their legal loan limits or are larger than the bank wishes to make. Under such circumstances a *participation loan* may be made. Two or more banks may cooperate in making the grant to a borrower. Agreements of this type are not common among small banks, but in 1955 about 50% of term loans with over five-year maturities made by the largest banks were participations.

In recent years about four fifths of the dollar amount of term loans have been made to incorporated businesses. This may be a reflection of the growth in size of business units or the realization that large long-term loans made to individual enterprises or partnerships carry a higher degree of risk because of the impermanence of operators. Yet, over 70% of the number of loans were made to small borrowers, many of whom were not incorporated. In fact, among the retail trade and service borrowers, over 80% were unincorporated. The growth in term loans to small and moderate-sized borrowers reflects in part their limited access to other sources of intermediate or long-term capital.

A limited survey of term loans by the 10 largest commercial banks in New York City indicates that term lending plays a more important role at large city banks than at smaller institutions and now constitutes more than one half of all business loan volume of the big city banks while at smaller banks they are approximately one third the volume of all loans.[4]

The greater importance of term loans in large New York banks reflects the fact that these banks service large companies located throughout this country and abroad. In recent years the relatively heavy demand for intermediate term credit has presented an opportunity for large commercial banks to aid in filling the void.

The dollar volume of term loans in New York City banks expanded from $3.5 billion to $5.9 billion between October 1955 and January 1961. Proceeds of the advances were distributed as follows: 31% to public utilities, 29% to petroleum, coal, chemical, and rubber companies, 19% to metal and metal product firms, and the balance—about 21%—to a variety of borrowers including construction, food, liquor, tobacco, textile, and others.

Commercial and industrial loans. Commercial and industrial loans are the traditional type of loans made by commercial banks. As noted, at the end of 1969 they accounted for 37% of total loans of all insured commercial banks. This class of borrowers has traditionally been the favored customers of commercial banks. Besides borrowing, businesses purchase

---

[4] "Term Lending by New York City Banks," *Monthly Review,* Federal Reserve Bank of New York, vol. 43 (February 1961), pp. 27–31.

a wide variety of other bank services and through their deposit balances supply a large fraction of total bank demand deposits.

The demand for commercial and industrial loans is highly cyclical, and so the volume of these loans fluctuates with the phases of the business cycle. Thus, banks must be prepared to meet the heavy loan demand of these favored customers during periods of strong business conditions. During periods of low loan demand, banks purchase short-term securities; when loan demand increases, these securities are sold and the proceeds are used to extend loans.

Security loans. Security loans are loans backed by stocks and bonds, made for the purchase or carrying of securities. Two classes of such advances are commonly recognized: loans to brokers and dealers and loans to individuals and others. Like other categories of loans in recent years, security loans have increased in absolute amount. The outstanding amount on December 31, 1969, was about $9.6 billion. These loans, however, accounted for less than 6% of total loans of insured commercial banks on that date. This class of loans accounted for approximately the same proportion of total bank loans at the end of 1940.

Loans to stockbrokers for financing margin accounts of their customers (customer loans from brokers to purchase stock) are ordinarily made on a demand basis. The most acceptable collateral consists of good quality securities traded on the New York Stock Exchange. Rates of interest charged on this type of loan tend to fluctuate with the prime commercial loan rate, which is the rate accorded to high-quality business borrowers.

Loans to dealers to finance their securities inventories or to carry new security issues during flotation have maturities normally ranging between 5 and 20 days. The difference in the regulation between brokers and dealers recognizes the difference in the operations of brokers and dealers. Brokers are middlemen between buyers and sellers and therefore require financing only for their buying customers. Dealers purchase and sell securities for their own accounts and must therefore finance their inventory of securities. The loan limit of dealers is determined by the quality of the issue being distributed. On government bonds the loan may be as high as 96–98% of market value, as much as 90% or more on high-grade state and municipals, 80% on Baa corporate bonds, and as much as 70% on common stock.

Bank loans to individuals and others for purchasing or carrying securities in recent years have been between 35% and 45% of all security loans.

To prevent a recurrence of the speculative movement in common stocks that developed in the late 1920s, the Board of Governors of the Federal Reserve System is now empowered to limit the amount that banks and others may lend to brokers, individuals, and others for the purpose of purchasing or carrying securities. Margin requirements have

5——Commercial bank credit, bank earnings, and credit expansion been changed many times since the Securities Exchange Act of 1934 placed security loans of banks under Federal Reserve control. As the amount of apparent speculation in the stock market drives price averages up, the Board of Governors tends to restrict lending in that sector by increasing the margin requirements.

In mid-1970 the margin requirement was 65%. This meant that banks could lend only 35% of the market value of a stock; the buyer's equity margin has to be at least 65%.

Consumer installment loans. Another class of noncommercial loans, but one of growing importance to commercial banks, is being made by personal loan departments. Although banks in rural communities have always made large numbers of small consumer loans, it was not until the late 1920s that metropolitan banks began establishing separate departments to process personal loan applications. The development became nationwide during the depression of the 1930s, when the demand for consumer credit was increasing and when declining earnings encouraged many banks to enter this field.

Personal loans of commercial banks are typically small, are usually repaid on an installment plan, and are made for a variety of purposes—chiefly consumption. In recent years installment loans have frequently been made with maturities of 36 months or more.

Information on the amount of consumer loans outstanding at the end of 1969 can be obtained from Table 5–1. Under the general classification of "other loans to individuals for personal expenditures," there are six subgroups: passenger automobile installment loans, credit cards and related plans, other retail installment loans, residential repair and modernization installment loans, other installment loans for personal expenditures, and single-payment loans for personal expenditures. The total outstanding consumer advances of all insured commercial banks on December 31, 1969, were in excess of $63 billion, approximately 22% of all loans of insured banks.

Growth in the totals of consumer installment loans, which encompasses three of the six categories listed above, made by commercial banks was from $43 million outstanding December 31, 1929, to $1.7 billion at year-end 1941. In December 1969, the total reached $39 billion.[5]

Although commercial banks were slow to enter the consumer installment lending field, by the end of 1969 they held 41% of the total outstanding installment credit in the United States. Recent developments suggest that in the future commercial banks will be even more important suppliers of this type of credit. In Table 5–1 the second subgroup of loans to individuals is listed as "credit cards and related plans." This is subdivided into two parts: retail credit card plans, and check credit

---

[5] The volume of consumer installment loans of commercial banks and other lending institutions is reported monthly in the *Federal Reserve Bulletin.*

and revolving credit plans. The two together account for only $3.7 billion of the more than $63 billion of consumer credit held by insured banks, but all indications point to a rapid growth in the use of bank credit cards.

Bank credit cards were first issued in 1951, but major expansion in their use dates back only to 1966. Prior to 1966, only 68 banks issued cards, but by the end of 1967, the number had increased to 197.[6] Moreover, the new entrants were on the average more aggressive than the banks which were already issuing cards, and since 1967, the rate of increase in the number of banks issuing cards has, if anything, accelerated. During 1968 and 1969, the individual banks and regional groups of banks issuing credit cards formed two nationwide systems, so that most bank cards are now acceptable in all parts of the United States.

In the typical operation, the cardholder is given a credit limit. He can make purchases from any establishment which accepts the card. In most areas, a large percentage of businesses now honor bank credit cards. Every 30 days a statement is sent to cardholders listing purchases and the debit balance. The cardholder has 25 days from the sending date in which to make payment with no interest charge. After the free period, interest typically is charged at 1.5% per month, or 18% per annum, on the unpaid balance.

The bank also receives a percentage of the dollar value of the sale from the vendor. In the early plans the size of this payment was fairly uniform at 5% or 6%. But as large numbers of banks have issued cards, this percentage has declined substantially. The size of the payment is determined in a bargaining process when the vendor agrees to honor the bank card. High-volume stores pay a lower percentage of sales and high-average sales items are usually charged a lower percentage rate.

Use of bank credit cards has great potential for businesses, banks, and consumers. It allows banks to provide credit for small purchases which could not be economically financed with prior forms of installment credit. It provides consumers with enhanced credit facilities and added convenience. It allows businesses to provide a broader range of credit to their customers, especially smaller businesses.

In addition to the attributes described above, bank credit cards have great significance as a first step in revolutionary changes that are expected to occur in the methods of transferring funds in the United States. We refer to the possibility of substituting electronic transfers in place of checks. The computer requirements for establishing and operating the credit card system require only the addition of remote terminals in the business establishment to accomplish electronic fund transfers.

Real estate loans. Real estate loans granted to individuals for the

---

[6] For a comprehensive description of the position of bank credit cards through the end of 1967, see *Bank Credit and Check Credit Plans,* Board of Governors of the Federal Reserve System, July 1968.

purchase and construction of homes have an important place in the loan portfolios of insured commercial banks. Data in Table 5–1 show outstanding real estate loans of $70.3 billion, or approximately 24% of the gross total of loans at the end of 1969. Like consumer loans and term loans to business, advances on real estate cannot be considered short-term, self-liquidating commercial credit. Many such loans have years to run, and they ordinarily add nothing to the borowers' income to assist in repayment.

Banks and other lending agencies suffered heavy losses in the collapse of the real estate market in the early 1930s. Defaults on outstanding loans were numerous, and few new advances were made. Real estate loans were stimulated a few years later, however, by the mortgage insurance program of the Federal Housing Administration. Following World War II the guaranteed loan program fostered by the Veterans Administration also contributed to the expansion of real estate loans.

Commercial banks have granted large amounts of credit on non-insured or nonguaranteed loans as rates on conventional mortgages have exceeded the maximum rates fixed by law for FHA and VA mortgages.

In the last several years one of the most significant developments has been the rise of commercial bank loans for real estate developments. Such advances are included in the "secured by other properties" category in Table 5–1. As can be seen, at the end of 1969 they amounted to more than $22 billion having grown 300% in the last six years. These loans are made to individuals and firms for the construction of apartment buildings and other residential property for rental, to contractors building homes for resale, and to mortgage companies carrying large inventories of residential mortgages.

Commercial bank loans to finance urban home development are discussed in Chapter 21.

Interest rates on loans

The income received by banks from loans has a double significance. Not only is it the largest source of revenue out of which current operating expenses of banks are paid, but when viewed from another angle, it is a price paid for the use of commercial bank loan credit.

The classification of loans provided earlier reflected the fact that bank income from loans and discounts is received from thousands of borrowers using bank credit for many purposes. Rates paid on various classes of loans often differ and are not the same for different borrowers on identical types of grants. Variations are commonly due to differences in the elements of risk, time, and size. Relatively lower rates are charged when the risk of loss is low, when the loan is for a very short time, and when the loan is for a large amount. Short-term rates are lower because the maturity date falls in the near-term or foreseeable future, and the entrance of unexpected risk factors is therefore at a minimum. Rates on large loans may be low because the character of the borrower is unquestioned and the costs of making a credit survey and administering the loan are relatively less than for a smaller borrower on whom adequate data may not be readily available. The effect of size differential is shown in Table 5–3.

TABLE 5–3

Weighted average bank rates on short term business loans, May 1970 (% per annum)

Center Reporting	All size loans	Loan size in thousands of dollars				
		1–9	10–99	100–499	500–999	1,000, or over
All 35 Centers	8.49	9.05	9.04	8.73	8.43	8.25
New York City	8.24	9.05	8.91	8.53	8.31	8.13
7 other Northeast ..	8.86	9.23	9.34	9.01	8.72	8.45
8 North Central	8.44	8.80	8.93	8.78	8.44	8.24
7 Southeast	8.44	8.70	8.77	8.49	8.31	8.15
8 Southwest	8.61	9.10	8.90	8.61	8.32	8.58
4 West Coast	8.42	9.49	9.13	8.72	8.50	8.13

Source: *Federal Reserve Bulletin*, July 1970, p. A32.

For example, for short-term business loans made in May 1970, in 35 major cities, an average rate of 8.49% was charged on all loans; but loans in the $1 million and over classification paid 8.25%. At the same time, 9.05% was charged on loans of $1,000 to $10,000.

The table also shows that rates vary from one geographical area to another at the same time and on the same size classes of loan. When the New York City rate on loans of less than $10,000 was 9.05%, the average in seven northeastern cities was 9.23% and in four West Coast cities, 9.49%. The discrepancies are due apparently to regional differences in the demand and supply of bank loans and the localized nature of banking markets.

Not only are there differences among rates at the same time, but the entire structure of interest rates on bank loans changes from one date to another. The causal factors involved include changes in the supply of funds available and in the demand for loans. It is possible, on the chart of money rates shown here (Exhibit 5–1), to note how changes in business conditions and governmental monetary policy are reflected in the changing rates of interest.

The stability of short-term rates at relatively high levels for the

EXHIBIT 5–1

Rates charged by banks on short-term loans to business (*averages by size of loans*)

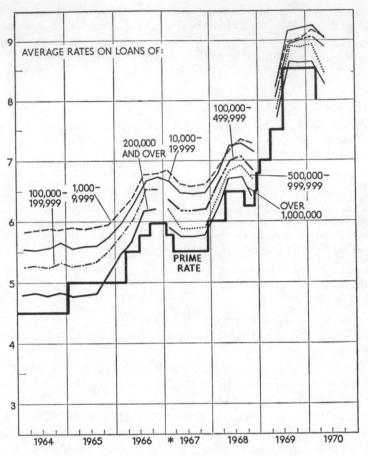

AVERAGE RATES ON LOANS OF:

100,000–499,999

200,000 AND OVER | 10,000–19,999

100,000–199,999 | 1,000–9,999

500,000–999,999

OVER 1,000,000

PRIME RATE

1964 1965 1966 * 1967 1968 1969 1970

* The break in the first quarter of 1967 is due to a revision in the series. Prior to 1967 the data were collected from 19 large centers. After the revision, 35 centers were represented.
Source: *Federal Reserve Bulletin.*

period 1960–64 was due to the absence of significant swings in the business cycle and, more importantly, to activities of monetary and fiscal authorities attempting to maintain short-term rates at levels competitive with foreign rates. It was hoped that maintenance of high rates in the United States would reduce the volume of short-term investment abroad, retard the outflow of gold, and exert a salutary effect on our balance of international payments. (See Chapters 25–26 for further discussion of U.S. balance of payments problems.)

The upswing in rates after 1964 reflects the increasing tempo of economic activity during the period. It is interesting to note the decline in lending rates after the Federal Reserve loosened credit by increasing reserves available to banks in the first and second quarter of 1967. The steady rise in rates from the third quarter of 1967 to the end of 1969 reflects the rising demand for credit during the period, the inflationary conditions in the economy, and the active policy of the Federal Reserve to tighten monetary conditions.

Within the structure of interest rates the various types of bank loans usually maintain their position relative to one another. The *prime* rate is the rate charged by a bank on its most riskless loans. Business firms that enjoy the prime rate are usually large, well-known, and well-managed concerns whose credit record is spotless. Prime loans to business are usually unsecured; other loans requiring security are made at higher rates, with the rate on stock exchange security loans being less than rates on those secured by inventory, plan and equipment, or pledge of accounts receivable. Long-term loan rates tend to be above rates on secured loans, and unsecured farm loans approach the usury limit established by law. Interest on consumer installment loans and credit card advances are commonly made at a rate of 1% or 1.5% a month on the unpaid balance.

Bank investments

Attention has already been directed to the principal earning assets of banks: (1) loans and discounts and (2) investments. These two types of assets differ in several respects. Loans and discounts, except those made in the open market, are made to regular customers who maintain deposit balances. These customers come to the bank for loans. In acquiring assets included in the investment category, however, the bank takes the initiative. As a lender, the bank has a personal relationship with the borrower and usually is the only creditor in the transaction. As an investor, the bank often deals as one of several creditors and does so on an impersonal basis. In a loan, the credit instrument is usually a simple promissory note; in an investment, it is more than likely a complex technical instrument in the form of a bond.

The average maturity of a loan is generally much shorter than that of an investment, and the purpose of the loan is usually to provide the borrower with circulating or working capital rather than fixed capital. But, in a more fundamental respect, investments and loans are alike. Each represents a channeling of funds into the hands of those requiring purchasing power for the conduct of their personal or business affairs. By making both types of advance, the banker is playing his part in maximizing the productive power of the country and raising its standard of living.

A commercial bank may extend credit by purchasing bonds for any of several reasons: it may want to reduce the risks of loss by diversifying its assets; it may want to space its maturities so that the inflow of cash will coincide with expected withdrawals by depositors or large loan demands of its customers; it may wish to have high-grade, marketable securities to liquidate if its primary reserves become inadequate. It may also be forced to invest because the demand for loans has decreased or is not sufficient to absorb its excess reserves.

None of the above reasons requires elaboration here; but anyone who examines bank statements and statistics may wonder at the changes in relative size of investments and loans through the years. Among national banks in 1913, loans were about 75% of all earning assets; invest-

EXHIBIT 5–2

Principal assets of commercial banks (*as reported in June 1914–46; and in June and December 1947–68*)

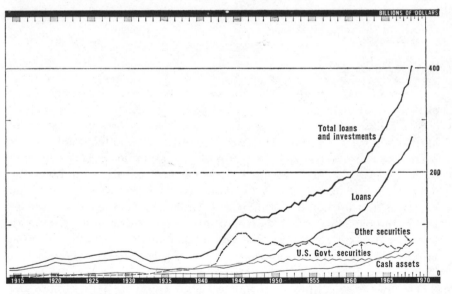

Source: *Historical Chart Book,* Board of Governors, Federal Reserve System.

ments were 25%. Gradually, and almost steadily, loans declined relatively, and investments grew until, in 1939, loans were slightly over 40% and investments almost 60%. Moreover, during these years real estate loans, which are similar to long-term bond investments with respect to maturity, increased from 1.2% of all loans to over 21%. An examination of banking data during the period of World War II shows that the trend away from loans and toward investments was accelerated after 1939.

In the years immediately following World War II, a reversal of the trend toward bank investments set in. The postwar boom and the expansion of private enterprise created strong demands for business and consumer loans. An additional impetus coming from the outbreak of the Korean War contributed to the movement, and by December 1950, loans had increased from 16% of total bank assets in 1945 to almost 32%; security holdings in the meantime had declined to approximately 46% of total resources.

The relative decline in the volume of investments in bank portfolios (and especially those of federal securities) has continued since 1950 with minor interruptions and setbacks. At the end of 1964, gross loans were approximately 50% of total insured bank resources, while securities of all classes accounted for 36%. With the continuing upswing in the economy spurred by the demands of the Vietnam conflict during the 1964–70 period, banks faced a continued growth in loan demand. At the end of 1969, loans had risen to 54% of total assets; whereas security holdings had declined to 23% of assets. The changing proportions of loans, securities, and cash in the total asset mix of banks from 1914 to 1969 can be seen in Exhibit 5–2.

Thus in large measure the changing proportion of investments to total bank assets is explained by changes in the demand for loans. Investments are liquidated when loan demand is strong and increased in periods of slack loan demand.

Yields on investment securities

Investment portfolios of commercial banks are established and maintained primarily with a view to the nature of bank liabilities. That is, since depositors may demand funds in great volume without previous notice to banks, the investments must be of a type that can be marketed quickly with little or no shrinkage in value. For that reason bond investments are largely in the form of federal obligations maturing within five years. The value of such obligations with a short term to maturity usually remains near par, thus assuring the bank of approximately full value if forced liquidation occurs before the redemption date.

On the other hand, investments of short or intermediate term normally yield less than long-term obligations and reduce the interest income of the banks. The two charts exhibited here (Exhibits 5–3 and 5–4)

EXHIBIT 5–3

Maturity classification of bank holdings of U.S. government marketable securities (*commercial banks reporting in treasury survey*)

BILLIONS OF DOLLARS

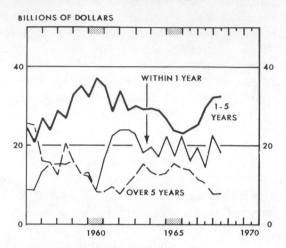

Source: *Federal Reserve Bulletin.*

EXHIBIT 5–4

Bond yields (*monthly averages*)

PERCENT PER ANNUM   PERCENT PER ANNUM

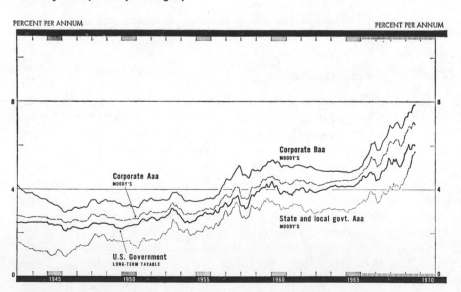

Source: *Historical Chartbook,* Board of Governors, Federal Reserve System, 1969.

Financial institutions

show: the maturity classification of bank-held government securities in the years 1956–68, and the yield on long-term government, compared to corporate and tax-exempt, bonds in the same period. It is to be noted that at the end of 1969 banks reporting to the treasury survey held more than 88% of their governments in the "less than 5-year" group, less than 10% in the 5- to 10-year class, and only 2% in the "over 10-year" group.

An interesting development in investment policy in recent years is the movement of commercial banks into tax-exempt state and municipal bonds. For the institution paying a 48% federal income tax, the purchase of a 4% municipal obligation will yield as much as a taxable security priced to yield 7.7%. Or a municipal with a 6% coupon will net as much as a taxable issue paying 11.5%.

As can be seen in Exhibit 5–4, yields on treasury, corporate, and tax-exempt bonds all increased after 1955. But because of the tax advantage, the tax-exempt bonds became relatively more attractive.

Tax-exempt securities in the portfolio of insured commercial banks increased from $17.3 billion in 1960 to $57.6 billion on December 31, 1969.[7] Thus, holdings of tax-exempt securities grew by more than 300% during a period when total bank assets grew less than 100% and bank holdings of securities only increased by 50%. This demonstrates the strong shifts in bank asset portfolios in response to changing earning opportunities on various types of assets.

Earnings of commercial banks

Total operating revenue of the 13,464 insured banks in 1969 was $30.8 billion. Interest earned on loans and discounts was $20.7 billion or over 67% of the total. Income on federal government obligations was $2.8 billion and from other securities, $2.8 billion. Thus income from security holdings accounted for about 15% of total revenue. Revenue from other sources, including $1.1 billion in service charges on deposit accounts and $1.0 billion for trust and other services, comprised the other 18% of earnings for the year.[8]

Earnings on total assets or on total capital accounts are more significant than the absolute figures noted above. In 1969 net current operating earnings before taxes were 1.3% of total assets. Banks earned 11.3% after taxes on total capital accounts. It is also interesting to note that dividends to total capital accounts were 4.6 or about 41% of net earnings.[9]

Exhibit 5–5 shows the ratio of current earnings to capital accounts

[7] Federal Deposit Insurance Corporation, *Annual Report* (1960), p. 142; *Annual Report* (1969), p. 264.

[8] Ibid. (1969), p. 276.

[9] Ibid., p. 278.

EXHIBIT 5–5

Earnings of all insured commercial banks

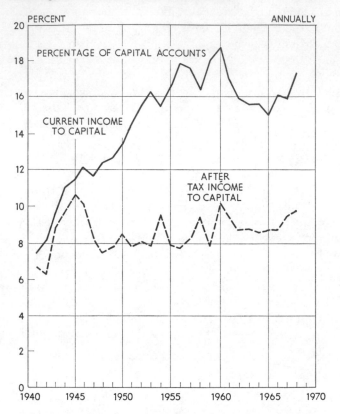

Source: *Annual Reports* of Federal Deposit Insurance Corporation.

and the ratio of net income after taxes to capital accounts annually from 1941 through 1968. As can be seen, the ratio of net current earnings to capital was relatively low during the early years of World War II. After 1943 these before tax earnings rose dramatically. During the 1960s this ratio fluctuated within the very narrow range of 15% to 19%. The ratio of after-tax earnings to capital, which was at very low levels during the 1930s, recovered during the early 1940s. In 1946 it reached a high point which has not been surpassed through 1968. As can be seen, through the years 1943–68, this ratio has been extraordinarily stable. The average after-tax return to capital in banking from 1941 through 1968 was 8.61%. This is somewhat below returns to capital in public utility companies and substantially below returns to capital in manufacturing. Even taking account of the great stability of earnings in banking, the return to capital in this industry is relatively low.

The relation of deposits, reserves, and loans

In our discussion of commercial banking to this point, we have considered the deposit function, maintenance of reserves, and the granting of loans as separate parts of bank operation. However, in explaining the monetary function of banks the interrelation of these operations must be stressed.

It will be recalled that one form of deposit, called *derivative*, is created or derived through loans or investments made by a bank. This type adds nothing to the bank's liquid assets or primary reserves; on the contrary, it forces a bank to tie up a larger amount of its assets as reserves and renders it somewhat less liquid. Because borrowers normally have the proceeds of the loan added to their deposit accounts and because such deposits are treated as money, as shown in Chapter 2, this process is a monetary function of commercial banks.

Reserves against deposits

Regardless of the origin of the deposit, whether primary or derived, each bank is forced by law to maintain a liquid reserve against its deposits. The present legal requirements in the United States are merely crystallizations of experience. Goldsmith bankers of 17-century England realized the necessity of keeping a reserve on hand to meet withdrawals of cash by depositors. The amount of the reserve was not a matter of law but was determined by the experience and judgment of the goldsmith.

Legal reserves. In the United States, legal minimum reserve requirements against deposits of commercial banks have been enforced for over a century. One of the most notable features of what has been viewed as a model banking law was enacted in Louisiana in 1842, and one of its most widely copied provisions was the requirement of a specie or cash reserve equal to one third of all the banks' obligations to the public. Many states incorporated a similar reserve provision in their banking statutes prior to the Civil War, and in 1863 the principal was written into the National Banking Act. Minimum-reserve requirements were included in the Federal Reserve Act of 1913, although details of the provision were modified.

Functions of reserves

Originally, the purpose of bank reserves was thought to be to assure noteholders and depositors of the ability of the bank to redeem its demand obligations in cash. It gradually became apparent, however, that legal minimum reserves had to remain in the vault or on deposit with a Federal Reserve bank. They could not be used, and and they gave little assurance to depositors that obligations payable on demand would be honored by the bank. Thus legal reserves seemed to be a form of frozen liquid asset. To be able to pay cash to depositors, or make loans when required by customers, the bank must maintain some liquid reserve and a secondary reserve that may be quickly converted into cash. The primary function of legal minimum reserve requirements today is to provide a restraining influence upon the freedom of banks to expand credit by lending and creating checkbook money. As we shall see later, altering the reserves of commercial banks is regarded as a means by which central banks influence the ability of their members to create deposit credit.

Loan expansion of a single bank

Since the subject of loan expansion and deposit creation is an important one, we shall develop the fundamental principles with the aid of a simplified illustration.

Suppose that we are first dealing with *one* bank that belongs to a system in which, to assume a hypothetical figure, the required reserve against deposits is 10%. If this bank receives new reserves that originate outside the commercial banking structure, i.e., from receipt of newly mined gold or from central bank credit expansion, the balance sheet entry recording the increase in reserve money would be as follows:

Assets		(1)	Liabilities	
+Reserves	$10,000		+Deposits	$10,000

Note that other items on the statement are ignored; the assumption is that existing deposits are adequately supported by a legal reserve and that working reserves are maintained as vault cash and balances with correspondent banks.[10] We are now able to center attention on the lending operation relating solely to the receipt of the new reserve money.

For the transaction illustrated above, the actual reserve ratio is 100%. That result is obtained by dividing $10,000 deposits into $10,000 reserves. But the law permits a bank to operate, in our assumed case, with as little as a 10% ratio. Knowing this, you ask: Would it not be logical for the banker to increase his earnings by making loans and investments to the

---

[10] Member bank funds held as vault cash and on deposit in Federal Reserve banks in excess of legal minimum requirements are called *excess reserves*. Excess reserves plus funds kept on deposit in other commercial banks are termed *working reserves*.

full extent permitted by his new reserve? In other words, would the bank not lend, at once, to one or more borrowers, enough to create deposits that would bring the new ratio down from 100 to 10%?

If this were done, the maximum loans granted and the derived deposits added to the bank's liabilities would be $90,000:

(2)

Reserves	$10,000	Deposits	$100,000
Loans and discounts	90,000		

Borrowers request loans because they have payments to make. Loans are seldom made at an earlier time or in a larger amount than needed. Hence, on the very day the advance is made by the bank, checks will be written against the borrower's derived deposit account. If some of these checks are paid to local citizens who deposit them in the bank on which they are drawn, then to this extent the bank will not lose either reserves or deposits. Title to that portion of the borrower's deposit account returned to the bank will be shifted to the account of the payee of the check. This bookkeeping transaction will cause the bank no problem; no reserve will be lost, and deposits will be maintained.

It is likely, however, that a much larger portion of the borrower's new deposit will get into the hands of others who do not patronize the bank on which the checks are drawn. Some checks may be deposited in other local banks; many may go to a distant area from which the borrower purchases inventory or supplies. Checks drawn by borrowers and sent to creditors in other communities will be cashed or deposited with other banks for collection. They will ultimately be presented to the drawee bank for payment. We may assume that checks are written for the entire amount of created deposits and that not a single dollar is redeposited in our bank. This means only one thing. The lending bank would be faced with claims for $90,000 and have only $9,000 in reserve that could be applied to settlement of the debts.

If the reserve-exhausting amount of $90,000 cannot be loaned, the question then is: How much can the banker lend on the basis of the original deposit of $10,000? The $10,000 may be thought of as being composed of two parts: one is the $1,000 (10%) necessary to act as reserve for the deposit; the other $9,000 is *excess reserves*. If it is assumed that the owner of the original deposit does not draw checks against his account, the bank may consider that it has $9,000 in free funds available for lending.

If the borrower placed the proceeds of the loan in his deposit account, the bank statement would show:

| Reserves | $10,000 | Deposits | $19,000 |
| Loans and discounts | 9,000 | | |

The reserve ratio at this point is more than 50% ($10,000 divided by $19,000); yet it may be as low as the individual banker feels is safe. Or, from his point of view as a lending officer, the banker's loans are as large as he can grant without risking a reserve deficiency.

The reader may wish to take issue with our statement that one bank will limit its loans to the amount of its excess reserves. He realizes, in the first place, that in each lending operation a partial balance will probably be unused, leaving some reserve with the lending institution. Moreover, he will assert that some checks drawn on the lending bank will be redeposited in it, thus allowing some reserves to remain as a basis for an additional expansion.

With these contentions we are in partial agreement. Banks not uncommonly do request lenders to observe "the 20% rule" of keeping an average deposit balance (compensating balance) during the term of the advance. Maintenance of an *average* balance does not mean, however, that the borrower refrains from checking out *all* his loan and having no balance at all during a portion of the loan period. With respect to the second objection advanced, it may be said that, while some checks are almost sure to be deposited in the drawee bank, no banker can accurately anticipate how many will return. In the absence of an accurate forecast, he will not create excessive deposits, for he dares not run the risk of being caught short of reserves. Moreover, we can strengthen our argument by noting that in a period of credit expansion the bank will experience a currency drain that will absorb some of its excess reserves and further limit deposit creation.

Expansion in a system of banks

If we agree that credit expansion of a *single* bank is limited to the amount of its excess reserves, our next question is: Why is it possible for the *system of banks* to expand deposits to a multiple of its reserves?

To explain this seeming paradox, we return to the commercial bank having new excess reserves and continue with the hypothetical illustration. Receipt of the deposit is shown as it appeared in transaction (1):

| Reserves | $10,000 | Deposits | $10,000 |

Granting a loan to the full extent of its excess reserves creates the following change when the borrower's deposit balance is credited. This is identical with (3) above:

(5)

Reserves	$10,000	Deposits	$19,000
Loans and discounts	9,000		

At this point it is necessary to introduce another bank of the system, a bank in which checks drawn against the lending bank are deposited. This we may designate as Bank 2.

If we now assume that all the derivative deposits of the lender bank are checked out and flow into Bank 2, the statement of the lending bank becomes:

(6)
Bank 1

Reserves	$1,000	Deposits	$10,000
Loans and discounts	9,000		

Bank 2 has acquired $9,000 of deposits and reserves from the original bank. Its statement shows the following changes:

(7)
Bank 2

+Reserves	$9,000	+Deposits	$9,000

The receipt of new deposits forces this bank to set up a minimum legal reserve of $900 (10% of the $9,000 deposits). But since this reserve is only a fraction of the new reserve received, an excess reserve is created. This is $8,100, the amount of total receipts minus the $900 in required reserve.

On the basis of the excess reserve so acquired, Bank 2 may grant loans to approximately the same amount. Assuming that borrowers deposit the proceeds of their loans, the position of the bank then becomes:

(8)
Bank 2

Reserves	$9,000	Deposits	$17,100
Loans and discounts	$8,100		

If the process continues, another bank, which we shall call Bank 3, will acquire new reserves from Bank 2. For example, checks aggregating $8,100, or the entire sum loaned by the second bank, may be deposited in Bank 3. As the checks are collected through the clearinghouse, the reserves and deposits of the third bank would expand by $8,100, as shown in (9):

(9)
Bank 3

Reserves	$8,100	Deposits	$8,100

This bank is now in a position to lend its newly acquired excess reserves. As loans of $7,290 are made, the new relationship of reserves, loans, and deposits will appear as in (10):

(10)
Bank 3

Reserves	$8,100	Deposits	$15,390
Loans and discounts	7,290		

After checks are written and paid against deposits of Bank 3, the final status of this bank will show it also to have a reserve ratio of 10%. Thus:

(11)
Bank 3

Reserves	$ 810	Deposits	$8,100
Loans and discounts	7,290		

As all banks in the system become participants in the diffusion, an ever-diminishing portion of the original deposit is passed from bank to bank until the amount involved finally becomes negligible. It is unnecessary to include added detail of computation to show expansion in successive banks. The upper portion of Table 5–4 indicates the changes resulting when 15 banks participate successively in such a transaction.

The process does not come to an end with the 15 banks shown in Table 5–4. As it continues and embraces a larger and larger number of commercial banks, expansion approaches its limit. At that point, the aggregate volume of deposits supported by the $10,000 new reserve is $100,000, and new loans (the expansion) aggregate $90,000. The limit of expansion in the system is the new excess reserve multiplied by the

TABLE 5–4

Multiple expansion of bank credit*

Bank	Additional deposits received	Additional loans made	Additional reserves retained
1	10,000	9,000	1,000
2	9,000	8,100	900
3	8,100	7,290	810
4	7,290	6,561	729
5	6,561	5,905	656
6	5,905	5,314	591
7	5,314	4,784	531
8	4,783	4,305	478
9	4,305	3,874	431
10	3,874	3,487	387
11	3,487	3,138	349
12	3,138	2,829	314
13	2,824	2,542	282
14	2,542	2,288	254
15	2,288	2,059	229
Total for 15 banks	79,411	71,476	7,941
Additional banks	20,589	18,528†	2,061†
Total all banks	100,000	90,000	10,000

* Assuming an average bank reserve requirement of 10% of demand deposits.
† Adjusted to offset rounding of proceeding amounts.

reciprocal of the reserve ratio—in this case 1.00/0.10, or 10. It is possible for the system to expand purchasing power in the form of deposits by a multiple of its excess reserves, whereas an individual bank is limited to a sum that closely approximates its excess.

The individual banker sometimes is resentful of those who contend that he can create money by granting loans. He always lends or invests only funds held in excess of legal requirements. To him this is not the creation of anything. It is merely a diversion from one form to another. Nevertheless, it is true that, because reserves are required to be only a fraction of deposits, deposits may be expanded throughout the system, as explained above, to several times the size of reserves.

Expansion through bank investment account

Although our illustration of bank credit expansion has been developed solely by considering loans, it may work with equal facility through an increase in any type of asset. A bank with excess reserves may experience no local demand for loan funds and may have to take the initial step in acquiring earning assets. It is of little consequence whether the bank makes a loan or purchases commercial paper, bankers' acceptances, or securities in the open market. In any case, the recipient of the funds deposits them in a bank, thereby increasing that bank's reserves and giving it a basis for lending or investing. The extent of ultimate expansion is not different from that in the case of the loans developed above.

Limitations upon full expansion

It must be admitted—in fact, we hasten to admit—that there may be limitations at work which will cause expansion to fall short of its theoretical maximum. One of the assumptions implicit in the process is that all banks that receive new deposits and reserves will be willing to expand credit. Some may, in fact, prefer to reduce outstanding debt at a Federal Reserve bank or to maintain greater liquidity in the form of larger reserve balances. Another limitation on full expansion may result because expansion is accompanied by an increase in the amount of coin and paper money held outside the banks. This reduces the reserve foundation for the support of created deposits.

A second assumption, also implicit, is that loan demand is sufficiently great. Clearly, banks cannot create money through loans (or through the investment account) unless there are clients who require additional funds for business or personal reasons. Usually, of course, this is the case, but multiple expansion is nonetheless dependent on demands for credit.

It should also be kept in mind that the amount of expansion which will occur is influenced by the ratio of demand deposits to time deposits in the system, the distribution of deposits in city and country banks, and the distribution of deposits between member and nonmember banks. These influences are felt because of different reserve requirements on these classes of banks and classes of deposits.

It is sometimes contended that all banks must be lending in step, or all at about the same rate, to make expansion possible. However, an unequal rate of lending or investing is not inconsistent with the process of deposit creation.

Contraction of bank credit

If momentarily we overlook the qualifications just mentioned and go bank to our original thesis, we can say that, under the conditions assumed, an increase in reserves may be followed by a tenfold increase in demand deposit accounts. By the same token, if full expansion existed, a loss of $1 of reserves would force a reduction of $10 of deposit credit. Loss of reserves may be due to any of a number of factors which will be discussed in Chapter 7. Regardless of the cause of contraction of basic reserves, it is almost certain to be followed by a multiple reduction in bank loans and investments, and in demand deposits.

An individual bank whose reserve falls below the legal minimum may draw money from other banks by sales of investments or by purchase of federal funds; may call loans payable on demand; and will allow earning assets of near maturities to run off, i.e., be paid in cash with no further reinvestment in similar assets. Contraction may not progress as fast as expansion because banks, hesitating to put the squeeze on borrowers by forcing them to pay loans at once, may borrow reserves from the central bank of the system. Later, as an orderly liquidation of the commercial bank's assets generates a flow of cash into the bank, the debt to the central bank is repaid, and contraction of credit occurs.

The 10% legal minimum reserve assumed in the illustrations in this chapter is, of course, hypothetical. Actually, required reserves in recent years have been close to 20%, or almost double the amount assumed. The effect of increasing required reserves is to reduce the potential limit of expansion. If, under our 10% assumption, $1 of reserve could support $10 in deposits, the $1 under a 20% requirement can act as a base for only half as much, or $5.

Reference has been made several times in this discussion to the credit-granting activities of the Federal Reserve System. Further treatment of the possibilities of credit expansion and the creation of demand deposits is postponed until the nature of central banking and its place in the process of expansion and contraction have been presented.

Questions and problems

1. Distinguish between "loans and discounts" and "investments." How may each account be subdivided?
2. What is the difference between customers' loans and open-market loans? Between discounts and straight loans?
3. What is the nature of a self-liquidating loan?
4. What is a secured loan?
5. Why do bankers favor stock exchange collateral as loan security?
6. Why are term loans said to be tailor-made?
7. For what reasons are rates of interest on short- and long-term loans often not the same?
8. In what respect are real estate loans similar to bank investments?
9. In your community, what is the average yield on commercial bank loans? On investments in mortgage loans?
10. Do banks in your community require borrowers to keep a deposit balance in the bank? If so, what percentage of the loan must be maintained?

11. What proportion of all commercial bank earnings are from loans and discounts, and what proportion from investments?
12. What is the secondary reserve of a bank? Why is it maintained, and what specific items does it usually contain?
13. Do the terms *self-liquidating* and *shiftable* mean the same thing when applied to bank assets? Explain.
14. Could the banking system as a whole ever be highly liquid?
15. What are two functions of the reserves of commercial banks?
16. Why are time or savings deposits not discussed in an explanation of bank credit expansion?
17. Explain and illustrate the process by which the system of commercial banks may achieve a multiple expansion of credit in spite of the fact that any individual bank in the system may lend or invest an amount approximately equal to its excess reserve.
18. If it is assumed that the legal minimum reserve against demand deposits of commercial banks is 16.5%, how much could be loaned if the following composite balance sheet data were given?

> Vault cash and reserves
>   held by Federal Reserve bank $120,000
> Deposits outstanding 675,000

19. What factors may limit credit expansion of commercial banks?
20. From sources of banking data, such as the *Federal Reserve Bulletin*, find figures showing the volume of commercial bank credit and the size of reserve funds. If expansion to the theoretical limit took place, how much would bank deposits increase?

Bibliography

The following texts, which can be found in the libraries of most colleges and universities, contain discussion of banking operation that elaborate the discussions in Chapters 3, 4, and 5.

Barger, Harold. *Money Banking and Public Policy.* 2d ed. Chicago: Rand McNally & Co., 1968.

Beckhart, B. H. *Business Loans of Commercial Banks.* New York: The Ronald Press, 1959.

Chandler, Lester V. *The Economics of Money and Banking.* 5th ed. New York: Harper & Row, 1969.

Hart, Albert Gailord, and Kenen, Peter B. *Money, Debt, and Eoconomic Activity.* 3d ed. Englewood Cliffs, N.J.: Prentice-Hall, Inc., 1961.

Kent, Raymond P. *Money and Banking.* 5th ed. New York: Rinehart & Co., Inc., 1966.

Klein, John J. *Money and the Economy.* 2d ed. New York: Harcourt Brace Jovanovich, 1970.

Klise, Eugene S. *Money and Banking*. 4th ed. Cincinnati: Southwestern Publishing Co., 1968.

Kreps, C. H., Jr. *Money, Banking and Monetary Policy*. 2d ed. New York: The Ronald Press, 1967.

Livingston, Homer J. *Management Policies in American Banks*. New York: Harper & Row, 1956.

Prochnow, Herbert V., and Foulke, Roy A. *Practical Bank Credit*. 2d rev. ed. New York: Harper & Row, 1963.

Prather, Charles L. *Money and Banking*. 9th ed. Homewood, Ill.: Richard D. Irwin, Inc., 1969.

Thomas, Rollin G. *Our Modern Banking and Monetary System*. 4th ed. Englewood Cliffs, N.J.: Prentice-Hall, Inc., 1964.

Whittlesey, Charles R.; Freeman, Arthur M.; and Herman, Edward S. *Money and Banking: Analysis and Policy*. 2d ed. New York: Macmillan Co., 1968.

For students interested in practical operations of banks and the limitations of deposit expansion, the following will be appropriate:

Crosse, Howard D. *Management Policies for Commercial Banks*. Englewood Cliffs, N.J.: Prentice-Hall, Inc., 1962.

Jessup, Paul E. *Innovations in Bank Management*. New York: Holt, Rinehardt & Winston, Inc., 1969.

Robinson, Roland I. *The Management of Bank Funds*. 2d ed. New York: McGraw-Hill Book Co., Inc., 1962.

Publications of the Board of Governors of the Federal Reserve System, the Federal Deposit Insurance Corporation, the American Bankers Association, and the 12 Federal Reserve banks provide a wealth of material covering the field of commercial banking and its relation to our economic system.

CHAPTER 6

Banking structure, supervision, and interrelations

Thus far we have discussed the functional aspects of banking —what the banking system does. Now we shall examine how the banking system is organized to perform its functions, some of the limitations imposed by banking laws and regulations, and the manner in which banking units cooperate with one another.

The structure of the banking system of the United States has many unique features. Our system is vastly different from the systems of Canada or Mexico, those of England and the European nations—or, for that matter, that of any other country. Differences are, for the most part, explainable in terms of our historical development. For example, most of our banks are "unit" operations—a system in which one corporation maintains only one office or place of business. This is in distinct contrast to the practice in other nations, which have a wide extension of the multiple-office branch banking system—a system in which one corporate organization carries on its banking operations at more than one office. Why? The reason is largely due to traditional American independence and a competitive spirit combined with apprehension with respect to the possible development of a "money trust." It is due in part also to the fact that our central government is one of delegated powers; states have always had the right to organize banks within their own borders and to grant charters of incorporation to individuals desiring to begin a banking business. The power to organize is accompanied with power to regulate. As a consequence, banking law and regulation in America have reflected local conditions, with a resulting diversity of detail.

The large number of banks in the United States as well as the geographic limitations on individual bank operations has imposed a need for interbank relationships. The broad development of a complex net of such relations between banks operating in various parts of the nation allows a smooth functioning of the banking system even though individual banks operate within narrow geographic confines.

Structure of the banking system

The preceding chapter has made it reasonably clear that commercial banks may be chartered by the federal government or by the individual states. This dual chartering practice is found in no other country; it is a feature of the banking structure carried over directly from our political system, which is characterized by a constitutionally divided sovereignty. Many other phases of American economic life are also marked by this division of authority.

Dual system of bank charter

A group of businessmen wishing to start a bank under federal charter make application to the Comptroller of the Currency in Washington, D.C. Application for a permit to incorporate under state law is made to a banking commission, auditor of public accounts, or other duly constituted state authority.

The data of Table 6–1 show that only 34% of the total number of commercial banks operate under national charters; yet they own 59% of

TABLE 6–1

Selected assets and liabilities of state and national banks in the United States, December 31, 1969 (*dollars in billions*)

	National	State	Total	Percent of total National	State
Loans	$177.4	$119.3	$296.7	60	40
Investments	70.1	55.0	125.1	55	44
Deposits*	256.3	177.8	434.1	59	41
Capital accounts	23.2	16.3	39.5	59	41
Number	4,668	8,993	13,661	34	66

* Excluding reciprocal deposits.
Source: *Federal Reserve Bulletin*, October 1970, p. A21.

total capital, hold 59% of all deposits, and make 60% of the loans and 55% of the investments.

Although national banks may be of larger average size, it is not difficult to find reasons for the continued existence of large numbers of state-chartered institutions. National banks must be members of the Federal Reserve System, whereas state-chartered banks can join or remain outside the system. The Federal Reserve banks perform services for members, such as clearing checks and transferring securities. Member banks can also borrow funds from their Reserve bank. The major cost of membership is the requirement that member banks maintain a specified proportion of deposits on reserve at the Federal Reserve. These reserves earn no income. Although almost all states also require the maintenance of a specified ratio of reserves to deposits, most states allow short-term security holdings and deposits in other banks to fulfill reserve requirements. Thus nonmember banks can keep a portion of their reserve requirements in the form of earning assets and receive valuable services in return for deposits kept at other banks. Moreover, the reserve requirements for many states are lower than those of the Federal Reserve.

Capital required to organize a state bank may also be substantially less than the requirement for a national charter. In addition, regulations on investment and lending activities and on operating procedures imposed on member banks tend to be much more restrictive than regulations imposed by state authorities.

An important operating restriction on member banks is the requirement that they pay all checks at par, that is, the full sum of the check. Exchange charges or deductions made from the face value of checks by the drawee banks may be made by nonmember state banks. These charges are very unpopular but account for a substantial portion of operating incomes of some small banks. At the end of 1969, 792 banks did not remit payment at par. However, it should be noted that nonpar banks operated in only 11 states and were concentrated mainly in the southern and the northwestern states. The importance of nonpar banking has been declining over the last decade. In the last six years, more than a third of the nonpar banks became par banks.

The greater freedom in use of funds, and smaller amount of nonearning assets required, as well as the lower capital requirements for starting a bank tends to enhance the earning power of state-chartered banks. As a bank grows in size, these advantages become less important relative to the advantages of membership in the Federal Reserve. These factors help explain both the fact that national banks tend to be larger on the average than state banks and also the fact that the larger state banks often choose to become members of the Federal Reserve.

American unit banking system

More than a third of the commercial banking offices in the United States are independent and individual units, each representing a separate business corporation. This situation contrasts with that of many other countries, where there are few banking corporations but many banking offices that are branches of a main corporation. In Canada, for example, there are only nine banks, but these operate several thousand domestic branch offices and many agencies in foreign countries. England has five leading banks and only a few of smaller size. The "big five" operate branches throughout England. In contrast, in the United States at the end of 1969 there were 13,662 incorporated independent banks. Branches of these banks numbered 20,208.

The prevalence of unit banking is, at least in part, attributable to a fear of monopoly in finance—sometimes called *money trusts*. During a large part of our history, while state banking laws were being crystallized, there was greater demand for credit than could be met with existing facilities. Many citizens feared that local branches would collect funds and would ship them to the head office for relending elsewhere. It was the constant fear of a money and credit shortage, as well as the desire to keep the control of local savings and credit facilities in local hands, that made the early frontier states prohibit branch banking. Well founded or not, this attitude left a permanent mark on our banking structure by retarding the development of branch and group organizations.

The trend toward branch banking

Although the United States is characterized as a *unit banking* country, the number of corporations is decreasing, and the number of branch offices is increasing. In 1947, 14,181 banking corporations maintained only 4,161 branch offices; branches numbered 22% of all offices being operated. In December 1959, 13,474 banking corporations had 9,652 branches. As noted above, by the end of 1969 almost 60% of all banking offices were operated as branches.

Nothing was mentioned in the National Bank Act of 1863 about branch banking although some states permitted this form of organization at that time. However, as an increasing number of states legalized branch banking, the national law was modified (McFadden-Pepper Act of 1927) to permit national banks to operate branches within the *city* of the parent organization if state laws permitted state banks to have such branches. Pressure for adoption of nationwide branch banking developed after 1927 but eased when the Banking Act of 1933 permitted national banks to establish statewide branches within those states where state banks operate branches. National banks in such states are bound by the laws that govern the operation of branches by state banks. If state law permits only citywide branches, national banks may maintain multiple offices only within the city; if state law permits statewide operation, national banks have that privilege also. National banks must have a minimum capitalization of $100,000 in order to establish branches regardless of the minimum capital provisions of competing state banks. A state bank member of the Federal Reserve System must receive approval of the Federal Reserve authorities before establishing branches outside of its home city.

Table 6–2 summarizes the branching regulations of the various states. Through the years many changes have been made in these regulations. In

TABLE 6–2
Summary of branch banking statutes of states

Areas having legislation on state or districtwide branch banking		
Permitted	Prohibited	Limited
Arizona	Colorado	Alabama*
California	Florida	Arkansas†
Connecticut	Illinois	Georgia‡
Delaware	Kansas	Indiana*
District of Columbia	Minnesota	Iowa§
Idaho	Missouri	Kentucky*
Louisiana	Montana	Massachusetts*
Maine	Nebraska	Michigan†
Maryland	Texas	Mississippi‖
Nevada	West Virginia	New Jersey*
North Carolina	Wisconsin	New Mexico#
Oregon		New York**
Rhode Island		North Dakota§
South Carolina		Ohio†
South Dakota		Pennsylvania†
Vermont		Tennessee*
Washington		Utah*
		Virginia*
		Alaska‖
		Hawaii††

Areas having no legislation		
New Hampshire	Oklahoma	Wyoming

* Permits branches within the city and county of head office.
† Permits branches within city, county, or county contiguous to county of head office.
‡ Permits banks in certain classes of cities to establish branches within limits of city of head office.
§ Permits only "offices," "agencies," or "stations" for limited purposes, as distinguished from branches.
‖ Permits branches within 100-mile radius of head office.
Permits banks to establish branches within the county or county contiguous to the county in which the parent bank is located, or within a certain distance of the parent bank.
** Permits banks to establish branches within the limits of the banking district in which the parent bank is situated.
†† Permits branches within certain zones.
There are no provisions as to branches of local banks, but banks not organized in the Virgin Islands may do business and establish offices in the Virgin Islands.
Source: Select Committee on Small Business, House of Representatives *Banking Concentration and Small Business* (Washington, D.C.: U.S. Government Printing Office, 1960), p. 35.

recent years the movement has in general been toward easing the restrictions on branching. In the past decade, New York and Pennsylvania have broadened branching privileges. However, the movement has not all been in this direction; Wisconsin, which allowed limited branching, changed to a unit bank state in 1947. Branches in existence at the time of the change were allowed to continue but no new branches can be approved.

The increasing importance of branches in the American banking structure has been stimulated not only by the liberalization of statutory limitations. A more significant force is found in the decentralization of industry, the mass movement of city dwellers to suburban areas, and the growth of shopping centers. In the period from December 31, 1947, to December 31, 1969, the number of banks decreased by 519, but in the same period, branch offices increased from 4,161 to 20,208. Although a substantial number of banks have been absorbed and converted into branch offices, the larger part of the growth in the number of branches reflects the establishment of new branch offices at locations not previously occupied by banks.

An examination of statistics for December 31, 1969, reveals that 4,669 national banks operated 11,727 branches and 1,202 state member banks maintained 3,477 branch offices. The 7,791 state nonmembers maintained 5,004 additional offices.[1] Six states contained more than 60% of all branch banks operating in the United States. California, home of the vast Bank of America system, led with 2,857, closely followed by New York with 2,294; Pennsylvania, Ohio, Michigan, and North Carolina were next in that order.

The power to establish branch offices is not limited to the domestic scene. At the end of 1969, 53 member banks had in active operation a total of 460 branches in 59 foreign countries and possessions of the United States. Of these, 428 were operated by 36 national banks, and the other 32 by 17 state member banks. The foreign branches were distributed geographically as follows: 235 in Latin America, 66 in continental Europe, 37 in England, 77 in the Far East, 6 in the Near East, 1 in Africa, and 38 in U.S. possessions overseas.[2]

In the last decade, overseas branch operations have become an increasingly important segment of the operations of major money-market banks. In addition to handling the overseas financial arrangements of their domestic customers, American banks have increasingly begun to compete with foreign national banks in the overseas markets. But over the last several years, the most important aspect of the overseas branch operations has been the deposits these branches provide to the home office in the United States. Operation of overseas branches does not fall

---

[1] *Federal Reserve Bulletin*, February 1970, p. A96.

[2] Board of Governors of the Federal Reserve System, *Fifty-Sixth Annual Report* (1969), pp. 312–13.

under Regulation Q. (This is a Federal Reserve regulation prescribing the maximum interest rates banks can pay on time and savings deposits. It will be discussed more fully in Chapter 7.) Thus, these branches can bid for deposits at rates above Regulation Q ceilings when domestic banks are unable to attract large depositors because rates on competing money market instruments are above the Regulation Q ceiling. At the end of 1968, these overseas branches provided more than $13 billion in deposits to their parent.

Advantages claimed for branch banking. Branch banking is said to provide the safety that results from wide diversification in the type of bank asset holdings. It is contended that loans made at the several offices would automatically provide a reduction in risk of loss which might accompany the practice of a single-office bank in placing too many eggs in one basket. This argument loses much of its force when the restricted nature of branch banking in the United States is considered. As we have just noted, most branches now being operated are in the city of the parent bank and are therefore subject to about the same commercial and industrial conditions. Thus a recession in business that impaired the credit worth of one borrower would probably exert a similar influence upon many borrowers in that city or county. The argument would have more weight if we had, or contemplated having, nationwide branch banking of the type existing in England and Canada.

A second claim favoring branch banking has somewhat more validity. Interoffice relations within a branch system make the transfer of funds quick and easy and promote mobility of banking resources. This flexibility has been of significance in Canada, where an office of a large bank may be set up in a frontier mining region or oil field and make large sums of bank credit immediately available to an area whose population would hardly justify the existence of a unit bank. Moreover, if the economic resources in such a location should be rapidly depleted, a local unit bank might fail, but a branch could carry on. The branch system may merely discontinue its office or have a representative on the site on a part-time basis. Reduction of the local service would entail no loss of banking capital. This argument is also most effective when branch banking is envisaged on a nationwide scale.

The greater concentration of capital provided by branch banking increases the amount that can be loaned to large businesses and may increase the services available to moderate-sized industrial concerns. Often the unit bank is unable to grant adequate advances because of the legal limitations on the size of loans to a single borrower.

On the other hand, it is widely maintained that the smaller unit banks can accommodate even the largest of firms by sharing loans with their correspondent banks. Moreover, those in favor of unit banking contend that the medium-sized and small firms are better served under a unit system because this business is more important to smaller banks than it would be to larger banks and so they compete harder for it.

It is also contended that branch banking can destroy the monopolies now enjoyed by unit banks in single communities. It is possible also that certain functions, such as trust and investment services, cannot be provided as well by a small unit bank as by the branch of a large metropolitan bank. It is maintained that branches may be operated more cheaply than small unit banks. Fewer spacious buildings are required, and fewer funds would be invested in fixed assets. Management may be more highly paid but is more capable at top levels, making for a more efficient organization. The larger number of minor positions in branch operation widens the choice of management in filling administrative positions in the home office. Thus the branch system is said to facilitate the training of officers.

Objections to branch banking. Always a prominent argument against branch banking is that it fosters monopoly. The broader the branching privilege, the fewer the number of competing banking organizations. But, the opposite relationship holds for the number of banking offices. The broader the branching privilege, the larger the number of banking offices. Unfortunately, it is not obvious whether competition is best served by many independent competing banks or by many offices with only a limited number of competing banks.

Also in the forefront of objections is the feeling that loans made to local borrowers will be administered by bankers not especially interested in the welfare of the local community or keenly aware of local credit needs. Representatives of branch organizations are said to operate on a much less personal basis than managers in unit banks. Doubtless there are many examples to illustrate these objections; yet it should be kept in mind that the long-run success of any banking system is dependent upon the prosperity of local communities. Moreover, perhaps more objectivity and less sentimental interest in promoting an individual local enterprise, irrespective of merit, should be encouraged.

When a large branch banking system is not competently managed and fails, the ensuing disaster is likely to be widespread. In fact, the failure of a large branch banking system may imperil the banking structure of a nation. This appears to have been true of the situation in Detroit that brought on the Michigan moratorium and the national banking holiday in 1933—the closing for a period of time first of all banks in Michigan and then of all banks in the United States. This incident lends support to a widely held objection to branch banking.

It is true that the unit banker is better able and more likely to make character loans, that is to lend money to an individual or business wholly on the ability and character of the person requesting the loan, than a branch manager would make. The unit banker considers himself, and rightly so, as a stable element in his community. Anything that helps the town helps the bank. His attitude and approach to a loan application are less impersonal than that of a branch manager who has been in the community a short time and who may be expecting to move to a more important post in the system very soon.

If we were to sum up the arguments regarding branch versus unit banking, we would conclude that both have favorable aspects. If our objective is to encourage small loans to be granted on a personal basis to individuals and small businesses, we favor the unit system. If the fear is that local funds would be siphoned out of the area in a branch system —contributing to greater monopoly and concentration of power in our large metropolitan banks—we would favor the unit system. On the other hand, if the free flow of money throughout a branch system proves able to alleviate the stresses and strains that accompany a money and credit shortage, we would favor a branch organization. This might depend upon the breadth of the area available for branching. Citywide or countywide branching would do little to relieve local crises. Statewide or nationwide branching could prove very valuable in overcoming local or regional credit stringencies. As we look about us, we are reminded that the nationwide branch systems of Canada and Great Britain, even in the years of greatest crisis, have had no bank failures. This may be attributable to better management or more conservatism, but it has been achieved under branch operation. Perhaps early adoption of nationwide branch banking in the United States would have resulted in substantial social saving if the failure of thousands of our small unit banks could have been averted in the decades of the 1920s and 1930s.

Both the unit and branch types of organization have relative advantages and weaknesses. The choice as to the most desirable form is not clear-cut. Both forms will continue to operate side by side in the United States, at least in the foreseeable future. The question of how and to what extent branching privileges should be changed is among the most difficult and perplexing of the problems facing banking supervisory authorities.

Mergers and consolidations

A recent development tending to modify the system of unit banking— and perhaps tending to reduce local bank competition—is found in the large number of bank consolidations and mergers. In 1952 a total of 100 mergers, consolidations, or absorptions occurred, the largest yearly number since 1939. As the movement increased, the figure rose to 115 in 1953, to 207 in 1954, and reached its peak of 232 in 1955. The move to merge abated somewhat after 1955, but still continued at a relatively high rate. The average was almost 150 in the years 1956 through 1969. In the 18 years 1951–69, over 2,600 banks were absorbed. The importance of mergers is seen when the number of mergers is compared to 14,132, the total number of operating banks at the beginning of 1951.

Motives for merger are varied. In states prohibiting branch banking, a merger can occur from the desire to increase legal lending limits or because one of the banks is located in a declining area that can no longer support a bank. In states that allow branch banking, the usual motive for absorbing a bank is the desire to add one or more branches. In recent years a very high proportion of merged banks have been converted to branches. Occasionally, the motive is desire of a bank to strengthen its management or desire of a strong bank to reduce the number of competitors. Some mergers are created when a bank lacking an important department, such as a trust or industrial loan division, consolidates with a second bank having these features. Some consolidations are implemented by the Federal Deposit Insurance Corporation to protect depositors of banks that would otherwise go into receivership. The favorable price at which a failing small bank may be purchased is doubtless a further motive for absorption.

Regardless of the reasons behind mergers, the reduction in the number of competing banks in some areas has caused increasing concern. In 1960 the Congress passed the Bank Merger Act setting more stringent requirements on bank mergers. Prior to the passage of the act, little formal control was exercised over bank mergers by banking authorities.

The Bank Merger Act requires banks to get approval from the appropriate banking authorities prior to a merger. The authorities are required to study each application for merger and to refuse those mergers which will tend to unduly diminish competitive forces in banking or adversely affect the so-called banking factors, such as the availability of banking services, the ability and depth of management of competing banks, and the financial condition of competing banks. Another important milestone came in 1963, when the Supreme Court, in the case of the proposed merger of the Philadelphia National Bank and the Girard Trust Company of Philadelphia, ruled that bank mergers are subject to antitrust legislation and prohibited this merger even though it had already been approved by the banking regulatory agencies.

Until recently much uncertainty existed among the bank regulatory agencies as to what the Bank Merger Act required them to do. During 1964 and into 1965, the Banking Committees of both houses of Congress held extensive hearings on revisions to the act, and in February 1966, a law was enacted that cleared up most of the uncertainties. The effect of the 1966 amendments is to substantially increase the weight accorded to the competitive factors by the banking authorities in judging the merits of a merger application.

Group banking

Group banking is an arrangement that brings two or more separately incorporated banks into the control of a holding company. The holding company usually exercises voting control by virtue of ownership of sufficient of the capital shares of each bank to dominate the individual institution. The banks within the structure may be unit banks or may be branch systems. Holding companies are always incorporated, and banks themselves sometimes act as the holding company where laws permit them to own the stock of other banks.

The statutes of a majority of our states make no direct mention of group banking, but 42 states prohibit or regulate the acquisition by commercial banks of the stock of other banks. About a dozen states retard the development of group banking by fixing a maximum limit on the proportion of a bank's capital shares that may be owned by one nonbanking corporation, trust, or other association. Mississippi is the only state specifically prohibiting group banking. Under federal law a holding company affiliate (which may be a bank owning the stock of other banks or may be a nonbanking corporation owning bank stock) is required to obtain permission from Federal Reserve authorities before voting the stock of member banks within its control. As early as 1935, federal law prohibited the purchase of bank stock by banks which are members of the Federal Reserve System.

The Bank Holding Company Act of 1956 defines a bank holding company as any company owning 25% or more of the voting shares of two or more banks or which in any manner controls the election of a majority of directors of two or more banks. A holding company is required to register with the Board of Governors of the Federal Reserve System and obtain consent to acquire more than 5% of the voting stock of any bank. No bank holding company is permitted to acquire ownership or control in any company other than a bank. Companies existing at the time of passage of the act were given two years to divest themselves of such ownership unless they received permission from the Board to retain their interest for five years after passage of the act.

Although group banking exists primarily in areas where branches are restricted or prohibited, the large size achieved by a few groups in states permitting branches renders any generalization quite inconclusive. Group banking is usually not considered to be of great significance in the United States. Federal Reserve authorities reported that 55 groups disappeared in the years 1932–36 inclusive, leaving 52 groups operating 479 branches and 1,326 offices. This number was 3.2% of all commercial banks; they held 14% of all deposits in the country. By 1945 the number of groups had declined to only 33 holding $18 billion, or 12% of aggregate deposits. At the end of December 1968, 80 holding company groups operating in

33 states and the District of Columbia included 629 banks with 2,262 branches and held approximately $58 billion in deposits. Holding company groups comprised about 8.9% of all commercial banking offices in the United States. Their deposits were greater than 16% of all deposits in the 33 states where they operate and only 8.9% of all deposits in the entire country.[3]

At the end of 1968, four bank holding companies each had deposits of more than $3 billion. The largest—Western Bancorporation—had almost $8.3 billion in deposits, 24 subsidiary banks, 591 offices, and operated in 11 states. The second largest, Marine Midland Banks, Inc., had deposits of more than $5.2 billion, controlled 11 banks with 229 offices, but operated entirely within the state of New York. The third largest, Northwest Bancorporation, had more than $3.5 billion in deposits, 78 subsidiary banks, 107 offices, and operated in eight states. The First Bank System, Inc., which was the fourth largest, had over $3.3 billion in deposits, 106 offices, 87 subsidiary banks, and operated in five states.

Chain banking

Another modification of the unit bank principle found in the United States is chain banking. It is very similar to group banking except that control of multiple offices is held by one individual or group of individuals or through interlocking directorates, i.e., the same men sitting on several boards of directors.

Chain banking has been predominantly a development in agricultural areas and has achieved greatest significance in a few middle western states where branch banking is prohibited. In only five states have chains accounted for as much as 10% of all banking offices. On December 31, 1945, 115 chains with 522 offices were in operation. Of these offices, 205 were national banks, and 50 were state member banks. Forty-five chains were branch banks, operating 74 offices. Total deposits held were $4.6 billion, or 3.1% of all bank deposits reported on that date.

The most recent survey of the extent of chain banking was conducted in June 1962. Unfortunately, the resulting data were not entirely comparable to those of an earlier series. Utilizing these data, it was estimated that if the ownership link is defined as holding 5% of total common stock or more, then 2,296 banks were members of chains in mid-1962. Under this definition the number of chain banks has more than quadrupled since 1945. The 5% ownership level was not defined consistently between the two surveys; it is therefore not certain that the increase in the number of chain banks was as strong as indicated. But there is little doubt that

---

[3] *Federal Reserve Bulletin,* August 1969, p. A96.

chain banking increased in importance in the United States in the period between 1945 and 1962.[4]

One-bank holding companies

The very substantial increase in the past several years in the number of one-bank holding companies is the outward manifestation of an extremely important development in banking. A one-bank holding company is a corporate entity which owns one bank and also owns other corporations that are engaged in a wide variety of activities. Thus the one-bank holding company is not legally considered a bank holding company for regulatory purposes.

By the definition given above, there have always been one-bank holding companies, since individual nonbanking companies have, in the past, held majority stock ownership of a substantial number of banks. The recent interest in one-bank holding companies, however, derives from the trend toward banks setting up a holding company and purchasing or organizing enterprises engaged in nonbanking, but in the main, financial service-oriented activities.

For banks an important impetus to the one-bank holding company form was the possibility of engaging in businesses from which they were excluded by regulations. But this was not the sole reason behind their formation. Many services, mainly computer based, that have been developed in recent years or that are now being planned can be more efficiently provided by a separate operating entity than by a department of the bank.

Some bank holding companies have diversified by setting up new activities, by purchasing companies engaged in other activities, or by doing both. Although this development holds the promise of increased efficiency in providing financial services, there is concern over how much regulatory control should be exercised over the expansion of these enterprises. It is widely expected that in the near future legislation will be passed which explicitly defines the areas in which one-bank holding companies can operate.

Bank supervision

In every phase of its existence, from the date of original incorporation until final liquidation, a commercial bank is closely supervised and regulated. In few countries are bank operations as carefully scrutinized by public authorities as in the United States. This may be due to the dual system of chartering and adherence to the principle of free banking that has resulted in a larger number of unit banks. It may partially be a reme-

---

[4] Jerome C. Darnell, "Chain Banking," *National Banking Review,* vol. 3, no. 3 (March 1966).

dial outgrowth of the many severe financial crises that have afflicted the nation periodically.

Strangely enough, in spite of the inherent dislike and general opposition of Americans to supervision, the regulation of banking activities has created little adverse comment. Perhaps the lack of criticism is due to the quasi-public nature of banking, to an awareness of the vulnerability to loss of millions of small-deposit holders, and to the recognition that special privileges had been granted to banks, such as the power to create money in the form of bank notes and deposit credit. However, in recent years there has been an increasing belief that the existing regulatory structure should be loosened, and a significant amount of loosening has actually occurred.

Banking supervision begins with the granting of charters and extends through regulations governing voluntary or involuntary liquidation. During the intervening life span of an institution, supervisory authorities maintain control by requiring periodic reports, by making unannounced examinations, and by forcing banks to take the steps necessary to correct abuses or inefficiences of management, particularly to maintain their liquidity and solvency.

Fifty-three agencies are actively engaged in the regular supervision of commercial banks. Fifty of these have responsibility for the supervision of banks in the respective states; several of them antedate federal supervision by many years. The three agencies directly responsible for bank supervision on a national scale are the Office of the Comptroller of the Currency (established 1863), the Federal Reserve System (1913), and the Federal Deposit Insurance Corporation (FDIC) (1933). For purposes of supervision, our commercial banks are divided into four classes: national, state member, nonmember insured, and nonmember uninsured. The words *national* and *state* refer to the chartering authority; *member* means membership in the Federal Reserve System; and *insured* refers to participation in the FDIC. At year-end 1969, there were 13,662 commercial banks in the United States: 4,669 were national; 1,202 were state member insured; 7,595 nonmember state banks were insured; and the remaining 196 were state nonmember uninsured.

The examination of commercial banks on the bank premises is one of the most effective controls exercised over bank operations. In the process, bank examiners evaluate the quality of the bank's asset portfolio, the ability of management, the adequacy of capital, and other operating characteristics of the bank. During the examination, examiners and management discuss bank practices and operating procedures. Bank officers and directors, as well as the bank regulatory authorities, are given a written statement and critique at the conclusion of the examination process. For the bank's board of directors, this document is used as an outside authoritative evaluation of management capability and of the appropriateness of management investment and loan policies. For the banking authorities, the examination report contains information necessary to evaluate the degree of bank compliance to laws and regulations, as well as the financial condition of the bank.

Examinations

Even though many banks are subject to regulation by more than one authority, there is virtually no duplication of bank examination in practice. Despite the fact that all national banks are members of the Federal Reserve System and are insured, they are examined by neither Federal Reserve authorities nor the FDIC. National banks are examined by the staff of the Comptroller of the Currency, and the reports are accepted by the Federal Reserve Board and the FDIC. It is the policy of the Federal Reserve authorities to make at least one regular examination of each state member bank, including its trust department, during each calendar year, by examiners for the Reserve bank in the district in which the bank is situated. Frequently, however, the Federal Reserve and state examinations are conducted concurrently. Insured banks which are not members of the Federal Reserve System are regularly examined by the FDIC. The FDIC may examine national banks only after obtaining written permission of the Comptroller of the Currency, and state member banks with consent of the Board of Governors of the Federal Reserve System. This it seldom does. Instead, it accepts reports prepared by the other two agencies. The FDIC does examine insured nonmember state banks but here also it often accepts concurrent or alternate examination with the state banking authorities. Thus 13,462 out of a total 13,662 commercial banks on December 31, 1969, were receiving regular examinations and other supervisory attention from at least one of the federal agencies.

Supervisory duties of the various banking authorities appear to be inextricably entwined, but careful consideration of the specialized functions of each agency shows a fair avoidance of actual duplication. An examination of Exhibit 6-1 reveals the many aspects of commercial bank operations that are supervised by federal and state authorities.

The Report of the Commission on Money and Credit recommended concentration of the examining functions of the three federal agencies in the hands of one of them, but Congress rejected this proposal. Opposition has been voiced unofficially by members of each of the federal regulatory organizations against such a move because each feels that its examination has a somewhat different objective than the others. In particular, it is avowed that the major goal of FDIC supervision is to keep the banks financially healthy, and to prevent the failure and the shrinkage of deposit credit that occur when banks fail. On the other hand, supervision by the Federal Reserve System points to regulation of banks' reserves in

EXHIBIT 6–1

Supervision of the commercial banking system (*principal relationships*)

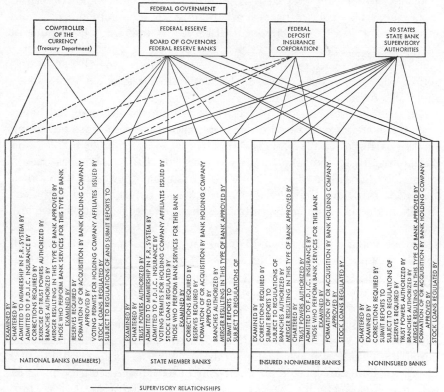

Source: *Bank Supervision*, Federal Reserve Bank of St. Louis, 1963.

such a way as to maximize productive capacity and prevent excessive fluctuations in the volume of business. (The manner in which Federal Reserve authorities determine policies and attempt to carry them to completion will be discussed in Chapter 7.) In view of the strength of the vested interests in the field of bank supervision, the small duplication of actual examination effort and general unwillingness of Congress to reorganize the executive branches of government, concentration of regulatory authority in the hands of one agency is not soon to be expected.

Regulation of commercial bank lending

Federal and state banking statutes place numerous restrictions upon the freedom of banks to grant loans. The basis for regulation is found largely in the desire of government to protect the bank depositors, the financial health of individual banks and the banking structure as a whole. Present also, as we shall see later, is the desire to exercise control over the volume of purchasing power existing in the form of bank deposits derived from loans. This control bears most directly upon the amount of liquid reserve required behind deposits, as it serves to limit the total volume of loans and investments the banks may make.

Although the pattern of loan limitations is similar for all banks, uniformity does not exist because of the separate jurisdictions of 50 states and the federal government.

In general until recently the restrictions under which national banks operated were as severe and often more restrictive than those governing banks chartered by the various states. However, beginning in 1960 and continuing up to the time this is written (late 1970) there has been a progressive loosening of restrictions governing the operations of national banks. At this time, the regulations for national banks are in many areas of banking activity much less restrictive than parallel regulations of many states.

In every jurisdiction the most important restrictions are those which force diversification of earning assets. A national bank may make unsecured loans to one borrower in an amount not greater than 10% of its unimpaired capital and surplus. Recent rulings by the Comptroller of the Currency which broadened the definitions of unimpaired capital and surplus have substantially increased the amount which national banks can lend to any one borrower.[5] If the borrower's note is adequately secured, the bank may lend an amount as large as 25% of its capital to that client. No limits are placed on extensions based on the security of drafts drawn against actually existing values, commercial paper of a third party owned by the borrower and endorsed over to the lending bank, bankers' acceptances, bills of lading on commodities in transit, and government obligations.

Real estate loans by national banks were prohibited before adoption of the Federal Reserve Act in 1913. This act and more recent amendments have placed national and state banks more nearly on the same competitive level in this field of lending. A national bank may now extend real estate loans in an amount equal to 100% of its total capital and surplus or to 70% of its time deposits, whichever is the greater amount. The philosophy that limits loans in relation to savings deposits or the invested capital of the bank is that these items are relatively stable, thus permitting a bank to extend a portion of such funds to borrowers on long-term notes.

Individual loans of national banks on real estate are limited to 50%

[5] U.S. Treasury, *One Hundred and First Annual Report of the Comptroller of the Currency* (Washington, D.C.: U.S. Government Printing Office), p. 6.

of the value of improved property if the note has five years or less to run; up to 66% if the note matures in 10 years, provided that no less than 40% of the loan will be paid in installments during that period. A recent modification of the law permits a national bank to grant real estate loans for periods between 10 and 25 years in an amount up to 80% of appraised value if the principal is completely amortized during the loan period. In all cases, the note is secured by a first mortgage on the property.[6] Exceptions to these provisions may be made when the loans are insured by the Federal Housing Administration (FHA) or guaranteed by the Veterans Administration (VA).

Other miscellaneous restrictions forbid a national bank to make loans to its own officers unless the loan is approved by the board of directors of the lending institution. If approved, the loan may be for no more than $2,500. Nor can a bank lend to an officer of another bank until the board of the employing institution has received a detailed report of the amount, purpose, collateral security, and date of the loan. No loan may be made on a note secured by stock of the lending bank. Examiners of national banks may not borrow from national banks, nor may state bank examiners borrow from the banks they examine. Maximum interest rates on loans are also stipulated in federal law. Rates may be as high as the legal or usury rate of the state in which the bank is located. In the event that the state has no legal maximum, 7% may be charged by the lending institution. Fees that increase total income earned above the legal maximum are allowed where the bank performs valuable and costly services related to credit investigation, title search, collections, and other operations closely associated with its lending activities. The lending regulations listed are enforced by bank examiners.

Government regulation of bank investments

Government regulation of the investments of commercial banks also lacks uniformity from state to state, although everywhere the idea of protecting the bank depositor by this means is accepted. National law on the subject changes from time to time. For example, in the year 1863, banks were forced to invest a certain percentage of their capital in federal bonds to be used as security for bank note issues. Real estate loans were prohibited in the same statute; and by implication, other long-term loans and bonds held for investment purposes were excluded. The provision regarding bonds was relaxed by subsequent ruling of the Comptroller of the Currency. The Federal Reserve Act of 1913 and the McFadden-Pepper Act, 1927, amended the law to permit national banks to grant real estate loans and to invest in "bonds, notes, or debentures commonly known as investment securities." The latter act also authorized the

---

[6] Public Law 88–560 (Act of Congress Approved September 2, 1964).

Comptroller to prescribe the nature of investment securities. His ruling was that banks might purchase securities that were marketable or those having "such a market as to render sales at intrinsic values readily possible." No suggestion was made of a method to determine intrinsic values.

In the 10 years after World War I, commercial banks not only expanded the volume of bonds held for their own account but became deeply involved in investment banking by establishing underwriting affiliates for the marketing of securities. The Banking Act of 1933 curtailed this activity. In fact, commercial banks are now forbidden to underwrite any issue of corporate investment securities. They are permitted, however, to underwrite state and local government issues that bear the full faith and credit of the governmental body that issued them and to deal in U.S. government bonds.

Diversification of the bond accounts of banks is promoted by the requirement (1935) that member banks cannot purchase securities of one obligor in an amount in excess of 10% of the bank's capital and surplus. Government obligations are exempt from this provision. Purchase of bonds convertible into stocks or low-grade bonds in which speculative, rather than investment, characteristics predominate is prohibited.

Because the experience of banks with investment securities during the depression of 1929–33 was often disastrous, the quality of bank investments for all members of the Federal Reserve System was made subject to supervision of the Comptroller of the Currency. The regulation, first issued in 1936, was revised in 1938 and jointly adopted by the Comptroller of the Currency, the Federal Reserve, and the FDIC. It is enforced by examiners of each of these supervisory agencies. The revision became effective only after extensive consultation among federal officials and state banking departments and, in practice, is now applied to virtually all banks.

The chief effect of the ruling is to prohibit purchases by banks of bonds not included in the four upper classes of securities as determined by investment rating services such as Moody's, Fitch, and Standard and Poor's. It has the further objective of penalizing banks for the continued holding of securities which have slipped down and out of the first four ratings. In short, the regulation provides that banks should purchase and hold only marketable bonds. Unfortunately, no very definite criterion of marketability is established.

In addition to corporate bonds, the investments eligible for ownership by commercial banks include federal government, state, and municipal issues, obligations of Federal Home Loan banks, Federal Farm Mortgage Corporation, Federal Land banks, and other agencies of the Farm Credit Administration, foreign bonds, and those of the World Bank if they meet the standards of quality established by the Comptroller of the Currency. Bank ownership of stocks is severely restricted, however. Only issues of the district Federal Reserve bank, the Import-Export Bank, safe deposit box subsidiaries, and a few other issuers specifically mentioned in the law may be held by national banks and state bank members of the Federal Reserve System.

Deposit insurance

Beginning in 1909, a few middle western states adopted deposit insurance or guaranty as an additional safeguard to depositors. Without exception, these systems fell into discard during the 1920s. The severely depressed conditions during 1929–33 and the chaotic state of the banking system served as the incentive for adoption of a nationwide plan for insuring bank deposits. This was originally provided in the Banking Act of 1933. The law has been in operation since January 1, 1934. Insurance is made available through the FDIC. As administered from 1934 to 1950, the law provided insurance for each deposit account of Federal Reserve members and qualifying nonmember banks up to $5,000. In September 1950, the insurance coverage was raised to $10,000 per account. In October 1966, coverage was raised to $15,000 and then to $20,000 per account on December 23, 1969.

When the plan was initiated, funds for reimbursement of depositors of failed banks became available from three sources: (1) a treasury subscription of $150 million in capital stock of the FDIC, (2) sale of stock to each Federal Reserve bank equal to half its surplus account, amounting to total to about $139 million,[7] and (3) from semiannual collections of premium assessments on insured banks equal in total to one twelfth of 1% of average deposits. Premium assessments in 1959 were still one twelfth of 1% of deposits subject to assessment. A credit arrangement in effect, since 1950, however, allows a reduction based on the preceding year's net assessment. During 1969 the effective assessment rate was about $\frac{1}{30}$th of 1% a year.[8]

The amount of funds collected and not required to settle claims of depositors or to meet current expenses of the FDIC must be invested in securities issued or guaranteed as to principal and interest by the federal government. Temporarily, however, such funds may be placed on deposit in the U.S. Treasury or in Federal Reserve banks. Since the beginning of its operations in 1934, the FDIC has been able to meet all insurance losses and operating expenses from earnings on its security holdings. Interest received on investments and other income becomes a more im-

---

[7] In the autumn of 1947, the FDIC began installment retirement of stock held by the U.S. Treasury and the Federal Reserve banks. Final settlement was made in September, 1948.

[8] Federal Deposit Insurance Corporation, *Annual Report* for the year ended December 31, 1969, p. 23.

portant source of current revenue as the security reserve is enlarged. In 1968 receipts from this account were more than $192 million, over $45 million more than the amount collected from assessments and more than five times as large as the total expenses of the FDIC for the year. Annual premium receipts and uncommited interest from investments have been credited to the Deposit Insurance Fund, which reached a total of $4,051 million at year-end 1969.[9]

The FDIC is administered by a three-man board of directors consisting of the Comptroller of the Currency and two other presidential appointees. It is empowered to conduct examinations of all insured nonmember state banks and may examine national and state members as noted above. It has other supervisory functions also, notably to prohibit payment of interest by banks on demand deposits, to limit interest paid on time and savings deposits of insured nonmember banks, and to pass on merger application of insured nonmember banks. The purpose of these provisions is to enhance earnings of insured banks to enable them to build up capital accounts and minimize the chance of failure. An indirect effect is to place almost all state-chartered commercial banks under federal supervision. The FDIC is appointed receiver of all failed national banks and accepts appointment as receiver of failed insured state banks if such receivership is tendered by state banking authorities.

When operating in the capacity of receiver, the FDIC liquidates assets taken over from failed banks as the opportunity for orderly conversion into cash presents itself. Balances held in insured accounts are made available to depositors as soon as possible. This is done either by transfer of the insured deposit to another insured bank in the same community, by depositing it in a new national bank organized by the FDIC for this purpose, or by giving checks in payment to depositors.

In recent years the plan of operation of the FDIC has been to preserve banks rather than to permit failure, after which it would act only as a receiver. By organizing a new national bank, administered by an appointee of the FDIC, to assume the insured deposits of a closed bank, or by transferring the business of the closed bank to an active insured bank in the same community, the FDIC has effectively insured or guaranteed payment of all deposit accounts in full, and not merely to the extent of the insurance coverage. From an economic or a social point of view, the FDIC's procedure in preserving the banking institutions in a community is far superior to any action it might take as merely a liquidating agent for an insolvent bank. In a reorganization, not only are all deposits fully protected, but business in the community is not interrupted; nor are there any undesirable repercussions on neighboring banks. Moreover, the costs to the FDIC of meeting depositor losses are kept to a minimum.

---

[9] Ibid., Table 14, p. 26.

On December 31, 1969, over 97% of all operating commercial banks were insured. On that date noninsured banks held less than nine tenths of 1% of total assets of the commercial banking system.

The degree of protection afforded to depositors of commercial and mutual saving banks is revealed in data released by the FDIC in its 1969 *Annual Report*. On December 31, 1969, 99% of all deposit accounts of insured banks were $20,000 or less. All such accounts were therefore fully protected by insurance. In the 13,462 insured banks, deposits totaled $496 billion. About $313 billion, or 63% of the deposits were insured. The relatively few accounts having an uninsured balance in excess of $20,000 contained approximately $183 billion. The portion of deposits that are in excess of $20,000 is afforded some degree of safety, however, by the existence of complete coverage on smaller amounts, and the prevention of failures makes the protection even greater. The insurance of 99% of all accounts reduces the likelihood and the severity of runs on banks.

In 36 full years of operation (1934–69), the FDIC paid the insured deposits of 287 banks for which it became the receiver. From 1934 through 1969, it made additional disbursements in the cases of 198 distressed insured institutions. In protecting the depositors of these 482 banks, the FDIC paid out over $475 million.[10]

In the 482 cases, almost 1.7 million depositors were involved, with total deposits of $879 million. The amount eventually made available to depositors was 97% in payoff cases and 100% when assets and liabilities of the weak banks were transferred to, and assumed by, a sound institution.

By the end of 1969, the FDIC had recovered, or estimated that it would recover, $419 million of the amount it had dispersed. This amounts to a loss of only $56 million in the 35 years of operation.[11]

The insurance of bank deposits by a federal instrumentality seems now to be generally accepted; in the minds of many individuals this is a firmly established institution occupying a permanent place in our banking structure. To many, the assumption of this responsibility by the federal government is considered only just. For years, bank notes have been guaranteed by the government, and extension of the same protection to depositors is not revolutionary in principle. Moreover, as long as the nation is committed to a dual system of free banking with thousands of unit banks in which the risk of loss has been relatively great, public safeguards are necessary to the preservation of the system.

Opponents of the plan have advanced several arguments against deposit insurance. One is that it will encourage bad banking and inefficient administration of local institutions by removing the necessity for

---

[10] Ibid., Table 3, p. 13.
[11] Ibid., Table 2, p. 12.

each bank to preserve itself through good management. Another, that the present plan of assessment places an unfair burden upon large metropolitan banks. That is, their likelihood of failure is less than that of smaller, less diversified rural banks, and so their contribution to the fund should be relatively less. Also, that a much smaller percentage of large city bank deposits is covered by the $20,000 limit, and the amount of the guaranty is insignificant to depositors with large balances. Although sentiment developed among some bankers for reduction of the premium or distribution of a dividend from the reserve already established, it is said in other quarters that the assessment is too small to provide a reserve adequate to meet the losses that would be incurred in a serious banking crisis. The counterargument (noted above) is that, if the plan creates confidence among depositors, they will not run on banks, and panic will be averted. Also, if the reserves should prove inadequate in settling claims of depositors of failed banks, the FDIC may use a $3 billion drawing fund available from the U.S. Treasury. It is interesting to note that the reserve of the FDIC in 1969 was more than $4 billion, more than three times as great as the $1.3 billion in losses suffered by depositors of over 9,000 commercial banks that failed in the 39-month period, January 1930 to March 4, 1933.[12]

There has been no opportunity to test the strength of the program in the years that federal guaranty has been in force. No one is able to determine at this time the validity of the contentions of either adherents or antagonists. We are safe in saying, however, that the FDIC has given our commercial banking structure a greater coherence and unity than it formerly possessed and, without doubt, has added stability to the system by increasing public confidence in the safety of deposits.

Interbank relations

In a country like the United States, where nationwide branch banking is prohibited and the independent unit bank is still typical, separate unit banks are forced to cooperate in providing the services demanded of them. Cooperation and joint action may be the result of legal compulsion, as previously observed in the requirement that all national banks must belong to the Federal Reserve System and that all members of that system must participate in the federal program of deposit insurance. But long before the advent of central banking and deposit guaranty, commercial banks had found voluntary cooperation both valuable and necessary. These interbank contacts are exemplified in the nationwide network of

---

[12] Board of Governors of the Federal Reserve System, *Banking and Monetary Statistics* (Washington, D.C., 1943), sec. 7, "Bank Suspensions," Table 66, "Commercial Bank Suspensions," p. 283; and the FDIC, *Annual Report* (1969), Table 9, p. 22.

correspondent banking relationships, in local clearinghouse associations, and such organizations as the American Bankers Association and the bankers associations in each state.

Correspondent banking

Early in the history of American banking, small banks in rural areas found it necessary to carry balances with other banks in the larger centers of trade. In no other way could banks finance shipment of goods into the local community and accommodate their customers in making payments at a distance. Small banks did not have adequate facilities for dealing in investment securities—either for their own portfolios or for the benefit of customers. They were often unable to transmit funds to remote places for financing foreign exchange transactions. They were at a competitive disadvantage, as compared to small banks in a branch system, in the clearing and collection of checks. As a consequence, long before the 20th century, there had developd a system of voluntary cooperation, known as *correspondent relationships,* to fill these gaps.

A country bank usually chose a bank in each of a number of larger cities as its depository or correspondent. The latter bank held a deposit account (interbank balance) for the smaller institution and usually, until the practice was outlawed by the Federal Reserve Act, paid what was then a relatively low rate of interest—frequently 2%—on the net balance. Correspondent balances were counted within limits as legal reserves against depositors' claims until the Federal Reserve banks become depositories of legal minimum-reserve requirements of member banks. The large city correspondent was constantly of assistance in check clearing and collecting and upon occasion would lend to its country correspondent.

It was expected, by some, that when the Federal Reserve banks established a nationwide system of check collection and provided rediscount facilities, thus minimizing the need for interbank borrowing, the correspondent banking system would be doomed but this has not been the case. If anything, correspondent relations have become more important and are destined to continue as long as our unit banking system exists.

Correspondent relations allow the small bank in a rural area, small city, or suburban area to offer the entire range of services available at a large city bank. City correspondents commonly provide foreign exchange, extend credit information, act as a depository for securities, or provide trust services for customers of smaller banks. In addition to clearing checks, correspondents act as a depository for liquid balances and oftentimes manage the investment portfolio of smaller banks. Because of the limit on the size of loan to any one borrower, loan participations are an important part of correspondent relations. Thus a small local bank which serves a large company can initiate a loan much larger that it can legally grant, knowing that one or a number of its correspondents will participate for the portion of the loan above its legal lending limit. Conversely, a small bank that has little loan demand can share in loans originated by its larger correspondent.

In recent years correspondent activity has broadened to include help with management recruitment, with marketing campaigns, and, of growing importance, help and advice in installing electronic data processing equipment. In this latter category many larger correspondent banks actually handle large portions of bookkeeping and data processing for neraby smaller banks. It is widely predicted that in the not too distant future the large city correspondents will handle the entire record maintainance, check clearing, and other data processing functions for their smaller correspondents through remote terminals. The smaller bank will have no on-site records; all data will be entered on the small bank's computer terminal and sent to the computer of the large bank. When records are needed by the small bank, they will be requested through the terminal and sent by the large bank's computer to the small bank's terminal.

The country clients or correspondents repay the city banks for their services, other than direct lending operations, by keeping sizable deposit accounts with them. On December 31, 1969, interbank balances totaled almost $28 billion for the country as a whole. Of this amount, $10.6 billion were held in banks in New York City and $1.7 billion in Chicago banks, indicating the importance of these two major banking centers.[13] In recent years, with the growth in the volume and variety of correspondent services, especially data processing, some movement has begun toward charging explicit fees rather than relying entirely on deposit balances.

Clearinghouse associations

Just as the correspondent relationship provides the vehicle for cooperation within the banking system among banks in various parts of the country, so the clearinghouse furnishes the means of cooperation for banks within a certain community. As the name indicates, the clearinghouse was originally an agency for the clearing of checks between banks in the same locality but in time it has come to be much more.

Clearinghouse associations conduct bank examinations supplementary to those made by legally authorized agencies. Some have assisted distressed member banks by arranging loans or temporary clearinghouse certificates in lieu of transfers of money in settlement of the claims cleared during periods of distress. They have become, in a sense, trade associations and, as such, exert pressure upon member institutions to pre-

---

[13] *Federal Reserve Bulletin*, October 1970, p. A20.

vent unfair practices, untruthful advertising, or unwise competitive methods. They provide for the interchange of credit information and aid the development of uniform methods or practices where standardization is of benefit to all concerned.

The clearing process. The checks that a bank receives on deposit are those that are drawn on itself, on nearby banks, or on banks some distance away.

The first kind of transaction is settled easily within the bank by adding to the depositing customer's balance and substracting the same amount from the balance of the customer who drew the check. The second class of checks may be collected by messenger or through the clearinghouse. The third kind will be collected either through a city correspondent or through the Federal Reserve System.

Collection by messenger. Collection by messenger is a cumbersome and costly arrangement, for, if widely used, it could place a large number of bank clerks on the streets at one time. If collections were being made in this fashion, each institution would send a different messenger to each one of the other banks to deliver the bundle of checks to be paid. The messengers would then return to their own banks with the settlements (officer's checks or checks in federal funds) they had collected.

Collection of local checks through a clearinghouse. If a clearinghouse association is substituted for a plan of clearing by messengers, as was done in New York City in 1853, the advantages of speed, economy, and reduced risk are realized. There are variations in the details of operation, but an example will illustrate the merits of any clearinghouse system.

For example, early each day Bank A will make up a bundle of checks drawn on each of the other banks of the city. The total amount represented by the checks in each bundle is noted, and at a certain time the messenger is dispatched to the clearinghouse. There he meets messengers from the other banks carrying bundles of checks received the previous day by their respective institutions. The bundles are then exchanged and calculations made to show how much Bank A should receive from each other bank. Also, it is necessary to compute the amounts owed by Bank A to the other banks that had received checks drawn by depositors of Bank A. It may be assumed that checks totaling $360,000 drawn against Bank A are presented by Banks B and C, whereas checks brought by Bank A drawn on Banks B and C total $385,000. In this case, Bank A has a favorable balance and is owed $25,000 more than it owes. But the amount due to Bank A must be owed by Banks B and C together. Those two institutions will have adverse balances totaling $25,000 due to Bank A. In the settling process, no funds are paid directly to a bank, nor are funds received directly from a bank. The respective debit and credit claims are offset on the books of the clearinghouse, and all receipts and payments are made by the manager of the association.

The accompanying exhibit (see Exhibit 6–2) may add clarity to our illustration. Let us assume that Bank A receives during the day claims of $175,000 against Bank B and $210,000 against Bank C; that Bank B receives claims of $115,000 on Bank A and of $150,000 on Bank C; and

EXHIBIT 6–2

Illustration of a clearing operation (*thousands of dollars*)

DRAWN ON	BROUGHT BY	BANK A	BANK B	BANK C	TOTAL
BANK A			115	245	360
BANK B		175		105	280
BANK C		210	150		360
TOTAL		385	265	350	1,000

	Bank A	Bank B	Bank C	Total
Total claims on other banks	$385	$265	$350	$1,000
Total claims presented by others	360	280	360	1,000
Difference—amount due	$ 25	$ —	$ —	$ 25
—amount owed	—	15	10	25

that Bank C claims $245,000 from Bank A and $105,000 from Bank B. The total of these claims, $1 million, can be settled by a transfer of $15,000 from Bank B and $10,000 from Bank C, or a total of $25,000 to Bank A.

When the calculations of amounts due and owed have been completed at the clearinghouse, the messengers return to their respective banks with the bundles of checks received from the other banks. Following that, bookkeepers in each institution deduct the proper amounts from the accounts of depositors who drew the checks. Canceled checks are then filed to be returned to the drawer at month-end or whenever the books are balanced.

Collection of out-of-town items. As already indicated, the collection of out-of-town checks is, in practice, effected either through a city correspondent or through the Federal Reserve. Since in both cases the process is very similar, we shall limit ourselves to a description of the general process and then add a few notes about the special problems of Federal Reserve collections.

Use of correspondent bank in collecting checks. Operation of the clearing process through the correspondent plan can be illustrated very simply. Small rural banks usually keep a correspondent balance in banks of several metropolitan centers with whom its customers have business. For a bank in a typical downstate town of Illinois, this may mean that deposits are maintained at Chicago, St. Louis, and Nashville. The total of these balances may be from 5% to 20% of the bank's deposit obligations.

Larger metropolitan banks, such as the well-known Loop banks of Chicago, may have from 100 to 1,000 correspondents in rural areas. In turn, these city banks have balances on deposit in New York and other large cities.

When a small bank in rural Illinois receives a check drawn on a country bank in Tennessee, it may forward the item to its Nashville correspondent for collection. If the Nashville bank also holds a deposit of the drawee bank in Tennessee, it may collect the check, after advice of acceptance, by merely adjusting the balances it holds for the two rural institutions. In the event that a check originates at a greater distance from Illinois, such as Oswego, New York, the check will be forwarded by the small Illinois bank to its Chicago correspondent for collection. The latter will send the item to a New York correspondent bank, which will in turn collect through its correspondent relations with a bank in Oswego.

Regardless of the distance between the point of origin and the bank in which the item is deposited, the network of correspondent relationships covering the nation makes collection relatively cheap and convenient. The system furnishes cohesion within the banking structure and introduces some of the natural advantages that would be found in a nation-wide branch system.

In some areas of the South and West, drawee banks do not honor at par checks presented by mail, but make a small deduction called an *exchange charge*. These are *nonpar banks*. The practice is usually confined to small banks in thinly settled areas. Before the Federal Reserve System was established, exchange charges were commonly made by national, as well as by state, banks. Checks being returned to the drawee bank were routed via a correspondent which would remit to the payee bank at par. The correspondent would bear the loss of nonpar remittance by the drawee bank unless it, in turn, was able to collect via one of its correspondents. The resulting system of indirect routing enlarged the volume of checks in the process of collection, called the *float*, and greatly increased the overall costs of the collection process. The Federal Reserve once tried to bring about universal par clearance. It failed, but by persuasion it has managed to reduce the nonpar fringe to a small number of remote banks.

Check collection through a Federal Reserve Bank. The process of check collection through the Federal Reserve is much the same as through a correspondent bank. The chief difference is that the Federal Reserve is somewhat more exacting about the way in which it insists that collection items be forwarded; on the other hand, since member banks must keep a reserve balance with the Federal Reserve bank whether or not they use its collection facilities, they can sometimes keep down the amount of idle cash by using these Federal Reserve facilities, thereby avoiding the need for a large correspondent account. Since all member banks are required to maintain deposits at the regional Federal Reserve bank, the balances can be used as a clearing account for members located in the same district. Checks drawn against Bank A and deposited in Bank Z, when sent to the Reserve bank for collection, are settled by increasing the reserve balance of Bank Z and reducing that of Bank A.

This system covers the entire nation; it works between Federal Reserve districts as well as within a single district. Each Federal Reserve bank maintains a balance in the Inter-district Settlement Fund in Washington, D.C. Here daily computations are made on the basis of telegraphic reports received from each Federal Reserve bank, indicating the amount of checks received during the day that involve collections in each of the other 11 districts. Net amounts due or to be received are calculated by computers, and the accounts of some district banks are reduced while an equal amount is added to the other district accounts.

Thus, when middle western businessmen make large payments to their creditors along the Atlantic seaboard, not only are deposits of member banks and Federal Reserve banks in the Middle West reduced, but the deposits of Federal Reserve banks of the Middle West held in the Inter-district Settlement Fund in Washington also decline. In contrary fashion, deposits of eastern commercial and Federal Reserve banks expand, as will balances in the Inter-district Settlement Fund held for the account of the eastern Federal Reserve banks. In short, settlements through this fund are correlated with member-bank deposits and reserve balances.

A few commercial banks that are not full-fledged members of the Federal Reserve System avail themselves of clearing privileges by maintaining a deposit, or clearing balance, with the regional Federal Reserve bank. Many others places themselves on the par list by agreeing to remit the face value of any legitimate check or draft on which they are the designated drawee.

When a check is sent to the Federal Reserve for clearing, the depositing bank receives a deferred availability credit. That is, depending on the distance of the bank on which the check is drawn from the Federal Reserve branch that receives the deposit, the bank will have to wait one or two days before it has collected funds credited to its account.

Deferred availability items at the Federal Reserve, and any check which has been deposited at the bank but has not been sent to the paying bank so that collected funds are available, represent unusable funds. Hence, banks place great emphasis on rapid and efficient processing of checks that have been deposited. Efficient processing means that checks are sorted and shipped through the quickest channel, either directly to the paying bank, to the clearinghouse, directly to a correspondent, or to the Federal Reserve for collection, whichever will minimize the time until the funds represented by the check are collected from the drawee bank.

The funds transfer mechanism described above has been and is operating with great efficiency. It is estimated that approximately 80 billion checks cleared through the banking system in 1969. The number of checks passing through the system has been growing at about 8% per annum, and this rate of growth is expected to continue.

In the last decade, the funds transfer system of banks has been automated to a considerable extent. Nonetheless, a very substantial portion of the manpower of commercial banks is involved in handling the physical tasks connected with processing checks. Considerable research is being undertaken within the industry, in the regulatory agencies, and by computer hardware and software manufacturers to develop a substitute for the present check system. This substitute has been widely discussed as the *checkless society* or the electronic transfer mechanism. There is a high probability that within 10 years a substantial fraction of fund transfers will be handled by direct electronic transmissions rather than through the present check system.

Summary

Despite the fact that nationwide branch banking is prohibited and that there are a larger number of competing unit-plan institutions than in any other nation, the United States has a fairly well-knit commercial banking system. The unity of policy and action found in the system rests upon a large body of statutory law and administrative regulations and on the high degree of cooperation found to exist among regulatory bodies and voluntary banking organizations and associations.

Without doubt, the system is now stronger than ever before. It is manned by a body of officials and private bankers who enjoy the full confidence of bank depositors because of their acceptance of the obligations imposed by their position as trustees of the public welfare.

Although minor modifications are being made constantly to reduce frictions that exist in such a vast machine, the successful operation of banks in recent years makes it unlikely that significant changes in the structure will occur in the near future.

Questions and problems

1. Name some of the unique features of the banking structure of the United States.

2. Distinguish between (a) national and state banks, (b) insured and noninsured banks, and (c) member and nonmember banks. Under whose supervision are the above-named banks administered?

3. Compare federal laws and the banking statutes of your state on these points: (a) minimum capital requirements, (b) minimum deposit reserves, (c) restrictions on real estate loans, and (d) limitations on investments.

4. What provisions regarding branch banking are found in the laws of your state? Does local sentiment favor the continuance of these provisions?

5. What do you consider the most significant advantages that would be realized from (a) statewide branch banking and (b) nationwide branch banking?

6. What do you consider the most significant disadvantages that would be realized if (a) statewide branch banking and (b) nationwide branch banking were allowed?

7. Describe the organization of a group banking system. What changes have occurred recently in the number of offices operated by the three groups discussed in the text?

8. How are bank examination functions divided among federal and state regulatory agencies?

9. Guaranty of bank deposits by state banking administrators was a failure. Why is there reason to believe that such a guaranty will succeed when administered on a national scale?

10. Describe the system of correspondent bank relationships of the United States. Why do these relationships persist alongside the cooperation provided by the Federal Reserve System?

11. Trace steps in collection of a check drawn on Planters State Bank, Salina, Kansas, and deposited in State National Bank and Trust Co., Evanston, Illinois. Both are member banks.

12. What is the difference between a one-bank holding company and a bank holding company?

13. How does a clearinghouse operate?

14. What is meant by the term *checkless society?*

Bibliography

Interesting accounts of the origins and development of banking are found in the following:

Barger, Harold. *Money, Banking and Public Policy.* 2d ed. Chicago: Rand McNally & Co., 1968.

Hammond, Bray. *Banks and Politics in America from the Revolution to the Civil War.* Princeton, N.J.: Princeton University Press, 1957.

Miller, H. E. *Banking Theories in the United States before 1860.* Cambridge, Mass.: Harvard University Press, 1927.

The administration and operation of banks is treated in the following text:

Robinson, R. I. *The Management of Bank Funds.* 2d ed. New York: McGraw-Hill Book Co., Inc., 1962.

The following volume written for the Commission on Money and Credit by the American Bankers Association contains an interesting description of the role, operation, and structure of the commercial banking industry.

American Bankers Association. *The Commercial Banking Industry.* A monograph prepared for the Commission on Money and Credit. Englewood Cliffs, N.J.: Prentice-Hall, Inc., 1962.

The bank merger movement and merger legislation is discussed in: Gerald C. Fischer, *American Banking Structure.* New York: Columbia University Press, 1968.

The nature and functions of commercial banking are discussed to some extent in standard college texts on money and banking. These include:

Chandler, Lester, V. *The Economics of Money and Banking.* 5th ed. New York: Harper & Row, 1969.

Hart, A. G., and Kenen, P. B. *Money Debt and Economic Activity.* 3d ed. Englewood Cliffs, N.J.: Prentice-Hall, Inc., 1961.

Kent, Raymond P. *Money and Banking.* 5th ed. New York: Holt, Rinehart and Winston, Inc., 1966.

Kreps, Clifton H., Jr. *Money, Banking and Monetary Policy.* 2d ed. New York: The Ronald Press, 1967.

Prather, Charles L. *Money and Banking.* 9th ed. Homewood, Ill.: Richard D. Irwin, Inc., 1969.

Pritchard, Leland J. *Money and Banking.* 2d ed. Boston: Houghton-Mifflin Co., 1964.

Current developments of a statistical nature may be found in monthly issues of the *Federal Reserve Bulletin* and in annual reports issued by the Comptroller of the Currency, the Federal Deposit Insurance Corporation, and the Board of Governors of the Federal Reserve System.

CHAPTER 7

Monetary roles of the Federal Reserve and the Treasury

Commercial banks have the power to expand and contract the amount of money in the economy, but their ability to change the quantity of money is strongly circumscribed by the actions of the Federal Reserve. Since a growing economy presumably needs a proportionately expanding money supply, not only is the power to control the quantity of money in the economy important but it can be a constructive economic force if used wisely. If used irresponsibly, it has a vast potential for disaster. As a famous English economist and journalist, Walter Bagehot, said a century ago, "Money will not manage itself."

Generally the power to regulate the quantity of money is so important that sovereign governments reserve it for their own use or undertake to regulate its use closely. The exercise of the power to regulate money is usually delegated to the central bank of a country, although in practice the Treasury is sometimes the dominant force in monetary policy. The delegation is provided for in the United States by our Constitution. In the United States, the Federal Reserve System acts as the country's central banking system. It is a creature of Congress and reports to Congress. It is independent of the Treasury in a legal sense. Although both agencies exercise monetary powers, the more important monetary powers are exercised by the Federal Reserve. Accordingly, most of this chapter will be devoted to monetary management by the Federal Reserve; the role of the U.S. Treasury Department will need to be considered only briefly. After reviewing both institutions as monetary agencies, the chapter will close with a discussion of the service functions of the Federal Reserve System.

Evolution of Federal Reserve monetary role

When the Federal Reserve Act was passed in 1913, its authors emphasized that they were not creating a central bank. They believed that they were merely correcting some of the defects that had been disclosed in this country's banking system. Nevertheless, they created more than they realized. Partly through new legislation, the role of the Federal Reserve System has been expanded, but present Federal Reserve powers have evolved mainly (without material change of law) by a clearer recognition and a subtler exercise of the powers that were granted in the very beginning.

Prior to 1913, this country had suffered from a series of financial panics, the principal ones occurring in 1873, 1884, 1893, and 1907. These panics showed that the national banking system was subject to a number of weaknesses. The most important were an inflexibility in the supply of paper currency and a lack of any means for making additional reserves available to banks in times of strain. Panics broke out when banks could not meet their obligation to pay legal tender currency on demand. The reason for these failures was essentially that banks could not supplement the reserves available to them and had no access to added bank notes when the public demand for currency exceeded their rather slender cash holdings. The Federal Reserve Act, as originally passed, was an effort to correct these two elements of inflexibility.

There was one other weakness—one that was more a matter of national monetary than banking arrangements. The pre-Federal Reserve national bank reserve requirements tended to scatter gold holdings among many banks and provided no means for the marshaling of these gold reserves when they were needed; hence these gold holdings were not available for international payments when called for by balance of payments needs (see Chapter 26).

The Federal Reserve System was designed to correct these defects. The Reserve banks were given the power of note issue, and the amount of notes issued was made responsive to the operating demands of commercial banks. In addition, the Reserve banks were able to make loans to member banks, which had the effect of adding to the reserves available to them. Finally, a large part of the nation's gold reserves was centralized in the Federal Reserve banks.

A central bank created

While the framers of the Federal Reserve Act set out merely to correct defects in our former banking system, they did more than they had intended: they created a central bank. They had been at pains to organize a regional system with Reserve banks in various areas, but they reckoned without the influence of money market economics.

A central bank or a central banking system uses its position to influence the extent to which operating commercial banks extend credit and expand deposit liabilities. This influence is made effective in a variety of ways. In the first place, member banks are required to keep their reserves in the form of deposit balances in a Federal Reserve bank. The ratio of reserves to deposits determines the amount of credit that can be extended. As was shown in Chapter 5, a 10% reserve requirement means that $1 of reserves will support $10 of deposit liabilities. But if the requirement is increased to 25%, then the $1 of reserves will support only $4 of deposit liabilities. In the beginning, the reserve percentages were established by law and could be changed only by new legislation. Since 1935, the required reserve percentages have been determined, within specified statutory boundaries, by the Federal Reserve Board.

The Federal Reserve, however, has a further channel of influence. It can manage the volume of its own deposit liabilities by expanding and contracting the amount of Federal Reserve bank credit, and the major use of bank deposits held at the Federal Reserve is as the cash asset reserve of member banks. The expansion and contraction of Federal Reserve bank credit is accomplished in two major ways: by direct lending to member banks and by the purchase or sale of U.S. government securities in the open market. The first method is usually called *rediscounting*, and the second is called *open market operations*.

Federal Reserve credit operations have a leverage effect because they have a multiplied effect on the volume of member bank deposits. Decreasing member bank reserve requirements by $1 or adding $1 of reserve deposits by rediscounting or by open-market operations makes possible the expansion of member bank deposits by $4 or $5 (see Table 5–4, Chapter 5). This is true because of the multiple expansion of deposits in banks.

This leverage effect made it possible for the Federal Reserve to correct the defects of the national banking system. The currency system was made flexible because whenever there was a demand for added currency, the Federal Reserve banks could issue several dollars of Federal Reserve notes for each dollar of reserves held. Member bank reserves were mobilized, because the total could be increased by exactly the same method.

Every modern commercial banking system has at its core a central bank. Most of these central banks are concerned with the control of monetary expansion or contraction. Some countries established central banks very early in their banking history. For example, the Swedish central bank, the Riksbank, was opened in 1656;[1] the Bank of England was organized in 1694; the Bank of France more than a century later in 1800. Other central banks have been organized more recently, for example, the Bank of Canada in 1935. Some central banks did not start business as central banks; they became central banks only by accident or slow evolution. In almost every case, the functions of central banks have changed greatly with the times. The degree of change has been particularly striking in recent decades.

Not only do modern central banks exercise greatly augmented powers, there have been just as great changes in the scope of their objectives. The Federal Reserve story illustrates this evolution. Although the original objective of the Federal Reserve System was primarily to correct the various defects that had been found in the banking system, bit by bit the system has looked toward more distant horizons. Now it takes the preservation of general economic stability as its central objective. During this evolution, however, it has pursued many other objectives: the accommodation of trade and industry; stabilization of the money market; during World War II, assistance of the Treasury Department in its program of war finance; and after the war, the Federal Reserve continued to support government security prices to stabilize interest rates. During 1950, the first years of the Korean War, the Federal Reserve abandoned its policy of interest rate stabilization because of its expected inflationary consequences. The stabilization policy necessitated large increases in the money supply which would have caused a rapid increase in the level of prices. Probably the greatest change has been that the nation and the Federal Reserve have come to recognize that prudent management of our monetary and credit system has a strong stabilizing influence on prices and employment and that these powers must be used to serve that end. Moreover, the role of monetary management in the economic growth of the nation is coming to be recognized, and the phrase "sustainable rate of growth" appears regularly in Federal Reserve documents. (Full consideration of this point will be found in Chapters 24 and 27). The unresolved question is whether the system can discharge the new obligations it has assumed.

Modern central banks perform many services for commercial banks in addition to their monetary responsibilities. For example, central banks use member bank reserve balances as the basis for check collection services; act as currency depots; examine and supervise member banks; collect, interpret, and dispense economic information relating to credit

[1] It did not exercise full central banking powers until 1897.

problems; and act as fiscal agents, custodians, and depositories for their treasuries and other governmental agencies. Monetary regulation, however, continues to be their biggest and most important job.

Structural organization of Federal Reserve

The Federal Reserve was superimposed upon an operating banking system; its structure was therefore built around the banking system then in existence. As time has passed, however, the Federal Reserve System has been modified to meet new needs. It is ordinarily thought of as consisting of the Board of Governors, located in Washington, D.C., the 12 Reserve banks, and their branches. But the system may be thought of as including, in addition, those commercial banks that are members. Other bodies may also be considered parts of the system: the Open Market Committee, the Federal Advisory Council, the President's Conference, and some other informal groups. The structural parts of the Federal Reserve System are described in the following sections.

Membership

Each national bank which is located in the United States is required to be a member of the Federal Reserve System and a stockholder in the Federal Reserve bank of the district in which it is located. State banks are free to join or not, as they wish; and most large state banks have joined. Smaller state banks have generally not joined; only 1,202 of the almost 9,000 state banks belong to the Federal Reserve System. But although less than one seventh of all state banks are members, state members have more than one half of the deposits of all state banks. Since there are slightly less than 4,700 national banks, total membership in the system of approximately 5,900 banks is less than half the number of commercial banks in the United States. Total deposits of member banks, however, are more than 80% of all commercial bank deposits in the country.

Board of Governors

The major policy-forming body of the Federal Reserve System is the Board of Governors, formerly known as the Federal Reserve Board. The board consists of seven members, known as *governors*, who serve 14-year terms, so arranged that a vacancy occurs every two years. The board members are appointed by the president of the United States with the advice and consent of the Senate. The executive head of the board is the member designated as chairman by the president. In practice, the chairman serves at the pleasure of the president. The board is primarily a policy-forming agency.

Federal Reserve banks

The operating functions of the Federal Reserve System are performed by the Federal Reserve banks (often called the "Feds" by bankers). There are 12 Federal Reserve banks located in the leading cities of the country, as shown in Exhibit 7–1, along with the 24 branches operated by Federal Reserve banks. These branches are more common in those areas of the country where distances are great and mailing time is long. The Boston Reserve bank has no branches, and the great New York Reserve bank has only one. On the other hand, the Dallas, Atlanta, Kansas City, and St. Louis Reserve banks each operate three branches; the San Francisco Reserve bank operates four. A clearly defined territory is marked out for each Federal Reserve bank and branch, as shown in Exhibit 7–1.

Each Reserve bank has a board of nine directors: three Class A, three Class B, and three Class C. Both Class A and Class B directors are elected by the member banks of the district. Class A directors must be bankers; Class B must be businessmen. In these elections the member banks are divided into three groups: the large, the medium sized, and the small; and each group elects one Class A and one Class B director. Class C directors are appointed by the Board of Governors. The chairman of the board is one of the Class C directors. Exhibit 7–2 shows the top organization of a Federal Reserve bank.

The capital stock of each Federal Reserve bank is owned by the member banks. Each member bank subscribes for capital in the Federal Reserve bank equal to 6% of its own capital and surplus. So far, only half of this subscription (3% of member bank capital and surplus) has been called. Each member bank receives a cumulative dividend of 6% on its Federal Reserve bank stock. Although profit is not a goal of the Federal Reserve System, large profits are made. At one time, excess earnings were paid to the U.S. Treasury as a franchise tax, but that has been discontinued. Federal Reserve earnings during World War II were large, and a part of these earnings was paid to the Treasury through a voluntary tax on Federal Reserve note issues. During 1969 the Federal Reserve had net earnings of $3,098 million. Of this amount, $39 million was paid in dividends to member banks. The Treasury was paid $3,019 million as interest on Federal Reserve notes. The remaining $39 million was transferred to surplus.[2]

The Federal Reserve banks are, to a very considerable extent, service

[2] Board of Governors, Federal Reserve System, *Fifty-Sixth Annual Report* (1969), p. 316.

EXHIBIT 7-1

Boundaries of Federal Reserve districts and their branch territories

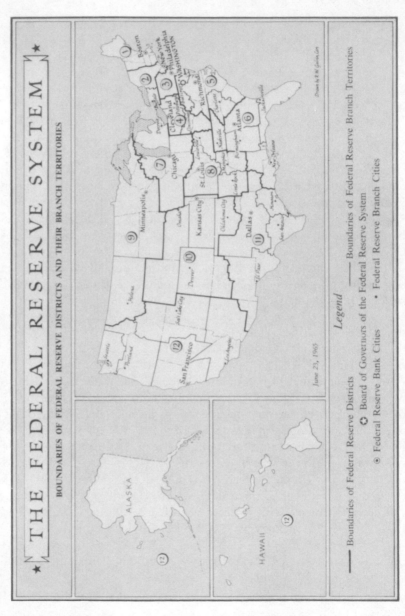

Source: Board of Governors, Federal Reserve System.

agencies: they clear and collect checks, count and ship currency, effect the wire transfer of funds, issue and retire government securities, and act as agents for the Treasury and other governmental offices in a variety of ways. These service functions, although less well known to

EXHIBIT 7–2

Top organization of a Federal Reserve bank

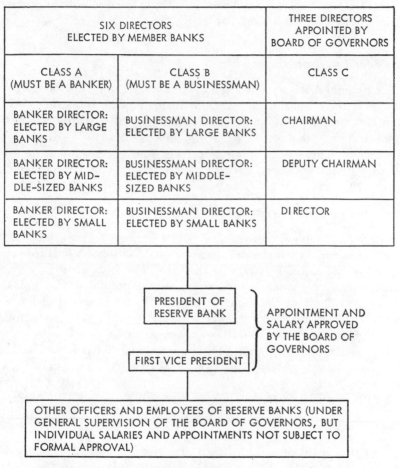

SIX DIRECTORS ELECTED BY MEMBER BANKS		THREE DIRECTORS APPOINTED BY BOARD OF GOVERNORS
CLASS A (MUST BE A BANKER)	CLASS B (MUST BE A BUSINESSMAN)	CLASS C
BANKER DIRECTOR: ELECTED BY LARGE BANKS	BUSINESSMAN DIRECTOR: ELECTED BY LARGE BANKS	CHAIRMAN
BANKER DIRECTOR: ELECTED BY MIDDLE-SIZED BANKS	BUSINESSMAN DIRECTOR: ELECTED BY MIDDLE-SIZED BANKS	DEPUTY CHAIRMAN
BANKER DIRECTOR: ELECTED BY SMALL BANKS	BUSINESSMAN DIRECTOR: ELECTED BY SMALL BANKS	DIRECTOR

PRESIDENT OF RESERVE BANK

FIRST VICE PRESIDENT

APPOINTMENT AND SALARY APPROVED BY THE BOARD OF GOVERNORS

OTHER OFFICERS AND EMPLOYEES OF RESERVE BANKS (UNDER GENERAL SUPERVISION OF THE BOARD OF GOVERNORS, BUT INDIVIDUAL SALARIES AND APPOINTMENTS NOT SUBJECT TO FORMAL APPROVAL)

Source: Board of Governors, Federal Reserve System.

the public than the monetary operations, require a large portion of the time and effort of the more than 20,000 employees and officers of the Federal Reserve banks. These functions are described below in greater detail.

Federal Open Market Committee

Decisions on the purchase and sale of U.S. government securities and related policies are made by the Federal Open Market Committee, which represents both the Board of Governors and the Federal Reserve banks. The committee consists of 12 members: the seven governors and five representatives selected by the 12 Reserve banks. Open market purchases and sales are conducted by a manager, who in practice is an officer of the Federal Reserve Bank of New York. This bank, because of the importance of New York as a money market, is the leading Federal Reserve bank.

The Federal Advisory Council

The Federal Advisory Council has 12 members, one appointed by each Federal Reserve bank. It advises the Board of Governors on economic conditions and banking problems throughout the country but has no administrative authority. It meets four times a year in Washington and recommends action both through private conferences and conferences with the Federal Reserve governors and through public statements.

Informal groups in the system

The actual influence on public policy of any agency, such as the Federal Reserve System, cannot be measured entirely by legal or formal organization. Informal groups within the agency are often very important—sometimes more important than the formal advisory bodies. The 12 presidents of the Federal Reserve banks have formed a Conference of Reserve Bank Presidents, a body not required or contemplated by law. This group has, nevertheless, considerable influence in forming Federal Reserve and general governmental financial policy. The chairmen of the boards of the 12 Reserve banks likewise have periodic conferences.

Interrelationships within the system

The maze of relationships already described provide an indication of the complexity of the Federal Reserve System. Later in this chapter, after the functional operation of the system has been described, the reasons for some of these structural arrangements will become more evident. Exhibit 7–3 shows in some detail the structural and the functional organization of the Federal Reserve.

As this diagram shows, the complexity of the Federal Reserve organization is due partly to the number of tasks involved in combining various credit controls with other more direct financial regulations.

Organization of Federal Reserve System with reference to instruments of credit policy

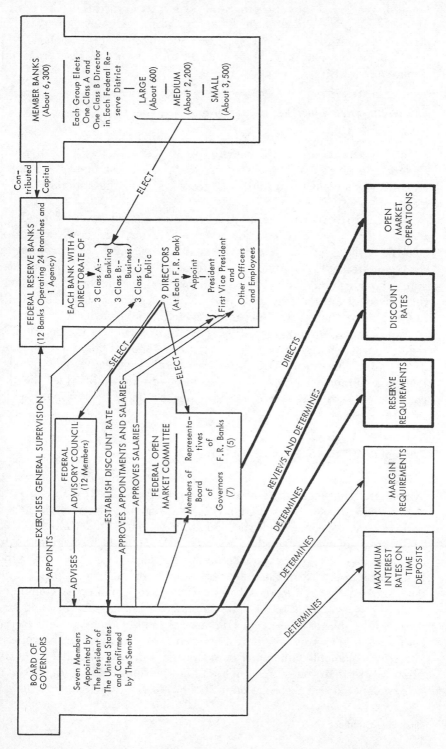

Source: *Banking Studies* (Washington, D.C.: Federal Reserve Board, 1941), p. 376.

Some of the complexity also grows out of efforts to distribute the power of the system among its various parts. Centralized power makes for simpler organization, but many fear centralization of monetary and financial power. The price of decentralization is in this case organizational complexity.

The public-private blend in organization

The Federal Reserve System is more a public than a private agency, but it has aspects of both. Ownership of the capital stock of individual Federal Reserve banks is vested in the private commercial member banks, and they elect two thirds of the directors of the Federal Reserve banks.

The Board of Governors is clearly a public body, as evidenced by the way it is selected. The major lines of monetary and credit authority stem from the Board of Governors. Its members constitute a majority of the Open Market Committee. The board establishes reserve requirements; and although the individual Reserve banks conduct discount operations, their discount rates are reviewed and, in effect, determined by the Board of Governors. The general rules under which member banks conduct discount operations are established by regulations issued by the board. The regulation of security loans, consumer credit, and interest rates on time deposits is vested in the Board of Governors. It might be said that the monetary authority of the system is centralized and public but that the conduct of service functions is more decentralized and responsive to private needs.

Principles of Federal Reserve banking

The monetary functions and responsibilities of the Federal Reserve System are what make it a true central banking system. It is the purpose of this section to show how Federal Reserve banking operations are used both to serve and to control the monetary system in the United States. The framers of the Federal Reserve System eliminated the inelastic note issue and immobile reserves of the national banking system by giving the Federal Reserve System the power to expand central bank credit. Chapter 5 showed that commercial banks are able to increase the volume of deposits by extending credit. The fractional reserve principle operates for central banks as well as for commercial banks. The Federal Reserve banks are able to provide a flexible currency and to regulate the volume of reserves available to member banks through their credit operations. In subsequent discussion of open market and discount operations, it should be remembered that these are credit operations.

As Table 7–1 shows, Federal Reserve bank balance sheets are roughly similar to commercial bank statements except that Federal Reserve notes form a large part of the liabilities of the Reserve banks. Commercial banks in this country no longer have note liabilities.

The dominant elements in the statement shown in Table 7–1 are, on the asset side of the balance sheet, the gold certificate account, open market (U.S. government) securities, and cash items in process of col-

TABLE 7–1

Combined statement of 12 Federal Reserve banks, December 31, 1969 (*billions of dollars***)**

Assets		Liabilities	
Gold certificate account	10.0	Federal Reserve notes	48.2
Federal Reserve notes of other banks	0.8	Member bank reserve accounts .	22.0
Other cash	0.1	Treasury, foreign and other deposits	2.2
Discounts and acceptances	0.1	Deferred availability cash items .	9.5
U.S. government securities	57.3	Other liabilities	0.6
Cash items in process of collection	12.9	Capital accounts	1.4
Other assets	2.7		
Total	83.9	Total	83.9

Source: Board of Governors, Federal Reserve System, *Fifty-Sixth Annual Report* (1969), pp. 326–27.

lection and, on the liability side, Federal Reserve notes, member bank reserve accounts, and deferred availability cash items (checks which have been deposited but not credited to member bank accounts).

The significance of reserves in modern banking

The role of banking reserves has been discussed in Chapter 5. A prudent banker tries to keep ample cash reserves to fullfill his needs. In our system the prudence of the banker is reinforced by laws requiring banks to keep minimum reserves. But any banker who keeps excess reserves fails to earn as much as he could safely earn. Thus banking reserves tend to fall between two limits: (1) they must be as high as prudence and the law require; and (2) they should not be higher, else profits will be missed.

Therefore, the amount of reserves available to banks is a direct limit on the amount of credit they can extend. The effectiveness of the Federal Reserve System depends on the operation of this principle. Since the ssytem can control the amount of reserves available to banks, it can control, indirectly, the amount of credit extended by banks and consequently the volume of bank deposits.

Federal Reserve notes

Most persons provide themselves with currency by cashing checks at commercial banks. Banks in turn obtain currency, directly or indirectly, from the Federal Reserve banks. Neither the government nor a Federal Reserve bank ever puts money into circulation in the sense of taking the initiative in issuing money. Deposits are convertible into currency to the extent the public demands; and the agency for making this conversion possible is the Federal Reserve System. But the amount of currency in circulation is determined by public demand, not by governmental manipulation.

When a commercial bank orders currency from a Federal Reserve bank, its reserve balance deposited with the Reserve bank is decreased by the amount of the currency ordered. Thus currency demands have a close and intimate effect on the amount of reserves available to banks. In recent years the policy of the Federal Reserve System has been to manage its credit so that these currency demands are met without straining the reserve accounts of member banks.

Federal Reserve monetary controls

The framers of the original Federal Reserve Act were not aware that they had created monetary controls. They were trying to correct the defects of the past; they felt that the Federal Reserve should service the banking system with adequate reserves but not control the banking system. But the margin between accommodating the banking system with such added reserves as it might need and controlling the banking system is a narrow one. The very act of judging just how great the need for bank reserves may be is itself an act of control.

The simple principles of Federal Reserve control of member bank credit expansion were outlined briefly in the opening of this chapter. Now that we have had an opportunity to learn more about central banking principles and organization, it is time to look more closely at the operation of the credit controls.

Federal Reserve rediscounting operations

It was originally intended that rediscounting would be the principal method for extending Federal Reserve credit. Member banks were expected to borrow at the Federal Reserve when in need of funds. These borrowings were rediscounts, because loans of a commercial nature, already discounted once by member banks, were the basis for rediscounting at the Federal Reserve banks. The rate of interest charged by the Federal Reserve is the rediscount rate.

In the early days of the Federal Reserve, rediscounting operations were of central importance, and the rediscount rate was the most vital single factor in the money market. Near the end of 1920, Federal Reserve rediscounts reached a peak of about 2¾ billion. This was more than one eighth of member bank demand deposits.

The rediscounting channel for making Federal Reserve credit available dwindled for a while as the importance of open-market operations grew. When the Federal Reserve System was originated, loans were the chief earning asset of commercial banks. It was only natural that banks should depend on rediscounting loans to secure added liquidity. But banks came to hold larger amounts of marketable securities, particularly government securities. Selling such securities was a much easier and more convenient way of getting added liquidity than rediscounting.

Rediscounts are recorded as follows: if the member banks should rediscount commercial paper with the Federal Reserve to obtain $1,000 added reserves, the following skeleton bookkeeping entries would be made:

Assets	Liabilities
Federal Reserve bank statement: (1) + Rediscounts $1,000	+ Reserve balances due member banks $1,000
Member bank statement: (2) + Due from Federal Reserve bank $1,000	+ Borrowings from Federal Reserve bank $1,000

With augmented reserve balances, the bank could then proceed with credit expansion, as will be illustrated in connection with open market operations. Similarly, pressure by the Federal Reserve to reduce discounts would cause multiple contraction in credit.

The effect of changing discount rates cannot be illustrated directly by skeleton entries similar to those used above but can be observed indirectly. Low rediscount rates naturally encourage banks to borrow; a low rate is an implied invitation by the Federal Reserve authorities to borrow, and the funds can then be reloaned at a profit. High rates, on the other hand, are an implied discouragement; furthermore, there is less profit in relending high-cost funds. Most banks have long-standing arrangements with many of their borrowing customers. They do not like to change rates charged these customers with every shift in the credit winds. But if the banks can lend or renew loans only by rediscounting, and at a rate which makes loans unprofitable, the banks will naturally be more reluctant to make loans and more likely to reject the marginal applicants.

In practice, discounting and discount rate changes have been effective Federal Reserve instruments roughly in proportion to the extent of member bank use of borrowing facilities. During much of the 1930s, during World War II, and during the early postwar period until about 1952, very few banks borrowed. Some banks developed a reluctance to borrow that has persisted even into periods of tight money markets. In 1952 and subsequently, however, because of cash needs caused by the increased demand for bank credit, banks started borrowing in greater volume. For a time the appropriate standards for use of rediscount facilities were in doubt, and the Federal Reserve is reported to have admonished some banks during that period for overuse of the rediscount window, particularly in 1953. In 1955 Federal Reserve Regulation A, covering these transactions, was revised. It enunciated the principles that borrowing is a privilege and not a right, and that it should not be engaged in for profit-making purposes or when other adjustments could be made to anticipate changes in availability of reserves.

During periods when the Federal Reserve is following a restrictive policy, that is, slowing the rate of growth of the money supply, discounts that add to bank reserves have the effect of countering the tightness of bank reserves which the policy is attempting to achieve. During such periods, interest rates are high, and commercial banks could profitably increase their loans if reserves were available. Under such conditions the privilege and not a right directive does not provide sufficient guidelines to either the member banks or the Federal Reserve discount officers as to which discounts should properly be made.

With the tight reserve positions and high interest rates that prevailed after 1965, banks made increasingly heavy use of the discount facilities of the Federal Reserve. Thus, over the last several years, much uncertainty existed among banks as to the conditions under which they could borrow and the amounts which could be borrowed.

Because of these problems, the Board of Governors in 1965 authorized a study "to reappraise and, where necessary, recommend redesign of the Federal Reserve lending facilities." The committee report was circulated in 1966, and it is expected that sometime soon the functioning of the discount mechanism will be substantially altered.[3] The major expected revision, if the proposals of the study are followed, is that banks will have a guaranteed loan limit, determined by the bank's capital, which can be drawn as a right. Banks will be able to borrow additional sums if emergencies arise. But, the discount rate, which was very sticky in the 1950s and 1960s, will be more responsive to other money-market interest rates. Thus frequent changes in the discount rate are envisaged under the new system.

---

[3] Board of Governors, Federal Reserve System, *Reappraisal of the Federal Reserve Discount Mechanism* (July 1968).

Federal Reserve open market operations

The original Federal Reserve Act permitted Federal Reserve banks to buy and sell U.S. government securities. When the public debt was small, the importance of this power was overlooked. But, as already shown in the analysis of commercial bank operations, the purchase of securities by a bank extends credit just as effectively as does making a loan. The same is true of the Federal Reserve.

The first important use of open market operations came in the early 1920s. By the time of the great depression in the early 1930s, open market operations were the chief instrument of credit control of the Federal Reserve System.

With the outbreak of World War II, open market operations became quite subsidiary to the requirements of treasury financing operations. Open market operations were used to make reserves available to banks so that they would be able to buy such treasury securities as could not be sold to the nonbanking financial institutions or to the public at large. Ultimately this use of open market powers was to assure the Treasury of an ample supply of funds at a reasonable interest cost. In other words, the objective of open market operations really became interest rate control.

For almost a decade, open market operations were hobbled by this responsibility. But, spurred by the inflationary threats induced by the outbreak of the Korean War, the system broke away from Treasury Department domination; starting with an accord in March of 1951 between the Treasury and the Federal Reserve, open market operations were restored to their primary importance as an instrument of general credit policy.

When Federal Reserve banks purchase U.S. government securities from a bank or an individual investor, they pay for them with a check drawn on themselves—a kind of cashier's check. When these checks are returned to the Reserve banks, they are added to member bank reserve balances. The skeleton entries for a Federal Reserve bank purchase of $1,000 of U.S. government securities on the books of the Reserve bank are:

Assets		Liabilities	
(3) + U.S. government securities	$1,000	+ Member bank deposits (reserve balances)	$1,000

If the securities were sold to the Reserve bank by a commercial bank, the commercial bank statement would be changed as follows:

7——Monetary roles of the Federal Reserve and the Treasury

157

(4) − U.S. government securities	$1,000		
+ Due from Federal Reserve bank	$1,000		

If the securities were sold to the Reserve bank by an individual who deposited the check he received for them in his bank, the skeleton entries on the books of the commercial bank would be:

(5) + Due from Federal Reserve bank	$1,000	+ Deposits	$1,000

Control of member bank reserve requirements

When the Federal Reserve System was inaugurated, the classification of commercial banks as central reserve city, reserve city, and country banks under the National Bank Act was retained. A distinction was made, however, between time and demand deposits. Reserves required against each type of deposit differ in size.

As noted above, the Federal Reserve can control member bank credit by varying the percentage rates of reserve requirements, as well as by controlling the amount of reserves available. The circumstances that led to the statutory introduction of this device were unique. Excess reserves in commercial banks have usually been considered abnormal. But in the early and mid-1930s, a combination of very low short-term interest rates and a gold inflow created a large volume of such excess reserves. It was feared that these excess reserves would ultimately lead to inflation. Increasing the cost of rediscounting by higher rediscount rates could not mop up these excess reserves because banks were not in debt to the Federal Reserve; neither could open market sales absorb the excess because the amount of securities owned by the Federal Reserve was less than the amount of excess reserves. Increasing reserve requirements, however, could do the job. So the power to double reserve requirements was added in the Banking Act of 1935.

Although the power to change reserves requirements was originally devised to absorb excess reserves created during a conjuncture of unusual events associated with a depression, its subsequent use has more often been to supplement other instruments of monetary policy. In practice, this authority has not been used very frequently, and it is considered the most clumsy and awkward of the instruments of credit policy.

A further revision of reserve requirement authority was made in

1959. The chief change in this new legislation was to authorize the Federal Reserve to allow member banks to count vault cash as an admissible reserve asset; to drop the distinction between central reserve city banks (only in New York and Chicago) and other reserve city banks after 1962; to permit the Federal Reserve to determine the reserve classification of individual banks on the basis of the bank's business characteristics rather than its location; and to change the top limit for reserve city requirements to 22%. (This last change represented a reduction for the New York and Chicago central reserve city banks but an increase for reserve city banks.) A summary history of Federal Reserve member bank reserve requirements is shown in Table 7–2.

TABLE 7–2

Federal Reserve member bank reserve requirements

	Original statute, 1917	Banking Act of 1935*	Reserve legislation 1959†
Net demand deposits			
Central reserve city banks (New York and Chicago)	13	13–26	10–22 until 1962; reserve cities thereafter
Reserve city banks (about 50 cities)	10		
County member banks ..	7	7–14	7–14
Time deposits	3	3–6	3–6

* For a brief period in 1948–49 somewhat higher requirements were authorized by Congress and were in fact enforced.
† Effective date for dropping central reserve city classification was July 28, 1962. The effective date set for the vault cash provision was November 24, 1960.

When the Federal Reserve Board makes a change in reserve requirements, that change by itself does not produce any discernible changes in banking statements, but the action may force substantial changes to be made. The effect depends on the existing relationship between reserves actually held by the banks and the amount they desire to hold. If reserve requirements are lowered when there is little demand for loans and few opportunities for investment by banks, the only change is that banks may have reserves in excess of desired reserves.

Likewise, an increase in reserve requirements, when all banks have excess desired reserves large enough to cover the new and larger requirements, might have no visible effect. But an increase in requirements that caught some banks short, i.e., found them with deficiencies in desired reserves, would necessitate credit contraction. For example, if an increase in reserve requirements were made which created a deficiency of $5,000, the member bank would be forced to liquidate assets of some kind and build up its balance in the Reserve bank, or effect a reduction in its deposits. Under present conditions the usual procedure is for the member to sell[4] government securities to the Reserve bank and have the sale price credited to its reserve balance:

Assets	
(6) — U.S. government securities	$5,000
+ Due from Federal Reserve bank	$5,000

Applying monetary controls

Federal Reserve use of monetary controls focuses on the reserve funds available to member commercial banks. The volume of these reserves, particularly the amount that is in excess of requirements, determines the ability of banks to lend and therefore create deposits. Rediscounting, open market operations, and reserve requirement control are not the only factors that affect the reserve positions of banks. Other important factors enter into the picture: the volume of gold reserves and the amount of currency in circulation are two numerically important examples. An increase in gold reserves increases the reserves available to member banks; an increase in currency in circulation has the effect of reducing member bank reserve balances. Thus, if the Federal Reserve System wishes to use rediscounting, open market operations, and reserve requirement control (separately or in combination) to influence member bank reserve balances, they must first offset the effects on bank reserves of gold movements or of changes in currency in circulation. If gold is flowing into the country, the offset is a reduction of Federal Reserve credit; if currency is flowing out of banks and into circulation, the offset is an increase in Federal Reserve credit. This does not mean, of course, that the Federal Reserve necessarily and regularly tries to offset the influence of these two factors. Quite the contrary, it may allow a gold or currency movement to continue without offset if it is having a desirable effect. If the Federal Reserve wishes to put pressure on member bank reserve positions when gold is flowing out of the country, it can simply do nothing and let the gold outflow produce the reserve effects they think are needed.

The sum total of technical factors influencing the reserve positions of

---

[4] Strictly speaking, the Federal Reserve buys from and sells to only a few specialized dealers in government securities, and these dealers in turn buy from and sell to member banks and others. The direct form of statement used here, however, is accurate for all analytical purposes—and it is simpler!

TABLE 7–3

Member bank reserves, reserve bank credit, and related items (*billions of dollars, monthly averages of daily figures***)**

Item	December 1960	December 1965	December 1969
Factors supplying reserve funds:			
Reserve bank credit			
U.S. government securities			
(open market)	27.2	40.9	57.5
Discounts	0.1	0.5	1.1
Float	1.7	2.3	3.2
Gold stock	18.0	13.8	10.4
Treasury currency	5.4	5.6	6.8
Total*	52.4	63.1	79.9
Factors absorbing reserve funds:			
Currency in circulation	33.0	42.2	53.6
Treasury cash holdings	0.4	0.9	0.7
Deposits (other than reserve balances)			
Treasury	0.5	0.7	1.2
Foreign	0.3	0.2	0.1
Other	0.5	0.2	0.5
Other Federal Reserve accounts	1.0	0.4	0.0
Member bank reserve balances	19.3	22.7	28.0
Total*	55.0	67.3	84.1
Memorandum items			
Reserves required	18.5	22.3	27.7
Excess reserves	0.8	0.5	0.3

*Totals do not add because vault cash has been counted as member bank reserve since November 1060. Thus, among factors absorbing reserves, currency in circulation should be reduced by $2.6 billion in 1960, $4.2 billion in 1965, and 4.9 in 1969 to offset currency held in bank vaults that is included in reserves.

Source: *Federal Reserve Bulletin,* March 1970, pp. A4–5.

member banks has been formalized in a balancing analysis of the sources and uses of member bank reserve funds, and this analysis is published weekly by the Federal Reserve System. These figures, a sample of which is shown in Table 7–3, are reprinted in the financial sections in the Friday morning editions of many daily newspapers and of some financial papers and are used widely by money-market analysts.

The various items we have emphasized in our discussion are shown in boldface in Table 7–3. The four factors that have been discussed are numerically large; however, the other factors are at times highly volatile, and their movements must be carefully considered by the Federal Reserve Board and more particularly the Federal Open Market Committee in determining monetary actions.

Coordinating the instruments of monetary control

How does the Federal Reserve choose among its three instruments of general monetary control in dealing with a specific circumstance? There are no universal rules for making such a choice; rather the problem is one of coordination.

In the first place, a change in reserve requirements is the most ponderous of the instruments of monetary management. As a result, it is the one least frequently employed. When reserve requirements are changed, their impact has often been cushioned during the transition period by open market operations.

During periods of monetary ease, most member banks abstain from borrowing at the Federal Reserve, so that the impact of changes in the discount rate tends to be more an indication of Federal Reserve sentiment than a direct cost-and-profit factor in the market. During periods of tighter money, a fair proportion of banks, particularly money-market banks, borrow quite frequently. During such periods the discount rate becomes a very practical element in the cost-and-profit decisions of such banks. The principal interest rate with which the discount rate is compared is that prevailing on treasury bills and federal funds, since many banks adjust their reserve position either by borrowing or by buying and selling treasury bills or federal funds.

Open market operations are the most continuously used of the monetary instruments. In many ways open market operations are planned to fit around both reserve requirement changes and changes in discount rates and member bank borrowing. At the same time, open market operations should not be viewed as merely a supplement to these other credit policy instruments; in most periods they are the principal, the most continuous, the most powerful, and yet, oddly enough, the most unobtrusive of these instruments. Their delicate and precise use is very much at the heart of successful central banking.

Part of the differences among these instruments lies outside the techniques of finance and in the area of psychology. The Federal Reserve sometimes seems to be guided by whether it wishes to make a public (and possibly dramatic) announcement, such as must accompany a change in reserve requirements or rediscount rates, or whether it wishes to be silent and inscrutable, as when conducting open market operations. This much can safely be said: the Federal Reserve almost always uses open market operations to offset seasonal or random variations in the factors that affect bank reserves, those listed in Table 7–3. An announced change in reserve requirements or the rediscount rate almost always represents a change, or at least an intensification, of monetary and credit policy. An area of doubt always remains, however. When the gossip of government security dealers first reports, and later the published weekly statement of the Federal Reserve confirms, open market purchases or sales by the system, one question is still unanswered: Is this just a routine operation because of present or anticipated seasonal factors or treasury financing operations, or is it a new direction to credit and monetary policy? Sometimes the very silence of the system becomes itself a powerful factor influencing the climate in the money and capital markets. The very act of keeping its official mouth shut is sometimes one of the Federal Reserve's most potent policy tools.

Monetary functions of the Treasury

While most of the domestic monetary functions of the U.S. government are performed by the Federal Reserve System, a few of them are performed by the Treasury Department. In general, the monetary arrangements of the two agencies are coordinated, but since the Federal Reserve is an independent agency while the Treasury is a part of the administration, lack of concord is always possible.

Treasury currency

Treasury currency consists primarily of silver certificates and silver coins, but it includes also a small number of greenbacks and national bank notes, which are remnants from earlier currency systems and have not been retired.[5] Treasury currency now represents about 13% of total currency in circulation. Treasury currency outstanding remains roughly constant. Treasury currency which consists of one dollar bills supplies much of the hand-to-hand or pocket form of currency; it is primarily a service portion of the money supply.

Treasury cash balance

The Treasury holds two forms of cash: one inert, and one quite active and important in its current operations. First, the Treasury is custodian for all gold either shipped to this country or produced by domestic producers. The Treasury pays for gold received with a check that is charged against its reserve bank balance. This charge is usually offset by a deposit of gold certificates, equal to the value of the gold purchased, to its account at the Federal Reserve. Thus an inflow of gold increases the amount of reserves in the banking system. Gold outflows are offset by the retirement of gold certificates. Thus an outflow of gold decreases the amount of reserves in the banking system. Insofar as the Treasury exactly offsets gold movements by the issue or retirement of certificates, gold has the same effect as changes in Federal Reserve credit. The Treasury has followed an offsetting policy for the last 30 years; but for a while in the mid-1930s, part of the gold inflow was sterilized as the

---

[5] Many suspect that the dollar volume of national bank notes and Federal Reserve bank notes actually in circulation is vastly overstated and that a large proportion of the amount listed as still in circulation has nevertheless been lost or destroyed or is dormant in hoards.

Treasury did not deposit gold certificates with the Federal Reserve. It paid for the gold by drawing down its deposit. Thus this inflow of gold did not increase bank reserves, which meant an active kind of monetary management by the Treasury Department.

The second and more active form of treasury cash is its deposit balances in both the Reserve banks and the commercial banks. All treasury expenditures are made by drawing checks payable on Reserve banks. The Treasury Department strives to maintain a relatively stable deposit in the Reserve banks as its working balance. However, because of the large sums which flow through the treasury account at the Federal Reserve, its working balance fluctuates very widely. Note that at the end of 1969, it had a balance of $1.2 billion at the Federal Reserve, and at the end of 1965, treasury deposits were $700 million (Table 7–3).

The amounts held in the so-called tax-and-loan accounts in commercial banks are drawn upon only by transfer to the Reserve bank. These balances represent the liquidity reserve of the Treasury Department and give it such latitude as it has in the management of its borrowings or other cash transactions. Since movements of both these active balances affect the reserves available to banks, these are factors of importance in determining the character of the nation's money market. If the size of these balances were managed with the objective of affecting member bank reserves, they would become an instrument of monetary control. Indeed, some have proposed that they be used in this way. Nevertheless, this policy has not been followed; hence the significance of these accounts is mainly mechanistic. In a short-run appraisal of the money market, however, the state of treasury finances and of its cash holdings is of considerable significance.

Treasury debt management

The Treasury is the largest borrower in both the money and the capital markets. The debt of the federal government represents about a third of all debts outstanding. One of the principal facets of debt management is control of the proportions of long-term and short-term debt in the total. The short-term obligations of the Treasury Department have a special significance because of their high degree of liquidity. They are treated by many as a quite satisfactory money substitute. It follows, therefore, that the proportion of short-term debt to long-term debt issued by the Treasury Department has a sizeable influence on the liquidity of the money markets. The policies followed by the Treasury Department in financing the public debt, therefore, influence the liquidity of the money and capital markets and thereby influence the monetary situation.

In Great Britain the amount of treasury bills issued is one of the principal vehicles used by the money managers in controlling the liquidity of the markets. Although the conventions of the money markets in the United States differ somewhat from those abroad, similar policies could be followed by the U.S. Treasury Department. Nevertheless, it cannot be said that the Treasury Department has regularly used debt management as a conscious tool of monetary management. All recent secretaries of the Treasury, however, have been fully aware of the monetary significance of this aspect of their function. Nevertheless, most of them have treated it as a part of their general economic and financial responsibilities and not as a detailed instrument of monetary and liquidity management.

Federal Reserve direct credit controls

In addition to the general monetary controls exercised by the Federal Reserve System, the system has been made responsible for the operation of a number of direct credit controls. The philosophy underlying each of these regulatory systems varies. Rather than generalize, it is better to explain each one in turn.

Stock market margin control

The Federal Reserve is empowered to control margin requirements on security loans. The control may be used to cut down the borrowing power of persons seeking credit for purchasing or carrying securities (stocks or bonds). As explained in the discussion of the organized stock exchanges, purchasers of stock may pay the broker only a portion of the purchase price of a stock and ask the broker to advance the balance. The broker may obtain the funds needed by borrowing from a commercial bank. This loan is secured by the purchased stock, or the stock purchaser may borrow funds directly from a bank to purchase the stock. In the 1920s, a stock could sometimes be acquired with a cash margin as low as 10–20%.

The Securities Exchange Act of 1934 gave the Federal Reserve Board the power to determine the maximum loan value (stated as a percentage of market price) at the time the loan is granted. As the margin requirement rises, the loan value decreases, and the amount of credit flowing into the exchanges tends to be reduced or stablilized. This regulation applies to the loans of banks to customers as well as to direct broker loans.

The philosophy of stock market regulation goes back to the belief that violent fluctuations in the stock market disturb business conditions. Margin trading made for violent fluctuations in credit and stock prices; it was argued, therefore, that margin trading should be regulated. The great collapse of stock market prices in 1929 certainly was hastened and possibly deepened by the liquidation of thin-margin trading.

At the present time, three regulations prescribe the maximum loan to market value of securities: Regulation T controls credit extended by brokers and dealers; Regulation U controls credit extended by banks; Regulation G controls credit extended by others. At the end of 1969, all three regulations required an 80% margin on loans for stock and 60% for bonds convertible into listed stock.

Control of consumer credit

During World War II and for a while thereafter, the Federal Reserve exercised control over consumer credit. Regulation W was in effect from August 1941 until November 1947. It was revived in August 1948 and expired again at the end of June 1949. Little more than a year later—in the fall of 1950 after the outbreak of hostilities in Korea—Regulation W was revived once more. The terms imposed were relatively mild; the regulation was kept in force for about a year and a half; it was suspended in May 1952. In 1955, when consumer credit expanded with unusual rapidity, the question was raised whether or not Regulation W should be revived on a standby basis for possible use in peacetime periods of rapid expansion. The Council of Economic Advisers asked the Federal Reserve to study the question, to report its findings, and to make a policy recommendation based on these findings. The Federal Reserve, while finding that consumer credit had sometimes been a fairly important cause of economic instability, did not recommend enactment of such standby authority in its 1957 response. Although general interest in such a regulation dwindled thereafter, the issue periodically comes up for public comment and speculation, particularly during periods when consumer credit expands rapidly. It is interesting to note that during the tight money periods in 1966 and 1968–70 this form of regulation was not favorably considered.

Regulation W, while in effect during World War II, required all consumer lenders and credit vendors to register with the regional Federal Reserve banks, to obtain a license, and to conform to details of the regulation. In general, it required a larger downpayment and a shorter maximum maturity than was customary on such contracts. Retail charge accounts were also regulated. The result was a reduction in the aggregate amount of credit extended for the purchase of consumer goods. But a more fundamental economic result was the reduction of the demand for goods at a time when they could not be produced in volume, when prices were tending to rise, and when citizens needed to refrain from competing with the military services for essential manpower and materials.

The philosophy of consumer credit regulation will be more fully considered in Chapter 20.

Control of interest paid on time deposits

Since 1933 the payment of interest on demand deposits has been forbidden by law, and the interest paid on time deposits has been subject to the administrative control of the Federal Reserve under regulation Q. During much of the time the regulation has been in existence, permissible rates have been well above the rates prevailing in the market; hence the regulation has not restricted banking operations. In recent years, especially during tight-money periods, permissible rates have sometimes been below market rates. The regulation of maximum interest allowed on time and savings deposits has reduced competition for such deposits among commercial banks, and it has opened up problems concerning the competitive relationship of commercial banks with other financial institutions, such as savings and loan associations and mutual savings banks.

Of great significance also, when regulated maximums are below rates on competitive money-market instruments, financial intermediaries such as commercial banks, savings and loan associations, and mutual savings banks experience large withdrawals of deposits. The owners of these funds *disintermediate,* that is, invest their funds directly in money-market securities. This has caused great alarm among managers of intermediary institutions and much pressure to rescind Regulation Q.

The philosophy underlying the regulation is this: If member banks, competing among themselves for deposits, paid a high rate for them, they would be forced to seek a high investment return. High yields and speculative risks go hand in hand; and so, by making it necessary to pay high rates, the pressure for risky investment is relieved. In recent years the soundness of this philosophy has been widely questioned.

Federal Reserve financial services

Although the Federal Reserve System is better known to the public for its monetary and regulatory functions, a large part of the time and effort of the system's personnel is devoted to providing the various financial services previously mentioned.

Clearing and collecting checks

When a check from a distant place is cashed or deposited in a bank, collection of the amount called for in the check requires rather more effort than the casual customer might think. Direct collection of each out-of-town check would be tedious and costly. Traditionally, this was done by a few city banks that specialized in this business. They were compensated by the balances that their country correspondents kept with them. When the Federal Reserve System was initiated, it required member banks to keep their legal reserves with the Federal Reserve banks. These balances could be used to settle the flow of clearings and collections, and as a result, the Federal Reserve was well situated to assume this function. Thus Federal Reserve banks offer collection services to their members and even to nonmember banks under limited circumstances.

While the Federal Reserve has not completely displaced the city correspondent in the collection of out-of-town checks, it has assumed a leading role. The major portion of such collections are now routed through Federal Reserve channels. To perform this service, the Reserve banks maintain large staffs of specialists and operate these transit departments day and night. They use airmail extensively and have developed other devices for the most expeditious handling of checks. A large proportion of bank checks now have on their face a routing symbol which is an instant indication of the location of the drawee bank and how items on it should be collected. For an example of such routing symbol, see Exhibit 7–4, which explains the meaning of the symbol

EXHIBIT 7–4

Check-routing symbols

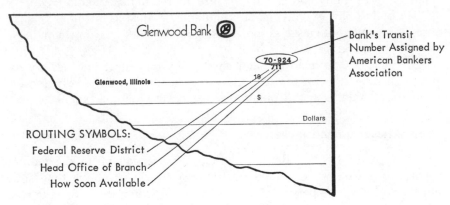

$$\frac{70-924}{711}$$ appearing on the face of the checks of a Glenwood, Illinois, bank.

These symbols are repeated at the bottom of the check in magnetic ink, which is easily read by computers at the Federal Reserve and at commercial banks. The magnetic coding has allowed the banking system to automate the check clearing function. Check processing within the banking system is now almost entirely handled by computers.

Because the Federal Reserve banks draw on each other for the collection of checks that must be sent from one district to another, they have amounts due to and due from each other to be settled. This is done through an interdistrict settlement fund, which operates according to the clearinghouse principle described in Chapter 6. In the interdistrict settlement fund, telegrams take the place of messengers and face-to-face calculation.

Currency supply and redemption

The notes of Federal Reserve banks now furnish about 87% of the currency in circulation. Thus Federal Reserve banks are directly the most important currency source. But, since the Reserve banks are also the agent of the Treasury in the issue and redemption of all other forms of currency, such as silver certificates and coins, virtually the entire currency business of the country is handled through the Reserve banks.

The Reserve banks maintain elaborate equipment for this service. They have complicated coin-counting machinery and experts to count bills and examine them for counterfeits. A visitor to a Reserve bank may see pennies, nickels, dimes, and quarters being handled by scoop shovels and deft-fingered clerks counting bills. Banks located near a Reserve bank can order and obtain shipments of currency in a matter of an hour or two; banks located farther away may have to wait for a day or two. In the past, currency has been flown in chartered planes or delivered by speeding armored trucks to meet emergency needs—often in a matter of hours.

When a member bank orders currency, payment is made by a deduction from the reserve balance of the bank; when the bank returns or redeems currency, the proceeds are added to the bank's reserve account. This illustrates what was explained in an earlier section: the Federal Reserve note and the reserve deposit liabilities of Reserve banks are interchangeable.

Issuing and retiring federal government securities

The Federal Reserve banks are the agents of the U.S. Treasury in virtually all public debt transactions. When the Treasury sells securities, the purchasers send their orders to the nearest Federal Reserve bank. The securities are issued by the Reserve banks. When the coupons on outstanding treasury obligations are presented to a bank for payment, the coupons are sent by the bank to the nearest Reserve bank. When the holder of a large-denomination treasury bond wants it replaced by several smaller-denomination bonds, the nearest Federal Reserve bank will do this quickly. Savings bond sales and redemptions channel through the Reserve banks. The great size of the public debt has made this function a mechanically large one. Reserve banks keep marketable federal government bonds in their vaults for member banks, and they will keep savings bonds in their vaults for individuals.

Fiscal agency for other government bureaus

The Federal Reserve banks act as fiscal agents, depositories, and custodians for the Treasury Department, the Commodity Credit Corporation, and other governmental agencies. They pay out the proceeds of loans made by these agencies; hold the notes, mortgages, or other documents that are pledged as collateral with them; and collect debts owed them.

In many ways these services performed by the Reserve banks for governmental agencies are similar to the services performed by the trust departments of commercial banks for their corporate customers.

Wire transfers of funds

Sometimes legal or other reasons call for prompt payment of funds at remote points. A businessman in New York may need to make a payment in San Francisco even faster than is possible by airmail. Through a wire transfer, the banker of the New York businessman can arrange to make this prompt payment. The Federal Reserve bank charges only the actual cost of sending the coded telegram. A reduction of the New York bank's reserve balance, an increase in the reserve balance of the San Francisco payee's bank, and a transfer of funds in the Federal Reserve interdistrict settlement fund are all that are needed to complete this transaction. Wire transfers have made the national federal funds market, discussed in the following chapter, a practical possibility.

Questions and problems

1. What was the "simple diagnosis" of monetary problems upon which the original Federal Reserve System was based?
2. What were the defects of the national banking system which the Federal Reserve System was expected to, and did, correct?
3. There are 12 Federal Reserve banks; yet they are called a "central banking system." What characteristics justify treating them as central banks?
4. Draw a rough organization chart of the Federal Reserve System.
5. Enumerate the factors in Federal Reserve organization that tend to make it a private agency and those which make it a public agency.
6. By what process does the Federal Reserve provide a flexible currency? How does it make bank reserves flexible?

7. Show how the limitation of bank reserves limits the amount of credit that banks can extend.

8. Why are bank reserve controls often called "money-market" controls?

9. What are the two leading ways in which Federal Reserve banks extend credit? Why is one of these ways more passive than the other?

10. Show the skeleton entries for the sale of $1,000 of U.S. government securities by the Federal Reserve to a commercial bank for both the Federal Reserve System and the commercial bank.

11. The nonmonetary controls are sometimes labeled "direct" controls. Why? (Clue: Price control is a direct control.)

Bibliography

Aside from the more arid reaches of the learned journals, some of the most important discussion of Federal Reserve affairs has appeared in congressional documents: the Douglas Committee inquiry in 1949, the Patman Committee inquiry in 1952, the Flanders hearings in 1954, and the hearings on the Federal Reserve after 50 years before the Banking and Currency Committee of the House of Representatives in 1964 are the most interesting. The annual appearance of the chairman of the Board of Governors before the Joint Economic Committee has given rise both to important Federal Reserve statements and to significant queries by committee members. The studies of the CED-Ford Foundation Commission for Money and Credit add enormously to the literature on this subject.

By far the best simple account of the Federal Reserve System is the one published by the system itself: *The Federal Reserve System: Its Purposes and Functions* (the fifth edition was published in 1964). In 1969 the Federal Reserve Bank of New York published a short pamphlet titled *Open Market Operations,* which describes the structure and decision-making process behind the Federal Reserve's open market operations.

For current discussion of monetary policy, the *Federal Reserve Bulletin,* published by the Board of Governors, and the monthly reviews of business and credit published by the various Federal Reserve banks are good sources. The *Review* of the Federal Reserve Bank of St. Louis, issued monthly, is especially interesting. The First National City Bank Letter on *Economic Conditions and Government Finance* frequently publishes excellent critical reviews of Federal Reserve policy. The Banking and Currency Committees of both Houses of the Congress also publish important testimony by expert witnesses on the subject matter in this chapter.

CHAPTER 8

The money market

As noted in a previous chapter, commercial bank advances are made as direct loans to depositing customers and as indirect and impersonal investments. The granting of customer loans is considered one of the primary economic functions of commercial banks. However, each bank must be sufficiently liquid to assure itself of being able to meet all cash demands that may be made on it. Furthermore, banks sometimes receive deposits that they know are temporary. It would be imprudent to invest such funds in long-term or nonliquid assets. For these reasons, banks resort to the facilities provided by the open money market. Money market instruments are also purchased by other financial intermediaries, nonfinancial corporations, and all types of institutions and individuals desiring to hold highly liquid assets for short periods of time.

Concept of the market

The term *money market* does not refer to a place in the sense that the market is housed in a single building, as is a stock exchange or a commodity market. It is, rather, a group of institutions and arrangements that bring lenders and borrowers together. It brings into focus all the forces of supply and demand for short-term funds. The distinguishing characteristics of the money market are, in fact, the dealing in short-term funds (usually defined with reference to obligations with one year or less to maturity) and an impersonal relationship between buyers and sellers.

Commercial banks are the chief source of short-term funds in the money market. As has been shown in Chapter 3, the highly volatile nature of bank liability structures requires them to maintain a substantial portion of their assets in a highly liquid form. Money market instruments, which have short maturities and are easily sold with little risk of capital loss, are an ideal medium to fulfill the need for liquidity and yet produce some income. Commercial banks are important holders of the whole range of money market instruments. Banks also are an important element in financing money market firms and traders.

A network of other institutions reaching across the country, such as the Federal Reserve banks, dealers in federal government obligations, savings banks, insurance companies, savings and loan associations, pension funds, and finance companies, also play significant roles in the money markets. Each institution at various times provides a portion of its funds to the market by purchasing money market instruments and withdraws these funds by selling the securities or not reinvesting when the securities mature and are repaid.

As in other free markets, the interplay of the forces of demand and supply largely determines prices in the money market. In the market for money, a single price does not prevail because money is loaned under various terms and contractual agreements by lenders with different investment requirements to debtors who use it for a wide variety of purposes. There are, for example, not only differences in the uses for which money is borrowed but differences in the collateral or security put up by the debtor as well as differences in the length of the term to maturity. For the creditor there may be differences in the tax liability on the interest income received, and there are known differences in the degree of liquidity of, and the risk involved in, various loans. As a result, there can be on one rate of interest; there is, rather, a complex structure of rates.

The New York money market

During World War I the United States became the greatest creditor nation, and New York emerged from the struggle as the financial center of the world. Its importance as a center of domestic and international trade since 1918 has permitted New York to maintain its key position as the most fully developed money market ever known. For that reason an ever-increasing number of financial institutions have offices in that city.

Money market operations in New York City are greatly influenced by the Federal Reserve Bank of New York, the largest one in the system. This institution is a correspondent of all leading central banks of the world. It acts as a fiscal agent for many foreign governments as well as for the United States. The bank holds legal reserve balances of commercial banks of the Second Federal Reserve District; it holds deposits of foreign central banks and governments, the International Bank for Reconstruction and Development (or World Bank), and the International Monetary Fund. The New York bank acts as a custodian of gold and securities of foreign banks and international institutions and deals in foreign currencies and bills arising out of foreign trade.

Not only are the large commercial banks in New York (the Wall Street banks) the hub of the domestic money market, they also perform the operations required to make New York an international financial center. Most large banks have well-developed foreign departments dealing in instruments involving foreign trade and investment. They extend credit to foreign banks, act as their U.S. correspondents, and hold deposits of foreign governments and corporations. These banks act as transfer agents and registrars for foreign corporations whose securities are bought and sold in American markets. They serve as custodians of bonds and stocks of American corporations owned by foreigners.

In addition to the Federal Reserve bank and numerous large commercial banks, New York has a large number of foreign exchange brokers and acceptance and discount houses dealing in bankers' and trade acceptances arising out of foreign and domestic trade. Investment bankers dealing in long-term credit and a host of brokers and dealers in corporate and government securities make New York the greatest capital market in the world. The city attracts the managers of trust and pension funds; it is the home of many savings banks, insurance agencies, and trust companies; it has the largest security exchange in the world.

The New York money market is really a combination of several markets that deal in different kinds of credit. For discussion it may be divided into the governmental and private sectors; or it may be considered as a customers' loan market and as an open market. These classifications also overlap the long-term capital market, in that the money market deals in some items whose payment dates fall rather far in the future.

For our purposes, the customers' loan market may be considered as that dealing in advances of a personal type made primarily by commercial banks to ultimate users of borrowed funds. These transactions are not included in the usual definition of the money market. The open market, on the other hand, operates on an impersonal basis through dealers or middlemen; the borrower and the lender do not meet to negotiate terms. The supply of and the demand for funds in this market may arise in any part of the nation (or of the world). The transfer is handled with complete objectivity as determined by market forces.

Since advances of commercial banks are often permeated with personal considerations for the borrower, because of a long relationship, the customers' loan rate is less sensitive than open market rates. As a result, the open market offers the keenest kind of competition to commercial banks in many kinds of loans that could be handled by either means.

Regional markets

The dominance of New York as a financial center is often overemphasized. This nation has hundreds of large banks, insurance companies, security brokers, and individual capitalists scattered from coast to coast and from Mexico to Canada. In Chicago, San Francisco, Dallas, and other large cities, there are replicas of the institutions that function in New York. Some of these markets continue to function after New York's business day is over; and San Francisco dealers are up before dawn getting reports of the activity in New York, Boston, and other East Coast cities. In a prosperous nation embracing more than 200 million inhabitants spread over four time zones, there is business enough for regional markets as well as the central money market.

Moreover, the various regional markets as well as large numbers of local markets are directly interconnected by a multitude of communication devices. The great improvement in communication because of new technology has both decreased costs and increased the ability of buyers and sellers to complete transactions anywhere in the country. Thus, a truly national money market exists, with buyers and sellers of funds in all parts of the country receiving virtually instantaneous uniform quotations on the purchase or sale of money market securities.

Principal money markets

The largest and most significant segment of the money market is concerned with the buying and selling of direct obligations of the federal government. The federal government issues three types of securities: treasury bills, which mature in one year or less, treasury notes which run for an intermediate term from one to five years, and bonds which include all obligations issued for five or more years. If we view the money market in its narrowest sense, only treasury bills are truly money market media; the others fall nearer to, or clearly within, the long-term or capital section of the market. However, as these longer term issues approach maturity, they are considered money-market issues. In addition to treasury bills and short-term bonds, money market instruments include government agency securities, certificates of deposit, bankers' acceptances, and federal funds. Each of these is discussed in this section.

Treasury bills

Treasury bills are bearer obligations of the United States, promising to pay a specified amount, without interest, on a specified date. They are issued on a discount basis and are obtainable in denominations of $1,000, $5,000, $10,000, $100,000, $500,000, and $1 million, payable at maturity. Income received by a holder is subject to all federal taxation.

Bills have a maturity of not more than one year. Generally they are issued with a maturity of 91 days. Since 1959, however, issues of six-month bills have been sold and, from time to time, the Treasury has sold series of special bills with maturities up to one year.

Issuance of treasury bills. Briefly stated, the mechanics of purchase and sale of treasury bills are as follows: Each week the Secretary of the Treasury invites competitive and noncompetitive bids on a forthcoming issue. Tenders are opened on Monday for 91-day bills at the Federal Reserve banks, and bids are arranged in descending order of prices and telegraphed to the U.S. Treasury. The Treasury combines bids and accepts them in the same order up to the amount of the offering. If identical bids are made, the amounts are allotted in proportion to the amounts requested in the bids. The Secretary of the Treasury announces the results of the offer, and the Reserve banks notify bidders of acceptance or rejection of their tenders.

Bills are issued each Thursday and are dated so that payment is made on a Thursday some specified number of weeks later. The weekly maturities in 1969 averaged over $2 billion. The total volume of bills outstanding at the end of 1969 was $81 billion. This represents a fivefold increase in outstanding bills since the end of 1947, whereas the total outstanding marketable debt of the federal government has increased by less than one half.

Noncompetitive tenders may be made by commercial banks wishing to purchase a small amount of bills—$200,000 or less. These are made without a stated price and will be filled at the average price of accepted competitive bids.

The fact that practically all government security dealers and many banks submit tenders for a new issue of treasury bills means that any issue may become widely distributed before maturity. Secondary purchases are made currently in most instances in the over-the-counter market by dealers and dealer banks. Dealers make a market by quoting bids and offers at prices they are willing to pay or receive for reasonable amounts of government securities. They are not brokers; they get no commissions. Rather, they make outright purchases and sales on their own account and collect their profit from the "spread" between their bid and offering prices.

Just prior to the maturity date of a bill, the nonbank investor will submit the security to his local bank and request that the bank collect and credit his deposit account. On occasion the investor may ask his bank to bid for an equal amount of the new issue. Unlike other securities, bills are never exchanged.

Position of treasury bills in the market. Treasury bills were first introduced in the United States as an instrument of federal finance in 1929. They were designed to attract short-term funds through a weekly auction market, as contrasted with the usual practice of issuing treasury certificates with fixed coupon rates. Within five years the bills had completely replaced certificates and had demonstrated that an issue sold at auction, on a weekly basis, at a discount, was particularly suited to meet the needs of a highly competitive money market.

From the point of view of the Treasury, bills provide a useful means of short-term borrowing. In addition, regular weekly issues afford the Treasury flexibility in adjusting its operations to current needs by increasing or decreasing the volume of bills offered each week. Interest rates on bills usually occupy a lower position in the money market rate structure than any other but have fluctuated widely in the postwar years.

The yield on treasury bills is very responsive to changing credit conditions. The yields at which new bills are sold at the weekly auctions are closely watched for signs of changing market conditions. Under the Treasury's plan to keep interest on the federal debt at the lowest possible levels during World War II, bill rates were maintained steadily at 0.38% from early 1942 to 1947. In 1948 market yields on bills rose to 1% and continued irregularly upward to 2.25% in 1953. In the recession period in 1954, bill rates dropped to 0.65%. In the following cyclical expansion, they rose above 4% in 1957; bill rates were again below 1% in the business contraction during 1958. In the 1958–61 business cycle, bill rates rose to 4.6% in 1959 and then fell below 2.3% in 1960; since then yields have generally increased. In December 1969, treasury bills yielded 7.91%.

Investors in the bill market. From the point of view of investors, the treasury bill market provides an outlet for idle capital that may be put to work for short periods of time with little risk of market loss. Moreover, if investors find it necessary to convert bills back into cash, the ever-present secondary market for these securities will absorb them immediately.

The depth of the treasury bill market is due to the nature and size of the demand for bills. Commercial banks are the heaviest institutional investors; they consider bills an ideal form of secondary reserves. Weekly redemption of maturing bills provides an automatic flow of cash, as the bills may be converted to cash or deposit balances by sale to Federal Reserve banks. Alternatively, they may be sold in the open market.

The second largest institutional purchaser of treasury bills is the Federal Reserve System. By far the largest volume of treasury bills is, however, absorbed by investors classified by Federal Reserve authorities as "all others." The classification includes U.S. government and trust agencies, foreign capitalists and banks, mutual savings banks, insurance companies, savings and loan associations, and business corporations. The last group—the nonfinancial corporations—are the most important bill investors by a wide margin.

Holdings of treasury bills by nonfinancial corporations have increased very rapidly since the end of World War II. This is attributable to several factors. The flow of funds through the corporate sector has greatly increased during this period. Thus, there has been a substantial increase in the demand for short-term investments as a temporary employment of funds reserved for such things as tax payments, dividend payments, capital expansion, and future working capital. Moreover, the higher level of yields available during the 1960s compared to the 1940s and 1950s and compared to noninterest-bearing demand deposits has increased the incentive for corporations to minimize cash holdings and invest excess funds. It is to be expected that the demand by nonfinancial corporations for bills will remain high as long as corporate liquidity persists and as long as corporation tax rates and profits are maintained at high levels.

The volume of corporation investment in the bill market fluctuates inversely with movements of the business cycle. During periods of high prosperity, corporation operations are profitable, and the rates earned on investment in operations exceed the yield on treasury obligations. As a consequence, bill holdings decline. But if recession occurs, as in 1957–58 and in 1960–61, corporations become liquid—they seek outside investments because their own operations are scaled down and bank balances pile up. A favorite place for these temporary balances is in the treasury bill market.

Treasury notes

Treasury notes are intermediate-term obligations of the U.S. government with maturities of one to five years. During World War II, notes were used sparingly in government financing, major emphasis being placed on the shorter term instruments already discussed. After the war, the supply of intermediate-term obligations became inadequate to satisfy the needs of commercial banks and other investors. In response to the growing demand and desiring to lengthen the average maturity of the public debt, the Treasury resumed the issuance of one- to five-year notes. For investors unwilling to incur the market risks that exist in the long-term bond market and for banks that prefer to arrange their government holdings with maturities spaced over a period of years, the treasury note is an ideal investment medium. The Treasury announces the rate of interest that it will pay on notes. The Treasury is under compulsion to make the rate sufficiently attractive to dispose of the issue but, at the same time, to keep the cost of financing at the lowest possible level. Ordinarily, rates on notes are higher than on the short-dated bills discussed above. Interest is usually paid each six months rather than at maturity.

Notes are acceptable for banks to hold as security for deposits of public money but are not acceptable in payment of taxes. Interest income to investors in notes is subject to all federal income taxes.

Commercial banks create the greatest institutional demand for notes. On December 31, 1968, they held $23.2 billion; approximately 50% of the $48 billion held by the public. Others in the market for notes include Federal Reserve banks, mutual savings banks, insurance companies, government agencies, and "other investors." The demand from banks is closely related to their desire to maintain secondary reserves. Almost all bankers consider notes of 12 months or less to maturity to be fully acceptable for secondary-reserve purposes, and many consider them good if maturity is two or even three years in the future. Because of the somewhat higher rates on notes than on bills the greater the proportion of secondary reserves held in this form, the greater the bank income.

Securities of government agencies

In recent years the outstanding volume of federal government agency securities has increased substantially. Moreover, all indications point to a continued growth in the future. These securities are not obligations of, nor are they guaranteed by, the federal government. Nonetheless, there is widespread agreement that in case of any problem the U.S. government would intercede. They are therefore considered to be virtually default riskless.

Table 8–1 shows the volume of securities outstanding of five major agencies at the end of 1960 and 1969. As can be seen, the outstanding securities of these five agencies more than quadrupled in the nine-year period. This growth implies an increasingly important role for agency securities in the money markets.

TABLE 8–1

Publicly held securities of government agencies (*in millions of dollars*)

	End of year	
	1960	1969
Federal Land Banks	2,210	5,949
Federal Home Loan Banks	1,272	8,422
Banks for Cooperatives	407	1,473
Federal Intermediate Credit Banks	1,262	4,116
Federal National Mortgage Association	2,190	10,511
Total	7,341	30,471

Source: *Federal Reserve Bulletin.*

U.S. government agency securities are issued periodically with both long and short maturities depending on market conditions and the needs of the agency. Thus not all of the outstanding securities can properly be considered money market instruments. But, at any time, a substantial fraction are dated to mature within a 12-month period.

The market for commercial paper

In the generic sense, the term *commercial paper* includes promissory notes, commercial drafts, bank acceptances, trade acceptances, and similar credit instruments issued by banking and business firms in financing their operations. In the narrow sense, as used in the money market, the term is restricted to unsecured single-name promissory notes issued in large denominations by large, favorably known business concerns. The minimum round-lot transaction size is $100,000; however, smaller amounts can be purchased (especially from direct sellers) as discussed below. Ordinarily, these notes are payable to the order of the issuing company and are endorsed by it to make them negotiable without further endorsement. Maturity dates are largely from four to six months. The notes do not carry a stipulated rate of interest but are sold to dealers at a discount which includes a small commission.

Open market rates on commercial paper. The rate of discount depends on the credit standing of the borrower, the quantity of similar paper available in the market, the general level of money market rates, and the strength of the demand. Only large firms with a national reputation use the commercial paper market as a source of working capital, and the cost of such funds is almost always lower than the prime rate charged by commercial banks. Rates in the open market, however, are much more volatile than customers' loan rates at commercial banks.

The business enterprises which depend on the commercial paper market for short-term working capital do so for a variety of reasons. As just noted, rates on prime commercial paper are usually lower than bank rates. Also, the maximum legal bank loan to one borrower may be less than the corporation needs. Moreover, funds borrowed in the open market are all at the disposal of the debtor; he is not required to maintain a compensatory deposit balance, as at a bank. Other restrictions, too, that banks often impose are avoided by borrowing in the open market. In addition to these cost factors, the corporation may enhance its financial reputation by disposing of its notes in the open market. This may enable it to finance its longer term needs more advantageously in other segments of the capital market.

Dealers who purchase commercial paper in bulk employ a staff of salesmen to retail the paper among individuals, nonfinancial institutions having excess funds to invest for short periods of time, and smaller commercial banks. The differential between the buying rate and the selling rate, plus a commission of one fourth of 1%, are the sources of profit to the dealers. Only a small number of dealers are active in this market; an even smaller number handle commercial paper exclusively. The others operate in the brokerage and securities business. To achieve wide distribution, the middlemen have established branch offices and correspondents throughout the country.

To facilitate their retail operations, dealers commonly make up lists of the paper available for sale. The lists include paper of various maturities, issues, denominations, and prices, so that a customer may select that which meets his particular requirements.

Direct placements of commercial paper. In recent years middlemen have faced intensive competition from several large finance companies that sell their commercial paper directly to investors. These companies use commercial paper as a primary source of working capital and as an alternative to direct bank loans. In December 1969, the total amount of commercial and finance company paper outstanding was $31,624 million. Of this amount, $19,807 million, or over 62%, had been placed directly by finance companies and bank holding companies. The selling of commercial paper by bank holding companies began during 1969. The two largest finance companies have sold their paper directly since the late 1920s, but in the 1950s a number of finance companies began direct selling, and by 1960 this was the dominant form of commercial paper sales. The expansion in direct placements is due to a number of factors: first, the tendency for the prime bank rate to remain above open market rates when rates fall. Second is the difficulty encountered by large banks in attracting funds during periods of tight money conditions when the maximum rate they are allowed to pay for deposits under Regulation Q is below the level of open market rates. The large banks are not able to supply the funds required by the large finance companies, thus forcing these companies to place greater reliance on the commercial paper market. Third, direct placement has the advantage of allowing the seller to tailor maturities to the exact date on which the purchaser requires funds. The recent entry of bank holding companies into the direct-placed market is due to the fact that rates offered on these securities are not subject to Regulation Q. Thus, bank holding companies can sell commercial paper at prevailing market rates and use funds received to purchase loans from its bank affiliates.

Commercial banks have been the traditional buyers of commercial paper. It is an ideal instrument for holding as a secondary reserve. The risk of loss is negligible; it is paid at maturity with no possibility of extension; and usually the diversity of issues provides convenient maturity dates. Also, if a bank wishes to obtain cash or build up reserves before the paper matures, it may resell in the open market or rediscount the paper at a Federal Reserve bank. In the latter case the paper must have no more than 90 days left before maturity.

During the last two decades, however, nonfinancial corporations have become increasingly important buyers of commercial paper, especially directly placed paper. A survey conducted during 1955 found that almost 55% of directly placed commercial paper was held by nonfinancial corporations.[1] Corporate treasurers have been attracted by the premium in yields usually available relative to treasury bills. In addition, flexibility in setting maturity dates, so that directly placed paper can be purchased to mature on the date funds are needed, is a very attractive feature. Thus, in recent years banks have held a very small portion of outstanding commercial paper.

Certificates of deposit

The increased participation of nonfinancial corporations as buyers and holders of money market instruments, especially commercial paper, has meant a loss of business for commercial banks. This is particularly true of the large money market banks. Large corporate deposits represent an important part of total deposits of these banks. To compete for corporate funds that would otherwise be invested in money market securities, commercial banks have developed a new marketable instrument, the certificate of deposit.

Commercial banks offer these negotiable certificates with tailored maturity at stipulated yields, which rise with maturity. An active secondary market has developed, in which they can be sold at very little cost. As do dealers of treasury bills, dealers in the secondary market for certificates of deposit maintain positions and earn their profit on the spread between bid and asked prices.

Most banks set minimum limits on the size of certificate they will sell. The limits usually are related to bank size. The largest money market banks will not ordinarily issue certificates in denominations below $0.5 or $1 million. Smaller banks issue certificates of $100,000 or less. It is felt that these relatively high dollar limits discourage large use of funds which would otherwise be kept as demand deposits in the banks.

Prime certificates of deposit, those issued by the largest money market banks, are usually sold to yield about one fourth of 1% more than treasury bills of comparable maturity. Although certificates of deposit are virtually riskless and easily converted to cash, this positive yield differential is required to entice buyers away from the treasury bill market. During periods of tight money conditions when treasury bill rates are

---

[1] See Donald P. Jacobs, "Sources and Costs of Funds of Large Sales Finance Companies," in *Consumer Installment Credit* (Board of Governors, Federal Reserve System, 1957), pt. II, vol. 1.

high, if the Federal Reserve does not increase the Regulation Q maximum, banks are not able to offer sufficiently attractive rates to sell substantial amounts of certificates of deposit. Such a condition occurred during 1966 and 1969. Large banks that had sold substantial amounts of certificates were unable to compete with other money market instruments. When outstanding certificates came due, they could not be replaced. Thus these banks lost large amounts of deposits during a period of heavy loan demand.

The acceptance market

A *banker's acceptance* is a credit instrument drawn by an individual or business concern on a bank and accepted, i.e., acknowledged as an order, by the drawee bank. It is an order for the bank to pay to a designated person or to bearer a certain sum of money at a stipulated time. When the bank accepts the draft, it literally becomes a cashier's check or a promissory note of the bank.

Origin of bank acceptances. Bank drafts originate mainly in the financing of foreign trade. As explained in Chapter 25, an importer asks his bank to issue a letter of credit indicating the bank's willingness to be drawn upon by an exporter of goods in a foreign country. This letter is also an authorization to the foreign exporter to draw drafts of a specific nature to finance a specific type of goods.

In the foreign market, the exporter places the product on an international carrier (boat, airplane, or railway) and obtains a receipt in the form of a bill of lading. The original bill of lading is a document showing ownership or title to the goods that will be transported.

With the bill of lading and the export letter of credit issued by a bank in the United States, the foreign exporter goes to his local bank. He draws a draft upon the American bank and attaches it to the letter of credit, invoice, bill of lading, insurance papers, and any other documents necessary to allow passage of the goods across international boundaries.

This sheaf of papers is purchased (discounted) by the exporter's local bank and forwarded to the importer or the drawee bank. At this point the draft is accepted by the American bank, and the documents required by the importer to obtain possession of the goods are released to him.

When he applies for the letter of credit, the American importer promises to pay the local bank at the time the draft matures. This will be on the date of acceptance if it is a sight bill, or a stipulated number of days after acceptance if it is a time draft.

Rates on acceptances. By accepting the draft, the drawee bank becomes the principal debtor, and the drawer becomes secondarily liable. The instrument thus becomes a liability of the bank for which a ready market exists. The payee, or any holder in due course, may sell the acceptance at a discount in the open market. The rate of discount is usually less than the rate on commercial paper and the rate to prime bank borrowers. At the end of December 1969, prime bankers' acceptances of 90-day maturity were quoted at 8.58%; prime commercial paper, to six months at 8.84%; and the prime bank rate commercial banks charge on the largest loans was 8.5%.[2]

Although bankers' acceptances are used principally in financing the movement of goods in international trade, they are used also for the domestic shipment and storage of goods. At the end of December 1969, of the estimated $5,451 million of acceptances outstanding, $1,889 million had originated in the financing of imports, $1,153 million in the export trade, and $2,408 million in the creation of dollar exchange, the shipment and storage of goods within the United States, and in the storage of goods in foreign countries and shipments between foreign countries.[3]

Dollar exchange. Under the Federal Reserve Act, member banks are authorized to accept drafts drawn by banks in foreign countries or in dependencies or insular possessions of the United States for the purpose of creating the dollar exchange needed to finance the trade of these areas. The object of making such credit available to banks abroad is to make it possible for importers to pay for goods received from the United States in periods when the sales of their products to the United States have declined because of the seasonal nature of production. Later, when the foreign goods are exported and sold in America, funds become available for paying the acceptances.

Volume limitations on acceptances. Because dollar exchange is based on anticipated shipment of commodities rather than on existing products, these credits are unsecured. In addition, acceptances drawn to meet the demand for dollar credits arising from transactions other than those growing out of the movement of commodities (finance bills) are unsecured. Both classes of bills are closely regulated by Federal Reserve authorities. Neither type of these acceptances creates deposits or other liabilities subject to reserve requirements, and in the absence of legal limitations, a bank could accept an unlimited amount. The Federal Reserve Act restricts the volume of a bank's outstanding acceptances, however, to 50% of the amount of unimpaired capital and surplus. If the aggregate amount of acceptances based on domestic transactions does not exceed 50% of capital and surplus, a member bank may accept drafts up to the full amount of capital and surplus. The rule that limits unsecured loans to one borrower to 10% of capital and surplus applies also to acceptances.

---

[2] *Federal Reserve Bulletin,* June 1970, p. A31.
[3] Ibid., p. A37.

Acceptances as secondary reserves. Bankers' acceptances are an ideal type of secondary reserves for commercial banks; they usually run from 30 to 180 days but may be sold in the open market or rediscounted at a Federal Reserve bank. If discounted, the maturity date must be no longer than 90 days. Federal Reserve banks seldom bid for acceptances on their own account but buy a great many for foreign banks for whom such investment sometimes has a tax advantage. The Reserve banks set the price to be paid; they hold all acceptances, except those obtained under a repurchase agreement until maturity. In the latter case, the selling bank agrees to buy back the paper prior to its maturity date. Acceptances bought outright and held among the assets of Reserve banks as of December 31, 1969, equaled $64 million. Acceptances purchased for foreign central bank correspondents are usually endorsed by the Reserve banks and appear as a contingent liability on Federal Reserve balance sheets. At the end of December 31, 1969, the amount shown was slightly less than $146 million.

The neutrality of Reserve bank policy in the acceptance market is more apparent than real. If they want to increase holdings, the Reserve banks may lower their buying rates and attract bills from commercial banks and acceptance dealers. Through a reverse action, they may repel acceptances. In recent years Reserve banks have not used acceptance buying to implement monetary policy actively. Nonetheless, the Federal Reserve continues its active policy of discounting acceptance to promote foreign trade by enhancing the liquidity of this important financial instrument. Policy actions have been carried out chiefly through changes in reserve requirements, treasury bill holdings, and the rediscount rate. The fluctuations in the volume of acceptances held by the Federal Reserve banks vary with changes in the method of financing domestic trade and in the volume of international transactions.

The market for federal funds

We have noted that commercial banks are required by law to maintain certain minimum reserves against their deposit liabilities. The legal reserves of member banks are maintained principally as deposit balances in Federal Reserve banks. Business and financial transactions cause a constant shifting of funds among the more than 13,000 banks, with the result that some have reserves in excess of their requirements and others have a deficit. The federal funds market provides a means of making quick adjustments and permitting banks with excess reserves to increase their earnings and deficit banks to avoid the penalty charged when reserves are below the legal minimum.

Origin and development. The federal funds market originated in New York in the 1920s, when the depression following World War I resulted in sharp disparities in the reserve positions of New York City banks. Members were able to borrow or rediscount at the Federal Reserve bank, but that was often considered costly because of the time and expense involved and at times because the rediscount rate was higher than rates in the short-term market. Deficit bankers naturally began purchasing (borrowing) funds from other members having excess reserve balances at the Federal Reserve. The transfer was usually accomplished by an exchange of checks. The lending bank drew a check on its reserve balance in the Federal Reserve bank, and the borrowing bank drew on itself. The former check was presented for clearing on the day drawn; the latter was payable through the clearinghouse the next day. Thus the borrowing bank was enabled by this overnight loan to avoid a reserve deficiency. If the borrowing bank needed funds for a somewhat longer period, the deal was renewed on a day-to-day basis. The operation of the market follows essentially the same pattern today.

The federal funds market was of little significance during the 1930s when practically all banks had excess reserves, and in the 1940s, when reserve adjustments were made readily through sales of treasury bills to Reserve banks at fixed rates. In the 1950s, especially following the Treasury–Federal Reserve accord, which freed the Federal Reserve to follow an independent policy, the federal funds market expanded and became very active. The growth in the federal funds market and its key position with regard to the transfer of reserves among banks has made the level of transactions and rates in this market as key indicators of money-market conditions.

Federal funds and monetary policy. The accord in which the Reserve System abrogated responsibility for purchasing government obligations to maintain a floor to prices and to hold down short-term interest rates restored the Reserve authorities to the status of a policy-making body. Since then there have been recurring periods of tight money, and pressure has been exerted on bank reserves. To the extent that deficit members have found it possible to make short-term adjustments in their reserve position by purchasing federal funds, the banking system is making more efficient use of its reserves. Widespread use of the federal funds market, however, has made the task of the Federal Reserve somewhat more difficult when it is following a policy of credit restriction. For example, in periods when the reserves of large commercial banks are subjected to pressure from business or the Reserve banks, the large commercial banks have found it possible to purchase federal funds from smaller banks in moderate-sized centers or from country banks. This relief from pressure by the larger banks may, of course, be only temporary. If the banks with excess reserves fear further pressure on their own liquidity position, they become reluctant to sell federal funds except at higher rates.

Despite the fact that the federal funds market forces the Federal Reserve Board to act more strongly to bring about a desired degree of credit stringency, its operation is on a whole beneficial. This market links banks in all sections of the nation, and therefore acts to spread quickly the effects of any changes in Federal Reserve policy. For example, a move to tighten credit conditions may have an initial impact on banks in New York or Chicago, through a Federal Reserve sale of bonds to a bank in one of these cities. This bank would then buy federal funds to augment its reserve position. The selling banks would have less excess reserves and so a part of the credit-tightening effect would then be felt by the selling banks. The opposite would happen if it were desired to make credit more easily available. The bank that sold bonds to the Federal Reserve bank might initially sell a portion of its added reserves in the federal funds market and so relieve the pressure on the buying bank. In this sense, changed credit conditions are transmitted more evenly throughout the system than would otherwise occur.

Nonbank investors. Although the major participants in the federal funds market are commercial banks of larger cities, a substantial number of medium-sized and small banks buy and sell federal funds when they have excess reserves or a reserve deficiency. Moreover, some government security dealers, agents of foreign banks, mutual savings banks, and a few business corporations are also active. A survey conducted by Federal Reserve authorities during the period from September 1959 to September 5, 1962, revealed that more than 90% of the dollar volume of transactions was accounted for by banks. The balance was accounted for mainly by government security dealers.[4]

Government security dealers were drawn into the federal funds market because bank customers of dealers insisted that all security transactions in short-term obligations be settled in federal funds.

Dealers finance their inventory of government bonds largely through loans from money market banks. Loans from banks outside of New York are transferred through the Federal Reserve wire transfer service and so are federal funds; the same is true of any financing provided by the Federal Reserve directly.

Corporations have found it to their advantage to use federal funds in payment to dealers for government securities. Their procurement, however, is largely a matter of bank-customer relationship. Ordinarily, corporation purchases are made so that maturities will fall on specific dates, and funds are borrowed for more than one day. The corporation needing funds to make payment for security purchases seldom actually receives the funds but directs the bank to handle the transaction. The bank takes

---

[4] Dorothy M. Nichols, *Trading in Federal Funds* (Board of Governors, Federal Reserve System, 1965), pp. 22–25.

delivery of the securities purchased, makes payment in federal funds against the corporation account, and places the securities in custody for the account. In the event of a sale of the securities, the procedure is reversed.

Rate determination in the federal funds market. Early each day, bids, offers, and inquiries for federal funds come from all over the country into two major brokerage firms and to a number of large money market banks that act as brokers in federal funds. Through this process, buyers and sellers of funds are brought into contact. In addition, many banks will buy and sell directly to their correspondents from their own reserve accounts.

When the market opens, attempts are made to match bids and offers, but if this is not possible, bid and asked prices are quoted, and transactions are consummated as customers revise their original bids and asking prices. Sometimes banks do not make bids at fixed rates but allow brokers to execute orders at their discretion within a rather narrow range of prices. Since the rate determined is an indication of the state of the money market, banks want to get the brokerage firm's quotation early in the day. The rate is widely quoted and is considered as *the* market rate.

Competition in the federal funds market. Although most banks outside of New York City accept the rate quoted in the city, some check rates of other dealers or shop around for more advantageous prices. At times a bank will lend at a lower rate than the market quotation to a correspondent; price is a secondary consideration. Rates on straight loans may be higher than rates on repurchase agreement contracts, in which the securities purchased are used as collateral security. There is a close relationship among the segments of the federal funds markets; the differentials are small, but it is not often that all rate quotations are the same at any given time.

The rate at which federal funds are bought and sold is very volatile. Substantial changes can occur during the week and also over the interest rate cycle. When there are substantial excess reserves in the system, the rate tends to be very low, sometimes as low as one fourth of 1%. Even during periods of tight money conditions, the rate during some days in the week may be very low if a temporary oversupply develops. Near the end of a settlement week, the period for which deposits are averaged to calculate a bank's required reserve, banks that have excess reserves will sell them for any price above the cost of the transaction. Before 1964, during periods of tight money, the rate usually was the same as the Federal Reserve discount rate. When the federal funds rate was equal to the discount rate, banks still preferred to buy federal funds rather than borrow from the Federal Reserve and it was believed that no bank would pay more than the discount rate for federal funds. During 1964 a new development in the market occurred when a major New York bank started to buy federal funds at one eighth of 1% above the prevailing discount rate. It is believed that this bank used these funds for dealer loans and could not borrow for this purpose from the Federal Reserve.

In recent years the discount rate has not been a ceiling for the federal funds rate. During the tight money conditions large money market banks faced serious deposit losses because of the low maximum rates they were allowed to offer under Regulation Q on savings deposits and certificates of deposit. To meet their loan demand for which they could not borrow at the Federal Reserve, these banks turned to the Eurodollar market for funds and bid up the federal funds rate to entice smaller banks to lend them funds. (See Chapter 26 for a description of the Eurodollar market.)

Interest rates and reserve adjustments

We have repeatedly noted that in the adjustment of their reserve positions, member banks patronize the markets for acceptances, commercial paper, treasury bills, and federal funds and may rediscount at Federal Reserve banks. There is obviously an interrelationship among the rates in these markets, and banks will shift operations from one market to another in seeking the least expensive, or most convenient, means of adjust-

EXHIBIT 8–1

Short-term interest rates (*monthly*)

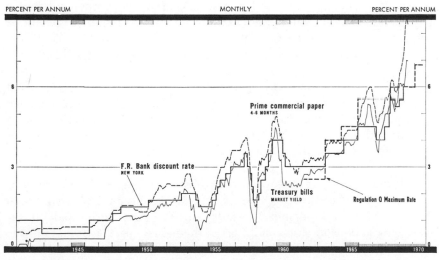

* Negative figure.

ing reserves. Ordinarily, the rate nearest the federal funds rate is that on short-maturity treasury bills. When the yield on bills is above other short-term rates, a bank with an excess of reserves will be inclined to invest in bills. A purchase of bills by a group of banks holding excess reserves will tend to bid up the price of bills and will reduce the available supply of federal funds. At the same time, certain other banks may have no excess reserves and may maintain rates for federal funds by competing for the reduced supply available. Many banks prefer to make day-to-day adjustments in their reserve position in the federal funds market rather than disturb their bill portfolios or go into debt at Reserve banks. The play of these forces tends to reduce differentials in rates between treasury bills, federal funds, and the rediscount rate. The close correspondence of rates in these markets is evidenced by the movements in the discount rate and treasury bill yields between 1953 and 1957; see Exhibit 8–1. But, this decision process and the close relationship between alternative borrowing and lending rates in the money markets is drastically disturbed when Regulation Q maximums are held below other market rates; this is shown for the periods 1962–63 and 1967–70 in Exhibit 8–1.

Interest rates in the money market

Exhibit 8–1 shows movements in the interest rates of treasury bills, certificates, prime commercial paper, and the Federal Reserve rediscount rate between 1940 and 1969. The horizontal movement during the World War II years reflects the policy of cooperation between the Federal Reserve System and the U.S. Treasury in stabilizing rates at low levels. About two years after the end of World War II, the prime commercial paper rate began to climb and was followed upward by other rates in an irregular advance until 1953. These movements were in response to the growing demand for short-term capital needed in financing expansion in the entire economy.

All rates fell substantially in the recession of 1953–54 but reversed themselves and continued upward until, in 1956, they achieved a peak not equaled since 1930. In the business recession of 1957–58, the rate on treasury bills again dipped below 1%; commercial paper slumped to 1½%, which was one fourth of 1% below the Federal Reserve rediscount rate.

The rise in interest rates from mid-1958 to early 1960 mirrors the upward movement of business activity. The slackening in business activity during 1960 was accompanied by falling interest rates as the Federal Reserve took actions to ease conditions in the money markets to help foster a return to prosperous conditions.

The downward movement of short-term interest rates in 1960 depicted in Exhibit 8–1 indicates the development of a new constraint in the framing and implementation of monetary policy. In the 1960 recession, short-term rates did not fall to the levels reached in the 1953–54 recession or the 1957–58 recession. The Federal Reserve was cognizant of the need to develop appropriate monetary conditions to help combat the recession in business activity but feared the implications of extremely low short-term rates on the nation's international balance of payments. (See Chapter 24 for an elaboration of this point.)

Short-term interest rates during the period 1961–1966 reflect the rising tempo of economic activity during those years. Of great interest is the rapid rise in rates in mid-1966. This rise came to an end when the Federal Reserve authorities, fearing a depression because of the extremely tight monetary conditions, aggressively added to bank reserves in the fall of 1966. Emerging inflationary conditions in 1967 caused the Federal Reserve to reverse its policies, and as can be seen, market rates again rose very rapidly until the end of 1969.

It is interesting to note that the Federal Reserve discount rate was substantially below the yields on commercial paper and treasury bills during most of the period after 1965. This reflects the decision of the Federal Reserve to maintain low Regulation Q ceilings and to discourage bank borrowing through rationing rather than by raising the discount rate.

The position of individual rates in the subsectors of the money market, i.e., treasury bills, commercial paper, and so on, are due to differences in maturity, in the credit worthiness of borrowers, and in the demand and supply factors in the several subsectors.

The force that keeps all short-term rates interrelated within this closely knit structure is that lenders are active in all subsectors and keep shifting their advances to the market that is most attractive. Adjustments, made by selling instruments with lower net yields and buying in those with higher yields, tend to keep rates in line with one another. Thus, if given time, pressure arising in one subsector will be transmitted to the entire market. As lenders adjust their purchases and sales of short-term obligations, a pattern of rates tends to be restored.

Relationship to the capital market

To this point in our description of the money market we have been concerned primarily with short-term private and governmental obligations and the place occupied by each as a part of the secondary reserves and earning assets of commercial banks. Chapter 9, which is devoted to an overview of the capital market, contains information on long-term debt and equity issues. At this point we shall summarize some of the features that tie these two markets together, leaving a more detailed discussion to Chapter 9.

Interest rate relationship

The primary tie of the two markets lies in the fact that many borrowers can chose between them in arranging some part of their financing. The choice is not a completely free one, as all borrowers must avoid too much short-term debt. But the degree of shiftability that prevails is great enough to keep a discernible relationship between the short-term money rates of the money market and the long-term rates of the capital markets. Not only is there some latitude in the borrowing choices of business and other debtors; some lenders can shift their investment operations between the markets, at least to some extent. Long-term lenders seldom invade the money market, but short-term lenders, such as commercial banks, do from time to time lengthen as well as shorten their maturity policies.

The term to maturity is an essential difference between money and capital market instruments. The prevailing term structure of rates, that is, the yield on obligations that are alike in all respects except maturity, is an important indicator of relationships between the two markets. The normal relationship is often thought to be that short-term interest rates are below long-term rates. History, however, has often contradicted this assumption. During a number of periods it has been reversed, i.e., yields on short-maturity securities were above those of longer maturity. Short-term interest rates, of course, can fluctuate and do fluctuate through rather wider ranges than do long-term rates since such movements do not involve large swings in capital values. In general, however, both long-term and short-term interest rates tend to move in the same general direction at about the same time.

Borrower-lender relationship

As already noted, most lenders stay within the maturity range of investment that seems to be in keeping with their institutional character. Life insurance companies are almost wholly long-term lenders; with trivial exceptions, the same could be said of savings and loan associations. Mutual savings banks sometimes shift the maturity structure of their assets moderately, but rarely in a drastic way. The only lender with a considerable degree of flexibility is the commercial bank, a point that has been made in earlier chapters.

Borrowers have more latitude in adjusting their financing to market conditions. Business corporations must keep short-term borrowing within the boundaries of prudence, but beyond this they can, and do, change the maturity structure of their debts. Individuals could exercise this privilege but seldom do. State and local governments borrow in serial form, so that they take funds from both the money and the capital markets. Perhaps the most eclectic borrower of all is the federal government.

The earlier sections of this chapter have shown the obligations used in treasury short-term borrowing. In addition, a great deal of treasury financing is done by long-term bonds. Many feel, however, that in practice the Treasury has failed to do enough long-term borrowing. In boom periods the Treasury has hesitated to borrow on this basis because of the high cost. In periods of recession, it has not wanted to preempt the supply of long-term funds that might stimulate private capital expenditures. Paralyzed by this paradox, a large fraction of the federal debt is in short-term form. Efforts to escape the paradox have unfortunately met with political resistance.

Questions and problems

1. What is the money market?
2. What services does the money market perform for (a) the business community and (b) commercial banks?
3. Appraise the relative merits of treasury bills, bankers' acceptances, and commercial paper as secondary reserves for commercial banks.
4. Discuss the market for federal funds and trace the effects of a transaction as it affects member-bank reserves.
5. Discuss the differences in the position or role of the dealers in subsectors of the money market.
6. Explain why interest rates in the open market are more volatile than bankers' loan rates.
7. List the media (or obligations) that are bought and sold in the money market.
8. What institutions are on the demand side of the money market? On the supply side?
9. Interest rates in the subsectors of the money market are often not at the same level. Why?
10. "In spite of the differences prevailing in interest rates of the various sectors of the money market, these sectors are closely interrelated and tend to resume their normal pattern after a period of disturbance." How do you account for this restoration of the normal pattern?
11. "The mounting number of Federal funds deals has increased the mobility of the reserves held by the nation's banking system." Do you consider this to be a true statement? Explain. What beneficial effects would you expect to result from "increased mobility"? Beneficial to whom?
12. Explain the two methods by which commercial paper comes to the money market. Obtain statistical evidence to show the amounts outstanding at each year-end since 1950.
13. Why do other countries have nothing closely resembling the American commercial paper market?

Bibliography

Beckhart, B. H., and Smith, James G. *The New York Money Market*. vol. II: *Sources and Movement of Funds*. New York: Columbia University Press, 1932.

Federal Reserve Bank of Cleveland. *Money Market Instruments*. 2d ed. 1967.

Federal Reserve Bank of New York. *Monthly Review of Credit and Business Conditions*.

————. *The Treasury and the Money Market*. May 1954.

Madden, Carl H. *The Money Side of the Street*. New York: Federal Reserve Bank of New York, 1959.

Nadler, M., Heller, Sipa, and Shipman, Samuel. *The Money Market and Its Institutions*. New York: The Ronald Press Co., 1955.

Nichols, Dorothy M. *Trading in Federal Funds*. Board of Governors of the Federal Reserve System, Washington, D.C., 1965.

Ritter, Lawrence. *Money and Economic Activity*. 3d ed. Boston: Houghton Mifflin Co., 1967.

Robinson, Roland I. *Money and Capital Markets*. New York: McGraw-Hill Book Co., 1964.

Roosa, Robert V. *Federal Reserve Operations in the Money and Government Securities Market*. New York: Federal Reserve Bank of New York, July 1956.

Willis, Parker B. *The Federal Funds Market*. Boston: Federal Reserve Bank of Boston, 1968.

PART III

CAPITAL MARKET INTERMEDIARY INSTITUTIONS

The following seven chapters comprise the book's next major section—capital market intermediary institutions. This section considers first the major sources of capital funds, the households, and then describes how household savings are accumulated and transmitted by capital market intermediary institutions to borrowers of the funds. The aim of Chapter 9 is to provide an overview of the functioning of capital markets, or markets for long-term funds, through a discussion of how the various economic units interacting through the capital markets are related to each other. Chapter 10, continuing the discussion, describes the process of channeling savings into financial investments in greater detail. Chapters 11 through 15 then provide detailed descriptions of the various types of capital market intermediary institutions: deposit type savings institutions, insurance companies, investment services, trustee services, and pension funds.

CHAPTER 9

Capital markets: an overview

This chapter begins with a discussion of what constitutes the capital markets and then considers problems involved in determining their size. Capital markets are defined as markets in which the lending and borrowing of money is effected, and the size of the markets is discussed both in terms of the amounts of loans outstanding and in terms of the amounts of new borrowing and lending over some annual periods. Discussion then turns to interest rates, the prices of capital market transactions. While interest rates in a given market are determined primarily by the supply of and demand for given types of loan funds, other factors affect rates. Such factors also determine the interest rate structure, or the rate differentials between different markets. Finally, the importance of financial institutions in transmitting funds from lenders to borrowers on terms satisfactory to both types of transactors is discussed.

Capital markets defined

It has already been indicated that the capital markets are markets in which long-term arrangements regarding the lending and borrowing of funds are established. Because loan arrangements can be made for any time period, a precise distinction between short- and long-term lending in terms of the length of time period for which the arrangement is made is of little help in understanding the types of transactions and institutions that will be encountered in our examination of the capital markets. Thus, even though long-term lending arrangements are established (usually) for a period of several years, any such definition of long term as "loan arrangements extending over a period of time greater than one year" is somewhat arbitrary. It is less difficult to classify the markets in terms of the kinds of lending which take place. The demands for funds from the capital markets can be categorized as demands for mortgage funds used to finance the construction of houses, apartments, and commercial buildings, for funds employed in the financing of corporations (raised both through equity and debt issues), for funds employed in the financing of federal, state, and local government operations, and also, for funds used for consumer credit.

The new funds flowing into the capital markets derive from consumer and business saving, but it is useful to indicate the major categories of financial intermediaries which supply funds to meet the demands just mentioned. The middlemen include life, fire and casualty insurance companies, privately and publicly owned pension funds, commercial banks, savings and loan associations, mutual savings banks, and investment companies.[1] The influence of governments also may be manifest in the supply as well as the demand for capital market instruments through transactions involving their securities.[2]

While the saving of corporations and households provides a measure of new funds entering financial markets, secondary transactions (transactions involving securities previously issued) also take place. Totals of outstanding instruments usually reflect issuance of several layers of claims against the same real assets. Some parts of the capital markets are regional in character, while others are at least partially separated in terms of the types of instruments employed. Distinctions between open and negotiated markets must be made. These aspects of definitional problems contribute to the development of a complete picture of the capital markets and will be discussed below.

Size of the capital markets

One measurement of the size of the capital markets is the stock of outstanding claims held at any specific time by different persons or organizations in the economy; a second measure is based on the flows of funds between different economic groups over a given period of time. Both kinds of measurements have advantages and limitations. These

---

[1] Other institutions whose operations are of lesser significance will also be discussed in the detailed account given below.

[2] As has already been seen, this influence is in one way manifested through treasury and Federal Reserve transactions in the money markets as well.

advantages and limitations have to do with the concepts underlying the measurements and with the availability of data.

Outstanding claims

It is impracticable to sum up all of the claims for all persons or organizations at a moment of time, but the Federal Reserve System does supply data that permit a totaling of claims held by groups of persons or organizations. Thus the discussion here is based on relationships among six groups:[3] households (including nonprofit organizations), businesses (farm, nonfarm, and corporate), state and local governments, the federal government, the financial sector,[4] and the rest of the world. Before looking at the figures for these groups, let us consider briefly how the claims arise and what they represent.

The ultimate determinant of wealth in the U.S. economy consists of its real assets. In order to develop this point without unnecessary complications, suppose for the moment that the economy has no financial transactions with the rest of the world. If we think in terms of a national balance sheet, then whenever such a balance sheet is drawn up, the identity:

$$\text{Real assets} + \text{financial assets} = \text{liabilities} + \text{net worth}$$

holds true. But since in a closed economy every borrowing (creation of a liability) is matched by an equal amount of lending (creation of a financial asset) it is clear that financial assets must be just equal to liabilities and that the net worth of an economy is therefore equal to the value of its real assets. Thus, it is important not to equate real wealth with totals of financial assets outstanding. This point becomes more relevant when it is recognized that the total of outstanding claims really depends on the number of times money is borrowed and re-lent.

In a closed economy in which every unit spent exactly what it earned, there would be no borrowing or lending and no outstanding financial claims. If, on the other hand, someone kept from spending a dollar of his personal income and deposited it in a bank, and if the bank were to re-lend the dollar, the economy's total financial claims outstanding would change from zero to two dollars. At the same time, if the borrower were to spend the dollar to acquire new physical assets, the

---

[3] This section is based on information presented in the Federal Reserve System, "Flow of Funds Accounts," *Federal Reserve Bulletin.*

[4] The financial sector, as the term is used in this chapter, includes commercial and mutual savings banks, savings and loan associations, credit unions, insurance companies, brokerage firms, finance companies, mortgage companies, open-end investment companies, and the Federal Reserve System. Nearly all the private institutions are described in later chapters; the Federal Reserve System is discussed in Chapter 7.

amount of tangible investment[5] (and the amount of savings) would equal just one half the total of new claims created. Thus, outstanding claims tell us very little about the economy's accumulated tangible assets or the rate at which these assets may be changing. Nevertheless, the totals of outstanding claims are useful in that they provide an indication of which groups in the economy are net lenders or borrowers of funds.

An aggregate amount of claims on others is displayed in Table 9–1. The figures then totaled $3,842 billion of which nearly half was held by households, and about a third of which was held by the intermediaries representing the financial sector. It will be noted that the households' claims on the financial sector, $848 billion, are approximately matched by the financial sector's claims on households and on business, $340 and $414 billion respectively. These figures indicate the flow of funds from

TABLE 9–1

Approximate amount of claims, December 31, 1969 (*amounts outstanding in billions of dollars*)

	House- holds	Non- financial business	Federal government	State and local governments	Financial sector	Rest of the world	Total claims by sector
Households	$ 13	$ 801	$105	$ 41	$ 848	—	$1,808
Nonfinancial business	29	198	13	6	175	—	421
Federal government	6	32	10	—	49	2	99
State and local governments ..	3	12	23	2	24	—	64
Financial sector	340	414	172	83	317	12	1,338
Rest of the world	—	20	40	—	52	—	112
Total claims on sector ..	$391	$1,477	$363	$132	$1,465	$14	$3,842

Note: Holdings of corporate stocks are valued at market prices.
Source: Prepared from "Financial Assets and Liabilities," Federal Reserve System, May 15, 1970, p. A71.10.

households through intermediaries to their final users. Other indications of the sectors that lend or borrow also are given by the table. Households lent $1,808 billion to other sectors (claims in this amount were held by households), while the claims of other sectors on households amounted to $391 billion. Thus, at year-end 1969, households were net lenders of some $1,400 billion to other sectors. Similarly, the financial sector was a net borrower of about $127 billion, and business a net borrower of about $1,056 billion.

The totals shown on Table 9–1 understate the actual total of outstanding claims because some categories, such as noncorporate trade credit, are excluded. On the other hand, as previous discussion has indicated, the fact that several layers of transactions are reflected in the outstand-

---

[5] Since the term *investment* is used primarily in connection with securities purchases in this book, the term *tangible investment* is employed to indicate the real capital formation process.

ing claims means that the reported total is greater than the economy's accumulated real assets; it means also that the economy's capital markets are both active and highly developed, and thus that the process of channeling funds from lenders to borrowers is both elaborate and sophisticated.

Flows of funds

Another way of measuring capital market activity is to study the rates at which claims of sectors on other sectors change, i.e., to study the new flows of funds between the economy's sectors over a given time period. The net flows of funds between sectors are measured by the Federal Reserve System's flow of funds accounts, for which recent data are sum-

TABLE 9–2

Approximate flows of funds for 1969 (*in billions of dollars as measured by lending transactions*)

	House-holds	Non-financial business	Federal government	State and local governments	Financial sector	Rest of the world	Total funds lent by sector
Households	$ 1.3	−$ 2.1	$13.1	$3.8	$34.2	—	$ 50.2
Nonfinancial business	1.8	30.2	−1.4	2.3	−7.3	—	25.5
Federal government	0.7	5.2	−1.3	—	1.0	1.4	7.0
State and local governments .	0.2	2.8	4.2	0.1	−5.3	—	1.9
Financial sector	32.6	36.3	−8.0	2.4	14.8	−0.1	78.2
Rest of the world	—	11.0	−2.1	—	1.2	—	10.1
Total funds borrowed by sector	$36.6	$83.4	$ 4.5	$8.6	$38.6	$1.3	$172.9

Note: Detail may not add to totals because of rounding.
Source: *Federal Reserve Bulletin*, November 1969.

marized in Table 9–2. The entries in this table show the net amount of lending by one sector to another for the calendar year 1969. Thus, during that year, the claims of households on the federal government increased by $13.1 billion, because the federal government borrowed that amount from households.

The aggregate figures in Table 9–2 give interesting information regarding the funds flow process. For example, the first row total indicates that in 1969 the household sector lent $50.2 billion, chiefly to financial institutions. At the same time, the household sector borrowed $36.6 billion, chiefly from the financial sector to which most of its funds were lent. Thus, during the year households were net suppliers of funds to the extent of $13.6 billion; financial institutions supplied a net amount of $39.6 billion, and the federal government $2.5 billion. Net demanders of funds were business ($57.9 billion) and state and local governments ($6.7 billion). Most of the funds flowed first from households to the financial institutions, which in turn directed the flows principally to households, business, and government.

Some unusual aspects of the figures—the negative numbers representing net reductions in certain types of lending—deserve special comment. An important negative figure is the $8 billion figure representing redemptions of federal government bonds by the financial sector as it attempted to offset the monetary restriction of 1969. Another important figure is the $7.3 billion figure attributable largely to the withdrawal of time deposits by business from the commercial banking sector in response to lower rates on these instruments, representative of the effects of Regulation Q ceilings which restricted rates on time deposits to levels below those prevailing on comparable instruments.

Only the difference between a sector's borrowing and lending is measured in the funds flow accounts data. This means that separate totals of funds flowing into and out of a sector are not available. Because only transactions between sectors are measured, business' internal financing of new capital formation is not reflected in the data, and the same can be true for consumers' financing of their purchases of durable goods. A second limitation is that funds flows are calculated from comparisons of balance sheet magnitudes, and therefore, any accounting revaluations affect the data reported. Thus, for example, revaluation due to mergers and acquisitions resulted in apparent funds flows to corporations from equity issues being reported as a smaller figure than it otherwise would have been.[6] Since the funds flow data reflect only changes in amounts outstanding, they reflect refinancing operations, or operations involving the maintenance of existing debts, only to the extent that these operations result in net flows between sectors.

Rate structures in capital markets

Supply and demand in financial markets

In capital markets prices for the use of borrowed money are established. The economic forces that determine capital market prices are basically the supplies and demands of loanable funds categorized according to types of lending arrangement. While the discussion is complicated by the differing characteristics of various lending arrangements (for example, the term of the loan, whether it is secured, the credit rating of the borrower, and so on) and by the extent to which the markets for these different kinds of transactions are interrelated, the economic forces

---

[6] See *Federal Reserve Bulletin,* May 1969, p. A69.4, and the discussion in Bankers' Trust Co. *Investment Outlook 1970.*

of supply and demand determine the general level of interest rates in any given portion of the financial markets.[7]

At any particular moment in time, there will be an amount of funds available for lending (on fixed terms), and the amount available will increase as the effective interest rate on this type of loan is increased. The schedule of rates and amounts is called a supply curve, in this case a supply curve of loanable funds. At the same time, the extent to which this type of lending arrangement will be utilized may also be represented as a schedule called the demand for loanable funds, and this schedule will generally show that the amount of funds demanded decreases as interest rate on this type of loan rises.[8] The interaction of the forces of supply and demand determines the number of dollars which will be lent (and borrowed) in any period, as well as the rates at which this lending will take place.

It is quite easy to discuss what occurs if demand or supply schedules shift. If potential borrowers become more eager to borrow than was previously the case, more funds will generally be borrowed at higher interest rates than formerly. Similar statements regarding a diminished eagerness of borrowers can be made.

Thus, demand versus supply analysis leads to general predictions that increases in demand for funds tend to raise interest rates and that decreases in demand for funds tend to lower rates. Not surprisingly, therefore, increases in supply of funds tend to lower rates; decreases in supply of funds tend to raise rates. However, while the principle of relations between interest rates, amounts of funds lent, and willingness to borrow or lend can be illustrated with the ideas of supply and demand, many other factors must be considered in explaining how interest rates are determined. One of these factors is suggested by the question: What happens to interest rates in a market if conditions change in another market?

Relationships between loan markets

In the previous section we considered how supply and demand for funds interacted to determine prices in markets for different types of

---

[7] The statement requires much more extensive discussion if all the factors determining interest rate levels in an economy are to be considered. This discussion, a topic in macroeconomics, is an elaborate one and would take us too far afield from our present topic. The interested reader should consult any of the standard textbooks in macroeconomic theory.

[8] These schedules are to be interpreted as assuming that all other variables which might affect this market (in particular such variables as the prices of other types of loans, lenders' and borrowers' expectations, and incomes, price levels, and so on remain unchanged). Such assumptions, while unrealistic from a practical point of view, are helpful in discussing the principles involved in the determination of an interest rate (or any other price).

loans. Clearly, the markets for different kinds of loans will be related at least to some degree. A potential investor in one-year government bonds could probably be induced to buy a two-year government bond if the price differential between these two markets were great enough. He might, on the other hand, be quite unwilling to buy a 20-year government bond at the same price differential. Some market participants who are already holders of bonds will be willing to switch from one issue to another if interest rate differentials become great enough. To some extent, loan markets are interrelated by these transactions and that becomes a factor in determining the relations between rates in different markets,

EXHIBIT 9–1

Yield curve for U.S. government securities

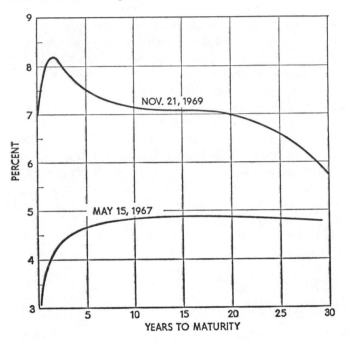

so that whenever supply and demand in a given market are examined, the effects on closely related markets must be kept in mind.

Charts of yield curves display relationships between interest rates on securities which differ only in their term to maturity but not in such characteristics as risk. Generally, yield curves show that interest rates increase with term to maturity, although there are exceptions as Exhibit 9–1 indicates.

Yield curves generally move up or down more at the short end than at the long. They are usually upward sloping. That can be explained either in terms of arbitraging transactions made on the basis of interest rate expectations or in terms of the different characteristics of short- and long-term loan markets. Downward sloping yield curves appear at or near the peak of a business cycle, and the slope can be explained either in terms of a scarcity of funds in the short end of a market or in terms of long rates expected to fall. The November 21, 1969, curve of Exhibit 9–1 reveals such a downward slope.

Negotiated and open markets

Financial markets are not ones in which there are many buyers and sellers capable of making good estimates of current and future prices.

TABLE 9–3

Schedule of approximate rates for long-term use of funds, 1969 (*percent annually*)

		Negotiated	
Form of agreement	Open market	To users	Intermediaries
Commercial bank savings	—	—	4.9
Municipal bonds	5.6	—	—
U.S. government bonds	6.1	—	—
Mutual savings bank deposits	—	—	4.9
Savings and loan deposit accounts ...	—	—	4.8
Corporate bonds—high grade	7.0	—	—
Corporate stocks—preferred	6.4	—	—
—common	3.2	—	—
Bank loans—prime credit	—	8.0	—
Corporate bonds—medium grade ...	7.8	—	—
Real estate mortgage loans	—	7.7	—
Bank loans-small business accounts ..	—	9.1	—
Credit card installment accounts	—	18.0	—
Consumer small loans	—	25.0	—

Source: Data derived from various publications and directly from lenders. The figures are imprecise in that they are averages. In particular, the larger figures represent averages of wide ranges of actual rates.

Open or auction markets are, however, markets where prices are set with the greatest sensitivity to changing expectations and the willingness of participants to borrow or lend funds. In contrast, rates on negotiated loans are partially insulated from the supply and demand forces that affect open market loan prices. Negotiated rates generally respond to changing conditions more slowly than open market rates, and the extent to which the adjustment takes place is usually not as great as in open markets. These differences can be seen in Table 9–3, in the smaller differentials on rates paid by intermediaries and in the larger differentials paid by final borrowers of funds.

Other factors affecting interest rates

Apart from supply and demand, and interrelationships of different markets for loanable funds, the major factors distinguishing different loan markets are the specific features of the lending arrangement, among which are risk, tax status of the loan's earnings, administrative costs, and regulation. The first of these features, risk, has itself a variety of aspects—money rate risk, default risk, and price level risk.

Money rate risk

Changes in interest rates cannot be forecast precisely. The securities of the federal government involve money rate risks whenever the buyer cannot purchase a security maturing exactly when he must disinvest, or whenever the buyer changes his mind about the period for which he wished to own the security. A lender desiring repayment in exactly three years, for example, bears a money rate risk unless he can find a security such as a treasury bond maturing at the end of the three years. Even if he can find a security with the desired maturity and can therefore calculate his earnings exactly, money rate risk is still involved to a degree if there is any possibility that the lender might wish to sell his security before maturity. To put the point another way, the interest rate that can be earned during the time period a security is held is not known with certainty.

The problem of money rate risk involves not only the risks in selling a security before its maturity, but also costs incurred as a result of making a fixed arrangement. The lender can usually fix the holding period yield rate (or interest rate on a loan) at a certain figure and thus avoid one kind of money rate risk. But this does not mean that the lender (or borrower) has entirely escaped money rate risk, because the fact that he enters into a fixed arrangement means that as soon as interest rates change from the levels prevailing at the time the arrangement was made one of the parties incurs an opportunity cost. Suppose, for example, the lender buys a one-year security, which he plans to hold for one year, and which if he does so will yield him 6%. If the day after he does so, interest rates rise to 8%, remaining with the original arrangement involves an opportunity cost for the lender.

Most of the time the yield curve is upward sloping. Yield curves reflect at least to some degree expectations regarding future interest rates. Should it then be inferred that both borrowers and lenders expect interest rates to rise continuously? A more appealing answer to the problem of the upward-sloping yield curve is to note that interest rate changes have proportionately greater effects on the prices of long-term securities than they do on the prices of short-term securities. In addition, the argument that forecasting rates over long periods is more difficult than forecasting them over short periods is a plausible one. For these reasons, money rate risk is generally regarded as being greater on long- than on short-term securities. It is also believed to be true that borrowers will pay more to avoid large risks than small ones and that lenders will charge more to undertake larger risks. Taken together, the last two points explain the generally prevailing upward slope of the yield curves.

Risk of default

Market rates for federal government obligations tend to provide a floor for other obligations because this type of obligation is free of one of the risks affecting others—the risk of default. Except in cases where a country is experiencing internal disturbances of such magnitude that its governmental structure is failing, it is unreasonable to believe that the federal government would fail to make payments when they are due. All national governments have the power to manufacture money with which to make payments.

Price level risk

Some price indexes in most countries have moved steadily upwards, although at widely varying rates, for many decades. More importantly, some price indexes have not moved when others have. Interest rates on long-term loans reflect expectations regarding price level changes. Consider, for example, a lender who wishes to advance a sum of money for a period of 10 years, and suppose that he expects the price level at the end of the 10 years to be 125% of its current value. Suppose also that he regards 8% simple interest paid with the principal at the end of the 10 years to be a fair return on money if money remains unaltered in terms of what it can buy. Then our lender, when making an advance of $100 today, would in the absence of a price level increase receive $180 at the end of the 10-year period. Since $180, 10 years from now, will have only four fifths of its present buying power, in order to maintain his real purchasing power the lender would have to receive $5/4 \times \$180 = \$225$ at the end of the 10 years. He can do this by charging 12.5% on the original loan. Risk is involved in these kinds of calculation also, because price level increases must be forecast, and the forecasts can be wrong. If in fact the price index in 10 years was to rise to 130% of its current value, the lender would not have earned what was judged to be the fair 8% return on the purchasing power of his money. The difference between rates actually charged on loans and rates measured in terms of constant purchasing power can be quite great, as reference to Exhibit 9–2 demonstrates.

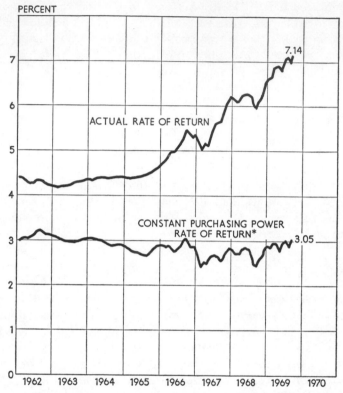

EXHIBIT 9–2

Yields on highest grade corporate bonds

PERCENT

ACTUAL RATE OF RETURN

7.14

CONSTANT PURCHASING POWER
RATE OF RETURN*

3.05

1962 1963 1964 1965 1966 1967 1968 1969 1970

* Estimates of "real" interest rates were obtained by subtracting the annual rate of increase in the implicit GNP price deflator in the preceding 24 months from the market rate on corporate Aaa bonds. The price deflator for the first and third months of each quarter was estimated by linear interpolation. Implicit price deflator for third quarter 1969 is estimated. While this is an important phenomenon, there is no perfectly agreed upon way of calculating and presenting it, and the series may be considered an illustration or approximation of what has been going on.
Source: Federal Reserve Bank of St. Louis, *Monetary Trends,* September 1969.

Tax position

High-grade municipal bonds yield earnings lower than those on U.S. government bonds. Since municipal bonds are subject to the same money rate risk as federal government bonds and in addition carry a risk of default, some other influence must have an effect on the prices of these bonds. The differential in this instance reflects the tax status of income from municipal issues. Interest received by investors from these issuers is exempt from federal income taxation. This tax advantage apparently has the effect of setting rates on the municipal issues about one half of 1% below those on federal obligations.

The differential actually seems quite small. A dollar of interest from a municipal bond means nearly the same net profit for corporate investors as two dollars from other debt instruments. The small size of the differential indicates that investors place quite a large value on the risk of default, present in the municipal but not in the federal obligations. This is clearer if we note that rates on medium-grade municipal bonds, on which the risk of default is not negligible, are higher than those on federal obligations in spite of the tax advantage.[9]

High-grade corporate bond issues have the disadvantages of municipals in relation to federal bonds without the tax advantage. Market rates on these bonds are higher than those on either the federal bonds or the medium-grade municipals. As the risk of default, or nonreceipt of expected income, increases, still higher rates prevail. This characteristic of the rate schedule is shown by the rates on high-grade preferred stocks, medium-grade corporate bonds, and the highly marketable common stocks of corporate issuers, as shown in Table 9–3.

Administrative costs

The relatively high rates on negotiated loans reflect another influence on interest rates: administrative cost. The management expense incurred in maintaining a portfolio of investments or loans is not negligible. Data for a number of intermediaries with marketable bond or stock portfolios indicate that management expense may represent one fourth to three fourths of 1% a year on the amount of funds invested. In relation to income from such investments, this expense may be from 5 to 18%.

Management expense rises with increases in the amount of work that must be done to make loans or investments, to keep records of and inspect properties pledged as security, and to collect payments due. In general, this expense is higher on secured obligations than on unsecured ones. The influence of management expense is reflected in the schedule of rates on negotiated arrangements in Table 9–3. The expense is relatively higher in each case on the ascending scale of rates. The most extreme instance shown is that of small consumer loans. For this form of credit operation, there are reasons for believing that management expense represents 50–60% of income. To illustrate, assume that a loan of $400 is made, repayable in 24 monthly installments. The average experience of a group of small loan lenders over a number of years indicates

---

[9] However, as indicated in Chapter 23, some of this differential is also attributable to the fact that there is less liquidity in the municipal bond market. That is, because the presence of fewer buyers and sellers makes the finalizing transactions somewhat more difficult, lenders can obtain higher interest rates to compensate for any difficulties they might have in selling the bonds.

that it would cost about $6 to make the loan, that an equal amount should be set aside to cover losses, and that the collection and recording of each payment costs $2. These figures add up to $60. Interest, at the rate shown in Table 9–3, would approximate $104. The difference is $44, or $22 a year. This "net" reward, which must cover the financial costs and taxes of the lender, is about 10½% a year on the average outstanding loan balance. The expense of this procedure reduces the yield from lending well below the rate charged. In each of the instances of secured lending—on real estate, inventory, accounts receivable—such expenses of management affect the rates at which funds are made available to users.

Importance of financial institutions

Earlier in the chapter, in the discussion of the sizes of outstanding claims and flows of funds (Tables 9–1 and 9–2), reference was made to the extent to which funds were directed *through* institutions to users. Of the $50 billion flow, for example, from households, $34 billion went to financial intermediaries. They in turn loaned $33 billion to households, mostly on mortgages and consumer credit agreements. Almost one half of all new lending was in the form of loans from financial institutions.

Consumer saving through institutional channels is built solidly into our economic system. People in the United States generally believe in the necessity for life insurance. Once an individual begins an insurance program, premium bills arrive with regularity and are paid. Many business organizations have established both insurance and pension plans for employees requiring automatic deductions from payroll checks. Individuals undertake to meet their own premiums on independent annuity and retirement plans. We have rules of thumb about adequate personal cash reserves which result in the creation of savings deposits and accounts or purchases of savings bonds. An appreciable amount of investment is made by individuals through the purchase of investment company shares. Habits and beliefs such as these have given the institutions serving the needs and requirements of individuals their position of dominance in the capital markets.

Referring back to Table 9–1, we see that about one third of the capital instruments of business, bonds, loans, or stock are held by the financial institutions. They hold nearly half the obligations of the federal government and about two thirds of those of state and local governments. These institutions, rather than individuals or businesses, direct so large a proportion of funds through the credit markets that the skills of their investment managers influence in an erratic way the precision with which rates are set and the directions in which money flows.

Questions and problems

1. What kinds of measurements of the capital markets were given in this chapter? Are they generally satisfactory measures for these markets?
2. Is the distinction between negotiated and auction markets significant? To whom? For what?
3. What are capital markets?
4. How do institutional investors influence or affect the markets?
5. How does the expense of management of a securities portfolio affect the availability of funds in capital markets?
6. What kinds of risks are accepted in the purchase of a security? How do they affect the price of the security?

Bibliography

No single reference covers the material of this chapter. All the bibliographies in Chapters 9–23 contain references which are of interest in this area. Attention perhaps should be directed to the three-volume *Study of Savings in the United States* (Princeton, N.J.: Princeton University Press, 1955–56) and *Financial Intermediaries in the American Economy since 1900* (Princeton, N.J.: Princeton University Press, 1958) by R. W. Goldsmith. The flow-of-funds information published in the *Federal Reserve Bulletin* provides current figures for relationships among groups of investors. The issue of August 1959 presents the definitions and concepts underlying the statistical series. Further information may be obtained from standard texts such as R. E. Badger, H. W. Torgerson, and H. G. Guthmann, *Investment Principles and Practices* (6th ed., Englewood Cliffs, N.J.: Prentice-Hall, 1969); Paul M. Horvitz, *Monetary Policy and the Financial System* (2d ed., Englewood Cliffs, N.J.: Prentice-Hall, 1969); J. Van Fenstermaker, *Readings in Financial Markets and Institutions* (New York: Meridith Corp., 1969); Ward S. Curran, *Principles of Financial Management* (New York: McGraw-Hill, 1970); William F. Sharpe, *Portfolio Theory and Capital Markets* (New York: McGraw-Hill, 1970). An excellent monograph on the subject is Herbert E. Dougall's *Capital Markets and Institutions* (Englewood Cliffs, N.J.: Prentice-Hall, Inc., 1965).

CHAPTER 10

Channeling savings into financial investment

This chapter describes the sources of savings and the arrangements involved in converting these savings to financial investment. It shows how the savings of households can be invested either directly in business or indirectly through the purchase of intermediary obligations. Attention is directed to the complexities of the direct investment process and therefore to the reasons for the importance of indirect investment through intermediaries.

An overview of savings sources

One of the distinguishing characteristics of a capitalistic society is the fact that decisions to save or to supply funds to the financial markets and decisions to demand funds from the financial markets for the purposes of financing tangible investment are generally made by different groups of economic units. Typically, the household sector of a capitalistic economy is a net supplier of funds, while the business sector is a net demander. Business is also a source of saving, but for the most part business savings provide only a part of the funds used in the operation of that business. The discussion of this and succeeding chapters will focus on the savings of households or individuals and on the flows of these funds into the financing of tangible investment.

Investment is of great importance. In order to provide for future growth more goods and services must be produced than are consumed. Both replacements of and additions to the stock of producers and other types of capital goods are needed. The more fully developed the process of providing additional tools of production, expanding plant facilities, increasing inventories, and expanding the stock of housing, the greater is the general well-being through a resultant higher standard of living.

It is the purpose of this chapter to serve as an introduction to Chapters 11 through 15, in which individual consideration is given to those intermediaries that channel savings into use by industry and government.

The present chapter first examines the size of the savings flows from the household sector and the various channels through which these funds flow to their ultimate users.

Alternative uses of savings are next examined. The types of risks to which businesses are exposed are then considered in order to set the stage for a discussion of the two most important ways in which savings are employed—through direct investment and through financial intermediaries. The discussion will show that investment is a specialized undertaking requiring training, experience, and seasoned judgment. Many savers recognize the complexity of the investment problem and are therefore ready to delegate responsibility for, or at least to seek assistance in, the management of their funds. As a result, financial intermediaries have a position of importance in the economy.

Saving: how much and through what channels?

A summary of the estimated accumulations of households' financial assets and liabilities is given in Table 10–1. The most striking aspects are the diversity of assets held, the continuous increases in the values, and the size of individuals' total net equity. Corporate stocks have been and remain the largest single form of personal assets and the $749 billion figure (estimated market value) represents the majority of the business equity investments in our economy. Assets held as currency, demand deposits, and savings accounts constituted the next most important category totaling almost $486 billion at the end of 1969. Next are the contractual types of savings—pension funds totaling $210.8 billion and life insurance reserves totaling $125.7 billion at year-end 1969. Federal, state, and local government securities follow, succeeded finally by mortgages, corporate bonds, and other assets. The major categories of illiquid assets represented in the table are, of course, pension fund reserves and mortgages; life insurance reserves usually are available in the form of policyholder loans.

The two major liabilities, mortgages and consumer debt, are discussed in the next chapter. The estimated net worth of households, $1,347 bil-

TABLE 10–1

Financial assets and liabilities of households* in the United States, 1960–69 (*amounts in billions at year-end*)†

	1960	1965	1969
Demand deposits and currency	$ 65.6	$ 93.5	$ 114.7
Savings accounts	165.3	277.7	370.9
Securities			
U.S. government	69.9	78.6	105.0
State and local governments	30.9	40.5	41.1
Corporate and foreign bonds	9.7	3.1	25.4
Corporate stock (market value)	394.2	668.7	749.3
Mortgages	31.8	10.9	39.7
Security credit	1.1	1.7	2.6
Life insurance reserves	85.2	105.2	125.7
Pension fund reserves	90.7	152.0	210.8
Other assets	13.3	15.5	23.7
Total Assets	$957.6	$1,477.5	$1,807.9
Home mortgages	$136.8	$ 203.3	$ 260.4
Other mortgages	9.2	14.1	18.9
Consumer credit	56.1	86.0	122.5
Bank loans not elsewhere classified	7.2	13.5	19.6
Other loans	7.0	13.5	19.6
Security credit	5.4	9.6	12.0
Trade credit	2.1	2.4	4.5
Deferred and unpaid life insurance			
Miscellaneous	2.4	3.2	4.7
Total Liabilities	$226.2	$ 342.2	$ 460.7
Total Households' Net Worth	$731.4	$1,105.3	$1,347.2
	$957.6	$1,447.5	$1,807.9

* Includes holdings by personal trusts and nonprofit organizations.
† Amounts may not add to totals because of rounding.
Source: *Federal Reserve Bulletin,* various issues. 1969 data from Federal Reserve System, "Financial Assets and Liabilities," December 31, 1969.

lion, is a residual figure which reflects the fact that households are major suppliers of funds to the rest of the economy.

As indicated in Chapter 9, understanding of the importance of the various kinds of lending arrangements being established in the financial markets involves a consideration not only of the amounts of assets outstanding but also the rates at which these amounts change in each time period. This kind of information is displayed in Table 10–2, which shows the annual flows of household savings and the fluctuating amounts of new savings directed into each category of financial investment from year to year. Table 10–2 indicates that during 1969, the household sector obtained disposable income of about $627 billion, which was augmented by new borrowing transactions totaling almost $39 billion. Of the $666

TABLE 10-2

Sources and uses of funds of households,* 1964-69

	1964	1966	1968	1969
Disposable income	$438.1	$511.5	$588.9	$626.7
Plus: increase in credit	32.2	28.3	43.4	38.9
Equals: total funds available	470.3	539.8	632.3	665.6
Less: spending on nondurable goods and services	339.8	393.0	447.3	480.1
Leaves: amount available for investment	130.5	146.8	185.0	185.5
Investments in tangible assets	82.2	92.0	107.9	116.8
Investments in financial assets	47.9	49.2	68.8	59.3
Statistical discrepancy	0.4	5.6	8.3	9.4
	$130.5	$146.8	$185.0	$185.5
Detailed statement of investments in financial assets				
Demand deposits and currency	$ 6.4	$ 1.9	$ 14.9	3.4
Savings accounts	23.9	19.2	27.6	11.3
Life insurance and pension fund reserves	19.9	23.1	25.9	26.9
U.S. government securities	1.9	8.0	4.1	13.1
State and local obligations	2.2	2.2	1.4	3.8
Corporate bonds	−0.8	1.2	3.9	4.9
Corporate stocks	0.7	0.8	−3.3	−5.1
Mortgages	−0.2	−0.4	—	1.3
Net investment in noncorporate business	−7.2	−7.9	−8.4	−4.8
Statistical discrepancy	1.1	1.1	2.7	4.5
	$ 47.9	$ 49.2	$ 68.8	$ 59.3

* Includes holdings acquired by personal trusts and nonprofit organizations. Portions of the table follow the form developed by the U.S. Savings and Loan League; see *Savings and Loan Fact Book,* 1969.
Source: *Federal Reserve Bulletin,* May 1969 and May 1970, p. A70.

billon so raised, spending on nondurable goods and services amounted to $480 billion, leaving $186 billion available for the purchase of durable goods and financial assets. Approximately $117 billion was invested in tangible assets, leaving (apart from a statistical discrepancy arising from various inaccuracies in the data sources) $59 billion for financial investment. These funds were directed into the categories shown in the second part of the table; for example, $27 billion into contractual savings (life insurance and pension fund reserves), $11 billion into savings accounts, and $3 billion into demand accounts.

Table 10-2 also shows the fluctuating amounts of funds directed to each savings category under different economic conditions. In 1964 there was a particularly heavy shift into the time and savings deposit and savings shares categories and away from marketable securities, as savers responded to changing yield differentials. The sharply smaller flows into savings deposits during 1966 and 1969 can be seen, as can the 1968 and

1969 shifts from corporate stocks to bonds in response to changing yield differentials. These shifts will be considered in more detail in the chapters which follow.

Finally, Table 10–2 indicates the large amounts of current income used by households to acquire nonfinancial assets. Perspective on the relative size of saving is gained by noting that the gross national product and personal income figures in 1969 were $932.1 billion and $747.2 billion, respectively. In the U.S. economy, the bulk of our national income accrues to individuals and a large proportion of this amount is channeled into the acquisition of consumer durable goods, real estate, and financial assets.

Relation of savings to the level of economic activity

Savings flows are closely related to the income measures of the level of economic activity. Historically, even though dollar amounts of savings have fluctuated substantially in response to such events as the Great Depression of the 1930s and to World War II, the ratio of personal savings to disposable income has remained quite stable for at least a half century. The relationship has been particularly steady during the postwar years. Analysis of the aggregate total of savings indicates that the amounts saved in each category have also been remarkably stable over long periods, with some movement between liquid assets and marketable securities during various changes in economic conditions. This characteristic is important for public and business planning in our society since it provides for the continuous accumulation of the investment funds needed for an expanding economy.

Exhibit 10–1 displays the percentage of personal disposable income saved for the last six years and confirms the stability of the ratio mentioned in the preceding paragraph. However, as the exhibit indicates, overall stability of savings does not rule out fluctuations. Indeed, small

EXHIBIT 10–1

Personal saving as a percentage of disposable income, 1962–68

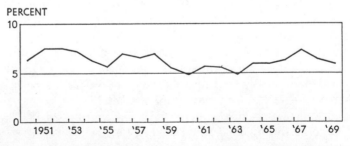

Source: U.S. Savings and Loan League, *Savings and Loan Fact Book*, 1970.

changes in it can imply quite large changes in dollar flows, as indicated in Table 10–2. As an example of change, the decline in the savings ratio that occurred in 1968 is partially attributable to increases in spending as a proportion of income following passage of the surtax legislation in mid-1968. Expectations of continued inflation probably explain a part of the same decline.

The stability of the relationship between personal savings and economic activity is highly important for the conduct of economic policy, but the relationship does not provide a complete picture of the decisions of the various types of households whose aggregative behavior is described by the relationship. Some further insight into variations in the saving behavior of households is provided in the following section.

Characteristics of individual savers

All kinds of people save—people with differences in their income levels, job classifications, ages, or marital status. However, some generalizations, which are on a less aggregative level than those of the preceding section, can be made if carefully hedged to recognize the wide variations in individual behavior. As indicated in Table 10–3, the economic status of a family, as measured by its net worth, is an important deter-

TABLE 10–3

Net worth components related to size of net worth, December 31, 1962 (*percentage of families reporting specified assets or debt*)

Component	All families*	Families with net worth of (thousands of dollars)			
		0–5	5–25	25–100	100 and over
Tangible assets	83	69	95	97	92
Own home	59	30	83	86	85
Automobiles	73	61	80	80	00
Business interest, profession	17	5	19	42	57
Life insurance, annuities, retirement plans	58	43	69	74	68
Liquid and investment assets	79	62	92	98	100
Liquid assets	78	60	91	98	99
Investment assets	29	6	33	68	93
Stocks	18	3	18	43	79
Marketable bonds	2	†	1	7	24
Other	15	3	17	39	52
Miscellaneous assets	12	7	15	18	30
Personal debt	50	51	52	23	20

*Includes families with negative net worth, not shown separately.
† Less than one half of 1%.
Source: "Survey of Financial Characteristics of Consumers," *Federal Reserve Bulletin,* vol. 50, no. 3, (March 1964), p. 287.

minant of the amount and type of savings. These figures, and the following conclusions, are based on field interviews conducted by the Federal Reserve System of a sample of families designed to be representative of all families in the United States.

As would be expected, the total amount of savings is related to the size of income. On the average, people with small incomes save very little and personal debt is more prevalent among this group. As income rises, net worth and the proportion held in liquid assets increases. The mean amount of assets held was $22,588 at the time of the study; however, the dispersion about this mean was very large and the median figure was only $7,500. For 25 families out of 100, the net worth reported was less than $1,000, while 7 out of 100 families owned assets in excess of $50,000. The type of assets held varied widely as did the proportion of family wealth invested in homes and automobiles. Only a small number of families owned an interest in a business, but this group reported a net worth well above the average figure. In the zero to $5,000 net worth category, only 5 families out of 100 held a business interest. A similar situation existed for ownership of stocks and marketable bonds. Investment in stocks is highly correlated with the level of family wealth. Ownership of life insurance, annuities, and retirement plans appears to be quite universal; whereas, investments in stocks, marketable bonds, and real estate investments are added to savings portfolios only after other liquid asset needs are covered.

The Federal Reserve study also indicates that savings tend to increase for each age category (age of the head of the family) until the over-65 age group is reached. The largest percentage increases in savings have occurred among older age brackets in the lower income and middle-income families. Home owners tend to report higher net worth values. Finally, with the exception of the South, regional differences in the net worths of families are minor.

Alternative uses of savings

Individual savers, who constitute the largest single source of savings, may make use of their current savings and their past accumulations in a number of ways, as described below.

Hoarding. Savings are sometimes hoarded by being placed in a safe-deposit box or cached in a mattress. Such disposition of savings benefits neither the saver nor society, because the money so saved earns no return and cannot be used for the financing of tangible investment. Most intelligent savers make more effective and profitable use of their funds, except possibly in times of stress, when confidence in the financial order may have waned. There is another possible exception, the person who seeks absolute privacy in his financial affairs, perhaps for such ulterior motives as concealing the amount of his income. Under usual conditions, however, only a small portion of total savings is sterilized in this way.

Reinvesting savings in one's own business. If the saver wishes ownership and management of his accumulations, he may establish or purchase a business, expand an existing business, or acquire real property. Such use of savings not only involves management responsibilities and requires knowledge of and preferably experience in the particular type of enterprise, but also exposes the savings to a high degree of risk because of lack of diversification, much being ventured in a single undertaking. More will be said about the factor of business risk as it relates to direct investment. However, the management of accumulations employed in one's own business becomes a broad problem of business administration which is not within the direct purview of our study.

Direct investment in publicly owned corporations. While most savers are not likely to be interested in becoming owners and operators of a business, they may still wish to have an interest in a business. They may be willing to lend money to or purchase stock in a company in order to obtain an investment interest without business management responsibilities. By dealing with one of the agencies or institutions discussed in Chapter 18—namely, investment bankers, securities dealers, or stockbrokers—individuals may obtain information and counsel as services supplementary to the purchase of bonds and stocks. Upon purchasing such securities, the supplier of funds becomes a direct investor in the enterprise, either as a lender if he purchases bonds, or as an owner if he buys common or preferred stocks. Usually the securities are bought in the name of the owner, who assumes the responsibility for deciding what to buy, what to hold, what to sell, and when.

Indirect investment. Many savers and investors recognize that the management of accumulated funds is a responsible undertaking not to be assumed lightly, that there are many hazards to be faced, and that adequate training, experience, and knowledge are essential to the pursuit of a successful investment policy. Individuals may, therefore, recognize their own inexperience or disinclination to shoulder the burden of investment management and may seek to shift the responsibilities of direct investment to more experienced individuals or corporations. An examination, later in this chapter, of the risks involved in investment and of the requirements for successful investment management will show why this is so.

Still, savers may wish to share, either as lenders or as owners, in the rewards that are expected to flow from participation in the nation's businesses. Such persons may become investors through a number of different types of financial institutions rather than lend their funds directly through the purchase of stocks and bonds. The purposes of the financial institutions are to assist the investor in attaining his goal of relative safety of principal with an income commensurate to the risk taken.

The types of financial institutions available are enumerated in Exhibit 10–2 and are discussed in the five chapters that follow. Savers' funds are channeled to productive employment in business and government through these institutions. Some, those classified as *thrift institutions*, are designed either for repositories of assets used for short-term liquidity purposes or for accumulation of a fund of investment proportions; others,

EXHIBIT 10–2

Classification of thrift and investment institutions

1. Thrift institutions
   a) Deposit-type institutions:
      Savings departments of commercial banks
      Savings and loan associations
      Mutual savings banks
      Credit unions
   b) Contractual-type institutions and securities:
      Life insurance companies
      Pension plans
      U.S. savings bonds
2. Investment institutions
   a) Investment companies:
      Open-end investment companies (also called mutual funds)
      Closed-end investment companies
   b) Investment counsel
   c) Investment bankers:
      Investment counsel services
   d) Trustees (individual or corporate):
      Individual testamentary or living trusts
      Common trusts (commingled funds)
      Investment counsel services
   e) Life insurance companies:
      Variable-annuity contracts

those classified as *investment institutions*, serve primarily those savers who already have an investment fund. What both types do amounts in essence to pooling the savings of many; then through the purchase of stocks or bonds or tangible property, these institutions make the pooled savings available for the use of industry and government. Thus, the agency rather than the individual saver assumes responsibility for investment management.

Risks and the financing of business

Some of the risks that must be faced by an investor derive from those faced by the businesses to which he entrusts his funds. In order to make good judgments about the types of business in which he should invest, the investor should have some knowledge of what business risks are, and of how these risks may be managed.

Types of business risks

Whichever avenue of investment is adopted—whether combined ownership and management of a business, the direct purchase of stocks and bonds, or indirect financial investment through thrift and other institutions—the savings that are employed will be exposed to varying degrees of risk. The owner-manager of a business, the purchaser of stocks or bonds, or the professional investment manager of a thrift or other indirect investment agency must cope with the risks involved in seeking to preserve principal, earn an income, and, in many instances, preserve purchasing power. Before reviewing the more specific problems of investment management it will be helpful to examine the nature of the risks inherent in all business and in property ownership generally.

Risk is pervasive and cannot be completely avoided. Any property that is acquired subjects the owner immediately to the possible loss or damage of his assets. Risk even affects life itself. From a pecuniary standpoint, the individual cannot know whether he will live the normal life span and provide anticipated income for his family, whether his life savings will be sufficient to maintain himself during the years of retirement, or whether he will live long enough to use up the sum that he has provided for his remaining years.

Of purely business risks, we find that writers have classified the uncertainties inherent in business operations in various ways, and we can recognize at least some of the categories without attempting to make anything like a full catalog:

1. Physical, tangible property may be lost or damaged through acts of God such as fire, flood, storm, hail, hurricane, unseasonable weather, too much or too little rainfall, lightning, or other incidents.

2. Individuals may not live up to the confidence placed in them, and as a result, property may be lost through embezzlement, defalcation, or unanticipated misconduct.

3. Groups of individuals may act violently and deliberately destroy property.

4. Production and distribution uncertainties may cause loss of income to a business. Delivery of essential materials may be delayed, goods may be partly processed before substandard qualities are detected, strikes may interfere with the prompt sale of physically perishable commodities, and seasonal merchandise may have to be sold at sacrifice prices because it did not reach the market in time.

5. Through a change in laws, certain businesses may be outlawed or

at least curtailed in activity. Many communities are now forbidding the sale of fireworks. The Volstead Act drastically curtailed the manufacture of liquor and strictly limited its sale. Many states have set up barriers to certain types of interstate commerce.

6. The tastes and habits of the public may change, or new industries or processes may replace the old. Today motion pictures are displaced by television. Freeways and widespread ownership of automobiles are favoring some market centers and harming others. Natural gas and fuel oil have partly displaced solid fuels and the diesel engine has largely replaced the steam locomotive.

7. Every business is constantly exposed to risks of market price changes. Prices of both inputs and outputs tend to fluctuate with general business activity. Risk of impairing profit margins may well increase as the time between production and the sale of output increases.

The reader will doubtless be able to supply many other examples (decline of the purchasing power of the dollar, for instance) and list still other categories of risk, but the enumeration just made will suffice to suggest that uncertainty besets the businessman and the property owner.

Coping with risks

As already noted, the businessman cannot completely eliminate all risks that confront him. It is possible, however, to minimize some risks, or to transfer the risk-bearing function in part to insurance companies. Our discussion is still concerned with protecting property and the income it generates against uncertainties and hazards, risks fundamental both to the investment process and to the owner-management of a business. Subsequently we shall consider dealing specifically with risk as it affects individual investors and professional and institutional investment managers.

Within limits, it is possible to minimize risk substantially by meeting it head-on. Distributors of gasoline and other highly inflammable fluids ground their trucks by means of a chain to avoid flash ignition due to static electricity. A well-designed fireproof building completely equipped with tested fire-prevention devices and containing appropriate structural features provides reasonably certain assurance against any serious fire loss. The steel and concrete construction of the safe-deposit vault of a metropolitan bank and the precautions exercised by the attending personnel provide reasonably good protection for the property of patrons. Cashiers' cages of bulletproof glass, equipped with siren alarms and tear-gas bombs, offer considerable assurance against robbery.

If we had all the facts with respect to a given risk, it would not be a risk. This is another way of saying that lack of understanding—or,

more bluntly, ignorance—is the basis for much uncertainty and consequent loss. Recognizing this fact, many businesses seek through research
to find the facts that will permit reduction of risk. Thus a great deal of
attention is being given to studying economic fluctuations and the effects
of these fluctuations on business' input and output markets. For example,
market surveys are made in a sample area to determine public taste and
public acceptance of a certain product before the manufacturer embarks
on a nationwide distribution effort, so that necessary adaptations to the
product line can be made or, if it seems expedient, the whole idea of
selling the product can be dropped without further cost. In this way, some
risks of fluctuating business incomes can partially be avoided. In another
field of forecasting, considerable progress is being made by meteorologists
whose efforts help many businesses (citrus-fruit growers or airline operators for example) to avoid heavy losses.

An excellent example of the transfer of risk to a specialized agency
established for the very purpose of spreading risk is found in the casualty
insurance field. A fire insurance company will, for a fee, insure many
individual property holders against complete loss of their particular
properties as a result of fire. In this way, a possible total loss is replaced
by a much smaller but certain expense, the annual insurance premuim.
Sharing of risk in this fashion is possible through a great variety of
insurance contracts that cover diversified fields of risk. For instance, fire
insurance companies also write policies protecting against loss by wind,
storm, rain, hail, and water damage as well as against loss by fire.
Casualty companies cover a great variety of risks, including automobile
fire, theft, public liability, workmen's compensation, use and occupancy,
accident, and health. Marine insurance companies offer protection against
loss of ships and cargoes, either on the ocean or in inland waters. Companies writing fidelity and surety contracts insure the employer against
losses growing out of the dishonesty or negligence of the employee. There
are many more types of insurance contracts to be purchased, including, of
course, life contracts. These types of arrangements are discussed in
Chapter 12.

Securities underwriting provides another illustration of the transfer
of risk. If the investment banker underwrites a new offering, he will
provide the specified amount of funds at a specified time, and the issuing
company can rely on having the money whether the new stock issue
has been sold or not. The flour miller transfers risk to a speculator when
he practices hedging by executing offsetting transactions, one in the
actual commodity and the other in the futures market. A loss on the one
contract is offset by a profit on the other, and the risk involved in possible
price change is thus reduced approximately to the amount of the brokerage commission that is involved. Any general contractor who has engaged

to complete a certain project at a stated price may reduce or spread the risk incident to possible price change by subletting parts of the project to other contractors.

There is still another method for dealing with risk, that of self-insurance. A large industrial company, such as the International Harvester Company, which has a great number of individual plants scattered throughout the United States and abroad, may in a sense provide its own fire insurance by setting aside each year a calculated sum to cover possible losses. Because the factory units are so widely distributed, there is little possibility of losing any substantial number through fire in any one year. The amounts set aside will gradually build up into a sizable fund that would provide for the replacement of any buildings lost through fire.

The risks we have been discussing confront every business, and business management faces the task of dealing with them. Risks and the manner in which management provides for them are of interest to every investor or investment manager, because these uncertainties affect the profitability of the businesses whose stocks and bonds are held.

The art of direct investing

In this section we consider exactly what problems are faced by the person seeking to administer an investment fund with the aims of maintaining the principal amount, realizing an income compatible with the risks incurred, and, if possible, garnering a gain in the form of capital appreciation. Some of the risks derive, as already mentioned, from the operations of the businesses to which funds are lent or in which ownership interests are acquired. Others, however, are peculiar to the investment management business itself.

Numerous decisions must be made in administering investment funds. This is true whether the fund is under the supervision of a professional adviser who gives full time and attention to financial investment problems or whether the fund is under the avocational direction of an individual who gives his major time and attention to other pursuits. More than a third of a century ago, a recognized writer in the field commented on the business of financial investment as follows:

the investment of funds is a real business subject to the true business foresight and the losses incident to attempts on the part of the poor business manager to invest funds. This is not self-evident. The school teacher, clergyman, lawyer, dry goods merchant, and the shoe manufacturer know enough about their own respective businesses to feel assured that the ordinary uninitiated could not succeed without long and specialized training. Yet these same men stand ready to embark on one of the most intricate of businesses—that of investment—requiring perhaps the most extensive specialized knowledge of any profession or business.

To compare intelligently, and with a degree of insight which makes the comparison something more than a guess, the credit obligations of São Paulo and the mortgages of the Chicago and Northwestern Railroad, the debentures of the Detroit Edison Company and the common stock of the General Electric Company, requires acumen and a breadth of knowledge compared with which the ordinary professional and business judgments are child's play. And yet it is just such specialized knowledge and acumen which constitutes the business of investment, a business which many, without training or aptitude, feel qualified to embark upon with their own savings and those of their relatives and friends.[1]

Complete development of the topic of investment management is hardly appropriate here, and only a few of the more important considerations are presented in order to point out the complexity of the problem.

Objectives

Every undertaking will have one or more goals and should have a plan to reach them, and this certainly is true of the problem of managing an investment fund. The procedure to be followed with respect to any given fund depends upon two principal considerations: the circumstances of the investor and his attitude toward risk.

A widow of 45 who has just received the relatively modest proceeds of her deceased husband's life insurance policy, representing her entire assets, will doubtless find it advantageous to emphasize safety of principal and to be satisfied with whatever income is consistent with such safety. On the other hand, the scion of a wealthy industrialist, a relatively young man who has a well-paying position, who has already acquired considerable property, and whose prospects appear excellent, may wish to accept the risk of following a much less conservative course. He might well buy a moderate, perhaps a substantial, amount of common stock in a new and speculative enterprise with the hope of realizing a large profit. If the venture is disappointing, he is able to absorb the loss with greater equanimity than the widow.

With respect to the circumstances of any individual investor, allowance should be made for the following: other property, other income, age, dependents, insurance program, and any other factors that have a bearing on his financial position.

No matter what the circumstances of the individual investor may be, attention must also be given to his personal attitude toward risk. Caspar

---

[1] Arthur Stone Dewing, "The Role of Economic Profits in the Return on Investment," *Harvard Business Review*, July 1923, p. 451.

Milquetoast, although his circumstances might justify an aggressive program, might not be so constituted as to withstand the vagaries of the stock market and business conditions. On the other hand, a less timid investor might be perfectly willing to accept the risks inherent in such fluctuations. Finally, an individual's attitude toward risk may change as his circumstances change: for example, he may become rather more sanguine about accepting risks as he becomes wealthier.

Most investors prefer more returns to less if the risk involved in earning the greater return is the same. Similarly, in most cases investors prefer to have as liquid a portfolio as possible if liquidity does not involve sacrificing return. However as return increases, risk generally does also, and maintaining liquidity usually does involve a sacrifice of potential returns. Accordingly, judicious investment management recognizes the existence of these tradeoffs, usually by specifying acceptable levels of one or more of these conflicting goals. Thus, the widow desires to earn as much income as possible given that the safety of her investment is reasonably assured; a fund portfolio manager may emphasize earning as high a return as is consistent with maintaining a specified degree of liquidity.

Business conditions

Having formulated his investment objectives the individual investor's next step involves an appraisal of current business conditions—of those economic conditions that have a bearing on interest rates and earnings trends, which in turn determine bond and stock prices. Fundamental factors include labor-management relations, monetary and fiscal policy, pending legislation, foreign developments, the imminence of war or peace, the temper of the business community, changes in the distribution of the national income and so on. The relative importance of these factors depends, of course, on the time period being considered by the investor. Whether to hold cash, to buy, sell, or hold high-grade bonds, to buy, sell, or hold common stocks, and in what proportions, will depend on the investor's appraisal of these fundamental forces.

Forecasting the trend of economic events with any degree of accuracy is itself a hazardous task beset by many pitfalls. To cite two instances: it was freely predicted that in the early postwar period there would be a large amount of unemployment and business recession, but that result never came to pass because consumers' pent-up demands were greater than had been anticipated. In another instance, it was quite widely believed that the 1968 surtax legislation would have a much greater effect in dampening consumer spending than that which was realized. Again, the forecasting error was probably due in part to the fact that changes in consumers' spending habits were not fully anticipated.

Industry analysis

With the objectives defined and the economic outlook evaluated, the next step in direct investing is the determination of those industries of investment caliber which are in the most promising position under existing conditions and in the light of the forecast. All industries do not present equally attractive opportunities at the same time, and to select the most promising the investor must be familiar with the fundamentals of each.

Under certain conditions, the heavy- or producer-goods industries may be favored; at other times, it may be the consumer-goods industries or the consumer durable-goods industries. A special set of conditions may at a given time single out a particular industry as one that offers striking possibilities. Government action, legislation, a Federal Trade Commission ruling, or antitrust activity may aid or hinder a given industry. Constant analysis of basic trends and specific industry trends is essential to sound selection of industry participation.

Another aspect of industry analysis should not be overlooked. Just as plant and animal life have cycles of growth, from infancy to maturity and old age, so industries (and companies) tend to have a life cycle. Businesses develop through successive stages from the formative and promotional phase of experiment, invention, and development, through early growth, established position and expansion, to maturity and, ultimately, decline. Industries in the early growth stages provide the capital appreciation element for the aggressive investment plan; more mature industries tend to provide certainty of income and relative capital stability for the more conservative investment program. Investment programs seeking to combine these goals will generally blend the securities of differing industry types.

Economic theory is of some help in the selection of industry. Depending on the market structures in which industry output is sold, typical profit levels will vary. Thus, for example, an industry which is monopolistic (or nearly so) is in the absence of regulation likely to post higher profits than an industry in which there are many different firms selling highly similar types of products.

Company analysis

Having determined the preferred industries, the next step is the selection of the preferred companies within an industry. In most industries there are outstanding leaders, other companies that tend to follow the leadership of the dominant units, companies that are definitely marginal, and companies that may be just entering the field. In selecting the preferred companies, many factors in addition to industry position should be considered. A few of these are caliber of management, financial structure, adequacy of capital, earning power in boom and depression, market acceptability of the securities of the company, the essentiality of the company activity, degree of integration, and vulnerability to government regulation. Within a certain industry there may be wide differences in company operation. In the oil industry, for instance, some companies are primarily crude producers; others are primarily distributors of finished products; and many in between produce and refine crude oil, buy and refine crude oil, or buy finished products in varying degrees and distribute the finished products over a wide area.

Selection of securities

The preceding steps in the formulation of an investment program prepare the investor for the final step in the process—the selection of the specific stocks and bonds to constitute the investment portfolio.

The investment objectives that have been formulated and the economic appraisal that has been made guide the investor in setting up an appropriate balance of cash, bonds, and preferred and common stocks. Industry and company appraisal have determined the preferred industries and the favored companies within these industries. In order to intelligently select the items that are to make up the investment portfolio, the investor should have a sound and comprehensive understanding of the investment function of the great variety of securities that are available to him. Some bonds perform much like common stocks; some common stocks act in the market more nearly like bonds. From an investment standpoint, the legal classification is often of little relevance; investment characteristics should usually be the predominant consideration.

However, it should not be inferred that legal characteristics are wholly unimportant. In Chapter 16 it will be indicated that there are (to the uninitiated) a bewildering variety of securities; simple classification into secured and unsecured bonds and preferred and common stocks is convenient but inadequate.

Diversification. It is usually the aim of the investor to maintain the principal value of his accumulations and to obtain a reasonable return, usually both income and capital gain, consistent with such preservation of capital. Risk can be minimized through diversification—not taking a 100% position in a single security at any time. The prudent investor distributes his investments over a variety of holdings: by balancing cash, bonds, preferreds, and common stocks; varying the maturities of bonds; holding securities in a variety of industries and companies; and through geographic diversification. Since not all types of business experience the same types of changes in their earnings as general economic conditions change, diversification means less risk from changes in portfolio value and earnings than would be experienced if the portfolio were concentrated in a single security issue, or in too small a number of securities.

The extent to which risk should be diversified depends partially on the time period for which a given security can be held. For example, if a security shows both rapid price growth and a good level of payout but varies quite substantially in price under different economic conditions, it could be very attractive to the long-term investor who can pick his sale date quite freely, but much less attractive to the investor who may have to sell the security on short notice.

If diversification is overemphasized, the problem of supervision may be increased to a burdensome point, and the performance of the investment fund may suffer. All companies and all industries are not equally promising, and the more items that are added to the portfolio, the lower on the list of preference must the investor reach. On the other hand, underdiversification, i.e., too high a concentration in too few items, tends to enhance risk. For instance, even if the investor's studies convinced him that a certain industry and the common stock of a particular company in that industry presented the outstanding investment at the moment, it would be generally unwise to place all of the fund in one security unless the investor's balancing off of potentially high gains against a substantial loss indicated that for his purposes such a risk was warranted. Otherwise, if the investor's judgment proved to be wrong, the loss might be disastrous.

Knowledge of markets. The investor should have an understanding of the capital and distribution markets discussed in Chapters 9 and 18, the technical procedures, and the terms, fees, and market action.

Continuous surveillance. The admonition to buy sound securities and put them in a strongbox (hold them indefinitely) has been at least partially discredited. In the economic world the only certainty is uncertainty. The level of business activity rarely remains constant, fundamental trends change, new industries are born, old industries decay, new laws and regulations affect industry and finance. The economy, the state of which determines business profits, has become increasingly sensitive to domestic and to international politics. Labor-management relations, social change, redistribution of national income, and international relations are significant factors in determining economic conditions.

To keep abreast of the myriad of factors that affect investment is a difficult undertaking even for those who give their full time to the task. In fact, professional investors tend to divide the responsibility by coordinating their activities and findings, and acting on a group basis. In addition to decisions with respect to holding, buying, or selling securities, there are other decisions to be made from time to time and clerical details that require attention. Bonds mature or are called, coupons must be clipped, and dividend checks deposited; rights and warrants should be exercised or sold, companies are reorganized or merged, proxies should be exercised or stockholder meetings should be attended, transaction confirmations should be verified, and at least a simple set of records should be maintained, particularly for the preparation of income tax returns. The investor who does not monitor his investments leaves himself open to a variety of possible losses.

Indirect investment

Investing is a complex business and, as has been indicated, is not an undertaking for the novice unaided. This is generally recognized by the financial community. Investment bankers, securities dealers, and brokers admonish prospective investors to investigate before investing; they make available the services of securities analysts and investment advisers; and they provide a variety of educational literature on various phases of investing. Seasoned investors take advantage of proffered assistance, and the novice would do well to heed the advice to investigate and accept the help that is offered.

Dealers and brokers stand ready to furnish much information about investments, but it is generally stressed that decision and action should rest on the individual investor's judgment. It is interesting to note that in an advertising campaign of one of the organized securities exchanges the discussion of purchase of stock was subordinated to home ownership, life insurance, and a savings bank account.

The individual investor who acknowledges his disinclination or lack of competence to assume the responsibility of direct investment or who does not have a sufficiently large accumulation to make direct purchase of stocks and bonds feasible may turn his funds over to one of the several thrift or investment agencies. In this way, he not only may obtain the advantage of the experience and specialized knowledge of professional investment managers but may also have the benefit of a wider degree of diversification than might otherwise be possible for a fund of modest proportions. In short, these agencies provide a means for transferring and minimizing risk; knowledge is substituted for lack of knowledge, diversification for concentration. But the individual investor still has the responsibility for selecting the agency to be employed. The success attained will depend on the ability, astuteness, and integrity of the management of the institution selected.

Thrift and other indirect investment institutions render valuable services both to their customers and to the economy as a whole. The individual saver gets specialized management and diversification of risk and is relieved of the problems of personal supervision and of making decisions of some complexity. This should mean relative safety of principal, relative certainty of income, and, in the case of some of the agencies, possible appreciation in value. Society, on the other hand, obtains more funds that are channeled into business use than would be available in the absence of these intermediaries, and this stimulus to the funds flow process results in an ultimate increase in producer and consumer goods and therefore in a generally higher standard of living.

Individual savers and investors are increasingly patronizing these indirect investment media. This is in part a reflection of high postwar earnings patterns and the high rate of saving, but it is also the result of the altered pattern of income distribution in our country. A larger share of the national income now flows to those persons in the lower middle-class brackets than did in earlier years. These persons are now able to save more and in seeking a haven for their savings, they turn in the main to those institutions with which they are familiar. For the most part, these savers are not traditionally buyers of stocks and bonds and therefore know little about investment bankers, securities dealers, brokers, and stock exchanges. As a consequence, there has been a marked expansion in the volume of funds entrusted to savings banks, the savings divisions of commercial banks, insurance companies, savings and loan associations, mutual funds, trusts, and pension funds, some of which agencies have been aggressive in their promotional activities. This channeling of funds into the various types of capital market intermediary institutions will be discussed extensively in Chapters 11 through 15.

Some aggregate effects of indirect investment practices

There are many who feel that if institutionalization of investing continues, it may present serious problems for the economy. In fact, some hold that these problems already exist. One such problem is that for reasons of law or tradition, savings banks and insurance companies are not substantial investors in equities, particularly not in common stocks. The funds they receive are invested mainly in government and corporate bonds and in mortgages. Little, if any, of these savings become available for the purchase of equity capital. Yet, a private enterprise society depends upon an adequate flow of venture capital.

The problem of institutional investment that does not flow into equities is accentuated by the fact that persons in the higher income brackets, who traditionally did most of the saving and provided most of the venture capital, apparently find stocks less attractive than formerly. Many factors account for this apathy, and one of them may well be the current income tax structure. Wealthy persons who might be expected to be in the best position to assume the risk of common stock ownership find that a tax-free income from a municipal bond may be more interesting than a common stock dividend subject to tax. In addition, there is relatively little risk in the municipal bond, whereas the income and market price of a common stock are both subject to wide fluctuation. It is therefore argued that the institutionalization of the savings of persons in the middle-income brackets, coupled with the effect of taxes on the incomes of persons in the higher tax brackets, has in the past and may continue in the future to retard the flow of venture capital.

It should be noted that if there is not an adequate supply of common stock or equity capital, there will not be a base to support additional bonds. For example, if a person wishes to buy a $20,000 home but has no funds to make a down payment, he is not likely to find a lender that will advance the full $20,000 purchase price. However, if the prospective home buyer has $8,000 of his own, representing his equity, he should have less difficulty in borrowing the other $12,000. By the same token, the extent to which a financial institution will loan money to a corporation, or buy the bonds of the corporation, depends upon the amount of ownership capital of the corporation.

Offsetting the trends of thrift and some other indirect investment institutions to channel funds away from equities, the flow of funds through such institutions as investment companies (including investment banking houses that render a counseling service), trust institutions,. and pension funds is increasing relative to total flows. In fact, investment companies as a group hold mostly common stocks, and investment counselors likewise make liberal purchases of stocks for the portfolios under their supervision. Similarly, pension funds direct a large proportion of their monies into common stocks.

An instance of potential problems with this newer type of institutional investment in common stocks is exemplified by the concentration of some securities in mutual funds portfolios. Although each mutual fund faces limits on the extent to which it can hold single stock in its portfolio, a small number of mutual funds still can hold a large proportion of a given stock issue. This concentration may pose particular problems when all mutual funds face, as they may from time to time, liquidity or other management problems or changes in their expectations regarding a stock's performance.

Certain observers point to still another possible problem growing out of the indirect investment that is fostered by some of the institutions under consideration. While these agencies render valuable services both to individual savers and to the economy as a whole, it is pointed out that savers and investors who do not have direct ownership of securities are likely to be unaware of, or at least indifferent to, fundamental sociological and political developments within the economy. It is stressed that direct stock ownership by a greater number of persons would provide greater sensitivity on the part of the public to such social needs and involves them, therefore, to the greatest possible extent in assessing priorities for the meeting of such needs. On the other hand, some fund managers are beginning to regard these matters as part of their responsibility.

Trends in stock ownership

In this section the trends in public and institutional holdings of stocks are briefly examined in order to provide some factual background for the issues just raised.

Broadened public ownership

Although tax considerations may have reduced the incentives for the very wealthy to invest in corporate shares, a great many middle-income Americans have joined the ranks of stock owners. Most of the great American corporations have shown a steady increase in the number of shareholders and a reduction in the average number of shares owned by individual holders.

Censuses of stockholders have been conducted regularly since 1952. The first indicated that 6.5 million Americans owned shares in one or more domestic corporations. In 1956, the number had grown to 8.6 million; in 1959, to 12.5 million; in 1962, to 18 million; in 1965, to 20.1 million; and in 1970, to 30.9 million. In the 1970 census, male shareholders outnumbered female shareholders for the first time since 1952. An interesting development is an apparent increase in the number of young shareholders. Several states have removed legal bars from the ownership of stock by minors. The 1970 data show that about 4.5 million persons under the age of 35 owned shares of stock. Of this number, about 2.2 million were under 21 years old.

The sobering fact is that this wider spread in stock ownership was for some time accompanied by a rapid increase in common stock prices and consequent decrease in yields. The high of the New York Stock Exchange Index in 1965 was about 3.5 times that of the high in 1952, when the first census was made, and the 1968 high was about 4.1 times that of the 1952 high. The 1968 high was 61.27, but by December 1969, the index had fallen to a level of about 51.20. Until 1969, it had been fair weather for the novice shareholders. It will be interesting to see if the 1968–69 decline has lasting effects on the holdings of this group.

A curious phenomenon that resulted from the rise in stock prices has been the opposite movements of common stock yields and those on high-grade bonds. For all but a few short periods in the past, common stock yields have been considerably higher than bond yields. In view of the protection of a bond return, this was viewed as the normal relationship. Since 1959, however, current yields on bonds have generally been above those on stocks, and since 1962, the margin between the two has been steadily increasing and quite sharply since 1967. In July 1970, Standard and Poor's dividend/price ratio stood at about 4.2%, while highest rated corporate bonds yielded approximately 8.9%. The factors that led to this reversal are complex. The increase in bond yields represented both a very strong demand for funds and, even more important, a growing reluctance of many investors to put funds in a fixed-dollar obligation. At the same time, they were tending to put more and more funds in common stocks. The fear of changes in price levels appeared to account for this change in preferences. Many believed that their long-run advantage was to be found in common stocks rather than in fixed-dollar obligations; indeed, many viewed such form of investment as being fundamentally more conservative or safer since it assured purchasing power preservation somewhat better than did bond investment. It will be recalled that Exhibit 9–2 showing bond interest rates on a constant purchasing power basis demonstrated that the real interest rates remained quite low.

It is important to note, however, that until 1969 common stocks were undoubtedly driven up in price and down in yield also as the result of economic policy. The success of economic policy in offsetting quickly the small postwar recessions in 1949, in 1953–54, in 1957–58, and in 1960–61 convinced many that prolonged cyclical downturns were unlikely in the future. This optimism was further indicated by the sluggishness with which expectations responded to contractionary monetary policy in 1969 and 1970.

A third factor, which has remained somewhat unnoticed, is the influence of taxes. When common stock yields are relatively low, the holders of common stocks may enjoy price appreciation based on retained earnings. Since this price appreciation, if realized, is taxed on a capital gains basis (which is considerably more favorable than for ordinary income), common stocks are quite desirable for investors in high-tax brackets. On the other hand, since corporations issuing bonds can deduct all the interest paid on bonds as an expense of doing business but cannot deduct dividends in computing taxes, they are disposed to seek their funds in bond form to the fullest extent possible. Thus tax considerations are moving from both sides to push for a reversal of the former yield relationships in which stocks offered higher yields than bonds.

The preceding discussion leaves untouched one basic problem: that of the newly formed corporation. The high prices of common stocks apply primarily to those of existing companies. Except for a few types of companies, such as space-age contractors for the federal government or electronic producers, new companies appear to have as great a problem of raising venture capital as in earlier periods; their problems have not been solved by the stock market boom. To some extent the financial problems to be outlined in Chapter 19 remain unsolved problems.

Ownership of institutional investors

To complete our overview of the funds flows in financial markets, the influence of financial intermediaries on the market for corporate stocks will be examined briefly. Since in later chapters the reinvestment activities of intermediaries will be closely examined, the purpose of the present discussion is to provide a broad picture of the aggregate effects of intermediary activity. Table 10–4 provides a part of this picture, showing that as of December 31, 1968, financial institutions owned more than 22% of stocks listed on the New York Stock Exchange, as contrasted to slightly less than 17% a decade ago. However, despite this long-run growth and despite the fact that institutions have recently been very active in the stock market, their holdings in relation to market value have grown rather

TABLE 10–4

Estimated holdings of NYSE—listed stocks by financial institutions (*billions of dollars*)

| | Year-end | | |
Financial institution	1949	1958	1968*
Insurance companies	2.8	8.1	22.0
Investment companies	3.0	14.6	42.5
Uninsured pension funds	0.5	10.3	57.5
Nonprofit institutions	3.2	11.8	28.9
Common trust funds	—	1.3	3.8
Mutual savings banks	0.2	0.3	0.6
Market value of all NYSE listed stocks	76.3	276.7	692.3
Estimated percentage held by institutions	12.7	16.8	22.4

* Preliminary.
Source: New York Stock Exchange, *Fact Book,* 1969.

slowly in the last several years. Thus, while institutions held 22.4% of the market value of the New York Stock Exchange's listed stocks at the end of 1968, the percentages at the end of 1966 and 1967 were respectively 21.8% and 22.0%.

Another point worth noting is that the figures in Table 10–4 do not include bank administered personal trust funds, although the New York Stock Exchange has estimated that institutional and personal trust holdings may account for about one third of the total value of all listed stocks.

The market activity of institutions as measured by their purchases and sales reached record levels in 1968, reflecting the institutions' emphasis on performance. In a 1966 survey, institutional volume accounted for about a third of the dollar volume traded on the New York Exchange, commercial banks and mutual funds being the most active institutional groups. Mutual funds have lately been turning over their portfolios at substantially increased rates, and their influence has been particularly apparent in some of the most heavily traded issues. Institutional trading in the 33 most actively traded issues observed during the July 1966 survey week ranged from 8.6% to 74.9% of the total trading in an individual issue.

The implications of increased emphasis on institutional performance and the size of institutions' trading in and holdings of individual issues remain still to be explored.

Questions and problems

1. Which uses of savings contribute to capital formation?
2. What is the distinction, if any, that can be made between thrift institutions and investment institutions? Give examples of both groups —institutions with which you are somewhat familiar.
3. Briefly indicate the various classifications of risk that confront the business enterprise.
4. What are the elements or steps in planning a sound investment program?
5. How do you account for the growth of thrift and investment institutions in recent years?
6. State what is meant by the "institutionalization of investment."
7. What are the advantages and the disadvantages of such institutionalization of investment?
8. There is much discussion about equity capital. What is the controversy?
9. Cite examples to show how investment aims or objectives might vary with individual investors.
10. Do you agree that the safest use of savings might be the retirement of a debt? Discuss.

Bibliography

For a comprehensive discussion on the risks inherent in business, see one of the earliest treatises on this subject, which, though old, is still considered authoritative: C. O. Hardy, *Risk and Risk Bearing* (Chicago: University of Chicago Press, 1931).

An interesting application of mathematical programming to the problem of investment uncertainty may be found in Harry Markowitz, *Portfolio Selection: Efficient Diversification of Investments,* Cowles Monograph No. 16 (New York: John Wiley & Sons, Inc., 1959). This seminal work has stimulated the development of a theoretical literature too vast to be cited here. Some of the more important articles can be found in such collections of readings as S. H. Archer and Charles A. D'Ambrosio, *The Theory of Business Finance* (New York: Macmillan, 1967), and in Wm. F. Sharpe, *Portfolio Theory and Capital Markets*

(New York: McGraw-Hill, 1970). On the classic approaches to risks confronting the institutional investor, consult the standard texts on investments; for example, the topic is well summarized in G. W. Dowrie and D. R. Fuller, *Investments* (2d. ed.; New York: John Wiley & Sons, Inc., 1950). This and other texts on investments, such as R. E. Badger, H. W. Torgerson, and H. G. Guthmann, *Investment Principles and Practices* (6th ed.; New York: Prentice-Hall, Inc., 1969) discuss the full scope of the problem of investing, including determination of objectives; economic, industry, company, and securities analysis; and thrift and investment agencies. Current articles on the equity-capital problem and on institutionalization of investment will be found in the periodical literature—particularly the *Harvard Business Review* and the *Journal of Finance*—and in reported addresses in the *Commerical and Financial Chronicle*.

Information on securities ownership is provided by L. H. Kimmel, *Share Ownership in the United States* (Washington, D.C.: Brookings Institution, 1952); *The Public Speaks to the Exchange,* Consumer Surveys (New York Stock Exchange, 1955); and the censuses of share ownership conducted by the New York Stock Exchange—the most recent of which is the 1970 census. Basic facts about tax-exempt securities may be found in Gordon L. Calvert, *Fundamentals of Municipal Bonds* (6th ed.; Washington, D.C.: Investment Bankers Association of America, 1968).

CHAPTER 11

Deposit-type thrift institutions; U.S. savings bonds

Introduction

The quest for economic security has created a variety of deposit-type thrift institutions for the accumulation of personal savings in the form of commercial and savings bank deposits, savings and loan association deposits, and credit union accounts. The earlier chapters of this part have discussed in a general way the economic determinants of household savings and the resulting flows of funds from households through intermediaries to their final users. The present chapter is concerned chiefly with the flow of funds from households to thrift institutions and the disposition of these funds by the thrift institutions and also discusses the flow of funds into U.S. savings bonds. Inasmuch as U.S. savings bonds resemble contractual savings arrangements about as closely as they resemble deposit-type savings arrangements, they could also have been discussed along with contractual savings institutions. Hence, their inclusion in this chapter is somewhat arbitrary. The remaining chapters of this part will examine in detail the flows of funds into corporate securities and contractual savings arrangements such as life insurance policies and pension funds.

General characteristics of thrift institution deposits

Thrift institutions assist in the accumulation of capital by enabling large groups of savers to channel their funds through financial intermediaries into productive financial investments while gaining the advantages of low risk, liquidity, convenience of both deposit and withdrawal, and the promise of a reasonable rate of return. The thrift institutions discussed in this chapter form a contract with savers to return the dollars entrusted to them plus any interest or dividends accrued. A saver's balance in a commercial bank or mutual savings bank has traditionally been called a deposit. Funds entrusted to savings and loan associations or credit unions were until recently placed in *share accounts* or *savings accounts*. Banks guarded their right to use the word *deposit* and resisted the efforts of other institutions to adopt this terminology. However, the Housing and Urban Development Act of 1968 permitted federally chartered savings and loan associations to issue accounts designated as savings deposits. The legislation is appropriate inasmuch as the operation, physical appearance, and promotional activities of the deposit liability operations of the institutions are quite similar, the differences for the depositor being chiefly the location of the institution, the additional services it offers, and the rate of interest paid on the deposit account. For accounts insured by the Federal Deposit Insurance Corporation or the Federal Savings and Loan Insurance Corporation, the differences in institutions' asset portfolios are not of great importance to the depositor because the safety of his assets is insured.

Closely related to the safety of principal offered by thrift institutions is the privilege of immediate withdrawal of savings, which provides for individual liquidity and convenience. In addition to wanting to earn some investment return, most savers with small accounts rely on their savings to meet emergency needs so the ability to withdraw funds immediately is vital. Wealthy investors can acquire proportionally less liquid assets because the proportion of their assets that would have to be liquidated quickly is usually smaller than for less wealthy individuals. Thus individuals with limited resources have difficulty investing in marketable securities because of the possible loss of liquidity and the risk that holdings might have to be sold at depressed prices when funds are needed. A large and growing number of individuals who save small amounts have therefore been attracted to thrift institutions by the twin incentives of safety and liquidity, at least unil recently when inflationary trends and high interest rates in the financial markets have tended to lessen the relative importance of these features.

The promised return of principal offered by savings institutions is certain and therefore differs from the uncertain yields on marketable securities with fluctuating prices. A higher average return is usually anticipated from investments with fluctuating values, but losses may also be suffered. Since the average person does not have the time, skill, or amount of money needed to invest wisely in marketable assets directly, thrift institutions provide an effective means of employing his funds while preserving safety of principal. Because the thrift institutions in turn reinvest the pooled funds of savers, they act both as risk absorbers and as agencies for enabling savers to invest indirectly in various types of economic undertakings. As we shall see, one of the most important types of indirect investment activity brought about by thrift institutions is the channeling of funds into mortgages on homes and apartment buildings.

It has been claimed that the upward trend in rates of return on savings and the stability of these rates have been major factors in the large flows of funds into thrift institutions which have been observed since World War II. The historical increases in rates shown in Table 11–1 are

TABLE 11–1

Average annual yield on selected types of instruments (*in percent*)

	Savings accounts in savings and loan associations	Savings deposits in mutual savings banks	Time and savings deposits in commercial banks	Corporate (Aaa) bonds
1930	5.3	4.5	3.9	4.5
1940	3.3	2.0	1.3	2.8
1945	2.5	1.7	0.8	2.5
1950	2.5	1.9	0.9	2.6
1955	2.9	2.6	1.4	3.1
1960	3.86	3.47	2.56	4.41
1965	4.23	4.11	3.69	4.49
1969*	4.78	4.85	4.87	7.03

* Preliminary.
Source: United States Savings and Loan League, *Savings and Loan Fact Book,* 1970, Table 6, p. 17. Savings and loan associations: effective rate of dividends; i.e., dividends distributed relative to average savings balances, based on data of members of FHLB system; mutual savings banks: "per deposit" rates reported by National Association of Mutual Savings Banks; commercial banks: effective interest rate, based on data of Federal Reserve Board and Federal Deposit Insurance Corporation; bond yields: Moody's Investors Services.

consistent with this view, but several other factors affecting funds flows must also be borne in mind. In the first place, total savings flows depend chiefly on the level of economic activity, as discussed in Chapter 9. Then, as the next section discusses, the proportion of total savings flow directed to a given category of financial investment depends, at least in part, on prevailing rate differentials between competing financial investments. (A variety of other factors which affect the process are also discussed.)

Following the discussions of the division and subdivision of savings flows attributable to interest rate and other factors, the remainder of the chapter considers in detail the historical development, industry structure, and operations of the several deposit-type thrift institutions. Finally, the last section discusses the importance of U.S. savings bonds as a repository for individual savings.

Flows of funds to deposit-type thrift institutions

As mentioned in Chapter 9, one of the primary determinants of the total savings flow is the size of the national income flow, because savings depend on the level of economic activity. The allocation of the savings flows determined by the level of economic activity then depends in part on the differential rates of return available on competing financial investments. Thus, Chapter 9 has noted that the flow of funds to all thrift institutions depends on the interest rate differentials beween savings deposits and such financial investments as bonds and common stocks.

These interest rate differentials can be seen by referring to Exhibit 11–1, and the fluctuations in rate differences shown in this graph tend to correspond to differentials in the proportion of total savings allocated

EXHIBIT 11–1

Average annual yield on savings and securities

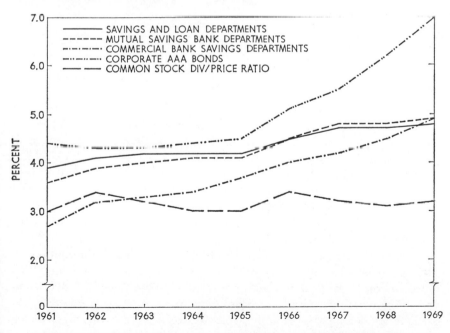

Sources: *Federal Reserve Bulletin,* various issues; *Savings and Loan Fact Book,* 1970.

to the thrift institutions. Thus, during 1966 and 1968 the unusually large rate difference between deposits and corporate bonds is associated with reductions in the thrift institution fund inflows.

The total flows of funds from households to deposit-type thrift institutions for the years 1960 through 1969 are shown in Table 11–2. Although the trend of these flows has been consistently upward since World War II, growth in them was almost zero for 1962 through 1965, and the flows show pronounced declines in 1966, 1968, and 1969. As already noted, these latter figures show the response of savings flows to differential yields in the financial markets; changes in the differential rates of return between deposits and other financial investments played an important role in the slowed growth rates of savings deposits.

In addition, the flows of funds into the individual types of thrift institutions deposits are also affected by rate differentials: differentials between commercial bank savings deposits on the one hand and the

TABLE 11–2

Households' supplies of funds to thrift institutions, 1960–69 (billions of dollars)

	1960	1961	1962	1963	1964	1965	1966	1967	1968	1969
Savings and loan association deposits	7.6	8.7	9.4	11.1	10.6	8.5	3.6	10.7	7.3	4.0
Mutual savings bank deposits	1.4	1.9	3.1	3.3	4.2	3.6	2.6	5.1	4.1	2.6
Time deposits at commercial banks*	2.8	6.2	10.3	7.9	8.2	13.3	11.9	15.8	15.1	3.3
Credit union accounts	0.6	0.7	0.7	0.8	1.1	1.0	0.8	1.2	1.1	1.4
Total flow	12.4	17.5	23.5	23.1	24.1	26.4	18.9	32.8	27.6	11.3

* Inclusive of large certificates of deposit.
Source: *Federal Reserve Bulletin*, November 1969, p. A71.2.

mutual savings bank (MSB) and savings and loan (S&L) deposits on the other. The effects can also be observed with reference to Table 11–2, where it will be noted that commercial bank savings deposits made relative gains, especially in 1966 and to a lesser degree in 1968. The changes in commercial banks' share of total household-owned savings deposits are displayed more prominently in Table 11–3. (These data do not include certificates of deposit issued by banks to business since the MSBs and S&Ls have not traditionally been regarded as competitors for this kind of savings business.)

Despite the emphasis to this point on interest rate differentials, it should not be concluded that rates are the only important competitive aspect of thrift institution operations. Other factors include advertising and promotional efforts, offers of different types of services, convenience of facilities, loan policies, and service charges. Our knowledge of the responsiveness of savings deposits to interest rates in comparison to the other factors just cited is inadequate at this time, since we do not know the relative importance of the different factors just mentioned with any degree of precision.

However, while precise knowledge regarding the comparative importance of these factors is lacking, the fact that savings flows do respond to interest rates is important for economic policy. Again referring to Table 11–2, the effects of the competitive rate disadvantages experienced by the thrift-type institutions in 1966 and 1968 were pronounced, particularly in the former year and especially insofar as funds flows to MSBs and S&Ls were concerned. (The same was true of banks' large certificates of deposit in 1969, because of Regulation Q restrictions on rates allowed on this instrument.) This means that funds available for mortgage lending by these institutions were in much shorter supply than has normally been the case. Since higher interest rates during both these periods were attributable to restrictive monetary policy, the effects of

TABLE 11–3

Time deposits and savings accounts liabilities (*billions of dollars*)

	1960	1961	1962	1963	1964	1965	1966	1967	1968	1969
Households' deposits with commercial banks savings deposits	62.2	68.4	78.7	86.6	94.8	108.0	118.7	134.5	149.6	155.4
All other deposit-type thrift institutions*	103.1	114.3	127.3	142.4	158.1	171.3	178.4	195.0	207.8	215.5
Total	165.3	182.7	206.0	229.0	252.9	279.3	297.1	329.5	357.4	370.9
Percentages held by commercial banks	38	37	38	38	38	39	40	41	42	42

* Includes credit union deposits not redeposited in savings and loan associations or mutual savings banks.
Source: *Federal Reserve Bulletin*, November 1970. 1969 data provided in *Federal Reserve System*, "Financial Assets and Liabilities," December 31, 1969.

that policy on the housing industry were qualitatively important ones.

During periods of high interest rates, banks have made deposit gains while other thrift institutions experienced proportional declines in their deposit inflows. The ability of MSBs and S&Ls to compete vigorously for funds during periods of high interest rates is impaired by the fact that while their liabilities are short term, their assets consist almost entirely of long-term mortgages. This means in times of rising interest rates that the mortgage lending institutions' ability to compete for funds is affected by the fact that their average costs rise faster than average earnings, an effect which is accentuated by the fact that rate increases on savings deposits are paid on all accounts rather than just on new ones. Inasmuch as during periods of low interest rates average costs also fall faster than average revenues, the problem is essentially a problem of survival during periods of tight money.

These facts together with the liquidity problems faced by MSBs and

S&Ls in 1966, 1968, and 1969 and liquidity problems resulting from individuals shifting funds from savings accounts into the securities markets and to bank deposits in response to changing rates of return, have led naturally to proposals for diversification of MSB and S&L operations. Diversification through such means as increasing their short-term lending in, for example, the field of consumer finance would partially offset the earnings difficulties faced when short-term rates are high and would therefore enhance their capability to compete for funds during such periods. A second type of diversification which has been suggested is increasing these savings institutions' proportion of fixed maturity deposits, thus stabilizing to a degree their sources of funds. Many other ideas involving diversification also are currently popular, but they all have in common an attempt to improve mortgage lending institutions' earning ability more rapidly when interest rates rise.

It is time now to turn to a more detailed examination of how the individual types of savings institutions operate within the environment of fluctuating savings flows which has just been described.

Savings and loan associations

Development of the savings and loan industry

The growth of savings and loan associations since World War II has caused many people to think of them as a new type of financial institution. Actually, the Oxford Provident Building Association was founded in 1831 in Philadelphia. The early associations were small, informal groups that pooled the funds of a few individuals to make housing loans to members. Operations were usually quite casual and were not subject to regulation. Growth was limited and many associations were disbanded after all of the members had received a loan. The number of associations increased rapidly following the Civil War and during the early 1900s, but the size of assets remained relatively small. Along with other financial institutions the S&Ls were hurt by the depression of the 1930s when withdrawals were heavy and loan repayments slow. The Home Owners Loan Act and the establishment of the Federal Savings and Loan Insurance Corporation (FSLIC) were significant developments during this period of strain. During the war the S&Ls shifted funds into government securities, which left them in a very liquid position to meet the tremendous postwar demand for housing. At this time, many associations changed from small cooperative enterprises, in which members slowly accumulated funds to purchase homes, into large savings institutions serving as intermediaries between masses of savers and mortgage borrowers. Progressive lending policies, including early entry into the veterans' housing loan market, plus heavy promotional efforts and emphasis on the attractiveness of physical facilities has enabled the industry to attract the large volumes of new savings indicated in Table 11–2.

The S&Ls continue to utilize aggressive promotional campaigns to make thrift an attractive concept with appeal to the growing numbers of savers in the lower and middle-income groups. The industry has spent more money on promotion and advertising than any other type of financial organization to create the image of an energetic, progressive, and friendly savings institution that can meet high standards of safety while offering a relatively high rate of return. As noted in Table 11–1, the savings and loans have paid an incremental yield differential that historically has ranged approximately 1% above the rate paid on commercial bank time deposits, although the differential has recently been almost entirely eliminated. In recent years, associations on the West Coast have been particularly aggressive solicitors of deposits in order to keep pace with the area's population expansion, and rates on deposits at some institutions have reached the permissible maximum of 5% for passbook accounts and 5.25% for savings certificates. Associations now emphasize the savings aspects rather than real estate financing as indicated by the evolution of names from "building and loan" to "savings and loan" associations. The concentrated efforts to make accounts as liquid as deposits in other savings institutions and the heavy promotional efforts have caused many savers to consider S&Ls equivalent to competing organizations in terms of safety, liquidity, and convenience, with the additional advantage of higher earnings.

Status of the savings and loan industry

The savings and loan industry has experienced unusually rapid asset growth since World War II. At year-end 1969, there were 5,898 associations with savings of $162.2 billion as compared to 5,983 associations with savings of $8.7 billion at year-end 1945. The extremely rapid asset growth has not been uniform from year to year, however, as indicated earlier in this chapter. Of the total savings held by the four types of deposit institutions at the end of 1969, the savings and loans' amount equaled approximately 32%, significantly larger than its 20% share in 1950, but lower than its 1963–64 share of 36%. Approximately 46.7 million accounts with an average balance of $2,898 provided the funds to make loans of over 10.7 million mortgage borrowers in 1969.

Associations are found in every state and in the District of Columbia and Puerto Rico. Few large communities are without an association. Pennsylvania had the largest number, 660, at year-end 1969, but California associations led in terms of total assets, $30.8 billion, followed by Illinois, Ohio, New York, and Pennsylvania. Growth has become the dominant consideration in management policies, and performance is frequently evaluated in terms of asset size and rate of expansion.

Associations may be chartered by a state or receive a federal charter from the Federal Home Loan Bank Board. Of the 5,898 associations, 3,827 were state chartered at the end of 1969. However, federally chartered associations held 54% of the assets. The governmental authority that grants the charter is in charge of supervision which includes an annual examination of accounts of the security for loans and of general compliance with rules. All federally chartered institutions are mutual in organization, while state-chartered companies may be either mutual or capital stock institutions. At the end of 1969 there were 736 stock associations, whose loans constituted about 20% of the industry assets.

TABLE 11-4

Statements of condition of savings and loan associations, 1968 and 1969 (*billions of dollars*)

	Year-end	
	1968	*1969*
Assets		
Demand deposits and currency	1.6	2.4
U.S. government securities	11.0	8.7
Mortgages	130.8	140.2
Other assets	9.5	11.0
Total assets	152.8	162.3
Liabilities		
Savings deposits	131.6	135.5
Mortgage loans in process	2.4	2.4
Borrowing from FHLB	5.3	9.8
Other liabilities	3.2	3.5
Reserves and undivided profits	10.3	11.2
Total liabilities	152.8	162.4

Note: Details may not add to totals because of rounding.
Source: *Federal Reserve Bulletin*, August 1970, p. A38.

The size distribution is typical of other industries with the majority of the associations falling into the "small" category. The average association held assets of $27.5 million in 1969 and only 172 savings and loans reported assets of $100 million or over. Nevertheless, the large associations do hold a disproportionate share of industry assets. There is also extensive use of branches in the 45 states where branching is permitted. California has the largest number of branches.

TABLE 11–5

Sources and uses of funds by savings and loan associations, 1968 and 1969 (*billions of dollars*)

	Annual fund flows	
	1968	*1969*
Sources		
Savings shares	7.3	4.0
Mortgage loans in progress	0.2	0.0
Borrowing from FHLB	0.9	4.0
Surplus and reserves	0.9	1.3
	9.3	9.3
Uses		
Demand deposits and currency	−0.4	−0.2
U.S. government securities	0.6	0.4
Home mortgage	7.2	8.0
Other mortgages	2.1	1.5
Consumer credit	0.1	0.0
Miscellaneous transactions	−0.3	−0.4
	9.3	9.3

Source: *Federal Reserve Bulletin*, May 1970.

Asset and investment structure

As indicated in Table 11–4, funds are provided largely by savings accounts and are invested primarily in mortgage loans. The competitive strength of the savings and loan association industry stems from its penetration of the mortgage financing field (which has continued to expand during the postwar period) plus its ability to obtain a larger share of this market. At year-end 1969 all associations combined held 45% of the outstanding mortgages on one- to four-family nonfarm dwellings $110 billion of $252 billion). This proportion was up substantially from the 29% share in 1950. The large market share of lending activity acquired by the savings and loans is reflected in the composition of their investment portfolios. In fact at the end of 1969, the associations had 86% of their total assets invested in mortgages and the bulk of these loans, 85%, were made on the one- to four-family residences, a much greater concentration than any other savings institution. The associations have added to their portfolios at a steady pace and during 1969 made net mortgage loans, after subtracting mortgage repayments, of $9.5 billion, as shown in Table 11–5.

The association's specialization in mortgage lending would probably have occurred even without the original legal restrictions which specify investments in home mortgages, U.S. government securities, limited property loans, Federal Home Loan Bank obligations, limited first mortgage loans on commercial properties and churches, and the extension of loans for land development by federally chartered associations. Following the disappointing experiences of the depression years of the early 1930s, state and federal regulations further restricted loans to a maximum of 80% of the appraised value of the mortgaged property, except for FHA-insured and veterans' guaranteed loans. Investments were also limited to rigidly defined geographical areas. In 1957 regulations were modified to allow FSLIC-insured associations to purchase participations in first mortgage home loans made by other insured institutions up to 75% (originally 50%) of the original loan regardless of location. This modification helps equalize the supply and demand for funds in different regions. Some federally chartered units have also been given the authority to make loans in excess of 80% of appraised value and to diversify their investments. The associations have experienced a rise in the proportion of loans for other purposes including home improvement and repair, use of open-end mortgages, and refinancing of existing loans and the creation of loans on debt-free property to provide borrowers with funds for education or unusual expenses, but despite these developments, associations continue to specialize in local loans for home ownership. Studies of potential housing requirements based on anticipated family formations and the replacement rate for present homes suggests that the savings and loan industry will have to continue aggressively to solicit savings capital, perhaps with the aid of subsidies, if it is to help fill the projected mortgage financing needs of the economy.

Regulation and safety

An important part of the savings and loan industry is the Federal Home Loan Bank (FHLB) system, established in 1932 to provide a nationwide credit facility to improve the liquidity of member associations. The FHLB system is modeled after the Federal Reserve System that serves the commercial banks. The 12 regional federal home loan banks are wholly owned by the member associations through the required purchase of dividend-paying FHLB stock. All federally chartered associations must be members and state-chartered organizations may join. The membership in 1968 included 81% of the number of associations and represented 98.5% of total savings and loan industry assets. Membership is also open to mutual savings banks and insurance companies, but only a few savings banks have joined.

FHLB advances to members may be in the form of short-term loans to balance a seasonal cash drain or long-term loans (up to 10 years duration). Long-term FHLB advances at below-market interest rates have been an important factor in keeping the flow of funds into mortgages as high as it has been during the 1968–70 monetary restriction.

Since 1966, the Federal Home Loan Bank Board has been empowered to fix the maximum interest rates which can be paid on association savings accounts; the rate ceilings apply to all associations which are members of the Federal Home Loan Bank system. The FHLB system can also require member associations to hold cash and government securities reserves of between 4% and 10% of their savings deposits. Members may decide to place demand or time deposits necessary for operations with the FHLB, just as commercial banks carry accounts with the Federal Reserve banks. Observers agree that the FHLB system has played an important role in the maturing of the industry.

The associations have tried to give their accounts all of the advantages of a bank deposit, including the safety of deposit insurance. Approximately 74% of the number of associations, representing 96.7% of industry assets, have their share accounts insured up to $20,000 by the Federal Savings and Loan Insurance Corporation (FSLIC), an instrumentality of the federal government supervised by the FHLB system. If an insured association becomes insolvent, the FSLIC settles each insured account either by payment of cash to the account holder or by making available a transferred account in a new insured institution. It should be noted that the definition of *default* varies materially from the rules governing insurance of commercial bank deposits by the Federal Deposit Insurance Corporation. The FSLIC insures against loss, but does not guarantee immediate withdrawal which is required for demand deposits, or even withdrawal within the 60- to 90-day period permissible for time deposits.

The FSLIC may make loans or grants to insured institutions, and FSLIC regulations govern the portfolio structures of the savings and loans associations whose accounts are insured.

Mutual savings banks

Development of mutual savings banking

Mutual savings banks were established early in the 19th century to promote the habit of thrift among the emerging class of industrial workers. The *mutual* form of organization means that there are no shareholders and that all earnings are distributed to the depositors after providing for reserves. The original savings banks were patterned after a Scottish institution established to provide an incentive and a place for persons to save and thus relieve the distress of poverty. Many of the early leaders in the movement had a missionary zeal and this spirit is still evident in the management and operation of modern savings banks. Since there are no stockholders to elect directors, the governing board of trustees of most organizations is a self-perpetuating body which generally serves for little or no remuneration. Control is literally kept in trust by the many outstanding business and professional men chosen to serve as trustees. The day-to-day operations are directed by a paid staff. The original nature of many savings banks is still evident in their colorful names: the Bowery Savings Bank, currently the largest institution with deposits of $2.7 billion in 1968; the Dime Savings Bank; Emigrant Industrial Savings Bank; Seamen's Bank for Saving; Boston Five Cents Saving Bank; Dry Dock Savings Bank; and so on.

TABLE 11–6

Location and deposits of mutual savings banks, December 31, 1969

State	Number of savings banks	Deposits (in millions)
Massachusetts	173	$10,480
New York	122	39,009
Connecticut	69	4,843
New Hampshire	31	1,086
Maine	32	836
New Jersey	21	2,651
Rhode Island	7	1,045
Pennsylvania	7	3,703
Maryland	5	823
Vermont	6	271
Indiana	4	103
Washington	9	1,194
Wisconsin	3	33
Delaware	2	320
Ohio	1	4
Alaska	2	39
Minnesota	1	554
Oregon	1	87
Puerto Rico	1	3
Total	497	$67,086

Note: Detail may not add to total because of rounding.
Source: *Mutual Savings Banking National Fact Book,* National Association of Mutual Savings Banks, 1970; number drawn from Table 6, p. 5; deposits drawn from Table 15, p. 11.

Almost all of the savings banks are located in the New England and Middle Atlantic states as indicated in Table 11–6. Three states, Massachusetts, New York, and Connecticut, account for three fourths of the number of institutions and about four fifths of the dollar volume of all mutual savings deposits. Savings banks are chartered by individual states and each state carefully regulates the operations and investments of each organization. The barriers against the issue of savings bank charters in some states partially explain the geographical concentration.

Other major reasons include the natural tendency to locate originally in the industrial areas to serve the working classes, the absence of economic incentives for promoters to form new units in other areas, the relatively difficult legal restrictions and the sizable capital requirements, and the early development of commercial bank and savings and loan association facilities in other areas to meet the saving needs of the population.

Status and growth of the industry

The major boom in establishing mutual savings banks occurred between 1850 and 1875 when 320 were organized. Between 1900 and 1960 only 36 savings banks were formed, including only 3 after 1940. A new Alaskan facility was opened in 1961. Recent physical expansion has been in the form of branches; at the end of 1969 there were 497 mutual savings banks in the United States. The mutual savings banks at that time operated a total of 1,483 offices of which 986 were branches. The early success of the savings bank movement is evident from the fact that by 1900 these institutions held three fifths of all savings deposits. However, in recent decades the relative rate of growth has been slower than the expansion of other savings facilities and the mutual savings bank share of savings deposits has declined to less than one fifth (see Table 11–2). Major reasons for this change in relative position include the concentration of facilities in the northeastern part of the nation which has not grown as rapidly as other regions, intensive competition for savings, particularly during the postwar period, a lower rate of return than that offered to savers by other savings institutions, reduced emphasis on promotional efforts, and restrictive regulations in many states. It is interesting that in the three most important savings bank states, the mutual savings banks hold more savings than the commercial banks and savings and loan associations combined.

These facts suggest that savings banks might well move into new areas and at various times there has been agitation for expansion, but these efforts have failed as indicated by the summary figures of new formations since 1900. The National Association of Mutual Savings Banks is currently advocating creation of a nationwide system of mutual savings banks using federal charters. Such a system would provide the desired opportunity for geographical expansion and would enable interested savings and loan associations to convert their charters to obtain the more diversified investment powers granted to savings banks. In the meantime, expansion efforts have turned to development of branch offices and in those states that permit multiple offices, such as New York, a sizable number of branches have been opened.

At the end of 1969 there were 23.6 million accounts in savings banks totaling $67.1 billion. This figure represents a large number of individual savers even after allowing for the duplication arising from the practice of maintaining multiple accounts. The average size of regular accounts in 1968 was $3,399 (excluding special club savings accounts). Since 1946 deposits have risen at a steady annual rate accompanying monetary restrictions except in such years as 1948, 1959–60, 1966, and 1969 when high returns on marketable securities distracted the flow of savings. In 1969 new deposits totaled $2.5 billion.

Savings bank depositors have the legal status of creditors and may withdraw their funds upon notice; in reality, withdrawals may be made upon demand. In keeping with the general expansion of activities, interest payments to depositors have steadily increased in recent years both in absolute amounts and in terms of the rate of return to savers. As indicated in Table 11–1, the rate paid was traditionally below the savings and loan association yield but above the return on commercial bank savings. In recent years MSB rates have slightly exceeded those of the S&Ls, and in 1969 the average MSB deposit account was earning 4.85%. In addition to providing savings facilities and a variety of other financial services, savings banks in Massachusetts, New York, and Connecticut are empowered to sell life insurance policies over the counter at a low cost to residents or to individuals regularly employed in these states. In 1964, the Savings Bank Life Insurance Company was formed as a legal reserve life insurance company with all the shares owned by savings banks to serve savings banks in all states where legislation permits the sale of this type of insurance. By the end of 1969 there were 1.1 million policies outstanding with a face value of $3.6 billion.

Asset and investment structure

The relative rate of growth of savings bank deposits for the last 10 years is shown in Table 11–2. The consolidated balance sheets in Table 11–7 give a detailed picture of the total assets and liabilities at the end of 1968 and 1969.

Savings banks place the funds received from depositors in long-term investments. At year-end 1969, mortgages comprised 76% of total assets, culminating a steady increase during most postwar years. In such years as 1966 and 1969, deposit growth and mortgage lending growth rates declined commensurately. Savings banks rank just below savings and loan associations in terms of the proportion of total assets placed in real estate mortgages. Loans on one- to four-family properties continue to dominate ($36.4 billion), but multifamily and nonresidential properties totaling $19.6 billion are also important outlets for funds. Mutual savings banks have been particularly important in the FHA and VA mortgage markets because geographical lending limitations on these types of mortgages are less stringent than on conventional mortgages and because most MSBs are located in capital surplus areas. Government guaranteed loans represent a majority of the mortgages held, although conventional loans continue to represent the largest single category (see Chapter 21). Savings banks concentrate on local loans, but in recent years they have increased their lending activities in states where these institutions are not located. In 1969, savings banks held mortgage commitments in all 50 states.

TABLE 11-7

Statements of condition of mutual savings banks, 1968 and 1969 *(billions of dollars)*

	Year-end	
	1968	*1969*
Assets		
Mortgage loans	53.3	56.0
Other loans	1.4	1.8
U.S. government securities	3.8	3.3
State and local government securities	0.2	0.2
Corporate securities	10.2	10.8
Cash	1.0	0.9
Other assets	1.3	1.3
	71.2	74.3
Liabilities		
Savings deposits	64.5	67.0
Other liabilities	1.4	1.6
General reserve accounts	5.3	5.5
	71.2	74.3

Note: Detail may not add to total because of rounding.
Source: *National Fact Book, 1970,* National Association of Mutual Savings Banks, Table 1, p. 2.

For many years prior to World War II, the assets of mutual savings banks were about evenly divided among bonds and real estate mortgages. The shift to mortgages resulted in a declining share for both U.S. government securities, which at year-end 1969 totaled $3.3 billion, and state and municipal bonds, $200 million. The dollar volume of corporate securities increased to $10.8 billion. Corporate bonds, particularly utility issues, are the most important form of investment in private marketable securities. Savings banks also purchase short-term treasury securities to provide liquidity. Borrowing for any purpose, even to cover short-term cash needs, is rare among these institutions.

In making generalizations about investment practices it should be emphasized that individual savings bank policies vary widely and many of the larger organizations have very diversified holdings. In fact, the ability easily to shift funds among various investments is a major advantage of the savings bank form of organization.

The investments of savings banks are closely regulated by state chartering agencies. In some states a *legal list* of authorized investment has been developed to regulate investment operations and hence protect the safety and liquidity of the funds entrusted by many individual savers. Under this system a state authority publishes and revises, from time to time, a list of eligible investments. In recent years mutual savings banks have been allowed to depart from the legal list rule and be guided by the *prudent man* principle, which has a long history of effectiveness in the trust investment field.

Regulation and safety of savings banks

Mutual savings banks have had an exceptional record of safety. In the few failures which have occurred, losses to depositors have been relatively moderate. Because of their investment concentration in railroad securities and real estate, savings banks had problems similar to other financial institutions during the 1930s. Fortunately, depositors did not withdraw deposits in panic to the extent that depositors in commercial banks did. With less pressure for liquidation, savings banks recovered with minimum losses and deposits actually increased despite the overall decline in activity throughout the economy.

Safety is also provided through membership in various insurance organizations. As of 1968, 67% of all savings banks were insured by the Federal Deposit Insurance Corporation, including all of the units in New York, New Jersey, Pennsylvania, and several other states. Massachusetts and Connecticut have their own state systems of deposit insurance. In addition, 48 savings banks belong to the Federal Home Loan Bank system. The New York mutual savings banks have also organized and own a commercial bank called the Savings Bank Trust Company which can provide the services of a central bank in a period of strain. The bank serves as a depository for the correspondent balances of the mutual savings bank members, which have received a return from these balances as a result of profitable operations. The Savings Bank Trust Company also assists individual savings banks in investment planning.

Savings departments of commercial banks

This section is concerned with the role commercial bank savings accounts play when regarded as a substitute for savings deposits in other types of thrift institutions. Savings deposits form only a portion of the commercial banks' regular business, but since commercial banks have already been discussed extensively in Chapters 3 through 6, the relations of savings deposit business to other aspects of banking are omitted here. For a discussion of bank regulation and its effects on the safety of bank savings deposits see Chapter 6.

Development of commercial bank savings accounts

Savings deposits in commercial banks are technically divided into two categories: *savings* deposits, the funds of individuals and non-profit organizations, and *time* deposits, held by businesses, state and local governments, and foreign banks as well as by individuals. Both terms are commonly used to also indicate the combined total.

Commercial banks did not actively solicit savings accounts until the 1900s, well after the development of the mutual savings bank movement in the eastern states. Prior to the establishment of the Federal Reserve System, national banks were required to maintain reserves against time and savings deposits at the same rate set for demand deposits. This regulation limited interest in acquiring savings accounts to the state-chartered banks. After reserve requirements for time and savings accounts were reduced, national banks aggressively sought to attract savings. By 1929 such deposits represented 44% of all bank deposits compared to a figure of 18% in 1899. Much of the growth resulted from the flexibility granted commercial banks to locate facilities throughout the nation, particularly in the more rapidly growing areas. The accumulation was halted during the depression years as total savings deposits contracted $8.2 billion, or 41%, between June 30, 1929, and June 30, 1933. Demand deposits fell $7.7 billion, or 33%, during the same period. This experience and the passage of the National Banking Act in 1933, which limited the interest rates that could be paid on savings deposits, diminished the attractiveness of this type of business. As a result the average interest rate paid on deposits fell from 3.4% in 1933 to 0.8% in 1945. As indicated in Exhibit 11–1, the accumulation of savings accelerated following World War II, particularly after the increases for maximum rates of interest granted in 1957 and 1962. During this phase, all time and savings accounts as a percentage of total commercial bank deposits increased from 24% in 1946 to approximately 53% by 1968 and declined to 44% at year-end 1969. Some of the changes are attributable to changes in banks' large certificates of deposit; households accounted for approximately 75% of total time and savings deposits at the end of 1968 while in 1955 they accounted for 86%. The totals for bank savings and time deposits are quite profoundly affected by movements in large certificates of deposit which occur when the maximum allowable rates on these instruments are below market interest rates. Thus, large certificates of deposit outstanding at large banks totaled

$23 billion on October 31, 1968, but only $11.5 billion on October 31, 1969, reflecting the fact that during most of 1969 the maximum rates permitted under the Federal Reserve Board's Regulation Q were considerably below prevailing market levels.

Growth in household savings has also occurred despite intensive competition from savings and loan associations and more recently from mutual savings banks and credit unions. The competitive situation is becoming even more intense as savers develop greater sophistication about yield differentials and services. In 1968, commercial banks were the leaders in the over-the-counter savings market, savings and loan associations were second, and mutual savings banks, third.[1] In addition to the upward trend in total savings deposits held at commercial banks, a number of variations in the rates of accumulation may be noted in Table 11–2. As already noted, the 1966 growth was relatively more rapid than that of savings and loan associations and mutual savings banks—a change which took place in a time of credit restriction and which was accompanied by the narrowing interest rate differentials displayed in Exhibit 11–1.

Growth of commercial bank deposits

The increasing national flow of savings and the efforts of commercial banks to obtain a larger share of the aggregate total are reflected in growth of bank time and savings deposits. Banks have initiated aggressive promotion and advertising programs in many areas to supplement the increases in interest rates permitted in recent years. Although the higher rate was partly offset by increases by other thrift institutions, savers have apparently responded favorably to the narrowing of the gap.

A second reason for the rising accumulation of bank savings is a shift in preferences from demand deposits to savings accounts. It should be remembered that banks are prohibited from paying interest on demand deposits. Thus, as interest rates on savings deposits have risen the implicit cost of holding demand deposits has increased. The comparable rates of growth and fluctuation in each type of deposit are shown in Table 11–8. Savings and time deposits are increasingly replacing currency and demand deposits as a basic form of liquid assets. Corporation treasurers in particular have attempted to replace demand deposits with short-term investments which offer some earnings return. There is also evidence that individuals have shifted funds from demand deposits and marketable securities into savings accounts.

A third factor stimulating the increase has been the development of

---

[1] Ranking measured as savings in millions of dollars as of December 31, 1968. See U.S. Savings & Loan League, *Savings and Loan Fact Book,* 1968, Table 4, p. 15.

large certificates of deposits to attract corporation funds. The certificates are negotiable instruments that pay interest on funds deposited for a specified period of time (often one year), designed to compete with treasury bills, commercial paper, and other short-term investments that have been siphoning away demand deposits. Such certificates offer a relatively high return on a safe investment and the development of a secondary market for trading also provides liquidity for the corporation. Between early 1961 and December 1968 a total of $23 billion in savings was attracted by banks using this new type of financial instrument. In addition, banks have expanded the use of this instrument to attract relatively small amounts of funds from individuals. These so-called consumer certificates of deposits now substantially exceed the large certificates of deposits in amount outstanding.

TABLE 11–8

Deposits in commercial banks at year-end, 1960–1969 (*billions of dollars*)

	Demand*	Time†
1960	115.6	73.3
1961	120.4	82.7
1962	122.9	98.3
1963	127.3	112.6
1964	132.2	127.2
1965	138.7	147.2
1966	167.8	158.8
1967	184.1	182.5
1968	208.9	203.1
1969	208.9	193.7

* Other than interbank and U.S. government.
† Excludes interbank time deposits; U.S. Treasury's time deposits open account; and deposits of Postal Savings System in banks.
Source: *Federal Reserve Bulletin*, various issues.

Effects of the rising total of savings deposits

Observers agree that the growing importance of savings accounts as a source of bank funds is one of the most significant developments in commercial banking. Costs, earnings, liquidity, and loan and investment policies are all affected by this development. The burden of meeting larger interest payments is significant enough to change many banking practices. In addition, bank officials must consider the impact on liquidity and the size of primary and secondary reserves. Since the annual turnover rate of savings accounts is much lower than that of demand deposits, loan and investment maturities can often be lengthened to take advantage of higher yields on long-term investments at a time when higher earnings are needed to meet increased interest payments. One example of this effect is the increased volume of real estate mortgage lending by commercial banks. The Federal Reserve Act includes a provision that allows national commercial banks to make real estate mortgage loans of up to 60% of the savings deposits held. Whereas commercial banks have been traditionally loan oriented, the new trend is making them more savings oriented.

Although savings accounts are much less active than demand deposits, experience indicates that commercial banks suffer more pressure for withdrawals of savings during depressions than do other savings institutions. Some states even require that savings funds be segregated and invested according to special rules. Except for such limitations, banks establish their own general policies and individually decide whether all types of deposits will be pooled or kept separate under the asset allocation approach in which each investment is related to a specific type of deposit.

Credit unions

Credit unions are nonprofit, mutual organizations in which the savings of members are accumulated and loaned to other members, usually at favorable interest rates. Participants are united by some occupational, educational, or residential bond. There is often a cooperative spirit reflecting the missionary ideals of the original founders of the credit union movement, which was introduced in America in 1909. Most of the saving and lending transactions are small, and credit union officials proudly claim that many people motivated to join such organizations would not otherwise accumulate liquid assets.

Credit unions are owned and operated entirely by the members under federal or state charters that provide for some examining and supervisory powers. Officials and advisory committees are elected by the members and usually serve without pay. Sponsoring organizations often provide physical facilities and absorb operating expenses, even to the extent of providing payroll deduction services both for additions to savings and payments on loans for members of the sponsored credit unions. Savers' accounts are technically shares, but redemption is normally immediate upon demand and most members consider their accounts to be savings. Dividends are paid on the shares at a rate which is often set by membership vote. In 1968, 80% of the credit unions paid dividends over 4%, and over 50% paid dividends in excess of 5%.

The initial growth of credit unions was slow, and many organizations had difficulty in finding loan and investment opportunities for accumulated savings, particularly during the war when consumer liquidity increased. This situation has changed and credit unions have experienced the most rapid percentage growth of any savings institution. Between 1948 and the end of 1968 growth occurred as follows: the number of credit unions increased from 9,329 to 23,563; membership from 3.8 to 20.2 million; total shares and deposits from $700 million to $12.2 billion; and loans from $400 million to $11.3 billion. The Credit Union National Association (CUNA) has also actively promoted the international growth of the movement and has a contract with the Agency for International Development and the Peace Corps to assist in the establishment of credit unions in developing nations.

Credit unions are another example of the creation of specialized financial institutions. Individual organizations have remained small during the rapid aggregate growth; about one half have assets of less than $200,000. Because of the small average size, it is probable that credit unions will continue to concentrate on small consumer credit loans where most of their assets are now concentrated.

U.S. savings bonds

During World War II and continuing to the present day, U.S. savings bonds have become familiar savings instruments for millions of people. At this time only Series E and H are sold, following the discontinuance of Series A-D, F, G, J, and K (there are also three old Series E issues.) The total value of all savings bond issues outstanding as of December 31, 1968, was $51.5 billion.

Series E savings bonds are the most familiar to most purchasers and may be acquired in various denominations ranging from $25 to $10,000. Since the bonds are sold at discount, the actual purchase prices begin at $18.75 and stop at $7,500. The bonds are issued in registered form to single owners, or two individuals as coowners, and may not be sold, transferred, or used as collateral. Series E bonds are completely liquid assets because the U.S. government redeems them virtually on demand any time after 60 days from the date of purchase. Interest accrues through increases in the redemption value at the end of each period, and the actual return is dependent on the length of time the bonds are held. If the Series E bond is held to maturity, the yield is 4.25%. The lower return in the early years was devised to discourage early redemptions. Since the yield rises to a level above 4% reasonably soon after purchase, the bonds are now competitive with other savings instruments. Since 1951, owners have been given the option of continuing to hold matured Series E bonds as interest-bearing obligations. The effective interest rate on bonds held beyond maturity is 4.25% compounded semiannually.

Series H savings bonds are purchased mainly by trust accounts and persons with large incomes. They are sold at par in denominations of

$500 to $10,000 in registered form to mature in 10 years. Current income is paid to owners by semiannual interest checks delivered through the mail. Series H bonds also have a progressive interest schedule that increases the yield as the bond matures, so that an average rate of 4.25% is paid on bonds held to maturity.

The Treasury Department, supported by financial institutions and various private groups, has heavily promoted savings bonds as a safe investment with a guaranteed yield that also benefits the nation by providing funds for national security. Financial institutions assist in the sale and redemption of savings bonds over the counter and by mail. Many companies participate by arranging payroll savings plans whereby voluntary deductions are made to purchase savings bonds for employees.

Considering the extreme promotional techniques used in selling the savings bonds, it was feared that a large volume would be redeemed soon after the war. Mass redemptions did not occur, although the amount of new money placed in savings bonds did decline and some premature returns of savings bonds have occurred as interest rates and dividends paid by other savings instruments have increased. The total outstanding of Series E and H savings bonds continues to increase each year, but the total of all issues of savings bonds outstanding is still lower than during the 1950s because of redemptions of other issues that were sold in previous periods.

Questions and problems

1. Why do so many people entrust their savings to specified savings institutions? How would you account for the rapid increase in savings at these institutions? Why have some thrift institutions grown more rapidly than others?

2. Using a *Federal Reserve Bulletin* and a *Survey of Current Business,* determine the current status of savings in our economy.

3. Does the rate of return on savings influence the flow of funds into competing institutions?

4. Why have mutual savings banks failed to maintain their relative share of the flow of savings? Are mutual savings banks dying or remaining active?

5. Why do mutual savings banks have different asset investments than commercial banks? Why are they different from those of the savings and loan associations?

6. Are all commercial banks interested in attracting savings accounts? How does an increase in the size and number of savings accounts affect bank policies?

7. Why do people continue to buy U.S. savings bonds when most sav-

ings institutions offer a higher return? Why does the government continue to sell savings bonds?

8. How would you explain the emergence of savings and loan associations? Is the growth the result of a higher yield? Will the growth continue?

9. What functions are performed by the Federal Reserve System, Federal Deposit Insurance Corporation, Federal Savings and Loan Association, and Federal Home Loan Bank Board?

10. With so many different savings institutions available, why are people interested in credit unions?

Bibliography

Two studies prepared by Raymond W. Goldsmith are basic sources for information on savings and financial institutions. They are *A Study of Savings in the United States* (Princeton, N.J.: Princeton University Press, vols. I and II, 1955; vol. III, 1956) and *Financial Intermediaries in the American Economy since 1900* (Princeton, N.J.: Princeton University Press, 1958).

Current data are found in the *Federal Reserve Bulletin* and the *Survey of Current Business*. The quarterly figures on flow of funds, saving and investment, and the annual surveys of consumer finance in the *Bulletin* are particularly important.

Additional current information is available in annual and special reports of trade associations representing the financial institutions. Among these are the American Bankers Association, the National Association of Mutual Savings Banks, the U.S. Savings and Loan League, and the Credit Union National Association. Information about U.S. government savings bonds, published by the Treasury Department, is available in commercial banks.

CHAPTER 12

Life and casualty insurers

A basic human motivation involves the search for security. Most people are concerned with what the future will hold if they become disabled or lose their income, as well as how their family will fare if they die. Insurance is one way to meet some of the financial uncertainty that arises under these conditions.

Insurance is an institutional device for accumulating a fund to meet losses. Individuals and organizations buy insurance to shift the risk of loss to the insurer. They accomplish this by making periodic payments into a fund. If a large number of people belong to the fund, the payments that they make into it can support the claims that are presented against the fund. The contractual promise to provide protection and service that is given by the insurer provides for restoration, entire or partial, of the insured to the economic position that existed prior to loss. Insurance does not remove the actual peril, but the uncertainties and consequences of large monetary losses are avoided by the insured.

Insurance companies then are one of the most important financial institutions on the economic scene. They not only help individuals meet contingencies, but because they hold substantial amounts of assets, they are capable of transferring funds quickly from one sector of the economy to another. Investments in 1969 amounted to about one third of the nation's total flow of funds, as shown in Chapter 9. This chapter can give only a few examples of the magnitude and economic importance of life and casualty insurers. The discussion will summarize some of the basic policy forms, the importance of reserves held by insurance units, and the investment practices of insurance companies.

Life insurance

It is often said that life insurance protects against dying too soon and against living too long. Well-planned insurance programs provide funds for debt repayment at the time of death and for sustaining surviving dependents, emergency funds for worthwhile projects during the middle years of life, and retirement benefits after family commitments have been fulfilled. The types of policies have changed over the years as social changes have occurred, creating the need for new forms of protection. In spite of these changes the basic goals remain the same: to provide immediate security, creation of a savings program, provision for emergency needs by having the ability to borrow against the accumulation of policy savings, and investment for retirement income.

The average amount of insurance owned per family in the United States at the end of 1969 was $19,500. Since the average disposable family income in that year was $9,600, the life insurance that the average family carried was equal to more than two years of its income. For the country as a whole, the amount of insurance in force was $1.3 trillion.

Most people are aware of the statistic that the expected length of life at birth for women living in the United States is 74 years and the comparable figure for men is 67 years. These averages are inadequate guides for life insurance firms responsible for the accumulation and investment of funds necessary to meet actual death claims. Because the length of human life is unpredictable on an individual basis, life insurers must rely on the statistical principle of the law of large numbers for forecasting death rates in terms of averages for the mass of individuals insured. Analysis of loss records enables insurance actuaries to predict losses with a high degree of accuracy. As long as the number of risk exposures (insured individuals) is large enough, the actual pattern of deaths will approximate, within definable limits of deviation, the underlying probabilities expected. Even when a catastrophe occurs, the diversity of insurers affected normally prevents any failures in the payment of claims.

The experience for life in the United States has been compiled for the years 1959–1961. Life insurance actuaries could use the data (as shown in Table 12–1 for some age groups) to predict that 143 of 100,000 persons, all 30 years of age and selected on a random basis, would die within the next year. It would be impossible to identify the individuals ahead of time, and it is probable that actual fatalities would vary slightly, but actuaries are concerned with average figures. State insurance regulatory authorities use such tables to compute required policy reserves and insurers use them to calculate premium rates.

Types of life insurance contracts

Three basic types of policies are available for protection against death: term, level premium, and endowment. Term contracts are those written for specific time periods although provisions may be made for automatic renewal at the end of the period or conversion into another form of contract without medical examination. No cash value is accumulated from the premium payments, and loans from the insurer are unavailable. All of the premium is devoted to meeting the pure cost of insuring the payment of loss claims plus insurer expenses and profits. No residual rights exist at the termination of the policy. The buyers of term insurance must also pay a progressively higher premium each time the policy is renewed because of the increased probability of death resulting from advancing age. Persons requiring protection for a long

TABLE 12–1

Mortality table—U.S. total population, 1959–1961

Age (years)	Alive at beginning of year*	Number dying during next year	Ratio of those who die to those alive at beginning of year
30	100,000	143	0.00143
31	99,857	151	0.00151
32	99,706	160	0.00160
40	99,042	300	0.00360
41	97,712	330	0.00338

* The number alive at the beginning of each year is the number alive at the beginning of the year before, minus those who died during the year.
Source: *1970 Life Insurance Fact Book,* Institute of Life Insurance, p. 118.

period of time would have to pay very high annual premiums later in life, and coverage is not even available beyond certain ages from many companies. Concentration on protection lowers the initial cost of term insurance below other forms of coverage as show in Table 12–2, but the buyer eventually pays a premium well above the annual rate of a permanent straight life policy. The need for protection during a specific period of time and the lower cost of term insurance relative to the coverage provided are major advantages of this form.

Group insurance plans in which life, disability, and retirement policies are sold to employees or members of an organization without medical examination under a single master policy are usually based on one-year term contracts. Coverage normally ceases when the individual leaves the organization although some policies permit conversion into permanent insurance. The master contract may require a flat premium for all members of the group, or the cost may be based on the amount of protection provided which is often linked to annual salaries. As a result of the interest in fringe benefits, $483 billion of group life insurance, averaging $6,450 per certificate, was outstanding in early 1970, which provided a low-cost base of financial security for many families. The cost to employees is usually lower because the employer may pay all or part of the premium and also absorbs administrative expenses under a single master policy arrangement with the insurer. In 1954 a group policy covering federal employees was started that covered 3 million employees for a total of $37.8 billion in early 1970.

TABLE 12–2

Comparative premiums for different policies, age 22

	Annual rate per $1,000 insurance	Amount of insurance purchased by $100	Cash value at age 65 per $100 premium	Monthly annuity 10 years certain at age 65 (men)
1. Term (5-year renewable and convertible)	$ 5.80	$17,241	$ 0	$ 0
2. Straight life	14.85	6,734	4,141	26.09
3. Straight life (20-year family income)	18.30	5,464	3,360	21.17
4. Life-paid-up-at-65	17.10	5,848	4,298	27.08
5. 20-payment life	26.75	3,738	2,747	17.31
6. Endowment-20 year ...	47.05	2,125	0	0
7. Retirement income at 65 (male)	27.15	3,683	6,095	38.40

Source: Jerome B. Cohen, *Decade of Decision,* prepared by the Educational Division, Institute of Life Insurance with the cooperation of the Health Insurance Institute, 1960. Material is adapted from a table on p. 26.

The absence of savings and the impermanence of the term insurance contract which must be renewed at progressively higher rates causes many insurance buyers to turn to straight life contracts, which are permanent as long as the policyholder fulfills the contract agreements. Since the probability of death increases as the insured grows older, straight life policies usually require a level premium be paid throughout the period of protection. The over-charge during the early years is accumulated and invested to provide the necessary funds to meet loss settlements when the amounts of level premium payments become inadequate. When the effects of compound interest rates on the cash values accumulated are considered, the total cost approximates the term insurance rate. However, under straight life contracts the policyholder has the right to receive the cash values saved and may borrow the entire amount from the insurer or convert the savings into retirement income rather than waiting for a death claim to be filed. Straight life policies, also referred to as *ordinary* and *whole life* contracts, continue to be the basic form. In 1970 ordinary life insurance in force in the United States totaled $679 billion. Purchases of this type of coverage amounted to $112.6 billion in 1969.

Many persons desiring the benefits of whole life insurance prefer to pay the total premiums required over a limited period of time to avoid the burden of payments in later years of life. Settlement of death claims may not occur for many years following the cessation of premiums. Since the fund of accumulated premiums must still be adequate to meet the claim when combined with the investment income, the size of the level premium over the abbreviated period must be larger.

A third type of insurance contract is the endowment policy which pays the entire amount of the policy at the maturity of the contract or immediately, if death should occur first. This form emphasizes the savings aspect of insurance because the premiums collected and invest-ment income earned must be adequate to make a settlement immediately at the end of the contract period. Endowment policies are often used as a forced savings device by persons with specific goals. For example, a father concerned about sending his newly born son to college might purchase a 20-year endowment. If the father died before the end of the period, the principal sum would immediately be available to his benefi-ciary or estate; if he lived, the sum would be available after 20 years to meet the expenses. Endowments are also used as retirement policies by people who accumulate retirement savings and then receive annuity settlement payments. The savings feature makes the premium very high relative to the protection provided.

There are many variations and combinations of the three basic contracts. *Family income* protection combines decreasing term and straight life insurance to provide a monthly income until a specified date when family responsibilities are expected to decline plus the face value of the contract. The number of monthly payments guaranteed decreases as the family matures until only the straight life protection re-mains. Family protection plans are also sold providing a small fraction of the husband's policy amount for each member of the family. Retire-ment income is often based on an endowment with an annuity agree-ment for payment of proceeds. Retirement benefits may also be created by conversion of cash values contained in whole life policies. Educa-tion insurance is similar to a regular endowment except the policy does not mature until the beneficiary is expected to start college even though death of the insured father occurs earlier (premiums would stop at the time of death). Somewhat the same purpose can be achieved by a straight life contract which would provide protection until the beginning of college expenses when the policy would be surrendered to collect the cash values. Mortgage-protection insurance is usually a nonrenewable term contract that decreases in size as the mortgage obligation declines. Credit life insurance designed to pay off the balance due on a loan if the borrower dies is the newest and fastest growing type of protection, which indicates the popularity of installment plan credit in the United States. Early in 1970 credit life insurance outstanding totaled $83.8 billion.

Other types of policies

The two other major types of protection also deserve brief discussion. Industrial life insurance has historically been sold to low-income workers unable to purchase the minimum coverage of $1,000 required by most standard life contracts. The average policy size was $490 at the beginning of 1970. Premiums paid in small coins are collected weekly or monthly through door-to-door visits. In 1970 there were 79 million industrial life insurance contracts in force totaling $38.6 billion. However, the expenses of premium collection and the costs of selling such small policies make this form of protection uneconomical. Prosperity has enabled many lower-middle income buyers to acquire standard life contracts, and the rise of group insurance now provides the minimum protection for many families that previously would have purchased small industrial policies. Industrial insurance policies are still sold; $6.5 billion of this type was sold in 1969; but a slight rate of decrease in the annual amount was observable in the latter 1960s.

Health and accident coverage is the second form which can only be referred to briefly despite the importance of this type of protection. A wide variety of policies may be purchased individually or as a package to provide weekly payments to replace a fraction of regular income lost from being unable to work, lump-sum payments for death caused by an accident, income payments for life where total or partial disability has been suffered, lump-sum payments for bodily dismemberment, costs of hospitalization, physicians and surgeons fees, and major medical policies for unusually serious medical problems. The high probability of suffering accident or sickness and the financial burdens of medical treatment and loss of income make health and accident coverage a vital part of all personal insurance programs. There are now over 150 million Americans covered by some type of protection described above. In 1968 insurance companies paid out $6.8 billion in claims, and the total continues to rise each year as the number of people insured and the size of policies increases.

The American public has continued to increase its ownership of life insurance until a total of $1,348.9 billion was outstanding at the beginning of 1970. Of this total, $1,284.5 billion was placed with mutual and capital stock companies known as legal reserve insurers; the balance was with various fraternal and assessment organizations ($22.8 billion), savings banks ($3.6 billion), and the veterans insurance program ($38 billion). The pattern of life for millions of policyholders in the United States has been deeply affected by the protective and savings aspects of life insurance.

Annuities

In annuity contracts the insurer agrees to pay an income monthly or annually for a predetermined period or, more commonly, for the remaining lifetime of the insured. Insurers average the life expectancy of buyers of annuities in the same way other life insurance commitments are determined, except that different mortality tables are used. However, the insurance risk is changed from protection against premature death to protection against outliving the savings set aside for old age. For example, assume that a couple aged 65 have saved $25,000. A return of 5% could be reasonably expected from a safe investment which would provide a monthly income slightly in excess of $100 per month. Withdrawal of any of the savings would proportionately reduce the monthly income. The same $25,000 could purchase an annuity which would provide monthly payments of about $120 until both husband and wife become deceased. If the annuity income is made contingent upon only the husband's life the amount would increase to about $165 per month. Because the obligations of the insurer cease at the time of death, it is possible that the couple might receive less than the purchase price of $25,000 if they die before the expected time; however, maximum income is available under this arrangement and protection until death is provided.

Annuities may be either immediate or deferred. An immediate lifetime income may be provided by a lump-sum payment to the insurer from the conversion of cash values in a straight life policy or from personal funds such as an inheritance. Persons with spectacularly large but temporary earnings, such as professional athletes, entertainers, and successful authors also purchase this type to avoid subsequent impoverishment after their earnings decline. Deferred annuities begin later in life, usually at retirement, after payment of a series of premiums. Under a joint life and survivor annuity the income is paid to two or more persons, such as husband and wife, until the last survivor dies. The income received is lower than in the case of a single annuitant. Arrangements can be made to set the payments at a higher rate prior to the death of one of the joint annuitants and special guarantees of a minimum number of payments may be added to meet the needs of dependents for a certain minimum period of time after the death of the insured. A refund annuity may also be arranged in which the estate receives a refund of the amount of the annuity purchase price not paid out in benefits at the time of death. The size of the periodic income payments are naturally lower under such special arrangements. Early in 1970 there were 9.1 million annuity contracts outstanding with life insurance companies (5.5 million in group annuity form) with an annual income obligation of $25 billion. Some payments under this obligation have already started and the remaining portion will be paid in the future.

Most annuities are created by group pension plans included in employee benefit programs, and the number of individual annuities has actually declined in recent years. An estimated 33 million people were covered in 1970 by privately financed pension plans which controlled pension reserves of $119 billion. The noninsured private plans discussed in Chapter 15 served about 23 million persons and controlled an estimated $81 billion in assets. Life insurance companies are also important factors in the pension field through the sale of insured pension plans involving special annuity contracts. The deposit-type plans whereby a fund is accumulated for the purchase of an immediate annuity at retirement and the deferred group annuity plans which require the continuous purchase of paid-up annuity contracts each year are described on page 330. Between 1930 and 1970 the number of persons covered by insured pension plans increased from 100,000 to 10 million, and the size of reserves jumped from $100 million to $37 billion.

Variable annuities

Proceeds of life insurance—both death claims and annuity-type payments—have been subject to erosion by inflation. Many people have been disappointed to find their life insurance and annuity proceeds, which were considered ample at the time of purchase, are inadequate because of inflationary trends. Regular insurance contracts cannot match increased living costs because policy claims are stated in fixed dollar amounts, and policyholder reserves are invested in bonds, mortgages, and other fixed dollar assets. The *variable annuity* is an attempt to meet the risk of inflation by investment of policyholder reserves in common stocks. The value of the annuity and the size of the monthly payment fluctuate as the value of the common stocks purchased changes. The policyholder is credited in numerical units based on actuarial rules of life expectancy. After retirement the amount of the annuity is computed by multiplying the number of units acquired by the dollar value of each unit, which is set according to the current value of the total investment portfolio. As long as fluctuations in the value of securities purchased match changes in the general price level the annuitant is protected against losses of purchasing power. Studies of long-term common stock price movements suggest there may be a rough correlation with changes in the cost-of-living index; but over short time periods the two statistical measures may actually move in opposite directions.

In 1956 two small firms began selling the new policies in the District of Columbia, and one major insurance company attempted to enter the field in the early 1960s. These companies met strong opposition from other life insurers critical of the fluctuating values of policies and from the securities industry, particularly the open-end investment companies. The question finally reached the courts where it was ruled that insurance companies selling variable annuities to the public are subject to regulation by the Securities and Exchange Commission as well as the various insurance regulatory agencies. An SEC ruling in January of 1963 affirming this jurisdictional power for a time discouraged the interest of many companies. The plans of one major insurer to sell such policies to self-employed persons, such as doctors, lawyers, and independent businessmen and their employees did receive SEC approval in July of 1964. By 1970, variable annuities were rather generally available. About 320,000 persons held such contracts and more than half of the contracts were with insurance companies.

Life insurance investment policies

In 1970 there were 1,820 legal reserve companies, of which 90% were organized as stock companies and owned by public investors. The oldest and largest life insurers are the mutual companies owned by the policyholders which explains why approximately 57% of the life insurance business and 71% of total assets are controlled by mutual companies. The largest 50 companies had insurance outstanding in excess of $1 trillion at the beginning of 1970. These large companies sell policies throughout the nation. Mutual policyholders *participate* in the investment income and excess premium collections through the receipt of dividends which may be collected or used to reduce premiums. Most stock company policies are nonparticipating.

The insurance dollar: income and disbursements

The life insurance company dollar at the end of 1969 was divided as shown in Table 12–3.

TABLE 12-3

Life insurance company dollar, 1969

Receipts:		Disbursements:	
Premiums	78.2¢	Benefit payments in year	55.2¢
Net investment earnings and		Additions to policy reserves	20.6
other income	21.8	Special reserves and surplus	1.5
		Commissions to agents	7.1
		Home office and	
		other expenses	9.9
		Taxes	4.5
		Dividends to stockholders	1.2
Totals	100.0¢		100.0¢

Source: Adapted from the *1970 Life Insurance Fact Book*, Institute of Life Insurance, p. 60.

The tremendous size of the life insurance industry is clearly indicated by the statistical summary in Table 12–4.

It is interesting that benefits paid to policyholders while still alive are much larger than death settlements paid to beneficiaries even though the primary reason for buying life insurance is to provide financial protection for dependents. Living benefits paid in 1969 included matured endowments of $953 million; disability payments of $205 million; annuity payments of $1.6 billion; policy surrender values of $2.7 billion; and policy dividends of $3.3 billion.

After paying benefits, taxes, dividends, and operating expenses, the remaining inflow of funds is added to policy and special reserve accounts. The discussion of types of contracts described how the payment of level premiums results in an overcharge in the early years relative to the risk of loss. Insurance regulatory law requires that reserves be maintained to meet the rising level of claims resulting from the aging of

TABLE 12-4

Life insurance industry statistics (*millions of dollars*)

	Life insurance in force*	Premium receipts	Investment and other income	Death benefits	Living benefits
1940	$ 115,530	$ 3,887	$ 1,771	$ 995	$1,669
1945	151,762	5,159	2,515	1,280	1,388
1950	234,168	8,189	3,148	1,590	2,141
1955	372,332	12,546	3,998	2,241	3,142
1960	586,448	17,365	4,642	3,346	4,772
1965	900,554	24,604	8,563	4,831	6,585
1969	1,284,529	33,996	11,632	6,758	8,766

* Life insurance in force does not include veterans, fraternal, assessment, and savings bank coverage as follows, stated in billions: 1940—$6.7; 1945—$105.8; 1950—$54.1; 1955—$53.2; 1960—$57.9; 1965—$19.5; 1969—$26.4.

Source: Adapted from the *1970 Life Insurance Fact Book*, Institute of Life Insurance, pp. 22, 47, 57, 101.

policyholders, and conservative companies usually maintain larger reserves than are legally required. Since the buyer of insurance is actually paying in advance for future protection, the cash surrender values represented by premium payments, plus interest at a guaranteed rate on the accumulated amount, belongs rightfully to each policyholder and may be collected by surrendering or converting the policy. The cash value of savings may also be borrowed from the insurer. The total protection specified by the policy, less the amount borrowed, remains in force during the loan period.

The savings aspect makes life insurers an important source of investment capital for private and public organizations. The flow of premiums, investment income, sales of assets and repayments of mortgages and bonds has created a growing pool of funds. Between 1920 and 1950 reserves increased from $5.5 billion to $53.6 billion; by year-end 1969 the total jumped to $147.5 billion.[1]

Despite the greater absolute total of life insurance reserves, the relative savings position of the industry has declined because of rapid expansion by the other financial institutions and a slowdown in the pace of life insurance savings accumulation. The slower growth is attributed to the emphasis on group term insurance which lacks savings benefits; increased surrenders of policies; more rapid withdrawal of policy proceeds by beneficiaries; policyholder loans; the effects of higher operating expenses; and the negative influence on the sale of new policies resulting from inflation and development of an inflationary psychology among the American public causing them to distrust long-term fixed dollar obligations. The life insurance industry is hopeful that the trend will be reversed by a vigorous emphasis upon the "living" benefits of cash value type policies and the reduced importance of inflation as a chronic threat. The growing affluence of some sectors of the general public is also a favorable sign for the industry because prosperity permits families to purchase insurance at an earlier age.

Distribution of assets

The accumulation of policyholder reserves and annual premiums to provide protection against risk creates a vast reservoir of funds which have made life insurance companies a large source of personal savings for investment in the public and private sectors of our economy. The size and diversity of these investments is shown in Table 12–5.

The assets fall into several major categories: corporate bonds, mortgages, government bonds, policyholder loans, income real estate, and

---

[1] Figure defined as reserves of life insurance companies, plus dividends left to accumulate, less premium notes and policy loans. Statistics drawn from *Mutual Savings Banking National Fact Book, 1970*, p. 36.

TABLE 12–5

Distribution of assets of U.S. life insurance companies, 1920–1969 (dollar amounts in millions)

	Bonds						Mortgages	Real estate	Policy loans	Stocks	Miscellaneous assets	Total
	U.S. government	Foreign government	State, provincial and local	Railroads	Public utility	Industrial						
1920	$ 830	$ 169	$ 350	$1,775	$ 125	$ 49	$ 2,442	$ 172	$ 859	$ 75	$ 474	$ 7,320
1930	319	160	1,023	2,931	1,631	367	7,598	548	2,807	519	977	18,880
1935	2,853	189	1,385	2,625	2,114	575	5,357	1,990	3,540	583	1,705	23,216
1940	5,767	288	2,392	2,830	4,273	1,542	5,972	2,065	3,091	605	1,977	30,802
1945	20,583	915	1,047	2,948	5,212	1,900	6,636	857	1,962	999	1,738	44,797
1950	13,459	1,060	1,547	3,137	10,587	9,526	16,102	1,445	2,413	2,103	2,591	64,020
1955	8,576	410	2,596	3,912	13,968	18,179	29,445	2,581	3,290	3,633	3,742	90,432
1960	6,427	437	4,576	3,668	16,719	26,728	41,771	3,765	5,231	4,981	5,273	119,576
1965	5,119	859	5,476	3,314	17,046	38,338	60,013	4,681	7,678	9,126	7,234	158,884
1969	4,124	647	5,463	3,608	17,963	49,968	72,027	5,912	13,825	13,707	9,964	197,208
						Percentage amounts						
1920	11.3	2.3	4.8	24.3	1.7	.7	33.4	2.3	11.7	1.0	6.5	100.0
1930	1.7	.9	5.4	15.5	8.6	1.9	40.2	2.9	14.9	2.8	5.2	100.0
1935	12.3	.8	7.3	11.3	9.1	2.5	23.1	8.6	15.2	2.5	7.3	100.0
1940	18.7	1.0	7.8	9.2	13.9	5.0	19.4	6.7	10.0	2.0	6.3	100.0
1945	45.9	2.1	2.3	6.6	11.6	4.3	14.8	1.9	4.4	2.2	3.9	100.0
1950	21.0	1.7	2.4	5.0	16.5	14.9	25.1	2.2	3.8	3.3	4.1	100.0
1955	9.5	.4	3.0	4.3	15.5	20.1	32.6	2.9	3.6	4.0	4.1	100.0
1960	5.4	.3	3.8	3.1	14.0	22.4	34.9	3.1	4.4	4.2	4.4	100.0
1965	2.9	.4	3.2	2.0	10.0	24.6	37.8	3.0	4.8	5.7	4.5	100.0
1969	2.1	.4	2.7	1.8	9.1	25.4	36.5	3.0	7.0	7.0	5.0	100.0

Source: Adapted from *1970 Life Insurance Fact Book*, Institute of Life Insurance, pp. 70–71.

various miscellaneous accounts. Corporate bonds comprise the largest single category, largely as a result of the rapid increase in the holdings of industrial and miscellaneous issues. A major factor in the historical shift to corporate bonds is the use of *direct placements,* in which corporate securities are sold directly to individual, or groups of, insurance companies rather than to the public. Direct placements enable life insurers to invest large amounts of capital for long periods of time at attractive yields backed by protective provisions in the lending agreement. It has been estimated that over two thirds of the corporate bonds held by life companies were acquired through direct placements. In dollar terms, the life insurance industry provided about one third of the net new debt money obtained by corporate enterprise in the capital markets between 1950 and 1969 for expansion, modernization, and working capital. These figures do not reflect the tremendous sums refinanced.

During the time period covered in Table 12–5, the proportion of railroad bonds continuously declined and even the dollar amounts have diminished since 1955. This trend demonstrates the historical shift of interest from railroad securities to utility and industrial company issues. Large amounts of utility bonds have been added to life company portfolios since 1945, and it is now estimated that two fifths of the long-term financing of privately owned utility firms is supplied by this group. For example, life insurance firms purchased the entire $15.3 million mortgage bond issue of the Yankee Atomic Electric Company, located in Rowe, Massachusetts, when it was formed by several New England utilities to develop commercial atomic energy. Life companies also make direct loans to corporations such as the financing provided several airlines for conversion to jet equipment. Some insurers have established special departments to facilitate lending to small business firms which cannot acquire long-term capital through public bond issues.

Life insurers have never held large amounts of common or preferred stocks, and until 1951 companies doing business in New York state were prohibited from making such investments. Modification of the law and rising stock market values stimulated increased interest in equity securities during the 1950s and 1960s, but the total remains relatively small because of statutory limits over the amount of stock that can be purchased and the portfolio management policies of individual companies which vary widely. Many insurers still believe the uncertainty associated with fluctuating stock market prices is an inappropriate risk for companies expected to meet fixed dollar contractual obligations. Nevertheless, many firms have a higher proportion of their assets in common stocks than the 4 to 5% average figure for 1969 would indicate.

Mortgages on residential, commercial, and farm properties are, by a small margin, the second largest category. During the 1920s and 1930s mortgages were the largest single form of investment for life companies. Total holdings at the end of 1969 amounted to over $72 billion, or 37% of total industry assets. In relative terms, life insurers have historically represented approximately 20% of the nation's sources of mortgage funds except during the depression years of 1932 to 1936 and the wartime period 1943 to 1945. It is expected that the upward trend indicated in Table 12–5 will be continued barring any major change in the demand for housing or in yields on alternative investments. A breakdown of the total indicates that close to two fifths of the mortgages are on one- to four-family residential properties under FHA insured contracts, VA guaranteed mortgages, or conventional contracts. Of the $7.5 billion in new mortgages acquired by life insurers in 1969, $6.1 billion were of the conventional type. Approximately one half of the mortgage holdings are on apartment buildings and commercial properties and the small remaining amount is invested in farm mortgages. The proportional amount of farm mortgages has declined since the beginning of the century although the absolute total has increased slightly since 1945.

During World War II the needs of the federal government dominated investment policies, and U.S. government bonds became the dominant category rising to a record level of 46% of total assets in 1945. The wartime experience, however, was unusual. Although U.S. government bonds have traditionally been a popular investment because of the liquidity and stability offered, the amount and relative proportion has steadily declined as firms have sought more attractive yields. Early in 1970, the industry held $4 billion of these bonds, which amounted to 2% of total assets.

On occasion, life companies buy short-term treasury bills and certificates while waiting for long-term opportunities to develop, but the dollar amounts of such temporary investments are usually small relative to the aggregate totals. The popularity of U.S. government securities has never extended to foreign government bonds and the total amount of such foreign investment, consisting largely of Canadian issues, remains very small. While investments in both U.S. and foreign government bonds have declined, there has been considerable interest in bonds issued by states, provinces, counties, cities, towns, townships, school districts, and public authorities. Continued increases in the population combined with growing demands for public services have rapidly increased the financial needs of these public organizations. Investment in this category by life companies is now more than equal to purchases of U.S. bonds and the upward trend will probably continue.

The remaining three asset categories are reasonably self-explanatory. Policy loans refer to borrowings from insurance companies by policyholders based on the accumulated cash value. Interest is charged on these loans because the company is deprived of the funds needed for investments to provide income to meet future claims. The total amounts of loans traditionally have varied inversely with economic activity, but the typical pattern has been broken in recent years as the amount of loans has increased during a period of prosperity. Policy loans have been taken at rates fixed in the insurance contract and the funds reinvested in higher yielding money market instruments. Real estate is another outlet for investment funds. Approximately three fifths of the 1969 total of $5.9 billion was placed in commercial income-producing properties including office buildings, department stores, shopping centers, and factories which are leased to tenants, and another 10% was invested in large housing developments. The remaining total represents ownership interests in home and branch office facilities. Miscellaneous assets include special equipment leased to other firms such as jet aircraft, railroad cars, trucks, and automobiles; cash; and premiums receivable.

Investment principles of life insurance companies

The investment practices of life insurance firms are shaped by financial considerations of safety, liquidity, diversification, maximization of income, and by regulatory commissions and public interests. It is assumed that the contractual arrangement will last for many years and that accumulated savings will be left intact until the death of the policyholder occurs or the exercising of various options at the time of retirement. On the average this period will last many years. Life insurance claims can be predicted with a high degree of accuracy using actuarial techniques. The extended time periods and the predictability of the pattern of losses enable life insurance companies to place investments in long-term assets such as corporate and government bonds and in real estate mortgages. Obligations with suitable maturities may be purchased to coincide with expected settlement claims. Beyond these basic assumptions, it must be emphasized that safety of the invested principal is of extreme importance because life insurance companies must be ready to settle claims quickly and in reality are investing the savings of the policyholders thus creating a fiduciary responsibility. Real estate mortgages, some of which are additionally secured by government agency insurance or guarantees, and high-grade bonds provide necessary safety.

Insurers must also consider liquidity needs even though policy reserves are not equivalent to short-term deposits subject to withdrawal, with the limited exception of policyholder loans. Cash is needed to meet normal receipts and disbursement transactions and to provide for unforeseen death and survival benefits, heavy cash value refunds resulting from policy surrenders, and policyholder loans. These cash needs are however capable of being predicted quite accurately, as are cash inflows in the form of premiums and mortgage and bond repayments. It has been suggested that insurance companies might maintain liquid assets to exploit unusually favorable investment opportunities; however, most life insurance portfolio managers follow the policy of investing available funds rather than waiting for changes in the marketplace. In general, safety and liquidity requirements are met by relying on the types of investments already described and through carefully diversifying holdings by industry and geographical location.

Life insurance and annuity contracts include an assumed rate of interest that insurers agree to pay on policyholder reserves on a compounded basis over the policy period. This commitment forces life insurance companies to seek investment returns that are adequate to cover the interest payments and provide a margin of profit for building reserves and making dividend distributions to stockholders or policyholders. Investments with fixed rates of return, regular income payments, and assured marketability are most appropriate for these purposes, but portfolio managers must balance the goal of safety against the benefits of higher investment income which reduces the net cost of insurance. As the large portfolio of U.S. government bonds acquired during World War II provided a return of approximately 2½%, life companies have had to replace them with higher yield issues. The demand for capital and the emphasis on acquiring corporate securities has improved the overall rate of return on life insurance company assets in recent years as follows: 1925, 5.11%; 1935, 3.70%; 1945, 3.11%; 1955, 3.51%; 1965, 4.61%; and 1969, 5.12%. The recent average rate of return adequately covers the guaranteed commitment.

Social goals also have some influence on the investment policies of life insurance companies. Since the U.S. economy relies mainly on the price system for the allocation of resources, life insurance investments contribute to society when the capital is channeled to opportunities with the greatest need. Demand and supply factors determine the price (rate of return) that must be paid to attract capital. To the extent that portfolio managers seek to maximize return on investment, capital is automatically directed to investments with maximum marginal efficiency of capital which improves the allocation of resources.

In specific terms, social and economic benefits have resulted from the support given to industrial development and expansion of housing through mortgage financing. Life insurance companies have also entered the housing field directly by building a number of large, multifamily housing projects. Insurance firms deserve recognition for many innovative financial practices including: sales-leaseback arrangements whereby real property is purchased from a company and then leased back to the selling corporation under a long-term agreement; oil and gas production loans based on expected revenues from proven underground reserves;

the financing of pipelines based on distribution contracts; cooperation with commercial banks in extending term loans; and the creation of mortgage loans for movable physical assets. Another innovation has been the support given to various state and area development agencies formed to attract industry to specific locales. These organizations rely on financial institutions, including life insurance firms, for credit to assist in the financing of the new industries attracted. Attempts have also been made to increase the number of loans to small businesses.

Regulation of the insurance industry

All states have laws covering the conduct of insurance business. Insurance statutes controlling investment policies prescribe permissible limits for determining how much of the firm's assets may be invested in each category. These laws are administered by state insurance departments that also license companies to sell insurance within the state. Many state laws are based on the regulations of New York state because of that state's early enactment of model legislation. In addition, the New York Superintendent of Insurance is empowered to require insurance companies domiciled in other states, but licensed to sell insurance in New York, to comply with the investment laws established for New York based firms. State laws also prescribe methods for valuation of securities and the preparation of financial statements and in general attempt to protect public interest by preventing discreditable sales and investment practices.

On occasion life insurance companies have become bankrupt—a socially, as well as economically, undesirable occurrence because of the nature of the contractual obligation and the expectations of policyholders. There is no way of determining how many failures would have occurred without regulation, but it appears that state commissions have been generally successful in preventing abuses which would be injurious to the image of the many reputable firms. Despite the basic protection created by regulation, buyers of insurance should carefully consider the financial status and business reputation of the insurer before purchasing coverage.

Fire, property, casualty, and other forms of insurance

The second field of insurance covers the risks of property and liability affecting businesses and individuals. Because of the more uncertain nature of physical risks, the timing and size of losses cannot be forecasted as accurately as in the case of life insurance; however, the statistical law of large numbers still applies. For example, it is possible to predict the number of fires that will occur by analyzing historical loss records when a large number of buildings are evaluated. In new forms of insurance, such as coverage of nuclear explosion risks, underwriters must use greater personal judgment because empirical evidence is unavailable. Because property losses are not inevitable, safety engineering efforts to lower the chances of injury and decrease the severity of losses are almost as important as the actual insurance protection provided, and insurers have concentrated on the prevention of fire and accidents. The following list summarizes some of the many forms of insurance available:

1. Insurance against damage by fire and related risks of lightning, wind, smoke, hail, riots, water, earthquakes, etc. Coverage of loss of earnings for a specified period following a fire may also be acquired.
2. Insurance of ocean marine transportation and inland marine risks including coverage of movable property such as clothes, cameras, etc. under personal property floaters.
3. Coverage of medical costs and loss of income resulting from accident or illness.
4. Insurance of legal liability and court costs for injury of persons or property caused by irresponsible acts. This liability is assumed by drivers of automobiles, owners of aircraft, sportsmen, owners of business and residential property, and parents.
5. Insurance of employers for workmen's compensation claims resulting from work-connected injuries and deaths.
6. Insurance against loss from theft, burglary, robbery, and forgery.
7. Insurance of losses arising from the infidelity of employees resulting in embezzlement of funds and stolen property.
8. Surety bonds which are related to insurance contracts because the bond guarantees that certain acts will be performed as contracted.
9. Title insurance is used to support the certification of a lawyer or title company concerning the title to real property.
10. Insurance against unexpected credit losses on accounts receivable.
11. Miscellaneous coverages including rain, crop, boiler explosion, glass, nuclear explosion, and any other type of risk an insurer will accept.

Capital stock companies comprised about two thirds of the total number of property and casualty insurers in the United States and accounted for approximately 70% of the business and 76% of industry assets in 1968. Until the late 1940s there was a sharp dividing line between life underwriters and property and casualty insurers. Even within the broad second category firms tended to specialize in the fire, marine, credit, and liability fields. In recent years there has been a trend toward diversification into many insurance lines through the creation of new departments and individual subsidiaries.

The greater degree of uncertainty requires that property and casualty insurance premiums contain a fairly wide margin of profit to meet unexpected losses from accumulated reserves. Insurers further protect themselves against localized catastrophes through a system of reinsurance whereby risks are split up and distributed among several insurance companies. Nevertheless, adverse loss experiences may occur and premiums charged must reflect the risk. Because actual loss settlements are often less than one half of the premiums collected, many mutual companies have been formed in an attempt to save the portion of premiums not required for loss claims and operating expenses. Many of these mutuals limit their membership to high-grade risks which are expected to have better-than-average loss experiences and then give large premium refunds to members with good records. Property and casualty insurance may also be underwritten by financially responsible persons individually or in syndicates. The famous Lloyds of London is an organization where individual members assemble to participate in syndicates formed to insure against marine transportation risks and a variety of miscellaneous perils including the famous examples of insuring the fingers of a violinist or the nose of an entertainer. The law of large numbers still applies because the underwriting of a large number of unique risks makes the probability of individual losses manageable.

Investment policies of fire, property, and casualty insurers

Property and casualty insurance policies are normally written for one, three, or five years, and the obligations of the insurer terminate at the end of the period. Any premiums collected in excess of loss settlements belong to the insurance company. The absence of cash accumulations equivalent to life insurance policyholder reserves reduces the absolute size of total assets of property and casualty insurers, but the industry is still extremely important as indicated by the latest published figures, the 1968 statistical summary, that show premiums of $26 billion and accumulated surplus of $19.1 billion. The total admitted assets of this group have moved upward as shown in Table 12–6 and the trend is likely to continue.

The distribution of aggregate assets and liabilities is shown in Table 12–7. The liabilities include two major categories: a reserve for actual and anticipated loss claims and an unearned premium reserve representing the portion of the premium paid in advance that is unexpired at the date of the financial statement. Although total loss claims will normally be less than the total reserves, the insurer is required to consider these two major obligations in establishing investment policies. Other liabilities include commissions, taxes, loans, and a variety of special claims. The capital and reserve accounts are roughly equivalent to the net worth account found in most firms.

The bulk of the assets are invested in securities, particularly in U.S. government, and state, municipal, and special revenue bonds to fulfill liquidity requirements. Further diversification is obtained by investing in railroad, utility, and miscellaneous bonds, but the size of mortgage, real estate, and collateral loan commitments is very small. Analysis of Table 12–7 also indicates that stock companies invest a sizable percentage of their funds in common stocks. The investment practices of individual companies vary widely, and these aggregate figures are only crude approximations.

TABLE 12–6

Total admitted assets of stock, mutual, reciprocals and American Lloyds property and casualty insurers, 1935–1968 (*millions of dollars*)

1935	$ 4,160	1955	$22,304
1940	5,145	1960	30,132
1945	7,851	1963	41,843
1950	13,477	1968	51,226

Source: *Best's Fire and Casualty Aggregates and Averages* (New York: Alfred M. Best Company, Inc., 1969), p. 1.

Four factors determine the investment policies of property and casualty insurers: (1) state insurance regulations; (2) diversification goals; (3) liquidity and safety requirements; and (4) incentives to maximize investment income. Insurance firms in this category are also regulated by state agencies that check on solvency, evaluate the quality of investments, and limit the size of individual investments. Amounts equal to minimum capital requirements must be invested in U.S. government, state and municipal bonds, and real estate mortgages. Insurers are also expected to hold investments equal to the total loss and unearned premium reserves in the categories listed above plus corporate bonds, mortgage loans, preferred stocks, and other high-grade investments. After meeting these minimum requirements, insurance firms may invest surplus funds in stocks and other bonds with certain limitations. The state regulations of New York have an important influence because insurers wishing to do business in New York must meet its requirements. Diversification is an important principle for all investors, but property and casualty insurers must be particularly careful to spread the risk of portfolio losses because of the short-term, contractual nature of insurance obligations. Most firms achieve diversification by investing in different industries and geographical areas and by limiting holdings in specific properties or institutions.

TABLE 12–7

Distribution of assets and liabilities of fire and casualty companies as of December 31, 1968 (millions of dollars)

	819 stock companies	%	326 mutuals	%	45 reciprocals	%	15 American Lloyds	%
Admitted assets								
Bonds:								
U.S. government	$ 3382.5		$ 1755.4		$ 109.9		$18.0	
Other government	196.5		81.8		3.3		.3	
State and municipal	4466.9		1969.4		570.2		3.0	
Special revenue	5224.1		1834.9		135.6		8.8	
Railroad	74.6		147.4		21.4		—	
Utility	1068.5		815.8		89.9		—	
Miscellaneous	1925.5		899.4		41.7		.1	
Total bonds	$16338.7	43.3	$ 7504.1	65.5	$ 972.0	67.4	$30.3	50.2
Common stocks	14318.8	38.0	2077.4	18.1	171.2	11.9	4.2	7.0
Preferred stocks	1050.2	2.8	330.9	2.9	58.5	4.1	.3	0.5
Mortgages	80.2	0.2	103.6	0.9	3.7	0.3	—	—
Real estate	485.0	1.3	252.8	2.2	29.5	2.0	.2	0.3
Collateral loans	43.6	0.1	4.2		.2		.0	0.1
Cash	1008.3	2.7	290.6	2.5	44.1	3.1	3.8	6.4
Premium balances	2763.9	7.3	567.9	5.0	113.0	7.8	4.5	7.5
Other assets	1602.1	4.3	326.7	2.9	50.0	3.5	17.0	28.1
Total Admitted Assets	$37690.9	100.0	$11458.3	100.0	$1442.2	100.0	$60.3	100.0
Liabilities								
Total liabilities	$22804.2	60.5	$ 8030.9	70.1	$1019.2	70.7	$38.1	63.1
Capital paid up	1499.8	4.0	—		—		—	—
Net surplus	10135.9	26.8	2941.6	25.7	353.4	24.5	18.8	31.2
Voluntary reserves	3250.9	8.7	393.5	3.4	58.1	4.0	.1	0.2
Guaranty funds	—		92.3	0.8	11.2	0.8	3.1	5.1
Subscribers deposits*	—		—		.3		.2	0.3
Total Liabilities	$37690.9	100.0	$11458.3	100.0	$1442.2	100.0	$60.3	100.0

* Referred to as underwriters deposit for American Lloyds.
Source: *Best's Fire and Casualty Aggregates and Averages* (New York: Alfred M. Best, Inc., 1969).

Liquidity, the ability to convert investments into cash for the settlement of claims, and safety are also vital factors in portfolio management because of the uncertain pattern of claims and the dangers of catastrophic loss. A company might be forced to default on claims despite the availability of adequate investments if the immediate marketability of specific securities is poor. This requirement explains the large size of cash and premium balances accounts and the emphasis on U.S. government, state and municipal bonds, and high-grade corporate securities. These insurers also maintain substantially more liquidity than life insurers because of the short-term characteristic of the contracts.

A fourth principle concerns the maximization of investment income through various portfolio policies. Some firms limit their investments to U.S. government and other riskless securities; other firms with free funds left after meeting basic requirements prefer to seek the higher yields and potential appreciation associated with equity investments. Capital stock companies in particular place a large proportion of their assets in common stocks. Profits of stock insurance firms are taxed at the normal corporate income tax rate, but only 15% of the total dividends received from domestic investments which have already been subject to the tax are included in the taxable income. The effective tax rate on total dividends is thus approximately $7\frac{1}{2}\%$ which compares favorably with the regular tax applied to interest income. The larger ratio of net worth to total assets in property and casualty firms relative to life insurers also enables this group to bear the risks of fluctuating market values associated with equity investments.

Property and casualty insurance firms also serve the dual role of providing risk protection and the services of financial intermediaries for the accumulation of capital. The nature of investments and obligations differs from other financial institutions, but the industry is a major part of our financial structure and will undoubtedly continue to be so in the future.

Questions and problems

1. What are the major types of risks faced in life? Which risks are insurable and why do they qualify for insurance?
2. How does the principle of insurance benefit society? Are any harmful effects created? If so, why?
3. Identify the major types of life insurance and justify the existence of so many diverse forms of policies.
4. What is the law of large numbers and why is it such an important principle in insurance?
5. How does a variable annuity differ from a regular annuity?
6. Why are life insurance companies now emphasizing the living bene-

fit of their policies? Why does the policyholder own the accumulated cash values and what rights does this ownership provide?

7. Identify the major types of asset investments of life insurers and the underlying principles justifying each type of investment.

8. Why have the life insurance companies avoided the purchase of common stocks?

9. How would you explain the variations in investment policies of various life insurance companies?

10. Why are life insurance companies regulated and how is the regulation enforced?

11. Can losses in the property and casualty fields of insurance be anticipated as accurately as in life insurance?

12. In what ways are the investment policies of property and casualty insurers the same as life insurance companies? In what ways are they different?

Bibliography

A large amount of information is published on the insurance industry and reference to a library card catalog will disclose many texts and technical materials. Two monographs prepared for the Commission on Money and Credit are useful: *Life Insurance Companies as Financial Institutions* (Englewood Cliffs, N.J.: Prentice-Hall, Inc., 1962) and *Property and Casualty Insurance Companies: Their Role as Financial Intermediaries* also published by Prentice-Hall, Inc., in 1962. The pamphlet by Jerome B. Cohen, *Decade of Decision*, prepared for the Institute of Life Insurance and Health Insurance Institute in 1960 is particularly informative.

Many trade and professional organizations publish statistical and informative material including the *Life Insurance Fact Book, Insurance Facts* relating to property and liability insurance and *Source Book of Health Insurance Data.* A very detailed annual publication on property and casualty insurance is *Best's Fire and Casualty Aggregates and Averages* (New York: Alfred M. Best Co., Inc.). Current articles frequently appear in the *Journal of Finance* and insurance industry journals.

Several books on the theory of risk and insurance are also of interest: A. H. Willett, *The Economic Theory of Risk and Insurance* (Philadelphia: University of Pennsylvania Press, 1951); F. H. Knight, *Risk Uncertainty and Profit* (Boston: Houghton-Mifflin Co., 1921); C. O. Hardy, *Risk and Risk-Bearing* (Chicago: University of Chicago Press, 1923); Irving Pfeffer, *Insurance and Economic Theory* (Homewood, Ill.: Richard D. Irwin, Inc., 1956); and J. D. Hammond, *Essays in the Theory of Risk and Insurance* (Glenview, Ill.: Scott, Foresman & Co., 1968).

A more general descriptive statement is in R. Riegal and J. S. Miller, *Insurance Principles and Practices* (5th ed.; Englewood Cliffs, N.J.: Prentice-Hall, Inc., 1966).

CHAPTER 13

Investment companies and investment counsel

In earlier chapters in this section, we examined the flows of savings of households through depository types of institutions in the capital markets. In the preceding chapter, the focus was on the functions of insurance companies. The investor may, of course, decide to conduct his own investment program and buy securities through one of the organized exchanges or in the over-the-counter market. If he feels the need for help, however, there are three types of investment institutions ready to assist him in acquiring common stocks as well as bonds and preferred stocks: investment companies; various kindred plans, including MIP, the monthly investment plan, and variable-value annuities; and investment counselors.

The investment company serves both large and small investors but is particularly advantageous to the person of small means because through it he can obtain both diversification and specialized management that would not otherwise be available to him. In contrast, investment counselors are useful mainly for persons with fairly substantial accumulations, who want highly individualized help in planning a program specifically designed to meet their particular situations. Increasingly, and particularly through the common trust fund, the corporate trustee is serving the investment requirements of the individual of modest means as well as the more opulent investor.

Investment companies

The terms *investment company* and *investment trust*[1] are used loosely and interchangeably to designate a variety of financial institutions through which the accumulated funds of a large number of savers and investors are pooled under centralized management to be invested in securities for the benefit of all the participants. It is the aim of the investment company to provide, particularly for the small investor, the same opportunity of spreading risk through diversification that is available to the larger investors and to institutional investors—a diversification that the individual small investor is usually not able to accomplish alone. Furthermore, it is the aim of these enterprises to give both small and large investors the benefit of trained, experienced, and specialized management, together with continuous supervision, neither of which the individual investor is, as a rule, qualified to supply himself.

Origin of the investment company

The investment company idea had its origin in Belgium (Société Générale de Belgique, 1822), and subsequently similar investment organizations were formed in Switzerland and in France. Still later in the 1860s the investment company movement started in England, expanded steadily for 20 years, and reached the height of its development in the boom period of the eighties. During the formative stage in England there was little regulation of the activities of these investment pools, and unsound and speculative practices were often followed. The Baring Brothers crash and the financial crisis of the early nineties were retarding influences, and there were investment company failures and loss of prestige. Those companies that stood the test thereafter followed more conservative practices. The British investment companies won public confidence and have, in the main, performed creditably since.

---

[1] The British investment companies were originally actual common-law trusts but subsequently changed to the corporate form, becoming limited-liability companies. Notwithstanding the change in legal form, the term *trust* was retained in England and was subsequently popularly accepted in America. It was applied to various pooled investment funds, whether they were legally trusts or not. Efforts are being made in the United States by those associated with investment company sponsorship to encourage the use of the term *investment company,* wherever applicable, rather than the misnomer *investment trust;* but it is difficult to change popular usage, and time will be required. Whether investment companies are organized as common-law trusts or as corporations has little effect on their operating policies or procedures. The difference is largely technical and need not concern us here. For a discussion of the common-law or Massachusetts trust form of organization see Chapter 14.

Development of investment companies in the United States

The 10 years prior to 1925 are generally regarded as the formative period of the investment company movement in the United States, although the idea took root before 1900. Only slight interest was shown in investment companies for a number of years, but development expanded rapidly in 1927 and 1928, followed by a period of high enthusiasm in 1929 up to the time of the October 1929 market break. Many of the American companies then only recently formed were at once subject to a market panic of serious proportions, an experience that closely paralleled the early days of the investment company in England.

Although the idea of pooling investment funds is basically sound, it was abused by many of the newly formed companies in this country. Organized toward the end of a bull market of vast proportions and influenced by the speculative fervor of the time, many of these companies bought mostly speculative common stocks and then faced a serious depreciation in the value of their portfolios in the ensuing collapse of the market.

Some of the so-called investment companies in America were really holding and financing organizations that acquired a major stockholding in companies in which they were interested. The holding companies were designed to effect rather long-term or permanent retention of substantial interests in given situations; the financing companies advanced funds for a relatively shorter time to assist a business during the developmental or perhaps a rehabilitation period, and then sold out and sought other commitments. Other companies engaged in trading operations and emphasized market profits on relatively short-term holdings of securities. Either speculative profits or control was the motivating factor in such companies. They lacked the diversification of a true investment company and, of course, followed more aggressive practices. The American investing public has learned to distinguish between the holding, financing, and trading enterprises, on the one hand, and the investment companies proper, on the other.

Following the lesson of the 1929–32 period, there were many mergers of investment companies, and numerous new affiliations were made. Stated or par values of both preferred and common stocks were written down; investment companies bought in their own senior securities at a discount; and objectives and operating policies were restated on a much more conservative basis.

The American investor was disappointed by the performance of the investment companies; management had not provided the expected safety of principal plus appreciation in addition to the expected income from interest and dividends. Investors eschewed discretionary management and turned to a cooperative investment device that provided for a minimum of management discretion and set up a relatively inflexible long-term investment program operated according to pre-established rules. This device became known as the *fixed trust* because policy was largely prescribed and little management decision was permitted.

Fixed trusts

Fixed trusts were established by sponsoring dealers who sold to the public redeemable shares (also called certificates of beneficial interest). Each of these fixed-trust shares represented a proportionate interest in a portfolio of securities deposited by the sponsor with a trustee. The securities were generally those of well-known companies, traded on the leading exchanges of the country; and the agreement (trust indenture) set out specifically the securities that might be included. Only limited changes were permitted in this block of underlying securities as indicated in the agreement, the purpose being to minimize management supervision. Some fixed-trust plans required the trustee to sell securities under certain conditions, yet permitted no substitution of new securities. The price of the fixed-trust shares to the investor was determined by dividing the number of shares into the market value of the underlying securities and adding to the quotient an amount to cover the selling charges. Income received on the deposited securities was distributed to the holders of the fixed-trust shares after the trustee's fee and the sponsor's expenses had been deducted. Fixed trusts were also called *unit trusts*, a designation that grew out of the fact that fixed-trust shares were issued against a block or *unit* of underlying securities. When the sponsor had sold all the shares pertinent to one unit, he would set up another block or unit and sell more shares.

The first unit trusts were probably created in 1924, but it was not until after 1929 that they attained the peak of their popularity. According to the Securities and Exchange Commission (SEC), sales of unit trusts from 1927 to 1936 totaled about $900 million, and about two thirds of these sales occurred in 1930 and 1931. Although more than 150 of these unit trusts were originated, probably a half dozen sponsors distributed most of the shares. In fact, two of the unit trusts together accounted for probably half the total flotations of this type of instrument.

As the SEC estimates indicate, the popularity of the unit trust soon waned after the very early 1930s, and no new ones were formed in those years. The further distribution of shares of already existing unit trusts ceased. Some of the unit trusts were subsequently converted into open-end investment companies.

Basically the original unit trust idea—to the extent that it sought to set up a rigid long-term investment program to be operated mechanically according to pre-established rules—was not sound. No one planning a program for future years can anticipate all possible developments and make provision for the action to meet such developments. Industries and companies change, as do the underlying economic fundamentals. This weakness was recognized, and the sponsors subsequently substituted for the fixed-trust plan a modified type of unit trust designed to permit some management discretion and therefore greater flexibility. These newer vehicles were described as semifixed or restricted management trusts.

Fixed trusts had another inherent disadvantage: possible loss of interest in the project on the part of the sponsor or possible withdrawal of the trustee if he did not find the arrangement adequately remunerative. Any premature dissolution of a unit trust would mean that selling charges would have to be absorbed over a shorter period of time than was originally contemplated (unit trusts were set up for varying periods—10, 15, 25 years, etc.).

A renewed interest in the unit trust form was observable, however, in the late 1960s when such trusts were formed to hold portfolios of state and municipal bonds or real estate mortgages, i.e., securities providing tax advantages and larger after-tax cash flows than alternatives.

Renewed interest in investment companies

Discredited in the years following 1929, the investment company later regained favor, and particularly since the early 1940s, there has been a wide public interest and resultant increase in the use of this type of investment. The SEC reported that 1,049 registered firms had total assets of $72 billion in 1969, in contrast to $2.5 billion in 1941.

Under authority of the Public Utility Holding Company Act of 1935 the SEC conducted a comprehensive study of investment companies and holding companies. On the basis of the findings, Congress passed the Investment Company Act of 1940, under which the firms referred to above are registered. This act, discussed more fully later, and the regulation of investment companies for which it made provision helped to engender again investor confidence in this form of investment device. The act served to codify many existing practices, modified others, and established some new requirements. According to one writer, who appraised the situation soon after the act had become effective: "Under the Act as it now exists and under the eyes of the Securities and Exchange Commission as its administrator, the buyer of investment company shares is about as nearly entitled as he ever can be to forget his anxieties about the honest care and administration of his funds."[2] This seems to hold true now; although investment company shareholders, in common with investors more

---

[2] A. B. Stevenson, *Investment Company Shares* (New York: Fiduciary Publishers, Inc., 1947), p. 13.

generally, have experienced from time to time the stresses of stock ownership in periods of major swings of stock prices.

The act applies to practically all investment companies and, in fact, makes registration under the act nearly mandatory because companies that do not register are drastically limited in their scope of activity. They may not use the mails for the purchase or sale of securities and may not engage in interstate commerce. Companies that qualify are called *registered* investment companies and fall into two main classifications: closed-end and open-end.

Closed-end and open-end investment companies

The most obvious and characteristic difference between the closed-end and the open-end investment company is the manner in which the investment company's own securities are bought and sold, but there is a distinction also with respect to capital structure, investment policy, and portfolio constituency.

Closed-end. Closed-end investment companies, much like industrial and other business corporations, have a relatively fixed amount of capital stock outstanding. Once distributed, shares are available only in the open market and can be bought either through one of the organized exchanges or through the over-the-counter market. Management may offer an additional block of shares; but this has happened infrequently and to only a small extent in recent years. There is no provision for issuance or redemption of shares on a day-to-day basis. The market price of shares depends not only upon the market value of the underlying securities but also upon the demand and supply of the investment company shares themselves in the open market. For this reason, shares of closed-end companies may often be purchased (or perforce sold) at substantial discounts below their asset or liquidating value. The discount tends to be greater in weak markets and to diminish, or even become a premium, in strong markets.

Many closed-end companies have only one class of capital stock outstanding; but some of them have pyramided capital structures, including preferred stock, debentures, and in some cases bank loans, in addition to common stock. Pyramided capital structures provide possible benefits of trading on the equity, also called *leverage*. A simple illustration of leverage: Assume that an individual with $1,000 invested in his business is able to earn a net return of 10%, or $100. Then, if he can maintain that rate of earnings on any capital additions, he should be able to realize a net return of 10%, or $100, on a second $1,000. If that second $1,000 was borrowed at a cost of only 5%, or $50, then there will be $150 net income for the owner of the business. This is equivalent to a 15% return on his $1,000 investment. He will have traded on his equity. The same principle applies to corporations that have senior securities outstanding. Leverage is effective with respect not only to income received from interest and dividends but also to gains realized from appreciation in value of the underlying securities of the investment company. It should be noted, however, that in a declining market, or with declining earnings, a capital pyramid accentuates adversity for equity holders.

Although most of the investment companies organized in the period of early growth during the 1920s were of the closed-end type, only a few such have been established since 1929. Total net assets of closed-end companies have increased but moderately in recent years, and the number of shareholders has decreased. This is in contrast with the growth of the open-end companies, as we shall see.

Open-end. Open-end investment companies generally sell their shares continuously on a day-to-day basis, either directly or through licensed securities dealers. The price to the buyer is the asset value of the underlying securities plus a selling charge or *load*, that ranges with exceptions, from 6 to 9% of the selling price. No-load fund shares are sold at asset value without addition of any selling charge. Shares will be redeemed by the open-end company at the asset value minus, in a few instances, a nominal redemption fee. The asset value of the shares is calculated at regular intervals, at least once daily, and is determined as follows: The market value of the underlying securities is added to the amount of cash and receivables on hand, liabilities are deducted, and the remainder is divided by the number of shares outstanding.

The prices at which shares will be either sold or redeemed are published in leading financial newspapers and on the financial pages of leading general circulation newspapers. As a rule, there is no over-the-counter trading in open-end shares. An exception is found, for example, in the shares of the State Street Investment Corporation, which are traded over the counter. State Street discontinued the sale of additional shares in 1944 but continued redemption of the shares at 1% below asset value. However, shares have rarely been presented for redemption; and because of the demand for shares, they have generally sold in the over-the-counter market at a premium above asset value.

Normally, because of the method of selling and redeeming open-end shares, the market price bears a direct relationship to the value of the underlying assets. This contrasts with closed-end shares, which may at one time sell at a substantial discount below asset value and at another time at a premium above asset value. For this reason and because of the acquisition cost (selling charge), open-end shares do not lend themselves to short-term trading—the fee would tend to absorb any possible profits.

With relatively minor exceptions the open-end companies have but one class of stock and have no bonds outstanding and no bank debt. The Investment Company Act of 1940 does not permit newly formed open-end companies to have more than one capital issue, and bank borrowing is permitted to only a limited degree. Accordingly, there is little opportunity for capital leverage in the open-end field.

Open-end investment companies are also called *mutual* investment funds. The open-end designation obviously can be traced to the fact that there is no fixed amount of capital, the number of shares outstanding varying from day to day with the flow of sales and redemptions. How the term mutual originated is not certain, although one sponsor, in testifying before the SEC, said that his open-end company was a mutual fund in equity securities analogous to a mutual savings bank.

Growth comparison. Open-end companies have had a very substantial growth in the last 10 to 15 years. Total net assets of member funds of the Investment Company Institute amounted to $48.3 billion at the beginning of 1970, which compares with $402 million at the end of 1941. The number of shareholder accounts in the same period increased from 293,251 to more than 10 million. The trend in net total assets and shareholder accounts for open-end companies is shown in Exhibit 13–1. Until some time in 1944 the net total assets of closed-end companies exceeded the assets of open-end companies, but since that time the reverse has been true; open-end assets early in 1970 were more than 16 times the assets of closed-end companies.

During 1969, sales of open-end investment company shares amounted to $6,718 million, repurchases were $3,662 million, and the net excess of sales over redemptions amounted to $3,057 million.

There are a number of explanations for this marked change in relative position. Over the years the shares of most closed-end companies have tended to sell fairly consistently at a discount. Not only does this preclude issuing additional shares without diluting the equity of existing shareholders, but many closed-end company managements have bought back their shares at a figure below asset value, a practice that serves to reduce total net assets. On the other hand, undoubtedly one of the important reasons for the demonstrated preference of investors for open-end shares is found in the fact that such shares may always be redeemed at approximately the market value of the underlying securities.

Probably the most significant explanation for the growth of open-end companies is found in the method of their distribution. Usually open-end investment companies arrange to have an individual or a securities house serve as the sponsor (wholesale distributor) of the shares. The sponsor is given the exclusive right to buy shares from the company at the net-asset value for resale to retail dealers, who, through their salesmen, sell the shares to the ultimate investor. Sponsors seek to set up a strong selling organization with representatives located throughout the country. Retail outlets include brokerage houses, investment bankers, securities dealers,

EXHIBIT 13–1

Open-end investment company statistics, 1940–69* (*total net assets and number of share-holders*)

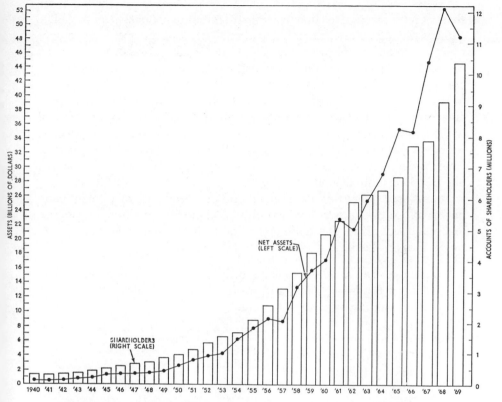

* The number of funds included may vary from year to year. Duplications not eliminated.
Source: Investment Company Institute.

and individual salesmen. Without active sales effort, redemptions might well exceed sales from time to time.

A 6–9% selling charge does not become a part of the fund but represents compensation to the sponsor or distributor, to the retail dealer, and to the dealers' salesmen. The commission paid the dealer is larger than on securities transactions generally and is sufficient to justify active selling campaigns, including person-to-person solicitation. Brokerage commissions and over-the-counter spreads on stocks and bonds generally are not adequate to permit similar selling effort. No-load funds handle the sale of their own shares directly.

With the new pattern of income distribution in our country, there are now many more persons who are able to save enough of their incomes to become potential securities buyers, but many of them know little about

13——Investment companies and investment counsel

stocks and bonds and securities markets. Person-to-person solicitation has served to inform many of these new investors and has undoubtedly been an important factor in the growth of open-end funds. Persons who might not otherwise buy common stocks have been interested in buying these shares on the strength of the diversification and management provided.

That the selling method and educational effort of the open-end companies are responsible factors in the expansion of mutual funds is evidenced by the fact that three mutual funds sponsored by investment counselors and established in the early days of investment company development have not enjoyed a growth comparable to that of many of the other open-end companies. The investment counsel funds bear no selling charge; and without sales effort, growth is relatively slow—this despite the reputation for creditable performance that is generally accorded these no-load funds. There are now several investment counseling firms each of which sponsors one or more mutual funds.

Investment policy. Whether open-end or closed-end, investment companies afford the investor a wide range of choice in investment programs and objectives. From the standpoint of portfolio content, investment companies can be classified as follows:

1. Common stock funds—predominantly or exclusively common stocks
2. Balanced funds—common and preferred stocks and bonds, the proportion varying from time to time
3. Specialty funds:
   a) Exclusively bonds
   b) Exclusively preferred stocks
   c) Speculative common stocks
   d) Single-industry common stocks
   e) Foreign securities

The objective and the expected performance of an investment fund are closely related, not only as to the nature of the underlying portfolio, but also as to the capital structure of the fund itself. Open-end companies, with one or two exceptions, have but one class of shares outstanding and therefore provide no leverage. Closed-end companies may have but one class of stock (nonleverage) or may have a multiple capital structure (leverage), including, in addition to common stock, preferred shares and bonds; in some cases they may have bank loans as well.

On the basis of the character of the investment portfolio, the nature of the investment company's own capital structure, and management policies, the following types of investment objectives are reflected:

1. Primarily capital appreciation, i.e., growth of share value
2. Emphasis on income

3. Moderate income and moderate appreciation
4. Maintenance of principal value and stable income
5. Unusually promising long-range opportunities, including perhaps a direct management responsibility (rare; never open end)

The performance of an investment fund is readily determinable for a given period by the appreciation in value per share, by the dividends paid from investment income, and by the dividends paid from profits realized from the sale of securities. Figures for a single year are not very significant and may actually be misleading; allowance must be made for the long-range objectives of the fund and the position of securities markets generally at the beginning and end of the period used for calculation.

How well a given investment management has discharged its stewardship on a relative basis presents a more difficult problem and is really a task for a specialist who is familiar with the investment company field and with securities and investing generally. In selecting other funds for purposes of comparison, he would take into account policy, underlying portfolio, and capital structure of the fund; he would appraise appropriately the accepted stock and bond averages that might be used as a gauge.

One factor in measuring the effectiveness of a given management is the cost of operation, although there is no relationship between such cost and actual investment performance. According to Wiesenberger's report for 1969,[3] operating expenses of the closed-end companies average about 0.60% of net assets and 10–12% of total cash income. Ratios for open-end companies were similar.

Some critics of the open-end investment companies hold the view that, because such companies represent continuous marketing operations, their investment policies may be influenced at times by the desire to encourage sales of their shares, and at other times may be conditioned by the need to plan for substantial redemptions. There is probably little validity to the first point; the established companies in the field are undoubtedly governed by more fundamental considerations in portfolio administration. With respect to the second point, in the more than a quarter of a century of continuous operation the need to generate cash for redemptions has probably not been an important factor in view of the steady, strong growth trend.

In the case of closed-end companies, because their shares are all outstanding, there is no continuing merchandising effort and no need to redeem shares.

It is also pointed out that, although the investment companies are, through their efforts, broadening the ownership interest in American en-

---

[3] Lucille Tomlinson Wessman, ed., *Investment Companies, 1969* (New York: Arthur Wiesenberger Services, 1969).

terprise, they are not contributing much equity capital for new industry because they tend to emphasize in their portfolios the "blue-chip" stocks, stocks of well-established companies with strong asset and earnings positions. In view of the very nature of the diversified investment company, it would appear logical to expect such a tendency. However, some of the investment companies, open-end and closed-end, are conscious of the equity problem. For instance, a number of investment companies of both types include among their holdings an interest in the American Research and Development Company, which was formed "to encourage research and to aid in the development of small new businesses into companies of stature and importance." Furthermore, because the funds buy investment-quality securities, they free other investment capital for more venture-some employment (new issues to provide equity capital).

Investment company legislation

The methods and policies of investment companies have been affected by various laws and by stock exchange regulations. Prior to 1929 there was no special stock exchange regulation, but the New York Stock Exchange in mid-1929 published requirements with respect to the listing of investment company shares and about two years later revised these requirements and set up regulations to govern member-firm participation in the fixed-trust movement. The blue-sky laws of several states, the Securities Act of 1933, and the Securities Exchange Act of 1934 all regulate the investment companies. Revisions in the federal income tax law, particularly the acts of 1936 and 1942, also affected the industry. Reference has already been made to the Investment Company Act of 1940.

Tax status of investment companies. Under the Revenue Act of 1936, corporations were taxed on dividends received from other corporations, and full application of this provision would have been harmful to investment companies because it would have meant triple taxation (the business, the investment company, and the individual would all have been taxed). Through conferences, special provision was made to favor with a tax advantage those open-end companies that would comply with certain operating procedures. Later the Revenue Act of 1942 (Supplement Q) established a special plan for the taxation of investment companies that agreed to comply with stated conditions. This applied to both open-end and closed-end companies that conformed and that were then called *regulated* investment companies, a term that is peculiar to the federal tax law and refers to registered companies that meet the conditions of Supplement Q, which are:

1. The company must elect to be a regulated company (irrevocable)
2. At least 90% of net ordinary income must be distributed each year

3. Gross income from the sale of securities held less than three months must be less than 30% of the total gross income
4. At least one half of the company assets must be in the form of cash or diversified securities
5. Not more than 25% of the assets may be invested in the securities of any one issuer.

If these requirements are met, the investment company pays no tax on the income or the capital gains distributed; but it does pay tax on both retained income and retained capital gains at the regular corporate rate. The holder of investment company shares treats the income received from a regulated investment company as though the income had been received on his own direct investments. The effect of the tax exemption granted to regulated investment companies is to encourage distribution of substantially all income and gains realized during the year.

Companies that do not elect to become regulated investment companies are taxed just as any other corporation is.

Investment Company Act of 1940.   Every investment company with 100 or more shareholders must register under the Investment Company Act of 1940. As already noted, this act grew out of an investigation authorized under the Public Utility Holding Company Act of 1935. The latter law, in turn, was enacted to regulate the holding companies (which are somewhat like investment companies) that had gained control over vast utility properties in the 1920s.

The Investment Company Act is administered by the SEC and was designed to regulate the practices of investment companies in order to protect the public against certain malpractices and abuses that characterized the operation of some of the investment companies in earlier years. A few of the more important provisions of the act can be summarized briefly as follows:

Management.   The law is intended to assure honest and independent management; persons who might be in a biased position (underwriters, etc.) may not constitute more than a minority of the board. Excessive commissions and self-dealing (an insider dealing with the fund as principal for his own gain) are prohibited. The SEC may sue in the event of misconduct. Embezzlement is made a federal offense. And the portfolio is to be maintained in the custody of a bank unless other arrangements are made with the SEC.

Investment policies.   Companies are required to file with the SEC a statement outlining precisely the investment policy that is to be followed, and such policy may be changed only with a majority vote of stockholders.

Shareholder participation.   At least two thirds of the directors must be elected by the shareholders. Management contracts are limited to a two-year duration and must have stockholder approval. Shareholders ratify selection of the accountants. All future stock issues must have voting power. And preferred stockholders must have the right to vote in the event of a default in dividends.

Capital. Minimum capital required is $100,000. Closed-end companies are limited as to capital structure. At least 50% of assets must be represented by common stock equity at the time new senior securities are issued. Only one class of bonds and one class of preferred stock may be issued by closed-end companies. Open-end companies may issue only common stock but may borrow from banks if assets are maintained at not less than three times the amount of the loan at all times.

Distribution. All sales of new securities by open-end or closed-end companies must be in compliance with the Securities Act of 1933, and sales practices are voluntarily regulated under the rules of the National Association of Securities Dealers, a self-policing body under the supervision of the SEC. Advertising and sales literature are governed by "A Statement of Policy."

Summary and evaluation

There was a time when the terms *investment company* and *investment trust* were confusing and encompassed a wide variety of organizations. Gradual evolution aided by legislation has brought about a clearer definition and understanding as well as a more precise terminology. The fixed trust or unit trust was but a passing phase. The intelligent investor is financially literate; distinguishes trading, holding, and financing companies; and recognizes that these organizations have particular functions to perform but that such companies are different from the open-end and closed-end investment companies.

All investment companies have the same general objectives: to provide for the small and large investor a diversification of holdings that might otherwise be impossible of achievement and to provide trained and specialized supervision, a function that the average layman is usually not competent to supply on his own. In short, investment companies provide a means of indirect investment in American industry.

This opportunity is made available in many forms. The indirect investor has many choices beyond that of selecting between open-end and closed-end companies. Some companies provide leverage, others are nonleverage. Some companies have balanced portfolios, including common stock, preferreds, and bonds, while others have concentrations in common stock, in preferreds, or in bonds. One management may seek to take advantage of business fluctuations to a major degree; another tends to be fully invested at all times and attempts little adjustment in portfolio during the course of a business cycle. It is possible to have industry diversification or industry concentration; capital appreciation or maintenance of principal; and maintenance of long-term purchasing power or current dollar income. Emphasis on established companies in proved industries is the policy of some investment companies, while others favor pioneering companies in new industries. These enumerated tendencies and policies are blended in varying proportions by different managements.

The investment company concept of distributing risk and providing continuous surveillance is basically sound. But the test is in the application of the theory; performance depends, in the last analysis, on management. And that is essentially what the purchaser of investment company securities is buying. It is reasonable to expect that the seasoned professional staff of an investment company should be able to show a performance superior to that of the average lay investor and sufficiently so to justify the fees entailed. The growth of the investment company movement tends to support this thesis.

In addition to serving the individual, investment companies serve society generally by providing another conduit for the flow of savings from the saver into industry. Through their sales and promotion efforts the open-end companies particularly try to inform and interest many potential new investors in investing, and they are meeting with obvious success. Because most investment companies emphasize, or at least include, some common stocks in their portfolios, the ownership base of American industry is being broadened.

Apprehension has been expressed that, with a continuation of the growth of investment companies, these organizations might ultimately come to control American enterprise and thus give a relatively small number of men—the investment company managers—great power over industry. There would seem to be no early or even remote danger of this sort, in view of the fact that total assets under investment company control are relatively small in comparison with the total income and wealth of the nation.

In the 23 years ending December 31, 1969, the member funds of the Investment Company Institute averaged an annual growth in net assets of $2.1 billion to bring the net total assets to $48.3 billion after some 35 to 40 years of operation. Assets of these companies at the end of 1969 represented 7.7% of the market value of all listed shares on the New York Stock Exchange. Holdings of stocks listed on the New York Stock Exchange made up 75% of the total and represented 5.5% of the market value of all shares listed on the exchange. Furthermore, the policy of broad diversification that is followed limits the extent of investment in the stock of any one company and thus serves to minimize the threat of control. It is noteworthy, however, that in the year 1968 alone, assets of the companies increased $8 billion. In 1969, as a result of market price declines, and despite net new investment of $3 billion by shareholders, asset values decreased $4 billion.

13——Investment companies and investment counsel

Admittedly, investment company managements might make their influence felt by bringing pressure to bear on corporate management, particularly if several investment companies collaborated. That this might become an important factor was suggested early in 1949. The managements of several investment companies became interested in the internal administrative problems of one of the leading mail-order houses in which the investment companies have sizable holdings. Opinions were publicly expressed by investment company officials, and shares were in some instances voted to protest the management policy of the mail-order house. As a general rule, however, investment company managers make no attempt to influence or participate in the management of companies in which they have security holdings.

Closely related to this problem of possible control is the question as to whether an investment company might become so large as to make liquidation of its sizable holdings in any given situation impracticable from a market standpoint. In 1970, the volume of trading by institutions on the New York Stock Exchange was over one half of the total volume of trading by all persons. Certainly, if managements of a number of large investment trusts all reach the conclusion simultaneously that it would be wise to sell a given stock of which they all held large amounts, it is obvious that the market might become seriously depressed. On the other hand, if many investment company managements independently decide to buy a certain stock, their combined action over a period of time might reduce the floating supply of that stock and exert an upward price pressure.

Further growth of the investment company field is favored by the increasing number of states (see Chapter 14, prudent man rule) that are recognizing investment company shares as suitable for trust fund (fiduciary) investments. About 15% of the share accounts at the end of 1969 were institutional accounts.

Kindred plans

There are a number of other investment procedures somewhat analogous to those of the mutual investment companies, insofar as they either are designed to serve particularly the needs of small investors or are adaptable to small investor participation. Such avenues of investment include the following: common trust funds, nonlife insurance company shares, investment clubs, monthly investment program (MIP) of the New York Stock Exchange, and the variable annuity fostered by certain insurance company interests. In varying degree each of these five schemes or practices has one or more of the attributes of mutual investment funds—such as diversification, specialized management, reduction of investment expenses, sharing of costs, commingling of funds, possibilities for dollar averaging, and availability in small amounts. The

MIP program of the New York Stock Exchange and the variable annuity are rather recent developments. Undoubtedly they were both inspired, at least in part, by the popularity and the rather phenomenal growth of mutual funds.

Common trust funds. The common trust fund makes available the services of trust administration to persons of small means, including investment service in many ways comparable to that provided by the open-end investment company (see Chapter 14).

Nonlife insurance company shares. Because nonlife carriers have a substantial margin of assets available for investment, shares of such insurance companies represent an interest in an investment portfolio and for this reason are regarded by some as akin to the shares of a closed-end investment company (discussed in Chapter 12).

Investment clubs. A year or two prior to World War II, a small group of young men banded together in Detroit for the purpose of raising a fund adequate to permit the establishment of a business in which they might all share. While the original objective was never attained—due to the war and other causes—individual members of this group or club continued pooling a part of their individual savings and then investing the accumulations.

Many similar clubs have been formed since that time. The members adopt bylaws, meet at regular intervals (usually monthly dinner meetings), and each member pays into a common investment pool each month an identical amount (generally in the range of $10–$25). There are no dues. The members listen to discussions on investments led either by a qualified club member or by an outsider (perhaps a representative of a brokerage house, an investment banker, or someone from another financial institution). Either on recommendation of an investment committee or by group selection, a decision is reached from time to time as to which stock or stocks should be bought.

Investment clubs are quasi-investment, quasi-social organizations made up of friends and acquaintances that have an interest in learning about investing in securities through actually participating in the formulation and execution of a program.

Obviously, these clubs are not a major influence in the capital markets, but they do provide an opportunity for thousands of interested persons to learn in a congenial atmosphere something about investing. The experience is undoubtedly inducing some of the members to embark on more ambitious programs of their own.

MIP program. In January 1954, the New York Stock Exchange announced its monthly investment plan designed to facilitate and encourage periodic purchases by small investors of stocks listed on the Big Board. Through the program, it is the hope of the exchange to interest a growing number of citizens in purchasing stocks so that they may have a stake in the tools of production and participate directly in the earnings of American enterprise.

Under the plan, the investor selects a given stock for investment. He agrees to pay as little as $40 a month or $40 a quarter, which is used to buy as many shares as the periodic payment will permit. He pays the quoted price for the stock plus an odd-lot differential and customary brokerage commission. The commission rate is 6% on investments up to $100, and $3 plus 1% on purchases over $100, with a minimum of $6. The New York Stock Exchange provides the following simplified illustration to show how the plan works (without indicating the odd-lot differential and the commission):

Say $50 of each of your payments is invested for you in XYZ stock. On the first purchase date the opening odd-lot price is $25 a share. So you get two shares. At the next purchase date it's at $20. You buy 2½ shares. At the third date it's down to $15. You get 3⅓ shares. The same for the fourth date—$15 a share, 3⅓ shares. But then it turns up. At the fifth purchase date it's $20; you get 2½ shares. At the end of six months it's back to $25 and you get 2 shares. Then it goes to $30 and you get only 1⅔ shares.

The average odd-lot price of the stock on those seven purchase dates was $21.43. But, if you total up the number of shares you've bought, you'll find you've acquired 17⅓ shares for $350. Each share, in other words, has cost you only $20.19.

The investor may receive the dividends or may arrange to have them reinvested automatically. There is no penalty for withdrawing from the plan or for skipping a payment. Upon withdrawal, the investor receives a certificate for all full shares registered in his name, fractional shares being sold and the proceeds mailed to the investor. All or part of the shares owned by the investor may be sold by him at any time.

Diversification may be achieved by arranging for three or more quarterly plans instead of a single monthly plan. Thus the investor may make payments for stock A in January, April, July, and October; for stock B in February, May, August, and November; and for stock C in March, June, September, and December. It will be clear from the foregoing illustration that the plan provides dollar cost averaging. The program is designed for long-term investing and not for short-term buying and selling.

On the 16th anniversary of MIP the plans in operation had accounted for the purchase of over 14 million shares worth $605 million. During 1969, an average of 500 new plans was opened daily.

Variable life income contract. The latest proposal for an investment plan based on common stocks and designed to serve large and small investors is the variable annuity, which is also called the variable life income contract. In the traditional annuity, the periodic payments received by the annuitants are fixed in dollar amount, and the recipient is penalized in periods of inflation because the purchasing power of his payments dwindles as the price level rises. It is expected that under the variable annuity the equal and fixed number of annuity units received periodically will rise in value in reflection of higher earnings and dividends and higher stock prices and thus provide an offset to the general price level. A more detailed description of the annuity is given in Chapter 12.

Mutual funds for institutions. The mutual fund idea for investment in common stocks is also being employed by institutions. The mutual savings banks in New York state, which were authorized several years ago to make common stock investments, organized a common stock mutual fund, *Institutional Investors Mutual Fund,* and by mid-1953, 60 of the 130 savings banks had pooled $3.5 million for investment purposes. By 1969, 129 banks had $238 million invested in the fund.

Such funds are restricted to the members of their respective sponsoring organizations and are not available to the general public. Sponsors of open-end funds may well regard the formation of such specialized investment companies as a tribute to their pioneering work.

Investment counsel

We have already noted that an investor is constantly confronted by a complex situation—a rapidly changing admixture of politics, business, markets, and international developments—and that any attempt to reach successful solution of his problems requires persistent study of the forces at work, continuous supervision, and an understanding of the available tools. One medium to assist the investor, which enables him to delegate responsibility for the management of his accumulations—the investment company—has just been discussed.

Investment counseling, likewise of recent origin, provides another avenue of assistance that makes available to the individual and institutional investor the services of investment specialists. The work of the investment counselor, who serves exclusively in this capacity, is purely advisory; he handles neither the money nor the securities of his clients. He receives a fee for his services graduated according to the size of the client's fund.

Origin of investment counseling

Investment counseling developed as an important independent occupation after World War I. Prior to that time, there may have been a few scattered individuals or organizations that furnished investment advice independent of any other activity and on some sort of fee basis. However, most investment advice was supplied as a service supplementary to another principal profession: by lawyers, personal trustees, banks and trust companies, brokers, security dealers, and, of course, investment bankers.

Up to the time of that war, there were relatively few securities in which there was a wide public interest, and securities buyers were largely of a professional type: banks, insurance companies, and trustees. Except for persons of wealth, individuals had little interest in stocks and bonds and gave preference to such investment media as savings accounts, mortgages, and local, familiar institutions. Wartime and postwar developments broadened interest in stocks and bonds. Such developments included the huge sale of Liberty Bonds for financing the war and the boom in the stock market.

To provide impartial, objective guidance for the growing number of investors, the then newly formed investment banking firm Scudder, Stevens & Clark of Boston decided to become exclusively professional advisers on a fee basis, on the theory that as merchants they could not be completely objective in their relationships with customer-clients. In investment counsel circles, this organization is generally regarded as the progenitor of investment counsel in essentially the form that it is practiced today.

Discussing the origin of the investment counsel concept, the late Theodore T. Scudder wrote as follows:

. . . I believe the beginning of investment counsel was more or less the result of my experiences and observations. . . . By 1912 or 1913, public corporate financing and corporate ethics had reached a point where some investors were beginning to recognize that common stocks held a real place in the individual investment program. But, generally speaking, most people still held to the old concept of conservative investment. . . . Recognizing that the average investor had no realization of how he should invest or the knowledge or experience to choose among the increasing number of stocks and bonds available, and, further, that there were no persons who were both experienced and impartial to advise him, I came to the conclusion that there was need for a new profession. . . . Therefore, in 1920 my partner, F. Haven Clark, and I decided to put these ideas into more concrete form. Recognizing that we were sailing uncharted seas, we felt that we would have to start on an experimental basis. Consequently I approached about 20 individuals to explain our ideas of conservative investment and our desire to deal with them on an impartial and increasingly expert basis. . . . We would then diagnose their situation and suggest to them what we believed to be a sound investment program to follow. . . . We suggested that they pay us 1 per cent of the money involved in each transaction. Hypothetically we figured this would pay the cost of serving them over an average period of years. Although many laughed at us in the beginning, we nevertheless found a ready reception of our ideas. The number of clients increased almost as fast as we could take them. In

1921 we invented the term "investment counsel" for the work in our office in Boston. The name was suggested by A. Vere Shaw, who was associated with us at that time.[4]

Within just a few years, and independently, E. P. Farwell in 1924 pioneered in the establishment of investment counsel services in Chicago and later joined with E. E. Sheridan and P. L. Morrison to form Sheridan, Farwell & Morrison, Inc., since absorbed by Scudder, Stevens & Clark. The Scudder organization not only is the pioneer investment counsel organization but is generally regarded as having the largest volume of funds under supervision.

Others followed the lead, and by 1929 there were about 70 investment counsel firms. The number expanded rapidly during the 1930s and subsequently, so that at the close of 1946 there were almost 900 investment adviser registrations reported by the SEC. The volume of funds under supervision is regarded as confidential information and is, therefore, not generally available. However, some indication of the magnitude of investment counsel operations was provided by a 1938 report of the SEC which showed that 50-odd investment counsel firms had approximately $4 billion under supervision in 1937. As of June 30, 1969, there were 2,476 investment advisers registered with the SEC.

Operation

Scope. Investment counsel service is available only for larger funds because most practitioners will not accept for supervision funds under $100,000 and in many cases $500,000 or more. Fees are usually payable quarterly at an annual rate ranging from 0.5 to 1% on the minimum principal sum and at a gradually declining rate for increments above the minimum. Smaller accounts are not accepted because the minimum work and costs entailed, whatever the size of the fund, would require a fee that the investor would probably consider excessive in relation to the principal and income. To serve the investor who has a smaller fund, some investment counselors sponsor investment companies under their own supervision. Such investment companies have the same management direction as the individual accounts of the counselor, but obviously the portfolio and policies cannot be adapted to the particular requirements of each of the participants.

Investment counsel serves, in addition to the more affluent individuals, a wide variety of institutional investors who do not have adequate funds under control to justify, on a cost basis, setting up a comprehensive in-

---

[4] Quotation from a signed statement supplied to E. W. Boehmler.

vestment organization of their own. Such institutional investors include commercial banks, trust companies, estates, insurance companies, pension funds, and educational and other endowment funds.

In addition to providing current investment advice, investment counselors often assist in estate planning through cooperation with the lawyer, accountant, and tax specialist of the client.

Procedure. Usually the investor who has decided to engage an investment counselor will sign a one-year contract, renewable quarterly thereafter at the election of either party. Then the procedure will generally be about as follows:

Determination of objectives. Agreement will be reached with the client on a specific statement of the investment objectives, as described in Chapter 10, including the policies to be pursued and any special arrangements to be made or conditions to be observed.

Fund analysis. The client will provide a list of his investment holdings and the cash that is to be included in the fund. He does not turn over the securities or cash themselves. The fund will be analyzed from the standpoint of suitability for the stated objective. It will be examined with respect to the nature and the quality of holdings. Specific recommendations will be made to sell, hold, or buy given securities, in the light of existing business conditions, in order to bring the fund into conformity with the investment aim. The reasoning that supports each recommendation is presented. The final decision as to what action will be taken rests with the client. However, if the client does not have confidence in the counselor and consistently fails to carry out recommendations, the relationship will probably be terminated at an early date by the counselor, unless the client takes the step himself.

Arrangement with the broker. Arrangements are usually made by the client with his broker to have confirmations of transactions in duplicate, one copy being sent direct to the counselor, the other to the client. On the basis of these confirmations, the counselor maintains an up-to-the-minute record of the client's holdings. If the client wishes to do so, he may give the counselor full discretion in managing the account and instruct the broker to execute the orders that are given by the counselor, rather than have the orders placed by the client himself.

Constant supervision. The account of the client is kept under close supervision and is periodically reviewed. Adjustments are recommended by the investment counsel as changing conditions dictate. Reports on the status of the fund are submitted to the client monthly or quarterly, showing for each item the cost, current market value, rate of income, and other pertinent information.

Recommendations are communicated to the client by telephone, letter, telegram, or in person; and clients are usually encouraged to call in person to review the business outlook and discuss the current attitude of counsel on investment policy.

Organization

There are three principal functions in the operation of investment counsel: administration and new business, counseling, and research. Administration is responsible for the overall business management and the development of new accounts. Counselors are responsible for account supervision; they communicate with the client on recommendations and review his account with him. Research is responsible for appraising fundamental economic and industry trends and for analyzing companies and specific securities. The findings of research are made available to the counselors, who use the information conveyed to them in supervising the accounts.

In large investment counsel firms the research function may be performed by a considerable number of individuals—some on economic research, others on government and foreign developments; some on heavy industry, others on consumer-goods industries; and so on. The findings of the researchers are coordinated into a composite opinion that constitutes the policy of the counseling firm with respect to economic fundamentals, industries, companies, securities, interest rates, earnings prospects, and related factors.

Performance

Client accounts are handled on a confidential basis, and results are not made public. However, it is usually possible for a prospective client to examine a few representative accounts. Satisfied clients may confide in friends and recommend investment counsel just as they do other professional help. If an investment counsel firm operates a mutual investment fund, the performance of the fund will give an indication of the effectiveness of the supervision.

Investment counsel is not infallible and cannot work miracles. However, it should be able to provide a reasonable rate of current income and some appreciation without undue exposure of the fund to risks. That investment counsel is justifying its existence is suggested by the retention of counsel over the years by many individuals and institutional investors and also by the growth in the volume of funds under supervision.

Regulation

Investment counsel is supervised by the SEC under the Investment Advisers Act of 1940, a part of the law regulating investment companies.

Subject to certain exceptions, all persons offering investment advice for compensation, either directly or through writings, must register under the act. Those who give advice incidentally and gratuitously are exempt and need not register. Others who need not register are those who do not advise with respect to securities dealt in on a national exchange; those who are consultants exclusively to insurance companies; and those who do not solicit business publicly and have fewer than 15 clients.

The use of the term *investment counsel* is limited to those who are registered; fees may not be based on capital gains realized; and registration under the act may not be held out as constituting government approval or sponsorship. The SEC may investigate violations of the act and may obtain information but may not examine books and records. The SEC may enjoin violators or may refuse or revoke registration.

A measure of control over investment counsel is also effected with respect to the members of the Investment Counsel Association of America, an association that has requirements more stringent than those of the Investment Advisers Act.

Other supervisory agencies

In contrast to the investment counsel firms discussed above, which engage only in investment counsel, there are other advisory and supervisory agencies that provide a similar service. In a census of the Investment Bankers Association of America made in 1940, 34 out of 368 members answered in the affirmative to the question: "Do you engage in the business of giving investment counsel for a fee?" Many of them continue to do so now. Trust companies and trust departments of commercial banks also render an investment supervisory service, and some sponsor common trust funds (see Chapter 14). Companies such as Moody's Investors Service and Standard and Poor's Corporation, which publish investment information and financial statistics, also offer investment advice on a fee basis. Some brokerage firms provide gratuitous investment advice through a special staff set up for the purpose.

Ancillary service

Investors who wish to transfer the responsibility for the physical care of their securities as well as the responsibility of making investment decisions may arrange for a discretionary account with investment counsel or for an agency account with a trust company. Under a discretionary arrangement, counsel is authorized to instruct the broker directly to execute transactions for the account. Under an agency account, the trust company holds the securities, receives confirmations from the broker, clips coupons, collects dividends, and provides related services.

1. In broad terms what is meant by *investment company?*

2. Distinguish between a fixed trust, an open-end investment company, a closed-end investment company, and a holding company.

3. What advantages are claimed for the investment company, particularly with respect to the investor of modest means?

4. What factors account for the rapid rise in net total assets of open-end companies in contrast to the experience of closed-end companies?

5. Explain through an illustration what is meant by capital leverage.

6. Are investment companies the answer to the venture-capital problem?

7. What is the distinction between a registered investment company and a regulated investment company?

8. Why is it difficult to make a comparative study of the performance of investment companies?

9. What is meant by *investment counsel?* How did the term originate?

10. Outline the general procedure followed by an investment counsel.

11. Who is served by an investment counsel?

12. What should the individual investor expect from an investment counsel?

13. In what respects are investment companies and investment counselors providing a similar service for individual investors? What are the elements of difference?

14. What is the economic justification for investment counsel and for investment companies?

15. Compare the portfolios of the following: an open-end investment company with a balanced fund; an open-end investment company with investments primarily in common stocks; and a closed-end company. Show in percentages the proportion invested in cash and government securities, in corporate bonds, in preferred stocks, and in common stocks. Obtain the portfolios from annual reports of companies or from one of the financial manuals.

Bibliography

In connection with the study of investment trusts and investment companies conducted by the Securities and Exchange Commission prior to the adoption of the Investment Company Act of 1940, the commission prepared a five-volume report, *Investment Trusts and Investment Companies* (Washington, D.C.: U.S. Government Printing Office, 1939–40). The SEC also published hearings on all phases of the industry and on related activities. *A Study of Mutual Funds,* which was prepared by the Wharton School for the SEC, was published in 1962 (Washington, D.C.: Government Printing Office), and *Public Policy Implications of Investment Company Growth,* a staff study, was published in 1966 (Washington, D.C.: Government Printing Office). A more recent study is the *Institutional Investors Study Report of the Securities and Exchange Commission* (Washington, D.C.: Government Printing Office, 1971) in 8 parts.

Discussions of investment policies of investment companies are presented in Douglas H. Bellemore, *Investments: Principles, Practice and Analysis* (2d ed.; New York: Simmons-Boardman Publishing Corp., 1962); R. E. Badger, H. W. Torgerson, and H. G. Guthmann, *Investment Principles and Practices* (6th ed.; Englewood Cliffs, N.J.: Prentice-Hall, Inc., 1969); and Harry Sauvain, *Investment Management* (3d ed.; Englewood Cliffs, N.J.: Prentice-Hall, Inc., 1967).

The Investment Company Institute publishes a number of statistical reports, some as frequently as monthly, concerning investment company asset values and share distribution. Data on portfolios and changes in them are reviewed quarterly by *Barron's*. Comprehensive information on individual investment companies and comparative statistics are available in a volume, published annually, by Arthur Wiesenberger, *Investment Companies* (New York: Arthur Wiesenberger & Co.; annually since 1941), which also suggests a method for appraising management results. J. K. Galbraith gives a vivid account of the investment company experiences, 1929–32, in *The Great Crash* (Boston: Houghton Mifflin Co., 1955).

CHAPTER 14

Trustee services

In an earlier chapter large metropolitan banks were characterized as department stores of finance. One of the departments of growing size and significance is engaged in the administration of trusts. Trust business is not, however, restricted to banks. Many nonbanking institutions have been organized to act as trustees and are serving thousands of customers. Nor are bank trust departments all found within the large city banks. More and more moderate- and small-sized banks are taking on trust functions as the benefits of trust operation become known to the public. There is no distinction to be made between the services of a trust company and the trust department of a bank. Nor can a distinction of significance be drawn between the trust departments of state and national banks.

The observing person will have noted that there is a wide variance in the titles of commercial banks. Some are merely named "bank"; others may be named "trust company"; and still others may combine both concepts and have a corporate title including the words "bank and trust company." Then, again, there are companies that have very similar-sounding names, but it is found that they are not commercial banks at all but do a purely trust business. There are, in fact, almost 60 different corporate titles represented among those institutions that engage in trust business either exclusively or in combination with some other business activity (usually commercial banking). These variations can be understood only in the light of historical development. But, first, what is a *trust?* What is meant by *trust business?* And what are *trust institutions?*

Concept of trusteeship

The *trust* is a legal device the concept of which can be traced back to antiquity. For present purposes, however, it is enough to know what it is and what it accomplishes. A simple example will serve best to explain this and to prepare the way for a definition of the term trust.

Assume that a businessman of means wishes to set aside a substantial sum of money for his son, the son to receive part of the income earned on the fund each year and to receive the principal sum when he reaches a certain age. The man then makes arrangements with a third person to have that person accept the money, invest it, pay the income as directed, and ultimately pay the principal sum to the son. A trust has then been created.

In this example the businessman is the grantor or creator of the trust. The third person who receives the money (the assets of the trust, or the body, or corpus, of the trust) and who then holds legal title or ownership is the trustee. The trustee holds the title for the benefit of the son, who is the beneficiary and who has a beneficial interest in the trust. The arrangment made by the businessman with the third person is the *trust agreement*.

A trust may also be created by means of a deed or a will. If the trust is created by a will, the creator is known as a *testator;* if the trust is created by a living person, the creator is variously known as *trustor, donor,* or *settlor,* as well as *grantor.*

The relationship between the parties to an arrangement such as has been sketched is one of confidence and trust. The creator of the trust places confidence in the trustee that the latter will act in good faith in carrying out the agreement as made. This arrangement is also referred to as a fiduciary relationship, and the trustee is called a *fiduciary.*

It should be noted, however, that a fiduciary is not necessarily a trustee. There are many other relationships of a fiduciary character: a member of a board of directors is a fiduciary for stockholders; a member of a partnership, for the other partner or partners; an attorney, for his client; and an agent, for his principal. But these persons are not trustees in the strict sense, even though they are in positions of trust and confidence.

What is the distinction? In the trust there is a transfer of ownership to the person who is trusted (the trustee), and he holds the legal title for the benefit of the beneficiary, who has the beneficial interest. In the other instances mentioned, there is no transfer of ownership.

A trust agreement may also be distinguished from a contract. In a contract there must be a *quid pro quo,* a consideration. In enforcing a trust agreement, it is not necessary to show that the trustee received a consideration; to enforce a contract, it must generally be shown that the party who made a promise received something in return. There is another important distinction: a party to a contract need perform only in conformity with the explicit stipulations in the contract; in a trust agreement, the law implies duties on the part of the trustee beyond those specifically stated in the agreement. (The student of law would sum up this significant distinction in this way: the contract is a creature of the common law, and a trust is a creature of equity.[1])

On the basis of this discussion a definition of a trust can be formulated: a trust is an agreement (trust agreement) under which the trustor or creator of the trust, having confidence in another, transfers the ownership of property to that other person (trustee) for the benefit of a third person (beneficiary) who has the beneficial interest in the property.

To expand the definition: the creator may be a beneficiary; the creator may be the trustee; the trustee may be one or more persons or a corporation; and the trust represents a fiduciary relationship that is characterized by the separation of the ownership and the beneficial interest.

Trust business

The term *trust business* as generally understood today was defined in 1933 by the American Bankers Association as follows:

Trust business is the business of settling estates, administering trusts and performing agencies in all appropriate cases for individuals; partnerships; associations; business corporations; public, educational, social, recreational, and charitable institutions; and units of government. It is advisable that a trust institution should limit the functions of its trust department to such services.

This statement will suffice for the present. The reader has already been introduced to the services that a trust company or a bank can provide for a corporation. In this chapter services performed for individuals will be considered in some detail.

Trust institutions

Any adult who is duly appointed by a person or court with authority to act may serve as a trustee and may engage in those activities that have been described as constituting trust business. He may be an agent, an executor named in a will, an administrator named by the court to settle an estate, a guardian of the estate of a minor, or a conservator of the estate of an incompetent. Lawyers and accountants give some time to the

---

[1] It is beyond the scope of this text to consider in further detail the distinction between a contract and a trust agreement and the distinction between the common law and equity. For such a discussion, consult treatises on business or commercial law and on trusts. See, for example, books listed in the bibliography of this chapter.

trust type of business. However, few individuals give their full time to such activity except in Boston, where some individual professional trustees, called *Boston trustees,* may be found. They are usually lawyers who devote much of their time to the settling of estates and the administration of trusts. They do not, however, engage in a comprehensive trust business.

As already noted, trust services are performed primarily by trust companies, most of which also engage in commercial banking, and by commercial banks that have established trust departments. Other corporations that do trust work include title-guaranty companies, mortgage bankers, and safe-deposit companies. This diversity of form explains why this chapter is headed "Trustee services" rather than "Trust institutions" or "Trust companies."

History of the trust business in the United States

In 1818 the state of Massachusetts chartered the Massachusetts Hospital and Life Insurance Company and gave the company the power, among other provisions, "to make all kinds of contracts, in which the casualties of life and interest of money are principally involved; and to make, execute and perfect such and so many contracts, bargains, agreements, policies, and other instruments, as shall or may be necessary, and as the nature of the case shall or may require." The grant was interpreted by the directors to mean that the company was empowered to accept trusts, and in 1823 the legislature confirmed this interpretation through an appropriate amendment of the charter.

The Farmers' Fire Insurance and Loan Company was incorporated in New York in 1822 to do a fire insurance business and to lend to farmers. A few months after incorporation the company applied for trust powers that were then specifically granted through an amendment to its charter. However, this company (which became the City Bank Farmers Trust Company and later merged with the First National City Bank of New York) did not accept its first trust until a number of years later.

In these two corporations are found the beginnings of the corporate fiduciary in the United States. Other states followed the lead of Massachusetts and New York and granted charters that authorized trust business. The Pennsylvania Company for Insurance on Lives and Granting Annuities was organized in 1812 and was expressly authorized to engage in trust business in 1836, but in the preceding year it had already accepted what is believed to have been the first living trust. This company continued doing business under the same name until several years ago. After a brief period of being known as the Pennsylvania Company, it merged and now operates under the title of the First Pennsylvania Banking and Trust Company.

Many reasons are assigned for the development of the trust business in the years 1820–40. The trust business is, in the main, a city rather than a country development; and the 20-year period witnessed a change in emphasis from such tangible wealth as farms, cattle, and related property to such intangibles as stocks and bonds. In the years to follow, this trend was accentuated by the establishment and growth of new industries and services, including railroads, steamboats, street railways, gas light, and many others. The populations of cities were expanding rapidly. Large family fortunes were being accumulated. The corporation was replacing the simple forms of business organization; and the introduction of various industries served to change the economy from one consisting primarily of farming and merchandising to an industrial one. Large accumulations of wealth and intangible property were undoubtedly the significant factors responsible for the inception and the early, moderate growth of the trust company movement.

Until after the Civil War the trust business was not of significant proportions. But thereafter, under the influence of steadily expanding industrialization, the mounting importance of the corporate form of enterprise, and consequently the growing complexity of business affairs, there was an increasing need for the type of service rendered by the corporate trustee. By 1900 there were about 300 trust companies. Trends have since been highly favorable to the rapid growth of the trust services offered by both trust companies and banks, and there are now more than 3,000 corporate trustees.

Trust companies versus trust departments

As already noted, the trust business was a development incidental to the insurance business; but soon corporations were chartered by various states for the express purpose of engaging in trust business, either by special charters granted by the legislature or under trust company statutes. These charters were generally so broad that the trust companies were able to engage in the commercial banking business as well, and did so, to the discomfiture of state banks. To meet this growing competition, state banks agitated for, and won, powers enabling them to engage in trust business. At first, national banks were not permitted to do a trust business; and in order to participate in the expanding volume of trust business, they organized separate affiliated trust institutions under state law. The First Trust and Savings Bank, created in 1903 by the First National Bank of Chicago, was one of the first of such affiliates to be established.

In 1913 national banks were authorized to serve as fiduciaries, and the Federal Reserve Act was amended in 1918 to extend their trust powers; but the authorization was challenged, and it was not until 1925 that a U.S. Supreme Court decision unquestionably established the right of national banks to do a trust business. National banks had difficulty in obtaining trust business, however, because their charters ran for only a stated 50 years. To remove this deterrent, the McFadden-Pepper Act, passed in 1927, gave the banks indeterminate life. Since that time, the trust business of national banks has grown rapidly.

Extent of the trust business

Annual data of the number of institutions engaging in trust operations are available only for national banks, but recent estimates indicate that the volume of assets being administered by both state and national banks is growing rapidly. At the end of 1946, of the 14,818 commercial and savings banks in the United States, 2,976 were trust institutions, of which less than 100 did no banking business. The 2,976 trust institutions had personal trust property under supervision amounting to approximately $36 billion. This business was concentrated in relatively few large institutions: about 4%, or 114 institutions, accounted for four fifths of the personal trust property under supervision; and 68 institutions accounted for almost 72% of the trust business in the country.[2] In 1952 the 1,513 national banks engaging in trust business had aggregate trust department liabilities of $39.7 billion, administered 60 common trusts, and served a total of 113,835 accounts. In December 1968, 1,671 national banks carried on fiduciary activities and had aggregate trust liabilities of $113 billion. Of these banks, 602 administered 1,429 common trusts and had 343,590 trust accounts.[3]

Assets worth more than $82.2 billion were held in *personal* trust accounts of all state and national banks and trust institutions as of December 1963, the latest date for which detailed information was published. Almost 66% was invested in common stocks; 14% in state and municipal obligations; 3% in U.S. securities; and the balance, about 17%, in preferred stock, mortgages, corporation bonds and debentures, real estate, participations in common trust funds, and cash. Of the $82 billion of assets, $48 billion were in nondiscretionary or depository trusts. The banks had full investment responsibility for the balance ($34 billion). An examination of Table 14–1 shows the banks' investments to be more conservative than those of the nondiscretionary type.

The significance of trust business in comparison with that of other financial intermediaries may be observed in Table 14–2. In this table the dollar values of investments of personal trust funds are compared with

---

[2] G. T. Stephenson, "Trust Business in the United States, 1947," *Trust Bulletin,* vol. XXVII, no. 8 (April, 1948), pp. 19–32.

[3] *Annual Report of the Comptroller of the Currency* (1968), Tables B-38, 39, pp. 237–38.

TABLE 14–1

Assets in personal trust accounts by type of investment responsibility, December 1963 (*in billions of dollars*)

	Sole responsibility		Shared or none	
Type of asset	Amount	Percent	Amount	Percent
Common stock	20.3	59.3	33.7	70.3
State and municipal securities	4.7	13.7	6.9	14.5
Participation in common trust funds	3.5	10.1	1.3	2.7
U.S. government securities	1.3	3.8	1.5	3.0
Corporate bonds and debentures	1.7	4.8	1.4	2.9
Preferred stock	.6	1.7	.7	1.5
Mortgages	.5	1.5	.4	0.9
Cash	.2	0.5	.4	0.8
All other assets	1.6	4.6	1.6	3.4
Total	34.2	100.0	48.0	100.0

Note: Detail may not add to total because of rounding.
Source: Gordon A. McLeon, "Report of National Survey of Personal Trust Accounts" *Trust Bulletin,* December, 1964, pp. 6–12.

the volume and disposition of savings and loan·associations, life insurance companies, and mutual savings banks. The investments of each intermediary are grouped into five general classes: federal government securities, other government obligations, industrial securities, mortgages, and all other assets. The last-named class often includes cash and real estate used in the conduct of the business and is not truly a part of investments as we use the term here.

Trust institutions are more fully invested in industrial stocks than are

TABLE 14–2

Investment assets of selected financial intermediaries, December 1965 (*in billions of dollars*)

	Savings and loan associations		Life insurance companies		Mutual savings banks		Trust institutions	
Item	Amount	%	Amount	%	Amount	%	Amount	%
U.S. government securities	$ 7.4	5.7	$ 5.1	3.2	$ 5.5	9.4	$ 6.9	7.8
Other government obligations	—	—	6.4	4.0	.3	.5	5.7	6.6
Industrial securities	—	—	67.7	42.6	5.1	8.8	65.7	75.1
Mortgage loans	110.3	85.1	60.0	37.8	44.4	76.3	—	—
All other assets	11.8	9.2	19.7	2.9	2.9	5.0	11.2	10.5
Total	$129.6	100.0	$158.9	100.0	$ 58.2	100.0	$89.5	100.0

Note: Details may not add to total because of rounding.
Source: *1969 Savings and Loan Fact Book,* p. 96; *Life Insurance Fact Book,* 1969, p. 65; *Mutual Savings Banking Annual Report,* May 1969, p. 2; *National Banking Review,* vol. 3, no. 4 (June 1966), p. 488.

other intermediary institutions. Investment policy of trustees is less subject to regulatory constraints.

Classification of trust services

Trust institutions undoubtedly render a wider range of services than any other type of financial institution, and this is certainly true of those metropolitan organizations that do both a commercial banking and a trust business. Corporate trustees are a significant segment of our financial structure not only in view of the volume of funds under their supervision but also from the standpoint of the approximately 80 separate trust services they perform. Trustees help the individual with his personal, financial, and business affairs and provide services that are highly essential, if not indispensable, to corporations and the business life of the nation. It can well be said that corporate trustees are ready to provide almost any service that has to do with the preservation and transfer of property—whether tangible or intangible, personal or real—and, in addition, are ready to assist the individual with personal problems that go beyond the pecuniary.

Some of the more important standard trust services may be classified under three main headings: those rendered only to individuals, those rendered only to corporations, and those rendered to individuals as well as to corporations and similar institutions. Services to corporations are described in Chapter 16. The services for individuals as described in the following paragraphs indicate how trust institutions contribute directly to the saving, conserving, and administration of individual funds and other assets.

Services rendered to individuals

Executor under wills. A trustee may be named as executor under a will or as coexecutor with one or more persons. It is the function of the executor to prove the will and receive court authority to distribute the assets in conformity with the provision of the will and to pay the debts of the estate.

Administrator of intestate estate. If the decedent left no will or if there is a will but no executor has been named, the court will appoint an administrator who is responsible for the settlement of the estate.

Ancillary executor. If the decedent owned property in a second state, then an ancillary administrator is appointed on court order to administer the assets in that state.

Trustee under will. If a person does not wish to have his estate distributed immediately upon his death but prefers to set up a trust for the benefit of his family, or others, he may create a testamentary trust, or trustee under will. There may be many reasons for creating such a trust: relieving the beneficiaries of the responsibility for property management; reduction of transfer costs; or the flexibility of the device. The trustee administers the trust in accordance with the provisions of the will, and he may be allowed considerable discretion.

Guardian and conservator of estate. Under order of a probate court a trustee may be appointed to administer the estate of a minor, in which instance the trustee serves as guardian, or to administer the estate of an incompetent, in which case the trustee serves as a conservator. In these capacities the trustee functions much like an administrator or executor. When the minor becomes of age, the estate is turned over to him.

Depository under court order. If an individual executor, administrator, guardian, or conservator wishes to transfer the custody of the assets of an estate, he may arrange for a trust institution to become depository under court order. He is thereby relieved of certain responsibilities and clerical detail, and the fee charged for the service of the trust institution will generally represent a saving, as compared with the cost of an individual surety bond.

Trustee under agreement. In contrast to a testamentary trust, a competent person may set up a trust during his lifetime. This is done under an agreement of trust which states the intention of the creator and outlines how the trust is to operate to achieve the objectives. There may be any of several motives: to transfer the responsibilities of property management; to make provision for members of the family in this way rather than under a will; to donate to charity, an educational foundation, or religious order; or to minimize transfer costs. There is a wide range of latitude in drawing up such an agreement. The creator may retain varying degrees of investment control or delegate full responsibility; and he may make the trust revocable and subject to amendment, or he may make the trust irrevocable.

Income and principal are paid by the trustee according to the terms of the agreement. The trustee may assume full management control, collect income, review the assets of the trust at intervals, prepare periodic statements, and provide information for income tax purposes. Such an arrangement is called a *living* or *voluntary trust*. If the trust is not revocable, the assets of the trust are essentially gifts.

Trustee under agreement—insurance trust. Another form of living trust that has some of the aspects of a testamentary trust is the life insurance trust. The creator deposits his life insurance policies with a corporate trustee under an agreement that provides for the distribution of the proceeds of policies which may be paid into the trust during the life of the donor or at his death. The trust is said to be inactive during the life of the creator; but upon his death it becomes active. Such a trust may be set up to provide liquid assets to meet the estate and inheritance taxes requiring payment after the death of the creator, particularly in the event that there are nonliquid assets in the form of a closely held business or substantial real estate. Much as in the case of a testamentary trust, provision may be made to have the trustee hold the assets of the trust for a considerable period after the death of the donor and to pay out income or principal periodically. The donor may, of course, reserve the right to control the deposited policies during his lifetime.

A life insurance trust may be funded (premiums are paid out of the income received on securities deposited with the trustee); partially funded (the premiums are paid in part from income on deposited securities, and the balance is paid by the creator); or unfunded (all premiums are paid by the creator).

Safekeeping. Trust institutions usually maintain safe-deposit vaults for the safekeeping of securities, jewelry, and other valuable property. In addition, trust institutions take custody of securities and other valuable papers and provide a limited amount of service in that connection, such as the collection of sums due and providing notices of maturing bonds, stock dividends, warrants, and subscription rights. Sales and purchases are made as directed by the client.

Supervised agency. Services in addition to simple safekeeping are also provided, including complete agency service plus investment advice, a complete record of all transactions and monthly statements showing the status of holdings, periodic review of the portfolio, and the requisite information needed for income tax returns. Such service may be rather comprehensive and may roughly parallel that provided by investment counselors, discussed in Chapter 13, but it includes the added feature of custodianship.

Escrow agent. Trust institutions serve as stake holders (escrow agents). Property may be placed with the trustee under certain conditions stipulating that the property is to be turned over to a third person in the event that certain conditions are met. If the conditions are not met, the property is to be returned to the party originally placing it with the escrow agent. Thus the deed to a piece of property may be placed in escrow along with the purchase price, pending the examination of the title. If the title is clear, the deal is consummated; if not clear, the parties are returned to their original positions. In this case, the seller receives the deed; the buyer has the deposited money returned to him.

The numerous trust institution services described in the preceding pages are by no means all-inclusive, and no attempt was made to discuss the many purposes for which trusteeship may be used. Some writers distinguish retirement trusts, spendthrift trusts, discretionary trusts, protective trusts, trusts for emergencies, sheltering trusts, rewarding trusts, common trust funds, and community trust funds.

Common trust fund

A *common trust fund* represents a single trust made up of many smaller fiduciary funds each one of which has a proportionate share in the income and assets of the common trust. It makes available to persons of small means the advantages of trust administration, which would otherwise be too costly in view of the size of the individual fund. In effect, the common trust is much like an open-end investment company. It makes specialized management and diversification feasible for modest accumulations of capital from the standpoint of both the trustee and the beneficiary.

Common trust funds, also called *commingled* or *composite trust funds,* are a means of collective investment. They were originated about 1930, when a number of banks, including particularly the City Farmers Trust Company, of New York City, the Brooklyn Trust Company, of Brooklyn, and the Equitable Trust Company, of Wilmington, Delaware, experimented with the idea. Double taxation under the revenue act was a handicap because the income of the fund itself was taxed, and then the income received from the fund by beneficiaries was taxed. The revenue act was amended in 1936 to exclude from taxation common trust funds organized by a bank or a trust company in states permitting commingled funds if the funds are operated in compliance with Federal Reserve requirements.

Various states passed the necessary enabling legislation in 1937 and succeeding years; and the Federal Reserve authorities, on December 31, 1937, prescribed regulations permitting three classifications of common trust funds: funds limited to not over $1,200 from a single account; funds limited to not over $25,000 from a single account, which limit was later removed; and mortgage investment funds. The two last-named funds are subject to strict regulation. In 1962, authority over trusts in national banks was transferred to the Comptroller of the Currency.

In 1964, a year for which data were published, there were 788 common trust funds in state and national banks. The market value of commingled funds was $5.9 billion and was distributed as follows: bonds, notes, and certificates, 46%; preferred stocks, 4%; common stocks, 47%; and the balance in real estate, savings accounts, and principal cash.[4]

Trust provisions

The trust agreement generally states the policies and outlines the activities of the trustee in the administration of the assets of the trust. The agreement may give the trustee full discretion; may designate spe-

[4] *National Banking Review,* March 1965.

cifically what property is to be held, sold, or purchased; or may make no provision, in which case the trustee is limited by the law governing trust investment. The agreement may, of course, specify that the trustee is to be governed by the state law. Thus there are three possible situations. The trust agreement may spell out the investment policy to be followed, and this governs the trustee. If the trust agreement stipulates that the state law shall determine investment policy, or if the agreement is silent with respect to investment policy, the state law governs.

Prudent man rule and legal lists

Trustees derive their investment powers and are governed by common law and state statutes, by the instructions in the agreement of trust, and by court decisions. Some states follow the prudent man rule, which permits the trustee (unless restricted by the trust agreement) to make such investments as a prudent man would make, having due regard for the preservation of principal and the regularity of income. This principle was first enunciated by the Supreme Judicial Court of Massachusetts in 1830 and is, therefore, often referred to as the *Massachusetts rule*. A few states adopted this rule by statute before 1942, in which year a model prudent man statute was proposed. Since then the District of Columbia and 38 states, including Hawaii, have adopted a prudent man rule, through either legislation or court decision. The prudent man rules in 15 states make specific reference to investment company shares eligible for trust investment subject to statutory limitations.

New York became the 20th state, when it adopted a modified prudent man statute effective July 1, 1950. Under the New York law the trustee is given discretion with respect to the investment of 35% of the value of a trust fund, and the remaining 65% must be invested in fixed-income securities as prescribed by the statute. The practical effect of this statute is that the trustee in New York may now invest up to 35% of a trust fund in other securities, including common stocks. When allowance is made for the fact that New York trust institutions have about one third of the personal trust property of the nation under their supervision, this change in the law may have an important long-run influence on equity prices, particularly in view of the expected growth in industrial pension funds.

States that do not follow the prudent man rule set out specifically the kinds of investments that may be purchased by a trustee, and the securities that meet the requirements under the law constitute what is called the legal list of the state. Under the prudent man rule, if not modified as in New York, there is no legal list.

In a legal list state, if there are losses to the trust fund because the trustee did not conform to the law or the trust instrument or because the trustee did not exercise a proper degree of care, the trustee must make good the loss. Under the prudent man rule, if there is a loss as a result of a transaction that a prudent man would have completed, the trustee is not liable.

Corporate versus the individual trustee

The corporate trustee, as opposed to the individual trustee, has a number of attributes, some of which are undoubtedly responsible to a large extent for the fact that the corporate trustee dominates the field.[5] The more important features for comparison are given in the following paragraphs:

Continuous existence. The term of a trust agreement may run for many years, and the individual trustee may not live to carry out the responsibility he assumed. Or he might become incompetent or otherwise be unable to serve. Administration of the trust might then be interrupted, pending the appointment of a successor trustee, or an accounting might become necessary, and there might even be legal proceedings—all involving a charge against the principal of the trust. The corporate trustee, on the other hand, has perpetual existence.

Continuous capacity. Even a trust institution cannot give assurance that a given trust officer placed in charge of a particular trust will be continuously able to serve, but the trust institution is in a position to make an immediate replacement with a qualified substitute.

Financial responsibility. The resources of the trust institution give assurance of financial responsibility, and this is recognized in most states, in that a surety bond is not required of a trust institution.

Responsiveness to obligations. Because administration of trusts and related activities constitute the principal business of a trust institution, the institution is almost certain to discharge its duties with dispatch and to the letter. There is not quite the same degree of assurance that an individual trustee will do so.

Specialization. The large trust company offering a comprehensive and wide range of services will usually have a well-diversified staff of specialists competent to handle in a coordinated way the various problems likely to arise in the administration of a trust or other fiduciary responsibility.

Group judgment. Not only does the corporate trustee have the advantage of the coordinated findings of staff specialists, but the action to be taken is generally subject to the review of administrative groups or of committees of officers. Regulation F of the Federal Reserve Board of

---

[5] Thomas H. Beacom, "Functions and Services of a Trust Department," in sec. 7, pt. II, of *Fundamentals of Investment Banking* (Chicago: Investment Bankers Association of America, 1947).

Governors requires bank board or committee action with respect to the acceptance or relinquishment of a trust account and requires periodic review of the account, as well as a review of day-to-day action with respect to purchase, sale, or retention of trust holdings.

Impartiality. The corporate trustee is able to act objectively and impersonally with respect to the parties in interest.

Adaptability. Metropolitan trust institutions generally have a staff that is equal to providing whatever experience, skill, or service may be necessary, no matter how diversified the requirements.

Obviously, the individual trustee can lay claim to certain of these attributes, too. He may well have an advantage in the personal administration of property, particularly with respect to relatively small estates. His close acquaintance with the decedent and his familiarity with the affairs and the family of the decedent may be advantageous. He may be able to keep down costs of administration, and his personal interest and attention may be definitely helpful in accomplishing the aims of the testator. The individual trustee may be more enterprising in exercising discretion and less restricted by rules and policies.

Often an individual is named as coexecutor or cotrustee to act with a corporate fiduciary. Such an arrangement combines the facilities of the corporate trustee with the advantage of having an individual trustee participating. The individual is relieved of much detailed responsibility, which is assumed by the corporate fiduciary, but he is able to supply the desired personal element.

Compensation of the trustee

At one time, persons accepted responsibility as executors, guardians, and similar fiduciary relationships as a matter of honor and did not expect to be paid, but it is otherwise in our country today. Fiduciaries have a right to receive reasonable fees for services performed, whether or not compensation is mentioned in the trust instrument. The fees may be based on principal or income, or both, and may be payable out of either income or principal, or both. The rate of compensation is not uniform throughout the country, and it is not even feasible to indicate a range of fees because there are too many variables—for example, section of the country, law of the state, size of city, basis of calculation, precise nature of service rendered, etc. Compensation may be stated in the will or trust agreement, defined by statute, or determined by a court, or may for certain services depend on custom in the area. Each trust institution has a detailed list of fees for all the various services offered, and this information may be had on request.

Only a few examples of compensation rates are cited for illustration:

In New York the compensation of an administrator is established by statute and is based on the value of the total estate, real and personal: first $50,000, one half of 1%; next $450,000, one fourth of 1%; and one fifth of 1% on the balance. In Washington the compensation, established by court on the value of the entire estate, real and personal, would be "reasonable." In both instances an executor, in the event that the will did not mention compensation, would receive the same compensation as the administrator.

In Georgia a trustee under a will would receive, under the statute, 2½% on all sums received and on all sums paid out plus 10% on all loans made by the trustee to the estate; whereas in Kentucky he would receive 5% of income and one fifth of 1% of principal, annually, and extra allowance for unusual services.

Trust institution charges for a full-management agency for a securities investment, including custody, continuous analysis, and constant surveillance, come nearer to being standardized and would probably be about as follows: if the principal is under $100,000, an annual charge of $5 per $1,000; if the principal is between $100,000 and $200,000, a fee of $250 and $2.50 per $1,000; if over $200,000, a fee of $550 plus $1 per $1,000.

The above sampling afford some indication of the rate or amount of trustee compensation and the variability and complexity of the fee structure which make generalization and comparison difficult.[6]

Summary

Trust institutions perform a great variety of useful services of economic and social importance, and on the basis of the foregoing discussion it should be apparent why the trust institution has been called an omnibus of finance. Conservation of wealth, in the sense of safekeeping and directing capital into productive employment, is undoubtedly the outstanding characteristic of trust operations. In fact, to the extent that the trust institution gives direction to the sound and constructive use of funds and thus avoids the wasteful use of assets, trust institutions might even be considered creative. Actually, there is an increasing tendency among trustmen toward the acceptance of responsibility not only for the traditional role of conservation but also for growth of the funds under their administration. To this end, common stocks are increasingly being recognized as appropriate for trust investment to a greater degree than in earlier years. The spreading adoption of the prudent man rule is indicative of this trend. The trust institution in its capacity as administrator, executor, guardian, and conservator aids in conserving and dis-

---

[6] The foregoing illustrations and discussion of compensation are based on more comprehensive exhibits of charges covering a great variety of trust services, as, e.g., reported in A. P. Loring, *A Trustee's Handbook* (Farr ed., Boston: Little, Brown & Co., 1962).

tributing property as it passes from one generation to another; and in the process, it protects the interests of minors and incompetents.

Trust institutions, as guardians and trustees, also serve individuals in a more personal and intimate way that transcends the purely financial. They provide guidance to minors and incompetents in meeting many of life's problems.

Questions and problems

1. What is a trust? Define and give an illustration.
2. Are a trustee and a fiduciary identical? Explain.
3. What does the term *trust business* encompass?
4. In what ways may a corporate trustee serve the individual?
5. What is the purpose of a legal list of investments that may be purchased by a trustee? Does the legal list contribute to the flexibility of investment policy by a trustee?
6. Discuss trusteeship and its relation to the flow of savings into investment.
7. Why is the trust business confined largely to metropolitan communities? What type of trust is most important in less populated communities?
8. Do you see any connection between the growth of trust business and the longer life span of individuals?
9. Do you favor the increasing purchases of common stocks for personal trusts? Explain.
10. In what respect does the trust company offer a service that might be considered competitive to the investment counselor? The open-end investment company?
11. Is your state in the group of states having a prudent man law?
12. Obtain a schedule of charges from a local trust institution and compare the rates with the few examples given in the text. Would you say that rates seem to be standardized?
13. What advantages, if any, are afforded by the corporate trustee as against the individual professional trustee? May a nonprofessional individual trustee provide any special advantage? How might the two sets of benefits be combined?

Bibliography

A comprehensive coverage of trust services for the individual is found in G. T. Stephenson's *Estates and Trusts* (rev. ed.; New York: Appleton-Century-Crofts, Inc., 1955), which is written for senior and graduate college students, not as a manual or text for professionals, but rather to provide the individual with the information that an informed person should have about fiduciary services offered by the professional trustee. A detailed history of trust institutions in this country is provided by J. G. Smith's *The Development of Trust Companies in the United States* (New York: Henry Holt & Co., 1928); and a review of trust institution business and practices in the United States is included in G. T. Stephenson's *Trust Business in Common Law Countries* (New York: Research Council, American Bankers Association, 1940), which emphasizes foreign trust business. The American Bankers Association, Trust Division, periodically publishes a *Bibliography on Trust Business*.

There are two monthly publications, devoted to estates and trusts and published primarily for trustmen, that frequently contain articles and analyses of a general nature of interest to nonprofessionals: the *Trust Bulletin,* published monthly, September to June, Trust Division, American Bankers Association, New York, and *Trusts and Estates,* published monthly, Fiduciary Publishers, Inc., New York.

G. T. Gilbert, who has written profusely on trusts, is also the author of *Drafting Wills and Trust Agreements: Dispositive Provisions* (Boston: Little, Brown & Co., 1955), which is a companion volume to his earlier *Administrative Provisions*. Both books are primarily for the lawyer and trustman but are also of value to the interested lay reader.

Some recent data are available in the *Institutional Investors Study Report of the Securities and Exchange Commission* (Washington, D.C.: Government Printing Office, 1971).

CHAPTER 15

Saving through pension funds

A pension, at its simplest, is an annuity paid to a retired person as long as he lives. In this form a pension is not appreciably different in its characteristics from an annuity sold by a life insurance company (and, indeed, many pensions are annuities carried with life insurance companies). This simple concept of a pension has, in practice, come to be modified in many respects. For example, many pensions provide a retirement income not only for the recipient but also for surviving dependents, mainly wives. Pension funds are also sometimes combined with various types of insurance, such as for survivors of the pensioner or annuitant if he should die while still working. Pension plans may also attempt to assure income for the principal as well as for his dependents in case of disability.

In recent years several types of savings institutions have grown rapidly. Among the leaders in rapid growth have been pension funds. The assets in these funds, if public funds are combined with private funds, passed the $100 billion mark in 1960 and are now estimated to be almost $240 billion.

The rise of pension funds illustrates dramatically the responsiveness of financial institutions to basic economic needs. The great depression of the 1930s caused many respectable people who had failed to provide adequately for their old age to suffer considerable privation. Accordingly, a demand grew for more systematic means of providing for the needs of old age and retirement. Some of these needs have been met through governmental social security programs, but a large proportion have been met through a variety of private or semiprivate pension plans. This chapter will deal with the public social security provision for old-age income as well as the private pension plans. Over the years, private pension funds have increased more rapidly than public funds. At present, private funds account for 53% of all pension fund assets.

The economic significance of private and public pension plans is that they are a means of meeting one of the commonest needs for individual saving: provision for income in old age. The fact that saving through pension funds accounts for roughly one third of total consumer saving is a demonstration of this feature. The point has even broader economic significance since the existence of these pension plans determines in part whether savings tend to be quite stable through all phases of business boom and business recession or whether they are volatile.

Another economic question of considerable significance is the extent to which pension plans provide protection against changing price levels. In countries that have suffered extreme inflation, even the most prudent and careful savers have sometimes been impoverished by the loss of purchasing power of their retirement funds. This issue is of considerable significance not only for the investment policies of pension funds in the United States but also for the terms and conditions under which benefits are established.

Pension funds also illustrate another quite significant factor in our economic scene: the effect of income taxes. The income tax law allows the amounts contributed by employers to pension funds to be treated as income by the individual only when he actually receives it in the form of a pension. This usually means that effective taxes on this portion of income are lower, since income is usually smaller after retirement. This tax factor not only has had the profound effect of shifting upward the demand for pensions but has also tended to increase the contributions of employers more than was initially contemplated when most pension plans were established.

Types of pension and retirement plans

Because pension and retirement plans have sprung from many individual circumstances, a great multiplicity of types of plans have evolved. Precise classification of these plans is not possible. The following descriptive account undoubtedly blurs many details of considerable interest. Nevertheless, private and public pension plans might be classified into the several broad categories or types shown in Exhibit 15–1.

EXHIBIT 15–1

Types of pension or retirement plans

1. Insured pensions
   - a) Conventional group annuities
   - b) Deposit administration annuities
   - c) Individual policy pension trusts
2. Trusteed or self-administered funds
   - a) Private corporate noninsured pension funds
   - b) Nonprofit, union-administered, or multicompany plans
   - c) Pension funds for government employees
     - (1) Civil Service Retirement Fund
     - (2) State and local government pension funds
3. Old Age, Survivors, and Disability Insurance
4. Railroad Retirement Fund

Insured pensions

Insured pension plans are administered by life insurance companies, generally as a special part of their annuity programs. Insured pension plans, by their nature, tend to be more fully funded, though the degree of vesting varies among contracts. (See the following section for an explanation of terms.) Most insured pension plans fall into one of the following three groups:

Conventional group annuities are paid-up annuity units purchased each year for the members of the group. These contracts, however, cover groups as such, so that the participants do not secure rights as individuals until the period of either vesting or retirement is reached. If an individual leaves employment before vesting or retirement, his contributions are usually returned to him, and the employer's prior contributions are used to reduce his current contributions.

Deposit administration plans (the fastest growing of insured pension plans) are programs in which the life insurance company administering the plan accumulates a fund based on employer and employee contributions, against which the cost of an annuity is charged as each covered employee reaches retirement age.

Individual policy pension trusts are used mainly by very small companies. An individual annuity contract is purchased for each of the members covered under these trusts.

In general, insured pension plans are used by companies somewhat smaller than those that administer their own pension plans.

The data presented in Table 15–1 show that the total book value of the assets in private insured pension funds rose from under $18 billion in 1959 to $35 billion in 1968, a doubling in 10 years.

TABLE 15-1

Assets of all public and private pension funds* *(billions of dollars)*

	1959	1960	1961	1962	1963	1964	1965	1966	1967	1968
Private										
Insured pension reserves†	17.6	18.8	20.2	21.6	23.3	25.2	27.4	29.4	32.0	35.0
(Separate accounts, included above)‡	—	—	—	—§	—§	.1	.3	.6	1.2	2.3
Noninsured pension funds	29.0	33.1	37.5	41.9	46.6	51.9	58.1	64.5	71.8ʳ	80.3ʳ
Total private funds	46.6	52.0	57.8	63.5	69.9	77.2	85.4	93.9	103.9ʳ	115.3ʳ
Government										
Railroad retirement	3.7	3.7	3.7	3.7	3.8	3.8	3.9	4.0	4.2	4.3
Civil service	9.6	10.6	11.6	12.7	13.8	15.0	16.2	17.3	18.4	19.8
State and local	17.1	19.3	21.7	24.3	27.1	30.2	33.5	37.3	41.3	45.8
Federal and Old Age and Survivors Insurance	20.1	20.3	19.7	18.3	18.5	19.1	18.2	20.6	24.2	25.7
Federal Disability Insurance	1.8	2.3	2.4	2.4	2.2	2.0	1.6	1.7	2.0	3.0
Total government funds	52.4	56.3	59.2	61.4	65.4	70.2	73.5	80.8	90.2	98.6
Total	99.0	108.3	117.0	124.9	135.2	147.3	159.0	174.7	194.1ʳ	214.0ʳ

* Book value, end of year.
† Statement value.
‡ Separate accounts of life insurance companies, set up for specific pension plans, allow greater investment latitude than is permissible under state laws for general life insurance assets.
§ Less than $50 million.
ʳ Revised.
Note: Figures may not add to totals because of rounding.
Source: SEC *Statistical Series*, release #2406, December 1969.

Trusteed or self-administered funds

Noninsured pension funds are substantially larger in terms of total assets than are the insured funds. In 1959 assets of these funds were $29 billion; by 1968 they had reached a total of $80 billion, an increase of 270%.

These plans vary greatly both in the generosity of their benefits and in the character of their investment policies. As mentioned in a later section, those plans in which the employer guarantees given benefits but does not fund the plan in full often tend to invest their funds rather aggressively in an effort to make investment income meet a considerable portion of the cost.

Corporate pension funds have usually been started voluntarily, but some were established as a part of union-negotiated employment contracts. Some funds include, or are even dominated by, union trustees, but if benefits are guaranteed, the funds tend to be controlled by trustees named by the employers. In industries marked by many small companies but with one large dominant union, the union-dominated type of multi-company pension trust tends to prevail.

A number of trusteed or self-administered pension funds for nonprofit institutions or for quasi-governmental administrative institutions also exist. For example, one of the more interesting and progressive of the self-administered funds is the Teachers Insurance and Annuity Association (TIAA), together with the associated College Retirement Equities Fund (CREF). TIAA was established originally on the basis of a grant from the Carnegie Foundation to help in the decent and orderly retirement of collegiate teachers. Another example of such funds is a large one for the retirement of Protestant ministers. Still another example of a large trusteed, self-administered fund on the margin between private business and government is the retirement fund of the Federal Reserve System, which covers mainly the employees of the Federal Reserve banks but also includes board employees.

Special governmental retirement plans

The Civil Service Retirement System covers federal government employees and had accumulated assets of $20 billion at the end of 1968. Since the assets in this fund were only $10 billion in 1959, the growth rate of this fund was comparable to that of the insured private funds.

This retirement fund is one in which the benefits are strictly governed by congressional legislation. The assets accumulated in the fund are considerably short of those required for discharge of the benefits set by Congress. In other words, the ability of the fund to discharge its liabilities depends on future congressional appropriations.

State and local government retirement plans command substantially more assets than the civil service plans. In 1959 these plans had assets of $17 billion, and by 1968 they increased to almost $46 billion. The rate of growth of these funds was comparable to that of the noninsured private funds.

These retirement plans employ a wide variety of methods for setting benefits and investing funds. In some cases the trustees of these plans are publicly elected officials, many without much knowledge of financial administration. As a result, the investment rules for these plans are frequently quite strict and simple, such as allowing investment only in obligations of the U.S. government or of state and local governments. In recent years the need for increasing the income from these funds has created a demand for more liberal investment provisions. Such liberalization, however, has not been as extensive as that of corporate investment funds.

The retirement benefits for a large number of state and local government funds are, like those of the Civil Service Retirement System, established by statute or by arbitrary rules. As a result, the funds accumulated are frequently inadequate to discharge their liabilities, so that the continued operation of these funds depends on future appropriations or supplements.

The Railroad Retirement System is a special fund administered by the federal government for the benefit of employees of the railroad industry. About a million and a half employees are covered, and about $4.3 billion of assets have been accumulated in this retirement fund at the end of 1968.

Old Age, Survivors, and Disability Insurance (social security or OASDI)

The most comprehensive of all of the programs providing pensions and other related benefits is the program of the federal government to provide pensions for the old, insurance for the survivors or dependents of those who die, and disability benefits. The program was initiated in 1934 and has since been expanded several times in terms of its coverage, while its benefits have also been materially improved.

Contributions to the social security retirement fund are made by both employers and employees. Participation is also available to some self-employed persons. The rates of contribution have been considerably less than the actuarial cost of the benefits provided, so that the fund is much smaller than its potential liabilities. Since 1954 the fund has grown hardly at all. In that year its assets were $20 billion, and in 1968 its assets were only $26 billion. Indeed, from 1959 through 1965, the size of the fund actually shrank! The ratio of those receiving benefits to those making contributions is now about six to one. When the fund has stabilized according to present life expectancy, the rate will be more nearly three to one. In other words, contributions will have to be doubled if the fund is to be made self-sustaining. This fact has been reflected in the increased rates of OASDI taxation of recent years.

To summarize, the total book value of the assets of all pension funds, both government and private, increased from slightly under $100 billion in 1959 to over $214 billion in 1968. During this period, the assets of private funds increased from $47 billion to $115 billion while the assets of the government funds increased from $52 billion to $99 billion.

Terms for accumulation and distribution of pension funds

Since pension funds have been established under diverse circumstances, the terms for both their accumulation and their distribution vary widely.

Contributions and payments

As indicated in the introduction, tax considerations argue for maximizing the contributions of employers to pension funds and minimizing those of employees. Most employees are better off in the number of dollars that they will receive if they get their pay raises in the form of larger employer contributions to their retirement fund rather than in cash. Of course, money that is received at a later date has a lower present value than money received immediately. The reason that the number of dollars to be received is greater is that the contributions of employees are

TABLE 15–2

Receipts and disbursements of private noninsured pension funds (*millions of dollars*)

	1964	1965	1966	1967	1968
Employer contributions	4,740	5,400	5,980	6,560	7,190
Employee contributions	600	660	690	750	860
Investment income	1,990	2,350	2,620	2,870	3,110
Net profit on sale of assets	390	570	490	980	1,350
Other receipts	40	50	90	50	90
Total receipts	7,750	9,030	9,870	11,210	12,600
Benefits paid out	2,320	2,650	3,140	3,380	3,880
Expenses and other disbursements ...	70	80	100	110	120
Total disbursements	2,390	2,730	3,240	3,500	4,000
Net receipts	5,360	6,300	6,630	7,720	8,610

Source: SEC *Statistical Series*, release #2406, December 1969.

taxed at the rate applying to the taxpayer at time of contribution, but the contributions of the employer are taxed at the rate applying at time of receipt, usually a considerably lower tax rate.

The contributions and payments (receipts and disbursements) of private noninsured pension funds in recent years is presented in Table 15–2.

Exhibit 15–2 illustrates the 10-year trend of the income account of all private noninsured pension funds. Within receipts, employer contributions were $7.2 billion in 1968 and made up almost 90% of combined employer-employee contributions—a slightly larger proportion than 10 years previous. Investment income has increased over the years proportionate to growth in total assets. Net profit on sale of assets and other receipts, combined in the exhibit, have shown considerable growth, but have a less predictable trend.

Total disbursements, almost entirely benefits paid out, were $4 billion in 1968. Disbursements were 32% of receipts as compared to 24% 10

EXHIBIT 15–2

Receipts and disbursements (*private noninsured pension funds*)

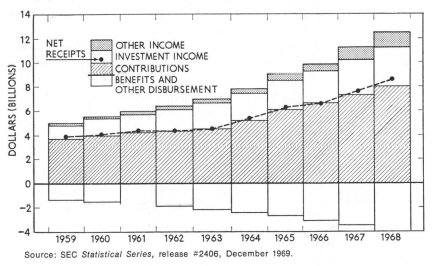

Source: SEC *Statistical Series,* release #2406, December 1969.

years ago. Net receipts of all private noninsured pension funds were $8.6 billion in 1968.

Funding

Actuaries can estimate the ultimate cost of a pension in the form of an annuity with considerable precision. On the basis of these cost estimates, the most prudent or conservative policy would be to accumulate currently funds equal to the annual increase in liability of a pension fund. Such a policy is called *complete funding*. The modal practice of pension funds with regard to funding is not accurately known; no comprehensive statistics have been compiled regarding this. Nevertheless, it appears that partial funding is quite common. Insured pensions are fully funded, but this is true of only a relatively few self-administered funds. As already mentioned, Old Age, Survivors, and Disability Insurance is funded to only a moderate extent. The same might be said of a large number of industrial plans that have been adopted as the result of union-management bargaining arrangements. On the other hand, TIAA and many nonprofit pension plans are fully funded, with the annuity contract always equal to the accumulated funds available.

The degree of funding depends to some extent on the matter of vesting (treated in the next section) and on employee turnover. A great many pensions are paid only to employees who work until retirement for the concern sponsoring the pension or complete a considerable period of service. Under those circumstances, only a fraction of the employees at a given time will ever qualify for pensions. If delayed vesting prevails, it is rather rare for a plan to be fully funded. On the other hand, if there is full vesting, complete funding is much more likely.

The contributions of employers to some pension funds are made by profit-sharing plans. Profit-sharing plans cover almost a million employees, and in about three quarters of these cases the shared profits are put into irrevocable trusts which are used for the payment of pensions. Money derived from profit sharing apparently accounts for about 5% of employer contributions to self-administered corporate pension funds.

Vesting

A pension is said to be fully vested in its ultimate recipient if and when he has full rights to its benefits without regard to his subsequent employment. (This does not mean he has access to the money involved. In fact, he may have no right to the funds until retirement, as is true in TIAA annuity contracts. However, he may change employers without losing any of his ultimate pension rights.)

Full and immediate vesting is comparatively rare. The Bankers Trust Company, which administers a large number of important private pension plans, has found, through frequent surveys, that only about 2–4% of pension plans provide for immediate vesting. Vesting on completion of some period of service, such as after 5 or 10 or 20 years, is far more common. In some plans vesting may be attained at some given age, such as 50 or 60. There are also vesting rules based on formulas combining periods of service with attained age. In general, most plans allow for some vesting of the rights of the annuitant after a period of service, though a few of them have no vesting whatsoever, so that members attain no rights until the actual moment of retirement.

The economic principle involved in vesting relates to the binding of the potential pensioner or annuitant to his place of employment. The Teachers Insurance and Annuity Association provided for immediate vesting as a matter of principle because it was felt that collegiate teachers should not be inhibited by virtue of a pending, but not yet completed, period for attainment of pension benefits in moving from school to school if their interests or their employing schools demanded it. On the other hand, many private employers feel that pension rights properly belong only to those who have stayed loyally with their company for a given period of time. This is viewed as an incentive for reducing turnover. At the same time, delayed vesting may have the disadvantage of tending to freeze into employment those who are ill-fitted for their tasks or are unproductive in them but who hesitate to change jobs and thus lose valuable pension benefits.

Variable annuities

As Chapter 12 on life insurance points out, most annuities are payable in a fixed number of dollars. However, the specter of inflation and of the changing value of money has attracted many to the idea that annuities or pensions should be first accumulated and then disbursed in units which would tend to vary in dollar value with changes in the price level, i.e., so-called variable annuities, which were discussed in Chapter 12.

Investment policies

The investment policies of pension funds depend, to a considerable extent, on the way in which benefits are determined. If benefits depend on the amount available in the fund and the employer discharges his liability to the pension fund by making a certain fixed and determined contribution, investment policy is likely to be conservative. On the other hand, in some self-administered pension funds pensioners have a right to a certain fixed dollar amount of pension. The employer must provide sufficient funds to pay such pensions. The investment policies of such pension and annuity funds are likely to be aggressive for if the assets of the fund can earn more, the employer contribution can be reduced.

Insured pensions are liabilities of the insurance companies that have assumed the business and in that regard are similar to the other annuity contracts sold by life insurance companies. There is no segregation of assets covering the pension funds by life insurance companies, so it cannot be said that there is a special investment policy applying to this sector of the business. The comments on general life insurance investment policy made in Chapter 12 are applicable to this particular part of the business.

The self-administered or trusteed type of pension fund that is fully funded, whether through the contribution of employers or those of employees, tends to follow relatively conservative investment policies. On the other hand, where there is a contingent liability in a pension trust that is not fully funded, there is a tendency for the administrators to try to maximize earnings. Thus there has been a movement into common stock investment even by pension funds that have fixed dollar liabilities. Exhibit 15-3 shows how the composition of assets of the private, noninsured

EXHIBIT 15-3

Distribution of assets* (*private noninsured pension funds*)

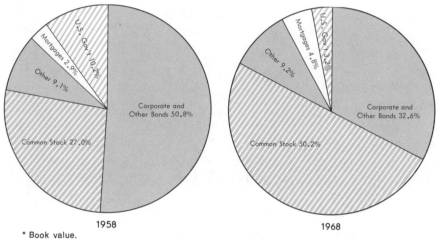

1958   1968

* Book value.
Source: SEC *Statistical Series*, release #2406, December 1969

pension funds has changed over the past decade. The growth in common stock holdings is striking.

The data supporting Exhibit 15-3 are presented in Table 15-3. These data are book value figures, which means that the actual purchase price of the asset is recorded, not the market value of the asset. Table 15-4 presents the market value of the assets of pension funds. The difference between book and market value in some cases is worth commenting upon.

Contrast for example the values of corporate bonds and stocks that are held by pension funds. The book value of the bonds—what was paid for them—was $26.2 billion in 1968. However, if these bonds were to be sold, they could only realize $21.7 billion; in short, $4.5 billion of value eroded. The reason for this was that interest rates rose, driving down the capital value of the bonds. The common stock then held had a book value of $40 billion, and a market value of $58 billion, a gain of $18 billion.

Assets of private noninsured pension funds, at book values* (millions of dollars)

	1959	1960	1961	1962	1963	1964	1965	1966	1967ʳ	1968ʳ
Cash and deposits	540	550	660	710	770	890	940	900	1,320	1,640
U.S. government securities	2,810	2,680	2,720	2,920	3,050	3,070	3,100	2,610	2,170	2,540
Corporate and other bonds	14,080	15,700	16,880	18,100	19,560	21,210	22,700	24,580	25,500	26,160
Preferred stock	770	780	760	750	710	650	750	790	980	1,320
Common stock	8,670	10,730	13,340	15,730	18,120	20,840	24,450	28,340	33,830	40,260
Own company	780	890	1,040	1,180	1,340	1,470	1,840ʳ	2,100ʳ	2,570	2,820
Other companies	7,890	9,850	12,300	14,540	16,780	19,370	22,620ʳ	26,240ʳ	31,260	37,440
Mortgages	990	1,300	1,560	1,880	2,220	2,750	3,320	3,810	3,940	3,910
Other assets	1,150	1,400	1,590	1,800	2,120	2,510	2,820	3,430	4,110	4,450
Total assets	29,050	33,140	37,510	41,890	46,550	51,910	58,090	64,470	71,840	80,280
Change in total assets	3,770	4,080	4,380	4,380	4,660	5,360	6,180	6,380	7,380	8,440

TABLE 15–4

Assets of private noninsured pension funds, at market values* (millions of dollars)

	1959	1960	1961	1962	1963	1964	1965	1966	1967ʳ	1968
Cash and deposits	500	500	700	700	800	900	900	900	1,300	1,600
U.S. government securities	2,600	2,700	2,700	2,900	3,000	3,000	3,000	2,600	2,100	2,400
Corporate and other bonds	12,500	14,600	15,900	17,500	18,800	20,500	21,500	21,900	21,900	21,700
Preferred stock	700	700	700	700	700	700	800	800	1,000	1,300
Common stock	13,800	15,800	22,100	21,200	27,000	32,900	38,900	37,800	48,500	58,000
Own company	1,800	2,000	3,000	2,600	3,100	3,800	4,400ʳ	3,600ʳ	5,100	5,700
Other companies	12,100	13,800	19,100	18,600	23,800	29,000	34,500ʳ	34,200ʳ	43,400	52,200
Mortgages	1,000	1,300	1,600	1,900	2,200	2,800	3,300	3,700	3,900	3,400
Other assets	1,200	1,400	1,600	1,800	2,200	2,600	2,900	3,400	4,100	4,200
Total assets	32,400	37,100	45,300	46,700	54,600	63,400	71,400	71,000	82,700	92,700
Change in total assets	4,200	4,700	8,200	1,500	7,900	8,700	8,100	−400	11,700	10,000

* Includes funds of corporations, nonprofit organizations, and multiemployer and union plans. End of year.
ʳ Revised.
Note: Figures may not add to totals because of rounding.
Source: SEC *Statistical Series*, release #2406, December 1969.

This then explains one reason for the investment policy that the funds have taken—the return was substantially higher in the purchase of stocks than bonds. Whether this will continue to be true in the future is, of course, a debatable point. It was not true in 1969.

Economic effects of pension funds

The sheer magnitude of the pension funds inevitably means that they have pervasive effects on the financial and economic structure of the country. In recent years, approximately 10% of the savings by households were directed to pension funds and 10% of the assets held by households are in the form of pension fund reserves. A more important but less measurable potential is their influence on individual economic behavior.

Effects of pensions on saving

Since provision for old age has always been one of the principal factors accounting for saving, it is natural to expect that pension funds should have an important influence on both the amount of other saving and its timing. Those who expect to receive a retirement pension might reduce their saving. It is extraordinarily hard to determine whether this is only a possibility or an actual result. When the OASDI was first initiated, it was widely thought that private savings might be reduced, but cross-section studies of consumer finance do not yield any evidence supporting this hypothesis. The rapid expansion of pensions occurred during a period of such general prosperity that the effects of pensions on saving cannot be separated from other effects. With increased income, a growth in aggregate saving might have been expected, but it has not occurred. It is conceivable, though not provable and certainly not measurable, that the existence of pension funds has reduced other forms of saving.

Influence of pensions on capital flow

The investment policies of pension funds doubtless have a great influence on relative interest rates and on the direction of capital flow. So far, pension funds have concentrated on acquiring high-grade marketable securities and so doubtless have increased the prices of bonds and of high-grade common stocks. On the other hand, pension funds have been unable to organize effectively the mechanics for acquisition of mortgages (except to the extent that life insurance companies administer pension funds), and so they may have retarded the flow of funds into residential mortgages. It is even conceivable that pension funds have had some influence on relative prices of common stocks—tending to increase the prices of conservative companies with growth prospects more than other types of common stocks. Although not demonstrable, it is conceivable that pension funds may tend to make for less export of capital and more domestic investment, since pension funds are clearly more limited in making external investments than are some other savings institutions.

Effect of pensions on number of persons in labor force

Pension funds make retirement possible at moderately early ages—typically at some age between 60 and 70. On the other hand, with medical science increasing longevity, we face the possibility of a growing proportion of older, retired persons in the population. In other words, the proportion of employed to total population may decline as a result of pensions. As a rich nation, one of our luxuries may be fewer years of work and more years of leisure for a substantial proportion of the population.

Pension-fund accumulation and interest rates

So far, the rate of accumulation of funds by pensions does not appear to have been sensitive to business cycle developments. Accumulations in the moderately depressed postwar years continued without visible slackening. On the other hand, a speeding up of accumulation in boom years cannot be detected. This means that pension funds tend to stabilize the flow of capital to the markets. If capital demands were also stabilized, the influence of pensions on interest rates would be moderate. If capital demands continue to fluctuate, as seems likely, the stability of pension fund accumulation could lead to greater instability of interest rates than in the past, when both the supply of and demand for capital funds tended to be positively correlated with the business cycle.

Questions and problems _____

1. What appears to account for the rapid growth of private pension plans in recent years at the same time that social security benefits have been liberalized?

2. Explain the influence of taxes on the introduction of pension plans and also on the division of contributions within existing plans.

3. What is the distinction between an insured and a self-administered private pension plan?

4. What implications do fixed benefits have for the investment policies of private corporate pension plans?

5. What influence has price level expectations had on such investment policies?

6. Explain vesting. Illustrate the incentive effects of delayed vesting.

7. Is delayed vesting good social policy?

8. Explain funding. Why do full funding and full vesting tend to be paired?
9. When is less-than-full funding prudent?
10. What evidence is there of any influence of pensions on other forms of saving?
11. What may have been the influence of pensions on interest rates?
12. What are some possible future effects of pensions on the size of the gross national product?

Bibliography

Our understanding of both public and private pension funds has been enriched by the studies of the National Bureau of Economic Research, under the aegis of Professor Roger Murray. These studies include Phillip Cagan's *The Effect of Pension Plans on Aggregate Saving: Evidence from Sample Survey* (New York: National Bureau of Economic Research, 1965) and Daniel Holland's *Private Pension Funds: Projected Growth.* (New York: National Bureau of Economic Research, 1966). The Brookings Institution study, *Industrial Pensions* by Charles L. Dearing (Washington, D.C.: Brookings Institution, 1954), remains significant. Two recent books are: D. M. McGill, *Fundamentals of Private Pensions* (Homewood, Ill.: Richard D. Irwin, Inc., 1964), and M. C. Bernstein, *The Future of Private Pensions* (New York: The Free Press of Glencoe, 1964). Figures on corporate pension plans are published in the *Statistical Bulletin* of the Securities and Exchange Commission and perspectives are provided by the flow-of-funds data published by the Board of Governors of the Federal Reserve System.

PART IV

BUSINESS FINANCE

Our attention to this point has been focused on money, commercial banking, the money market, and capital market intermediary institutions. In the next four chapters attention shifts from the suppliers to the demanders of capital market funds; in particular to the most important user of capital market funds, the business firm. Consumer finance, public finance, and international finance will be discussed in the three parts following the present one. The four chapters of this part discuss the financial aspects of corporate organization, the financing of large business, the characteristics of securities markets, and the financing of small business—the most important segments of the capital markets insofar as business finance is concerned.

CHAPTER 16

Financial aspects of corporate organization

The objective of this chapter is to describe the financial aspects of the corporate form of business organization. This form of organization characterizes America's larger business firms. By purchasing the securities that these companies issue, both individual and institutional investors can participate in the financing of business ventures. The widespread popularity of this form of organization is therefore a significant factor in the development of the American capital market.

The dominance of the corporation

To many people the terms *corporation* and *business* are almost synonymous, and it is easy to understand why this is so. Corporations produce most goods and services, account for a substantial part of the sales volume of the nation, hire most of the gainfully employed workers, and utilize most of the funds made available to business.

While there are a large number of small and medium-sized businesses organized under the corporate form, most small firms are either single proprietorships or general partnerships; and a much smaller number of firms use one of the less common legal forms of organization: special forms of partnership, including limited partnership, limited partnership association, joint venture, and mining partnership; joint-stock company; Massachusetts (common-law or business) trust; and cooperative.

TABLE 16–1

Businesses—number and receipts—selected years (*numbers in thousands, dollar figures in millions*)

	1939	1960	1967*
Number			
Proprietorships	1,052	9,090	9,126
Partnerships	271	941	906
Corporations	470	1,141	1,534
Business receipts			
Proprietorships	23,505	171,257	211,372
Partnerships	14,763	74,308	78,023
Corporations	132,878	849,132	1,285,000

* Last year for which summary data were published.
Source: U.S. Treasury Department, *Statistics of Income, Business Income Tax Returns,* various issues.

The data in Table 16–1 show the trend in the number of proprietorships, partnerships, and corporations since 1939. Note that between 1939 and 1967, the number of proprietorships increased nine times while the number of corporations increased threefold. The total sales of corporations, however, continue to be roughly six times that of proprietorships.

The data in Table 16–2 provide additional perspective on the three forms of business organization. Note that proprietorships are heavily concentrated in agriculture, retail trades, and services. Corporations, however, are more evenly distributed throughout all forms of business.

What accounts for the dominance of the corporate form of enterprise

TABLE 16–2

Businesses—number, by form of organization and industrial division, 1967 (*in thousands*)

	Proprietorships	Partnerships	Corporations
Agriculture, forestry, and fisheries	3,196	125	32
Mining	46	13	14
Contract construction	680	52	123
Manufacturing	170	34	197
Transportation, communication, electric, gas, and sanitary services	278	15	66
Wholesale trade	260	31	143
Retail trade	1,544	187	316
Finance, insurance, and real estate	549	245	399
Services	2,328	166	221
Total*	9,126	906	1,534

* Includes business firms not classified by industry.
Source: U.S. Treasury Department, *Statistics of Income, Business Income Tax Returns,* 1967.

Financial institutions

in terms of size and the dominance of the proprietorship in terms of number? A brief description of the individual proprietorship and the general partnership and comparison of both with the corporation will provide the explanation.[1] We will show the relative status of the corporation, explain how it raises permanent capital, and point out some of the social and economic problems that grow out of the wide use of the corporate form of organization.

Characteristics of major business forms

Individual proprietorships and general partnerships are in many ways comparable. Both have very little in common with the corporation and are of secondary importance in terms of aggregate value added to the economy's output and compensation of employees. There are four basic differences between the corporation and the other two major business forms: ease of starting the business; evidence of ownership; liability of the owners for the obligations of the business; and length of life. Of these four differences, the liability feature transcends all others in significance.

Inception

There is little, if any, formality in connection with the establishment of either the single proprietorship or the general partnership (unless articles of agreement are drawn up in connection with the latter). The organizer, or organizers, need merely start in business without obtaining sanction from anyone. Capital is usually self-provided or obtained from family, friends, or acquaintances. Some funds may be obtained from banks, small business investment corporations, or professional friends. There is usually little, if any, attempt made to obtain permanent capital from the general public. Until the business is established as a going and profitable enterprise, there is little likelihood of getting much capital from such sources unless the organizers have means outside the business to give them adequate credit standing.

In organizing a corporation, on the other hand, certain formalities must be observed, and the process is more expensive. The organizers (incorporators) must apply to the state for a charter by filing a certificate of incorporation, the contents of which must meet the requirements of the corporation statutes. They must also pay the fees or charges for incorporation. After the appropriate state official has approved the charter (the

---

[1] A discussion of the legal characteristics and the advantages and disadvantages of the several forms of business organization will be found in most textbooks on business organization and particularly in texts on business finance or corporation finance. For a comprehensive presentation see H. G. Guthmann and H. E. Dougall, *Corporate Financial Policy* (4th ed.; New York: Prentice-Hall, Inc., 1962).

articles of incorporation), the bylaws are adopted. The latter supplement the charter in outlining the working regulations of the corporation.

Evidence of ownership

In neither the single proprietorship nor the general partnership is there any formal evidence of ownership. In the proprietorship, the owner takes all the risk, owns all the assets, and is responsible for all obligations of the business. In the general partnership, ownership interest in the business and the right to the profits depend on the arrangement between the partners, an arrangement that need not be in writing, although self-interest would dictate that it should be.

Ownership in the corporation, however, is represented by shares as provided in the charter and is evidenced by stock certificates. These certificates may be for one share or for hundreds of shares. A stockholder has an interest in the assets and earnings of the corporation in direct proportion to the number of shares he owns. A corporation may have but one class of stock (common stock); or it may have, in addition, one or more issues of preferred stock, which is differentiated as to claims to assets, earnings, dividends, or voting power, or a combination of these factors.

If the corporation has long-term debt, it is usually in the form of a bond issue. In the event of liquidation of the business, the bondholders have a claim prior to that of the stockholders.

Thus, in obtaining their permanent capital, corporations may use credit instruments (bonds) or special classes of stock, and they must use common stock. The very nature of the individual proprietorship and the general partnership makes issuance of stocks and bonds infeasible.

Liability of owners

The individual proprietor is responsible for all his business debts. He risks his entire estate, including assets not used in the business. If the business is liquidated and the assets of the business venture are not sufficient to pay off all the obligations, any property the individual holds is subject to levy.

Any general partner is likewise subject to unlimited liability for debts of the partnership. His liability is not limited to his proportionate share or to the amount of his investment. Partners are jointly and severally liable for all the debts of the partnership. For example, assume that a millionaire invests $10,000 for a one-tenth interest in a general partnership and that the partnership ultimately fails, with net obligations of $100,000. Creditors of the partnership must sue all the partners but may collect the entire amount from any one, in this instance, possibly the millionaire. He may, in turn, recover from the other partners if they have any assets.

In contrast, the loss of the corporation stockholder is limited to the amount of his investment. This is one of the most important distinguishing features of the corporation and it is one factor that accounts for the popularity of the corporate form of organization in big business. It should be noted that it is possible in most states to limit the liability of some partners through formation of a limited partnership; but even in this case, there must be at least one partner who has unlimited liability.

Advantages of the corporate form

There are a number of advantages other than limited liability that help to explain the predominance of the corporate form of enterprise.

Legal entity. The corporation is a person in the eyes of the law; it has identity apart from that of the owners. Legal action is brought against the corporation and not the stockholders. In a partnership, however, legal action is directed at the partnership and the individual partners.

The stockholder's management responsibility is limited principally to electing directors and voting on policy questions at occasional stockholders' meetings, whereas general partners are usually the operating heads of the business, responsible for day-to-day operations, as well as for setting long-run policies.

Permanence. Unless the business fails or the stockholders vote to dissolve, the corporation may go on without interruption for the term indicated in the charter—usually a period of years subject to renewal. An individual proprietorship ends at the will of the owner or when he becomes disabled or dies. A partnership is dissolved by the withdrawal of a partner or by his legal disability, bankruptcy, or death.

Transferability. A stockholder may transfer his stock to others; and in the case of well-known stocks having a public market, such transfer may take no longer than the time required to telephone a sell order to a stockbroker. The life of the corporation is not affected by the death, incompetence, or bankruptcy of a stockholder.

A partner may transfer his interest only with the consent of the other partners, and even then the old partnership is dissolved.

Administrative efficiency. Responsibilities in the corporation are fairly definitely established. The enabling legislation and charter delimit the nature of the business and its activities; stockholders elect the directors; directors elect the officers; officers define the duties of intermediate management; and so on down to the lowest echelon.

The individual proprietor is master of his business, and his success depends on his effectiveness as an administrator.

In the partnership, each general partner is a general agent and has a part in the administration of the enterprise. Unless there is complete understanding and cooperation, confusion may arise.

Ease of raising capital. All the preceding characteristics facilitate the raising of capital by the corporation. As already noted, limited liability is of paramount importance. It enables the corporation to raise far larger amounts of capital than would be possible under the unlimited liability of the partnership. The divisibility of ownership into many small units enlarges the source of capital to include persons of moderate means and also facilitates diversification of investment by investors.

The variety of corporate capital issues appeals to persons of widely differing temperaments, from the daring speculator in high-risk common stocks of new enterprises to the buyer of highest grade investment bonds of established industries.

Disadvantages of the corporate form

There are certain weaknesses or disadvantages inherent in the corporate form of business; but obviously, in view of the large number of corporations that have been established and the large volume of business they do, these handicaps have not been widely preclusive.

It is more troublesome and costly to organize corporations than other forms of enterprises. Being a creature of the state, the corporation is subject to a greater amount of regulation and is recognized only in the state of incorporation unless steps are taken to qualify in other states. The corporation is more likely to be subjected to investigation because it is listed and easily traced in official records. It is required to make periodic and special reports to public agencies.

The corporation is less flexible than the individual proprietorship and the partnership, in that certain time-consuming formalities must be observed to effect fundamental changes, and there are generally a larger number of parties that have an interest and whose consent to the changes must be won.

The credit of a corporation is more limited, in that creditors may look only to the assets of the corporation, whereas the creditors of the individual proprietor and of the partnership have the additional protection of all the assets of the owners of the business.[2]

Whether the corporate form is a tax handicap or benefit cannot be answered with a generalization but depends on the circumstances of the business and the circumstances of the owners, as well as the tax provisions at the time. Large-scale businesses have little choice of form; they are almost always corporations. Small businesses may be organized as corporations or may adopt one of the other forms, and the relative tax

---

[2] The officers of many small corporations are asked to personally sign notes when the corporation borrows money. Through this means, the creditor retains the ability to collect from corporate officials the funds loaned in the event the company fails, thus safeguarding himself against the corporation's limited liability character.

advantage may be an important factor in the decision. Under such circumstances the prospective tax would be calculated both ways, making due allowance for the individual tax status of each of the owners. The income tax law may, of course, be changed from time to time, so that in any given situation the partnership form may have the advantage at one time and the corporate form at another.

Stockholders inarticulate. A very large proportion of stockholders are inarticulate as owners. They do not seek to have a voice in management, do not attend stockholder meetings, and often do not trouble to send in a written authorization (called a *proxy*) delegating some other person to vote the stock for them at the meeting. Their motivation for investment is undoubtedly found in the hope of income and appreciation in value rather than in managerial ambitions. In effect, the great mass of stockholders behave more nearly like creditors than like owners. In fact, this is but a manifestation of the separation of ownership and control (management) that has so frequently been noted as characteristic of our time. For this reason, some writers have called stocks "investment *credit* instruments." The legal nature of stocks should, however, be clearly understood —they represent ownership, not credit.

During recent years there have been a number of proxy fights, often involving nationally prominent companies, news of which is reported on the front pages of the daily newspapers. As a result, not only the stockholders directly concerned but the public generally have become acquainted with the power that rests with the ultimate owners of American industry if only they can be shaken out of their lethargy. Proxy contests may be inspired by minority stockholders of long standing who have become dissatisfied with the management or by new interests that see an opportunity to improve operations or raise the market's appraisal of the enterprise. Sometimes those who start a proxy contest hope to acquire control of an undervalued company and make a quick profit, perhaps through distribution of liquid assets or even through liquidation of the property. In still other instances, proxy fights develop when one group of shareholders wants to merge with one company while another group of shareholders wants the company to retain its individual identity or merge with a different company. In any event, many actual and potential stockholders have learned of their rights and capacity for action in such instances.

Instruments of corporate finance

Corporations provide their long-term, permanent capital funds through the sale of shares of stock to persons who thereby become the owners of the business and have an equity interest to the extent of the number of shares purchased. Corporations also raise long-term funds through bor-

EXHIBIT 16–1

Instruments of corporate finance

Debtor-creditor relationship:
  Secured bonds
    Represent a claim against specific pledged assets of the corporation
  Unsecured bonds (*debentures*)
    Represent a claim against the general credit of the corporation
  Other loans
    Represent claims arising from a variety of direct credit arrangements
Ownership:
  Preferred stock
    Represents ownership and is generally preferred as to assets or dividends, or both
  Common stock
    Represents ownership—the residual interest in the assets and earnings of the corporation

rowing (see Exhibit 16–1). Money obtained in these two ways is used to acquire fixed assets, such as land, buildings, and equipment, and to provide working capital. Such a provision of long-term funds contrasts with the use of commercial credit instruments, already discussed, to provide short-term, temporary funds.

Common stock

The corporation charter, issued by the appropriate official in the state of incorporation, indicates the number of shares and the classes of stock that the corporation is authorized to sell in order to raise ownership capital. In the simplest situation, there would be but one class of capital stock. For example, the charter may authorize the corporation to sell 1,000 shares of stock at $100 a share to provide $100,000. An individual investor may then buy one share, ten shares, or many more shares and will receive a stock certificate (engraved, in the case of larger corporations and particularly if the stock is listed on an organized exchange) indicating the extent of his ownership in the business. If an individual purchases 100 shares, he will receive a single certificate for the 100 shares and will then be a one-tenth owner of the corporation because he will be in possession of 100 out of the total 1,000 shares authorized and outstanding.

It should be noted that the corporation is an entity apart from the owners or shareholders. In contrast are the sole proprietorship and the partnership, in which the business assets are owned by the proprietors and the business units are not entities apart from the owners. The corporation holds ownership of the business assets, and the shareholders in turn own the corporation and are entitled only to a pro rata interest in the aggregate assets and income of the corporation.

EXHIBIT 16–2

Common stock certificate

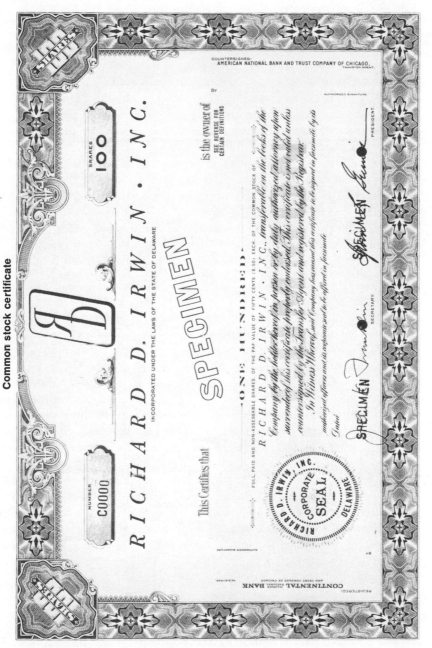

Rights of stockholders. The stock certificate is essentially a contract between the corporation and the stockholders, and the terms of the contract are stated in the stock certificate and in the charter of the corporation. Some of the principal rights of the individual stockholder can be briefly summarized as follows:

1. The right to have a certificate evidencing the ownership of shares of stock
2. The right to transfer the stock certificate at will
3. The right to receive notice of and attend stockholder meetings and to vote the stock standing in his name (usually one vote per share)
4. The right to buy additional shares of stock issued by the corporation in proportion to his present holdings
5. The right to share in the assets in proportion to stock held in the event of dissolution of the corporation
6. The right to share pro rata in the profits of the corporation that are distributed as dividends
7. The right to examine the books of the corporation under certain circumstances
8. The right to seek redress through court action in the event of malfeasance on the part of corporate officials

Collectively, the stockholders elect the directors, who are responsible for shaping the policies of the corporation, and elect and supervise the work of the officers; may amend the charter and bylaws; may vote to dissolve the corporation; and may vote on matters fundamental to corporate welfare, such as the sale or mortgaging of important assets.

Stock certificate. The stock certificate (see Exhibit 16–2) shows on its face the name of the issuing corporation, the number of shares it represents, and the name of the owner of the certificate. On the reverse side, a form for assignment of title is printed. This facilitates transfer. The name of the owner is kept on the stock record book of the corporation: he is the *holder of record* who is entitled to vote the shares, receive dividends, and exercise the other rights of stock ownership. The owner may transfer his shares by completing the assignment form on the reverse side of the certificate. The old certificate will then be canceled, and a new certificate will be issued to the new owner, whose name will be recorded in the stock record book. Such transfer is often effected through the services of a transfer agent and a registrar.

Preferred stock

Up to this point we have been discussing one class of capital stock, common stock, which represents the residual ownership claim to the earnings and assets of a corporation. Its claim is met only after all other claims have been met. Every corporation has common stock outstanding in effect, if not in name. (One of the rare exceptions for many years was the Great Northern Railway Company, which had a $6 noncumulative preferred stock as a residual issue.) Some corporations have a preferred stock issue outstanding in addition to common stock, and as the name implies, preferred stock has some degree of preference over common stock. This preference usually is a prior claim to dividends or assets, or to both dividends and assets. Because shares of stock do not grow out of a debtor-creditor relationship, a stock certificate is not a credit instrument but rather a capital or ownership instrument. This is true of preferred, as well as common, stock.

A preferred stock issue is usually offered in order to give the buyers a claim to earnings and dividends prior to that of the holders of common stock; and this is, as a rule, the outstanding characteristic of preferred stock. Preferred stockholders are generally entitled to a stated dividend payment, limited in amount, before anything may be paid on the common stock. On the other hand, common stockholders are entitled to all earnings of the corporation remaining after the payment of interest on bonds and the dividend on preferred issues. However, no dividend is payable on either preferred or common stocks until declared by the directors.

Assume that a corporation has outstanding 1,000 shares of preferred stock entitled to a quarterly dividend of $1.25, or $5 a year, and that there are also 1,000 shares of common outstanding. If the income (after taxes and interest) available for dividends amounted to $20,000 in a given year, the preferred stockholders, in the aggregate, would be entitled during the year to receive $5,000, and there would then remain $15,000, out of which the directors also might declare dividends on the common stock. If the income available for dividends in another year amounted to but $6,000, there would be only $1,000 left for the common stockholders after the preferred dividend of $5,000. Obviously, the earnings available for distribution to holders of common stock may fluctuate widely with the fortunes of the corporation. They are absent or low in poor years and high in good years. In contrast, no matter how prosperous the corporation and how large the earnings, the preferred stockholders receive at most the stipulated amount. To this extent they have a claim prior to that of the owners of the common stock. If in the judgment of the directors the continuing welfare of the corporation precludes dividend payments on either or both the preferred stock and the common stock, such payments may be omitted entirely. This is not true of interest on bonds, as we shall note later in this chapter.

Cumulative preferred. There are several different features which preferred stock may have. If the stock is cumulative, unpaid dividends accumulate, and the accumulated dividends must be paid before payments may be made on the common stock. For example, if the $5 dividend on a cumulative preferred share is passed for three years, the accumulations would amount to $15. If the directors of the corporation decided to pay a dividend, up to $15 would be paid to holders of each of the preferred shares before any dividend was paid to common stockholders. If a preferred issue is *non*cumulative, a dividend not declared in a given year is lost; no claim is carried forward. Typically, preferred stock is cumulative.

Participation. Some preferred stock issues include provisions for dividends in excess of the preference amount. For instance, holders of preferred stock may be entitled to a preferred annual payment of $5 a share and, if that is paid, may be entitled also to share in further dividends with holders of common stock. This right to participate in further dividends appears in different forms. Preferred stockholders may share with common in any further payment, in payments after the holders of common stock have received some specified dividend per share, or in some proportion of payments above a specified amount. Typically, however, preferred stock is *non*participating and very few participating issues have been distributed in recent years.

Convertible. Corporate bonds and preferred stocks may be convertible, at the option of the holder, into other securities. There are a few issues outstanding which are convertible at the option of the corporation, but the disadvantage of such an option precludes general use. In either case, it is usual for the issue to be convertible into common stock. The security holder, upon surrender of his bond or preferred stock, will be given a specified amount of common stock in exchange. The conversion privilege is not common, but it is more frequently granted than is the right of participation. Convertibility is offered to increase interest in an issue. Since the convertible issue may be exchanged for common stock, the market price of the common stock will have an influence on the price of the other issue. If the market price of the common rises, holders of convertible securities may be enabled to take capital gains which they would not ordinarily obtain on a nonconvertible issue of bonds or preferred stock. Issuers may find the conversion privilege useful in another sense: in general, the number of common stock shares into which an issue might be converted is less than would be required to raise the same amount of cash if sold directly at the time of the financing.

Voting power. Preferred stockholders may or may not be granted voting power. Even if they are granted it, since they have preferences as to dividends and as to payments on principal in the event of liquidation, they usually do not have voting power proportionate to that held by the common stockholders. In general, preferred stockholders share in ownership but do not participate effectively in control.

Call option. Quite commonly, preferred stock issues are callable in part or whole at the option of the issuing corporation. The issuer may require the holder to surrender his shares in exchange for cash at a specified price per share. The investor must then find a new investment outlet for his funds. To overcome the costs of such reinvestment, it is usual for the call price to exceed the price at which the stock was issued.

Sinking fund. The call option may be used also to permit the orderly retirement of a preferred stock issue. The corporation may be required to meet sinking-fund provisions that lead to repurchase and retirement at regular intervals of a portion of an outstanding issue. Thus, although preferred stocks have no maturity, regular calls for sinking-fund purposes may actually have the effect of introducting dates of payment leading to final extinction of the issue.

Par and no-par. Stock, whether common or preferred, may have a par value (a dollar amount stated on the face of the certificate) or may be without par value (no-par). In either case, each share represents a pro rata fractional ownership interest in the business.

If a preferred stock is of par value, the face of the certificate will generally show the dividend preference of the stock, if any, in terms of percentage of par. Otherwise dividend preference will be stated as a dollar amount.

Position of preferred stock. Bondholders have the first claim on the assets and earnings of a corporation, but the amount of income is limited to the coupon rate. Common stockholders, on the other hand, have the residual claim on assets and earnings, but the possible income return is without limit and depends only on the success of the enterprise. Accordingly, bonds provide a limited appreciation potential, whereas common stocks have virtually unlimited growth possibilities.

It is apparent that preferred stocks are, in a sense, a cross between bonds and common stocks. They have the limited income and appreciation possibilities of the bond but are without the benefit of an equivalent asset protection. Their asset position is just above that of the residual common stock. Preferred stockholders do not share, however, with the common stockholders in the prosperity of the corporation. Thus, in periods of adversity, preferreds have a weaker position than bonds; in times of prosperity, they yield no share in the good fortunes of the common stock.

This characterization of preferred stocks is, of course, a broad generalization and should not be interpreted to mean that a preferred stock may not be a sound investment. Quite the contrary is true. If a financially sound and prosperous company has no funded debt outstanding prior to its preferred stock issue and if the preferred issue is outstanding in relatively small amount in relation to the common stock equity, then the senior stock issue might well be a high-caliber investment. That would certainly be true of a company that is adequately financed and has a comfortable cash and working capital position, earnings that cover dividend requirements by a good margin, a favorable long-term outlook, and net assets equal to many times the amount of preferred outstanding. It is not the legal description of an investment item that determines its quality, but rather the economic position of the corporation. For example, the common stockholders of the American Telephone and Telegraph Company received a regular dividend every year since 1881. This common stock is undoubtedly a better investment than the first-mortgage bond of an industrial company in a weak financial position that has lost money steadily over the years and may become insolvent at any moment.

Other forms of stock

In addition to common and preferred, there are several other kinds of stock that are found much less frequently. Two kinds will be described briefly. Some corporations classify their common stock into *class A and class B*. The two classes may be identical except with respect to dividends —for example, it may be permissible to pay dividends on the A stock without payment on the B, or it may be permissible to give a dividend in stock to the holders of the B issue when cash is paid to the A holders. Still another kind of stock is the *guaranteed stock*, the dividends of which are guaranteed by a corporation other than the one issuing the stock.

Rights and warrants

Under certain conditions, corporations may give their present stockholders the privilege of buying additional stock in the company in proportion to their present holdings. Stockholders then receive a transferable certificate called a *subscription warrant*, evidencing a certain number of rights to buy additional shares. Rights are issued in connection with current financing, as against warrants, which evidence a similar privilege to buy additional shares but which are options usually forming part of a long-term financing program and likely to be exercised only in the more remote future. (A specimen subscription warrant is reproduced in Exhibit 16–3.)

It is common-law doctrine that the owner of common stock in a corporation has a preemptive right to purchase his pro rata share of any additional stock issued by the corporation (or he may sell that right). This principle permits the shareholder to preserve his relative voting power and also to preserve his share in the corporate surplus in the event that the new stock is being issued at less than its current value. Some states do not recognize this common-law doctrine, and others permit the limitation of the preemptive right by appropriate provision in the articles of incorporation. The New York Stock Exchange regards as one right the privilege accruing to one existing share of stock.

EXHIBIT 16–3

Subscription warrant

BELL SYSTEM

000-000
of Debentures

AMERICAN TELEPHONE AND TELEGRAPH COMPANY
Warrant for subscription to Convertible Debentures dated March 19, 1951

VALUELESS IF NOT USED ON OR BEFORE MARCH 19, 1951
SEE DIRECTIONS AS TO USE—ACTION ON YOUR PART IS REQUIRED

Subscription
Warrant for

This is to
Certify that

which is

the number of Rights
needed to subscribe for

SPECIMEN

Transfer Clerk

, or assigns, upon surrender of this warrant to the Treasurer of American
Telephone and Telegraph Company at 195 Broadway, New York, is entitled to the subscription rights set forth above, upon the terms and
conditions specified in the Prospectus relating to the Debentures.   JANUARY 29, 1951

_____ Treasurer

DO NOT DETACH

FORM 1

AMERICAN TELEPHONE AND TELEGRAPH COMPANY
195 Broadway, New York 7, N. Y.

I wish to subscribe as stated below for Convertible Debentures dated March 19, 1951, upon the terms and conditions specified in
the Prospectus relating to the Debentures, receipt of a copy of which is hereby acknowledged.

Amount of Debentures subscribed for . . . . $_____

Total Rights required for this subscription (7 Rights for each $100 of Debentures) _____ Rights

Total Rights represented by this and any other warrants submitted herewith _____ Rights

Please request Bankers Trust Company to purchase for me any additional rights required to complete
my subscription or to sell any rights in excess of the number required for my subscription.

Date_____

Subscriber's Signature _____

Address
for Delivery
if Other
than Above

DO NOT DETACH

FORM 2

AMERICAN TELEPHONE AND TELEGRAPH COMPANY
195 Broadway, New York 7, N. Y.

Please request Bankers Trust Company to sell all of the rights
represented by this warrant and send me a check.

000-000

SPECIMEN

Date_____

Owner's Signature

DIRECTIONS AS TO USE

1. To Subscribe: Fill in and sign Form 1 and send Warrant together with the necessary payment for the Debentures to the Company in the return envelope sent to you with the Warrant. Be sure that it reaches the Company by March 19, 1951.

If you do not have exactly the number of rights required for your subscription, any additional rights needed should be purchased or any excess rights sold. By signing Form 1 you authorize this to be done through Bankers Trust Company. If you wish to make other arrangements for the purchase of additional rights or the sale of excess rights, you should do so before entering your subscription.

2. To Sell All of these Rights Through Bankers Trust Company: Sign Form 2 and send Warrant to the Company in free return envelope sent to you with the Warrant. Be sure that it reaches the Company by March 19, 1951.

3. To Sell Rights Through Your Bank or Broker: Sign Form 3 on back of Warrant and deliver to your bank or broker in ample time so that the rights sold can be used by March 19, 1951.

4. To Transfer Rights or Divide Warrant: Fill in and sign Form 3 on back of Warrant. Warrant should reach the Company in ample time so that rights can be used by March 19, 1951.

DO NOT DETACH

000-000

Corporate bonds

Bonds are credit instruments used in raising long-term funds. They represent a borrowing-lending relationship. There are two principal kinds: *secured bonds,* secured by a mortgage on tangible property or by a lien on intangible collateral; and *debentures,* or unsecured bonds, which are a claim against the general assets of the corporation and whose holders rank with other unsecured creditors, including trade creditors.

Many descriptive designations are given to bonds to indicate their nature, and one author once listed more than 160 different types of bonds.[3] However, a simple classification can be made on the following bases:

Nature of the issuer—government, municipal, corporate, railroad, industrial, special revenue, etc.
Nature of security—mortgage, collateral trust, debenture, assumed, guaranteed, income, etc.
Maturity—long term, short term, perpetual, etc.
Termination (payment and redemption)—convertible, redeemable, serial, sinking fund, etc.
Form of instrument—coupon, registered.
Purpose—refunding, construction, development, equipment, improvement, purchase money, unifying, etc.

Bonds, whether secured or unsecured, may also be classified with respect to the payment of principal and interest, as follows:

Coupon bonds have interest coupons attached. Principal is payable to the bearer, and interest is payable upon surrender of the coupons. Because title passes without endorsement, these bonds are also called *bearer bonds.*
Registered bonds have the name of the owner on the face of the instrument and cannot be transferred without endorsement. Interest checks are mailed to the holder of record.
Registered coupon bonds are registered as to principal only, and the attached coupons are payable to the bearer.

A specimen coupon bond is reproduced in Exhibit 16–4.

Denomination; interest. Bonds are usually for a principal amount of $1,000; and unless there is a specific indication to the contrary, the term *bond* is assumed to refer to an instrument of that denomination. The nominal or coupon rate of interest is shown on the face of the bond, and holders are entitled to this payment, usually semiannually, whether or not it has been earned by the corporation. If payment of principal or

---

[3] W. E. Lagerquist, *Investment Analysis* (New York: Macmillan Co., 1922), Appendix A.

EXHIBIT 16–4

Coupon bond

interest is not made when due, the secured bondholders have the right to foreclose; debenture holders may sue and get a judgment. Bonds are often referred to as *funded debt,* and the interest thereon as a *fixed charge.*

Corporation note. The corporation note is a promissory note, often less formal than a bond but more formal than a commercial promissory note. It has a maturity of from 1 to 10 years and may be secured or unsecured. Except for the shorter maturity, it is much like a corporation bond. In contrast, the commercial promissory note usually has a maturity of 30 days to six months and is customarily used in connection with short-term borrowing from a bank.

Corporate mortgage. The corporate mortgage is a legal document used to pledge real property to secure a loan. It is a much more complex instrument than the mortgage given by the home buyer, which will be discussed in Chapter 21. A detailed consideration of the corporate mortgage is beyond the scope of our immediate interest, but a brief treatment appears appropriate here.

The borrower who pledges the property remains in possession. The lender either holds title to the property by virtue of the mortgage or has a lien against the property until the loan is repaid, depending on the law of the state in which the property is situated. (This is primarily a legal and not a financial distinction.) The mortgage describes the pledged property in detail and lists the obligations assumed by the borrower, such as the payment of interest and principal, maintenance of the property, payment of taxes, insuring the property, etc. When all interest and principal payments have been met, the title is restored to the borrower, or the encumbrance is removed. On the other hand, if there is a default on the mortgage, the lender may start reorganization proceedings. If the property has value, the lender receives a settlement on termination of the reorganization proceedings.

Trustee and the trust agreement. Corporation bond issues, whether secured or unsecured, are frequently issued to raise substantial sums of money, running into many millions of dollars. Bonds of a given issue may be sold to a large number of investors living in various parts of the country; these investors are not acquainted with one another and would find it difficult to take collective action. For this reason, it is expedient to appoint some third person as trustee to act for the bondholders and look after their interests because it would be impractical for individual bondholders to act independently. Such a third person is usually a corporate trustee (see Chapter 14).

The borrowing corporation enters into an agreement with the trustee, called a *trust agreement* or *indenture.* This agreement outlines the obligations of the trustee to: authenticate the bonds that are issued to preclude overissue; hold the mortgage or the collateral pledged to secure the loan; enforce the provisions of the indenture; submit periodic reports; notify bondholders of any default; bring suit in case of default; and generally represent the bondholders.

In the case of mortgage bonds, the indenture includes the mortgage; in the case of bonds secured by collateral, such personal property as stocks or bonds, the securities are deposited with the trustee or may be pledged by means of a chattel mortgage, as distinguished from a real estate mortgage, which is applicable only to real property.

Retirement of bonds. Corporate bonds may be retired through *con-*

version, exchanging a new security, usually a preferred or common stock, for the outstanding issue; through *redemption,* or payment of cash; or through *refunding,* replacing the outstanding bonds with another issue of later maturity, with perhaps some alternation in the provisions and rate of interest.

There are two common redemption plans designed to retire the bonds gradually over the life of the loan rather than have the full amount of the original obligation come due all at one time upon maturity. The borrowing corporation may include a *sinking-fund* provision in the indenture, stipulating that a certain sum is to be set aside each year out of earnings, the appropriation to be used either to retire outstanding bonds immediately or to be invested and used to retire the bonds at maturity. A second method is the issuance of a *serial* bond issue, under which a portion of the bonds mature each year so that a substantial portion, if not all, of the bonds may be retired by the end of the loan period.

Determinants of corporate capital structure

Corporations, as we have noted, meet their long-term capital requirements through the sale of common and preferred stocks and by borrowing through the use of one or more bond issues; but they may also add to their capital by the retention of earnings. The outstanding stocks and bonds of a corporation, together with surplus, make up its capital structure, and the nature of this structure depends on a great variety of factors, both internal and external.

It will be recognized that a company that uses bond financing assumes a fixed charge for interest and the obligation to pay the principal. In times of depression and adversity such obligations might prove burdensome, if not embarrassing. It is otherwise in the case of stock financing, because dividends are but a contingent obligation. Accordingly, only those corporations with a well-established and fairly stable level of earnings are likely to resort to bond financing. Furthermore, corporations with substantial fixed-asset requirements are more likely to use bonds than companies with low fixed-asset needs. This is true because bond buyers seek the protection of a good margin of asset coverage as well as sustained earning power. Public service companies provide a good example of an industry that meets these conditions, and the utilities obtain much of their capital through bonds.

Industrial companies, on the other hand, operate under competitive conditions rather than under franchise, as do the utilities. Their earnings tend to fluctuate widely and therefore do not provide as good a base for bond financing. Thus the earning and asset positions of companies vary from industry to industry, and these factors influence or condition the capital structure for the companies in any given industry.

Forces in the securities markets are an important factor in determining the type of financing that is to be used. At any given time, is the investing public receptive to bonds, to convertible issues, or to preferred or common stocks? There tend to be fashions in securities just as in other areas. The trends in corporate earnings, in interest rates, and in the price trends of stocks and bonds are all elements of influence.

The judgment and policy of management and the extent to which management may wish to increase or decrease debt or increase or minimize stockholder interest also have some weight in determining capital structure, whether the company will have simply common stock or a pyramid structure consisting not only of common stock but of preferred stocks and perhaps several classes of bonds as well.

The federal tax on corporate income also influences to some extent the form of capital structure. Interest on debt is deductible as an expense before computing the tax; earnings and dividends on stock are not. Some corporate managements have found it useful to sell bonds and retire stocks with the proceeds from this sale. Savings are of two kinds: interest rates on bonds are generally lower than stock dividend rates, and bond interest is a tax-deductible expense whereas dividends are not. Such savings sometimes have been great enough to meet interest and sinking-fund payments on the debt without any larger payment of cash than was needed to meet dividend requirements alone.

Changing techniques for marketing securities and negotiating loans, together with the substantially increased amounts of money flowing through intermediary investment institutions, have also affected the extent to which debt financing is used. The opportunity to obtain funds in substantial amounts through credit channels has made the use of these channels more attractive. The institutions effective here will be discussed in later chapters.

Questions and problems

1. Distinguish the three major forms of business organization from the following viewpoints: ease of starting a business, evidence of ownership, and financial responsibility of the owners.

2. What advantages does the corporation have that are not shared in equal degree by the other two forms of business organization?

3. How important is the corporation in the American economy in terms of the number of business units, the dollar volume of business, and the employment opportunities offered?

4. Classify the instruments of corporate finance.

5. In what sense is it appropriate to say that stockholders are inarticulate?

6. With respect to bond issues, what do the terms *sinking fund* and *serial maturity* mean?
7. What are the typical provisions of a preferred stock?
8. What factors influence decision as to the form of the capital structure of a corporation? Why do some corporations have only common stock outstanding while others have one or more bond issues and preferred stock?
9. What are some of the more important rights of common stockholders? Do you view them as equally important?
10. Bond and preferred stock issues may have the feature of callability. What is this? Is this a feature that investors should weigh heavily in their investment decisions today?

Bibliography

Textbooks in business or corporate finance provide more details as to the nature and use of corporate securities. Some texts which are widely used are H. G. Guthmann and H. E. Dougall, *Corporate Financial Policy* (4th ed.; New York: Prentice-Hall, Inc., 1962); J. C. Van Horne, *Financial Management and Policy* (Englewood Cliffs, N.J.: Prentice-Hall, Inc., 1968), and E. M. Lerner, *Managerial Finance: A Systems Approach* (New York: Harcourt Brace Jovanovich, Inc., 1971).

Important theoretical contributions to discussions of determinants of corporate capital structures, such as the Modigliani-Miller theorems and cost of capital discussions, are collected in such books as Stephen H. Archer and Charles A. D'Ambrosio, *The Theory of Business Finance: A Book of Readings* (New York: Macmillan, 1967).

Business population figures are published from time to time by the U.S. Department of Commerce in the *Survey of Current Business*.

CHAPTER 17

The financing of large business

Firms must be profitable if they are to continue in business, and they must have liquid resources if they are to pay their bills as they fall due. This chapter discusses some of the liquidity problems that face corporations. The patterns of the overall sources and uses of funds characterizing business firms are discussed first. It is important, however, to go behind some of these flows and to determine how they arise.

The sources and uses of funds

The funds that are available to a corporation can be thought of as originating from either of two sources: they can be generated by the operations of the firm itself (internal sources) or they can be generated from sources outside of the firm (external sources). The uses to which a firm can put the funds it raises can also be divided into two categories. The first is the purchase of physical assets, such as buildings, machinery, and inventory. The second is the acquisition of financial assets, such as cash, securities, and receivables. The data in Table 17–1 indicate the size of these flows over five years. These data show that roughly two thirds of the funds available to nonfinancial corporations are generated internally and that one third of the funds are generated from external sources. Internally generated funds arise from normal business operations, i.e., they are equal to the firm's profit plus depreciation charges. External sources are the funds raised through selling bonds or stocks, or through other long-term borrowing.

Of the two inflows, external sources are most volatile. They declined 20% in 1967 and rose 80% from then to 1969.

Roughly 70% of the funds available to a corporation are used to purchase physical assets, such as buildings, equipment, and inventory. The figures in Table 17–1 indicate that in 1969 corporations invested $87 billion in physical assets. This figure is almost three times as much as the

TABLE 17–1

Sources and uses of funds, nonfinancial corporate business, 1965–1969 (*billions of dollars*)

	1965	1966	1967	1968	1969
Sources					
Internal					
Undistributed profits	21.3	22.9	19.1	19.7	18.4
Depreciation changes	35.2	38.2	41.2	44.3	47.4
Other*	.1	.1	.9	−.9	−3.1
Total	56.6	61.2	61.2	63.1	62.7
External					
Sale of stock*	.0	1.2	2.3	−.8	4.3
Sale of bonds	5.4	10.2	14.7	12.9	12.1
Other long-term borrowing ...	15.1	13.5	12.3	19.0	21.6
Accounts payable increase ...	9.1	7.8	2.6	5.7	10.9
Miscellaneous	6.8	6.7	1.1	3.2	7.3
Total	36.5	39.4	33.0	47.3	56.2
Total sources	93.1	100.6	94.2	110.4	118.9
Uses					
Construction of plant	54.9	62.7	66.0	70.3	80.0
Additions to inventories	7.9	14.4	6.4	6.5	7.4
Additions to cash and securities	1.7	1.9	.0	10.1	2.3
Extension of credit to customers	16.3	12.5	9.7	16.5	18.6
Other uses	5.1	1.0	3.8	.1	3.4
Total uses	85.9	92.5	85.9	103.5	111.7
Statistical discrepancy	7.2	8.1	8.3	6.9	7.2

* Negative figures arise from loss of market value of inventories on hand or stock outstanding.
Source: Adapted from *Federal Reserve Bulletin*, May 1970, p. A71.4.

amount spent a decade earlier. Some of this rise in outlays reflects the fact that prices of materials rose. But the increase in construction and material costs that took place during this period is not the major reason that plant and equipment outlays increased. Rather the rise in outlays occurred because the economy was larger and stronger. And the increased outlays in turn helped contribute to this strength.

It is important to stress that as impressive as the $87 billion figure is, it is an understatement of the amount of investment that can be attributed to business firms. The figure does not include the outlays that proprietorships and partnerships undertook. Moreover, it does not include the outlays that private individuals, pension funds, insurance companies, and other financial corporations made for plant and equipment. These groups could then lease the facilities they built to business firms.

The increase in financial assets that is reported in Table 17–1 was represented by changes in the holdings of demand and time deposits, short-term securities, trade credit, and so forth. This increase in corporate liquidity was necessary to accommodate the larger volume of business that was being carried on.

Internal sources

As indicated in Table 17–1, internal funds have been the dominant source and have consistently provided approximately two thirds of all corporate funds. The advantages of internal sources and limited access to public financial markets have also caused sole proprietorships and partnerships to rely heavily on these types of financing.

Retained earnings

Companies that sell their products and services at prices sufficient to cover all expenses earn profits which may be disbursed to owners or retained for internal investment. The postwar pattern of corporate profits, federal tax liabilities, dividends, and undistributed profits is shown in Exhibit 17–1.

The amount of profits that firms earned before taxes grew from roughly $62 to $92 billion over the period 1964–1969. Firms paid a portion of this in taxes, a portion to stockholders in the form of dividends, and retained a portion in the firm. Taxes increased from $24 to $37 billion over the period, dividends remained roughly constant at a rate of $15 to $18 billion, and retained earnings grew from $20 to $24 billion.

Exhibit 17–1 shows that profits before taxes increased by roughly 50% over the period 1964–1969. The graphs in Exhibit 17–2, however, indicate that this rise in profits came about through an increase in the volume of goods and services produced rather than through an increase in operating margins. Though the prices of goods and services grew rapidly after 1965, the compensation of employees and other costs advanced more rapidly. As a result, profits per unit of goods and services sold actually declined after 1965. The graph presented in Exhibit 17–3 shows that the profit margins in 1969 were close to the level that they were at in 1961.

The concern in this chapter, however, is not with gross profits but rather with retained earnings or undistributed profits, for these are the

EXHIBIT 17–1

Corporate profits

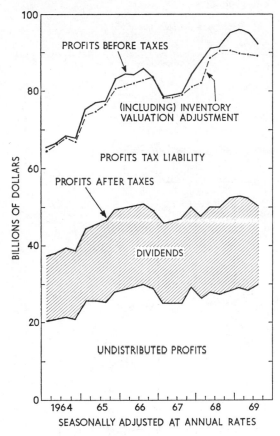

BILLIONS OF DOLLARS

PROFITS BEFORE TAXES

(INCLUDING) INVENTORY
VALUATION ADJUSTMENT

PROFITS TAX LIABILITY

PROFITS AFTER TAXES

DIVIDENDS

UNDISTRIBUTED PROFITS

SEASONALLY ADJUSTED AT ANNUAL RATES

Source: Adapted from *Survey of Current Business*, vol.
49, no. II, p. 12.

funds that firms have available to them for investment. The fact that
aggregate dividend payments have remained fairly stable and that many
companys have a stable dividend policy means that the fluctuations that
take place in profits will be reflected in fluctuations of retained earnings.
An extreme example of this occurred during the depression of the 1930s.
During the period 1929–39, dividends actually exceeded profits by a substantial margin: the ratio of dividends to profits was 166%.

During the postwar period annual ratios hovered around the 50%
mark, but in recent years higher dividends have pushed this measure well
above 60%. The stable dividend policies followed by many corporations
suggest that definite target payout ratios exist in many industries. Never-

EXHIBIT 17–2

Prices, costs, and profits per unit of real corporate product

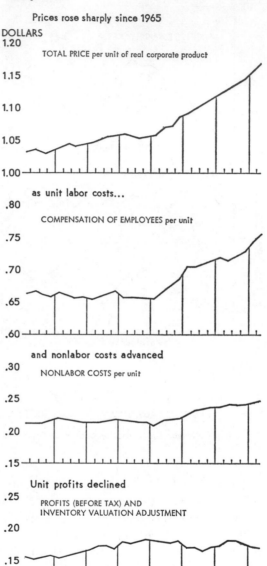

Prices rose sharply since 1965

DOLLARS

TOTAL PRICE per unit of real corporate product

as unit labor costs...

COMPENSATION OF EMPLOYEES per unit

and nonlabor costs advanced

NONLABOR COSTS per unit

Unit profits declined

PROFITS (BEFORE TAX) AND INVENTORY VALUATION ADJUSTMENT

QUARTERLY, SEASONALLY ADJUSTED

Note: Nonfinancial corporations only.
Source: Adapted from *Survey of Current Business,* vol.
49, no. 11, p. 12.

EXHIBIT 17-3

Shares of profits and employee compensation in corporate gross product (*since late 1965, profits have been declining relative to output while employee compensation has been increasing*)

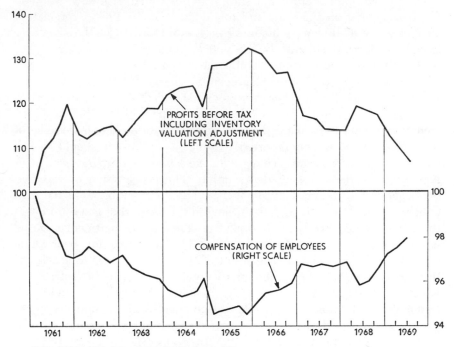

Note: Index, 1961 1st quarter distribution = 100.
Source: Adapted from *Survey of Current Business,* vol. 49, no. II, p. 13.

theless, the payment of dividends is still a discretionary act which preserves some flexibility for management in meeting the needs for funds. A number of important factors influence each individual company's dividend policy, including: contractual and legal requirements, liquidity needs, the availability of alternative sources of funds, future financing plans, the tax status of stockholders, and management attitudes concerning the dangers of diluting control and earnings through the use of other types of financing.

The financial effects of depreciation charges

Profitable firms have an excess of income over total expenses including depreciation charges. The accounting entry to record depreciation allocates the original cost over the expected lifetime of the asset acquired. In other words, the original capital investment is gradually recovered by a series of depreciation charges against earnings. There is no outflow of cash associated with the accounting entry; the cash expenditure is made when the asset is acquired. Because the depreciation entries reduce reported earnings, analysts frequently add the depreciation charges to net profits to determine a crude measure of the expected cash flow available for the payment of dividends and for investment. In 1969, depreciation charges were $47 billion, an amount that is more than twice the size of retained earnings. It should also be noted that depreciation charges for noncorporate enterprises also exhibit an upward trend.

The increasing volume of depreciation charges is the result of the expanding value of assets being depreciated and the liberalization of accounting and regulatory policies. It may seem paradoxical that businessmen would want to increase the size of depreciation charges because of the depressing effect on reported earnings; however, it should be remembered that corporate income taxes are levied against business earnings *after* the deduction of depreciation. The acceleration of reported depreciation thus reduces taxable income *without* creating an actual *cash* outflow. Indeed, it reduces cash outflow in the sense that taxes are lower than they would have been. In 1962, the Treasury Department released new guidelines which substantially reduced the length of time over which assets may be depreciated. The result of this adjustment is to accelerate the rate of depreciation even though the total asset value to be depreciated is not changed. The faster rate of depreciation benefits companies that frequently replace old assets, a typical practice in the modern, competitive business world. For all manufacturing industries combined, the average depreciation period for assets was dropped to 13 years which is 6 years shorter than the average period previously allowed.

The use of accelerated depreciation formulas, such as *double-declining-balance* and *sum-of-the-years'-digits* has also influenced the rate of depreciation charges. Under the old *straight line* method, only one half of the depreciable value of an asset could be written off during the first half of the asset's expected life time. Approximately two thirds of the value under the double-declining-balance and three fourths of the total under the sum-of-the-years'-digits may now be charged off during an equivalent period.

The development of accelerated depreciation reporting methods has an obvious significance for management, investors, economic planners, and tax authorities. Some observers have attributed part of the slow growth of corporate profits, relative to other forms of income, to the depressing effect of new reporting methods for depreciation on reported profits. This viewpoint ignores the multiplier and accelerator effects of the incremental funds made available for investment and other company needs. The flow of depreciation funds will undoubtedly become even more important in the future as national and international patterns of competition become even more intense.

External sources

In general, business firms do not rely entirely on internal sources of funds. A variety of external sources are available as indicated in Table 17–1. The external types of financing described in this chapter are frequently used because of the flexibility and convenient terms available from creditors. Debt funds also avoid the dilution of ownership control and earnings associated with the sale of equity securities to outsiders. Nevertheless, the disadvantages of frequent maturities, higher financing costs, and the risks of overindulgence because of the informality of some of the credit arrangements must be considered in evaluating the alternative sources of funds available.

The data in Table 17–2 indicate the percentage distribution of the assets and liabilities of all manufacturing firms during 1968, by quarters. While frequent mention will be made of these data in this chapter, it should be noted here that liabilities finance 42% of total assets and equity 58%. The breakdown of debt is that 23% is short-term debt and 19% is long-term debt, i.e., debt maturing in longer than one year.

Trade credit

The universal use of trade credit in modern business operations makes this form of financing the most familiar source of funds. Trade credit is created automatically when one company sells its products to another firm under an arrangement permitting payment at a later date. Credit facilitates the sale of goods without the complications of immediate cash settlement and enables companies to separate the production and distribution functions from the problem of obtaining financing. This process is so commonplace that it may correctly be considered a permanent source of funds despite the short time periods allowed for settlement specified in most trade credit transaction terms. In 1969 the total amount of trade credit extended reached almost $200 billion.

The credit process. Delivery of goods by the seller and acceptance by the buyer establishes the trade debt which becomes an account receivable for the seller and an account payable for the buyer. In most sales, the debt is handled on an open account basis; there is no formal written evidence of the agreement such as a draft or promissory note. Except for a few specific industries where the use of written documents is customary and acceptable, most companies would resent attempts by sellers to obtain formal drafts or notes. Promissory notes are occasionally used for individual customers in weak financial condition or when debts have become delinquent.

Companies selling on open-book credit terms naturally investigate the credit worthiness of customers and avoid prospects which would obvi-

TABLE 17–2

Financial statement in ratio form for all manufacturing firms

	1968 by quarters			
	1st	2nd	3rd	4th
Assets				
Cash on hand and in bank	4.8	4.9	5.0	5.2
U.S. government securities, including treasury savings notes	1.8	1.5	1.4	1.6
Total cash and U.S. government securities	6.6	6.5	6.4	6.8
Receivables from U.S. government, excluding tax credits	1.0	0.9	0.9	1.0
Other notes and accounts receivable (net)	16.3	16.9	17.1	16.6
Total receivables	17.3	17.8	18.0	17.5
Inventories	23.9	23.6	23.6	23.3
Other current assets	3.5	3.5	3.4	3.6
Total current assets	51.3	51.4	51.3	51.2
Property, plant, and equipment	76.7	76.4	76.2	75.4
Deduct: Reserve for depreciation and depletion	36.7	36.4	36.4	35.8
Total property, plant, and equipment (net)	40.0	40.0	39.8	39.6
Other noncurrent assets	8.7	8.6	8.8	9.1
Total Assets	100.0	100.0	100.0	100.0
Liabilities and stockholders' equity				
Short-term loans from banks (original maturity of 1 year or less)	3.9	3.9	4.0	3.9
Advances and prepayments by U.S. government	1.3	1.3	1.3	1.3
Trade accounts and notes payable	7.8	8.1	8.1	8.5
Federal income taxes accrued	2.5	2.3	2.3	2.5
Installments, due in 1 year or less, on long-term debt				
(a) Loans from banks	0.4	0.4	0.4	0.5
(b) Other long-term debt	0.6	0.6	0.6	0.6
Other current liabilities	6.6	6.9	6.9	6.7
Total current liabilities	23.2	23.5	23.6	23.9

Long-term debt due in more than 1 year

(a) Loans from banks	3.0	3.1	3.1	3.2
(b) Other long-term debt	12.9	12.9	13.1	13.1
Other noncurrent liabilities	3.2	3.4	3.4	3.6
Total liabilities	42.4	43.0	43.2	43.8
Reserves not reflected elsewhere	—	—	—	—
Capital stock, capital surplus, and minority interest	19.9	19.6	19.3	19.2
Earned surplus and surplus reserves	37.7	37.5	37.4	37.0
Total stockholders' equity	57.6	57.0	56.8	56.2
Total Liabilities and Stockholders' Equity	100.0	100.0	100.0	100.0

Annual percent rate of profit on stockholders' equity at end of period—

Before federal income taxes	19.4	22.4	19.7	21.8
After taxes	11.5	12.6	11.4	12.8
Ratio of current assets to current liabilities	2.21	2.19	2.17	2.14
Ratio of total cash and U.S. government securities to total current liabilities	.28	.28	.27	.28
Ratio of total stockholders' equity to debt	2.76	2.72	2.67	2.65

Source: SEC-FTC Quarterly Financial Report.

ously be unable or unwilling to make payments according to customary terms. Many factors, however, make commercial vendors more willing to accept credit risks than other types of lenders. In fact, the comment is often made that a credit manager who reports a record of no credit losses is not properly performing his job. In the modern business environment, companies seek to gain new buyers and make repeat sales to established customers by using trade credit as a competitive tool. By taking calculated risks on some buyers, the seller can distinguish between those customers which are really poor credit risks and other firms which are able to continue prompt payments for purchases despite apparent financial weaknesses. Credit managers who forbid the extension of credit to marginal customers without such evidence often unnecessarily limit the expansion of sales. As long as the net profit from selling to marginal buyers exceeds the occasional credit losses incurred, the company will benefit.

The gross profit margin on the sale of business products is a second motivation to accept greater credit risks. Financial institutions extending loans must cover expenses and provide for profits entirely from the interest income, which is normally limited by competitive and regulatory pressures. The larger margin of income on commercial activities permits the business firm to take greater risks of loss without endangering its ability to earn a profit or its technical solvency. (Even though a firm may have more than enough assets to cover all debts, if given time to convert these assets into cash in an orderly manner, situations may arise where maturing debts exceed available liquid assets. Inability to make immediate payment when due is referred to as *technical insolvency*.)

Business customs and competitive pressures also force most companies to sell products on a trade credit basis even though terms vary according to the type of industry and the status of the seller. Retailers and distributors located away from the financial centers in particular have required liberal trade credit terms. In most industries, unless a customer's credit is accepted on normal terms, reluctant sellers will lose business to competitors. The financial position of the seller is a fourth factor influencing the amount of trade credit available. Large companies with adequate financial resources and access to the financial markets are in a good position to assist smaller companies by accepting orders with delayed payments. To the extent that larger firms acquire funds in the public markets and then sell to other companies on a credit basis, the users of trade credit gain indirect access to public sources of funds.

Cash discounts and cost of trade credit. It is customary to allow discounts for prompt payment when credit sales are made. These discounts —usually called cash discounts—are required in most industries by competitive pressures. The seller also derives benefits from quick collection by gaining more immediate use of funds for investment and by elimination of the financing burden created by the physical transfer of valuable goods to a buyer without cash receipts. Prompt payment further removes the danger that an account will become delinquent or uncollectible. If the cash discount is not taken by customers the additional income to the seller above the gross profit resulting from the sale constitutes compensation for the financing service offered and provides a buffer to help absorb any credit losses. Buyers occasionally abuse the credit system by seeking to take cash discounts after the discount period has elapsed or by deferring final payment beyond the specified maturity date.

Competitive pressures to expand sales often prevent measures that might limit abuses, such as refusal to accept additional credit and insistence upon written evidence of indebtedness.

The terms of trade credit usually refer to two periods: a brief period, frequently 10 days, during which the buyer may take a discount on the face amount of the purchase billing, and a second, longer period, that represents the number of days permitted until maturity when the full amount of the bill is expected to be paid. Typical terms are: 2/10, net/30, or some variation of the time periods (in this example a 2% discount is permitted for payment within 10 days; the total amount is due in 30 days). Other familiar terms are: 10 e.o.m. (full amount due 10 days after the end of the month in which the transaction took place—the usual terms of personal charge accounts at retail stores) and c.o.d. (cash on delivery). When the 10 e.o.m. and c.o.d. terms are used there is no explicit measure of the cost of credit to the buyer because the financing charge is concealed in the purchase price. Terms such as 2/10, net/30, clearly imply a cost. If the cash discount is lost, the buyer must pay 2% for the privilege of deferring payment of 98% of the invoice amount until he does pay. He is expected to pay the bill, in any event, within the next 20 days. The payment of 2% for deferment is a definite cost. On an invoice for $100 which remains unpaid until the end of the agreed period, the cost is $2. This cost may be converted into an annual rate of charge as follows: $2 × 360/20 equals $36—i.e., payment for the use of money for 20/360 of a year is equivalent to payment of $36 for the use of the same amount of money for a full year. Since the amount of money conserved by deferring payment is $98, the annual rate of charge is slightly greater than 36%. Similarly, the annual rate of charge for deferring payment to the 60th day under terms of 2/10, net/60 would be approximately 14.5%.[1] Business firms that fail to take cash discounts pay a high price for this privilege, although the deferral may be necessary for survival or to conserve funds to exploit opportunities with returns above the cost involved. Companies that can use other, less expensive types of financing normally do so, but alternative sources are not always available.

---

[1] If the debtor defers payment beyond the maturity date, the effective annual rate of charge declines.

Use of trade credit. Although the use of trade credit varies with the availability of other short-term sources of funds and business conditions, this type of financing is still the most important form of current liabilities. The data in Table 17–2 indicates that it accounts for a third of all short-term liabilities. Statistics on trade credit also show that smaller companies depend more on trade credit, despite the high cost, because of the convenience and barriers to the use of other sources available to larger companies. Intercompany payables are an extremely significant source of funds for sole proprietorships, partnerships, and corporations, and they will undoubtedly continue to be so as business competition increases.

Sources of creditor funds. As emphasized above, business practices require that most companies make credit sales to customers. Because new accounts continuously replace paid-up bills, a portion of the funds of a business are tied up in accounts receivable at all times. The permanent nature of this minimum investment in receivables indicates that these funds should be obtained from long-term sources. Additional investments in receivables, such as occur during the Christmas and Easter sales periods at department stores, should be financed by funds obtained for a short period from commercial banks and other short-term sources, even to the extent of deferring payment to trade creditors if this procedure is necessary.

Loans secured by current assets

In addition to obtaining funds by unsecured short-term loans (as discussed in Chapter 5), business firms may arrange loans from banks and finance companies by pledging various types of current assets. These arrangements require promissory notes secured by the pledging of current assets which may be seized in cases of default. Although the individual notes have short-term maturities, the common procedure is to renew the commitments to create a continuous source of funds that may last for several years.

Pledging of accounts receivable. When accounts receivable are pledged as security for a loan, the methods and contracts used generally follow a standard pattern. The lender first audits the borrower's business with special attention given to the outstanding receivables including verification with the actual customers. An agreement is then created giving the lender the right to seize the accounts receivable if default occurs. Customers may or may not be notified of the arrangement, and the borrower continues to pay all costs of collection, bad debts, and credit investigation. The agreement may specify acceptance of all accounts or only those receivables that meet certain credit standards. The borrower is required to replace uncollectible accounts with new obligations to maintain the quality of the security behind the loan.

The lender usually agrees to advance some fraction of the face value of the receivables pledged. The margin of excess security must be large enough to protect the lender against losses on bad debts or shrinkage from returns and allowances. Lenders also prefer not to prepay the borrower's gross profit on sales. Between two thirds and four fifths of the face amount of receivables pledged is advanced to borrowers. As the receivables are paid, the borrower forwards the proceeds—often the customer's actual check—to the lending institution. These proceeds are applied to the reduction of the loan balance, or if a continuing agreement is in force, the funds are made available to the borrower as new receivables are submitted to replace those that have been paid. Most borrowers attempt to switch to simpler and less expensive sources of funds as soon as possible. However, reports indicate that average arrangements last from $3\frac{1}{2}$ to 4 years and may continue in existence for even longer time periods.

Pledging of inventories. Receipts for goods stored in bonded public warehouses or field warehouses and certain other forms of title to physical inventories may be used as security for loans. When a field warehouse arrangement is used the inventory is stored in a segregated area on the borrower's premises under the control of an independent warehouseman. This procedure is simple and convenient because it avoids the physical movement of goods to and from public warehouses. The bonded custodian issues a receipt for the stored inventory and the lender advances the loan against the inventory claim used as security. The actual loan is usually some fraction of the collateral value, usually two thirds to five sixths. The margin is expected to cover potential losses arising from price declines and physical deterioration in those distressed situations where the lender must liquidate the inventory to settle the loan. As inventory is withdrawn from the warehouse by the borrower, it must be replaced by satisfactory substitute goods, or its value must be offset by a reduction of the loan balance.

In some instances, the lender permits withdrawal of inventory on a trust receipt which gives the borrower physical possession acting as a trustee for the lender. The borrower may possess and sell the goods, but they are held in trust for the lender as are any receipts obtained from sales until applied against the loan balance. Inventory loans are normally seasonal and self-liquidating; however, revolving agreements may be created to prolong lending arrangements for several years.

Other current assets that may be pledged as collateral for loans include marketable securities, special receivables such as claims against a government agency, cash values of life insurance policies, and other miscellaneous assets. The principles of creditor investigation and control, fraction of collateral value loaned, and credit terms are similar to the pledging of accounts receivable and inventory.

Nature of borrowers. Many borrowers that are unable to meet the standards of credit established for unsecured loans and that lack the types of fixed assets required for mortgage loans are able to obtain funds by pledging current assets. Some companies even find this approach to be the most advantageous. For example, certain industries that must tie up large sums in inventories and accounts receivable find these assets are a convenient means for obtaining secured loans in excess of the lines of credit that most lenders would grant on an unsecured basis. Companies in the wine, lumber, food, furniture, machinery, and similar fields often utilize such secured notes in order to enlarge their borrowing capacities or to borrow the same amount at lower interest rates with fewer restrictions.

Other industries, characterized by seasonal peaks and troughs of business activity, require increased investments in inventories and receivables for short periods. The proportion of the increased investment obtained by borrowing may be increased by the pledging of inventories or receivables. Such industries as canning, seed distribution, and clothing fall into this category.

Still other businesses use secured notes because their financial condition appears weak as a result of declining business operations or rapid expansion. The first example suggests the use of collateral as a protective device to establish priority in case failure occurs. In reality, many companies can continue to meet their obligations during periods of reduced activity through the liquidation of assets that are not replaced and the curtailment of expenses. Under these conditions, whatever funds are available may be used for debt repayment. Business firms also experience financial strain during periods of rapid expansion. To meet rising sales demands, companies must usually acquire larger inventories and sell to customers on credit. The investments in fixed assets and the expenses of operation may, and usually do, increase before the receipts from sales are available. In the interim, especially if the production process is long and payments by customers are slow, the expanding concern tends to move toward technical insolvency. Such firms find it difficult to borrow on an unsecured basis and welcome the opportunity to obtain funds using as security the temporarily excessive inventories and receivables.

Unfortunately, comprehensive data on the amount of loans secured by current assets is not available; changing patterns of short-term debt and occasional reports on business practices indicate that the use of accounts receivables and inventory as loan collateral have increased in recent years. It is also apparent that this type of borrowing is a particularly flexible device that can be used to adjust to changing business conditions.

The borrower's cost. Estimating the actual costs of borrowing is difficult because the borrower may be required to make expenditures not included in the interest rate payments, the full amount of funds committed may not actually be available for use, and other services may be provided by the lender. On the other hand, the borrower may receive important services from the lending agency in the form of credit information, market analysis, financial management assistance, and production advice. The proper adjustments for indirect costs and benefits of other services are so difficult to make that it is probably reasonable to measure the cost in terms of the nominal payments made for the use of funds. Accounts receivable loans often require a payment at a specific rate per day on the total amount of receivables pledged, even though the actual loan is only a fraction of this figure. Typical rates range from one twentieth to one fiftieth of 1% per day. The actual rate is determined by the quality of receivables, the volume of advances, the handling costs, and the type of lender involved. For example, if the actual loan approved is 70% of the receivables pledged and the rate is one fortieth of 1% a day, the effective rate of interest would be $360 \times 1/40 \div 0.70$, which equals 13% a year. Another common method of charging for such loans is to establish a service fee of 2% (or some other figure) of the value of receivables handled to cover the sizable administrative costs involved and then to require an annual interest charge of 6 to 8% on the actual loans outstanding. There are several other types of agreements, which vary in procedures and definitions; however, the normal range of costs is from 10 to 20%. Commercial banks making loans against pledged accounts receivable typically charge the lowest rate.

Inventory loans also involve an interest charge on the amount of funds borrowed plus the costs of warehousing arrangements. The charges for warehouse services naturally vary widely. Typical charges for a field warehouse arrangement amount to $350 to $600 for installation of the facilities plus a percentage of the value of goods stored and the handling charges. The warehousing costs represent a charge of 1.5 to 2% a year on most loans which should be added to the variable interest charges on the funds borrowed to determine the total cost.

Wholesale, or floor-plan financing. In the distribution of high-value consumer and producer durable goods, two distinct forms of receivables financing are important. One is the sale of consumer time-installment contracts to specialized financial institutions by retailers (see Chapter 20). The other is wholesale, or floor-plan, financing developed to meet the receivables financing problems of manufacturers and the inventory financing problem of dealers.

The discounting process. When goods are shipped by a manufacturer, payment often is expected before the dealer is able to sell the product. Dealers must thus pay for the goods from their accumulated cash balances or borrow from one of the finance companies, commercial banks, or other types of lenders that make these types of loans. Under the floor-planning arrangement the dealer executes a note and a trust receipt. The dealer has physical possession of the goods and may display and sell them, but actual ownership, evidenced by the trust receipt, remains with the lender. The dealer possesses the goods as trustee for the financing agency and collects the proceeds of cash sales to periodically make payments on the loan balance and accumulated interest. When the dealer makes a sale on credit, the installment contract is frequently discounted with the lender to reduce the loan as described in Chapter 20. Under a revolving credit arrangement, dealers are continuously receiving and paying off loan advances based on the turnover of inventory. The lender normally advances 80 to 90% of the wholesale price of the goods and the interest is charged on a discount basis. The rate of discount and the maturity of notes depends upon the type of products, the financial condition of the borrower, and the type of financial institution making the loan. Since the borrower retains physical possession, the lender must be particularly careful to avoid the fradulent sale of inventories without settlement of loan balances.

Function performed. The process of floor-planning or wholesale financing has a dual benefit. The manufacturer is relieved of the burden of financing customers through trade credit. As fast as goods are produced they can be shipped and payment received without tieing up funds in inventories and receivables. Dealers avoid the investment of their limited capital in inventories. This freedom is particularly important if goods are shipped according to the manufacturer's production schedule rather than the dealer's selling schedule.

This financing procedure is particularly commonplace in the distribution of automobiles, home appliances, and other relatively high-priced goods. The arrangement is often supported by franchise agreements or licenses to sell the products of a well-known manufacturer to encourage the dealer to undertake the problems and expenses of arranging for financing.

Commercial finance companies

Among the more important specialized financial agencies developed to help finance business enterprises are the *commercial finance companies* which: advance funds on a revolving basis against the security of current trade receivables, inventories, and other assets; finance industrial time-sales contracts of buyers when equipment is purchased on installment terms; factor accounts receivable; rediscount receivables offered by other financing institutions; and lease industrial equipment, retail store fixtures, and a bewildering variety of other assets. Commercial finance companies are distinguished from consumer-oriented sales finance and personal loan firms by their concentration on business loans; however, many sales finance companies also make receivable and inventory loans, factor receivables, advance short-term credit to businesses, and arrange for wholesale or floor-plan financing.

The types of businesses that use commercial finance companies span the range of American industry. One small company, Lakeshore Commercial Finance Company, includes in its annual report to shareholders an industrial classification of its customers. A small sample of this list includes hospitals, automotive pattern manufacturing, research equipment, steel erection, lumber, spacecraft components, automatic conveyor systems, plumbing contractors, furriers, and industrial fork lift manufacturers. In 1968, the total assets of Lakeshore Finance were only $5 million. The range of loans of larger finance companies—and many of these approach $1 billion in assets—is even wider.

The key to commercial finance company operations is their ability to borrow from banks and other lenders at low interest rates and then lend the money at higher rates to companies with limited access to other sources. Approximately one half to two thirds of the resources of the large finance companies are borrowed from banks and an additional one quarter to one third of the amount is obtained by selling debt obligations, usually in the form of straight and subordinated debentures. The small ownership contribution consists largely of retained earnings. In the case of the smaller finance companies, the relative importance of equity is increased.

Although much of the business handled by commercial finance firms is considered too marginal for banks, this does not mean the borrowers are unsound risks. Typical customers are rapidly growing firms that need capital for expansion but can't present the record of earnings and financial condition usually required by banks. Companies experiencing temporary financial embarrassment because of specific problems or declining business conditions also frequently turn to this source of funds. It is common for commercial finance companies to finance the initial growth or recovery of a company and then lose the customer to a bank that is happy to fill its credit needs after financial strength is established. In this sense, these specialized agencies indirectly extend the resources of commercial banks into many business situations where banks are unable or unwilling to lend. The constant stream of new companies and new types of loans for shell homes, vending facilities, mobile homes, leasing, etc. provide the customers for commercial finance companies.

Despite the types of loans handled, losses through liquidation, defaults, and fraud have been low because of the wide diversification of borrowers, rapid turnover of loans, and basic quality of receivables as a form of collateral that can be collected in 30 to 60 days. For example, one major company typically reports losses of only six to twelve hundredths of 1% of total receivables processed.

Captive finance companies. In addition to the large-sales finance companies, several other competitive financial institutions have been attracted to the financing field served by commercial finance companies.

Many banks have increased their receivables and inventory secured and chattel mortgage loans by establishing special departments, and a number of major corporations have created captive finance subsidiaries to handle the notes receivables that result from parent company sales on time installment terms. One authority notes that at least 125 such subsidiaries to handle the notes receivables that result from parent company sales on time installment terms. One authority notes that at least 125 such subsidiaries were in operation at the end of 1961,[2] and since that time the number has increased sharply. Companies in the electrical machinery, nonelectrical machinery, transportation equipment, farm equipment, and certain retail industries have been particularly active in forming these organizations. Most captive subsidiaries do business only with customers of the parent company.

It is claimed that creation of a finance subsidiary allows the pyramiding of debt on top of minimum equity investments to a much higher degree than would be possible for the parent because of the acceptance of receivables as a suitable form of security and the limited scope of financing activities. It is also suggested that captive units stimulate the sales of the parent company, that the financial appearance of the parent is improved, and that benefits result from the separation of sales and financing functions. The growing volume of business credit, pressure on large manufacturers and retailers to help carry the financial burden of smaller customers, and the reputed success of the financing subsidiaries has attracted the interest of many corporations and the criticisms of other financing agencies that recognize the emergence of another strong competitor.

Direct placements

One important method of obtaining long-term funds is through the sale of new securities issues to the public or by direct placements with a single or small number of investors. Direct negotiations between the issuer and buyer result in the sale of securities to purchasers who are willing to hold investments that are not readily marketable in return for a higher rate of return than would be received on the purchase of a public issue. The issuing corporation may also benefit from lower financing costs resulting from the elimination of various expenses associated with public issues. The growth in size and financial sophistication of investors and corporations has made this type of financing a major source of funds.

Motivations for the investor. Direct placements are not a new financing technique. Short- and long-term credit needs have traditionally been

---

[2] Victor L. Andrews, "Captive Finance Companies," *Harvard Business Review*, vol. 42, no. 4 (July–August 1964).

arranged by direct negotiations between the borrower and lender. Nevertheless, bonds and stocks have been sold largely to the public or to existing owners through subscription offerings. The increasing sales of securities through private placement resulted from the limited volume of public financing during the 1930s and the low rates of return on new issues, coupled with an extraordinary growth of investment funds available to life insurance companies and other financial institutions. Since the 1930s, the proportion of new securities placed privately has fluctuated widely, but the amounts have increased steadily. When it is noted that railroad and many public utility issues must be sold publicly through competitive bidding, the growth of private placements is even more impressive.

Life insurance companies are clearly the largest single market for direct placements. The tremendous size and stability of cash flows into life insurance companies, many of which have assets in excess of $1 billion, makes these institutions particularly well suited to absorb large blocs of securities without violating principles of investment diversification and liquidity. Commercial banks, individuals, investment companies, pension funds, and various funds controlled by universities, foundations, and private groups also are active buyers of private placements. These investors are usually attracted by the advantages of higher yields and direct contact with the organization selling the securities. Many institutions have staffs of specialists to handle the negotiations and supervise the many protective provisions usually included in a private placement agreement. The low volume of new public security issues at various times has also made direct placements attractive to financial institutions that must continuously invest large accumulations of capital.

The major disadvantage to the investor is the lack of ready marketability. In some institutions, such as commercial banks, this is a serious drawback, and accordingly bank participation in private placements is limited in amount and normally to short maturities. Life insurance companies and certain other institutions do not have the liquidity problem faced by banks and can invest more heavily in less liquid assets and accept longer maturities. To some extent the lack of marketability is partially offset by the greater influence that a single investor can wield if the corporation gets into financial difficulty. However, since all investors require some degree of marketability, there is a limit to the volume of direct placements that any one investor will accept. Some institutions, particularly pension funds, have also been restricted in purchasing private placements because of regulations forbidding investments in nonrated bonds. The various agencies that evaluate the quality of bonds have recently started rating private issues when requests are made.

Motivations for the seller. Companies that can meet the investment standards of private placements have a large source of funds available and many corporations have turned to this financial device to take advantage of the benefits discussed below.

During certain periods of business fluctuations when the outlook for corporate earnings is poor, new securities are often not salable to public investors except perhaps at substantial price sacrifices. In these situations the costs of acquiring the funds relative to the returns expected from investment projects make public sales of securities unattractive. The use of private placements avoids some of the emotional aspects of the general investment market and permits the company seeking funds to deal directly with more sophisticated investors.

The size of a corporation, the nature of its business, and the size of the prospective securities issue may also prevent a public sale. A large, well-known corporation can usually market its securities through public sales much more easily than a small firm. Direct negotiations enable smaller companies with good potential to overcome this public market bias. It is also common to have investment fads develop whereby certain industries attract unusual attention and others fall into extreme disfavor. Companies in the downgraded industries may have difficulty obtaining funds despite their adequate individual records because of investor bias. These factors of size and sales appeal also influence institutional buyers; however, such investors usually have research staffs capable of appraising the strong qualities and weaknesses of specific companies. Many of the psychological market factors affecting public sales may be ignored by institutional purchasers where satisfactory financial strength is evident and the rate of return is satisfactory. A corporation that finds it difficult and expensive to raise funds through public sale may convince a small group of institutional investors of the soundness of its credit and obtain funds with less difficulty and at a lower cost.

Many companies have turned to direct placements to eliminate or reduce some items of expense associated with the public sale of securities in which investment bankers assume and charge for the risks and costs of distribution (see Chapter 18). Investment bankers frequently serve as intermediaries in arranging private placements and charge a fee for their services. This fee seldom exceeds 1% which is much lower than the usual compensation required when the underwriting risk is assumed. Distribution costs on a privately sold preferred stock issue offer even greater savings because the middleman's fee and other expenses are likely to be roughly equivalent to the costs of a private placement, whereas the underwriting spread on an equity issue is usually increased to reflect the greater risks and efforts involved in the selling process. The practice of serving as an agent in private placements is naturally a controversial subject among investment bankers.

The exemption of private sales from registration with the Securities and Exchange Commission is a second source of savings. The major items of expense in registering an issue with the SEC are printing and engraving costs for the prospectus and securities and legal, accounting, and engineering fees for the expert opinions set forth in the registration statement. The actual registration fee and costs of meeting state blue-sky laws are usually nominal. New issue expenses can easily total several thousand dollars and since most of the costs are the same for varying sizes of issues, the burden becomes heavy for small companies attempting to sell securities publicly. Savings also result from avoidance of the federal transfer tax on securities and the possible elimination of corporation trustee expenses. Even if a trustee is required, private sales of debt do not have to qualify under the Trust Indenture Act administered by the SEC which substantially reduces the trustee fees.

Another advantage of private placements is the elimination of the waiting period required by SEC registration procedures. The prices of securities may change materially during such periods as demonstrated during several recent bear markets when many companies had to drop planned public sales. In private sales there is only a short time period between agreement on terms and delivery of the securities.

Critics of direct placements claim that the savings are offset by two major financial considerations. First, the claim is often made that financial institutions are much sharper bargainers than most investors and that companies often have to pay a higher return that wipes out any savings. This claim is somewhat controversial and the wide variance of actual experiences make any empirical proof difficult. Second, corporations relying on private placements lose the opportunity to purchase obligations at a discount in the open market when prices are depressed. If a $100 par preferred stock is purchased for $75 in a depressed market, the company eliminates a $100 claim that is senior to the common stock position and increases the book value of common shares by $25.

Dominance of debt in direct placement financing. Most direct placements involve debt securities that are attractive to institutional purchasers because of the contractual promise to pay interest currently and the principal at maturity. In recent years, however, there has been a growing tendency to have these debt securities convertible into common shares or to have warrants attached to the bonds. The provisions are designed to give the lender an opportunity to share in any increase in the prosperity of the company that may result from use of the funds they made available.

Many classes of institutional investors are legally limited in the purchase of equity securities which further increases the supply of funds available for absorbing direct sales of debt obligations. Commercial banks are prohibited from buying equities, and life insurance companies are restricted to small purchases.

Preferred stocks have also been used for private placements because

of the higher rate of return and various protective provisions that prohibit common stock dividends and provide for preferred stockholder voting rights if preferred dividends are not paid. The fixed dividend rate
and the desire of most companies to keep payments current to protect
the corporate image also add to the strength of preferred stock and help
offset the fact that the payment of dividends and return of principal to
stockholders are contingent upon company decisions.

Common stock is usually not attractive for private placement because
of the absence of a public market in which investors may realize capital
gains by selling stocks that have appreciated in value. The uncertainty of
dividend payments, residual priority position of common shares, and
lack of provisions for systematic retirement generally eliminate common
stock from consideration for private sale to institutional investors. However, some companies called venture capital firms specialize in extending
precisely this kind of money. These firms purchase the equity in the
expectation that the firm will eventually sell its shares to the public, and
then they will realize a capital gain.

Term loans

An important form of direct financing is the *term loan*, which is an
obligation repayable in installments over a period of 1 to 15 years. Such
loans are usually made by commercial banks, life insurance companies,
pension funds, and government agencies. Characteristics of this type of
loan were reviewed in Chapter 5; however, it should be noted in this
section on the financing of business that term loans provide several major
advantages: flexibility of a long-term source of funds, convenience of
direct negotiations with the lender to preserve secrecy and to create a
personal relationship; avoidance of the irritations and risks of constantly
renewing short-term loans; and the suitability of installment repayments
of loans used to finance plant expansion in situations where the returns
from the investment provide the funds to pay off the loan. Banks typically
limit maturities to three- to five-year periods, whereas life insurance companies and pension funds prefer longer lending periods to keep assets
active and to avoid the churning of investments.

Single banks and life insurance companies may handle a term loan
independently, but it is also common for several financial institutions to
band together to form lending syndicates. When a commercial bank and
an insurance company combine to share a loan, the normal procedure is
for the bank to receive the early installment repayments. Examples of
recent term loans include: large loans to major commercial airlines to
assist in the financing of new jet aircraft; small term loans to businesses
by the Commercial and Industrial Loan Department of the Prudential

Life Insurance Company of America under its special program for reaching the small business market; and numerous term loans by major commercial banks to foreign borrowers.

Commercial real estate loans[3]

Loans on retail store locations, shopping centers, office buildings, large apartment buildings, and other commercial properties are usually made by life insurance companies, commercial banks, and mutual savings banks. Savings and loan associations also occasionally finance commercial properties. There is no provision for government guarantees or insurance of loans on commercial properties similar to the arrangements on residential commitments, except that large apartment buildings can be financed with a government-insured loan if certain qualifications are met. The making of commercial property loans is a highly specialized business requiring a thorough knowledge of commercial real estate values, trends in business districts, utilization of buildings, operating expenses, and the credit status of prospective borrowers.

Life insurance companies and banks are limited to lending only a fraction of the appraised value of the property. Substantial down payments are thus usually required to purchase commercial real estate. Most of these loans are made on an amortized basis, although the repayment schedule may leave an unpaid balance to be refinanced or settled with a balloon payment. It is also common to have the amortization rate decline over the lifetime of the loan. Maturities usually run from 5 to 30 years, depending on the condition, use, and location of the property and the credit standing of the borrower. If the property is rented under long-term leases to reliable tenants, favorable lending terms and larger loans may be demanded by the borrower. This bargaining process forces financial institutions making such loans to carefully adapt the loan repayment schedule to the expected gross and net incomes expected.

Industrial loans. Many small, and some nationally known manufacturing companies, use ordinary real estate mortgage loans instead of bond and equity issues to finance the purchase or construction of factory buildings, warehouses, or offices. The field of industrial real estate financing and property appraisal is also a particularly complicated and specialized business. Many of these types of loans are made by life insurance companies that are often represented by mortgage banking firms, which serve as specialist intermediaries between the borrowers and lenders. The loan departments of life insurance companies also may have staff members

---

[3] See Chapter 21, "Residential Real Estate Finance," for a more detailed description of instruments and institutions in this field.

that specialize in such loans. The diversification of commercial bank lending practices in recent years has also increased the role of banks in this field.

The rates and terms on industrial real estate loans vary widely. Here too, as in the direct placement market, there has been an increase in the use of instruments that combine both debt and equity features. For example, the mortgage on a shopping center may have an interest rate that has two parts: a fixed minimum plus a percentage of the gross rentals if the rentals exceed some specified levels. Alternatively, the loan may call for a direct equity interest in some land adjacent to the shopping center.

Special agencies

From time to time, emergencies have given rise to formation by governments of special agencies to facilitate financing. Some of these have persisted for long periods. During World War I loans were made to business firms by the War Finance Corporation, a federal agency. It was liquidated in 1929. The Reconstruction Finance Corporation was created by Congress in 1933 to help combat depression conditions. It was liquidated in 1954, 22 years later. In the interim, it supplied funds for other federal agencies, to foreign governments, for agricultural loans, and to state and municipal authorities. Need for rapid expansion of production facilities during World War II and the Korean War was met in part by authorizing the Federal Reserve System to guarantee loans to defense contractors in excess of the amounts private agencies were willing to grant. In 1953 Congress authorized formation of the Small Business Administration and in 1958, of small business investment corporations. Both the federal agency and the private companies were designed to provide funds for small business organizations unable to obtain sufficient amounts otherwise and to provide management counseling services (see Chapter 19 for more information about these special agencies). A number of states have established development corporations to attract industries to their areas with the expectation that more, or different, industries will facilitate regional economic development. Some of them have made moves into the area easier by issuing municipal securities to provide funds for construction of plants which are leased to the new business firms.

Some private venture capital firms have been formed expressly to lend money to or to buy stock in new small businesses. Over time, it is expected that some of the firms will prosper and that their securities will appreciate sharply in value. One of the earliest and most successful of these companies is American Research and Development Corporation of Boston, which has its common stock listed for trading on the New York Stock Exchange.

Transferred financing

Opportunities to avoid or transfer the burden of financing may also be properly considered a means of acquiring access to assets without immediate payment of the full capital cost. In some situations the use of certain resources may be possible without any outright purchase. Since the financial reserves of most companies are limited, the elimination or postponement of cash outflows associated with the purchase of assets frees funds for investment in other company activities.

Any device which allows a company to acquire needed resources without immediate payment may be considered an example of transferred financing. New companies often begin operations by selling products manufactured for them and then add the assembly function later. At the next stage of development the manufacturing process may be added. The final step, undertaken by only a few firms, is to extend direct control of operations from the retail level back to the basic acquisition and processing of raw materials.

The dependence of business firms on others for absorption of part of the financing burden is difficult to identify and measure. Nevertheless, evidence of this process may be seen in many business practices such as subcontracting, the use of public facilities by private companies, the ordering of goods for delivery on short notice to shift the inventory investment back to the supplier, joint ventures in which one of the participants supplies the ideas and others provide financial support, and many other common business activities. In the following section three specific means of transferring the financing burden of investments in receivables, equipment, and buildings and equipment are described.

Factoring

The outright sale of accounts receivables to factors is sometimes used to meet financial needs rather than pledging the accounts as collateral for a loan. The factor assumes the entire credit risk at the time of purchase and does not have recourse to the client for uncollectible receivables. Credit customers of the client are notified that the receivables are being factored and payment is remitted directly to the factor. The factor must approve the credit purchase arrangements on all invoices the client expects to have factored before the sale. After approval is obtained, the client forwards a copy of the invoice to the factor and is credited with the value of the invoice, less a small reserve to cover the factor's commission and the possibility that customers will take cash discounts or return part of the shipment. The factor must settle with the client by a predetermined payment date regardless of whether or not the account is collected. The client may also withdraw the amount credited to his account immediately even though the factor does not expect to collect from the customer until the payment date.

Factoring provides a means of transferring the credit function, including the collection process, to a specialist institution. The client either collects the amount of its sales, less the factor's commission, within a short period following the end of the cash discount or average collection period, or funds may be advanced immediately following the reporting of sales. If an advance is made prior to a payment date, interest is charged by the factor on a daily basis on the borrowed amounts until the payment date. The client also shifts to the factor burdens of credit investigations of customers and bad debt risks in return for payment of a predetermined fee on the receivables handled. Factoring provides a flexible, self-perpetuating arrangement in which the cost is variable and declines whenever sales volume drops.

Factoring developed within the textile industry early in history when manufacturing operations were performed by a large number of small mills producing similar products. The mills were located at sources of water power in the New England states, but sales were made in the financial and commercial centers, particularly in New York City. It became a common practice for both foreign and domestic producers to sell through agents located in the major cities. These agents also assumed the credit investigation and risk bearing functions for clients. In recent years the selling function has been largely divorced from financing although extensive marketing and financial advice is still given by factors to clients. The bulk of factoring still occurs in the textile industry; however, the arrangement has been used by companies in the lumber, paper, shoe, clothing, fur, electrical appliance, fuel, oil, furniture and glassware industries. Clients fall into all size categories and there is a tendency for the amount of individual receivables to be somewhat larger than in the case of pledged receivables loans.

Factoring is done by specialized financial agents and by many commercial and sales finance companies through factoring subsidiaries. A few banks also buy accounts receivables without recourse to the selling firm.

Cost to the client.   There are two charges for factoring: a rate of discount, typically 6 to 8%, applied to the amount of funds advanced to clients from the date of withdrawal to the agreed date of payment (usually 10 days after the cash discount or average collection period); and a commission between three fourths of 1% and 2% on all receivables handled. Factoring costs range from 15 to 22% a year on receivables which are outstanding an average of 50 days, assuming the client withdraws the funds immediately after the sale. Actually, the effective cost may be considerably lower because the factor usually pays interest on balances left on deposit after the date of payment. The client also eliminates the bad debt losses and expenses of operating a separate credit and collection department. Nevertheless, the spread of factoring has been limited by the reluctance of clients to have customers notified that their accounts are being factored and by the relatively high cost.

Reserve-plan discounting

A form of financing that deserves attention is reserve-plan discounting, a compromise between the receivables loan and the factoring process. This hybrid arrangement provides for the sale of receivables to a financial agency without recourse as would occur in a factoring agreement. The difference is that the lender assumes only the unusual or extreme credit risks. The client is required to maintain a deposit with the lender of 8 to 15% of the amount of receivables discounted. As receivables are paid, the client is permitted to draw against the reserve, provided it does not fall below the amount specified in relation to receivables still outstanding. Any bad debts or returns are charged against the deposit. Credit losses are absorbed by the client unless the amount exceeds the deposit total. The lending agency must cover the excess losses. The cost to the client tends to be an annual rate of 5 to 10%.

Equipment financing

A large proportion of the average company's needs involves the acquisition of equipment. Many companies, particularly small and medium-sized firms, purchase equipment on installment contracts that require periodic payments, often for extended periods, following a down payment by the buyer (often 20%). The creditor retains title to the equipment as security during the amortization of the debt. Manufacturers and distributors may provide the financing by retaining the receivables, but many prefer to shift the burden to a bank or finance company. After settlement with the seller, the bank or finance company receives title to the equipment and the buyer makes payments directly to the financial institution. Banks may also make direct loans to customers for the purpose of obtaining equipment.

Railroad rolling stock has traditionally been provided through the use of special equipment securities. One approach involves the use of conditional sales contracts arranged with commercial banks. The banks hold the title to the railroad cars until the monthly installment payments eliminate the obligation and accrued interest. In the second approach, the railroad agrees to rent equipment from a trustee. The trustee retains the title to the equipment and raises funds to pay the manufacturer by selling certificates, known as equipment trust certificates, to banks and other investors. After the final payment the title is transferred to the railroad. These methods have been used because of the simplicity of arrangements and cost savings resulting from direct negotiations. Similar methods of equipment financing have been developed for acquisition of buses, boats, airplanes, and some types of industrial equipment. Contractual arrangements vary widely, but the basic principle of periodic payments to a long-term creditor while the equipment is being used is common to all of the different agreements.

The rental of equipment as a substitute for direct ownership has expanded extremely rapidly during recent years. Fleets of autos and trucks, office machines including computers, shoemaking equipment, bowling pinsetters, machine tools, and almost every other conceivable type of equipment may now be leased. Small companies can even rent time on computers at various service agencies. Out-of-pocket costs of rental generally exceed those of direct ownership, but if company resources are limited, the rental approach provides an effective device for obtaining immediate use of equipment for expansion without large capital outflows.

Leases may be arranged in several different ways. A *service lease* requires the lessor to cover all the costs of repair, maintenance, taxes, installation costs, etc., as part of the rental agreement. In the *financial lease* the rental covers only the use of the equipment. The lessor's profit is the sum of the rental income and the residual value of the equipment at the end of the lease less the costs of providing the equipment.

Leasing remains one of the most controversial subjects in the financial field following several years of argument among businessmen, economists, tax officials, and leasing companies. Advocates have claimed leasing provides many advantages, including: the risk of owning equipment subject to technological obsolescence is avoided through short-term or cancelable leases and stipulations that new equipment must be provided when obsolescence occurs; needed equipment is provided without large cash outlays which preserves working capital; elimination of the down payment provides for complete financing; lease charges are tax deductible and may permit a faster and more complete write-off of equipment values; service may be improved; lessors may be able to pass on their economies of purchasing to users; and the appearance of the balance sheet and certain financial ratios is improved by elimination of liabilities associated with acquiring equipment.

Critics of leasing respond with the following arguments: the cost of leasing is usually 0.5 to 1% higher than borrowing costs; rental payments do not build up equity in the equipment; long-term leases may restrict flexibility; the tax status of lease payments may be questionable if certain types of repurchase options are available; and despite the accounting illusion of eliminating a liability, leases do create a stream of fixed charges requiring future payments. Many accountants believe the present value of the obligated payments should be capitalized and entered on the balance sheet. In view of the strong controversy, it is important for individual business enterprises to consider the specific terms of the lease agreement in analyzing the value of this financial device in each unique situation.

Sales-leases

A relatively new form of private financing is the sales-lease or sales leaseback arrangement which has proven attractive to business and investors. This procedure results in the sale of land and buildings by a company to an insurance company or other institutional investor while simultaneously entering into a long-term lease to rent the facilities from the investing institution. The monthly or annual rentals, which may be fixed or variable, are designed to amortize the amount of the investment and provide a predetermined rate of return over the long-term contractual period. An annual rental of about $7\frac{1}{2}\%$ of the principal, paid in monthly installments, is adequate to completely recapture the purchase price and earn interest at a rate of $4\frac{1}{2}\%$ over a 20-year period. Options for extending the lease at reduced or negotiated rates are often included in the terms. Ownership belongs to the investor but the selling company may be granted options to repurchase the properties.

Sales-leases are often used by companies to eliminate investments in land and buildings to provide funds for other business activities. The arrangement is particularly attractive where the land value is a relatively high percentage of the value of fixed assets. Property owners cannot charge depreciation on land, whereas all the rental charge, including the portion for the use of land assets, may be considered a tax deductible expense. The tax savings created and the release of funds for working capital are important advantages. Sales-lease plans are often used for retail stores, office buildings, service facilities, hotels, and other forms of real estate. Industrial plants have not used this device as frequently as retail stores, but there are examples such as the sale and leaseback by Lockheed Aircraft Corporation of its missile manufacturing facility in Sunnyvale, California, to a large insurance firm that worked closely with Lockheed throughout the construction period. The sales-lease method has also been used for equipment, such as trucks, in plans similar to the equipment financing arrangements described above.

Changing patterns of financing business

The financing of business involves continuous bargaining among prospective investors and companies in need of funds for expansion or survival. Internal sources continue to dominate. Reliance on retained earnings, depreciation funds, and other internal sources has had a large impact on the capital markets, management policies, and the status of investors. Companies also utilize a variety of external sources of funds including familiar trade credit and lending agreements. The flexibility of arrangements provided is an important part of the business system and demonstrates the strength of financial institutions in adapting to changing business conditions. Patterns of change have been created by many new business practices and by the growing concentration of investment funds in financial institutions that serve as intermediaries for the collection and investment of funds. The demands of business enterprises will cause continued use of the financing techniques described in this chapter, but the forces of change will also create new forms of institutions and financing arrangements.

Questions and problems

1. If maturities on current liabilities are normally very short term, why are these liabilities considered permanent sources of funds suitable for financing permanent assets?

2. Why have internal sources of funds become such an important form of financing business? Is depreciation actually a source of funds?

3. Why is trade credit so prevalent in American business operations?

4. If the cash discount offered for prompt payment reduces the total amount paid, why does failure to take the discount create a cost?

5. Describe the processes of lending on accounts receivable and factoring and explain how the two practices differ.

6. What types of financial institutions make receivables and inventory loans? What factors influence the amount borrowed and the cost? Why do companies use these types of loans if the cost is higher than for other sources of funds?

7. How does wholesale or floor-plan financing differ from loans secured by inventory?

8. Develop a list of the various sources of funds available to business arranged according to the cost to the business firm. How would you explain the large variation in costs?

9. Why do specialized finance companies flourish when commercial banks are so well established? What relationship exists between these two institutions? Why have many corporations established their own finance companies?

10. If you were an investment banker, how would you react to the growing volume of direct placements? What arguments can be used against this practice? Do you believe direct placements will increase in importance?

11. Why are real estate loans for business purposes so complex? Are these loans the same as a term loan?

12. How do you feel about the creation of government agencies to finance private business firms? Have these agencies been successful?

13. Do you expect equipment financing to increase? If so, what financing techniques will be important?

14. Does leasing improve the credit standing of companies by releasing working capital and eliminating liabilities from the balance sheet?

15. Since selling companies lose their ownership equity in a sales-lease arrangement, why did this form of financing increase during the 1960s?

Bibliography

The large number and broad scope of publications on the subject of financing business prevents any detailed listing here. The 1964 publication, *Corporate and Business Finance: A Classified Bibliography* compiled by Gordon Donaldson and Carolyn Stubbs for Baker Library, Graduate School of Business Administration, Harvard University, is particularly useful. Many finance textbooks also contain extensive bibliographies. For example, see Harry G. Guthmann and Herbert E. Dougall, *Corporate Financial Policy* (4th ed.; Englewood Cliffs, N.J.: Prentice-Hall, Inc., 1962) and J. C. Van Horne, *Financial Management and Policy* (Englewood Cliffs, N.J.: Prentice-Hall, Inc., 1968). Current publications may be found in the *Business Periodical Index, Reader's Guide to Periodical Literature,* and *Public Affairs Information Service.*

Several journals carry articles on business finance including: *Journal of Finance, American Economic Review, Journal of Business, Harvard Business Review,* and *Financial Executive.* The *Wall Street Journal, Financial and Commercial Chronicle, Barrons,* and *Business Week* also frequently contain articles on business financing. Several trade associations and individual companies publish magazines and pamphlets which are useful. For example, the pamphlet, *How to Finance Business by Field Warehousing Inventory; Facts and Information for Borrowers, Banks, and Lending Agencies* is available from the Douglas-Guardian Warehouse Corp. Another useful publication is Clyde W. Phelps, *Factoring and Accounts Receivable Financing as a Method of Business Finance* (Baltimore: Commercial Credit Co., 1957).

Particular attention should be given to the Business Finance Series of monographs published by the National Bureau of Economic Research. Several major contributions have been made by this series. Current statistical information and occasional articles may be found in the *Survey of Current Business* and the *Federal Reserve Bulletin.*

CHAPTER 18

Securities markets

In the preceding chapter a number of permanent or continuing sources of funds for large business was considered. Public markets for securities of corporate business were not included, however, and interest in these markets warrants discussion in a separate chapter. Since there are two kinds of markets—the market for new issues and the market for securities already outstanding—and differences among procedures in these markets are substantial, each is described separately in the following pages.

Public distribution of new securities issues

The best-known intermediaries in the public market for long-term funds for business are investment banking houses. They distribute securities issued by corporations and public bodies to their customers, the nation's investors. Investment bankers derive their income from the difference between the price paid to the issuers and the price received from investors.

Throughout the early history of the United States, business was financed largely through private subscriptions. In the 18th and 19th centuries, substantial amounts were obtained through sale of securities abroad. The need for raising a large volume of funds to finance the Civil War led, however, to the development of agencies that specialized in the rapid distribution of government securities over a broad area—the prototype of the modern investment banking firm. In later years the great size of many issues necessitated the use of *syndicating,* a device for pooling risks among several firms. Today, through syndicating and using modern methods of communication, investment bankers are able to distribute very large blocks of securities widely and rapidly and can guarantee successful distribution to the issuing entities. Without such organizations and their services, many of our present-day corporations probably could not have obtained so readily the sizable amounts of funds necessary for their present scale of operation.

Investment banking functions

Securities houses provide a variety of services to investors and to securities issuers. A typical concern may serve in the following capacities:

1) *Originator.* Negotiate with the company seeking new capital and assist in the preparation of an issue of stocks or bonds for underwriting.

2) *Underwriter.* Buy outright an entire stock or bond issue or agree to buy any portion of an issue not otherwise subscribed.

3) *Distributor.* Purchase new or already outstanding stocks or bonds for sale to investors. In originating, underwriting, and distributing, an investment banker may act alone or, particularly in the case of large issues, in participation with other investment banking houses.

4) *Dealer.* Buy and sell outstanding securities. He may hold an inventory of such securities to facilitate trading in them. He will deal in particular issues because he was an underwriter or distributor of the issues initially or because he regards them as otherwise attractive for his investor customers.

5) *Broker.* Act as an agent for investors in the purchase or sale of securities, whether the securities are listed on an organized exchange or traded over the counter.

6) *Financial adviser.* In addition to advising issuers of securities, may serve in other financial counseling capacities. He may advise businesses on problems of a financial nature, including assistance in effecting consolidations or in acquiring and selling capital assets; he will furnish information and investment advice when requested; and he may aid individual and institutional investors in determining the value of securities for which there is no adequate public market. Origination, underwriting, and distribution are considered below. Dealer and broker functions are treated later in this chapter.

Investment banking industry

Some measure of the scope of the investment banking industry and securities business structure is provided by the membership of the Investment Bankers Association of America (IBA) and the membership of the National Association of Securities Dealers. There are about 680 members of the Investment Bankers Association, who maintain about 2,400 branch offices in addition to the main offices, or a total of more than 3,000 places of business. Members of this association are primarily originators and underwriters of securities with a national market and houses that participate in the distribution of such securities as well as local securities. Included among these IBA members are a number of the larger commercial banks.

Commercial banks may underwrite and deal in municipal bonds and may deal in federal government bonds; they are precluded from underwriting and dealing in corporate securities, either stocks or bonds. The general-obligation municipal bond is payable from the full taxing power of the issuing unit and depends upon the faith and credit of the community. In contrast, revenue bonds are issued to acquire income-producing properties such as toll bridges, water plants, and turnpikes; payment of principal and interest must be met solely from the revenues of the particular project; such bonds are not the obligation of a special group of taxpayers.

With the exception of the municipal houses and the commercial banks, practically all IBA members also belong to the National Association of Securities Dealers, which has a total membership of about 4,800, including many smaller houses that do a largely local business. Securities houses employ 180,000 persons. Half of them are registered employees, those who do business with the public.

The nature of the National Association of Securities Dealers is discussed more fully later in this chapter.

Preliminary investigation

The first step in the issuance of new securities by public distribution may be taken by an officer of a corporation who seeks the assistance of an investment banking house, or by a banking firm which contacts the businessman to suggest an issue. After the initial interview with the representatives of the business, the investment banker will make a thorough study of the particular business and the industry of which it is a part, to determine the feasibility and advisability of contracting to handle the financing. Such specialists as accountants, lawyers, engineers, and industry and management consultants will be called in to assist in the investigation. This study will include a careful review of the history of the company, its operations, financial record, managerial policies, position in the industry, the competition that the enterprise must meet, and any other factors that may aid in appraising the soundness of the operation and the ability of management.

If the decision is reached that the company requires financing and that fundamental conditions, internal and external, justify the raising of additional funds, an agreement will be made by the investment banker and the issuer. The choice of the form of security will depend on the needs and wishes of the management and the temper of the market, i.e., what type of security will appeal at that time to investors. Agreement must be reached on a price at which the security can be sold and, if a bond or preferred stock, the interest rate or the dividend; whether the issue should be designed to appeal to institutional investors or to individuals; and whether the responsibility for the distribution of the securities will be shared with other investment bankers who might then join in signing the agreement.

Underwriting

One decision emerging from such investigation is whether or not the investment bankers will underwrite the issue. Investment bankers are often called *underwriters*, although this is a term which is usually associated with insurance. The marine insurer agrees to compensate the owner of goods placed on a ship if the ship fails to make port; the accident insurer agrees to pay costs resulting from accidents. In much the same way the underwriter of a securities distribution assures the company seeking funds that the funds will be available regardless of the success of public distribution. This assurance is usually provided by agreement that the underwriters will pay for the securities issued whether or not the investment bankers are able to sell the issue to their customers. On a date set in the underwriting or purchase contract, each member of the underwriting syndicate delivers to the managing house a certified check for its share of the issue. The managing house thereupon delivers the funds to the corporation or a designated agent. Under these conditions the issuing firm is insured against failure of the distribution process. It can depend upon receiving the funds it needs at the time needed.

Underwriting contracts. Two forms of underwriting contract are common: a firm contract and a stand-by agreement.

A *firm contract* is one by which the bankers bind themselves to pay the corporation as indicated above. This contract may be cancelable: up to a certain date the bankers may withdraw from the agreement. On or after that date, however, they are bound by the contract.

A *stand-by agreement* is one by which the bankers bind themselves to purchase all the securities which the issuing corporation may be unable to sell through some other distribution channel. For example, the corporation may offer a new issue to its present security holders. Under a stand-by agreement, the bankers underwrite the success of the issue by standing ready to purchase any securities that the present security holders do not buy. Regardless of whether or not the old security holders give the new issue enthusiastic reception, the corporation will receive the needed funds. The banker assumes the problem of marketing unsold securities.

"Best-effort" distribution. The facilities of banking firms are sometimes employed only for distribution, and the bankers do not underwrite the issue. They contract simply to employ their best efforts to obtain purchasers for the new securities. The bankers receive a commission for their efforts; they do not commit themselves to purchase or distribute the entire issue; they do not depend for income on the sale of the new issue in total to the public. If any part of the issue remains unsold at the end of the contract period, the issuer has little alternative except to withdraw the remaining portion. The issuer loses to the extent that it fails to obtain the amount of funds desired. Best-effort contracts are requested by issuers whose investment appeal is so great that the need for insurance (underwriting) is negligible, and such contracts are preferred by bankers if they undertake distribution of issues so difficult to sell that underwriting does not seem feasible. Thus best-effort contracts are used for very strong and very weak issues. Stock issues, especially of new firms, are frequently offered on a best-effort basis.

Risks of underwriting. Examples of losses to underwriters are numerous. Although other and perhaps more spectacular cases might be cited, a number of sticky or slow-moving issues appeared in 1946. In October of that year, owing to an unexpected fall in securities prices, a syndicate of 46 investment bankers found themselves unable to sell at their offering price the 125,000 shares of Willys-Overland Motors, Inc., $4.50 preferred stock, which they had purchased at $100 a share in June for resale at $102.75 a share. They finally disposed of these shares at $53 to $68 a share. The huge offering of 1,445,000 shares of Cincinnati Gas and Electric Company common stock purchased by 156 investment banking firms at $26 a share was finally distributed at prices as low as $21.75. In 1950, about two thirds of an issue of Potomac Electric Power Company bonds, for which underwriters had paid $100.80¼, was sold at a price of approximately $100.50. With about $12 to $14 million of General Motors Acceptance Corporation bonds unsold, the syndicate in September 1959 let the bonds find their price on the market. The price dropped promptly from $100 to about $96½. On a 1.5 million share offering of Atlantic Richfield stock in July 1969 the offering was made at $115¼, the underwriters paid $112, and much of the issue was marketed at prices around $107. The risks of marketing are not, of course, confined to issues sold under firm contract or stand-by agreement. In 1939, Shell Union Oil Corporation completed the sale of bonds on a best-effort basis at 96 rather than the desired 100. On the other hand, many issues are sold within a few minutes because they are priced attractively for the market at the moment of offering.

Purchase syndicate. An issue of securities is usually distributed in two steps: wholesale and retail. After an initial contact has been made between the issuing corporation and investment bankers, one or several firms make an agreement to purchase the issue from the corporation. In times past, if two or more firms were involved, they formed a joint venture, a kind of partnership created for the definite limited purpose of purchasing the specific issue. The joint venture, in turn, sold the issue to other bankers at the retail level or direct to investors. The full advantage of gain or the full weight of loss fell on the venture and was distributed according to the agreement between the members. In more recent years, it has become usual for each member of a syndicate to sign a separate contract with the corporation and assume responsibility only for a specific amount of the issue. In a divided account of this kind, losses fall directly on the firms that fail to market their particular allotment successfully. Another advantage of this separation of liability lies in the unknown potential loss arising under the federal law regulating the issue of securities, the Securities Act of 1933. Under the terms of this act, any individual responsible for a misstatement or omission of a material fact in information concerning a new issue might be asked to pay damages sustained by purchasers. In a joint venture, any one firm might be asked to pay damages as great as the full amount of the issue; with separate contracts, the damages for which a firm may become liable probably would not exceed the amount of that part of the whole issue which the firm contracted to distribute.

Small issues may be handled by a single concern. When, however, purchase syndicates are formed, the number of members and the constituency of the group are separately determined for each issue. Syndicates may include as few as two or three or as many as 200 or 300 houses. The firms may be concentrated in a small geographical area or spread nationwide. There is, therefore, a great deal of flexibility in arranging a syndicate operation.

Most syndicates have one member firm acting as manager. This firm is usually the *originating house,* the one that made the initial contact with the issuer and that, as syndicate manager, assumes certain responsibilities for the venture as a whole. It will often handle business dealings between the syndicate and issuer, among syndicate members, and between the syndicate and a selling group. Occasionally two or more houses cooperate in performing the management function. In any event, responsibility for coordination of activities among members is a requisite of successful purchase and subsequent resale operations.

Selling group. A purchase syndicate usually contracts with a second group of banking houses to provide for retail distribution—i.e., sale to individual investors. Some or all of the purchase syndicate members will also engage in the retail distribution. However, utilization of additional firms increases the number of investors who can be reached quickly. The retail organization may take the form of a syndicate but usually is a less formal selling-group arrangement. The number of houses in the selling group varies with the issue, and many smaller dealers may be included. A selling group made up of dealers in all parts of the nation tends to broaden distribution. Selling-group members purchase outright a participation in the new issue at an established discount from the public offering price, and their risk is limited to the extent of their participation. If a dealer is unable to place the entire allotment, the manager of the underwriting syndicate may, at his discretion, repurchase all or part of the allotment without penalty to the dealer. The ultimate aim of the selling group, of course, is distribution of the entire issue to investors.

Market support. The prices of securities in public markets are subject to sudden and marked change. Fluctuations may occur for temporary and rather insubstantial reasons. As a new issue of securities is sold to investors by the selling group, the salesmen seek to place the securities in the hands of individuals who will retain ownership for some time—i.e., in "firm hands." Some buyers, however, will turn about and reoffer the new securities in the public markets. If a fairly large number of the securities are thus offered in a short period of time, the market price may well decline. This in turn would have an adverse effect on the continued distribution of the new issue. If securities offered in the public market can be reacquired by the bankers and redistributed—this time into firm hands —the price is less likely to drop. For this reason, the purchase syndicate may agree to maintain a trading account. The manager will place a bid to purchase all securities offered at a certain price. This price usually is slightly below that at which the new issue is being sold to investors. Securities repurchased are then distributed again to members of the syndicate for sale to the public.

This procedure of price support is known as stabilization and has been a center of controversy as a possibly socially undesirable practice. However, the Securities and Exchange Commission, the federal agency regulating securities market practices, ruled in 1939 that price stabilization is an essential part of securities distribution if proper disclosure of the fact is made to the public. It prevents early buyers of a slow issue from being penalized and, conversely, prevents underwriters from holding back for a better price on an issue that is readily marketable.

Secondary distributions

Owners of large blocks of securities often find that sale of their holdings cannot be easily accomplished through the usual channels for securities marketing. A secondary distribution, as the term is usually employed, is a sale of a large block of outstanding securities off the organized exchanges. A syndicate is formed to underwrite the distribution to the public, and it purchases the block at a given price. It then sells at a fixed price, which is usually established by the latest available market quotation for the issue prior to the sale and to the public offering. The spread between purchase and sale price is similar in amount to that for a primary public distribution of a new securities issue. The British government used this procedure in 1940–41 to sell the holdings of its citizens; the Mellon and Rockefeller interests have also used this method to reduce their investment in some companies; and it continues to provide an effective procedure for marketing large holdings. One of the largest secondaries was the distribution of 6.8 million shares of Trans World Airlines stock in May 1966 for $587 million.

In 1942 the New York Stock Exchange established a procedure for *special offerings* of securities ordinarily sold on the exchange. The minimum quantity is 1,000 shares of stock or $25,000 market value, whichever is greater, or $15,000 principal amount of bonds with aggregate market value exceeding $10,000. The block is offered at a fixed price on the exchange, and efforts are made to place the securities with buyers in much the same way as for a secondary distribution. This method was used for some years after its introduction, but has been used very infrequently in recent years.

In 1954 the first of a different type of offering—an *exchange distribution*—occurred on the New York Stock Exchange. Under this procedure also the block of securities is offered for sale on the floor of the exchange. However, prices are established in the regular auction market, and the buyer pays the usual commission on the transaction. In 1968 this method was used almost to the exclusion of the special offering, as the following figures show:[1]

Type of distribution	No.	Shares sold (millions)	Market value ($ millions)
Special offerings	1	—*	—*
Exchange distributions	35	2.67	93.53
Secondary distributions	174	36.11	1,571.60

* Less than ½ million.

Each of the two newer methods for distributing stock have counterparts in methods for acquisition of large blocks, such as an institutional investor might wish. These are called, respectively, the *exchange acquisition* and *special bid*. In addition to these methods there are procedures for

---

[1] Securities and Exchange Commission, *35th Annual Report* (1969), p. 194. *Statistical Bulletin,* November 1964, p. 8, and February 1965, p. 11.

specialist block purchase and *specialist block sale.* These govern the purchase or sale *off* of the exchange by the specialists in particular issues of large blocks to be distributed or which have accumulated bit by bit in the ordinary trading on the exchange.

Types of clients

The investment banker serves medium- and large-sized corporate businesses and state or local governments primarily. It is essentially the breadth and magnitude of securities distribution that investment banking firms are prepared to achieve which gives them their specialized place. Sole proprietors and partnerships do not have securities to offer. On the other hand, certain forms of securities—e.g., U.S. government bonds, which receive wide distribution—are marketed through other channels, such as the commercial banking system or special selling organizations. Of the corporate securities offered for cash sale in the United States in 1969 about 80% moved through investment banking channels. In that year, $24.3 billion of securities were offered by the following broad industry groups: manufacturing, $5,770 million; mining, $1,636 million; electric, gas, and water, $6,137 million; railroad, $276 million; other transportation, $1,710 million; communication, $1,911 million; financial and real estate (excluding investment companies), $3,884 million; and commercial and other companies, $2,929 million.

Cost to clients

The cost of obtaining funds is reflected in the bankers' spread and the expenses paid by the client himself. The bankers' spread—commissions and discounts received—covers charges for underwriting and distribution. In the aggregate, the spread tends to be small relative to the amount of money received by the issuer. On the securities offered for cash sale for the account of the issuer and registered with the Securities and Exchange Commission in its fiscal year ending June 30, 1964, commissions and discounts equaled 1.21% and other expenses, 0.54% of the gross proceeds expected from the issues. More detailed estimates of costs to issuers per $100 received during the years 1951–55 are shown in Table 18–1. These figures, however, are not indicative of the costs that a particular issuer might pay. There are several weaknesses in the use of aggregates to show individual costs. The data cover issues that were underwritten, as well as issues sold on a best-effort basis. The amount of commissions and discounts per $100 tends to be greater when the latter form of distribution is used. Then, too, some of the costs in any distribution are fixed or nearly fixed in amount. They must be covered by proceeds from sale of the issue, whether large or small; but they tend to increase the comparative cost of small issues over that of large. The common and preferred stock issues were, on the whole, smaller than the bond issues. Thus some of the apparently higher cost of issue for these classes of securities is really a measure of the difference in cost between small and large issues and between methods of distribution rather than between classes of instruments.[2] However, some common and also preferred stocks require considerable selling effort, whereas many bond issues readily go out the window.

TABLE 18–1

Cost to issuers per $100 received from new securities issues, 1951, 1953, and 1955, combined

Type of security	Total cost	Commission and discount	Other expense
Bonds	$ 1.49	0.80	0.59
Preferred stock	4.34	3.34	1.22
Common stock	10.28	8.75	1.85

Note: detail does not add to total because of rounding and use of median figures.
Source: Securities and Exchange Commission, *Cost of Flotation of Corporate Securities 1951–1955* (Washington, D.C.: Government Printing Office, June 1957), p. 37.

The "other expense," which ranges from $0.59 to $1.85, as shown in Table 18–1, is a measure of the expense per $100 received that the issuing corporation usually must pay directly. It refers to the costs of printing and engraving, registration and recording, taxes, legal, accounting, and engineering costs, and the costs of listing the issue on an organized exchange—to the extent that these expenditures are required for any particular issue.

Long-term relationships with clients

The investment banker cannot afford to dispose of his merchandise and then forget about its existence. As long as the securities he sells are outstanding in the hands of the public, the reputation of the banker is linked to the success or failure of the enterprises he helps to finance. In a very unusual case reported in 1955, one firm gave a quarter of a million dollars to the state of Iowa to pave a road leading to a toll bridge, the revenue bonds for which had been sold by this firm and had been defaulted for lack of revenues from tolls. In another case in an earlier year, a small investment banking firm, which had advised its customers to purchase

---

[2] More detailed figures are available in the report cited for Table 18-1, and much more detail for different types of equity issues is to be found in a later study, SEC, *Cost of Flotation of Registered Equity Issues, 1963–65* (Washington, D.C.: Government Printing Office, 1970).

stock in a local company that subsequently failed, returned to those customers the full value of their shares at the original purchase price. The investment banker stands in relation to his customers as an adviser, a fiduciary. Prudence, caution in acceptance of new approaches to old ideas or markets, and a capacity for seeing the economic significance of the companies whose securities he distributes are expected of him by his customers. Failure to maintain their regard is tantamount to failure in this business.

On the other hand, close connections and cooperation with business firms are necessary. Opportunity to sell new issues arises from acquaintance with firms requiring new capital. His knowledge of securities markets may lead to recommendations for distribution of new issues at times when the usefulness of new financing is not apparent to managers of business firms. Often the investment banker serves on the board of directors of firms he helps to finance. Firms may use the same underwriters year after year as needed because of the banker's intimate acquaintance with the affairs of the corporation. If the investment banker were to act imprudently or fail to serve effectively, the corporation would replace him with a competitor eager to serve in a more efficient manner. Similarly, when an investment banker is dissatisfied with the management of a firm that he has helped to finance, he may voluntarily relinquish his underwriting position.

Sources of bankers' funds

A successful distribution of a security issue results in a flow of funds from investors to the issuer. The investment banker provides the channel through which these funds flow and diverts a small amount—his spread—to himself in payment for his services. In any event, excepting best-effort distributions, whether or not the public buys the entire issue, payment of the principal amount to the issuer will be made by the banker at the time set in the contract, and this is usually before the investors have paid the banker for securities they have purchased.

If the banker is to pay the issuer before funds are obtained from investors, he must supply them from his own assets or borrow. In general, the greater proportion will be obtained by borrowing from commercial banks. Here we can observe how the capacity of the commercial banking system to supply money for short-term use facilitates the consummation of a long-term activity. The commercial bank can lend against the investment banker's note—probably secured by the deposit of the issue in question as collateral—for the length of time needed to collect funds from a multitude of individual investors. This loan bridges the time gap between issue and sale in a successful distribution. The investment banker need commit only so much of his own funds to an issue as the commercial banker requires for a margin of protection on the loan.

An attempt at distribution that fails places the investment banker under financial strain. The loan at the commercial bank may be continued as long as there is adequate collateral to support it, but an inventory of unsold securities held by the investment house not only ties up the investment banker's own funds but limits his capacity to borrow more to carry other issues. It blocks the continued turnover that is fundamental to his business. Therefore, in many cases, the investment banker will lower the price at which the issue is offered to the investing public to a point where he can sell all the securities, take the loss, clear the loan, and free funds so that he may engage in future distribution.

Under a best-effort agreement, the investment banker advances nothing. The banker is acting simply as an agent on a commission basis and does not supply any funds of his own for the operation. He channels money from investors to the issuer and does not underwrite success.

Investment banking firms may engage in the distribution of many millions of dollars of securities in a given period—say, a year—and yet have relatively small amounts of owner investment in the business. Only in rare instances and in recent years have investment bankers sought funds for their own use in the market they serve.

Regulation

The nature of the business that the investment banker conducts has led to a certain amount of regulation of securities distribution and of the activities of persons engaged in this distribution. Investment securities are intangible. A bond or stock is merely a bundle of rights on which it is very difficult to place a precise value at any particular time. The strengths or weaknesses of these rights may not be apparent for years. Even the elements of strength or weakness that appear to be obvious at one moment may prove to be otherwise at some future period, owing to changes in the economy generally and in the securities markets in particular. In a dynamic world, the forecast of the future implied in the pricing of a security is, at best, an informed estimate. Since few persons are in a position to make an intelligent appraisal, they may be acting under a considerable misconception when they acquire securities. Public interest has dictated that willful exploitation of this possible weakness in the investor's ability to understand the nature of a security shall not be condoned. Regulation is directed at restraint of practices that magnify the risk of ownership through misunderstandings between the purchaser and the seller of securities. In a sense, a useful analogy might be drawn with the regulation of sellers of foods and drugs.

Governmental attempts to control the sale of new securities issues are based on the existence of a public offering. Statutory definitions of *public sale* are usually not given; but by construction, a public offering may be defined as one made to the public generally. Thus the sale of an issue to one person is a public sale if the offer might have been accepted by any individual or group. In practice, a sale to fewer than 25 persons has been presumed a private, rather than a public, sale. These definitions are important because all laws on securities sales, of outstanding as well as of new issues, as noted, are based on a public offering. The laws are designed to protect the *public* against fraud or deceit.

The development of restrictions on the marketing of new securities issues has followed the familiar pattern of many other kinds of regulation: first, it is initiated by the states; second, state laws have been found ineffective to control interstate transactions; and finally, there is subsequent federal legislation.

State regulation. The various blue-sky laws were the first attempts at state regulation of the marketing of security issues. Their title has been attributed to an early court decision that commented on "speculative schemes that have no more basis than so many feet of blue sky." The first state act was adopted in Kansas in 1911, and other states followed. Such blue-sky statutes afforded some protection to the investor against outright fraud; but because of variations in type and enforcement, the state laws are not uniformly effective and are applicable only intrastate. Nevertheless, blue-sky laws are now in effect in all states except Nevada.

The blue-sky laws may be classified into three types: fraud laws, licensing laws, and registration laws. Only Delaware, New Jersey, New York, and Maryland have fraud laws in their true sense. They do little more than provide for penalties and for enjoining those who are guilty of fraud in the sale of securities. These laws apply equally to the sale of new securities and the exchange or trading of outstanding issues. Licensing laws, of the type found in Maine, place emphasis on the dealer rather than on the securities sold. This type of law, requiring licensing of all securities dealers, may be combined with a required registration of securities, as in Illinois, Indiana, Ohio, and Wisconsin. In many states such registration of dealers has become a rather perfunctory detail, with little scrutiny of the character and ability of applicants. The registration laws, as in Massachusetts and Ohio, resemble the federal Securities Act of 1933, being intended to prevent deceit and fraud before it occurs, rather than, as is the case under the fraud laws, to punish after an act has been committed. Under such a type of law, for instance, Wisconsin has often prohibited the sale of securities where bonuses to promoters or underwriters, in the form of rights, have appeared excessive; and Ohio prevented the sale of a second large original offering of Kaiser-Frazer Corporation stock because of a legal technicality precluding a second offering before operations had actually begun and before routine financial statements reflecting operations were available for scrutiny.

While state securities laws are reasonably good, their enforcement is difficult, owing to weak administration at times and always to lack of control over interstate transactions. A promoter in one state might sell stock to residents of another state and be able to avoid, or at least delay, his prosecution under the law of that second state for a considerable period of time.

Securities Act of 1933. The two principal federal acts regulating securities distribution and markets are the Securities Act of 1933 and the Securities Exchange Act of 1934. The latter is discussed in the next section since it is directed primarily to the regulation of practices in markets for outstanding securities. The Securities Act of 1933 is concerned mainly with public offerings of new securities issues. It provides for full disclosure in a registration statement of all pertinent information regarding a proposed issue and for penalities following violations of the act. It assumes that disclosure of pertinent information, together with access to digests thereof by investment services, will enable prospective investors to appraise the security more effectively. It thus does not attempt directly to prevent sale of speculative (or perhaps even worthless) issues. It does not guarantee the investment merit of registered securities, but it does require full and truthful disclosure of all pertinent information.

Specifically exempt from the provisions of the act are issues of the federal government, municipalities, government corporations, and banks; commercial paper with maturity of not more than nine months; issues of nonprofit organizations and cooperatives; railroad securities; receivers' certificates; insurance and ordinary annuity contracts; and new securities issued pursuant to reorganization.

Other exemptions from registration apply to enterprises that sell issues not exceeding $300,000 ($100,000 in some instances) and thus have only limited public offering; sell issues wholly within a single state; or sell a complete issue of securities to a limited public. This last exemption applies particularly to the direct placement of an issue with institutional investment agencies.

It is significant to note that the last-mentioned exemptions from registration do not constitute exemption from civil and criminal liability in case of actual fraud in the public sale of securities of any corporation, municipality, state, or the federal government, regardless of the size of the issue. The promoter of a small enterprise who offers to sell a security to more than a limited number of persons, therefore, can protect himself against subsequent claims of fraud only by filing with the Securities and Exchange Commission an informational statement about the issue.

The *registration statement* under the Securities Act of 1933 must be signed by the principal officers of the corporation and a majority of the board of directors and filed at least 20 days before any public offering is to be made. The Securities and Exchange Commission (SEC) may shorten this waiting period (accelerate the registration date) for a particular issue under certain conditions if warranted. But most issues are actually in registration for more than 20 days. In 1969 the average waiting period was 65 days. A registration fee based on the aggregate proceeds of the offering must be paid. The written consent of all experts who prepared parts of the statement, such as accountants, engineers, and lawyers, must also be filed. In the form must appear a full disclosure of the name, location, and state of incorporation of the issuer and the purpose of the issue, as well as the names and addresses and amount of securities owned by and remuneration paid to directors, officers, promoters, underwriters, and all who own more than 10% of any class of stock of the issuer.

Detailed information on the new security must be given, including the underwriting agreement, estimated proceeds, net offering price, underwriting spread, and costs. Additional information on the relation of the company to the promoters and principal stockholders must be submitted, together with certified financial statements, in a prescribed form for the preceding three fiscal years. The SEC has the power to ask for additional information, if necessary, to give a complete public disclosure of all material facts on the company and the security issue.

The SEC is empowered to refuse to permit a registration statement to become effective if it believes that the statement is inaccurate or incomplete in any material respect. If a registration that has become effective is later found to be false, misleading, or incomplete, the SEC may issue a stop order suspending the effectiveness of the registration statement. These steps were taken, for example, in the case of the Tucker Corporation, an automobile manufacturing company which did not actually reach the production stage before attempted reorganization.

Registration is required also of all secondary distributions in which outstanding stock is being sold by a principal stockholder or stockholders through an underwriter, with proceeds exceeding $100,000.

A *prospectus* must be delivered to each customer at or before the actual sale or delivery of new securities. The prospectus is in reality an abridged form of the registration statement described above but usually is, nevertheless, a lengthy document.

Competitive bidding. In order to assure arm's-length bargaining between the managements of railroad and public utility corporations issuing new securities and the investment banking firms that undertake the marketing, both the Interstate Commerce Commission (ICC) and the SEC have adopted the device of compulsory competitive bidding. Under such regulation, a corporation is required to obtain bids from a number of individuals or purchase syndicates. The securities are then sold to the bidder making the most favorable bid.

The use of the competitive bidding device has been traditional in the marketing of municipal bonds. In 1926 the ICC made this a requirement in the issue of railroad-equipment trust certificates, special issues sold to provide funds to purchase rolling stock for the railroads. The SEC ruled in 1941 that securities of public utility companies under their jurisdiction were to be offered by competitive bidding. In 1944 the ICC extended its ruling to cover all railroad bond issues amounting to $1 million or more. Approximately 25% of all corporate securities and over half of all securities (exclusive of federal government issues) offered for sale in recent years have been sold subject to competitive bidding rules.

The principal argument in favor of competitive bidding is that the issuer receives a better price for a given issue than it would otherwise. It is probably true also that the decisions of management are less influenced by the interests of investment banking firms. On the other hand, there are likely to be only a few bids placed for quite small or quite large issues, and this lack of bids suggests that the device is not very competitive in such cases. Some evidence indicates that, on other issues where competition is a factor, the bankers' spread is too narrow to permit the careful investigation by the bankers needed to provide a safeguard on the quality of securities marketed to the public. In practice the SEC has found it necessary to exempt issues from its own ruling at times when it was fairly clear that an issue could not be marketed successfully under competitive bidding. Industrial corporations have shown no tendency to adopt the device voluntarily for their own use. The mere fact, however, that competitive bidding has been invoked by the rules of these two federal agencies suggests that within their jurisdictions it probably will be continued.

Other regulatory agencies. Two other agencies play a part in the control of practices in the sale of securities: the National Association of Securities Dealers (NASD) and better business bureaus. The NASD is a trade association for persons in the securities business, and it performs a number of functions, including self-regulation of trade practices. The association has established rules of conduct that are said to be of assistance to the industry in following paths of useful service. Not all securities dealers are in agreement as to the value of NASD: many are strongly critical; others are staunch supporters. The organization and operation of this association will be discussed further in the next section. Better business bureaus play a part in restricting the activities of fly-by-night or itinerant sellers, who enter a territory to offer securities for sale by other than the regular channels.

Securities exchanges, brokers, and dealers

If the public is to invest its savings in stocks and bonds, it is important that some investors have the means provided for recalling funds at will without undue loss of principal. In other words, in addition to the origination and the initial distribution of securities to investors there must also be markets in which it is possible for investors to dispose of security holdings and obtain cash. Without such fluidity, many savers would be loath to make their accumulations available for investment. Fluidity for a considerable amount of invested funds is attained through the operations of the nation's securities brokers and dealers and the markets in which they operate.

Brokers and dealers

In popular usage, anyone in the securities business is considered a securities dealer. But the various kinds of dealers range from large investment banking houses, interested only in the distribution of new issues, to the one- and two-man offices engaging in a brokerage business and the occasional fellow who may keep his office files in the breast pocket of his coat. In the United States about 4,800 broker-dealers are registered with the Securities and Exchange Commission. An uncounted additional number, who do only a local business, are not registered. To some, the securities business is only a part-time adjunct to selling insurance or real estate; to most, it is their principal, and usually only, work.

Broker-dealers operate in several markets and in different capacities: they may facilitate the distribution of securities either as underwriters or as members of selling groups, as noted in the preceding section; they may buy and sell outstanding securities on an organized exchange; and they may conduct their securities business in that nebular, indefinite area called the over-the-counter market. They may serve as brokers or as dealers, i.e., as agents or principals in securities transactions.

Broker. A broker is, first of all, an agent for his customer. As such, he does what his customer instructs him to do, for which he makes a charge, called a commission. As an agent he is obligated to do his best for each customer—i.e., to buy at the lowest possible price or to sell at the highest possible price. Failure to do this is a breach of his position of trust as agent. When a broker confirms the fact that he has completed transactions for a customer, he sends him a written statement. A confirmation of a purchase, for example, carries a notation as follows: "As broker, we have this date bought for your account [a given number of shares of a given stock at a given price]." This notation reflects the relationship of the broker to his customer. The confirmation slip will also carry information with respect to brokerage or commission charges and transfer taxes. A

EXHIBIT 18–1

Broker's confirmation of purchase for customer (*machine bookkeeping form*)

(front)

(reverse)

confirmation slip adapted for machine bookkeeping is shown in Exhibit 18–1. The significance of the data is clearly indicated by the titles to the columns of the statement. The relation between the securities house and its customer is revealed, however, only by the figure in the column headed "Symbol." A figure 1, 2, 5, 8, or 9 in this column indicates that the security house acted as broker for the customer in the transaction confirmed. Other symbols are defined, and certain agreements between the securities house and its customer are stated on the reverse side of the confirmation slip, also shown in the exhibit. Nearly all transactions executed for customers on most organized exchanges are on a commission-agent basis.

Securities dealer. A securities dealer in the technical sense is one who buys and sells on his own account. He meets his customers presumably at arm's length as a principal. He does not receive a commission; his income is the difference between the price paid and the price received for

EXHIBIT 18–2

Dealer's confirmation of sale to customer (*manual bookkeeping form*)

		INVOICE
THE MILWAUKEE COMPANY	#30	4432
EDGAR, RICKER & CO. INVESTMENT SECURITIES		
207 E. MICHIGAN ST. MILWAUKEE 2	Dec. 21,	

Mr. John C. Canter

2148 N. Prospect Avenue

Milwaukee 2, Wisconsin

AS YOUR AGENT WE HAVE { BOUGHT FOR YOU ☐ / SOLD FOR YOU ☐

AS AGENT FOR ANOTHER WE HAVE { SOLD TO YOU ☐ / BOUGHT FROM YOU ☐

AS PRINCIPAL WE CONFIRM SALE TO YOU OF ☒

AS PRINCIPAL WE CONFIRM PURCHASE FROM YOU OF ☐

TRANSACTIONS EXECUTED FOR YOUR ACCOUNT BY US AS AGENTS, ARE SUBJECT TO THE RULES OF THE EXCHANGE ON WHICH SUCH ORDERS ARE EXECUTED. NAME OF THIRD PARTY, DATE, AND HOUR OF EXECUTION WILL BE FURNISHED UPON REQUEST.

SHARES	SECURITY	RATE	MATURITY	PRICE
100 PAR VALUE	R. H. MACY & COMPANY, INC.	Common		32

AMOUNT	BROKERS COMMISSION	TAX	INSURANCE & POSTAGE	SUB TOTAL	ACCRUED INTEREST OR DIVIDEND	TOTAL
$3,200.00						$3,200.00

PAYMENT IS DUE ON   Dec. 27   Chk. by: *b·v*

ADDITIONAL INTEREST OF   Fig. by: VM

WILL BE ADDED FOR EACH DAYS DELAY

DELIVERY INSTRUCTIONS

B-1

securities passing through his hands. Although he may make some profit (and, of course, experience loss) on the inventories which he holds, his profit margin frequently is only the difference between bid and ask quotations. For example, a dealer may stand ready to buy a security at $23\frac{7}{8}$ and sell it at $24\frac{1}{4}$. On such $\frac{3}{8}$ spread he would expect to cover his expenses and make a profit. It should not be assumed, however, that the dealer realizes a profit equal to the full amount of the spread. With a spread of $\frac{3}{8}$ on an actively traded stock selling at about 25, the dealer is more likely to make a profit of $\frac{1}{8}$ to $\frac{1}{4}$ point than $\frac{3}{8}$ of a point. In maintaining a market for the issue, his cost will probably average higher than the $23\frac{7}{8}$ bid, and his selling price will probably average lower than his $24\frac{1}{4}$ offer.

It is generally expected in the securities business that the dealer will make a profit equivalent to about half the spread on an actively traded issue and a profit equivalent to less than half the spread on an inactively traded issue.

In contrast to a broker, the dealer confirms a transaction to a customer as follows: "As principal (or as dealer), we have this date sold to you [such and such shares]."

Another example of a confirmation of the purchase of stock by a customer in which the securities house itself was the seller is shown in Exhibit 18–2. The relationship is indicated on this form, which was used in a manual bookkeeping system, by the "X" in the appropriate square at the upper right side of the slip. Both the type of confirmation slip shown in Exhibit 18–1 and that shown in Exhibit 18–2 may confirm a transaction in which the securities house acted as dealer or one in which the securities house acted as broker.

Under rules of the Securities and Exchange Commission every confirmation must set forth the capacity in which a securities house has acted with respect to a particular transaction. Securities dealers, so far as the public is concerned, operate only in the over-the-counter market. Of course, stock exchange specialists and odd-lot dealers, as indicated below, are distinctive varieties of securities dealers, but the public has no direct dealings with them as such.

The combined activities of brokers and dealers constitute the securities market. It is the purpose of this section to discuss the two principal subdivisions of this broad market through which the transfers of outstanding securities are effected, namely, the organized securities exchanges and the over-the-counter market.

Organized securities exchanges

At the present time there are 14 organized exchanges active in the United States. Their major service is that of facilitating the sale of preferred and common stocks by one holder to another. Bond trading, which also takes place on some exchanges, is of much less importance. These securities exchanges are referred to as the organized market because of their formal organization characteristics.

Security trading in the United States had its inception in Philadelphia, which was the leading city in the colonies. The New York area, however, grew in commercial importance, and securities trading became established there soon after the adoption of the Constitution. Trading was carried on informally among interested parties, who would assemble at a public place, such as a coffeehouse. In 1792 the first formal steps toward organizing a brokers' association were taken in New York when 24 brokers who "met under the shade of a buttonwood tree in Wall Street," where they had been rendering their services for a commission, agreed that "we will not buy or sell from this day for any person whatsoever, any kind of Public Stock at a less rate than one quarter per cent Commission on the Specie value and that we will give preference for each other in our Negotiations."[3] As would be expected from the character of business at

---

[3] Birl E. Shultz, *The Securities Market and How It Works* (rev. ed.; New York: Harper & Bros., 1963), p. 2.

the time, trading took place mainly in shares of shipping companies, banks, and insurance companies and government obligations. At this time the brokers had no established place of business, and much of the trading was carried on out of doors. It was not until after the War of 1812 that a more formal organization was set up in a place of business of its own.

The New York Stock Exchange

With the exception of a few months at the beginning of World War I and a few days on other occasions, the New York Stock Exchange, the major organized exchange in the United States, has been in continuous operation providing trading facilities to the financial community, not only in this country but in the world at large. In 1929 the membership was increased from 1,100 to 1,375. In 1952 provision was made to reduce the membership to 1,325 but only nine memberships were retired. As of January 1970, the membership was 1,366. During the 1920s the volume of shares sold ran between 2 and 6 million per day, and even reached a one-day high of 16 million shares in October 1929; recently, 10 to 20 million share days have been common.

After a severe stock market break in 1937, the governing rules as set forth in the constitution and bylaws of the New York Stock Exchange were revised to streamline organization and trading procedures. The stock exchange is no longer looked upon as a private club existing for the benefit of the members but as a public institution with commensurate duties and responsibilities. Its objectives, as set forth in Article I of the revised constitution, are: "to furnish exchange rooms for the convenient transaction of their business by its members; to furnish other facilities for its members and allied members; to maintain high standards of commercial honor and integrity among its members and allied members; and to promote and inculcate just and equitable principles of trade and business."

The exchange is managed by a Board of Governors consisting of 33 men. Their terms are staggered, and they represent different interests: active brokers and traders, partners of members (officially called allied members, some of whom come from outside New York City), and prominent men selected to represent the general public. There is an elected, nonsalaried chairman, who presides over the board. The president—the chief salaried administrative officer of the exchange—is selected by the board and is not otherwise engaged in the securities business.

The functions of the Board of Governors are to draw up, adjudicate, and enforce rules governing the conduct of day-to-day trading. These rules are designed to maintain fair and orderly markets and adherence to just and equitable principles of trade. Failure to observe them may involve a member in a disciplinary proceeding before the board. Severe sanctions may be invoked, and a member may be subjected to suspension or expulsion.

Trading on the floor of the exchange is limited to members of the exchange and is not open to the general public. The public is invited to view trading activities from the visitors' gallery. The privilege of membership, the right to participate in trading, is termed a *seat*, a name carried over from earlier days when the members sat at tables during trading sessions. These seats are valuable business assets commanding a substantial price, which tends to vary with the volume of trading and the profits which may be derived therefrom. The price paid for a seat reached a high of $625,000 in 1929, declined to a low of $17,000 in 1942, and is currently about $300,000. Membership is limited to individuals over 21 years of age, with adequate financial resources, who carry on trading for their own account, for companies of which they are a member, and customers.

The members of the exchange may be classified into several groups according to the function they perform. An individual member may act as commission broker, two-dollar or floor broker, registered floor broker, specialist, odd-lot dealer, or a combination of the foregoing at different times.

Commission brokers are members who, as individuals, partners, or officers of commission brokerage houses, execute orders as agents for customers of their companies. These brokers, or the firms they represent, maintain offices for the convenience of their customers. At these offices there is usually a room which is called the customers, or board room, where the customer can watch a board on which stock-price quotations are recorded as they come in on the ticker tape. This tape carries a continuous record, reproduced telegraphically throughout the nation, of the transactions taking place on the exchange. The tape itself is usually reproduced on a large screen (Translux), so that anyone in the room can watch it. The Dow-Jones news ticker (broad tape) may be projected on another screen. The board and the two ticker tapes provide valuable information for those who need it and know how to use it. Information about individual issues or general market averages also can be obtained by keyboard inquiry on any of several desktop devices supplied by information service firms. Here, too, so-called customers' men or account executives greet the public. In many cases these account executives are relied upon by customers for information about companies and their securities and for suggestions as to purchases and sales. A number of the major houses make a practice of issuing suggestions with respect to certain securities in the form of market letters, memoranda, and financial analyses.

In addition to being a member of one or more stock exchanges, the broker or other members of his company may also have a seat on some commodity exchanges for the purpose of broadening the type of service available to his customers. For example, the firm of Merrill Lynch, Pierce, Fenner and Smith, a merger of several financial houses, holds more than 75 seats on various stock and commodity exchanges and maintains branch offices in more than 100 cities throughout the United States. This firm is the largest of its kind.

The schedule of minimum commissions charged by commission brokers for their services on round-lot transactions in stocks priced at one dollar or more a share follows:

Money value of a round lot	Commission
Less than $100.00	As agreed
$100.00 to $399.99	2% + $3
$400.00 to $2,399.99	1% + $7
$2,400.00 to $4,999.99	$\frac{1}{2}$% + $19
$5,000.00 and above	$\frac{1}{10}$% + $39

The commission schedule can be presented in another way—in terms of the round-lot cost per share for stocks selling at various prices. Selected commission charges on this basis are as follows:

Price of stock per share	Commission per share
$ 5	$0.12
10	0.17
20	0.37
30	0.34
50	0.44
75	0.465
100	0.49

On transactions involving more than 1,000 shares, the rates on accounts over the first 1,000 are substantially lower.

In 1969, a service charge of $15, or up to one half the commission, if less, was added for each order executed.

A *round lot* is the unit of trading. It is generally 100 shares; but in the case of high-priced or inactive stocks, the exchange may designate 10 shares as the unit of trading. In the case of odd lots (amounts less than a round lot), the minimum commission is $2 less than is indicated in the above schedule. In addition to the broker's commission, the seller in any transaction on a New York exchange must pay New York State transfer taxes. The seller also must pay the SEC fee, $\frac{1}{2}$ cent per $500 involved.

Other trading may be carried on by members assisting the commission-house brokers who are not able to execute their entire volume of business themselves. These men are referred to as two-dollar brokers because in earlier years they charged a flat two-dollar commission per transaction to fellow stock exchange members for handling their business on the floor.

The floor broker, of course, does not have the overhead cost of maintaining customers' rooms and branch offices.

In addition to regular brokers who live on their commissions, the exchange membership includes a few persons who buy and sell for their own account. These members, called registered or floor traders, may also serve at times as commission or floor brokers; and some commission or floor brokers, if registered to do so, may trade for their own account from time to time.

The activities of floor traders have been under study by the Securities and Exchange Commission for some time. There has been agitation for the elimination of their activities on the theory that they contribute to instability of the market in individual securities. Floor traders not only transact business at a reduced rate of commission but have the additional advantage over the general public that, in an active market, they may be in a position to sense the direction of price changes and promptly take advantage of the small fluctuations. There was much opposition, however, to expelling the insiders in order to turn the exchange into a completely public market, and such a change has not been adopted. However, a requirement for registration as a trader and prohibition of the right to trade for one's own account after such registration were added to the rules in 1964. It is argued that, although the floor trader may make a profit from small changes in security prices, he contributes at the same time to the continuity of pricing as prices change. This continuity of pricing, i.e., the absence of abrupt fluctuations as the demand for and supply of securities shift in response to orders from the general public, is an important attribute of an efficient market.

Security trading is scattered over a wide area in a very large combination of three rooms called the *floor* of the exchange. It is physically impossible for a broker to be everywhere; yet customers' orders must be executed promptly. Brokers, therefore, frequently engage the services of fellow members who specialize in the buying and selling of securities of a limited number of issues at a given post. These members are known as specialists. They accept the obligation of remaining at the posts where the auction for the issues in which they are specializing is held. It is the responsibility of a specialist to see that orders are executed whenever either buyers or sellers are available or, in the case of orders to buy or sell at specified prices, when prices reach such designated levels. To aid him, he keeps what is known as the specialist's book, a record of buy and sell orders. The data in this book are not available to others because the book's contents might give important information not generally known as to market conditions and might stimulate unethical pricing practices.

Despite the fact that quotations and deliveries are based on round lots, many people want to buy or sell securities in amounts less than the unit of trading in order to avoid a large commitment of funds. This odd-lot trading, on the part of customers sometimes picturesquely termed *small fry,* may aggregate 5–10% of the total volume of trading. In recent years securities dealers generally have sought to encourage securities buying by these investors and to cater to their needs for information and service.

Standard commission houses execute odd-lot orders through an odd-lot dealer firm that specializes in this business. The odd-lot dealer stands ready to buy or sell odd lots at a price usually one eighth (of $1) away from that of the next round-lot sale in the same stock issue, if priced under $55 per share on the exchange, or one fourth (of $1) away from the price of stock selling at $55 or more per share. If, for example, a customer wishes to buy 63 shares of the U.S. Steel Corporation common stock through his regular commission house, the commission house turns the order over to an odd-lot dealer. If the price on the next sale on the exchange is, say, 56⅝ ($56.625 a share), the dealer then sells 63 shares at 56⅞. If the customer were selling, the sale would be completed at 56⅝. The odd-lot dealer derives his income from the ¼ differential plus or minus gains or losses which may be sustained on the relatively small inventory that he may carry.

Requirements for listing securities

Not all securities are traded on the Big Board. Shortly after the Civil War the members of the exchange decided to restrict their trading to a particular list of securities and to require that, in the future, all additions to the list be issues which conformed to certain requirements. As a prerequisite for this privilege, an issue must be judged acceptable by the Department on Stock List, registered for trading with the SEC, and admitted to trading by the Board of Governors.

Requirements for listing have gradually become more stringent as the country has developed financially and industrially. The forward-looking administration of the exchange endeavored early, and with some success, to effect dissemination of vital financial information to the general public by requiring, as a condition of listing, that each company publish annual financial statements. In addition, applicants are required to file copies of their articles of incorporation and bylaws, copies of the contracts behind securities issues, and information relating to the number of stockholders, the percentage of stock publicly held, and the geographical location and size of individual holdings of their securities. The latter data especially provide information about the character of the distribution of the securities. Stock of a company closely held might have too narrow a market, making it difficult to buy and sell its securities. Furthermore, such securities might become subject to manipulation and artificial price influences. Since 1926, nonvoting common stock and, since 1943, preferred stock without voting power adequate to protect its position have been refused listing.

As further protection to the public and to facilitate the safe transfer of securities, companies are required to use certificates engraved from steel plates, which cannot easily be counterfeited. Provision is made for cross-checking transfers through separate registrars and transfer agents (see Chapter 17) with offices in the financial district on Manhattan Island.

From a public point of view, much of the original function of listing has been superseded by the more rigorous requirements of the SEC acting under the Securities Exchange Act of 1934. Companies with a national reputation, in whose securities there is a nationwide interest, encounter little difficulty in qualifying their securities for trading. At the present time there are listed on the New York Stock Exchange approximately 3,500 stock and bond issues of about 2,000 issuers.

Managements of many corporations list their securities because they feel that it promotes good public relations for the company, that they achieve a better distribution of their stock, that it increases the marketability of outstanding securities, that new financing is facilitated, and that the securities often tend to sell at a higher price by virtue of the larger market growing out of listing.

Securities may be delisted for the following reasons: they do not continue to meet the requirements for listing; public interest in the issue is not sufficient for an active market; the issuing corporation is merged, becomes bankrupt, or is in process of reorganization; the issue is retired; or the company requests delisting (with stockholder approval).

Bond trading

The New York Stock Exchange also provides a market for bonds. Nearly 2,000 bond issues, mostly convertibles, are listed for trading on this exchange; but because of the highly specialized nature of the securities, the institutional character of the market, and relative lack of speculative appeal, most bond trading takes place in the over-the-counter market.

Trading on the stock exchange

Security trading on the floor of the New York Stock Exchange is highly organized. Under usual conditions, if, at the same moment, a man in San Francisco should place an order to sell and a man in New Orleans an order to buy 100 shares of an issue, they would each have confirmation of execution of the transaction a few minutes later. Orders are sent by wire and telephone from commission house offices to open booths on the floor of the exchange, where clerks make notations and send the orders to the appropriate broker for execution.

Trading in each security is assigned to a definite location at a horse-shoe-shaped booth called a post. Here the brokers, through a series of bids and asks, make a market.[4] This market has been called a double-auction market. Both the bidders (buyers) and the askers (sellers) are constantly varying their respective prices either up or down. Sales take place when the highest bidder meets the price of the lowest asker. This is in contrast to the usual auction, in which the bidding is all on the buying side. The actual auction process, of course, is not open directly to the public; but individuals, by watching the ticker tape and getting quotations that in a normal market are only a few seconds old, take a direct and active part in the determination of price by submitting their orders to buy or to sell to a commission broker.

When a sale has been made, the two brokers (buying and selling) each make a brief memorandum as to the security traded with whom, the price, and the amount. This information is immediately phoned back to the commission house, from which the customer obtains a confirmation of the transaction. He may receive the confirmation immediately in person, by telephone, or by telegraph; but in due course, he will receive a written confirmation through the mail.

At the time the transaction takes place, a record of the number of shares and price per share is forwarded to the market data computer, and usually in a matter of seconds, the transaction is recorded on the stock ticker tape, which taps out a continuous record of all round-lot transactions. Occasionally, however, trading becomes so heavy that even modern high-speed tickers fall behind by a few minutes.

Under the rules of the New York Stock Exchange, transactions that are executed on the floor must be settled in five days. Settlement procedure is similar to that employed by banks in clearing checks. The New York Stock Clearing Corporation is set up specifically to expedite this procedure, which may involve many millions of shares and worth over $500 million a day. Settlements are made every business day but, as indicated above, are five days delayed. The five-day delay allows time for necessary bookkeeping, comparisons of records of each transaction at offices of the buying and selling firms, and delivery of certificates and funds. When a broker buys or sells, he merely clears or delivers to the Clearing Corporation the balance of what he owes in stock or money. Thus purchases and sales of stock of the same issue may leave the broker no balance to be received in the form of stock, but there might be a balance of money owing because the transactions were executed at differ-

---

[4]For another explanation of this term, see p. 430.

ent prices. In contrast to our prompt procedure, European bourses follow the practice of cumulative fortnightly settlements.

The purchasing broker's customer, if he elects to hold in his own possession the stock he has purchased, will receive a certificate by mail after the lapse of several more days, during which the transfer of the stock will be recorded on the books of the corporation. Many customers do not themselves receive their certificates but leave them on deposit with their brokers. Sellers usually deliver certificates to their brokers at or before the time of placing any order to sell unless the broker already has them on deposit.

There are several types of *orders* that may be entered by customers as well as types of security *transactions* that may take place on the floor of the exchange. The most important order is the market order, which directs the broker either to buy or to sell at the market a given number of shares at the best possible price then obtainable.

Limited orders are entered by customers specifying that a given number of shares of a given stock be purchased or sold at a specified (limited) price. When the market price reaches the specified level, the limited order must be executed promptly by the commisssion broker or a specialist at the specified price or a better one (i.e., a lower price on buy orders or a higher price on sell orders). Limited orders may be for a specified time (a day, a week, until a given future date, a month), after which they are canceled unless renewed. Others may be good until canceled (G.T.C.).

To protect a profit one who holds stock but is not able to watch the ticker tape constantly may enter a stop-loss order to sell his shares if a specified price below current quotations is reached or passed through. Then, if the price of the security should decline to the specified level, the order becomes a market order, the stock is sold, and the investor has limited the extent to which profit may be wiped out by price decline. Stop-loss orders may also be entered in an attempt to limit further losses from adverse price movements. Some traders also use stop-loss orders to buy shares if the price rises above a limit set by the trader.

The type of security transaction most frequently effected is the outright purchase or sale. The buyer of a stock in this case is said to have assumed a long position. His usual aims are to make a profit through market appreciation, receive income through dividends declared, or both. Through such a purchase he becomes a part owner of the corporation and shares in its fortunes.

Some security buyers wishing to make as large a commitment as possible with a given sum of money buy securities on margin. This means, in effect, that they borrow part of the purchase price from the broker in order to meet the daily settlement. The amount deposited or placed with the broker by the customer is called margin; and it protects the broker, who has advanced the balance of the purchase price, against loss resulting from price decline. In 1969, customers of the New York Stock Exchange member firms were borrowing $6 billion, an amount equaling about 1% of the value of all securities listed on the exchange.

During the early 1920s a customer's margin frequently might be as low as 10% of the market price. The broker's margin clerk kept a careful check on the prices of issues against which loans were outstanding, and if prices dropped, the customer was required to put up additional collateral (securities) or reduce the loan. If this was not done promptly, enough of the customer's securities would be sold to protect the broker's loan. In declining markets, thin margins frequently contributed to distress and even panic selling, which made for a disorderly market and contributed to further decline of prices.

To remedy the consequences of such action, Congress, in the Securities Exchange Act of 1934, gave to the Board of Governors of the Federal Reserve System the power to fix minimum margin requirements. This power has been exercised to regulate the flow of credit and to prevent an unhealthy speculative boom in the securities market. The Federal Reserve authorities first indicated a minimum initial margin requirement that varied between 25 and 55%, depending on security price. However, in the light of credit conditions, they saw fit, for the 12-month period beginning January 1946 to eliminate the purchase of securities on credit by requiring full payment—i.e., 100% margin—for long purchases and short sales. The requirement has fluctuated between 50 and 90% in postwar years. It was 80% in the stock market boom of 1968–69. To date, no regulations have been made by the Federal Reserve Board with respect to margins which must be maintained after purchase. Nevertheless, the Board of Governors of New York Stock Exchange has a rule for the guidance of its members that customers must maintain an equity in their account at all times of at least 25% of the current market price. Furthermore, small traders, with an aggregate equity in their accounts of less than $2,000, must pay cash.

The securities owner who wants to clear his account merely gives his broker an order to sell. The loan is repaid from the proceeds of the sale.

A very different type of transaction is a short sale. The essence of a short sale is that the seller does not intend to deliver the stock from his own account. An individual may feel that the market is about to decline and may wish to take advantage of his judgment. He therefore gives his broker an order to sell stock at the current price, with the hope that he may buy shares at a lower price later and pocket the difference. In order to make delivery to the buyer, who is entitled to receive his certificate at settlement date five days later, the customer's broker borrows the securities from a fellow broker or from a customer and delivers borrowed stock to the buyer.

To protect the lender from whom the stock is borrowed, the lender is given cash equal to the current market price, and a margin in cash or collateral is deposited with the broker to assure the lender that stock can be purchased if the price rises. The owner (lender), of course, is entitled to dividends on the stock which he still owns, but the buyer of the loaned stock also expects the dividends. Therefore, the short seller must pay the lender an amount equivalent to any dividend paid while the shares are borrowed. When money rates were high, in past years the stock lender, rather than the borrower, paid interest for the use of the money turned over to him as security. If the borrowed stock is scarce, however, the borrower may even pay a premium for the privilege of borrowing the stock.

In due course the short seller covers his position by buying an equivalent amount of stock and turning it over to the lender, who then returns the money. If the seller buys the stock at a price sufficiently lower than his prior short sale, he will be able to pay brokerage, transfer taxes, and other expenses and make a profit in a period of falling prices.

A short seller may enter with his broker at the time of sale a stop-loss order to buy the stock in order to protect himself against loss, should the price rise rather than decline.

There has been considerable controversy over short-selling operations. Some contend that short selling is uneconomic, unethical, or even immoral. That it may at times contribute to a disorderly market seems fairly well established, despite the argument that the short sales offset buying by overoptimistic bulls and later create support buying in depressed markets. Continued short sales, when there is an absence of market support, would accelerate the decline. In 1930 the New York Stock Exchange adopted a rule that short sales could not be made at a price less than the last long transaction. After the market break of 1937 the Securities and Exchange Commission adopted a very stringent rule which limited short selling to prices at least one eighth above the last transaction. A year later the rule was modified so that short sales could be transacted at the level of the last transaction but only if the level of that last transaction itself represented an advance over the last previous different price.

If a corporation declares a dividend and shares change hands at about the time when the corporation makes up the official list of stockholders to whom dividends are payable, a question may arise as to whether the buyer or the seller should get the dividend. The New York Stock Exchange follows the practice of having a stock traded on an ex-dividend basis four full business days before the date of record, i.e., the date on which the official list is prepared. Thus, if the date of record for a dividend is, say, Friday, August 21, 1970, the share will sell ex-dividend beginning with the sale opening the market on August 17. This allows for the five-day settlement delay. The new owner (buyer) does not get the dividend; the seller does. The price of the security may be expected to decline from the last sale on the previous day to the opening sale on the ex-dividend date by approximately the amount of the dividend unless other influences on security prices offset or increase it.

At the turn of the century, Charles H. Dow, a broker and newspaper publisher, was interested in presenting for his readers an indication of the daily fluctuations of securities prices on the stock exchange. To give a better picture of the day-to-day movement of the market, he computed an average of the prices of the leading stocks, which at that time were mostly rails. Since then, stock market averages have undergone considerable change. At the present time, the best-known averages are the Dow-Jones Industrial Average, based on the shares of 30 leading industrial corporations, and the Dow-Jones Transportation and Utility Averages, based on 20 transportation company and 15 utility stocks, respectively. Other stock market indexes—e.g., those of the Standard and Poor's Company—are based on considerably broader lists of stocks. Both the New York and American stock exchanges compute indexes using information about all issues traded on the exchange. These indexes may be found on the financial pages of most large city newspapers and are followed with great interest by securities buyers.

Other exchanges

Securities which are not on the trading list of the Big Board may be listed and sold on other exchanges. As mentioned above, there are 15 organized exchanges: 13 are registered with the SEC, and 2 have been exempted from registration by the SEC because of the small volume and local nature of business transacted. A list of these exchanges and an indication of the volume of business transacted on them are given in Table 18–2. Note that one registered exchange, the Chicago Board of Trade, is inactive.

There is considerably more volume on the Big Board. The American Stock Exchange, which is second in dollar volume, handles only about one quarter and the Midwest Stock Exchange only 2% as much business as the Big Board.

The services of these other exchanges have value for the financial community. The securities of companies which, for one reason or another, are not listed on the Big Board are marketed here. New companies without established records of operations, or companies that are too closely held or do not have large enough issues outstanding to meet the requirements for listing on the Big Board, or companies for which a regional market is logical, gain the advantages of organized markets that would otherwise be unavailable. Regional investors are more adequately served. A point of technical importance to investors in stocks, say, of midwestern compa-

TABLE 18–2

1969 volume of sales of organized securities exchanges in the United States
(in millions)

Name of exchange	Stock transactions Market value	No. of shares	Bond transactions Market value
Registered:			
New York Stock Exchange	$129,603	3,174	3,550
American Stock Exchange	30,074	1,341	929
Midwest Stock Exchange	5,988	146	—*
Pacific Coast Stock Exchange ...,	5,422	157	21
Philadelphia-Baltimore-Washington Stock Exchange	2,528	61	—*
Detroit Stock Exchange	217	6	0
Boston Stock Exchange	1,191	26	0
Cincinnati Stock Exchange	19	—*	—*
Pittsburgh Stock Exchange	47	1	0
Spokane Stock Exchange	11	13	0
Salt Lake Stock Exchange	18	12	0
National Stock Exchange	180	25	0
Chicago Board of Trade	0	0	0
Total	$175,298	4,963	4,501
Exempt:			
Honolulu Stock Exchange	$ 12	1	$ 0
Richmond Stock Exchange	2	*	0
Total	$ 14	1	$ 0

* Less than ½ million.
Souroo: Soouritioo and Exohango Commiooion, *Statiotioal Bulletin*, March 1970, p. 11.

nies is the fact that the New York state taxes on securities transfers are not applicable to transactions on the midwest exchange. Nearly half the securities listed on the Big Board and a quarter of those listed on the American Stock Exchange are also traded on the other exchanges.

Over-the-counter trading

Securities houses not only engage in brokerage transactions on the organized stock exchanges and distribute newly issued securities, but they constitute the core of the over-the-counter markets. The majority of securities are neither listed nor traded on the organized exchanges. In fact, of the estimated half-million corporations of the United States, the securities of only 3,000 are traded on organized exchanges. The securities of as many as 50,000 others, however, find their major market in the bid and ask trading through security dealers who *make a market* in particular issues.

Making a market

A market in the securities of a given corporation is made by dealers who stand ready to buy or sell these securities. In doing so, they act as a sort of sponsor. This sponsorship may stem from the fact that they participated in the original distribution or may reflect a personal or professional interest in these securities as trading items.

Trading in the over-the-counter market is not so highly organized as on the exchanges, but nevertheless it is effective for many issues. A customer who wants to buy unlisted securities places an order with his securities dealer. The dealer will then either supply the securities from his own inventory or find the best place to buy them for resale to the customer.

The process of finding the best place to buy is facilitated by a system for publication of bid and ask prices. The dealers throughout the nation who maintain inventories or who can buy securities readily from local investors furnish daily quotations to the National Quotation Bureau. The bureau, in turn, publishes daily, for distribution to subscribers, quotations on as many as 8,000 issues. The quotation sheets also indicate the amounts of securities available and the dealers' interest in each issue. The quotations are bid and ask prices, the prices near which the dealers stand ready to buy or to sell the security quoted. It should be recognized that bid and ask prices are not prices at which actual sales or purchases have been made and are, therefore, not comparable to sales quotations for transactions on organized exchanges. They are, rather, offers; securities may never change hands at the quoted prices; offers are subject to change without notice.

When a firm which itself does not hold an inventory of a given security issue seeks to buy securities for a customer, one of the firm's traders will probably consult the quotation sheet for information concerning approximate prices and the dealers who are prepared to sell these securities. The trader will then call one or more of the dealers in the issue to obtain current quotations and quantities of the shares offered. With these in mind, he will call the customer for confirmation of his interest in buying at a price which he will have to pay to get the securities. If the customer agrees, the firm, acting as broker, will call back the house offering the securities at the lowest price and arrange for the purchase. It may, however, acting as a dealer, buy the securities for its own account and then sell them to the customer at the agreed price.

The idea of making a market, which means buying, selling, and trading in a given issue, must not be confused with that of maintaining a price. Securities prices change frequently with the passage of time. A dealer, of course, is not able to maintain a price in the face of alterations in fundamental conditions. And an attempt to maintain a price in the face of outside influences would undoubtedly be construed as a form of market manipulation.

Types of securities traded

Securities may be traded over the counter because they do not qualify for listing: the issue may be closely held or there may be insufficient public interest. On the other hand, the management of the corporation may not wish to comply with listing requirements. A recent change in the Securities and Exchange Act, however, requires registration and reporting similar to listed companies of large, unlisted companies with stock held by 500 or more shareholders. Some types of securities, like many preferred stocks and most bonds, because of the small amounts available for trading and lack of general public interest in the issues, are traded, if at all, only intermittently in the over-the-counter market. The stocks of many insurance companies, banks, and trust companies are traded over the counter. Although the securities of many of these companies are suitable for listing, it is not the custom for them to be traded on an organized stock exchange.

It should be stressed, however, that markets may be made over the counter for securities listed on organized exchanges. This is referred to as the *third* market, i.e., the third procedure for effecting transactions in an issue. The first two are trading in the primary market, usually the New York or American Stock Exchange, and trading in the secondary markets on other national stock exchanges, such as the Midwest or Pacific Coast exchanges. A *fourth* market is sometimes identified as the procedure by which a buyer and seller are brought together directly to negotiate a trade. In this fourth market, middlemen neither make a market nor handle securities; they engage in the business of identifying buyers and sellers that can negotiate trades directly for themselves.

Dealing in governments

The dealers in federal government and municipal obligations constitute a very specialized over-the-counter market. Some securities dealers handle municipal bonds exclusively. Most securities dealers will buy and sell U.S. government bonds, but those who really make the market are a small number of the bigger banks and a small group of highly specialized houses operating in New York and Chicago. The big houses may buy and sell in lots of a million dollars or more at a time. Their bid and ask prices are close together and are made in terms of one thirty-second and sometimes even one sixty-fourth of a dollar. The market for U.S. obligations is extremely sensitive and is probably the most efficient securities market in the world.

The market prices of these securities are determined primarily by the supply of and demand for investable funds; large savings institutions, life insurance companies, savings banks, and, of course, the commercial banking system are the leading customers. The buying and selling is influenced strongly by both the controls on credit markets exercised by federal agencies and the changing financial problems of the federal government.

Federal regulation of securities trading

On September 3, 1929, the Dow-Jones Industrial Average, after an almost continuous rise from 65 in 1921, reached 386. Three years later it had dropped to a depression low of 40. The bankruptcies and hardships which followed in the wake of the depression caused the New Deal candidates in the 1932 campaign to pledge, among other things, a program of financial reform. With respect to securities markets, the proposed program was designed to improve trading and the quality of the market by requiring public dissemination of all material information with respect to a security and a company, the elimination of manipulative pools and artificial market influences, and the regulation of credit used for speculative purposes.

The objectives of the regulation of securities markets as set forth in the Securities Exchange Act of 1934 are attained through four different regulatory techniques or approaches: registration of persons, of places, and of things—i.e., brokers, exchanges, and securities—and limitation of the use of credit.

Registration of securities

All nonexempt securities traded on organized markets or, if of sufficient size, over the counter, must be registered with the Securities and Exchange Commission through its Trading and Exchange Division. Registration requires the filing of much more complete and detailed information than has heretofore been available with respect to the history and current operations of the corporation. Annual audited financial statements must be made promptly available, and interim quarterly reports on sales are now required. The SEC checks these statements as a protection to the public. Furthermore, the proxy solicitations are now more informative; and trading by insiders—i.e., officers, directors, and major stockholders— is subject to report and review.

Registration of exchanges

The securities exchanges themselves must register with the SEC by filing their constitution, bylaws, and regulations governing the execution of transactions. These rules and regulations must be so designed as to insure a fair and orderly market and adherence by brokers and customers to just and equitable trading principles and practices. The trading rules of the registered exchanges have undergone considerable change. Particularly important have been rules with respect to the handling of customers' securities, the execution of orders, and the audit of brokers' financial affairs. Manipulative and deceptive devices are prohibited. Stabilization to aid in the distribution of a special offering or of an additional new block of an already outstanding issue is severely restricted by rules of the commission to protect the inexperienced investor whose funds are being solicited.

Registration of broker-dealers

As originally passed in 1934, the Securities Exchange Act was designed primarily to control trading on the organized stock exchanges. By amendments added in 1936, broker-dealers using the instrumentalities of interstate commerce or the mails are required to register with the commission. In filing a registration statement, they must show that they are men of reputable standing, with a record free of security fraud convictions. In addition, they must conform to certain capital requirements.

In this relatively unorganized over-the-counter market the Securities and Exchange Commission has had considerable difficulty in maintaining standards of business conduct at a level deemed essential to protect investors and the general public. Price quotations and information of the true character of the market have not always been accurate. Broker-dealers in their semifiduciary capacity and as recipients of the confidence and the money of uninformed investors could and sometimes did take advantage of their inside position to buy and sell at prices materially out of line with the market.

It is fraudulent for a dealer to sell securities to customers at prices bearing no reasonable relation to the prevailing market without disclosing this fact. This was first established in a proceeding as a result of which the registration of a dealer was revoked.[5] The commission held in this and in other cases involving similar business conduct that the dealer assumes special obligations by virtue of the inherent characteristics of the securities business. The dealer represents himself as having specialized knowledge and skill. He cultivates the customer's trust, his reliance on the dealer's skill, and his confidence in the dealer's integrity. There is a presumption in this confidential relationship that the dealer will deal fairly. The duties and obligations of the dealer are not to be measured by the ordinary standard of arm's-length bargaining.

---

[5] Duker & Duker, 6 SEC 386 (1939).

National Association of Securities Dealers. The technique of regulatory control by registration of persons, i.e., broker-dealers, has not proved entirely satisfactory. Considerable difficulty is encountered by the governing authorities in controlling the detailed, daily, semiprivate practices of about 4,800 registered broker-dealers, to say nothing of the fringe who are not registered and who do an intermittent, part-time, or intrastate business. The commission works closely with a special trade association to police the activities of securities dealers. The members of the industry know better than anyone else what is going on. In 1938, to give more adequate protection to the public and to protect reputable securities dealers from competition with financially irresponsible individuals, the Securities and Exchange Commission joined with members of the industry in sponsoring an amendment to the Securities and Exchange Act:

To provide for the establishment of a mechanism of regulation among the over-the-counter brokers and dealers operating in interstate and foreign commerce or through the mails, to prevent acts and practices inconsistent with just and equitable principles of trade, and for other purposes.

Pursuant to this amendment and under combined industry and government sponsorship, the National Association of Securities Dealers, Inc. (NASD), was formed. In 1969, its membership included 4,100 firms, with 159,000 registered representatives. The association's objectives are as follows:

To promote through cooperative effort the investment banking and securities business, to standardize its principles and practices, to promote therein high standards of commercial honor, and to encourage and promote among members observance of Federal and State securities laws;

To provide a medium through which its membership may be enabled to confer, consult, and cooperate with governmental and other agencies in the solution of problems affecting investors, the public and the investment banking and securities business;

To adopt, administer and enforce rules of fair practices and rules to prevent fraudulent and manipulative acts and practices, and in general to promote just and equitable principles of trade for the protection of investors;

To promote self-discipline among members, and to investigate and adjust grievances between public and members and between members.

This code of fair practice is now enforced by the NASD through 13 district committees. Complaints filed by the public, by other members, or by the district committees themselves are heard, and penalties are imposed if they appear warranted. Decisions of the district committees may be appealed to the Board of Governors of NASD, then to the Securities and Exchange Commission, and finally to the federal courts.

Through a staff of examiners the NASD is constantly making spot inspections and field investigations at unannounced times, to check adherence to the stated objectives.

The principal power of the NASD derives from the enabling act, which allows the association to provide that no member may deal with any nonmember broker or dealer except at the same prices, for the same commissions or fees, and on the same terms and conditions as are accorded the general public. Therefore, from a practical business point of view, it is necessary that broker-dealers be members in order to participate actively in securities distribution or over-the-counter trading because preferential trade discounts are important to the net profits of houses dealing in securities.

Security markets and the economy

Both the formally established, listed securities market, as found in the organized stock exchanges, and the amorphous and widespread over-the-counter securities market provide an essential service in facilitating the easy transfer of stocks and bonds. They make possible a high degree of liquidity in investment, without which funds would much less freely find their way into productive channels. They permit the wide distribution of new issues accomplished by investment banking procedures. Unless the saver and investor has reasonable assurance that he may sell his holdings and receive cash promptly, he will be less willing to advance his accumulations in the first instance. With a broad and active market, it is possible for an investor to shift his investments from one type of security to another, from one industry to another, from one company, and from securities to cash, as his judgment may dictate. Such flexibility makes it possible to adapt an individual investment fund to the needs of the moment as fundamental trends may dictate.

In former years, but much less so now, speculative trading and distribution of speculative issues rather than investment operations made up a very substantial portion of the volume in the securities markets. Speculative excesses and rapidly fluctuating markets lured many uninformed buyers into the markets in search of quick gains. Much of this activity verged on gambling, based, as it was, on the hope of profit through rapid price change rather than on intelligent buying predicated on fundamental analysis. The uninitiated often not only experienced loss rather than gain for himself; but even worse, he helped create an unsound market condition that, as a rule ultimately proved disturbing to the entire economy.

There are many reasons why speculative trading has dwindled, including, among others, broader dissemination of more complete information about new issues of securities and outstanding, listed securities issues, virtual elimination of price manipulation, the elimination of stock pools, the income tax structure and resulting altered distribution of national income, the search for security, and memories of past debacles.

With a reduced volume of trading in the 1940s and 1950s the organized exchanges sought to broaden the base of prospective customers in order to build up volume. They are also finding that, to a considerable extent, listed securities are being traded over the counter rather than through exchanges. The schedule of commissions has been altered in order to make the use of the exchanges more attractive to institutional investors and thus win additional volume for the exchanges. There also has been the consolidation of organized exchanges in various cities into regional exchanges. In this, the Midwest Stock Exchange, a merger of five smaller exchanges in midwestern cities (the Chicago, Cleveland, St. Louis, New Orleans, and Minneapolis–St. Paul exchanges), is an outstanding example. In 1953, the Washington (D.C.) exchange merged with the Philadelphia-Baltimore exchange; and in 1957, the San Francisco and Los Angeles exchanges joined their facilities. The purpose is to enlarge the market, reduce costs, improve efficiency, and, of course, increase profitability.

Questions and problems _____

1. What is investment banking? Why do the services of an investment banking firm have value to an issuer? A buyer?
2. What is underwriting? How does it differ from selling?
3. What is a purchase syndicate, and how long do syndicates last?
4. Are there risks in investment banking? What kinds, if any? Are risks introduced or altered if best-effort contracts are substituted for firm contracts?
5. How does federal regulation affect sales of new issues of securities?
6. What are the differences between the operations of brokers and those of dealers?
7. How can you distinguish the organized exchanges from the over-the-counter markets? Describe the process of over-the-counter trading.
8. What are the various kinds of members of an organized exchange according to their functions?
9. Name and describe the different types of orders which a customer may give his broker.
10. Describe a transaction for purchase of stock on margin. List advantages and disadvantages of margin trading.
11. Describe a short sale. List advantages and disadvantages of short selling.
12. What does listed mean? Why are some securities listed and others unlisted? Why are so few listed?
13. What are the major features of federal regulations of securities markets?
14. Compute the commissions that you might expect to pay on the purchase of stock selling at $0.75, $8, $25, and $50 per share.

Bibliography

The stock markets described in this chapter are the subject of a voluminous literature. Some description of activities in these markets is to be found in almost any book on corporation finance, investments, or banking. Pamphlets and reprints of articles are published by many commission brokerage houses. Academic journals—e.g., the *Harvard Business Review* or *Journal of Business* —may be consulted for articles on almost any phase of the securities business. Diverse aspects of the work of securities houses are covered in *Fundamentals of Investment Banking* (Englewood Cliffs, N.J.: Prentice-Hall, Inc., 1949). A book by Birl E. Shultz, former director of the (New York) Stock Exchange Institute and designed for use by New York Stock Exchange employees, *The Securities Market and How It Works* (rev. ed.; New York: Harper and Row, 1963), provides the reader a detailed picture of the operations of the Big Board. Historical and statistical information concerning the over-the-counter markets is available in a collection of monographs by Irwin Friend, B. W. Hoffman, and W. J. Winn, *The Over-the-Counter Securities Markets* (New York: McGraw-Hill Book Co., 1958). More comprehensive studies of exchanges are those of Leffler and Farwell, *The Stock Market* (3d ed.; New York: The Ronald Press, 1963), and F. G. Zarb and G. T. Kerekes, eds., *The Stock Market Handbook* (Homewood, Ill.: Dow-Jones Irwin, Inc., 1970). The most significant recent source of detail and critical comment on the securities markets is the *Report of Special Study of Securities Markets of the Securities and Exchange Commission* (in 5 parts; Washington, D.C.: Government Printing Office, 1963).

Students who wish to extend their knowledge of securities and securities markets usually find it helpful to gain facility in reading and digesting financial news as it is presented in daily newspapers. A booklet written to assist readers to this goal is *How to Get More out of Financial News* (New York: Barrons, 1963).

Both historical and current information about many companies and their security issues are available in services such as *Moody's Manual of Investments* and *Standard Corporation Records* (Standard and Poor's Corporation). Descriptions of corporate operations, records of prices, dividends, and earnings, and summaries of securities contracts are among the data to be found here. Current information about individual companies or securities issues and articles of general interest are found in periodicals such as *Barron's* and the *Commercial and Financial Chronicle*. The basic source of information on new securities issues is the *Statistical Bulletin* of the Securities and Exchange Commission.

The items referred to in the bibliography of the previous chapter will also provide information on the institutions described in this chapter.

CHAPTER 19

Small business finance

The image of a small businessman working to serve his community while retaining personal control over his own destiny is familiar. Economies of scale and rigors of competition, the financial power of large firms, and the presence of central government have not stifled the economic role or political power of this group. In many communities the small businessman really represents "business" in an economic, political, and sociological sense.

The small business category includes a great number and diversity of firms: job-lot manufacturers; tiny retail and service establishments; franchised shops; satellites of larger firms; pioneering ventures intent on exploiting new ideas; part-time operations; intermediate-sized companies evolving into corporate giants; one-desk operations; stagnant family enterprises; dynamic syndicates. In terms of numbers of units, small businesses dominate the American environment; large firms, however, account for the majority of sales, products produced, income, assets, and employees in most industries. Nevertheless, the economic impact of small firms measured in absolute dollars and influence upon public policy is large. Small companies create competition in some industries lowering prices and stimulating efficiency.

During the 1950s much was written about the status of small business and particularly the problem of providing adequate capital to preserve free entry and growth opportunities. The dating of tables in this chapter reflects that spurt of interest and subsequent abatement. Unfortunately, much of the discussion has generalized about the subject by referring to a single, homogeneous group without recognizing the diversity of sizes, ages, goals, and abilities of the several million companies involved. These differences complicate the problem of description in this chapter which will focus on the characteristics of small companies, the factors influencing the financing of these firms, and the variety of sources of funds and financial institutions involved.

Definitions of small business

There is no conclusive definition of a small business. Various measurements have been used by government agencies and independent researchers to identify this broad group, including: number of employees, gross volume of sales, number of outlets, net income, total assets, total current liabilities, inventories, value added, and dependence on short-term financing. One of the most useful definitions was set forth in the Small Business Investment Act of 1958 where a small business concern is defined as one which is independently owned and operated, not dominant in its field, without a public market for its common stock, and possessed of total assets of less than $5 million, net worth under $2.5 million, and average annual net income after taxes of $150,000 or less for the preceding three years (subsequently changed to $250,000 during the preceding two years). A second definition based on the number of employees in manufacturing firms considers firms employing fewer than 250 persons to be "small" and those employing 1,000 or more as "large" with intermediate-sized companies classified by other industry characteristics. One study found that only 5% of all firms analyzed employed more than 20 workers, but that this group accounted for 77% of total employment, whereas the 75% of the business population which employed three persons or less represented only 6.3% of the total.[1]

The statistics in Table 19–1 indicate that corporations comprise only 13% of the population but receive four fifths of total business receipts. It is only in the manufacturing, wholesale trade, and finance categories that corporations represent a significant portion of the number of firms and even in these fields sole proprietorships and partnerships maintain a numerical majority. When business receipts figures are examined the pattern is reversed, even in the retail trade category where 75% of the firms are unincorporated. Sole proprietorships and partnerships dominate the agricultural industry, as would be expected, and continue to claim a large share of the activity in the retailing and service fields where flexibility and location are particularly important.

A great majority of corporations should also be considered small ac-

---

[1] Betty C. Churchill, "Size Characteristics of the Business Population," *Survey of Current Business,* May 1954, Table 2, p. 18.

TABLE 19–1

Number of firms and total business receipts by industry; sole proprietorships, partnerships, and corporations; 1967

	Total	Number			Percentage of total		
		S/P	Partnerships	Corporations	S/P	Partnerships	Corporations
Number of firms (in thousands)							
Agriculture, forestry, and fisheries	3,353	3,196	125	32	95.3	3.7	1.0
Mining	73	46	13	14	63.0	17.8	19.2
Construction	855	680	52	123	79.5	6.1	14.4
Manufacturing	401	170	34	197	42.4	8.5	49.1
Transportation, communication, electric, gas, and sanitary services	359	278	15	66	77.4	4.2	18.4
Wholesale trade	434	260	31	143	59.9	7.1	33.0
Retail trade	2,047	1,544	187	316	75.4	9.1	15.4
Finance, insurance, and real estate	1,123	549	275	299	48.9	24.5	26.6
Services	2,715	2,328	166	221	85.7	6.1	8.1
All categories	11,566	9,126	906	1,534	78.9	7.8	13.3
Business receipts (billions of dollars)							
Agriculture, forestry, and fisheries	$ 49.6	$ 35.3	$ 5.4	$ 8.9	71.2	10.9	17.9
Mining	15.1	1.3	1.0	12.8	8.6	6.6	84.8
Construction	92.2	18.3	7.1	66.8	19.8	7.7	72.5
Manufacturing	588.7	6.5	5.6	576.6	1.1	1.0	97.9
Transportation, communication, electric, gas, and sanitary services	106.0	5.5	1.3	99.2	5.2	1.2	93.6
Wholesale trade	213.2	19.7	10.8	182.7	9.2	5.1	85.7
Retail trade	320.7	81.1	23.3	216.3	25.3	7.3	67.4
Finance, insurance, and real estate	86.6	6.7	8.1	71.2	7.7	9.4	82.9
Services	94.7	34.8	14.7	45.2	36.7	15.5	47.7
All categories	$1,574.3	$ 211.3	$ 78.0	$1,285.0	13.4	5.0	81.6

... the U.S. Treasury Department, Internal Revenue Service, July 1970.

cording to Table 19–2. Nevertheless, when total asset values are analyzed, major corporations are still dominant with 80% of the total held by companies larger than the $5 million cutoff point. The extremely large corporations with assets in excess of $250 million are particularly important in shaping the inverse distribution of assets relative to the number of firms.

Depending upon the standard selected, small businesses represent 90 to 99% of the business population. A combination of the assets held by sole proprietors and partnerships with the figures reported by the smaller corporations would represent approximately 35% of total business assets.

TABLE 19–2

Number and total assets of U.S. corporations by asset category based on tax returns for 1966

Asset category	Number of firms			Total assets		
	Number	Per-centage	Cum-ulative	Billions	Per-centage	Cum-ulative
Zero assets	43,634	3.0	3.0	$ 0	—	—
$1–50,000	575,963	39.2	42.2	11.3	.6	.6
$50,000–100,000	244,880	16.7	58.9	17.6	1.0	1.6
$100,000–250,000	291,520	19.8	78.7	46.7	2.5	4.1
$250,000–500,000	144,699	9.9	88.6	50.6	2.7	6.8
$500,000–1,000,000	78,652	5.4	94.0	54.5	3.0	9.8
$1,000,000–5,000,000	63,988	4.4	98.4	132.5	7.2	17.0
$5,000,000–10,000,000	11,048	.8	99.2	78.0	4.2	21.2
$10,000,000–25,000,000	7,792	.5	99.7	121.1	6.6	27.8
$25,000,000–50,000,000	2,954	.2	99.9	102.7	5.6	33.4
$50,000,000–100,000,000	1,576	.1	100.0	109.6	5.9	39.3
$100,000,000–250,000,000 ...	1,137	.1	100.1	174.9	9.5	48.8
$250,000,000 or more	882	.1	100.2	945.3	51.2	100.0
Total	1,468,725			$1,844.8		

Note: Total does not add correctly due to rounding.
Source: Adapted from Table 1, *Corporation Income Tax Returns, Statistics of Income, 1967*, U.S. Treasury Department, Internal Revenue Service.

Business turnover and life expectancy

In an economy where individuals are free to establish a business after meeting minimum requirements, it is not surprising that over 400,000 new firms are initiated annually and that the number of discontinued companies is only slightly smaller as shown in Table 19–3 for the immediate postwar years. More recent data indicate a continuation of both the rate of formation and the rate of discontinuance.

Some large companies are started and discontinued each year, but most of the turnover involves small firms. Despite the faith and personal moti-

TABLE 19–3

Number of business firms in operation on January 1, new formations and discontinued units, 1946–1963 *(figures in thousands)*

Year	In operation	New	Discontinued
1946	3,242.5	617.4	208.7
1950	4,008.7	348.2	289.6
1955	4,286.8	408.2	313.8
1960	4,658.0	438.0	384.0
1961	4,713.0	431.0	389.0
1962	4,755.0	430.0	387.0
1963	4,797.0	—	—

Source: *Business Statistics,* 1963 ed., Supplement to the *Survey of Current Business,* U.S. Department of Commerce, Washington, D.C., 1963, pp. 10, 11. Figures in Table 19–1 and 19–2 are not comparable because different definitions are used. It is estimated that there were 4.9 million firms in operation by the third quarter of 1964.

vations of the founders, many new firms are discontinued soon after their organization. One study of the experiences of business firms conducted by the Department of Commerce in the early postwar years discloses that new firms have had about a 2 to 1 chance of surviving the first year; one third have remained in existence 4 years; and a fifth have lasted 10 years or more (Table 19–4). Some of the changes were caused by the sale or

TABLE 19–4

Percentage of firms surviving to specified age, based on figures for years 1947–54

Category of firm	Number of years surviving (in percent)										
	0.5	1.5	2.5	3.5	4.5	5.5	6.5	7.5	8.5	9.5	10.5
All industries	77	54	41	34	29	26	24	23	21	20	19
Mining and quarrying	79	55	42	34	30	26	24	22	20	19	18
Contract construction ...	82	62	51	44	40	37	35	33	31	30	29
Manufacturing ...	82	60	46	38	33	29	26	24	23	22	20
Transportation & other public utilities	76	51	38	31	27	25	23	21	20	19	19
Wholesale trade ..	85	67	56	48	43	40	37	35	34	32	31
Retail trade	74	39	36	29	25	22	20	19	18	17	16
Finance, insurance, real estate	84	66	54	47	42	38	35	33	32	30	29
Service	77	53	40	33	28	25	23	22	21	20	19

Source: Betty C. Churchill, "Age and Life Expectancy of Business Firms," *Survey of Current Business,* December 1955, p. 17.

transfer of successful businesses; however the overwhelming majority resulted from lack of success. A second study analyzing business failures between 1934 and 1957 reported that firms with liabilities of $25,000 or less accounted for over three fourths of the failures and that companies that had been in existence for five years or less were responsible for 60% of the number. It is clear that success in business is not as easy as most aspiring entrepreneurs believe.

Analysis of the business population indicates no perceptible change in the relative position of small business during the past 70 years although cyclical swings and shifts within industry classifications have occurred. In some fields business activities have become highly concentrated, but small firms have developed in other areas to offset this trend. For example, in the 1920s there were 111 automobile manufacturers compared to the three major and two smaller firms (plus several other manufacturers that produce special-purpose vehicles) operating in the 1960s, but thousands of small companies have been created to supply parts, materials, and services. Furthermore, numerous studies have indicated that no generalization can be made about the relationship of size and efficiency. In certain industries there are economies of scale associated with large size, but such relationships change for each type of business. It is also apparent that the cost savings do not increase indefinitely as size increases and that the curve flattens out, or drops, at a level which leaves considerable opportunity for small firms. It appears that small business will remain a basic segment of the economic environment. Failures and terminations will continue to afflict the new and established small companies, but the apparently indomitable spirit of entrepreneurs will supply candidates for creation of new ventures and continuation of existing small enterprises.

Financial problems of small business

Business management is a demanding occupation requiring marketing, production, personnel, and financial skills. Many businessmen with such professional abilities as salesmen, engineers, or accountants, for example, are unable to achieve the necessary balance of abilities. At the same time, complaints are frequently made by small businessmen, trade associations, and politicians that small companies are restricted by a serious lack of long-term debt and equity funds which are not readily available to this group. In appraising all of the alleged problems it must be noted that an aspiration gap will always exist between the desired availability of capital and the amounts that can realistically be provided. A gap between the desired amount and the amount actually obtained does not prove that small businessmen are unfairly treated or that our allocation of capital through a competitive pricing system should be altered. It is also meaningless to refer broadly to the financial problems of small business without recognizing that this category includes dormant fix-it shops with assets of a few thousand dollars and growing chemical or computer service firms with assets of $5 million. The popular literature and personal testimonies of some frustrated businessmen have developed a folklore concerning the difficulties of tapping sources of capital which psychologically prevents many companies from taking any action to obtain funds. These complex relationships emphasize the importance of analyzing specific conditions in various industries.

Four problem areas are apparent: providing venture capital for new firms; providing funds for companies that have outgrown the personal resources of the original founders but are not large enough for a public sale of securities; facilitating the transfer of ownership; and specific management problems and institutional limitations.

The problems of the new entrepreneur in obtaining financing are familiar ones. Financial inexperience of the managers, the unproven qualities of the new idea, inadequate equity contributions from the owners, and the time lag of receipts that follow expenditures for materials and expenses combine to discourage prospective lenders and investors evaluating new ventures. Many of the complaints about the nonavailability of long-term capital refer to examples of small innovators for proof while ignoring the great majority of firms with routine activities which have no need for outside capital. Small companies introducing innovations do have difficulty attracting funds from financial institutions, but this situation is a result of the risks involved and does not necessarily represent a bias against small size alone. The problem requires improving the system of contacts between small firms and specific sources of capital willing to bear the higher risks in return for higher returns rather than general condemnation of the entire financial system.

Growth also creates financial strain when: demands for investment of new funds exceed the retained earnings and regular sources of short-term credits; unexpectedly good sales tie up working capital in accounts receivable and inventory; or owners are unable or unwilling to solicit outside funds because of resentment against dilution of ownership control and possible indirect pressure by creditors. This problem is particularly acute for firms that must add facilities to obtain economies of scale and protection of their competitive position. Most companies must pass through a period when internal funds and short-term borrowing arrangements become inadequate. Small businessmen usually prefer the use of long-term debt at this stage to avoid loss of ownership; however such sacrifices must often be made or creditors will not loan funds. The alternative is to curtail growth and accept the competitive repercussions.

The transfer of ownership at the death or retirement of the owner or major stockholders is a third difficult problem. The loss of a key figure,

TABLE 19-5

Relative frequency of various reasons for rejections of small business loan applications, by size of area and size of bank* (*percentage of banks citing each reason as "relatively important"†*)

Reasons for loan rejections involving small business	All banks	Size of area (population in thousands)			Size of bank (deposits in millions)		
		Under 50	50 to 500	Over 500	Under $20	$20 to $100	Over $100
Reasons involving credit-worthiness of borrower:							
Not enough owner's equity in business ..	93	90	96	96	91	97	97
Poor earnings record	85	83	83	88	81	89	90
Questionable management ability	84	83	84	87	83	85	89
Collateral of insufficient quality	73	70	75	76	72	74	75
Slow and past due in trade or loan payments	69	66	74	71	68	74	67
Inadequacy of borrower accounting system	51	41	59	65	42	66	68
New firm with no established earnings record	48	40	49	57	42	55	59
Poor moral risk	41	45	36	40	46	36	33
Other reasons‡	6	3	10	7	3	11	14
Reasons involving bank's overall policies:							
Requested maturity too long	71	60	71	75	70	69	81
Applicant has no established deposit relationship with bank	49	42	50	52	45	57	53
Applicant will not establish deposit relationship with bank	36	27	42	51	30	41	49
Type of loan not handled by bank	33	32	30	35	38	25	25
Line of business not handled by bank ...	21	21	22	20	25	18	11
Loan portfolio for type of loan already full	19	18	24	17	21	15	17
Other reasons§	4	1	5	7	2	5	10
Reasons involving federal or state banking laws or regulations:							
Loan too large for bank's legal loan limit	23	30	17	17	32	13	4
Other reasons¶	9	8	8	12	8	10	12

* Based on views expressed by banks during interviews on small business financing in late 1957.

† Each bank was asked to rate the relative frequency with which each reason for rejection occurred as follows: "Frequent, occasional, rare, or never." For each reason above, the percentage of banks indicating that it was "relatively important" consists of those that checked the reason as "frequent" or "occasional." The balance of the banks indicated that the reason occurred "rarely" or "never." The responses covered rejections of formal applications as well as informal inquiries.

‡ Additional reasons cited by the banks, involving the credit-worthiness of the borrower, related to the condition of the specific enterprise, the general nature of the business, or the proposed use of the proceeds of the loan, e.g., overexpansion by the firm, speculative venture, too many firms in the field, tax problems, bad health of owner, obsolete product, duplicate borrowing, and the owner's reluctance to reinvest earnings.

§ Other reasons involving the banks' overall policies which were cited included such things as borrower located at too great a distance from the bank; too many banking connections; split line of credit.

¶ Other reasons involving federal or state banking laws or regulations, and the percentage of banks citing each of them as "relatively important" in loan rejections, were as follows:

	Percent
Regulations or limitations on real estate loans	5
Restrictions on loans on personal property	1
Criticism by examiners	1
Other restrictions	2

Source: Board of Governors of the Federal Reserve System, *Financing Small Business*, April 1958, p. 415.

one who has often provided the major driving force or organization, confuses the company's prospects and may discourage creditors and potential investors, particularly if a large drain on company resources is necessary to settle estate and inheritance taxes. Some of these risks may be met through use of buy-and-sell agreements available in business life insurance contracts.

In addition to the specific problems which affect only part of the small business population at any given time, the existence of management weaknesses often creates serious financial difficulties. Contrary to common beliefs, numerous studies have shown that inadequate financing is not a major cause of business failure. In fact, most failing companies have access to more capital and credit than they can manage efficiently. Dun & Bradstreet, Inc., a well-known source of information on business failures, reports that managerial weaknesses are the underlying cause of the great majority of failures as follows: managerial incompetence, 41.4%; unbalanced experience in all management areas, 19.2%; general lack of managerial experience, 18.8%; lack of experience in specific line of business, 12.8%; neglect, 3.6%; fraud, 1.7%; disaster, 1.2%; and unknown, 1.2%. Such managerial inadequacies are particularly dangerous if the internal generation of funds is curtailed because this source is the basis of a growing ownership position and provides a cushion of protection for creditors, particularly in short-term loans. This factor is highlighted in Table 19–5, which reviews the findings of a Federal Reserve System survey.

The Federal Reserve System in its exhaustive study was unable to find any definitive answer to the question of adequacy of capital for small business. It is unlikely that any satisfactory solution can be obtained from statistical studies because the problem affects individual businessmen, and the continuous debate among lawyers, economists, professors, and legislators is somewhat meaningless to the specific firm experiencing unfilled needs. One analyst has argued that adequacy cannot be examined in terms of availability, but is best measured by equity of treatment among candidates for funds.[2] Professor Guttentag's suggestion is that equity exists when investments are based on prospective rates of return properly adjusted for risk and that variations in the costs of obtaining credit are based on risk differences among prospective borrowers and expenses of investigation and administration of loans rather than arbitrary barriers to certain companies based on size and lack of knowledge about risk differentials.

---

[2] Jack Guttentag, "Adequacy of Financing Facilities for Small Business: Some Conceptual Problems," Board of Governors of the Federal Reserve System, *Financing Small Business,* April 1958, pp. 192–95.

Actual financing experience

Studies of the actual financing experiences of small firms are unfortunately sparse and usually concentrate on aggregate totals and broad generalizations. Some analysts have attempted to show the financing resources of small firms have been adequate by referring to the high postwar incomes of sole proprietorships and partnerships; the high rate of new business formations; the large amounts of personal funds being channeled into small firms; and the fact that the use of long-term debt by small companies as a proportion of total debt and relative to equity amounts has been increasing at a faster rate than the comparative figures for large companies. Such conclusions ignore the adequacy of funds available, the problems of small businesses in obtaining such capital, and the results which might have been achieved if different conditions had prevailed.

One study which did attempt to analyze the actual experiences of

TABLE 19–6

Size of company and type of financing related to financing experience
(percentage of all manufacturing corporations in each size group)

Financing experience	Small	Medium	Large
	Short-term credit		
Total in scope	100.0	100.0	100.0
Total response	81.8	83.9	94.5
No need for funds	44.5	38.7	45.3
Needed funds	37.3	45.2	49.8
Needs met satisfactorily	26.3	39.9	48.3
Experience not satisfactory	11.0	5.2	1.5
No financing efforts made	4.3	1.2	0.5
	Long-term credit		
Total in scope	100.0	100.0	100.0
Total response	81.7	84.0	94.5
No need for funds	64.1	66.0	70.1
Needed funds	17.6	10.0	24.4
Needs met satisfactorily	5.9	11.7	20.9
Experience not satisfactory	11.7	6.4	3.5
No financing efforts made	8.4	3.6	2.0
	Equity capital		
Total in scope	100.0	100.0	100.0
Total response	81.8	83.9	94.5
No need for funds	68.2	69.9	52.7
Needed funds	13.5	14.1	42.3
Needs met satisfactorily	1.4	6.2	36.3
Experience not satisfactory	12.2	7.9	6.0
No financing efforts made	10.7	6.7	3.0

Note: Details may not add to totals because of rounding.
Source: "Small Business Financing," *Federal Reserve Bulletin,* vol. 47, no. 1, January 1961, p. 12.

small companies was the Federal Reserve System interview survey of 3,000 manufacturing firms (Table 19–6). This study reported that the financing needs of individual companies vary widely by size category; two fifths of the smaller companies indicated a need for external financing compared with one half of the medium and three fourths of the larger companies. The proportion reporting satisfactory results in filling needs also increased with size. The experiences of smaller firms varied according to the type of financing sought. Most small firms desiring short-term credit were successful in arranging satisfactory terms, although not to the same degree as larger companies. Results in the other two categories were not as good. Of the 17.6% requiring long-term credit, only one third were satisfied with their financing experience. Success in obtaining equity investment was even more limited, particularly when compared with the very satisfactory record of larger companies. A basic reason for dissatisfaction on the part of small firms was their failure to solicit financing because of anticipated rejections; four fifths of the small firms expressing a need for equity made no effort to get it. The survey also found that the most profitable firms in the sample relied on retained earnings and expressed the least need for external financing. There was a positive relationship between profitability and success in obtaining financing, particularly among the smaller firms. Companies with the highest liquidity and highest equity as a proportion of total capital also had the most successful experiences. Once again, this relationship was particularly important among small enterprises. One extensive study has shown that even though the ratio of losses is higher for banks making a large number of loans to small businesses, the higher gross interest earnings on loans more than compensates for the extra losses.[3]

Information on the financing of small firms in other industry categories is not as complete; various publications, however, indicate that the great majority of small service and retail trade establishments with routine operations rely on internally generated funds with some supplementary seasonal credit from commercial banks and other specialized lenders.

Although generalizations are dangerous, it appears that the short-term financing needs of small firms are adequately met, but that inadequacies appear as the time period involved becomes longer. Specific problems still exist in providing venture capital for new firms and in meeting the financial strains created by rapid growth and transfer of business ownership.

---

[3] Geoffrey H. Moore, Thomas R. Atkinson, and Edward J. Kilberg, "Risks and Returns in Small Business Financing," Board of Governors of the Federal Reserve System, *Financing Small Business*, April 1958, pp. 40–101.

Sources of financing for small business

Small companies are usually organized without established sources of capital and must depend upon investments by the owners and their relatives and friends. In some situations wealthy private investors may also be attracted. Once operations have started, interbusiness financing in the form of trade credit becomes the largest source. Trade credit is created by selling on terms which permit payment at a later date, frequently stated as 2/10, net 30, which means that settlement need not be made for 30 days and that a 2% cash discount is available if payment is made within 10 days. Failing to take cash discounts seriously depresses net profits, particularly if the margin of profit is small. Nevertheless, many small companies with inadequate liquid funds are forced to use the entire credit period despite the high effective interest costs and injury to company prestige. It is ironic that firms that would benefit the most from taking the cash discounts are often the least able to marshal the necessary resources.

Even the newest and smallest enterprises are able to obtain trade credit without the careful scrutiny typical of institutional lenders because of business customs and the convenience of such arrangements. Sellers use trade credit as a competitive tool to increase new and repeat sales, and selling prices contain a larger element of profit than most loans so the occasional absorption of losses in the quest of larger sales can be justified. Trade credit frequently flows from large companies with access to national financial markets to smaller businesses which provides them with an indirect contact with external sources of financing. Several large manufacturers have even established captive finance companies to facilitate the sale of their products on long-term credit contracts. Small businessmen may also receive financial assistance from prime contractors and other customers through advance payments, loans, and the providing of equipment and materials.

Financing the organizational stage may be further simplified by leasing equipment, fixtures, office equipment, vehicles, and even real estate and buildings which reduces the immediate outlay of capital required when assets are purchased.

Financing of seasonal and expansion needs

Retained earnings are the basic source of expansion capital supplemented by additional advances of capital from the original investors. These contributions are adequate for many companies with routine operations and slow growth rates, but others must turn to external suppliers of funds such as the various venture capital firms that provide consulting service and capital. Investments by such firms usually take the form of purchases of convertible debentures or common stock providing a share in potential capital gains. Protective provisions usually provide some control over the operating policies of the companies receiving assistance. Examples of such firms include the American Research and Development Corporation, J. H. Whitney Company, and various family groups such as the duPont and Rockefeller interests. Officials of investment banking firms may also direct small companies to sources of venture capital and often join investing syndicates as individuals. Commercial bankers and financial consultants may serve as finders arranging such contracts.

The commercial banking system is the oldest and largest source of short-term loans (one year or less) to meet seasonal and temporary credit needs. These loans are considered to be self-liquidating because the proceeds from the investment financed are expected to provide the repayment. Small businessmen also make heavy use of short-term bank loans as a substitute for long-term credit. The continuous renewal of outstanding loans is a dangerous process, particularly during changing business conditions, but many small businessmen use the technique effectively. The extent of financing provided is indicated by the extensive Federal Reserve System survey of member bank lending experiences in 1957 that disclosed that firms with assets of $5 million or less accounted for 94% of the number and 49% of the dollar value of total bank loans. Most analysts report that established small businessmen tend to be well accommodated through short-term, general purpose loans provided by local banks. Even some relatively new enterprises may borrow on occasion, although banks usually require some record of demonstrated managerial competence and earning power. From the banker's viewpoint, such loans are advantageous because they keep assets active; small borrowers often grow into sizable customers and maintain the original banking relationship; deposits are increased; a higher rate of interest may be charged to offset the increased risk and the fixed costs of loan investigation and administration; and an image is created of a progressive lender concerned with the economic needs of the local community. Commercial banks are also the major supplier of long-term credit to small companies in the form of term loans.

Most loans to small firms are secured by mortgages or claims against inventories, accounts receivable, life insurance cash surrender values, saving accounts, stocks, and cosigners (see Chapter 17). The use of modern lending techniques provides the security desired by lenders to reduce risk while avoiding many of the frictions caused by earlier practices. Commercial finance companies are a second major supplier of short-term credit through the sale or assignment of accounts receivable, inventory collateral loans, and the floor planning of retailer inventories of durable goods. Many of the loans are made to companies not eligible for bank credit. Although the cost to the borrower is usually higher, comparisons should consider the importance of funds for survival and the returns to be obtained from business investments made possible by such credit. The extension of credit to small business by commercial finance companies continues to increase each year.

Long-term sources of funds

Insurance companies make many mortgage loans on commercial and industrial properties to small firms and it is probable that many individual loans made to policyholders are used for business purposes, but only a limited number of nonmortgage business loans have been granted to small enterprises. Chapter 12 discusses the new departments established by several insurance companies to solicit loan applications from firms in the under $1 million in assets category. Despite these good intentions, many problems still remain. First, the size of even the minimum loan limit, although extremely low by life insurer standards, is still far beyond the needs of most small businesses. Second, arranging the loans requires special effort and expenses which reduce the incentive and increase the interest rate charged. Many analysts believe the higher interest rates still fail to cover the incremental risks and expenses. Third, many states require that long-term, unsecured loans by insurance companies should have the interest charges covered at least $1\frac{1}{2}$ times by average earnings of the borrower during the five years preceding the loan agreement which automatically excludes new companies lacking the necessary collateral. Other states prohibit the making of unsecured loans to unincorporated businesses. Most loans require a number of protective covenants affecting additions to assets, additional debt, maintenance of working capital, expenses, dividend payments, etc. Borrowers often balk at these restrictions. Fourth, the field agencies of insurance companies are sales oriented and are not particularly qualified to make complicated loan arrangements.

The experiences of the special loan programs emphasize that it is difficult for insurance companies to generate a substantial volume of nonmortgage loans to small businesses of an acceptable quality, although reasonable success has been achieved in making loans of $250,000 to $1 million to companies in the $1 to $5 million asset category.

The public sale of bonds by smaller companies is virtually impossible. On the demand side, the flow of savings is increasingly into financial institutions which invest the accumulated funds according to their needs for safety, liquidity, and investment income (see Chapters 11 and 12). Life insurance companies; corporate, state, and local pension funds; trustees, savings and loan associations; savings banks; and other financial institutions are limited by regulation and their own portfolio policies to large blocs of high-grade securities with enough marketability to provide resale opportunities in national financial markets. None of these private institutions has any specific motivation to seek out the public bond offerings of smaller firms. From the supply side, it is apparent that the high costs of registration and selling have become prohibitive for small issues. Because such expenses are relatively fixed, the costs as a proportion of the total proceeds increase sharply as the size of an offering declines. Investment bankers may also avoid the underwriting of small, unknown bond issues to protect their reputations.

Sole proprietors and partnerships have always had difficulty in finding investors willing to contribute equity funds because of the managerial problems of adding partners and the dangers of unlimited liability for business debts. Many smaller, incorporated firms rely on term loans and continuous renewals of short-term credit to fill needs which would be better met by the addition of equity funds. The many advantages of equity capital for small businesses include: permanent working capital is provided; the risks of fixed interest payments and frequent loan renewals are eliminated; a base is provided for future borrowing; the development of public interest in the shares of a small firm benefits the original shareholders by providing a sales outlet when diversification and liquidity are needed; and the potential number of future investors is increased. There are also a number of disadvantages, including: dilution of ownership control by the founders and of the amount of earnings and dividends allocated to original investors; the shares may have to be sold at a discount from their true value because of the many risks associated with small companies; and the costs of selling a small issue of stock are high. One study by the Securities and Exchange Commission of the costs of equity financing during four years found that expenses as a percentage of total financing receipts rise as the size of an issue declines, as follows: $1 to 2 million category, 11.5%; $500,000 to $1 million, 15%; and under $500,000, 22%.

The SEC has attempted to reduce the barriers to small firms by exempting public issues not in excess of $300,000 from filing the detailed registration statement required when larger amounts are involved. Under Regulation A filings a simplified disclosure statement is permitted, and some of the mechanics of distribution are simplified. Such issues must also comply with individual state blue-sky laws in areas where the shares are sold publicly. Despite the simpler procedures, many fixed costs remain including legal and accounting services, registration fees, printing and engraving costs, miscellaneous federal and state taxes, and the underwriting expenses if investment banker services are used. Some small issues are sometimes sold directly to the public without investment banker support when local investment appeal exists or the services of an underwriter cannot be obtained. Special restricted offerings to residents within a single state at the time of incorporation are also permitted under simplified regulations.

Experience indicates that very few small companies attempt to sell common stock publicly (see Table 19–6). A more common procedure is to interest employees and officers in stock purchase plans although this source may be limited, particularly if the officers have already invested heavily. Some analysts have suggested that a minimum standard for a small firm attempting to sell stock might be to have earnings of $100,000 to $150,000 and net worth of $400,000 to $500,000 plus an upward growth trend of sales and profits and favorable future prospects. Many small firms have been successful in raising money in this way, particularly in certain glamorous industries such as electronics during the late 1950s and the 1960s.

Government agencies

In 1953 Congress authorized the creation of the Small Business Administration (SBA) to: facilitate the acquisition of government contracts by small businesses; provide managerial and technical consulting services for small firms; provide debt funds for eligible companies unable to obtain private financing at reasonable terms; and administer special government financing programs including disaster loans for rehabilitation of destroyed and damaged businesses. The SBA is currently the only federal government agency specifically charged with the financing of small businesses. The Smaller War Plants Corporation which assisted war-oriented manufacturers during World War II has been liquidated. Small businesses in the war and in immediate postwar years also obtained credit from the Reconstruction Finance Corporation, Veterans Administration, Federal Reserve Board, through V-Loans, and Federal Reserve Bank working capital loans, but these agencies were never specifically directed to meet the needs of small companies. The total amount of such loans was low and eventually the granting of these loans declined.

The Small Business Administration cooperates with the Department of Defense in designating particular orders to be placed with small firms and assists these companies in acquiring subcontracts from large prime contractors. The SBA has also been instrumental in establishing training classes in business management and in publishing a series of pamphlets on management, production, and technical problems designed specifically for improving managerial techniques of small businessmen.

In fulfilling its financing function, the SBA makes medium-term working capital loans and long-term loans for the acquisition and renovation of equipment and plant facilities. To be eligible for such assistance, the borrower must meet the various size and income standards reviewed earlier in this chapter. The maximum loan size is currently $350,000 to a single borrower and the interest rate is 5 to 6%. The average SBA loan has been $47,000, and it is significant that over one half have been made in the $10,000 to $50,000 range. Regulations specify that all loans must be of sound value, and usually collateral is required as security. There have been complaints about the red tape involved and the possible negative influences on overall credit standing of small firms required to pledge assets for secured loans, but the requirement is normally enforced. The maximum lending period is 10 years and the average maturity of loans so far has been 5 years. In keeping with the concept that SBA credit is intended to supplement, rather than compete with the established financial institutions, tangible proof must be supplied by the prospective borrower that funds are not available from private sources. The agency also requires an elaborate application procedure and offers considerable financial counsel during the investigation stage as part of its management service.

The regulations and financing techniques of the agency are constantly changing to meet the different problems created by our complex business system. An interesting example of adaptation occurred in May of 1964 when an experimental program to lend small amounts up to $15,000 to grocery stores, repair shops, beauty and barber shops, and other small retail and service establishments employing no more than four workers was announced. It is anticipated that loans will be made at the regular interest rate of $5\frac{1}{2}\%$ (4% to businesses in depressed areas) and that security requirements will be relaxed if adequate earnings prospects can be shown. Another program initiated in 1964 is the "6 by 6" plan to make loans of up to $6,000 for as long as six years. It is hoped that this program will be of particular help for businessmen from minority groups.

The Small Business Administration may extend loans directly to applicants, but the required approach is to first offer to share the loan with a commercial bank or other private financial institution on either an immediate or deferred basis. Under the immediate participation plan the SBA grants a share, up to 90%, of the loan simultaneously with the private lender. When the deferred approach is used, the private financial institution loans the entire amount and the SBA agrees to purchase, on demand, a predetermined share of the loan (up to 90%) from the private lender. Under both types of participation the private institution administers the loan for a fee of 0.5%. The lending experience of the SBA is shown in Table 19–7.

In absolute terms the lending activities of the SBA have never represented a large proportion of the total loans to small business. A survey by the Federal Reserve System of bank loans to small business outstanding at the end of 1955 indicated that the loans of the Small Business Administration and Veterans Administration combined amounted to only 2% of the total ($118 million of $6.3 billion). Loans made by the SBA have increased since 1955, but it is estimated that the total amount is still less than 4% of all loans made by member banks of the Federal

TABLE 19–7

Loan applications and approvals of the Small Business Administration, September 29, 1953, through December 31, 1963 (*dollars in millions*)

Appli-cations	Approvals		Direct loans		Participations			
					Immediate		Deferred	
	Number	Amount	Number	Amount	Number	Amount	Number	Amount
102,301	50,754	$2,440.9	20,075	$685.7	24,105	$1,453.5	6,574	$301.5

Source: SBA, *Annual Report,* 1964, p. 16.

Reserve System to small companies. It is also significant that a sizable proportion of the applications have been rejected, as the figures for early years show, and that government loan programs have not been financially self-sufficient if all administrative costs of making and servicing the loans and the cost of funds loaned by the agencies are considered. This result is not an unexpected one since the goal of the SBA is to provide catalyst capital at reasonable interest rates to small firms unable to obtain funds on acceptable terms from private sources. Nevertheless, it should be noted that the high costs of acquiring and servicing such small loans and the greater risks associated with many of the small borrowers would make it impossible for private financial institutions to cover their full costs, by charging an interest rate of only 5 or 6%. Political and sociological considerations, as well as the economic goal of preserving small firms as a segment of the competitive business system, apparently justify continuation of this government lending program.

Development corporations

In order to attract and hold industry, a number of development corporations have been formed. Many of these organizations limit their activity to disseminating information, but a growing number assist in the financing of companies. The efforts of development corporations have resulted in some relocation of industry. These transfers create rejoicing in the receiving areas because of the new employment opportunities and needs for retail and service facilities and accusations of piracy from the areas losing industry.

The six New England states have been particularly active in organizing state development corporations, since 1949, when Maine established one. Lending and consulting operations have been successful and some profits have been reinvested. Many other states now have such organizations and a few have even authorized creation of credit corporations which may use state funds for financial aids to industry. The Pennsylvania "100% financing" plan is one example. Hundreds of other development corporations have been formed at the regional and community level under the sponsorship of utilities, railroads, and various business and civic groups.

Services include consulting and assistance on plant site selection and construction, help in hiring and training labor, direct financing and arrangement of contacts with local financial institutions, and various cost-saving inducements such as free or low-cost physical facilities, tax exemptions, and lowered utility rates. The capital is provided by selling stock of the development corporation to individuals, commercial and savings banks, insurance companies, and other groups interested in the economic condition of specific areas. Revenue bonds may also be sold with the intention of retiring the obligations through various sources of income created by the attraction of new business. Local financial institutions further give support by pledging to make low-cost loans to selected borrowers which expands the financing capacity of the development corporation. Such loans frequently carry greater risk but the capital of the development corporation serves as a cushion to absorb losses. Loans with maturities of 5 to 10 years are typically made to established firms interested in moving or expanding into a new area, but new ventures and local companies experiencing difficulties also may receive assistance. Since 1958, development corporations have been able to acquire funds from the Small Business Administration through the "Local Development Company Loan Program." The typical procedure is to have the local group provide about 20% of the funds and then to request the support of private lenders and the SBA.[4]

The volume of lending by development corporations has never reached substantial proportions because of the limited financial resources and the practice of spreading available funds among as many borrowers as possible; many companies, however, have benefited from such seed capital loans, and the various sponsoring groups appear satisfied that industrial production and employment have been stimulated in certain areas.

Small business investment corporations (SBICs)

In theory, new institutions and financing techniques should be constantly evolving to meet the needs of business. In reality, the supply of long-term capital for small firms is limited by imperfect competition among lenders and inadequate information concerning types and degrees of risk associated with certain types of loans. Beginning in 1950, many bills were introduced in both houses of Congress calling for creation of a new institution to provide long-term capital for small firms. Finally, the

---

[4] *How 233 Communities from Coast to Coast Have Benefitted from SBA's 502 Loan Program* (Washington, D.C.: Small Business Administration, 1963).

Small Business Investment Act of 1958 was passed "to improve and stimulate the national economy in general and the small business segment in particular by establishing a program to stimulate and supplement the flow of private equity capital and long-term loan funds which small business concerns need." To establish an SBIC, the private individuals or organizations sponsoring the company are required to obtain a charter from the state in which they expect to operate and raise $300,000 as minimum paid-in capital and surplus. The Small Business Administration is charged with general supervision of the act including the granting of federal charters, if necessary, and approval of officers, major stockholders, and investment policies.

The SBA is authorized to assist in the providing of capital by buying up to $700,000 of subordinated debentures issued by a new SBIC. Once formed, an SBIC is authorized to borrow amounts up to four times total equity from any sources willing to lend. The potential leverage prompted a flood of articles predicting magical capital gains and large investments in such ventures. Experience has shown that such fantastic leverage is unreal because the SBA has carefully limited its loans, and private lenders have not extended large amounts except to captive SBICs sponsored by commercial banks, real estate firms, and other financial institutions. Smaller SBICs have not pushed for additional loans and the larger firms have either sold stock publicly or formed a working arrangement with private lenders. Banks have formed many of the largest SBICs and are permitted to make investments of up to 2% of their capital and surplus in the stock of an SBIC, which enables the bank to indirectly make equity investments and certain loans that might otherwise be rejected. Other SBICs have raised capital from the public. Electronics Capital Corporation, incorporated in 1959 with capital of $305,110, has sold an equity issue of $18 million to public investors. At various times other SBICs have had successful offerings and in 1969 there were 46 publicly owned firms. The largest 13 companies controlled 26% of the capital resources of the entire industry. However, attempts to sell SBIC shares following the stock market declines of 1962, 1966, and 1969 have been difficult because of the large market price losses of SBIC stocks and of the shares of many small companies whose securities were held by these investment companies. In the last several years, SBICs have borrowed funds from a variety of sources to support expansion.

The act also granted certain tax privileges including the right of investors owning SBIC shares to write off losses on these investments against ordinary income, rather than capital gains which is the normal procedure. A similar right was granted to SBICs to cover losses sustained on investments in small businesses. In addition, dividends received by SBICs from taxed corporations are fully exempted from the corporate income tax, whereas, most firms are allowed only an 85% deduction.

In the original act, SBICs were authorized to buy convertible debentures or make term loans to small firms meeting the eligibility requirements referred to in the chapter introduction. Amendments are continuously being made to the 1958 act, and investments are now permitted in the equities and stock purchase warrants of incorporated firms. SBICs may also provide consulting and advisory services on a fee basis. The emphasis on convertible debentures and equity securities excludes sole proprietorships and partnerships as candidates for such investment, but term loans are available to attractive unincorporated firms (see Table 19–8).

Convertible debentures are particularly appealing to SBICs because of the potential capital gains resulting from conversion into equity securities at one of the predetermined ratios established at the time of purchase. The bonds are made callable at the option of the borrower with proper notice to permit conversion, and some limitation is required to prevent the SBIC from gaining control through direct purchase of equities or conversion of debentures. Whenever control is obtained through some market development, there must be a provision for divesture within a reasonable time.

TABLE 19–8

Loan and equity financing of licensed small business investment companies as of September 30, 1969* (dollars in millions)

Loans	Debt securities	Capital stock	Total
$133.7	$139.6	$345.0	$618.3

* Based on 362 reporting companies.
Source: SBA, SBIC Industry Trends, March 31, 1970.

Term loans with maturities of 5 to 20 years often are made on a secured basis. The interest rate is determined in the borrowing negotiations. The maximum rate allowed is 15%, or the legal limit of the state where the loan is made, whichever is lower. Actual rates seldom fall outside of the 6 to 12% range and the average rate is typically 8 to 9%. These charges may seem high compared to the prime borrowing rate at commercial banks; however, the higher risks involved and the rates charged by other private lenders must be recognized. In fact, it is anticipated that SBICs must use interest and dividend receipts to cover operating expenses and losses and rely on capital gains from equity securities to provide profits.

Within the specific definition limiting the size of companies eligible for assistance, wide investment latitude is granted. Individual investments and loans were originally limited to $500,000 with a few technical exceptions or 20% of the SBICs combined capital and surplus, whichever measurement was lowest. The maximum dollar limitation has now been deleted. For a minimum-sized firm this rule restricts transactions to $60,000 for any single client. A breakdown of the types of equity investments and loans by industry is shown in Table 19–9.

Following passage of the act industry developments moved slowly. By midyear 1959, the SBA had committed only $5 million among a few of the 15 SBICs organized, and as late as the end of 1960 there were only 117 companies. Beginning in 1961, there was a surge of organizing activity and by year-end 1962 there were 606 companies holding assets of $588 million with active business investments reported as follows: 3,910 loan transactions, $138 million; 1,910 debt security transactions, $185 million; and 1,117 capital stock investments, $37 million. The 6,937 transactions reported involved average outlays of $53,000. For one SBIC, an investment of $750,000 in a small growth firm increased in market price to $11 million following a successful public offering by the electronics company. The market price of this SBIC's stock, which had traded at $10 in 1959, moved into the $60 price range following this favorable development.

TABLE 19–9

Outstanding balances of 362 SBIC financings of major groups of industries as of September 30, 1969 (*dollars in millions*)

Category	Amount	Percent
Manufacturing	$153.6	37
Wholesale trade	19.4	4
Retail trade	46.9	8
Other nonmanufacturing industries	227.7	51
Totals	$447.6	100

Source: SBA, *SBIC Industry Trends,* March 31, 1970.

Many publicly held SBICs were swept up in a splurge of investor interest, and one investment service reported that a price index of 12 SBIC stocks reached 250% of the original issuing prices at a time when the companies had only 30% of their assets invested. The stock market fall in 1962 hit glamor stocks particularly hard, hurting SBIC shares both directly and indirectly. The natural tax advantages to investors of being able to write off losses on SBIC shares directly against ordinary income created additional selling pressure. By the end of 1962 the pendulum had swung to the opposite extreme and many SBIC shares were selling at approximately 60% of their original offering price. During this troubled period many grandiose expectations concerning SBICs were readjusted.

An analysis of the industry in 1964 indicated that during the years of rapid growth, the number of financing transactions and the amounts invested and loaned continued to increase, particularly in certain fast-growing geographical sections. It is also significant that SBICs distributed $96 million in 2,476 transactions during the first six months of fiscal 1964 compared to a total of $50 million in 1,368 transactions in the comparable 1963 period. A recapitulation of industry experience as of July 1964 indicated that of the 1,144 applications to organize an SBIC, there were 766 active firms, 103 approved for activation, 34 under review, and 43 canceled licenses. The active firms were spread across the country with the largest number located in New York, California, Texas, Massachusetts, and Florida. Thereafter, activity and the number of SBICs declined. In 1969, there were 460 licensed SBICs, of which 362 were reporting activity. Both the financing done by them and the capital resources committed to their operation were down from mid-decade levels.

From a qualitative viewpoint a number of trends can be determined after the first dozen years. A sharp dividing line exists between minimum capital firms and the larger companies. Although 90% of the firms had capital of less than $1 million at the end of 1962, this group controlled only 35% of the industry total. Analysts believe that high operating costs and the difficulties experienced by many smaller companies in making investments will stimulate the trend toward larger units. There appears to be greater interest in servicing the needs of companies at the top of the size scale permitted and in the formulation of syndicates to permit several SBICs to pool their resources to handle large transactions in excess of the old $500,000 transaction limitation that was repealed in 1964. Many companies have even turned to specialization in term lending and real estate investments. A few mergers have occurred as part of the trend toward consolidation.

Few financial institutions have received as much attention as the SBICs, and few have been given such unfavorable publicity. Many analysts have been particularly critical of the interest in larger loans, creation of syndicates, specialization in loans only, and the growing real estate investments. These critics claim that such policies ignore the basic purposes underlying the creation of the SBIC program. Industry spokesmen responded that 1,200 of the 1,496 transactions completed in 1962 involved amounts under $100,000, but the general impression persists that very small businesses have not been helped. Critics have also pointed to the small capital structures of many companies as proof that SBICs cannot solve the major problems, particularly during the waiting periods immediately following the initial investments. Many smaller SBICs have simply held their resources in government securities and cash because of difficulties in locating attractive opportunities. Other criticisms include: SBICs are economically unsound without the government largess; the leverage claims are unrealistic and serious problems would result if such techniques were actually used; the tax incentives are available only if losses occur; operating expenses are high; small businessmen are often resentful of the potential loss of part of their ownership interest through direct sale or conversion; excessive red tape exists in meeting SBA regulations; some unqualified promoters have been attracted by the speculative claims made at the beginning of the program; and a poor job has been done in describing the services of SBICs to most small businessmen.

Other analysts have made optimistic appraisals in direct contradiction to the gloomy predictions cited above. This group refers to the many favorable factors in the industry, including: the consolidation of assets in the larger firms; attractive tax incentives for wealthy investors; the growing number of SBICs and the infrequent cancellation of licenses despite the severe trials of the early years; the continued interest of banks and other financial institutions; the opportunity for small firms to indirectly tap the national capital markets by selling securities to SBICs, which in turn sell their securities to public investors; the possibility of establishing a capital bank for SBICs where securities could be sold to obtain increased liquidity; the fact that some of the established companies are achieving the goal of meeting expenses and losses out of interest and dividend receipts; and the elimination of many of the unqualified sponsors as the industry continues to mature.

It is impossible to generalize about an entire industry that is only a few years old and which contains so many diverse members with regards to size, investment policies, and managerial abilities. The first round of investments has not even been completed and many regulations are still being modified. As is the case in most appraisals of new financial institutions, it is probable that the extremist claims of optimism and pessimism will prove to be exaggerated. The SBICs apparently are filling a small gap in the structure of institutions serving small business, particularly for larger firms with equity securities offering potential capital gains.

Questions and problems

1. Why does small business get so much attention in Congress, newspapers, and classrooms?
2. How would you explain the annual increase in the number of firms despite the high mortality rate among small companies? Is it true that corporate giants are squeezing out the little firms?
3. What is the aspiration gap? Is the problem it represents typical of small business?
4. How does growth in sales volume create financing problems? Is it logical for small businessmen to expect profits from increasing sales volume to meet these problems?
5. Has small business had adequate access to external funds during the postwar period? How would you define adequacy?

6. Why do small businessmen usually prefer long-term debt rather than the sale of common stock to meet expansion needs?
7. Why are commercial banks such a prominent source of short-term debt financing for small firms? What is the role of insurance companies in small business financing?
8. How does the Small Business Administration assist in the financing of small firms?
9. What are small business investment corporations? How do they operate?
10. What type of financial institution would you suggest for meeting the financing problems of small business?

Bibliography

A basic source is *Financing Small Business: Report to the Committees on Banking and Currency and the Select Committees on Small Business of the United States Congress by the Federal Reserve System*, pts. 1 and 2, April 1958. Various subsequent hearings before these two committees often involve small business topics. Other basic sources include A. D. H. Kaplan, *Small Business: Its Place and Problems* (New York: McGraw-Hill Book Co., Inc., 1948); George D. Summers, *Financing and Initial Operations of New Firms*, Ford Foundation Doctoral Dissertation Series published by Prentice-Hall, Inc.; and numerous articles in various business journals, particularly the *Harvard Business Review, Duns Review and Modern Industry, Journal of Finance*, and *Law and Contemporary Problems*. The National Bureau of Economic Research also publishes occasional studies on small business subjects.

The Survey of Current Business often contains reports of staff studies as does the *Federal Reserve Bulletin*. Activities of the Small Business Administration are summarized in its annual reports. The SBA publishes numerous pamphlets on small business management including a *Handbook of Small Business Finance*. Information on small business investment corporations may be found in Richard E. Kelley, *The SBICs: Source of Venture Capital* published by the Keyfax Publications of Los Angeles and the *National Directory* from the same organization. The National Association of Small Business Investment Corporations publishes a newsletter containing pertinent information. Several other trade associations issue pamphlets including *Equity Capital for Small Business Corporations* and *Initial Public Financing for Small Business* published by the Investment Bankers Association of America.

PART V

CONSUMER FINANCE

Since for consumers the main demands for financing are related to purchases of homes and the furnishing of them, this part on consumer finance has two chapters. Chapter 20 is directed to the forms of transactions usually arranged in the purchase of consumer durables; Chapter 21 is on residential real estate finance.

Consumer credit

Nature of consumer credit

Consumer credit is just what the name implies: it is credit granted to consumers for consumption purposes. When an individual buys a new car on an installment basis, this is a consumer credit transaction. When a family head borrows some cash from a small loan company or a bank, it is a consumer credit transaction. The charge accounts that a family runs at department stores or elsewhere are another kind of consumer credit. Credit for the buying of homes may be thought of as consumer credit, but its character is so specialized that many persons consider it a separate type. In this text, residential housing credit will be treated separately in Chapter 21, but the credit for repair and modernization of houses is included here. While repair and modernization credit is related to real estate credit in many respects, it is generally classed as consumer credit. For our purposes we may say that *consumer credit* is debt with a maturity of less than five years owed by consumers for consumption purposes.

Even though many individual consumer credit transactions are for trivial amounts, the aggregate amount is large. In January 1970, it was estimated by the Federal Reserve to be $121.1 billion. This amounted to more than eight month's income of the total population.

In medieval times the church banned the charging of interest or usury.

The practice of lending for consumption purposes was thought to be exploitive. But consumer credit is now a respected institution; the concerns that grant the credit occupy a recognized position in the financial community; individuals borrow or become indebted openly and without shame.

Until late in the 19th century, most consumers could borrow only from loan sharks. Such lending was not wholly legal, but it was practiced with little concealment. The persons borrowing were usually ashamed of doing so and conspired in the secrecy, which was the protection of the loan sharks. The history of the loan shark extends right up to modern times. The need for financial aid is so common and often so urgent that legal prohibition of lending at usurious rates has never been very effective. In very recent times, loan sharks have been known to operate more or less openly in the courthouses where their fellow practitioners were being prosecuted. The modern practice has been not to prohibit the granting of consumer credit but to recognize the need for consumer loans, bring most of the lenders into the open, and enforce rules and regulations that protect both borrower and lender.

The great recent growth of consumer credit is related, however, to another modern development: the widespread purchase of automobiles and many durable household appliances. The use of consumer credit for reasons of desperation has been largely displaced by its use for purposes of pleasure and comfort. Modern incomes are spent more and more for the so-called big-ticket purchases which many people cannot pay for in one lump sum. The big-ticket purchase has opened the way for vast growth in consumer credit.

Who uses consumer credit?

Because consumer credit has achieved respectability rather recently, it is often assumed that such credit is used largely by lower income groups. Research studies show that this is not true. They show that consumer installment credit is used not so much by persons in the low-income class as by persons in middle- and high-income classes. The poor do not have the financial standing to qualify for installment credit. Data summarized in Exhibit 20–1 show that few users of consumer installment credit are in the poverty income class (under $3,000 annual income).

Within the consumer finance industry it has long been recognized that the factors that make applicants credit-worthy are relative stability of income and employment rather than size of income. Schoolteachers, for example, have long been considered prime outlets for consumer credit, even though their incomes (until fairly recently and even now, to some extent) are on the slender side.

EXHIBIT 20–1

Number of loans made: percentage distribution by monthly income classes

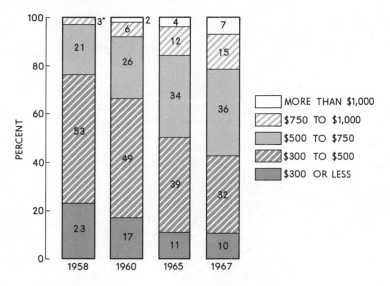

* More than $750.
Source: Adapted from *Finance Facts Yearbook*, 1969, p. 58.

Classification of consumer credit

Forms of consumer credit are so diverse that there are several ways of classifying these debts. One of the commonest is the division between *sale* credit and *loan* credit. Sale credit refers to a transaction in which the consumer gets a product (an automobile, furniture, or the like) or a service (electricity or gas, or medical attention) and promises to pay later. Loan credit refers to a transaction in which the consumer gets cash and undertakes an obligation to repay cash at some later date.

Another classification can be made: *installment* and *noninstallment*. An installment credit is one in which the amount owed is repaid in periodic (weekly, monthly) and usually equal amounts. Noninstallment loans are those which are due in one lump sum, such as charge accounts or a note at a bank. Noninstallment consumer credits are not always repaid in lump sums but may be paid off in driblets, in much the way that some slow charge accounts are settled.

The division of consumer credit between installment and noninstallment forms is shown in Exhibit 20–2. This diagram shows not only this major division of consumer credit but also the major subsections of consumer credit and the types of lenders that extend credit. It will be used

EXHIBIT 20–2

Short- and intermediate-term consumer credit, December 31, 1969 (by type of credit and institution, millions of dollars)

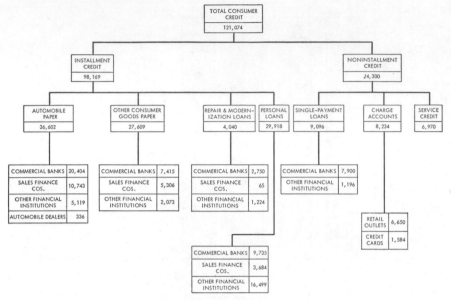

Source: *Federal Reserve Bulletin*, March 1970, pp. A54–A56.

later in the chapter when we are dealing with the different financial institutions that are involved in the consumer credit business.

A third way of classifying consumer credit is by purpose. Here we meet with almost insuperable obstacles in getting data for such a breakdown. A consumer cash loan may be for the same purpose as a sale credit. For example, a consumer borrows from a bank in order to pay cash for an automobile rather than arranging installment payments to the auto dealer. Sometimes the purpose of consumer credit is said to be remedial. This means that the purpose is urgent—medical or hospital needs, or consolidation of outstanding and pressing debts that break down the consumer-debtor's morale. This is an ambiguous basis of classification at best. In general, the purposes of consumer credit are as broad as consumption itself; the way in which the consumer gets credit may be more a matter of convenience than an indication of real purpose. A consumer might let his charge accounts run in order to make medical outlays from current income, but the figures would show that he was borrowing to finance purchases on credit.

As a practical matter, the classification of consumer credit has been statistically possible only on rather general grounds. The data in Table 20–1 were first assembled by the National Bureau of Economic Research and are now compiled by the Federal Reserve.

TABLE 20–1

Consumer credit in the United States, January 1970

	Billions of dollars	Percent
Consumer credit—Total	121.1	100
Installment	97.4	80
Automobile sale	$36.3	30
Other sale*	31.3	26
Installment loan	29.8	24
Noninstallment	23.7	20
Charge accounts	7.5	6
Service credit	7.0	6
Single-payment loans	9.1	8

* Including repair and modernization loans.
Source: *Federal Reserve Bulletin*, March 1970, p. A54.

Consumer credit transactions and their terms

It is not possible to generalize about the character and terms of consumer credit because the transactions assume so many forms. For this reason, the major types of consumer credit are examined separately in the following sections. The terms under which each type is usually extended and the implicit or explicit cost of the credit will be discussed. Classifications will be the same as in Exhibit 20–2.

Installment sale credit

Automobile purchases, more than any other consumer expenditure, have been the basis for the extension of consumer credit. Consumer credit appears most frequently when the unit size of the transaction is large relative to the income of those undertaking the transaction. The automobile is one of the largest unit expenditures ever made by families. It was the growth of automobile use and financing of automobile purchases that led consumer credit from the fringe to the center of respectability.

About 60 to 65% of all new car transactions are financed by consumer credit, and about 55 to 60% of the deals in used cars (except junkers) are on a credit basis. Sewing machines were among the very first household articles sold on an installment basis; more recently the electrical type of household appliance—television, for example—has come to be of relatively greater importance and is the basis for much consumer credit. More than half the purchases of furniture and appliances involve credit today.

The terms of a typical installment sale transaction include three elements: the down payment, the monthly payment, and the carrying or interest charge. The "truth-in-lending" act now requires all to be stated on a contract.

Down payments assume a special importance in most installment sale transactions because the security for the credit is the buyer's equity in the article purchased. The larger the down payment, the larger the buyer's equity in his purchase, and the lower the ratio of the payments to that equity. Down payments vary considerably among various classes of merchandise, depending in part on the custom in the trade.

In some installment sale transactions—on an automobile, for instance —the down payment is made by the trade-in of an older item. Where this is true, the expected down payment is customarily fairly high (partly because an overvaluation of the trade-in means that the real cost of the article purchased was not so great as it appeared). In some lines, such as furniture, trade-ins are much less common, and down payments are correspondingly lower.

The *maturity* of an installment credit determines the size of the monthly (or periodic) payment. If a one-third down payment is required on a $4,500 car, and the balance is to be paid off in a year, this means monthly payments of $250 plus interest and other charges; if the credit can be spread out over 15 months, the monthly payments are only $200 plus interest; if carried to 18 months, the payments are $167 plus interest; for 24 months, $125 plus interest. Many buyers are not much impressed by the length of the contract, but they may be concerned about how much they must pay out of income each month. The student may have noted how often advertisements will say: "Can be had for monthly payment of $——."

The maturity of consumer installment sale contracts is of considerable importance in another respect. As we shall find out, the amount of business done on an installment basis varies a great deal. It is large in some periods, small in others. The longer the maturity of installment debt contracts, the longer they overhang the financial affairs of the indebted persons.

The *cost* of installment credit is difficult to determine. The "truth-in-lending" act now requires that an annual interest rate be shown on a contract, but a buyer still should consider computing the effective rate for himself in order to decide whether the stated rate is acceptable to his plans for commitment to future payments. The cost of credit may be expressed as an explicit interest charge, or it may be concealed in higher prices. For example, let us assume that a buyer is considering the purchase of a bedroom suite. One store offers it for $200, stating that no charge is made for 12 months credit. Another store sells an identical set for $190 but makes a charge of $6 per $100 per year for the credit privilege. Each store requires a cash down payment of $30, so that in the first instance there is a balance of $170 to be repaid in 12 equal payments and in the second case the balance is $160 plus the credit charge of $9.60 (0.06 × $160), which makes the total obligation $169.60. In other words, although the first store states that it makes no charge for credit, the buyer actually pays more than he does in the store that charges for the credit privilege!

We should look at our illustration carefully for yet another reason. Note that the charge was said to be $6 per $100 of credit, which sounds like 6% per annum. Since the credit is gradually reduced, the average amount outstanding is not the full amount initially advanced but slightly more than half this amount. In a very real sense, the interest cost is not 6% but rather between 11 and 12%. In the supplement to this chapter we shall examine a formula for computing such rates.

This example shows that the cost of sale credit may be difficult to evaluate, since there are several ways in which this cost may be passed on to the debtor, including any one of the following:

a) The cost of the credit may be included in the price of the merchandise.

b) Part of the cost of the credit may be included in the price of the merchandise, and there may be a nominal additional charge.

c) The full cost of the credit may be assessed as an additional charge to the purchase.

The dealer may hold the credit instrument; or he may elect to sell it to, or discount it with, one of the specialized financial agencies discussed in Chapter 17 and later in this chapter. The financing agency may or may not require the dealer to guarantee the consumer's payments. The charges made by the dealer for the credit may be the exact amount that the financing agency in turn charges for its services, or it may be greater or less than that amount. The usual procedure is for the financing agency to furnish the seller with a chart of specified charges for definite maturities, so that, in the preparation of the contract, the exact amount to be charged by the credit agency may be added to the contract as part of the total price.

It is obvious that if the merchant has sufficient capital to carry his own paper, he derives income not only from the sale of the merchandise but also from the finance charges. In addition, some stores prefer to have the customer make the payment to them, in the hope that he will buy additional merchandise that is on display at the time he visits the store to make his periodic payment. In the field of automobiles and, to some extent, appliances, it is customary for the dealer to sell his installment paper to a finance company. In the furniture field it is more common for the merchant to handle his own paper. But there are variations within fields. For example, the two leading mail-order houses for many years followed differing policies: Sears, Roebuck and Company discounted installment paper it received from sales; Montgomery Ward and Company kept its installment paper. The financing agencies that discount installment paper are, for the most part, sales finance companies and commercial banks.

Installment sale credit agreements usually make the goods sold security for the credit. It follows that the normal recourse of the creditor when payment is defaulted is to repossess the article and resell it. Credit grantors do this when necessary, but they are very reluctant to take this step. They dislike the ill will that such incidents create, and the amount recovered is often not great enough to cover the unpaid balance.

The installment loan

The installment loan differs from the installment sale credit in that it actually puts cash in the hands of the borrower. The installment borrower may elect to buy something with his money, so the end effect of the loan may not be greatly different from sale credit. The principal difference is that the agencies extending installment loan credit are quite different from those extending sale credit, as shown in Exhibit 20–2. The original objective of installment loan credit was to remedy the plight of hard-pressed, poverty-stricken people, who might otherwise fall into the hands of loan sharks or other unscrupulous lenders. The theory of the remedial loan still finds some substance in modern practice as the bill payer loan, one used to pay past debts and consolidate them in a single obligation. Most installment loans, however, serve about the same purpose as other forms of installment credit: financing the purchase of what the borrower does not have enough cash on hand to buy.

As with sale credit, the question of maturity is determined largely by the capacity of the borrower. The longer the terms the lender will grant, the larger the debt burden that the borrower may assume. The institutions extending loan credit have not been as variable in their policies as have installment sellers; the maturity terms have been more nearly constant from good times to bad times.

The cost of loan credit is more readily determinable than the cost of sale credit. In transactions involving a loan of money the borrower knows how much money he receives; when the transaction is completed, he knows how much he has repaid in interest in addition to the principal. Thus it is easy to compute an equivalent rate of interest that was charged for the loan, although the borrower may not always know in advance what his total cost will be. Since the supplement to this chapter presents a formula for approximation of this cost, it will be discussed only in general terms here.

On installment loan transactions there are two commonly accepted methods for stating charges: the *discount basis* and the *percent per month basis.* On the discount basis, a flat sum in dollars or a flat percentage is charged for the loan. Service and insurance charges are also sometimes added. The dollar amount of the charge is then deducted in advance. On the percent per month basis, a monthly rate of interest is quoted, which rate is applied to the declining unpaid principal each month that the loan is outstanding.

Almost all installment sale credit plus a large share of the loan credit is handled on the discount basis. The percent per month plan is usual for small loan companies and credit unions. Under the discount plan, the borrower knows the dollar cost of his loan, but it is difficult for him to determine the equivalent annual rate of interest that he is paying for the money borrowed, whereas if the loan is on the percent per month basis, the borrower may readily determine the annual rate by multiplying the monthly rate by 12. It is less easy, however, to compute in advance the total dollar cost of the loan.

In some cases, where a flat charge is made for a fixed period of time, there may be additional charges assessed against the borrower if the obligation is not paid according to its terms. If the interest is on a monthly percentage basis, the total cost of the loan increases automatically if payments are not made according to their original terms.

The security for installment loans varies from case to case. In the past it was common practice to require one or two additional signatures on installment loans. Sometimes cash lenders take a chattel lien on the borrower's personal possessions, such as furniture or an automobile (although the transaction is not sale credit, since it is not for the purpose of purchasing these goods). Wage assignments are sometimes obtained. The modern tendency is for lenders to rely more on the credit-worthiness of the individual and less on more specific forms of security. Unsecured notes are quite common. It is now widely recognized that consumer loans are generally repaid; the losses on them are very low. Some of the more extreme safeguards of the past have been found unnecessary.

The noninstallment loan

For many years, persons of means have been getting loans from banks for consumption purposes but in a form not materially different from business loans. Because banks prefer short-term loans, the ordinary or single-payment loan is very common. A businessman or a doctor or some other responsible person might, although temporarily short of cash, want to buy a car. He might be unwilling to borrow on an installment basis but be willing to borrow on a single-payment basis. What is more, if the bank, as a matter of accommodation, charged its ordinary business loan rate, the cost of the credit would be materially less than the installment loan rate.

While many of these short-term loans are retired promptly, many are often renewed and become, in fact, rather long-term credits. The frequently renewed single-payment loan has come to be viewed rather unfavorably by the banking community and seems to be on the way out.

These single-payment consumer loans are often secured just like any other bank loan. The persons of property who are considered satisfactory credit risks for this type of credit by banks are often the owners of securities that make very acceptable and easily manageable collateral.

In January 1970, the amount of credit in this form was estimated by the Federal Reserve to be $9.1 billion.

The pawnshop loan is another, but vastly different, form of noninstallment consumer credit. It is secured by the pledge of personal chattels, usually small and fairly high-value objects with a ready resale value. This type of credit has had a long and not always respectable history, but it is of small and shrinking importance. Other agencies are, more and more, displacing the pawnshop.

Still another type of noninstallment credit is the loan-shark payday loan. Those who have been in the Army will recognize the 4 for 5 or the 9 for 10 loan: you borrow $4 now and repay $5 on payday, or you borrow $9 now and repay $10.

The Uniform Small Loan Law and the small loan companies, which will be discussed later, were devised to meet the social need for credit that the loan shark disclosed. Loan sharks now operate mainly in states where there are no regulated small loan companies or where the money is needed for illegal activities.

Although often pictured as a vicious and degraded character, the loan shark has sometimes deserved a better reputation. Under circumstances that encouraged competition and in closely knit communities, such as foreign language groups, where social approval or disapproval conditioned his policies, the traditional loan shark appears often to have been a fairly useful citizen who performed many of the functions now undertaken by the regulated small loan company. Many modern loan sharks, however, deserve no such approbation.

Life insurance companies are required to lend their policyholders amounts which are equal to, or a large percentage of, individual policy reserves. (For an explanation of policy reserves, see Chapter 12.) These loans are not included in the statistics of consumer credit shown above, nor have they been elsewhere considered. They can, however, be looked upon as a form of consumer credit. For many families they are the best and cheapest source of such credit. Where families have control of their finances so that they can borrow on their insurance without jeopardizing the insurance protection, there are many great advantages in the use of this source of funds.

The record of insurance policy loans shows them more likely to be remedial in their use than the so-called remedial loans. Unlike the consumer loans, which increase in good times (when remedial needs are presumably least) and decrease in bad times (when remedial needs are presumably the most), insurance policy loans do the reverse. They hit a peak of $3.8 billion in 1932. This was more than 21% of total policy reserves. The dollar volume of such loans dwindled for a time but then rose. In relation to total insurance reserves, loans in 1969 at a level of $11.5 billion were only 8% of policy reserves.

A form of credit procedure that has gained wide acceptance in recent years involves the credit card. A retailer, bank, or financial company may issue a credit card to a customer. When the individual makes a purchase, he hands the card to the seller. A record of the transaction is made. If the card is acceptable to the seller but is issued by another organization, the effect is to turn the transaction into a cash sale for the seller. It is a credit purchase for the buyer. The terms of credit card transactions usually call for payment in full at the time of billing without an additional credit charge. The buyer, however, usually has the option to decide to pay the price in installments over a number of months. If he selects that option he agrees also to pay a charge, often of 12 or 18% per annum, on the outstanding balance over the period he chooses to pay installments. The extent of use of this credit procedure is obviously widespread, but separate data on the amount outstanding are not available.

The noninstallment sale credit

The commonest form of noninstallment sale credit is the familiar charge account at the department, grocery, or clothing store. Other and closely related forms are the credit extended by public utilities—telephone, electric light and power, and gas companies—and also the credit extended by doctors and dentists. There is even some credit of this type extended by such nonprofit institutions as colleges and hospitals.

A great deal of short-term sale credit is extended for the mutual convenience of the creditor and the debtor. For example, a monthly charge account at a department store eliminates the necessity of paying for individual purchases in cash and permits settlement of the entire month's business by one payment when the bill is rendered.

Although much of this credit is for convenience, it often involves a very real anticipation of income. Only slightly more than half the charge accounts in city department stores are paid the first time the customer is billed; almost half wait for the second or subsequent billing. The average period outstanding is about 60 days. In rural areas of the country the collection of charge accounts is even slower; and in some cases, such as the sharecropper credits of the South, the consumer is carried for substantial periods on charge account credit.

There are also some kinds of charge account credit that lie in the twilight zone between charge and installment credit. Some stores advertise: "Charge your spring clothing purchases and pay your bill in three installments."

The dollar figure of noninstallment sale credit is sizable; in January 1970 it was $10.3 billion.

Institutions that advance consumer credit

The student may now find it convenient to refer once more to Exhibit 20–2 appearing on page 468. As this diagram shows, several types of agencies extend consumer credit; some agencies are active in more than one field. The commercial banks, for example, are shown in five different places; sales finance companies in three; and even retail stores in two different roles. Consumer credit is the major business of some of these lending agencies; with others it is just a sideline, usually undertaken in order to facilitate the use of credit in promotional selling.

The institutions that make cash loans to consumers usually carry these loans themselves. Those who sell goods or services and use credit as a supplement to their main business of selling often dispose of the credits they originate; they transfer them to specialists in that business. The major institutions that either discount or lend on consumer credit receivables are the sales finance companies and the commercial banks.

Sales finance operations

Some sales finance companies were operating prior to World War I, but their real growth did not take place until after 1915. During the years 1915–29 these companies expanded with the automobile industry. The major ones were, indeed, subsidiaries of the automobile manufacturers. The major one still so connected is the General Motors Acceptance Corporation. Automobile paper still represents the largest portion of the business handled by sales finance companies. There are both large and small sales finance concerns. There are a few national companies with hundreds of branch offices, a number of regional companies with branches, and many individual companies with single offices. It should be remembered that sales finance companies do not lend money but, instead, discount (buy) paper acquired by merchants and dealers.

By purchasing this paper from the merchants, sales finance companies are not ordinarily affected by usury laws. Their discount charge, reduced to a true interest rate basis, is usually in excess of the maximum legal rate of interest.

It is customary for the sales finance company to furnish its dealer-customers with conditional-sale contract forms and rate charts and also to procure insurance in connection with the financing of installment sales. The merchant makes his contract with the purchaser and then offers the installment purchase contract to the finance company. If the deal is satisfactory to the finance company, it purchases the contract from the merchant.

This discounting may be on a recourse basis, whereby the merchant assumes the risk of bad debt losses and takes back from the credit agency any delinquent paper; or it may be on a nonrecourse basis, whereby the merchant has no liability and the credit agency assumes any bad debt losses. A third plan is a combination of these two: the merchant and the credit agency may share the credit losses, with a limit being placed on the loss of one or the other. As an inducement to the merchant to discount the obligation with a particular financing agency, it is a common practice for the financing agency to rebate to the merchant a portion of the original amount charged to the buyer of the merchandise for the credit accommodation.

Most retail-sales financing operations are combined with a closely related function—financing of the dealer. For example, the sales finance concerns that buy installment paper from automobile dealers will also finance the dealer's inventory of cars. There are various plans of wholesale financing or floor planning. Usually these credits are secured by the automobiles or other merchandise financed, and the dealer obtains custody through a trust receipt.

The field of sales finance is not dominated by a single leader. Because these concerns do not deal so directly with the public, their names are not as well known as some other names in finance. The General Motors Acceptance Corporation, affiliated with General Motors, is an almost pure sales financing operation. The Commercial Credit Company (CCC) and the CIT Financial Corporation are largely sales finance concerns, but they also engage in other financing operations.

Sales financing operations have not been regulated for as long as direct consumer lending. They still are not regulated in many states, but regulation is becoming more common. The usual form of regulation is to require full disclosure of all charges, and sometimes the circumstances in which collateral security may be repossessed is subject to control.

The sales finance pack, which was often met in earlier years, is now much less common. The pack was an amount added by the seller to the ordinary financing charges and retained by him so that he might make a larger amount on a credit sale than on a cash sale. Thus there was an incentive to sell credit wherever possible—that is, induce the buyer to take merchandise on time rather than pay cash for it.

Commercial banks

It was mentioned earlier that commercial banks were rather slow in entering the field of consumer installment credit. However, since 1934 their activities have expanded rapidly, and it is estimated that today nearly 90% of the commercial banks have some stake in installment credit. Some commercial banks extend installment sale credit by virtue of discounting dealer paper, but many commercial banks also make direct installment cash loans. Banks were attracted to this field for two principal reasons: first, to provide income when commercial loans were at a low point and, second, as a means of improving their public relations. The banks have found that by meeting the credit needs of the average individual they build goodwill in the community.

Once the banks became active in the field, they grew faster than the other lenders for a while. This is natural because of the large number of banks and their wide dispersion. The fixed charges of banking can be spread over their entire business, and commercial banks sought out the larger and safer consumer loans. The rates quoted by banks for installment loans tend to be somewhat lower than those quoted by other credit agencies—the range of discount charged by banks has been from $4 to $6 per $100 per year. In the high interest period of 1969 and 1970, it might have been $9 per $100 per year. Many commercial banks have established separate consumer credit departments to make direct loans.

Commercial banks are also active in the sales finance field. They operate in much the same way as sales finance companies through the discounting of paper in the hands of merchants. Since 1934 they have acquired an increasing portion of the business, and in general they operate at rates slightly lower than those charged by the finance companies.

Small loan companies

The small loan company was an almost direct outgrowth of the effort to curb and regulate the loan shark. Since the efforts at prohibition of extortionate lending practices usually failed, the alternative was to bring the business into the open and regulate it. These regulations were aimed at allowing rates that covered the cost of this business but that outlawed the exorbitant charges loan sharks had sometimes made. Pennsylvania, New York, Massachusetts, New Jersey, and Ohio all played a role in the development of this type of experimental legislation. The Massachusetts law was one of the first to be considered workable by the professional lending companies. The plans for making small loans in this early legislation were soon copied, with variations, by several other states. The Russell Sage Foundation, established in 1907, sponsored studies and issued a report that led to the drafting of the first Uniform Small Loan Law. This law, or a modification, has been enacted by 49 states. The original law required interest to be quoted on a percent per month basis. This feature has been retained in all revisions of the model small loan law. The original act recommended a rate of $3\frac{1}{2}\%$ per month (42% a year) on unpaid balances and a limit of $300 for initial loans. The small loan limit of $300 prevailed for many years, but with higher price levels, this limit has been raised in most states.

The rate of interest has been the subject of legislative action in several states. Lenders claim that if the rate is set too low they cannot do business; a rate between 2% and 3% a month is now common. Some states set a rate of 3% a month on small loans of $100 or less, with 2 or $2\frac{1}{2}\%$ on the portion of the loan over that amount. The interest charge is calculated on the unpaid balance. If the borrower pays his loan in advance, he reduces the amount of interest paid proportionately. On a loan of $100 in Illinois, repayable in 12 months, the amount of interest collected at the legal rate of 3% a month, with uniform monthly payments, is $20.56. Small loan companies are not allowed to make any additional charges in the way of delinquency fees, fines, or other handling charges.

Recently there have been upward revisions of the $300 loan limit, some states permitting as much as $5,000. In most states where such high limits are set, the legislation provides for a lower interest rate on the larger portion of all loans.

Small loan companies make secured and unsecured loans. The unsecured loans are based on the borrower's character and ability to repay. The secured loans are usually made on a chattel mortgage basis against furniture or automobiles or electrical appliances.

It is necessary under the small loan laws for companies to obtain a license for each office they intend to operate. Usually some state officer supervises the activities of the various licensed offices. State regulation of small loan offices usually has the primary goal of curbing practices that exploit borrowers. Many offices are controlled by a single company. In fact, two leading small loan companies control several hundred offices throughout the country. About one quarter of the capital for small loan companies is supplied by the owners. Some companies have debenture bond issues outstanding, and many borrow from commercial banks.

Small loan companies are mass marketing operations; to succeed, they must attract business from many individuals. For this reason they use the advertising vehicles appropriate for mass merchandising. They have spot commercials on television: "Need money? Call the Blank Loan Company, Farmers 6–6666, for prompt service. No endorsers required; if you have a steady job you can have up to 24 months to repay. Remember, Farmers 6–6666 for prompt loan service." They also use classified advertisements, streetcar poster advertisements, and neon signs.

There are many small loan companies, but the biggest and best known is the Household Finance Corporation. This concern and its subsidiaries operate over 1,500 offices in 31 states and in Canada. At the end of 1969 it had $15½ billion outstanding in installment loans. The Beneficial Loan Corporation is another large small loan company.

Industrial banks and industrial loan companies

In 1910, Arthur Morris of Virginia organized the first industrial bank. The Morris Plan spread to other cities under local ownership. Fundamentally, the Morris Plan provides that the maximum legal rate of interest will be charged for the term of the loan. Certain additional fees for credit investigation or for recording of necessary documents are often added. By the terms of the agreement the borrower is obligated to make uniform deposits at regular intervals in a savings account so that, at the maturity date of the loan, there will be on deposit an amount sufficient to pay the loan.

This plan, with modifications, is the basic one used by all industrial banking companies. It worked so well that many commercial banks adopted it. In some states special legislation was passed to permit the operation of industrial banks, although ordinarily they operate under the regular statutory interest limit. The courts have usually found that the deposit contract that results in a higher effective rate does not violate the usury limit. Originally, industrial banks made the bulk of their loans on a comaker basis and confined their operation within the limits of the Morris Plan. The industrial loan companies and banks used to be a distinct type of institution. Many of them included the words *Morris Plan* in their corporate title, but this practice has dwindled. Some have changed their name and dropped the old title. Through the years their activities have broadened, and many have become commercial banks specializing in the consumer credit field, while others have become, for all practical purposes, either sales finance companies or small loan companies.

Charges for loans quoted by industrial banks and industrial loan companies are usually on an annual discount basis, the rates ranging from 5 to 9%. In addition, there is usually a handling or investigation fee of 2% for each loan. Unsecured single-name loans usually carry the highest rate, with comaker and secured loans being given more favorable rates. A typical transaction would be a loan of $100 for 12 months at an interest cost of $6 plus a $2 investigation fee, making the total cost $8. The borrower signs a note for $108 in such a case but receives $100 in cash. Since the $108 is repaid in equal monthly installments, the borrower has an average indebtedness of about $54 over the entire year. Thus the interest cost is not 6% but somewhere between 14 and 15%. Additional fees may be collected from the borrower if he is delinquent; these fees may range up to 5% of the amount of the delinquent payment.

Industrial banking companies usually are banks of deposit, so that a large part of their funds represent the savings or checking accounts of their customers, who in some cases may also be borrowers. The industrial loan companies may, in some states, sell certificates of deposit; and in effect, they are somewhat similar to savings banks in this regard. However, they usually cannot extend checking account privileges, and supervision is not so detailed as it is in the case of savings and commercial banks.

Credit unions

Credit unions originated in Europe and were introduced to this country around 1909. They first spread widely in Massachusetts. Credit unions are now authorized by special legislation in most states. There are 24,000 credit unions with consumer loans of $11 billion. They charge various rates on loans, but most use a rate of 1% per month on unpaid principal balances.

Credit unions are in some ways similar to savings and loan associations in that they have savings share accounts; and they are similar to small loan companies in that they are allowed to charge rates for loans usually in excess of the normal legal rate. They are mutual organizations and may be organized under either federal or state charter. The first credit union in the United States was chartered under state authority (New Hampshire). During the next 25 years the movement spread slowly, with more and more states enacting permissive or charter legislation. Edward A. Filene, the philanthropic Boston merchant, was deeply interested in the movement and helped it in many ways. The most rapid period of expansion came after 1934, however, when legislation for the federal chartering of credit unions was adopted.

Participating or shareholding members of credit unions receive dividends. Credit unions often vary their dividends considerably from year to year, depending on earnings. In this they are more like industrial corporations, in which dividends vary, than like savings and loan associations or mutual savings banks, in which efforts are made to keep dividend rates steady, to change them only infrequently.

The most fertile ground for the organization of credit unions has been among those working for the same employer. While a church or neighborhood or trade union is often the basis for organization, the plant or place of business is the most common unit.

The affiliated organization (such as the employer or labor union) often provides the credit union with operating facilities and assumes many of the routine expenses, so that credit unions normally have a relatively low cost of doing business. One basic weakness of any credit union organized within one industry, more particularly when limited to employees of one concern, is the lack of diversification of risk. Ordinarily, nearly all the members will have excess funds when the industry or concern is prosperous, and nearly all may need funds when the industry suffers or when the plant closes down. (For a further discussion of the credit union industry see Chapter 11.)

The pro and con of consumer credit

Installment credit has been the target of much criticism. The main argument of the critics used to be that installment credit is a mortgage on the future of families with limited means. But families are faced with economic emergencies from time to time that require the borrowing of money. Lending agencies should be available to meet this need at a reasonable cost. If legitimate lenders are not accessible, history has shown that people will borrow money when they need it, wherever it may be available, and will pay any rate necessary to get it. It is from such experiences that we get the term *loan shark*. Emergency credit extended for the liquidation of existing indebtedness or for purposes such as hospital and medical expenses (and other items of similar nature) is generally considered to be remedial credit and is regarded as a necessary type of borrowing.

Many families find it difficult to accumulate large amounts of cash with which to make major purchases, whereas they will meet obligations incurred as the result of purchasing a major item, such as an automobile or a refrigerator; and in addition, they have the benefit of the use of the article while they are paying for it. In other words, installment purchasing is, in effect, a form of forced saving into which people willingly enter to acquire ownership of furniture, automobiles, appliances, and other household goods. Although installment credit does not include residential real estate credit, most families purchase their home on the installment basis; they also acquire a life insurance estate through making monthly or annual payments on a policy. It is easy to see the effectiveness of a periodic payment program when we realize that most people receive their income on a weekly or monthly basis.

It has been argued that the cost of the credit extended reduces the purchasing power of the family and that, as a result, the members of the family do not obtain as many goods as they would if they had accumulated the money and paid cash. However, without installment selling, the total production of many of these articles presumably would be lower and the price higher. Installment sales create a wider market and perhaps lower the cost of production. Although there is a charge made for the credit, the net cost of the article purchased may be no higher than it would be in a market without consumer credit.

Another major criticism of consumer credit is that it costs too much.

The per month rates of small loan companies, put on an annual basis, shock many who have become accustomed to reading the prime rate figures for business credits and investment returns. These rates are not comparable however.

The making of loans involves fixed charges; each loan, no matter how small, costs some minimum amount. If an interviewer sees the applicant for half an hour; if a credit investigator spends an hour checking the application; and if a bookkeeper puts in no more than a few minutes setting up the account, the minimum first cost for a loan is likely to be at least $6 and other costs, as much as $30. This amount would be only a small fraction of a sizable loan; but it amounts to more than 65% of the average principal balance of a loan that starts out at $100 and is paid off in equal installments in one year.

The above factors should be kept in mind when consumer credit rates are compared with rates for other types of loans. Because of these factors, the net return to the lender on funds invested in consumer credit loans is generally not excessively higher than the net return on commercial loan transactions, even though there is a wide difference in the quoted rates of interest for the two classes of business.

With respect to installment sale credit, the seller may quote a comparatively low rate for credit as a means of attracting customers. However, since he cannot escape the basic cost of handling installment credit transactions, the actual rate is usually concealed in a higher price for the merchandise or a discount statement of interest.

The many important advantages of consumer credit must be balanced against its possible disadvantages. Devices of promotion and advertising work so effectively that many persons are persuaded to become more indebted than may be prudent. Improvidence is as old as frail human nature, and the relative ease of getting into debt may aggravate this situation. The concerns that grant credit cannot be particularly blamed for this; to call them merchants of debt, as some do, exaggerates their responsibility. They cannot be expected to be the financial guardians of their clients, even though many responsible firms try to serve this purpose too. Only in connection with general economic stability does consumer credit raise serious problems.

Economic stability and consumer credit

Perhaps the most important, but much disputed, charge made against consumer credit is that it contributes to economic instability. All credit permits the borrower to make purchases that he might not make at that time without credit. If credit is extended freely during good times and then the credit grantors press collection of outstanding credit during bad times, there is a tendency for buyers to bunch purchases when times are

EXHIBIT 20–3

Relation of consumer installment credit to disposable personal income*

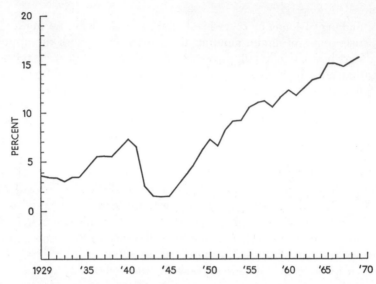

* Amount of consumer installment credit outstanding at end of year as percentage of disposabie income for the year.
Source: Computed from data published by the Board of Governors of the Federal Reserve System and Department of Commerce.

good and curtail them excessively in bad times. The record of the past shows that many forms of credit have this characteristic. There is nothing about consumer credit that makes it necessarily a worse performer or a better one than other forms of credit; the test is in its record. But repayment of consumer credit, extended freely during good times, has been made during bad times at the expense of other needs. Consumer purchases of durable goods fluctuate more violently over various phases of the business cycle than some other kinds of consumer buying.

There is no doubt that the volume of consumer credit itself has fluctuated widely and corresponds in some degree to other economic fluctuations. The examination of only the dollar figures of consumer credit, however, tends to exaggerate the degree of variability. When viewed as a proportion of disposable personal income, consumer installment credit has varied quite widely, as shown in Exhibit 20–3. This chart shows a range of from 0 to 15½% in the ratio of credit to income, but in the recent years, it shows remarkable stability about a growing rate, reflecting higher purchases of durable goods in our society.

Nevertheless, there is doubt at times about the necessary virtues of consumer installment credit. During the automobile sales races of 1955 and, again, to some extent in 1959–60, sales were influenced almost certainly by the extensions of maturities and reductions of down payments offered by installment sellers. In 1955, in particular, maturities were extended from 24 months to 36 months, and in a few instances to 42 months. Down payments—often through overvaluation of trade-ins—were reduced to zero. The extent to which the public committed itself in that year to payments during the next three years, 1956–58, probably influenced economic trends in those years. Irresponsible merchandising, together with public gullibility, could turn a useful financial institution into a source of social danger, even though the fundamental reasons for believing that consumer credit contributes to economic instability are very weak.

Regulation W

During World War II, consumer credit was subject to special control as a means of fighting inflation. With the supply of consumer goods scarce, the administration elected to limit the extension of credit to buyers able to make larger than usual payments so as to take some pressure off prices. Credit was particularly restricted for those types of goods in short supply, but all credit was curbed to some extent by raising minimum down payments and shortening maximum maturity requirements.

In the postwar period this type of control of credit was continued until November 1947. It was then allowed to lapse. Less than one year later— August 1948—in the special session of Congress devoted to inflation, control of consumer credit was reinstated on a temporary basis, but this provision was permitted to lapse without renewal on June 30, 1949. Again, because of the inflationary spurt stimulated by the Korean War, the control of consumer credit represented by Regulation W was imposed in October 1950. The regulation was continued for about a year and a half and was suspended in May 1952.

For a while during the postwar period, the Federal Reserve was involved in trying to support treasury security prices and at the same time preserving some semblance of credit control (see Chapter 7). While it was attempting these difficult and conflicting roles, there was some sentiment for the use of Regulation W as a permanent measure for economic stabilization. Since the Federal Reserve has been freed of the obligation to support treasury security prices, however, this sentiment has dwindled and largely vanished. From time to time, it has been pointed out that increases in the volume of consumer credit were high, perhaps dangerously high, but few have proposed governmental regulation as a measure to cure this situation.

Supplement: Computation of consumer credit interest rates and charges

The precise computation of consumer credit interest charges and monthly payments involves more complex techniques and difficult questions of definition than can be introduced here. Satisfactory results, however, can be obtained by simple methods. A single approximation formula, in two forms, is adequate for the calculation of almost all consumer credit interest problems. The formula in both forms is:

$$R = \frac{2 \times m \times I}{P(n+1)}$$

or, transposed,

$$I = \frac{R \times P(n+1)}{2 \times m},$$

where:

R = annual simple interest rate (in decimal form),
I = dollar cost of the credit (interest),
m = number of payment periods in a year (12 if monthly, 52 if weekly),
n = number of payments scheduled, and
P = net amount of credit advanced (principal).

Application of the formula may be illustrated as follows:

Example 1. Suppose you should apply to a bank or an industrial loan company for a loan of $100 to be repaid over a period of one year. You are told that the discount charge is $6 and that a service fee of $2 is also required. This makes a total cost of $8. The problem: Find the rate of interest. The solution is obtained by using the first of the forms shown above:

$I = \$8,$
$m = 12$ (12 monthly payments in a year),
$n = 12$ (number of payments on this loan),
$P = \$100,$
$R = \dfrac{2 \times 12 \times 8}{100 \times (12+1)} = 0.148 = 14.8\%.$

Example 2. The interest rate at a credit union is 1% of the unpaid balance. You wish to find the dollar cost of borrowing $100 for one year. For this purpose use the second form of the formula:

$$P = \$100,$$
$$m \text{ and } n = 12,$$
$$R = 12\% \ (1\% \text{ a month}),$$
$$I = \frac{0.12 \times \$100 \ (12 + 1)}{24} = \$6.50.$$

Example 3. You note from an advertising poster in a streetcar that a small loan company will lend you $100 for one year for a monthly payment of $9.96. You want to find out the rate of interest. The formula to be used is the first of the two forms shown above. But first some preparatory computations must be made. A monthly payment of $9.96 multiplied by 12 means that the annual payments are $119.52. The interest cost is, therefore, $19.52 (since you subtract the $100 from the total annual payments). Since $19.52 is I, you can compute the rate thus:

$$R = \frac{2 \times 12 \times \$19.52}{\$100(12 + 1)} = 0.360 \text{ or } 36\%.$$

Example 4. You are dickering for a new car. Your present car is considered a satisfactory down payment. You are trying to determine the interest rate cost of buying on time. The cash payment you have to make would be $1,500 in addition to the car you turn in. You are offered the privilege of paying for the car over 18 months at the rate of $100 a month. The monthly payments would also include the cost of the insurance ($180 for 18 months). The first form of the formula shown above will supply the answer, but certain preparatory computations must be made. The 18 monthly payments ($1,800) less the cost of the insurance leaves a "time payment" total cost of $1,620. This is $120 more than the cash cost. This amount is I. The other parts of the formula are as follows:

$$m = 12,$$
$$n = 18,$$
$$P = \$1,500,$$
$$R = \frac{2 \times 12 \times \$120}{\$1,500(18 + 1)} = 0.101 \text{ or } 10.1\%.$$

Questions and problems

1. Clip advertisements from a current newspaper illustrating as many kinds of consumer credit as you can find. Identify each type according to the plan of classification used in this chapter.
2. Why is it hard to prosecute loan sharks?
3. Why did the growth of automobile sales and usage depend on the availability of consumer credit of an appropriate kind in adequate amounts?

4. What is the security behind most installment sale credits?

5. What is the security behind most installment loans?

6. Rate the various sources of consumer credit with reference to the average cost of credit.

7. How free is installment sale credit, even though there may be "no carrying charge"?

8. Do you favor the peacetime regulation of consumer credit to reduce economic fluctuations? Why?

9. A credit jeweler advertises a watch for $50 with "no down payment, no carrying charge, and only $1 a week." The same watch can be purchased for $45 in a department store. What is the implicit annual interest rate involved in buying the watch from the credit jeweler?

10. A $200 loan from a small loan company at 3% a month is to be repaid in equal installments over a 15-month period. Approximately what are the monthly installments?

11. In buying a car a $1,000 balance needs to be financed. The dealer offers to finance this for $50 monthly payments over the next two years. The dealer also declares that the finance charge is $6 a year per $100. Is there a pack in this deal? If so, how much approximately?

12. An industrial bank charges a discount of $4 a year per $100, and also a service fee of $2 regardless of the maturity of the loan. What is the approximate rate of interest for a one-year loan? For a two-year loan?

Bibliography

The most important recent study—and a very comprehensive exploration of all kinds of information on consumer credit—is the six-part *Consumer Instalment Credit* study of the Federal Reserve Board, released in 1957. Prior to this time, the National Bureau of Economic Research staff had published 10 monographs on the subject. Of these, the summary economic study by Gottfried Haberler, *Consumer Instalment Credit and Economic Fluctuations* (New York: National Bureau of Economic Research, Inc., 1942) is probably the most interesting. All of them represent basic contributions to the knowledge of the subject, however.

Current information is made available most conveniently in each issue of the *Federal Reserve Bulletin*. The same information is reproduced later in the *Journal of Marketing* and the *Industrial Banker,* among other trade publications. A basic study of historical importance is that made by Rolf Nugent, *Consumer Credit and Economic Stability* (New York: Russell Sage Foundation, Inc., 1939).

CHAPTER 21

Residential real estate finance

Although the financing of housing has much in common with the other fields of financing discussed thus far, and especially with other consumer financing, it nevertheless has distinguishing characteristics. The social and political implications of housing, for example, are so broad that they cannot be discussed in detail in this chapter. We are a nation of homeowners: 6 of 10 nonfarm families own their own homes. Public interest in housing is one of the factors that distinguishes this field of financing from others.

The size of investment in real property—i.e., land and property permanently affixed to land—and the size of the markets for such property also affect financing in this field. More than half the wealth of the United States is invested in real property. In 1960, the market value of the investment in owner-occupied homes was estimated to be $450 billion. Roughly 10% of the national income originates in construction of real property, rentals and interest on real estate indebtedness, and payments for the services of brokers, lawyers, insurance companies, and others who assist buyers and sellers in the real estate markets.

The median price for houses transferred in 1969 was about $30,000. Four fifths of the transfers involved mortgage financing. The average mortgage was $21,500, about seven tenths of the purchase price of the house. The estimated value of houses was, on the average, slightly over twice the income of owners. Approximately 20% of the income of the average spending unit was spent on housing and household operation.

The problems that most directly influence the methods of financing in this field, however, stem from two important characteristics of the financing: as noted above, more than 75% of all single-family homes are purchased on long-term credit; and the price of real estate is subject to some fluctuation. The long-term nature of real estate credit transactions emphasizes the necessity for security behind loans. The type of security usually taken is the right to repayment from the proceeds obtained from the sale of property owned by the debtor. The security is, however, no better than the opportunity afforded the creditor to recover amounts due by this sale of property. Sharp swings of real estate prices become of considerable importance to a creditor in attempting to determine how secure his position actually is.

In this chapter we shall discuss the credit principles and practices now in use, the extent to which credit is used in real estate transactions, the types of institutions that supply funds to the real estate market, and the agencies of the federal government that are active in the financing of real estate.

Credit principles and practices

In making secured loans, creditors must place emphasis on both the nature of the assets securing the loan and the characteristics of the borrower to whom the loan is made. Generally, the longer the term of a loan, the greater the emphasis that must be placed on an analysis of the security behind the loan.

Appraisal

Analysis of security begins with an appraisal of the property, i.e., a determination of its value. Real estate loans are generally for a large proportion of the value of the property against which they are made. Loans of from 80 to 95% of the market value of the property are quite common in residential financing. When the margin between value and amount of loan is as narrow as these figures indicate, the creditor must appraise the property carefully before he can safely advance funds.

The appraisal of real estate values is not easily accomplished. Each unit has individual characteristics. The appraiser does not have the guide offered by comparison with exactly similar units currently sold, as might be the case in, say, the market for automobiles. It is possible to make an estimate of the cost that would be incurred to construct a similar building on the same land—that is, to estimate reproduction cost—and then estimate the extent to which existing real property has depreciated from "new." This approach, however, is obviously more easily applied to property recently constructed than to property of considerable age, and it does not provide a useful guide to the measurement of the value of land on which other property is constructed. Another approach to appraisal is the estimate of all the future benefits—for example, rentals—which the owner will get and the present price that such a stream of future benefits should command. In other words, the appraiser can look at past, present, and future. He can estimate past costs, adjusted to present conditions; he can estimate present selling price, based on current market prices for other real estate; and he can estimate the present worth of the future stream of benefits that an owner would receive. At best, an appraisal value is the summation of informed opinions. Real estate evaluation is a field that calls for specialists.

Legal documents

A second phase of analysis of the security behind a loan is the determination of the legal position of the debtor. If the creditor, in case of default, is to depend for protection on taking possession of property, it is important to establish the debtor's ability to provide the security. This involves knowledge of the instruments of real estate finance and inspections to see that all legal steps have been properly taken.

The instruments of real estate finance are more detailed in character than for most other credit transactions because of the nature of real estate itself. Real estate is immobile; each parcel is unique. Possession does not indicate ownership. Ownership of real estate is transferred not by change of possession but by the passing of a legal document called a deed. Because relatively large sums of money are involved in the ownership of real estate, parties to a transaction take precautions not typically found in other dealings.

Evidence of title. Before anyone may safely loan money on the security of real estate, he must make certain that full ownership of the property is actually in the name of the borrower, and he must further make certain that no other claims to the property are outstanding.

There are a number of systems followed to assure the validity of a person's title, the most common of which is to have a lawyer examine an abstract or make a search of the records filed in the county recorder's office. In many cities there are title companies, which insure the owner of real estate against the risk that title to the property may not be in his name and which promise to compensate him for loss if some other person later proves to have title to the property. In a few areas, the county government issues a certificate of title known as a Torrens certificate, which is a guaranty of the validity of title to property.

The mortgage instrument. A real estate loan is, in almost every case, accompanied by a mortgage (or by a trust deed, which is used in some states as a substitute for the ordinary mortgage). A mortgage, briefly defined, is a transfer of title to property, given by a debtor to a creditor as security for the payment of a debt—with the provision that the transfer is void if the debt is paid by the day named and if interest payments are made as promised. The debt itself is always evidenced by a note similar in its essential parts to any promissory note except that it includes a reference to an accompanying mortgage.

In the very early days of the use of mortgages in England and early in the history of this country, the lender could immediately take possession under the transfer of title given in the mortgage if the borrower failed to make his interest and principal payments on the exact due date. Frequently the lender might even take possession of the property at the time the loan was made and might retain it until the loan had been paid. Such stringent interpretations of the transfer of title have been greatly modified by statutes and by court decisions. The law now generally takes the view that it is unreasonable for the lender to retain full value of the property when it was merely transferred as security for a debt. A mortgage in many states is simply a claim to proceeds from the sale of specific property when a court orders such a sale to satisfy creditor claims under debt agreements. The creditor has a right only to proceeds from the sale of the property up to amounts owing to him. Present-day law in most states also provides that borrowers have a right to redeem pledged property within a reasonable time after the debt has been defaulted and the property has been forfeited to the lender. This right is known as the equity of redemption.

A typical instrument used in home loan financing includes the date, names of the borrower and lender, exact legal description of the property, brief statement of the amount of the debt, and the promise to repay the debt according to the agreed schedule with interest payments on agreed dates. Such an instrument usually includes promises or covenants as follows: to pay all taxes, special assessments, and other charges levied by the local government upon the property; to keep the property in good repair and not to permit any waste of the property; to keep the property fully insured against fire, windstorm, and other hazards as the lender may require; not to permit the property to be used for any unlawful purpose; and to allow no substantial changes, alterations, or additions to the property without the creditor's permission. Finally, the instrument is signed by the borrower, witnessed, and notarized.

Land contract. Sometimes people buy property without paying the full purchase price in cash but by signing a long-term land contract. This is a form of installment sales contract whereby the purchaser agrees to pay for the property in installments, frequently running for as much as 20 years with interest paid on the unpaid portion of the contract price.

In essence, the land contract performs the same function as the combination of mortgage and mortgage note just described above.

Costs. Because of the detailed nature of title verification and the necessity of either a title insurance policy or careful examination of an abstract by an attorney, together with the charge for recording a mortgage in the county recorder's office, it may cost from $100 to $500 to cover legal, title, and recording fees alone. Typically, these closing charges are paid by the borrower.

The complexities of mortgage loan laws and protection granted borrowers under state laws give rise to substantial expenses on the part of the lender if the borrower defaults on his loan and it becomes necessary to foreclose on the mortgage property and acquire title by purchase at the foreclosure sale. In some states—for example, Illinois and Kansas—it may take from 14 to 20 months to acquire possession and a marketable title to property through a foreclosure sale. In Illinois, the state with the highest foreclosure costs, the expenses of acquiring property through payment of attorney's fees, sheriff's fees, court costs, costs of title search, etc., may run to $500 or $1,000 or more on a home foreclosure. In only about half the states may a lender acquire a marketable title to property through foreclosure in less than one year and at a cost of $250 or less.

Adaptation of loan to borrower's capacity

If the creditor is assured that the security is good, then he must also assure himself that the terms of the loan agreement are adapted to the borrower's capacity to meet future payments.

Loan terms in the 1920s. During the 1920s the emphasis placed on the borrower's ability to meet the payments stipulated in a loan contract was not so great as it is today. Most real estate loans were loans for which the note and mortgage provided the entire principal amount that would be due on one final maturity date. Interest payments were usually made at six-month intervals. The final interest payment and the maturity date were commonly five years from the loan date. During the interim, no payments on principal were acquired. The borrower was expected to make provision for the accumulation of a sum sufficient to meet the payments when due. In practice, loans were frequently renewed because, at the maturity date, the borrower could pay some, but not all, of the principal of the loan and it was necessary to negotiate a new loan for the balance. As a result, loans on a creditor's books were seldom shown to be in default, but there was often little information as to the borrower's ability to meet the final payment when it fell due.

The relation between amounts loaned and the value of property securing loans in the 1920s appears conservative at first glance. Because of law and custom, few first-mortgage loans amounted to more than 50 to 60% of appraised value. On the other hand, few borrowers were in the position to make down payments amounting to 40 or 50% of the purchase price of property. Therefore, in the 1920s a substantial business in second- and third-mortgage loans developed. A person buying a house at a purchase price of $12,000 would borrow $6,000 on a first mortgage, $3,000 on a second mortgage, and pay the remaining $3,000 from his own savings. If he did not have as much as 25% of the purchase price saved, he might even borrow the remaining $3,000 on a third mortgage. The interest rate on the first mortgage would probably have been 6%, and the second- and third-mortgage loans would bear interest at rates within the range of 10–20% a year. Unlike first mortgages, second and third mortgages would probably require payments of both interest and principal at monthly or quarterly intervals. The principal of these junior claims would be repaid before the maturity date on the senior mortgage.

Depression experience. In the general depression of the early 1930s, weaknesses in real estate credit practice became apparent. Borrowers did not accumulate sufficient funds with which to meet the final payment on mortgage debt within the five-year periods for which loan agreements ran. They depended upon renewal. Even those who had saved a considerable portion toward repayment of mortgage indebtedness found their savings dwindling as the depression continued. Creditors could not collect amounts as they fell due, and yet the creditors themselves were under pressures to meet their own expenses. The rate of foreclosure increased rapidly as creditors tried to enforce their rights. The ensuing debacle aroused public attention and caused a number of states to pass laws by which debtors were relieved of the immediate necessity to pay off the principal of loans, although, as a rule, they were expected to continue paying interest. This type of remedial action weakened the position of creditors, who then had no way in which to withdraw funds invested in real estate loans. Congress took steps in 1933 to bring relief to both debtor and creditor by establishing an agency to buy and hold mortgages. Steps were also taken toward adaptation of loan terms to borrower capacity to pay.

Current practice. The lessons of depression are reflected in current almost universal acceptance of amortized loans which are common not only in residential real estate financing but also for commercial and industrial credits. By the terms of an amortized loan, the borrower agrees to make regular payments on principal as well as of interest. The loan is gradually reduced and finally paid off within an agreed period of years. At the same time, the loan period is much longer than formerly, so that the borrower may be expected to make the necessary payments and retire the loan without seeking renewal and without borrowing on junior mortgages. Under current practice, a first-mortgage loan may amount to as much, in proportion to the value of the property, as combined first and second (and perhaps third) mortgages did in the 1920s—that is, 80 to 90%.

Residential loans

Interest rates on home mortgage loans in the period since 1937 rose from 4 to 7% and declined to 6% and rose to 9% in 1969 before declining somewhat in the following year. In the 1930s, the usual amortization periods was between 10 and 20 years, but in the postwar era, final maturity dates 30 years removed from the loan date have become common. On a level monthly payment basis, the portion of the payment representing interest becomes smaller as time passes, and the loan principal is reduced. Terms on an amortized mortgage loan are illustrated in Table 21–1.

TABLE 21–1

Terms on an amortized mortgage loan of $1,000 at 5¾% for 18 years

		Monthly payment			
Year	Month	Total	Interest portion	Principal repayment	Balance due on loan
0	1	$7.45	$4.79	$2.66	$997.34
0	2	7.45	4.78	2.67	994.67
0	3	7.45	4.76	2.69	991.98
3	1	7.45	4.47	2.98	929.54
6	1	7.45	3.91	3.54	812.07
9	1	7.45	3.24	4.21	672.59
12	1	7.45	2.45	5.00	506.98
15	1	7.45	1.51	5.94	309.87
17	10	7.45	.09	7.36	11.68
17	11	7.45	.05	7.40	4.12
Final		4.14	.02	4.12	0.00

Some idea as to the monthly payment required on loans of various maturities and at various interest rates is given in Table 21–2. This table shows the monthly payments required to amortize a loan of $1,000 during the indicated term. It shows, for example, that a person can pay off completely a $10,000 loan at 6%, extending over 20 years, with payments of $70.40 per month. On a $20,000 loan, the figure would be $141.40 per month. This is less in most instances than the amount for which a person can rent equivalent property, although, of course, the amount of the monthly payment on the loan is not the only out-of-pocket expense involved in owning a home.

To the monthly payment required to pay interest and amortize the principal, many lending institutions will require that the borrower add

TABLE 21–2

Monthly payment required to repay an amortized mortgage loan of $1,000

Maturity (years)	Rate of interest (%)			
	4	6	8	10
10	$10.09	$11.02	$11.99	$12.98
12	8.72	9.68	10.67	11.70
15	7.36	8.35	9.40	10.48
18	6.46	7.49	8.58	9.72
20	6.02	7.07	8.19	9.37
25	5.24	6.35	7.53	8.78
30	4.73	5.89	7.14	8.46

an amount equal to one twelfth of the annual fire insurance premium and annual property tax bill. Depending, of course, on the type of property and the city, the additional payment for taxes and insurance will range from $60 to $90 per month on a house valued at $15,000 to $25,000.

The down payment required for conventional loans—that is, loans neither insured nor guaranteed by federal agencies—on homes and small apartments varies greatly, depending on the policy of the lending institution and on business and real estate conditions. In periods of housing surplus, when homes sell for an amount approximating the cost of reproduction less depreciation, creditors will make loans with 20 to 30% down payment. In periods of great housing shortage and inflationary prices, as in the years 1945–49, practically all lending institutions require at least a 35–40% down payment, with a 50% down payment being quite common. On loans insured or guaranteed by federal agencies, the down payment tends to be smaller (in fact, under the present law, the down payment on a $15,000 house may be smaller than that usually asked on a $4,000 car) since the lender is protected by the government against substantial loss on the loan.

The procedure followed by a person seeking a loan on a home will vary a great deal, depending on the individual case and the custom of the community in which he lives. If an individual is buying a house, he will most frequently purchase the house through a real estate broker. If, like most purchasers of homes, he is unfamiliar with real estate and real estate financing, he may rely on the broker to help him get the necessary loan. The broker will direct the individual purchaser-borrower to a lending institution and, in many cases, arrange the details of the loan with the institution on behalf of the purchaser-borrower. In other cases, the individual will contact a lending institution of his choice directly.

Where a house is to be constructed or is under construction for sale, the contractor may arrange for a loan from a lending institution which disburses funds to him periodically as the house is being built. At the time the house is sold, the purchaser may assume the loan,[1] and the lending institution would release the contractor from any further obligation on it.

The procedure generally followed is outlined in the following steps:

1. Borrower signs loan application, which includes:
   Data about borrower
   Location of house
   Some details of house
2. Lender investigates the borrower's credit
3. An appraisal of the value of property is made (the borrower must usually supply or pay for a survey of the property)
4. Loan is approved by the loan committee, and the borrower is notified
5. Title investigation is made
6. Mortgage is recorded
7. Loan is "closed":
   Note signed
   Money disbursed to borrower or to some other person designated by him

Lending institutions in some areas, depending on the competitive situation, give 24- to 48-hour service in approving loans and notifying borrowers that the loan will be made as requested or subject to some modification. The subsequent steps in making the loan may take from one week to many weeks, depending upon the complexity of the title and the speed of service given by the local title insurance companies, abstract companies, or attorneys employed to investigate titles.

Extent of urban real estate financing

As already indicated, more than 75% of residential real estate transactions are completed through credit arrangements. The relative importance of real estate financing in the United States is indicated in Table 21–3, which shows a classification of the amounts of indebtedness outstanding at the ends of the years, 1930, 1940, 1950, 1960, and 1968. Figures for corporate debt include some mortgage debt, but the comparison between urban mortgage debt outstanding and the total gives a reasonable picture of the relationship of urban real estate loan credit to all credit. It is interesting to note that the proportion of urban mortgage debt has been rising. Twenty percent of all credits to private borrowers outstanding on December 31, 1930 and 1940, 24% of those outstanding on December 31, 1950, 30% of those outstanding on December 31, 1960,

---

[1] In some instances wholly new loans are made, and construction loans are retired. Costs of making loans preclude general use of this procedure.

TABLE 21–3

Estimates of net private debt in the United States; amounts outstanding at year-end, 1930, 1940, 1950, 1960, and 1968 (*billions of dollars*)

	1930	1940	1950	1960	1968
Corporate	$ 89.3	$ 75.6	$142.0	$302.7	$ 605
Noncorporate, urban mortgage ..	32.0	26.0	59.4	174.5	286
Noncorporate, nonmortgage	29.7	20.5	43.4	99.2	219
Farm mortgage	9.4	6.5	6.1	12.8	27
Total private debt	$160.4	$128.6	$250.9	$589.2	$1,137

Source: *Statistical Abstract, 1969*, p. 394.

and 26% of those outstanding on December 31, 1968, were based on urban mortgages.

A second indication of the extent of real estate financing is provided by a comparison of new financing for different types of users. For the year 1969, for example, about $16 billion was advanced on home loans; $25 billion was the total amount of new issues of corporate securities; and the total of funds obtained by corporations from all sources was $48 billion. States, counties, cities, towns, villages, and districts of the United States borrowed $8 billion, part of which was used to pay off existing debts. Although not strictly comparable, these figures serve to show the approximate relative importance of real estate financing.

TABLE 21–4

Urban real estate mortgage debt; amounts outstanding at year-end, 1930, 1940, 1950, 1960, and 1968 (*billions of dollars*)

	1930	1940	1950	1960	1968
One- to four-family residential	$18.9	$17.4	$45.2	$141.3	$251.5
Multifamily residential and commercial ...	6.5	12.6	21.6	52.7	117.9
Total urban mortgage debt	$25.4	$30.0	$66.7	$194.0	$369.4

Source: *Historical Statistics of the United States*, p. 397, and *Statistical Abstract, 1969*, p. 394.

The totals for urban real estate mortgage debt for the years 1930, 1940, 1950, 1960, and 1968 were, respectively, $25.4 billion, $30.0 billion, $66.7 billion, $194.0 billion, and $369.4 billion. In order to compare the relative amounts of residential and business real estate financing, these figures have been broken down into subclasses in Table 21–4. Of course, multifamily residential properties represent housing. The proportion of financing of individual housing to the total for urban real estate is greater, therefore, than is evident from the data for one- to four-family residential properties alone. Yet, this class accounted for nearly one quarter of the total of all private indebtedness, as is shown in Table 21–3 for 1968.

Private sources of real estate credit

The principal sources of real estate credit are private investment agencies: savings and loan associations, commercial banks, insurance companies, mutual savings banks, individual investors, and firms making occasional investments in real estate, although not principally engaged in real estate financing. Only a small amount of actual financing is handled by federal agencies—but federal agencies play an important role in this field, as the next section will show. The amounts invested by different lenders in the credits outstanding at the ends of 1960 and 1968 are shown in Table 21–5. The relative importance of savings and loan associations,

TABLE 21–5

Sources of urban real estate credit; amounts of debt held at year-end 1960 and 1968 (*billions of dollars*)

	1960	1968
Savings and loan associations	$ 60.1	$130.8
Life insurance carriers	38.8	70.0
Commercial banks	27.2	65.7
Mutual savings banks	26.9	53.5
FNMA	2.5	6.9
Individuals and others*	38.5	42.4
Total urban mortgage debt	194.0	369.3

* Including some debt held by federal agencies, excluding the Federal National Mortgage Association (FNMA).
Source: *Statistical Abstract*, 1969, p. 451.

commercial banks, and insurance companies as creditors has changed since 1940. These agencies now supply two thirds of the total funds, whereas in 1940 they supplied 40%. The size of debt held by individuals and others indicates the extent to which individual investment is important in this field. Many properties are sold on the basis of a down payment, with the seller himself taking a mortgage and note to cover the balance of the purchase price. A fact that Table 21–5 does not reveal is the dominance of the savings and loan associations in residential financing and of insurance companies in commercial and industrial financing. Savings and loan associations accounted for about 40% of the loans on residential properties, and insurance companies for about one third of commercial and industrial financing in recent years.

Savings and loan associations

Savings and loan associations have already been discussed in Chapter 11 as savings institutions. In 1969, these associations advanced $21.8 billion on urban real estate, nearly one half the total from all sources.

Commercial banks

Most commercial banks today make real estate loans through their trust departments and as a part of their regular lending activities. Banks usually have special departments to handle real estate loans. They have specialized personnel familiar with the legal and technical aspects of real estate finance. Commercial banks make all types of real estate loans, including loans on homes, on apartments, both large and small, on retail store properties, on office buildings, and on small factory buildings. Loans are generally limited by law to 60 to 75% of the value of the property and to a maturity of 20 years (except for loans insured or guaranteed by federal agencies). Today most loans made by banks are amortized loans. In the case of loans on homes, banks may prefer to make loans insured by federal agencies because they are permitted to make larger loans—up to 90% of the value of the property, with amortization to be completed over 20 to 30 years.

Currently, commercial banks and trust companies originate approximately 17% of all urban real estate loans. In 1969, they loaned $6.7 billion on home mortgages, and at the close of the year they held approximately $45 billion of such loans plus $22 billion of other urban real estate loans in their portfolios. Most of these loans are on property in the banks' own or neighboring communities. Some banks, however, purchase government-insured loans on homes in distant cities.

Mutual savings banks

Mutual savings banks (described in Chapter 11) are found mainly in Massachusetts, New York, and Connecticut. Their real estate lending activities are confined largely to those areas, although recently they have greatly increased loans on properties in other states. At the end of 1969, mutual savings banks had $56 billion, or about three quarters of their assets, invested in real estate mortgage loans. In 1969, they advanced $3 billion on urban real estate.

Life insurance companies

As shown in Table 21–5, the participation of insurance companies in the urban real estate field has increased. At the end of 1969, these companies had $66 billion invested in urban real estate mortgage loans and about $6 billion in real estate directly owned. More than one third of all insurance company assets were invested in real estate. In the year 1969, they advanced $9 billion in mortgages.

A definite preference is shown by life insurance companies for larger loans. Some companies actually exclude loans below a certain size—say $10,000. Their loans are made on the whole range of urban land improvements from large office buildings to single-family homes. They are generally limited by law as to the percentage that the loan may bear to the value of the property, and the actual percentage loan is generally much lower than is the case for other lenders. For about half the companies the maximum ratio permitted is 60%. Only a small number of the companies can make a loan as high as 70% of the value of property if there is no government guarantee or insurance of the loan.

The loans made by life insurance companies on real estate security are frequently among the lowest interest-rate loans made by any type of lender. The rate at which these companies can afford to make real estate loans depends largely on the interest rates on their alternative forms of investment, mainly corporate, municipal, and government bonds. Eight percent loans on office buildings, retail store properties, and small factory buildings are profitable when yields on high-grade corporate bonds are as high as 6%. When yields on high-grade bonds are as low as 2¾%, insurance companies can afford to make loans on individual homes at rates as low as 4%, with even lower rates for large loans on commercial property or large apartment developments. When rates on bonds rise, as in 1969 and 1970, rates on insurance company loans rise also.

A number of the larger eastern life insurance companies have financed the building of large apartment developments, such as Parkchester and Stuyvesant Town, in New York City, and Lake Meadows, in Chicago. In these cases they own the apartment buildings and the land outright, as permitted by special laws. They also have invested directly in the related field of shopping centers. The ownership of real estate by lending institutions is a quite recent departure from the traditional methods of real estate finance, and more will probably be done along this line in the next several decades. As mentioned above, at the end of 1969, life insurance companies owned more than $6 billion of urban real estate.

Early in 1951 the Prudential Life Insurance Company acquired the air rights over a portion of the railroad tracks (about the area of a city block) of the Illinois Central Railroad to Chicago, together with the title to enough small parcels of land to permit the sinking of caissons for a large office building to house the middle-western operations of Prudential and to provide additional office space as well. Other substantial acquisitions of air rights have been made since that time, and it is probable that air over railroad right-of-ways will be an important site for future building in large cities. It is the largest unused space available in many areas.

The mortgage correspondent system

Life insurance companies active in the mortgage field lend over a wide area—that is, in several states. This program necessitates special methods of obtaining and keeping in touch with their mortgage loan investments, including direct purchase of loans, use of salaried local agents, or appointment of exclusive loan correspondents, known generally as *mortgage brokers* or *mortgage bankers.*

The last-named method is most commonly used by the larger insurance companies and works somewhat as follows: A local real estate broker or mortgage banker in a community is selected by the mortgage lending officer of an insurance company to solicit loans and take applications in his community. The applications are checked by the loan correspondent and then submitted to the home office for final selection and approval. When an application is approved, the funds are disbursed by the insurance company, and the correspondent is charged with servicing the loan, that is, looking after the loan until it is fully discharged. He must see that interest and principal payments are made when due, that the property is kept in good repair, and that taxes and insurance payments are kept up to date. If the loan has to be foreclosed, then that, too, must be handled by the loan correspondent, who will frequently rent the property or manage it for the life insurance company and later arrange its sale to a new buyer.

The correspondent is compensated for his services by sale of the loan instrument to the life insurance company at one or more points above par. For example, a $10,000 loan might be sold at a price of 102, where par is 100. This would mean that the insurance company would pay the correspondent $10,200, the additional $200 covering the costs of making the loan and possibly some profit on the transaction. In addition, the life insurance company would typically pay its correspondent one half of 1% of the loan balance annually. For example, if the loan were written at an interest rate of 5%, the correspondent would collect this interest charge from the borrower and remit 4½% (or 90% of the total interest collected) to the life insurance company and keep the remainder as his fee.

Individuals

In contrast to most other major fields of credit, individuals, including trust and endowment funds, also engage in financing real estate. In 1969, home loans from individuals amounted to about $41 billion, approximately one seventh of the total from all sources.

Federal agencies

When the depression emphasized a number of fundamental weaknesses in the mortgage field, particularly in financing homes and apartments, the federal government, in the closing days of the Hoover Administration, initiated a broad program for strengthening and improving the facilities for mortgage finance and for improving housing conditions. Implementation of the program is reflected in the activities of the federal agencies created to do the job.

Department of Housing and Urban Development

The Housing and Home Finance Agency was established by Congress in 1947. It had the job of coordinating activities of five agencies: the Federal Housing Administration (FHA), the Federal National Mortgage Association (FNMA), the Public Housing Administration (PHA), the Community Facilities Administration, and the Urban Renewal Administration. The last of these had limited functions, as their titles indicate. We shall not describe the activities in detail in this chapter. In brief: the Community Facilities Administration handles special programs, such as college housing loans, and the Urban Renewal Administration made grants and loans to cities redeveloping slum areas. The Public Housing Administration was responsible for committing funds to low-cost rental projects which are included in redevelopment plans of cities. In effect, the federal government was committed to pay the costs of the buildings so that tenants need pay only current, direct operating costs. In 1965, the functions of this agency were transferred to the Department of Housing and Urban Development (HUD), which was created by executive order in that year.

HUD is responsible for coordination and administration of a wide range of activities under programs established by Congress. These include concern for home ownership and rented housing, urban systems and renewal, disaster area redevelopment, and assurance of housing availability in financing distressed areas.

Federal Housing Administration

The government agency, now an organization in HUD, that has received the most publicity in home mortgage operations is the Federal Housing Administration. It was created by the National Housing Act of 1934. Contrary to popular conception, the FHA does not make loans. It insures payment on loans made by private lending institutions on homes and rental apartments. In effect, the FHA is an agency for placing the credit of the federal government behind the credit of individuals who borrow to buy or build residential property.

The agency was created by Congress at a time when the residential construction industry was lagging, and the new legislation was designed to stimulate it to greater activity. It was the theory that, by providing government insurance against loss on home mortgage loans, more credit would be made available for the financing of homes with lower down payments and longer maturities and thus make it possible for more people to buy or build homes.

Other objectives of the act include certain reforms in mortgage lending practice, an improvement in housing standards and conditions, a system of mutual mortgage insurance, a national market for mortgages, and increased liquidity of mortgages. These changes and reforms did bring more capital into the mortgage market, particularly from commercial banks, and did effect substantial improvement in small house design and construction.

The FHA carries on several rather distinct activities under different titles of the National Housing Act. The most significant are described below.

Insurance of loans made for the repair and modernization of homes was provided under Title I of the act. Under the terms of this title, lending institutions are insured against loss on loans made for the repair, improvement, or modernization of property, such as repairing the roof, installing a modern heating and plumbing system, building a garage, or painting and redecorating the house. These loans are generally limited to $5,000 in amount and are not secured by a mortgage. The maximum term for most loans is five years. They are discount loans and carry an effective interest rate as high as 9.72%. In 1969, $693 million of such loans were insured.

The FHA insurance of home mortgage loans for the construction or purchase of a home or the refinancing of an existing mortgage debt under a system of mutual mortgage insurance was created under Title II of the act. A mutual mortgage insurance fund was created with the initial capital subscribed by the RFC and the fund built up by premiums paid to the FHA by borrowers on FHA insured loans. Any loss from defaulted loans is met out of this fund, with the lender in effect trading the defaulted loan for a debenture of the FHA, which is guaranteed as to principal and interest by the federal government.

Briefly, the insured mortgage plan works somewhat as follows: An individual borrower applies for a mortgage loan at a savings and loan association, bank, or other approved FHA lending institution. The necessary application papers are sent to the local FHA office for approval. The loan is an amortized direct-reduction loan: the borrower makes monthly payments of principal and interest on the loan plus the insurance premium, which the lender in turn pays to the mutual mortgage insurance fund. This premium is one half of 1% of the unpaid balance of the loan.

Whenever an insured mortgage is in default, the lender must notify the FHA and start foreclosure proceedings according to FHA regulations or otherwise acquire title and possession of the property. Having foreclosed a defaulted loan and taken title to the property, the lender may transfer title and possession of the property to the FHA and obtain, in exchange, debentures of the mortgage insurance fund with a maturity the same as that of the mortgage in exchange for which they were issued. The debentures are issued for an amount covering the unpaid principal amount of the loan plus the payments made by the mortgagee for taxes, special assessments, insurance premium, and also foreclosure costs to a maximum of $75.

To be eligible for insurance under Title II of the act, the loan must meet certain detailed requirements. The security must be a first mortgage on a property designed principally for residential use for not more than four families; the note may bear interest at a rate not greater than $5\frac{1}{4}\%$; and the property must be located in an approved section of a city in a neighborhood that meets certain standards. A loan must not, in most cases, exceed $16,000, or 80% of the appraised value of the property, or have a maturity longer than 30 years. The loan on houses priced at less than $10,000, however, may be as much as 97% of the value.

Most of the loans insured under Title II are on small residences. Under a special section of this title, provision is made, in addition, for insuring, under certain conditions, amortized mortgage loans up to $5 million on rental and cooperative housing projects; such insured loans are limited to a maximum of 90% of the value of the property and may have a term as long as 30 years. From the time of the passage of the National Housing Act in 1934 through 1968, a total of 10.5 million loans on one- to four-family residences and multifamily units has been insured. These loans amounted to $128 billion, and about 50% of them were on newly built homes.

The impressive size of these data does not mean that all real estate loans are backed by federal guarantee however. As Table 21–6 indicates,

TABLE 21–6

Outstanding home mortgages by type (*billions of dollars*)

Year end	Total	"Conventional"*	FHA insured	VA guaranteed or insured
1950	46.0	32.5	7.0	6.5
1955	90.1	52.0	16.6	21.5
1960	143.6	92.1	25.5	26.0
1965	238.0	172.5	38.7	26.8
1968	283.1	213.2	42.2	27.7

* Difference between total and sum of FHA and VA figures.
Source: Data derived from *Statistical Abstract, 1969*, p. 451.

most residential real estate loans are conventional loans, and less than one quarter are insured or guaranteed by either the FHA or the Veterans Administration (VA), as described in the next subsection.

Title VIII permits insured loans to builders of rental housing for military personnel on or near military posts.

Initiated as a purely temporary agency to stimulate the home building industry, the FHA is now well established as a permanent mortgage insurance agency of the federal government. It was partly the effect of the FHA to broaden the scope of real estate markets, which had been local in operation. Through the use of the indirect government guarantee, generally lowered interest rates on home mortgage loans have been achieved, and a measure of unity in both interest rates and requirements for acceptable mortgages has been brought into the home mortgage market. A much higher degree of standardization of mortgage loan terms, lending plans, and borrower requirements exists now than previously.

As a result of these changes, the liquidity of home mortgage loans has been increased considerably, and the vast resources of the commercial banking and insurance companies have been brought into the mortgage market. The commercial and savings banks and life insurance companies hold in their portfolios approximately 60% of all FHA loans outstanding.

Federal National Mortgage Association

As one more move to enhance the flow of money through real estate markets in the 1930s, Congress, in 1934, authorized formation of national mortgage associations. The federal government offered to supply funds to back private investors who were willing to engage in the business of buying and selling federally insured or guaranteed mortgages. Congress intended to encourage development of a secondary market in which creditors could adjust their investment portfolios by adding or subtracting amounts of mortgages as they could add or subtract amounts of government or corporate bonds. There was no immediate interest shown by private investors in the proffered opportunity. However, in 1938, one association was formed by government officials—and subsequently named itself Federal National Mortgage Association.

Until 1954, the association bought mortgages at par. The mortgages offered were those bearing low interest rates in periods of rising rates. They would not have been priced at par in a free market. Thus FNMA, in practice, became a means for direct investment in real estate mortgages for the federal government. Its holdings reached $2.6 billion. Mortgages acquired in this early period and still outstanding in 1954 were placed under a management and liquidation program. Monthly amortization was to reduce the portfolio gradually.

After 1954, the association engaged in secondary market activities in a more realistic fashion. From time to time it set prices on the different mortgages, classified by interest rate, at which it would buy or sell. The prices were as low as $90 (for $100 face value) on 4½% mortgages. Under this program, in 1959, the association bought $1,907 million and sold $5 million. In 1963, in contrast, the figures were $290 million and $1,114 million, respectively. In 1968, the association adopted the free market system for pricing. Under this system, it states the amount of dollars it is willing to commit and sellers then turn in offers. Over the period 1955–69, purchases exceeded sales, repayments, and other credits by $8.3 billion, but sales totaled $3 billion. At the end of 1969, the total amount of mortgages held was $11 billion. The association was committed to the purchase of $3.5 billion more, if offered by prospective sellers.

A third activity of FNMA was a special assistance program. Under this program it bought mortgages of types specified by Congress at uneconomic prices. Activity under this program increased in 1959 and was fairly stable after that.

The original concept of private investment, assisted by federal funds, has only recently been carried into practice. It was intended that, as creditors sold mortgages to FNMA, they would invest in the stock of the association. In 1969, $140 million of stock had been sold. As an offset to the $11 billion of assets, this is a small amount. In 1968, subordinated debentures were issued and the proceeds used to retire the preferred stock issue owned by the U.S. government. At that point the ownership of FNMA was clearly private. Larger amounts of private funds have been obtained from sale of debentures. At the end of 1969, the outstanding FNMA debenture issues held by private investors aggregated $10.5 billion.

Government National Mortgage Association

In 1968, the Government National Mortgage Association (GNMA) was formed. It is a wholly owned government corporation administered by HUD. When it was formed, the liquidation, management, and special assistance programs of FNMA were transferred to it. At the close of 1969, GNMA held $6 billion of FHA and VA mortgages. GNMA provides a guarantee of payment of interest and principal on mortgages which are security for instruments sold to the public.

Veterans Administration guaranty and loan programs

The most significant measure enacted to provide home mortgage loans to veterans of World War II is Title III of the Servicemen's Readjustment Act of 1944, commonly known as the "GI Bill of Rights." This act with subsequent amendments required the Veterans Administration, backed by the U.S. Treasury, to guarantee or insure loans to veterans made by private financial institutions, savings and loan associations, banks, and insurance companies. Within the first three years of operations, up to December 31, 1947, over $6,107 million of home loans to 1,056,000 veterans had been made under its provisions. This compares with loans of $1,100 million insured in the first three years of the FHA programs and with the $3,093 million in loans made by the Home Owners' Loan Corporation in the three years it was actively lending. At the end of 20 years, $57 billion of loans had been made pursuant to the provisions of the act.

The law offers a guaranty for real estate loans to qualified veterans of World War II, the Korean War, and the Vietnam conflict up to $12,500, or 60% of the total loan, whichever is less. The cutoff dates (1964) were July 1970 for World War II and January 1975 for Korean veterans. This

TABLE 21–7

Relationships of conventional and guaranteed loans

	Ordinary loan	Veterans loan
Purchase price of home	$12,500	$12,500
Amount lending institution would be willing to lend *at its own risk* ...	$ 7,500	$ 7,500
Amount actually loaned	$ 7,500	$12,500
Amount of down payment	$ 5,000 in cash	None
Assuming loan defaulted immediately after being made and property was sold for	$ 8,000	$ 8,000
Loss to lending institution	None, since only $7,500 was loaned	$ 4,500, but lender is reimbursed by the VA to the extent of its guaranty
Loss on down payment or guaranty ..	$ 4,500 loss to borrower	$ 4,500 loss: VA loses unless it can later collect this amount from veteran
Actual loss to lender	None	None

guaranty is unusual in that, through it, the Veterans Administration takes the first risk on the loan. The guaranty is designed to take the place, up to the amount of the guaranty, of the usual cash down payment ordinarily associated with mortgage lending.

The nature of the VA guaranty can be most easily understood by reference to what might happen in a case involving a default and subsequent foreclosure, as outlined in Table 21–7. As can be seen by studying this table, lenders can make larger loans to veterans than they can to nonveteran borrowers on the same house. The Veterans Administration endorses the veteran's credit up to the amount of the guaranty in such a manner that the veteran can substitute this guaranty for cash.

The *insurance* of loans (as distinguished from *guaranty* of loans just described) provided by the Veterans Administration under a different section of the act offers a type of insurance in which lending institutions are reimbursed for all losses on loans to qualified veterans up to 15% of the aggregate of principal amount of such veterans' loans made. This means that if a lending institution made $15 million in insured veterans' loans, it would have to its credit an insurance reserve of $2,250,000. If the losses of this lending institution on the total of these $15 million loans amounted to only $2 million, the lender would be reimbursed by the Veterans Administration in full for its losses on these loans. Lenders make either insured or guaranteed loans. The guaranty privileges are used more frequently. The Veterans Administration also has the authority to make direct loans of $10,000 or less in areas where veterans are unable to borrow at the maximum legal interest rate. The total for direct loans made since 1944 represents only about 3% of the total of VA loans however.

Toward the end of 1947 and in subsequent months, following a rise in yields on government and corporate bonds and an increase in the operating expense of lending institutions, many lenders became reluctant to make veterans loans under the 4% rate then authorized. The permissible rate of change on these loans was increased in later years. In 1969, it was $8\frac{1}{2}\%$. Under the impetus of rate increases together with the restrictions of Regulation X, the volume of veteran loans rose for a few years after World War II to a substantial proportion of the total for home financing but has not retained this position. Although there was some increase in lending under the provisions of the act in the 1960s (see Table 21–6), loans in 1969 were $4 billion.

Federal Reserve Board Regulation X

The Defense Production Act of 1950 empowered the president of the United States to regulate certain aspects of real estate financing. Under this authority, as expressed in Regulation X of the Federal Reserve Board, down payments were increased and time to maturity was decreased for mortgage financing of real estate purchases. These restrictions had the effect of decreasing activity in real estate markets. The authority to invoke this regulatory power ceased in 1953, but its exercise in the earlier emergency may indicate a form of selective credit control to be used in future emergencies.

Present problems and outlook

Developments in the real estate mortgage market, both as a result of federal and of private actions, have encouraged the assumption of debt by individuals. The general shift from straight to amortized loans has added an element of strength. Creditors learn more promptly whether debtors are able to pay up mortgage debt because that ability is reaffirmed monthly. The budgeting of consumer incomes resulting from the regular payments of principal and interest probably has had a salutary effect on debtor recognition of their responsibilities as debtors. On the other hand, a schedule of regular payments has the disadvantage of making more difficult the problem of the debtor in bridging even a short, sharp break in the flow of his income; and the rate of building up owner equity in real estate is probably slower under the present type of amortized debt plan than it was under the accelerated amortization enforced by the types of second- and third-mortgage terms prevailing in earlier years.

A substantial element of strength is added also by the mere existence of agencies such as the FHA, the Federal National Mortgage Association, and the Government National Mortgage Association, which can take mortgages over from lenders and in this way relieve the lending agencies of some of the dangers of credit restrictions. The existence of an agreement such as that with the FHA, however, does not relieve creditors of the disagreeable and locally unpopular task of foreclosing defaulted mortgage notes.

Over the past several years the flow of funds into mortgages has varied inversely with the rate of interest. When interest rates have risen—when we have experienced tight-money markets—major institutions have reduced the flow of investment in real estate credits and increased the flow in other directions. The rigid ceilings on rates on federally guaranteed mortgages and state usury laws have at times intensified these moves. It becomes wise to direct funds to the forms of obligations that are free to reflect the higher interest rates of such markets. In a rough sense this has tended to place housing investment in a countercyclical role. The funds available to support housing construction have been restricted in booms and are more freely available in recessions. It is possible that this has contributed to economic stability in recent years, but the housing industry has been continuously conscious of its inability to participate with other industries in some of our periods of prosperity. Moreover, the sharp contraction of flows of funds to mortgage markets in periods of tight money has lowered construction of housing below levels popularly believed to be socially desirable. This has prompted large-scale increases in government programs to increase flows of funds to housing.

A point of interest to students of real estate finance is the approach to marketability for mortgage instruments. Until recently, mortgages have not had markets as securities. However, several practices have been developed in the 1950s and have become more nearly a part of institutional routines. These were not discussed in the chapter. The extent of development is not yet great but in 1969 and 1970, it increased decidedly. Nevertheless, commercial banks are warehousing mortgages for mortgage companies in much the same way as they supply funds to investment bankers while securities issues are in process of distribution to individual investors. Banks and insurance companies enter into agreements to buy mortgages which have not been placed by a certain time—an agreement paralleling the underwriting agreement of securities distributions. Secondary markets, with active dealers—for example, FNMA and GNMA—are reflecting increasing activity. The action of FNMA in exchanging mortgages for federal government bonds indicates somewhat broadened interest in these instruments as investment media. Mortgages are becoming marketable securities.

In the early 1970s, because of constricted flows of funds caused by tight money conditions, the federal government has entered even more fully the real estate market. Housing has cabinet status. Over half of the financing of residential real estate came from federal agencies in 1970. Plans referred to in the press and in academic journals would lead to considerably more influence on the kinds of properties built and the places where development takes place. Rent supplements, concern for housing for senior citizens, metropolitan planning, and urban renewal programs bring government into housing more often and more importantly.

Large housing projects can be and have been carried out with private financing. The question as to the advisability of governmental financing arises when the cost of housing to occupants is considered. The debate is fundamentally one of what minimum standards of housing are acceptable in a society such as that of the United States and whether privately financed projects can supply minimum housing requirements at prices that occupants can afford to pay. In effect, the suggestion that public financing is required is a suggestion that the nation must subsidize the families at low-income levels if they are to be suitably housed.

Questions and problems

1. Why is the financing process of great importance to the market for real estate?
2. What does amortization mean?
3. What are the leading legal formalities of the real estate finance deal? Why do these tend to be of greater importance in real estate than in other personal transactions?
4. What are the differences in practice in financing commercial and residential properties?
5. What factors may be considered by a lender in judging a real estate loan application?
6. Outline the functions of the Federal Housing Administration.

7. Distinguish between the insurance and the guaranty features of Veterans Administration operations.

8. Why do bank and insurance companies hold a large proportion of the federally insured loans? Why do savings and loan associations and individuals refrain from insuring the loans they make?

Bibliography

There is a wide range of differences in the kinds of materials written about real estate finance. Two general texts are those by Henry E. Hoagland and Leo D. Stone, *Real Estate Finance* (4th ed.; Homewood, Ill.: R. D. Irwin, Inc., 1969) and by Maurice A. Unger, *Real Estate Principles and Practices* (4th ed.; Cincinnati, O.: South-Western Publishing Co., 1969). Detailed treatment of special aspects are found in such books as Henry A. Babcock, *Appraisal Principles and Procedures* (Homewood, Ill.: Richard D. Irwin, Inc., 1967); Robert Kratovil, *Real Estate Law* (5th ed.; New York: Prentice-Hall, Inc., 1969); and J. E. Morton, *Urban Mortgage Lending: Comparative Markets and Experience* (Princeton, N.J.: Princeton University Press, 1965). There are five other monographs in the National Bureau of Economic series, of which Morton's is primarily a summary. A second, more recent book concerned with appraisal is that by Sanders A. Kahn, Frederick E. Case, and Alfred Schimmel, *Real Estate Appraisal and Investment* (New York: The Ronald Press Co., 1963). Two other special sources are the books by Paul Edward Anderson, *Tax Factors in Real Estate Operations* (2d ed.; Englewood Cliffs, N.J.: Prentice-Hall, 1965); and Janice B. Babb and Beverly F. Dordick, *Real Estate Information Sources* (Detroit: Gale Research Co., 1963). The latter is a detailed bibliography.

The annual reports of the Department of Housing and Urban Development are sources of information about federal activity in the real estate field and statistics on real estate markets. These reports also list other publications of the agency.

PART VI

PUBLIC FINANCE AND PUBLIC POLICY

Government has been mentioned frequently throughout this book a reflection of the fact that it has become an element of great significance in our economic and financial life. This may be observed in dozens of ways. Government—whether federal, state, or local—is one of the most important buyers of goods and employers of persons; the results of government expenditures may be observed at almost every turn. Government collects taxes from almost every paycheck. Government is a debtor of magnitude: it owes money to millions of its citizens and to almost all financial institutions. But, at the same time, government is an important lender and banker. Most notable of all, government has assumed a major responsibility for assuring the stability of economic activity and the growth of national income.

In order to cover all these types of government activity and economic influence, three chapters will be needed. In Chapter 22 the finances of the federal government will be given detailed attention. Chapter 23 is devoted to the financial problems of state and local government. Chapter 24 combines a discussion of monetary and fiscal policy in which the descriptive treatment of public finance in Chapters 22 and 23 are applied to the problems of public policy formation.

Public finance: federal government

The account of public finance that follows in this chapter will begin with a review of federal government expenditures. It is followed by a general treatment of federal government revenues. The third section of the chapter deals with public debt problems; the fourth, with an institutionally oriented description of federal government finance and its effects on financial markets.

Federal government expenditures

Expenditures of the federal government represent the outlays decided on through the processes of a political democracy. Appropriations are made by the legislative branch of the government; the actual spending is done by the executive branch. The purposes of expenditures are often explainable only in terms of the way in which the legislative process works—or the way in which executive departments of governments operate. The formal titles used in budgets and appropriation bills are not entirely revealing, and it should be recognized that a certain amount of inaccuracy mars the classification of governmental expenditures. For example, the national security expenditures include the substantial sums spent on atomic energy, military stockpiling, civil defense, space research, and foreign aid. While atomic research and weapons have an important role in national defense, a substantial part of the funds appropriated and spent in this area are aimed at peaceful uses quite distant from the category in which they are listed. Another example is the inclusion of "area redevelopment" under expenditures for "commerce and transportation"; these items could probably rationally be included with the expenditures for "housing and community development." These examples suggest that governmental accounting is often as imprecise as private accounting.

In declining order of general importance, government expenditures are categorized in terms of national security; health, education, and welfare; general government; commerce, transportation, and housing; agriculture and national resources. The general pattern of federal expenditures for the years 1954–1969 is shown in Exhibit 22–1. This chart illustrates the dominance of national security expenditures, the emerging expenditures

EXHIBIT 22–1

Federal expenditures by function

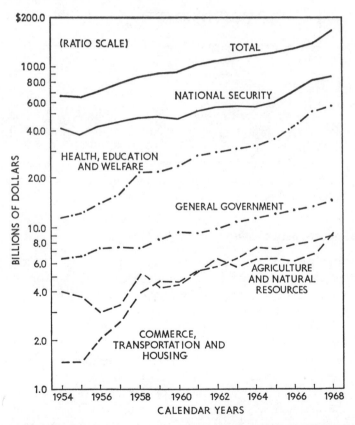

Source: Department of Commerce, Office of Business Economics, *National Income & Product Accounts* (Washington, D.C.: U.S.G.P.O., August 1966) and *Survey of Current Business,* July 1970; presentation follows that in *The Federal Budget,* an annual publication of the National Industrial Conference Board.

of the "great society," and the importance of agriculture. This pattern of expenditures is roughly the one that has prevailed since 1952, when the Korean War convinced the nation that it must provide itself with a never-ceasing readiness to strike back with nuclear weapons should we be attacked.

The pattern differs greatly, however, from the one that prevailed between the two world wars and for a while after World War II. In these periods national defense expenditures were a relatively much smaller part of the total. In the 1920s the entire federal budget was small and was devoted mainly to the regular operating functions of the federal government. In the 1930s various kinds of welfare or transfer payment expenditures came to be more important. Then, for obvious reasons, World War II brought a great bulge in federal government outlays. Federal government expenditures reached a high of $98 billion in fiscal 1945, or nearly half the gross national product. The reduction of expenditures after World War II brought them to the low point of the postwar period in 1948—$33 billion.

National security

By all odds, war causes the greatest volume of government expenditures, and national defense expenditures presently constitute almost one half of total federal expenditures. In peacetime we maintain costly departments of national defense—army, navy, and air. In wartime, government expenditures grow rapidly, not only for the military services but for many other purposes—for a merchant marine, for raw materials, for public health, and the like. The great peaks in governmental expenditures are easily identifiable as the result of war.

Virtually all war expenditures represent activities of the federal government. Not only is war the direct cause of a large share of federal government outlays, but the aftermath of war is expensive. Pensions, bonuses, and benefits for the veterans of wars are important costs. Aid to our allies did not end with World War I, World War II, or the Korean War. The cost of the later aid may be charged to defense, however, since outlays abroad are justified as helping to reduce the chances of future war or to increase our chances of winning those we must fight.

As shown in Exhibit 22-2, the types of expenditures which comprise the national security category are military defense, defense-related activities, international affairs, and space research. From 1954 to 1964, this order also reflected the relative sizes of the expenditure categories, but more recently space research has become the second largest category, and spending on international affairs (mainly foreign aid programs) has become more important than defense-related activities (atomic energy, military stockpiling, and civil defense) because the former has remained

EXHIBIT 22–2

National security

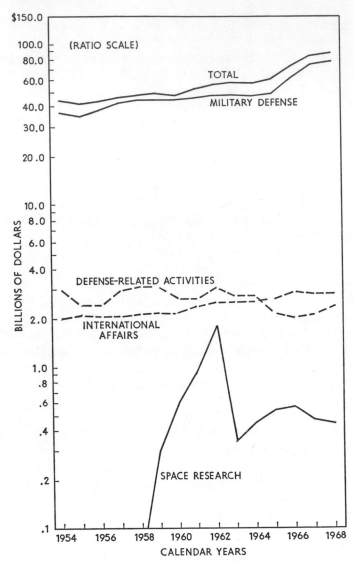

Source: Department of Commerce, Office of Business Economics, *National Income & Product Accounts* (Washington, D.C.: U.S.G.P.O., August 1966) and *Survey of Current Business,* July 1970; presentation follows that in *The Federal Budget,* an annual publication of the National Industrial Conference Board.

stable at a level of about $3 billion while the latter has declined in importance to about $2 billion. The recent declines in defense-related expenditures are attributable to reductions in all three categories composing that total—atomic energy, stockpiling, and civil defense. Space research expenditures grew at an extraordinarily rapid rate from 1957 to 1966 but were cut back sharply in 1967 and in 1968.

Health, education, and welfare expenditures

Health, education, and welfare expenditures currently account for about 32% of federal budgeted expenditures, and this category includes many kinds of outlays. In order of relative importance, the various types of outlays are social insurance, veterans programs, programs for the needy, health, and education. (See Exhibit 22–3.) While these orders of importance remained stationary for roughly the last 15 years, recently expenditures for the needy have exceeded those for veterans, and educational expenditures have exceeded health expenditures. About 80% of total health, education, and welfare expenditures represents the redistribution of income to individuals, either directly through social insurance programs or indirectly through public assistance programs.

Over the last 15 years, health, education, and welfare expenditures have increased in relative importance to about 29% of current federal spending. The annual rate of growth of this expenditure category in the period 1954–1968 has been approximately 10.7%. Federal programs for veterans are the only category that has grown slowly—at an annual rate of 3.4%. Social insurance and other programs for the needy constitute the largest nondefense expenditure categories and have increased at annual rates of 12.8% and 12.3%, respectively. Health expenditures on research and hospital operation have grown rapidly, but this category currently represents a small proportion of total health, education, and welfare expenditures. Federal education and manpower expenditures have grown more rapidly than any other category during the last few years, the impetus stemming primarily from programs to provide additional education for the disadvantaged.

Commerce, transportation, and housing expenditures

In order of importance as they are reflected in the budget, spending on transportation, commerce, and housing comprise the total of this category, which accounts for about 5% of total expenditures.

Commerce, transportation, and housing expenditures showed rapid growth rates through 1960, declined in 1965, and increased somewhat more slowly in 1966 through 1968, as shown in Exhibit 22–4. The transportation category of these expenditures represents highway construction,

EXHIBIT 22-3

Health, education, and welfare expenditures

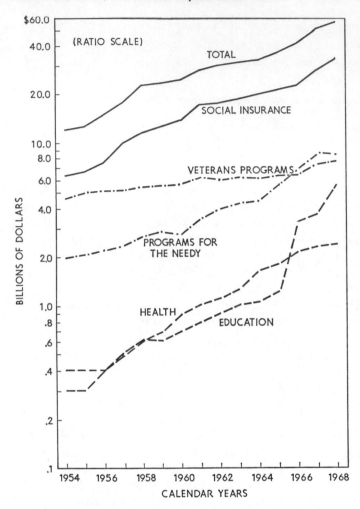

Source: Department of Commerce, Office of Business Economics, *National Income & Product Accounts* (Washington, D.C.: U.S.G.P.O., August 1966) and *Survey of Current Business*, July 1970; presentation follows that in *The Federal Budget*, an annual publication of the National Industrial Conference Board.

subsidies to airlines and shipping, and the navigation services provided by the Federal Aviation Agency and the U.S. Coast Guard. The chief item is the continuing development of the interstate highway system. The post office deficit accounts for a major portion of commerce expenditures; the rest of this category represents services to business and regulation of business. Expenditures on housing, which currently total $1 billion, under-

EXHIBIT 22–4

Commerce, transportation, and housing

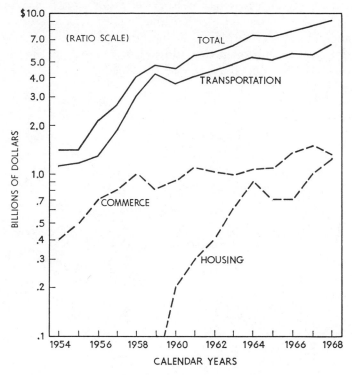

Source: Department of Commerce, Office of Business Economics, *National Income & Product Accounts* (Washington, D.C.: U.S.G.P.O., August 1966) and *Survey of Current Business,* July 1970; presentation follows that in *The Federal Budget,* an annual publication of the National Industrial Conference Board.

state the role played by the federal government in this area as much of its activities consist of loans and loan insurance programs.

Agriculture and natural resources

Expenditures on agriculture and natural resources constitute another 5% of federal expenditures. The largest single item in the category is expenditure for farm price stabilization; spending for natural resources represents the category second in size (see Exhibit 22–5). The major current thrusts of federal agricultural programs are the provision of low-income rural housing, expansion of loan programs (chiefly to aid financing technological change in agriculture), aid to rural communities, and public investments for the health care, education, and training of the rural labor force.

The background of government welfare expenditures for agriculture is an involved one. The federal government went to the economic rescue of agriculture in the otherwise prosperous 1920s, when programs for agricultural aid were started. At that time, money was appropriated for purchasing agricultural surpluses. While the kind of policy pursued by the federal government to aid agriculture has changed, as the preceding paragraph indicated, the purpose has remained constant—to keep the farmer happy and prosperous.

EXHIBIT 22–5

Agriculture and natural resources

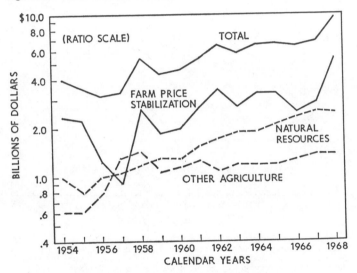

Source: Department of Commerce, Office of Business Economics, *National Income & Product Accounts* (Washington, D.C.: U.S.G.P.O., August 1966) and *Survey of Current Business*, July 1970; presentation follows that in *The Federal Budget*, an annual publication of the National Industrial Conference Board.

The conflicting characteristics of alternative proposals for supporting agricultural income illustrate one of the subtle problems of measuring the cost of governmental operations. Some devices raise the price (or support the price) of agricultural products on the open market. In these cases the cost to the public is not fully reflected in direct government costs; it also includes higher prices at the grocery store. Other means for support of agricultural income involve letting agricultural prices find their market level and then paying direct subsidies to those farmers who cooperate with the government by appropriate programs of crop limitation. This second sort of scheme might cost the government more in direct outlays than does the first, but it might cost the public less in total than the first plan. How is cost to be measured? And, which groups in the private sector ought to bear those costs? Tax levies have different impacts on consumers than do higher prices on some agricultural products.

More than half of agriculture and natural resources expenditures is currently attributable to farm price support programs. The "other agriculture" category includes expenditures on projects involving improvement or recovery of agricultural land or the supply of irrigation water. Rural electrification and rural telephone loans fall under this category, as do farm ownership and operation loans. And, while spending substantial amounts to support the prices of agricultural commodities, which because of enlarged production would otherwise be low, the federal government also spends a modest amount on research for further improving agricultural productivity.

Expenditures for natural resources arise chiefly from developing land and water resources; smaller amounts are spent on conservation and recreational activities. Doubtless many of the former class of expenditures are important and useful in aiding commerce and providing safety devices and services for the protection of navigation. But development expenditures also include some items that have cynically been labeled *pork barrel*, such as the dredging of harbors which are used by few ships but which happen to fall in the home district of a powerful congressman. However, expenditures for preservation of public forests and parks and the conservation of water resources have much merit.

General government

Expenditures on general government, amounting to approximately 10% of total expenditures, constitute the major remaining category of federal outlays. Two thirds of the expenditures in this category represent interest on the public debt—debt which has increased only moderately since World War II. Thus, in a real sense, interest on the public debt is an expenditure category resulting from previous wars and might properly be accounted for as a national security outlay. Although the actual overhead costs of running the government are included in the general government category, the major part of expenditures represents not direct outlays but transfer payments—the redistribution of incomes. As Exhibit 22–6 indicates, the single category next in importance to interest on the public debt consists chiefly of pensions to civil service employees.

How extensive should government services be?

Although federal government expenditures as a proportion of national income have remained relatively constant over the last 15 years, accounting generally for a little less than 20% of GNP, certain categories of expenditures have shown rapid growth. Over the 15 years, national security

EXHIBIT 22–6

General government

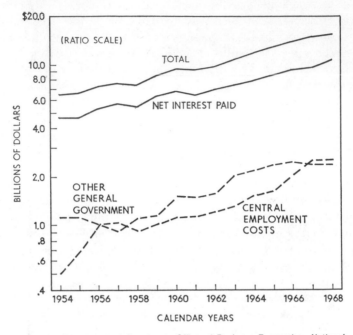

CALENDAR YEARS

Source: Department of Commerce, Office of Business Economics, *National
Income & Product Accounts* (Washington, D.C.: U.S.G.P.O., August 1966) and
Survey of Current Business, July 1970; presentation follows that in *The Federal
Budget*, an annual publication of the National Industrial Conference Board.

expenditures have shown the greatest average decline as a proportion of
total expenditures, while the health, education, and welfare category has
shown the greatest proportional increase. A much smaller increase has
been posted by commerce, transportation, and housing.

To a large extent, the changing importance of expenditure categories
is aimed at achieving solutions to problems which could be characterized
as being both economic and social in nature. Examples of such problems
include poverty, blighted areas (both urban and rural), inadequate educational facilities, and the quality of the environment.

Problems such as poverty are not new, and there is a real question as
to whether governmental support programs can be designed in such a
way as to provide individuals with the freedom and incentive to change
their station in life if they should choose to do so. Nonetheless, better
educational facilities and subsidized training programs appear to provide
a long-run solution to the poverty problem, and it should be recognized
that to the extent the productivity of a society is increased through such
programs, the economic benefits redound to all.

The problems of blighted areas and of the quality of the environment concern another aspect of the question of motivating individuals freely to choose actions which are in accord with the good of the society in which they live. These problems are symptomatic of the fact that in some types of markets as they are presently constituted, the workings of our major allocative and motivating mechanism, the price system, can lead to results which many judge to be socially undesirable.

A major reason for an economic system's exhibiting these undesirable properties is that prices do not always reflect adequately the costs, both to the producer and to society, of producing and trading certain commodities. Thus, prices paid by consumers do not presently recompense society for the costs of keeping the air clean, or of the destruction of ecological balance through the use of pesticides or through waste disposal. In such instances there is a growing body of opinion which argues that the quality of life could be improved by ameliorating these problems, and that natural resource usage taxes aimed at controlling environmental pollution or at financing the cleaning costs are thereby justified. Since these taxes would be passed on to consumers, commodity prices would then reflect the costs of repairing the damage caused by production and consumption of these commodities.

Since the American economic system relies heavily on individual motivation, it is useful to recognize that increased legislative activity or larger government expenditures may, while seeming to provide easy answers to some of the previously mentioned social problems, have long-run undesired effects unless they utilize individual motivation to a high degree. For example, members of the economy may spend large amounts of time and effort attempting to evade legislative constraints. There is thus a very real question concerning the efficacy of legislative constraints as compared to tax mechanisms for offsetting the effects of market failure discussed above.

Another aspect of the question of whether to use individual motivation or the workings of government to achieve social goals is that the seeming remoteness of government accentuates the tendency to have government assume more functions—to build more school buildings, increase social security benefits, and so on. But "having government do something about it" does not per se make the activity cost less. The desirability of what we want government to do can be debated, but there is no magic by which government can do away with cost. Indeed, one point of view argues that governmental operations are frequently less efficiently conducted than they would be by private business. Legislation to make the U.S. Post Office Department an autonomous corporation was based partially on this line of thought.

The fact that government cannot do away with cost does not mean, however, that because a project is not privately profitable it has no special virtue; it may be highly profitable in a social sense. For example, if government can reduce the severity of depressions through deficit spending, the net gain in social good is worth vast sums. If, through projects such as the Tennessee Valley Authority, government can turn eroded, underproductive areas into productive areas, the net gain is very great indeed. If public health measures can improve the national well-being, the benefits would exceed anything that money can measure. If the Job Corps were able to increase the productivity of substantial numbers of youth who would otherwise be unproductive or even socially destructive, these expenditures would have a worthwhile rate of return economically and in addition would produce substantial social dividends.

Government revenues

When government needs money, it generally obtains funds through taxing or borrowing although there are other revenue sources as well. For example, some government revenues come from partial cost-covering fees, such as postal fees or tuition at state universities. The federal government obtains revenues from the sale of public power and incidental receipts from activities such as the sale of war-surplus goods. It is also possible for government to obtain funds simply by printing money. However, in a well-managed economy financing through printing money is seldom resorted to because it creates inflationary economic conditions. Finally, sources other than taxes are usually unimportant ones in terms of their relative contribution to total revenue.

The principal elements in federal revenues are shown in Exhibit 22-7. The individual income tax is now, as it has been for a full generation, the most important source of revenue. The corporate income tax provides the next largest source, with excise taxes following.

Since the federal individual income tax is marked by a sharp progression of rates from low incomes to high incomes, it raises questions about economic incentives. Nevertheless, circumstances have required revenues so large that the federal tax on personal incomes is collected largely from what are ordinarily considered middle-income persons.

The corporate income tax is at a flat rate except for a modest reduction for smaller corporations. The rate was 52% on corporate taxable income from the period of the Korean War to March 1964. At that time the rate was reduced to 50% for 1964 and then 48% thereafter.

The federal government depends largely on income taxes for revenue, and the yields from individual and corporate income taxes are both quite sensitive to changes in business conditions. When national income declines, the revenues of the federal government are likely to decline more than proportionately (the income elasticity of tax revenues is greater than unity); when national income increases, the revenues increase more

EXHIBIT 22–7

Federal government budget receipts, 1959–70

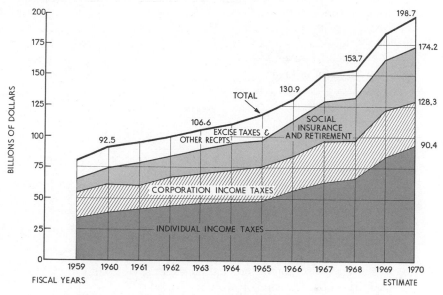

Source: U.S. Congress, *The Budget of the U.S. Government, Fiscal Year 1970.* (Washington D.C.; U.S.G.P.O., 1970).

than proportionately. The significance of this point will be developed at greater length in Chapter 24 where the subject of fiscal policy is discussed.

With rather high levels of income taxation, various kinds of exemptions have been sought and obtained by many groups in the population. For example, long-term realized capital gains (profits on sale of capital assets held more than six months) are taxed, but at rates below those applying to ordinary income. As a result, a variety of devices has been used for transmuting what would otherwise be regular income into some form of capital gain. For example, popular public entertainers form producing or recording companies which sell their services rather than working directly for wages. Ultimately these companies may be sold and the increase in value taxed as a capital gain. Petroleum producers and the owners of other extractive industries have sought and received depletion allowances which shield them from a considerable amount of taxation. Depreciation allowances for tax purposes have been the subject of considerable legislation.

Tax-exempt interest, such as on state and local government obligations, dealt with in the next chapter, becomes of more consequence to investors when marginal tax rates are as high as those now prevailing.

Types of taxes

Many different types of taxes are assessed, the following being most widely used in modern times:

Income taxes
  Personal income taxes
  Corporate income taxes
    Regular
    Excess profits
    Employment taxes
Death and estate taxes
Excise taxes
Property taxes
  Real estate
  Personal property
Sales taxes
  General sales taxes
  Excise taxes
Import duties (also sometimes called excises, although they do not
    depend on the transfer of property by sale)

In order of their current importance, receipts from individual income taxes, employment taxes, and corporate taxes account for about 85% of total federal receipts.

Why are there so many other kinds of taxes? One of the reasons, probably the leading one, is that too much reliance on one type of tax could be unfair or have undesirable economic effects. A second reason is that because our tax system represents, to a very great extent, an improvised system, many elements in it cannot be explained logically without regard to the circumstances which prevailed at the time when the taxes were adopted. Furthermore, sometimes new taxes have been introduced simply through expediency. For example, the general sales tax did not have widespread usage until the depression of the early 1930s. Although the sales tax has many undesirable features, particularly during a depression, it has one obvious merit—it is easily collectible. The most important undesirable feature of a sales tax is that when it is added to goods purchased by all income groups, its impact in terms of proportion of income is generally largest for those groups which have the lowest incomes.

Who pays the taxes?

The question "Who pays the taxes?" is much harder to answer than might be expected. It is not hard to find out who is billed for the taxes in the first place, but are the real economic costs of taxes borne by the one who makes the payment? Not necessarily.

For example, corporation taxes are an important source of tax revenue. Who bears the burden of a tax paid by a corporation? A few moments' reflection shows that the corporation itself, as a legal entity, cannot absorb the ultimate burden of the taxes it pays. Is it borne by the shareholders of the corporation, or is it passed along to buyers in the prices charged by the corporation for its products? If corporate taxes are passed along in product prices, as many think they are, then the ultimate bearers of these taxes are those who buy the products of the corporation. An analytical answer to the question of whether the taxes are passed on is that the division between shareholders and purchasers of the product depends on the type of market in which they are sold. If demand for a product is relatively insensitive to changes in its price (technically speaking, if it is relatively inelastic), it is generally easier for the corporation to pass the full burden on to its customers. Since some prominent economists now argue that to a great degree demand depends on advertising, the corporation's ability to shift taxes to consumers may depend on the extent to which some corporations are able to shift demand in this manner. In their final effect, corporate taxes may be far less equitable than they first appear to be. They may be as objectionable, on grounds of social equity, as are sales taxes.

Who should pay the taxes?

The commonest answer to the question "Who should pay taxes?" is: "Those able to pay." It is usual to assume that those able to bear the burdens should do so. The physically able expose themselves to the risks of battle, while the physically weak are sheltered.

Rules, however, have relevance only if they serve some purpose. Is the ability-to-pay rule, for example, a good tax rule? Taxes affect the economy in many ways. Owning a home, buying a security, taking a job—all of these acts are influenced by the taxes that bear on each transaction. Some taxes, while apparently fair, may have an undesirable economic effect.

For example, it might be assumed that a rich man is able to pay more taxes than a poor man—and should. But suppose that the rich man is rich by virtue of operating a productive business. Suppose that a high tax burden induced the rich man to ask himself "Why bother?" and to place his money in tax-exempt[1] municipal bonds and go fishing. It is conceivable that a relatively higher tax on the poor man, if a lower tax induced business expansion by the rich man, might benefit the poor man; his

---

[1] Income from securities issued by state and local governmental units is exempt from federal and sometimes from state income taxation.

income after taxes might be higher by virtue of the better wage opportunities offered by the rich man. However, it is probably fair to state that most economists would judge this type of effect to be relatively insignificant in our economy.

The illustration has still another bearing. The existence of tax-exempt municipals shows the pervasive influence of government finance. At first glance, it seems highly desirable to promote economy in government expenditures, as appears to be done when municipalities issue tax-exempt securities. But if these securities offer a tax-exemption haven for the rich investor, they may cost the economy much more revenue than they appear to save. (This point is discussed further in the next chapter on state and local government finance.)

How large should the total tax bill be?

In its attack on both inflation and depression, government has a potent weapon in fiscal policy—the adjustment of government revenues and expenditures according to economic conditions. (More will be presented on this subject later.) It deals not only with the appropriate kinds of taxes and who should pay them but with the size of the total tax bill and when it should be changed.

It is obvious that when individuals or businesses are taxed more, they can spend less for other things; when they are taxed less, they can spend more. Consequently, it is averred that the total tax bill should go down during depressions so as to encourage spending and that it should go up during periods of inflation in order to discourage spending.

This principle would seem easy to follow, but it is far from that. We have further questions, such as: Whose taxes should go up in inflation and down in depressions? Should the authority to vary taxes be delegated to some administrative agency which could change them promptly when economic conditions warrant change; should the tax authority continue to be exercised solely by legislative bodies; or should the executive branch have authority to effect temporary tax changes? How can the principles of fiscal policy and fairness be reconciled? For example, a sales tax is an effective weapon in curbing inflation, but it would be opposed by many if it were a regressive tax which took a larger percentage of the income of the poor than of the rich. Even so, some sales taxes, such as a tax on the sale of luxuries, need not be regressive in nature and the question becomes in part one of the appropriate design of the taxation system.

Government debt and its effects

The level of the public debt depends on the budgetary balance or on the balance of receipts and expenditures: when expenditures exceed receipts, the public debt grows; an excess of revenues over expenditures reduces public debt.

There is an enormous difference in the way in which federal government debt and state and local government debt come into being. State and local governments now adhere rather closely to the practice of keeping their current budgets in balance. In other words, they borrow mainly for capital improvements such as roads, schools, sewers, or similar projects. The service of this debt (the interest cost and the repayment of principal) then becomes a part of current costs and is met out of current revenues. State and local government debt is seldom refunded.

The federal government debt has been contracted mainly for war or during depressions and can be considered to have financed current outlays just as much as capital outlays. More importantly, the principles governing the management of the federal budget have come to be viewed chiefly as a matter of public concern with economic stabilization. However, the fact that government deficits can offset recessionary developments in the economy does not argue for fiscal imprudence; clearly, if a deficit is to be incurred the economy will be better off if the money spent is directed to creating useful rather than useless output, or if it is directed to building up rather than to destroying other economies.

The federal debt is continuously refunded, and the policies that govern its creation and handling are aimed at creating prosperity in the economy rather than at stabilizing the size of the federal government obligation to the exclusion of economic goals. Taxes are deflationary; expenditures, inflationary. Movements of the public debt are therefore an approximation to an index of the net inflationary or deflationary influence of government. An increasing debt (indicative of an excess of expenditures over revenues) is inflationary in its implications; a declining debt, the reverse, providing that the judgment is made in terms of whether the debt would be declining or increasing when the economy is operating at full-employment levels. For example, the federal budget during the early 1960s was deflationary even though it was showing a deficit, because if the economy had been at full employment in that period the budget at those full-employment levels would have shown a surplus.

Growth of the public debt

Largely as the result of wars, but also because of depression expenditures during the 1930s, the United States has a huge public debt—about $502 billion at the end of 1969. The public debt owed by the federal government was $368 billion, while state and local government debt amounted to $134 billion. It is hard to realize just how large this debt is —what the dollar figures mean. Some try to demonstrate it by reducing it to per capita terms. For example, net public debt is now equal to about

$2,300 for each man, woman, and child in this country; or—another demonstration of size—the public debt is one third of total debt obligations of the nonfinancial sector of the nation (promissory notes, mortgages, bonds, and so on).

The ratio of federal to total debt has been declining steadily since World War II, as reference to Exhibit 22–8 shows, so that despite its increase in absolute terms, government debt is not growing in relation to the size of the economy. Nonetheless, the debt is certainly large enough to warrant an examination of its effects on our economy, in order to understand just what the implications of its existence may be.

Effects of an existing public debt

A large public debt has some dangers to it, but these are not usually the dangers that people attribute to its existence. First, it is important to realize that the size of the debt has been declining steadily in relation to both total debt and GNP since the end of World War II, and that over this same period interest charges as a proportion of GNP have been relatively constant. Thus, the huge size of the debt or of the interest charges on it have little meaning or importance by themselves. This argument is strengthened by the recognition that domestically held government debt is like debt owed to oneself, something quite different from owing money to a third party because, in the latter case, the third party has a claim on the obligant's future income.

It is important also to recognize that the size of interest payments on the debt does not itself constitute an economic hardship, since interest payments represent not a cost but a redistribution of income between members of the economy. A possible source of real cost, though probably a small one, is the disincentive effect that taxes levied to pay the interest charges may have.

Similarly, the fact that the federal budget shows a deficit in some years does not mean we are saddling our grandchildren with burdens of consequence just because the size of the government debt is being increased. What does matter is the purpose for which the deficit is incurred—the economy will be better off in the future if the money is spent on useful rather than on useless projects. It is important in making this judgment also to ask whether spending by government reduced private sector investment spending. That is to say, spending by government may be productive or nonproductive, and at the same time it may or may not reduce business or household spending on capital formation. If the future productivity of private capital formation which would have taken place in the absence of government spending is greater than the productivity of the government expenditure which replaces it, a burden is passed on to future generations. Thus war imposes burdens on our grandchildren because it usually reduces the amount of productive capital formation that could otherwise have taken place. Deficit spending to build dams or highways, on the other hand, could create benefits if the spending were to reduce private sector capital formation and the output from governmental spending were to create more economic well-being than the private sector capital formation it replaced.

Still another possible effect of an existing government debt concerns whether the management of its average maturity has important economic consequences. The average maturity of the debt constantly shortens with the passage of time unless refunding operations are regularly carried out. Obviously, sharply varying refunding policies could disrupt the financial markets, and government borrowing to a great degree through these markets can also have a serious impact on private sector borrowing for capital formation purposes. But small variations in the maturity structure of the debt (i.e., whether it is outstanding on the average for 10 or for 12 years) are now thought to have little importance insofar as economic policy is concerned.

Financial markets and the federal government's budget

The growth of the federal government's functions means that its financial affairs and their management constitute important influences on the rest of the economy. Spending by the federal government is an important part of the business picture. Some business concerns sell their products or services primarily to the federal government, and most large corporations have either entered into contracts with the federal government directly or serve such contracts indirectly.

Government raising of funds, chiefly through taxes, also penetrates almost all levels of economic activity. The financial officers of some corporations spend more time on federal tax matters than on any other single matter of business policy, while at the other extreme a large proportion of the residents of this country devote many hours each spring to personal income tax returns.

The debt of the federal government is diffused through the structure of financial institutions and changes in the debt's size or distribution dominate both the money and the capital markets—often in ways that seem to upset the functioning of these markets. The purpose of this section is to follow the course of these influences in a quantitative way.

Effects of federal government borrowing and refunding

The pattern of federal government finance has gone through a great many stages. As recently as 1929, the budget expenditures of the federal government were less than 4% of gross national product. In later years

EXHIBIT 22-8

Federal government's share of total economy, 1929-68 (ratio of federal expenditures to gross national product and ratio of federal debt to total debt)

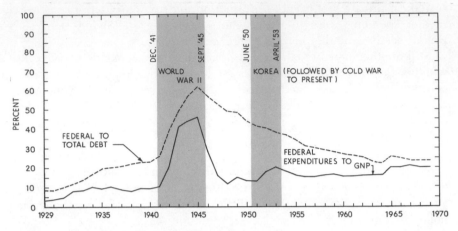

Source: *Federal Reserve Bulletin*, various issues.

they have run from 15 to 18%. During World War II, they rose to over 40% of the gross national product. As a proportion of GNP, federal debt held by the public has been declining since World War II. This pattern is displayed in Exhibit 22-8.

Changes in the outstanding amount of the government debt are constantly occurring because the expenditures and receipts of the federal government are seldom in balance. (A balanced budget is not necessarily desirable from the viewpoint of economic policy, as Chapter 24 will show.) Over most fiscal years, a budget balance has been uncommon. From fiscal 1939 through fiscal 1969 the difference was less than $2 billion in only six years. (Two billion dollars is used as the cutoff point in this illustration since this is an amount by which cash balances might reasonably fluctuate.)

The cash balance of the Treasury (partly in the Federal Reserve banks and partly in commercial banks) can take up some of the difference between receipts and expenditures. As already intimated, $2 billion is about the amount of variation from expectations that the Treasury Department can normally absorb through its cash balance. Since this amount normally represents only about 6-8 days' expenditures, the Treasury Department does not have much margin for strategic maneuver. Thus one can say almost categorically that the Treasury Department must engage in some financing in almost all years, whether the budget is balanced or not.

If the imbalance is a temporary one, the Treasury can borrow on a short-term basis, expecting to repay the loans later, or it can repay short-term loans and later borrow anew. But if the budget imbalance is for a longer period of time, then the Treasury Department must consider long-term borrowing or the possibility of retiring outstanding longer term debt. These kinds of transactions can have a major impact on the amount of funds available for financing the capital expenditures of the business sector, the building of homes, and the capital expenditures of state and local governments. This is because at any time the amounts of funds lenders will supply at given interest rates are limited, and if government borrows unusually large amounts of these funds, less will be available for borrowing by the private sector. If government repays debt, funds are added to supplies otherwise available in financial markets.

The problems of the Treasury Department also involve debt management. As the legacy of two great wars and a deep depression, the debt of the federal government judged in relation to total debt has been very large, as shown in Exhibit 22–8. At its wartime peak it was more than three fifths of all net debts. Even now, 25 years after the end of the war, the debt of the federal government still is about 24% of all debt, and a very large part of it has a short maturity. Because of this legacy, the Treasury Department constantly faces the problem of debt refunding. While it would be possible to repay maturing debt with cash and then sell new issues for cash, the dollar amounts are so great that exchange offerings are required. Thus, the Treasury Department is constantly engaged in managing the debt. While the technical problems of carrying out these operations in a way which does not disrupt the financial markets are quite difficult, the prevailing maturity structure of the debt does not appear to be of great importance for economic stabilization. In fact, many economists argue that a large government debt improves the functioning of financial markets by enhancing the trading activity in the markets and thus providing more nearly representative prices for different kinds of credit instruments.

The securities of the federal government are for practical purposes without default risk. In addition, its shorter term bills and certificates are considered to be very liquid securities that can be used by their holders as a reserve almost as good as cash. The market in which these short-term obligations are traded is fluid, and large amounts can be and are bought and sold daily. The dollar volume of this trading far exceeds stock exchange trading; for example, the amount often exceeds a billion dollars in one business day. Thus any one holder can sell (or buy) large amounts without much effect on the market.

Control and management of federal finance

In Chapter 24 the fiscal policy of the federal government and its relationship to the general economic policy of the government will be considered in detail. In this section the process of management and policy formation will be considered.

Formation of the federal budget might be considered the first step in the managerial process. This responsibility falls on the president of the United States and is, in fact, discharged for him by the Bureau of the Budget, which is a part of the executive office of the president. The Bureau of the Budget gathers plans from the various branches of government and then, under the direction of the president, negotiates such changes as seem needed for overall budget policy. The budget contains not only the expenditure proposals but also any proposals for tax changes that the president recommends.

Since this country does not operate on a parliamentary basis and since party discipline is relatively lax, the president's budget may be substantially altered before it emerges from Congress. (Under parliamentary governments, the executive officers are drawn from the legislative branch and hold office only so long as they command a legislative majority. They rise and fall, but as long as parliamentary governments remain in office, they can get their budget expenditures and taxes enacted. Of course, the issue of the budget can cause a parliamentary government to fall. If, however, the ruling party is strong, that is unlikely.) Congressional influence on both expenditures and receipts is likely to be great. The history of budgets as they have gone into Congress and as they have emerged shows considerable variation in form and pattern. Although generalizations are unsafe, Congress has more often than not tended to increase the amount of spending proposed by presidents and has tended to resist tax increases recommended. There have been exceptions, and some Congresses have been economizers.

Once an appropriation has been passed, the actual spending is usually in the hands of some one of the executive departments: defense, agriculture, etc. That means negotiating contracts to purchase military equipment, hiring of personnel to carry out projects, building government buildings, transferring funds to states and to local governments, or whatever other action may be indicated by the authorization. All expenditures are subject to the review of the Comptroller General of the United States, an office that is considered a kind of auditing branch of Congress. When expenditures have been made, the actual disbursements of payments are effected by the Treasury Department.

One might expect that the funds appropriated by Congress would automatically be spent. Such is not always the case. Congress has sometimes appropriated funds not asked for by administrators, and executive officers of federal government departments have been known to drag their feet in spending funds available to them. Furthermore, the spending process often takes time, and there are thus raised the complex problems involved in carrying over from one fiscal period to another the authority to obligate funds implicit in a congressional appropriation. Some items, such as public housing or military equipment, go through long preliminary periods of planning and design.

The role of the Treasury Department in expenditures is primarily that of accountant and bill payer. In the matter of revenues, the Treasury Department plays a much larger role: it is not only the tax collector but the chief technical branch advising the president and ultimately Congress on the many technical problems of tax and revenue legislation. Interpretation of tax laws is complex, and the standards set by the Treasury Department have great weight with tax courts. Although all taxpayers can seek ultimate relief in the courts if they feel the Treasury Department's interpretation of the tax law has been unfair, the presumption of validity is on the side of the Treasury.

The influence of the Treasury Department in the formation of tax legislation is even more pervasive. Most presidents have had to depend primarily on the Treasury Department for help and advice when the tax portions of the budget were being formulated and at other times when tax problems arose. The same is also true of Congress. While various finance committees of Congress have retained their own tax experts, in the long run the prime source of technical competence on tax matters has been the Treasury Department. The drafting of legislation and the making of revenue estimates generally is done in that department.

The Treasury Department also dominates the management of the public debt. While Congress sets the general rules and while some presidents have taken some interest in the process, this has been one of the main and central roles of the Secretary of the Treasury. Because the Federal Reserve has both expert knowledge of the money and capital markets and great influence in these markets, it is often an important adviser of the Secretary of the Treasury, but the final responsibility is his, and his alone.

The balance of financial power in the federal government shifts as the power and prestige of individuals change. A strong president, aided by a competent Secretary of the Treasury, may both sway Congress and strongly influence the Federal Reserve. A weak or indifferent president is likely to lose most of this power to Congress. A strong Secretary of the Treasury is not enough to save a weak or indifferent president, although he can have some independent influence. Strong individuals in Congress may have a range of influence that exceeds the normal boundaries of their office. The judgment of political scientists on this point might be divided, but Congress seems to have increased its financial role in recent years.

Events also influence the balance of financial power. War is sure to reduce the role of the Federal Reserve and increase that of the Secretary of the Treasury. War is also likely to increase the role of the president and reduce that of Congress. Any sharp or unexpected economic development, such as a recession or a period of international tension, may create something of a power vacuum into which the strong leader moves whether from the side of the executive or the legislature.

Managing the federal trust funds

The federal government operates a number of trust funds, having asset holdings of $89 billion at year-end 1969 and with annual receipts and disbursements of nearly $45 billion in 1969. The principal trust account is the Old Age Survivors and Disability Insurance (OASDI) account, which administers all social security payments. The unemployment insurance account is second in size. (Unemployment benefits are distributed through state agencies, but the asset account is administered by the federal government.) Other trust accounts include hospital insurance, veterans life insurance, federal employees retirement, railroad retirement, the trust account for federal aid to highways, and a number of smaller accounts.

Federal trust accounts are invested almost wholly in the securities of the federal government. These investments are the principal reason for the difference between gross and net federal debt. Most of them are non-marketable obligations issued to the trust accounts at fixed rates of interest, but some of the trust accounts buy and sell marketable treasury obligations in the open market.

Questions and problems

A. General

1. List criteria that distinguish good from doubtful government expenditures.
2. List the factors that have tended to increase the expenditures of the federal government.
3. List the factors that have tended to increase the expenditures of state and local governments.
4. What general principles govern the choice of an equitable tax?
5. If these principles are simple, why do we have so many taxes?
6. Why is public debt different from private debt?

B. Federal government finance

7. Cite a few figures from the most recent *Economic Report of the President* illustrating the relative importance of the federal government in the economy.

8. If you wanted to reduce the expenditure budget of the federal government, where would you start?

9. What obstacles would you probably face?

10. If you set out to revise the federal tax system, where would you start?

11. Why is too much short-term financing by the Treasury Department considered dangerous?

12. Draw a rough diagram illustrating the division of financial management functions within the federal government.

13. Compare management of federal finances in the United States with that in most parliamentary governments.

Bibliography

A student wishing to consult a general reference text on governmental finance may select among several excellent ones. Two are especially recommended:

Due, John F. *Government Finance: An Economic Analysis.* 4th ed. Homewood, Ill.: Richard D. Irwin, Inc., 1968.

Groves, Harold. *Financing Government.* 6th ed. New York: Holt, Rinehart, and Winston, 1964.

Basic statistical facts on federal finance may be secured from the *Treasury Bulletin* and the federal budget documents. *The Federal Budget in Brief,* which is published each January a few days after the budget message goes to Congress is a compact and authoritative survey of federal finances. Another useful document (which this chapter follows in its analysis of federal expenditures and presentation of graphs) is the National Industrial Conference Board's annual publication *The Federal Budget: Its Impact on the Economy.* State and local government finance is less well reported. The government's Division of the Bureau of the Census publishes a number of pamphlets on city and state finances, but the summary of governmental finances published each year appears late and covers only a relatively few basic facts.

CHAPTER 23

Public finance: state and local government

The federal government, which was dealt with in the last chapter, is concerned with national defense and international affairs and has a conscious fiscal and monetary policy. The kind of government dealt with in this chapter is often rather closer to our daily lives: state and local government. The streets that run in front of our homes and the sewers that service them are provided by such governments. Police and fire protection are functions of local governments. Many hospitals and most libraries and some museums are built and maintained by state or local governmental units. Some states and a few cities operate liquor stores. Very much in the center of political controversy is the public operation of utilities such as light and power plants. The operation of public transportation systems, such as subways and street railways, is less controversial only because many of these systems failed to operate successfully as private utilities. Considered essential, they have been taken over and operated as public services. Somewhat more recent among state-sponsored ventures are toll roads and toll bridges.

Education, however, is the single largest and most costly function of state and local government. Although some excellent private primary and secondary schools operate in the United States, the great majority of schools at this level are public or publicly supported. Six out of seven students in primary or secondary grade attend public schools.

At the collegiate level, the ratio is much lower; some of our greatest universities are private institutions. The numerical balance is nevertheless weighted on the side of state-supported colleges and universities. For example, of the 87 institutions that used an earlier edition of this textbook, 59 were publicly supported institutions. On the basis of numbers of students, the balance was even more extreme. In other words, the chances are three to one that you, the student reading these words (we hope you read them carefully), are attending an institution of higher education supported by public funds. It is at least a 50 to 1 bet that at some time in your primary or secondary school education you went to a public school; possibly the odds should be even higher.

State and local governmental operations are an important part of our economic structure. In 1969 such governments employed about 10% of the labor force. As Exhibit 23–1 shows, the expenditures of state and local

EXHIBIT 23–1

Relative importance of state and local government expenditures and debt

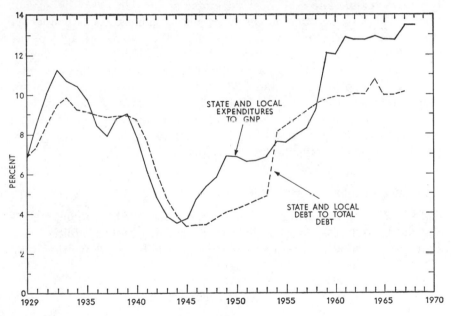

Source: U.S. Department of Commerce, Bureau of the Census, *Government Finances in 1968–69* (Washington, D.C.: U.S.G.P.O., September 1970).

government are becoming a larger part of gross national product; during 1968–69 the proportion was more than 13%. The debt of state and local government was almost 10% of all kinds of public and private debt. Obviously, the financial practices and policies of state and local government can and do have a profound influence on the economy.

A great diversity of policies makes it difficult to generalize about state and local government finance. This diversity is due partly to the great number of local governmental bodies. Over 80,000 different state and local governmental units were functioning in the United States in 1967. School districts were the most numerous; about 22,000 were active. In addition, over 18,000 municipalities and 17,000 townships were in legal existence. Over 21,000 special districts function: sewer districts are the best illustration of such entities. A total of 3,000 counties are contained in the 50 states.

The range in size of state and local governmental units is extreme. Several of the great states have budgets and debts as large as major foreign powers. At the other extreme, some special districts have no elective officers and exist only as small subsidiaries of cities.

The function of this chapter is to generalize about the finances of state and local government, a task greatly complicated by the diversity in size and circumstance just mentioned. The first major topic to be considered is the character of state and local government expenditures. The second topic is a discussion of the sources of revenue—mainly taxes—upon which the expenditures depend. Since a more general economic analysis of tax principles appeared in the preceding chapter, we shall not dwell long on this issue here. The third major section of this chapter considers borrowing and debt repayment by state and local governmental units. The major emphasis in this section is on the unique feature of state and local government securities: their exemption from federal income taxation. The final part of the chapter is devoted to a brief analysis of the general financial policies pursued by state and local government units.

State and local government expenditures

In 1969, state and local governments spent almost $117 billion, including the gross transactions of their trust accounts, public utilities, and liquor stores. Table 23–1 shows these expenditures broken down according

TABLE 23–1

State and local government expenditures, 1968–69

Expenditure by function	Percent*
Education	39.9
Highways	18.4
Public welfare	16.0
Health and hospitals	6.9
Other	18.8
	100.0%

* Total dollars represented by percentages: $117 billion.
Source: U.S. Department of Commerce, Bureau of the Census, *Government Finances in 1968–69* (Washington, D.C.: U.S.G.P.O., September 1970).

to their functional purpose. This section will discuss the functional expenditure classification, the division of expenditures between current and capital outlays, and the expenditures of utilities and liquor stores.

The purpose of spending

The expenditures classification in Table 23–1 shows that education accounts for the largest percentage of state and local government direct spending. Most education expenditures are incurred for primary and secondary education; these expenditures are generally made at a local level but supported by extensive grants-in-aid. Public educational institutions at the higher level are generally state operated.

Highways are the second most important element of cost in state and local government operations, accounting for more than $15 billion in 1968–69. States tend to dominate the direct expenditures and also support highway expenditures by cities and other local governmental units through grants-in-aid. The federal government in 1968–69 was allocating almost $4 billion to state and local government to aid in highway construction. However, most highway expenditures are to some extent tied to the revenue from various automobile and gasoline taxes.

The third most important category of state and local government expenditures is welfare outlays for the sick, the aged, and the indigent. During 1968–69, $12 billion was expended for these purposes. Since unemployment benefits and other benefits related to the federal social security programs are not included in these tabulations, these welfare expenditures are for state and locally originated programs.

Hospitals and other health expenditures—the fourth most important category—accounted for $8.6 billion in 1968–69. Institutions for the aged and for mentally disturbed people account for a considerable part of this total. Provision of county or visiting nurses is another kind of health service. Public health programs, such as mosquito eradication, also fall into this category.

Other lesser but not unimportant state and local government expenditures include fire and police protection, sanitation, parks and reservations, public housing, and interest on state and local government debt.

Capital versus current outlays

One of the impressive facts of state and local government finance is that such a large fraction of expenditures is of a capital nature. About 22% of outlays is so classified. This is a much larger proportion of capital expenditure than is made by the other major sectors of the economy: the consumer sector, the business sector, and the federal government.

Expenditures for highways, the brick-and-mortar part of educational programs, and public housing account for the fact that capital expenditures are relatively high. As a result, state and local governments are the owners of one of the largest segments of wealth in the national economy. Goldsmith estimated that in 1949 the depreciated value of capital assets (including highways) constructed by state and local government was $52.4 billion, and the holdings of land had a value of $22.5 billion.[1] Later figures suggest that by 1958 state and local governments administered capital assets having a depreciated value of close to $125 billion. No doubt this total has continued to grow at a rapid rate.

Assistance and subsidy payments of state and local governments are similar to the transfer payments dealt with in the federal budget in the preceding chapter. These transfer payments, at about 5% of state and local government expenditures, are of an importance almost equal to those in the federal budget. Interest on state and local government debt accounts for about 3.4% of expenditures.

State liquor stores, public utility expenditures

The statistics presented in the capital versus current outlays section on state and local government expenditures include gross expenditures of state and local government business ventures, the chief of which are light and water utilities and liquor stores, in the percentage calculations. Both gross and net revenues from these ventures are reported in the following section, because these kinds of operations are intended either to be self-financing or to provide funds for the governments operating them.

State and local government revenues

In contrast to their importance in providing about 87% of federal revenues, taxes account for approximately 60% of the revenues of state and local governments. Other important sources are therefore also considered in this section: intergovernmental grants-in-aid, charges for the use of various facilities, and profits from state-operated business enterprises such as liquor stores and public utilities. Table 23–2 gives the broad pattern of revenue sources.

Taxes

The taxes collected by state governments in 1968–69 amounted to nearly $42 billion; about $35 billion was collected by local governmental units. The details are shown in Table 23–3. Although the totals are similar, the sources are quite different. Property taxes were once the

---

[1] *Study of Saving* (Princeton, N.J.: Princeton University Press, 1956), pt. III, p. 56, Table W-16.

TABLE 23–2

State and local government revenue sources, 1968–69
(*millions of dollars*)

Taxes	$ 76,712
Charges and miscellaneous general revenue	18,686
Utility revenue	5,931
Liquor stores	1,909
Insurance trust revenue	9,764
Federal government grants (net)	19,153
Total	$132,154

Source: U.S. Department of Commerce, Bureau of the Census, *Government Finances in 1968–69* (Washington, D.C.: U.S.G.P.O., September 1970).

principal source of tax revenue for both state and local governments. "Real" property—land and buildings—is the principal property taxed. In course of time, however, the property tax has been turned over to local governments for their sole use. State governments look to other sources for revenue. The most productive tax of state governments now is the sales tax. The most important state sales tax is the general sales or gross receipts tax, but sales taxes on gasoline are almost as important a source of revenue. The *sumptuary* taxes on tobacco products and on liquor account for a large part of the remainder. A sumptuary tax is one aimed at limiting, but not prohibiting, the consumption of potentially dangerous but cheap products. The idea of consumption limitation has probably vanished from the minds of most tax authorities. The unusually heavy rates on these products, however, even heavier than the so-called luxury taxes (as on perfume), probably are accounted for by this vague but persistent objective.

TABLE 23–3

Kinds of taxes used by state and local governments, 1968–69
(*millions of dollars*)

	Total state and local	State	Local
Property	$30,673	$ 981	$29,692
Individual income	8,908	7,527	1,381
Corporate income	3,180	3,180	—
Sales and gross receipts	26,519	24,050	2,470
Automobile	2,841	2,685	157
All other	4,590	3,508	1,082
Total	$76,712	$41,931	$34,781

Source: U.S. Department of Commerce, Bureau of the Census, *Government Finances in 1968–69* (Washington, D.C.: U.S.G.P.O., September 1970).

23——Public finance: state and local government

The income tax is of only moderate importance as a revenue producer for state governments. Income taxes on corporations are avoided for fear of losing industry to states that impose no income taxes. But, without a corporate income tax, an income tax on individuals is often viewed as unfair. While individuals have less opportunity of moving away from state income taxes, this factor has not been without some influence. In any event, individuals with high incomes probably would avoid living in states with excessively high rates, so there is seldom very much progression in the income tax rates imposed by states.

Local governments depend primarily on the property tax, and while there is token taxation of personal or intangible property in many areas, the bulk of the property tax burden is borne by real estate. Taxation of real estate produced almost $30 billion for local government in 1968–69 and was the principal source of revenue for the support of primary and secondary schools, fire and police departments, and other local governmental services. Sales taxes have been imposed by a few cities, but this has been done with caution; a sales tax is too likely to shift trade to surrounding untaxed areas.

Because of the growing demand for state and local government services and because of the increased cost of these services, there has been a scramble to invent new taxes that would not drive business away but would be easy to administer and would produce revenue. State and local governments have applied taxes such as on theater admissions, on racetrack betting, on hotel rooms, and on payrolls. The automobile has come to bear a number of taxes, including both local license fees and state license taxes.

Although it is hard to judge precisely (experts debate the point), state and local government taxes appear to be more evenly spread over all income groups and less concentrated on high-income groups than is true of federal taxes. The extent to which this is thought inequitable depends, of course, on one's views of how the costs of government should be divided—and what effects taxes have on incentives.

Intergovernmental revenues

Local governments depend partly on grants-in-aid or tax remissions from state governments, while state governments in turn depend on grants from the federal government. For example, most states give aid to local school districts. The purpose of these grants may be to equalize the educational expenditures of the poor and the better-off communities. Some of them, however, are used as tools for enforcing minimum education standards. (A school may not qualify for state aid unless it passes inspection or has certain minimum facilities.) A leading example of

TABLE 23–4

Intergovernmental grants-in-aid, 1968–69 (*in millions of dollars*)

Federal government grants
To local governments .... $ 2,245
To state governments $16,907

Total $19,153

State government grants
Gross amount of grants to local governments $23,837
Less: grants from local governments
to state governments 868

Total $22,969

Source: U.S. Department of Commerce, Bureau of the Census, *Government Finances in 1968–69* (Washington, D.C.: U.S.G.P.O., September 1970).

federal government grants is its payments to state governments for highway construction. The purpose of these grants is partly to control the type and character of highways built by states, so that something like a national highway system is created. The structure of intergovernmental grants-in-aid is shown in Table 23–4.

As this table shows, the federal government distributed $19 billion of such grants in 1968–69, about nine tenths of it to state governments. The state governments distributed $24 billion in grants to local governments, and local governments paid back $0.8 billion to the states.

Put in net terms, the federal government spent $19 billion on such grants; state governments added a net $4 billion to this amount and passed the whole along to local governments. Looking at these amounts as net flows, however, might be misleading because the states that were beneficiaries of net federal receipts were not necessarily the states that passed along aid to local government. Indeed, in the poorer areas of the United States, federal aid to the states frequently is in excess of amounts passed along to local government. In wealthy states, state aid passed along is often many times larger than amounts received from the federal government.

Net revenues from liquor stores and state-operated public utilities

The liquor stores operated by states and a few cities produced about $1.9 billion of gross revenue during 1968–69; an amount which exceeded current expenditures by $0.4 billion. Since these profits are often an alternative to a state tax on liquor sales, they should not be viewed as the equivalent of profit in a privately operated business.

Most publicly owned utilities are operated by local governments, either by cities or by small special districts. Water systems are the most important ones. An estimated 80% of water systems are publicly owned and operated. Electric power and gas utilities are far less important relatively, except in a few areas of the country. Intraurban transit systems, however, have more often than not failed in private ownership and are now being publicly operated. In 1968–69 government-owned public utilities produced revenues of $6 billion and had current costs of $4.1 billion. Capital expenditures amounted to $2.5 billion.

The policy of having state or local governments operate business ventures is disputed, as is the accounting for profits and losses. At the present time, no clearly established trend of either increase or decrease in the number of publicly owned utilities is discernible. State liquor stores can be viewed partly as regulation of an industry whose social value is questionable and partly as a means of getting revenue from a state monopoly. Water, electricity, and gas utilities operated by municipalities face up more directly to the issue of economic policy—state versus private operation of business. Water utilities are more often publicly owned than are other types of utilities because of their very slow capital turnover. Since interest on outstanding debt is often the chief cost of running a water system, tax exemption provides a greater incentive for public ownership of water systems than is the case with other types of utilities.

Charges from revenue projects: toll roads, bridges, sewers, etc.

Charges are made for some governmental services, although frequently at rates which fail to pay the full cost of the facilities offered. Such charges include tuition at state-supported educational institutions, hospital charges, admission fees for state or local parks, rents on air terminals, and charges for school lunches.

One charge of increasing importance is the fee or toll for use of a public facility, such as a toll road or bridge, or the fee paid for use of public docks or warehouses. Revenue-producing projects, such as sewer districts or special toll facilities, generally only pay for themselves; they do not yield revenues for general governmental purposes. When these facilities are fully paid for, they are usually put on a no-charge basis.

State and local government borrowing

All levels of state and local governments borrow. The most common purpose of borrowing is for capital expenditures. It follows, therefore, that most of the borrowing done is by those units of state and local government that have unusually heavy capital expenditures. Thus school districts are frequently important as borrowers.

Because the chief purpose of borrowing is for capital outlays and since state and local governments rather rarely have budget deficits on current account, it follows that the securities offered are mainly in long-term form. At June 30, 1969, the end of the 1968–69 fiscal year, state and local government long-term indebtedness totaled nearly $107 billion, of which $27 billion was incurred for provision of local schools and $17 billion for local utilities.

Most state and local government obligations are the debt of the unit issuing them and are based on the full faith and credit of the issuing body; in other words, they are general obligations. They are backed up by the taxing power of the governmental unit issuing them. In recent periods, however, state and local governments have created an increasing number of special districts or special authorities for a fixed purpose, such as to build and operate a toll road, a sewer system, or airports and terminal buildings and bridges, such as the Port of New York Authority. Such authorities generally do not have taxing power but do have the power to borrow and to secure the borrowing by the revenue from the project being undertaken. These revenue obligations furnish a somewhat special market for state and local government obligations, though they enjoy the same privilege of tax exemption (discussed below on p. 550). Although revenue obligations are frequently in serial form, as is true of general obligations, they are more often in term (single maturity) form. The investment analysis of revenue obligations has a striking parallel to that of corporate obligations, and indeed, the investment banking methods of marketing revenue obligations frequently parallel those of corporate obligations. In some areas where debt limits have inhibited the use of general obligations, special forms of revenue obligations have been created for such purposes as building public schools.

Purpose of state and local government borrowing

The purpose of state and local government borrowing is generally to finance capital outlays. Schools lead as a cause of borrowing, but utilities run a close second. Sewer and water installations have been numerous and costly in this period, particularly because of the extension of urban communities into suburban areas. The amount shown for roads and bridges was used mainly to construct toll facilities. The amount shown as housing represents primarily public housing projects, many of them under federally sponsored programs. Nevertheless, a number of states have their own public housing programs not related to federal subsidies or support.

Since most state and local government obligations are issued in serial form, they are seldom refunded. Accordingly, the proportion of new debts sold for refunding purposes is small.

Tax exemption of state and local government obligations

The unique characteristic of state and local government obligations is that they are exempt from the income tax of the federal government. Many of them are also exempt from income taxation by the states in which they are issued, though they are seldom exempt from the income taxes of other states. This circumstance evolved in U.S. constitutional history. Before the Sixteenth (income tax) Amendment was passed, the Supreme Court had held that the securities of the federal government could not be taxed by the states and that the income from securities issued by state and local government could not be taxed by the federal government. Although the Sixteenth Amendment seemed to remove this second bar (the federal government was given the power to tax income from whatever source derived), this practice was preserved in the form of a statutory exemption by the federal government of state and local government securities from the income taxation of the federal government. The power of the federal government to tax state and local government security interest thus has not been adjudicated. Constitutional authorities continue to debate the question whether the exemption rests solely on this statutory basis or whether it also has a constitutional foundation. The point is academic, since only a few obscure fiscal economists keep alive the movement for repeal of the tax-exemption statute. Their general argument is that the rich escape their just share of taxation by investing in tax-exempt obligations. Since the federal government ceased making its own securities tax-exempt in any degree in 1941, state and local governments have had a monopoly of this privilege.

The exercise of this monopoly by state and local governments works to reduce somewhat the cost of borrowing by state and local governments. The exact amount cannot be estimated precisely because state and local government obligations are not exactly comparable to either corporate or U.S. treasury obligations. Nevertheless, a rough comparison can be made. Exhibit 23–2 compares corporate bond yields before and after taxes (at the corporate tax rate) and indicates the part retained by investors and the part that reduces state and local government borrowing costs.

As this chart shows, much of the advantage of tax exemption was retained by state and local governments in the early postwar period. In later parts of the period, however, most of it went to investors. In other words, the loss of tax revenues to the federal government can be considerably greater than the reduction of costs of state and local government.

The facts in this chart illustrate a principle that could also have been arrived at by marginal analysis. Presumably, an investor will buy a tax-exempt security at a yield less than a comparable fully taxed security only

EXHIBIT 23–2

Division of revenue lost by tax exemption between state and local government and investors

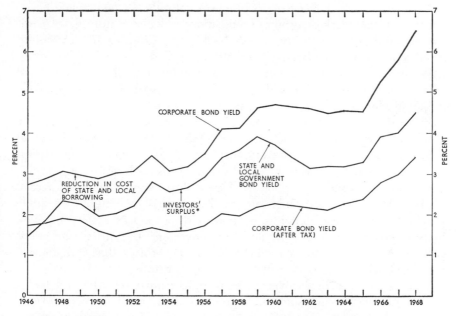

* Advantage to investor paying taxes at corporate income rate over a fully taxed corporate bond. All yields are Moody's annual averages.

Source: Moody's annual averages as reported in *Federal Reserve Bulletin*.

when he can secure a tax advantage of a greater amount by doing so. In other words, the saving in the taxes he pays must be at least as great as the reduction in yield that he accepts. Since this must be true of the *marginal* investor, it follows that the tax saving will be greater than the yield reduction for intramarginal investors. To sell tax-exempt securities, government as a whole must forego more income than it saves in lower borrowing costs. Exhibit 23–2 illustrates this fact. The portion retained by investors can be viewed as a kind of investors' surplus—something extra that they gain beyond what they would receive by investing in fully taxable obligations.

Marketing practices

Almost all state and local government obligations are sold by public bidding. A few are still offered at open auctions, but the public sealed bid is now the much more common form. Occasionally, the securities issued by such revenue-producing ventures as toll roads or bridges are sold by direct negotiation to investment bankers, but this practice is still relatively uncommon.

The firms that underwrite and market these securities and, accordingly, bid for them when they are offered include not only the investment banking houses that market corporate obligations but also a number of commercial banks. (Review investment banking in Chapter 18.) Although commercial banks are barred from acting as underwriters of corporate obligations, they may underwrite general obligations of state and local governments. Commercial banks have also recently obtained the privilege of bidding for and marketing revenue obligations.

Since state and local government issues range all the way from very small amounts such as $50,000 or $100,000 up to massive issues of several hundred million dollars, the organization of the underwriting groups selling the securities varies greatly. Very large issues require large syndicates, sometimes numbering several hundred investment and commercial bankers. At the other extreme, very small issues may be bought by a single purchaser or, more commonly, by two or three houses acting together. Since the median size of state and local government security offerings is only about a quarter of a million dollars, the groups that bid for and reoffer most issues consist of two, three, or four firms.

Since state and local government securities must be sold to a larger number of investors and since the individual sale typically involves a small amount, these offerings cannot be disposed of quite as rapidly as can corporate obligations. The underwriters of a large issue of corporate obligations can sometimes sell it completely in 10 or 15 minutes by a few telephone calls. Such speed would be the exception rather than the rule in selling a state or local government issue. Occasionally, quick sellouts occur, but more often than not even a successful issue may be held for several days by the syndicate buying it. It is not uncommon to hold syndicates together for several weeks. As a result, more inventory of state and local government obligations is typically held by investment bankers and commercial banks than is true of corporate obligations. This inventory may be the cause of losses and occasionally can also be made the source of unusual profits.

Because of the greater marketing problems in selling state and local government obligations, the marketing costs are somewhat higher than those of corporate obligations. The spread on very high-grade obligations represents about 1% of the gross amount sold; on intermediate-grade obligations the cost of marketing may be 2% or even higher in some cases. Most corporate bonds are sold for a cost of from one half of 1% to 1%. Marketing costs, however, seldom exceed 3–5% of the total even for very small issues or for the somewhat more speculative revenue bonds.

Investors in state and local government obligations

As would be expected, most state and local government obligations are bought by investors who can take advantage of tax exemption. The principal investors in these obligations, accordingly, have always been individuals with high incomes. Individuals buy tax-exempt securities when they wish a conservative, income-protected investment. Rich men who are aggressive portfolio investors are more likely to seek capital gains in equities or oil-producing royalties, both of which are to some extent protected from the full impact of income taxes. In other words, even though high-income individuals are the principal natural market for them, only some individuals are interested in state and local government obligations. Presumably, this circumstance accounts for the fact disclosed in Exhibit 23–2 that investors demanded and got a larger part of the advantage of tax exemption in the postwar decade. A booming equity market draws investors away from fixed-dollar tax-exempt obligations.

Since most commercial banks are exposed to the full corporate income tax rate, they are likewise natural investors in tax-exempt obligations and are the second most important group of buyers. Part of their interest is due to the fact that they can also underwrite them and act as dealers in these securities. This, however, is not the sole explanation, since even nondealer banks are important investors in tax exempts. Since these obligations are usually sold in serial form, most offerings include some short- and intermediate-term obligations which are the natural investment choice of commercial banks. In other words, when an underwriting syndicate offers a serial issue, it is likely to find that individuals buy the longer term obligations and that commercial banks buy the short- and intermediate-term obligations.

Casualty insurance companies are another important group of investors in tax-exempt obligations. These companies are subject to the full corporate income tax, and they have still another reason for interest in tax-exempt bonds. Since their other principal investment vehicle is common stocks, they tend to alternate between purchase of common stocks and purchase of tax-exempt obligations.

Most other institutional investors pay only limited amounts of income tax and therefore are not as interested in tax-exempt obligations. Until a few years ago, life insurance companies paid modest income taxes, as did mutual savings banks and savings and loan associations. Accordingly, none of these groups bought many tax exempts, though life insurance companies occasionally purchased revenue bonds.

Since the secondary market in tax-exempt obligations is not very active, an investor may find the cost of disposing of his holdings before maturity relatively high. It is high particularly for investors who hold odd lots (less than five bonds or $5,000 par value).

Financial policies of state and local governments

In times gone by, the management of state and local government finances was often inept, and it was sometimes dishonest. Financial management, however, has become both more rational and more honest. Many states have rather complex requirements for the financial management of the local governmental units they charter. Debt limits are also sometimes imposed on these local governmental units. Several states themselves operate under constitutional debt limits. The small governmental units frequently are managed by part-time officials, and so rather simple practices are followed. However, in the larger cities and for many of the special projects, such as toll roads and other public authorities, financial management is in the hands of competent specialists, who follow practices comparable to those of large businesses.

Almost all state and local government units now operate under some form of budget. Unlike private business, they do not always make a clear distinction between current outlays and capital outlays. Increasingly, however, the two types of outlay tend to be budgeted separately.

State and local governments have developed almost no conscious countercyclical or compensatory fiscal policies (see Chapter 24 for a full account of this idea). There are exceptions, and the financial managers of some large cities and states try to manage their affairs so as to take up the slack in short-term changes in revenues without being forced to make parallel changes in expenditures. Aside from such rare cases, most state and local governmental units aim at the annually balanced budget. This annual balance is between cash receipts (not including borrowing), and current outlays plus debt service (interest and principal repayments) and some capital outlays. Most capital outlays are consciously and specifically financed by borrowing. There is occasional short-term borrowing in anticipation of tax revenues, but it is frowned on by many managers of state and local finances.

In state and local government finance, as in federal government finance, the line of causation tends to run from expenditures to receipts. Public expenditures are made in response to a variety of public or political pressures.[2] These pressures may represent widely supported demands (such as for adequate fire protection) or sharply disputed demands, such as for a proposed swimming pool for a new school, or quite parochial demands, such as for a new road which will make a real estate developer's land more valuable.

After expenditures have been authorized, the problem is then to secure

---

[2] This is not to suggest that *political* is a nasty word. A democracy's business is transacted through the political process. When a PTA circulates a petition to build a new schoolhouse, it is engaging in a form of political activity.

the necessary revenue. Taxes (or other receipts) must be generated. There is often a considerable lag in time between the authorizing of the expenditure and the levying of the tax that pays the bill. In the long run, however, the limits imposed by the tax base do tend to influence expenditures. Poorer states generally do not spend as much for schools, not because they want to spend less but because they are forced to do so. Tax revolts have not been unknown in local governmental affairs. On the other hand, a bulge of prosperity which increases receipts is likely to make the budget makers a little more generous.

The benefits of state and local government projects tend to be more closely related to the kind of tax used to finance them than is true of federal government outlays. Citizens use the schools, enjoy the parks, and drive on the roads for which they pay taxes. The benefits of national defense or of adequate statistics in the Department of Commerce may be just as important to the nation, but they have a remote quality. The benefit theory of taxation tends to have a much closer application in state and local government finance than in federal finances.

Questions and problems

1. Cite examples from the state or locality in which you live illustrating why state and local government expenditures have risen in recent years. Is this increase likely to continue?

2. List the various governmental units that function in the area in which you live. (*Hint:* unless you live in a remote rural area, it should be easy to identify at least four or five such units.)

3. If possible, locate the budget of your home city (or state) and analyze it in terms of functions.

4. Analyze this budget in terms of revenue sources.

5. What has been the recent history of taxes and tax rates in this area?

6. If you find grants-in-aid in the sources of revenue, trace them back to their source.

7. In answering problem 3 above, you presumably divided expenditures between current and capital outlays. (If not, go back and do so.) To what extent were capital outlays financed by borrowing?

8. What was the interest cost on any recent borrowing that you encountered?

9. Through what channels were these securities marketed?

10. Locate at least one type of local institution that owns tax-exempt securities. (Individuals also probably own them, but it would be prying into personal business to attempt to locate such ownership.)

11. What are the tax factors that make such ownership logical?

12. Tax exemption presumably has lowered the borrowing cost of the

local government unit you are using for your case study. For government as a whole, including the federal government, such tax exemption has almost certainly reduced the net revenues of government. Why?

Bibliography

(Bibliography for government finance at end of Chapter 22.)

CHAPTER 24

The attack on economic instability through monetary and fiscal policy

The U.S. federal government has assumed a very great responsibility—that of assuring a satisfactory rate of economic activity, of providing the kind of economic environment that fosters sustainable growth, and of discharging this responsibility while keeping the value of money reasonably stable. This responsibility is so great that as yet it is not completely clear that the federal government can successfully do all these things.

The major weapons used by the federal government in trying to discharge this responsibility, monetary and fiscal management, have already been considered: in Chapter 7 the principal tools of monetary management were reviewed, and the management of federal finances and debt (i.e., the management aspect of fiscal policy) was considered in Chapter 22. The function of this chapter is to provide a general discussion of economic instability and then to discuss experience with the two principal tools of economic stabilization as they have been applied since 1945.

Government policy to stabilize output, employment, and price levels

Of government's many tasks in our complex economy, that of economic stabilization occupies an important place in the minds of many.

Extreme business fluctuations are a source of great social waste. During slowdowns in economic activity, some individuals cannot get jobs and, being without income, go hungry. At the same time, farmers and businessmen cannot sell what they raise or produce at prices that cover their marketing costs. Not only is unemployment wasteful, but it also results in other serious consequences. Welfare payments can demoralize individuals and families and undermine the working habits of those who receive them. The fear of job loss haunts those who are working, and the fear of poor business conditions affects business management. Even when business is good, the fear that economic activity may subsequently deteriorate has damaging consequences. Businessmen cannot plan as boldly as they would like; they are beset by the fear that if they launch new business ventures, these ventures may be unprofitable. Worst of all, the output losses experienced during a depression can never be offset, so that as the result of a slowdown in economic activity society is permanently worse off than it otherwise would have been.

The evils of rising prices or inflation are not necessarily so severe nor so immediately evident. A prosperity that improves income and increases prices seems pleasant and stimulating to almost everyone except recipients of fixed incomes. But if price rises become excessive, a hectic race develops in which everyone tries to keep even—and nobody seems to win. When inflation is allowed to get out of hand, as it has sometimes in other countries, the results are devastating. In cases of extreme inflation, trade breaks down because traders resort to barter rather than being willing to hold money. The chief difficulties created by moderate but unanticipated inflations are the disruption of debtor-creditor relationships caused by the fact that the dollars used to repay loans are not worth as much, in terms of buying power, as were the dollars originally lent; also, the distribution of income is away from fixed dollar income groups.

Because of the difficulties created by fluctuations in business activity, government has acknowledged its responsibility for mitigating their effects. The Employment Act of 1946 provides that the maintenance of adequate employment opportunities shall be one of the goals of public finance. Government undoubtedly can do a great deal to influence the level of employment, but one may reasonably ask just how much they *should* do. Should government guarantee employment opportunities? Will government expenditures waste economic resources, destroy or compete unfairly with private enterprise? These questions lie at the core of what is, and for some time doubtless will be, one of the greatest issues of difference among citizens of goodwill.

The feeling that government ought to do something about depressions is deep-seated. During World War II it was widely feared that a serious depression might develop in this country after the war. It turned out to be a groundless fear, although it also prevailed in other countries; in England the relatively conservative wartime coalition government adopted a full-employment policy in 1944. The victory of the Labour Party in 1945 was taken as evidence that the earlier employment policy was milder in sentiment than popularly desired. In Canada full employment has been declared an objective of policy, as it has in Australia and Sweden. Many other governments, while not adopting an explicit full-employment policy, have given the idea commendatory blessings and their policy actions suggest a strong adherence to its tenets.

In the United States the idea of governmental support of full employment has been endorsed by both major parties. There are different kinds of views on the means for achieving full employment and of definitions of that term, but the general objective seems to be beyond political dispute.

Even though the issue is accepted as settled in general terms, there nevertheless remain great differences of opinion about the desirable extent and character of government programs to support such a policy. It is to be noted, for example, that the word *full* was deleted from the title of the employment act. But it was, nevertheless, implicitly dedicated to creating and encouraging a high level of employment through governmental policy. The language of the policy section of the act was debated and revised many times, and its final form shows the marks of compromise:

SECTION 2. The Congress hereby declares that it is the continuing policy and responsibility of the Federal Government to use all practicable means consistent with its needs and obligations and other essential considerations of national policy, with the assistance and cooperation of industry, agriculture, labor, and state and local governments, to coordinate and utilize all its plans, functions, and resources for the purpose of creating and maintaining, in a manner calculated to foster and promote free competitive enterprise and the general welfare, conditions under which there will be afforded useful employment opportunities, including self-employment, for those able, willing, and seeking to work and to promote maximum employment, production, and purchasing power.

The act presumably was not just a cure for depression and without application to problems of inflation. However, implicitly and unavoidably, the emphasis of the employment act and its tools of policy are more significant as depression cures. That assumption grew out of the belief that depressions are more probable and damaging than inflations. However, bills have been introduced into Congress which would make the injunction to fight inflation an explicit part of the employment act, and in recent years the government has accepted the goal of price stability as a legitimate policy goal. The difficulty with attempting to deal with inflation is that the known methods of cure lead to rising unemployment, that expectations which lead to a continuance of the inflation may not respond to restrictive monetary or fiscal policies, and that a strong anti-inflationary policy is likely to lead to recession. It is, therefore, by no means a simple matter for a government to deal with inflation.

The problem of economic instability

As citizens of the United States, we are justifiably proud of our economic system. It is strong, has grown rapidly, and has increased our standards of material comfort by rapid improvements in productivity. All this has been accomplished in an environment of economic and political freedom.

Unfortunately, free economies can be beset with very difficult problems, among them the fact that they are not always wholly stable. Sometimes business is good, sometimes it is poor. During some periods it is easy for anyone to find work; there seem to be more jobs than persons to fill them. Then, again, job openings seem to disappear; even good, experienced, and diligent men cannot find gainful employment. During some periods, business profits are high, and most businesses get along very well; at other times, almost all businesses suffer difficulties, and profits dwindle or even disappear. The prices of commodities exhibit different rates of increase; securities prices rise and fall by relatively large amounts in response to changes in economic conditions.

Although all these kinds of fluctuations by no means coincide exactly, a great deal of similarity may be found among them: the favorable events which characterize a period of prosperity come at about the same time, and the events associated with depressions seem to bunch. Fluctuations in economic activity are pervasive; they are reflected throughout the economy in employment, prices, and profits.

The fact that economic activity fluctuates is confirmed abundantly by a study of the past. The volume of economic goods produced has varied widely. Price levels and therefore the value of money have moved up and down. High levels of employment have been followed by periods of considerable unemployment. The income for the nation as a whole has fluctuated widely, and for some persons the range of swing has been wider than for others.

It is because these fluctuations are roughly simultaneous—that is, the various economic factors rise and fall at about the same time—that the problem is a social one and not just one of isolated or special interest.

From 1854 to 1961, 27 complete cycles in business activity, from trough to peak to trough, have been cataloged by the National Bureau of Economic Research (as shown in Table 24–1).[1] Exhibit 24–1 shows four important economic series that reflect business fluctuations over the last 10 of these cycles. The shaded areas represent periods when economic activity was declining, light areas, economic expansion. Since 1961, economic output has moved continuously upward, and the modest pauses in

EXHIBIT 24–1

How business cycles affect various types of economic activity (*indexes 1957–59 = 100*)

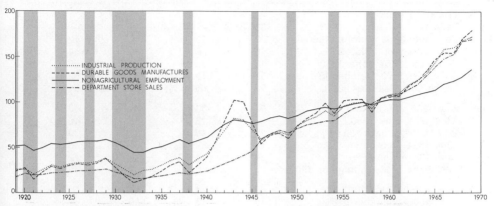

Source: U.S. Department of Commerce, Bureau of the Census, Business Conference and Joint Economic Committee, *Economic Indicators*.

activity which occurred to the end of 1969 do not qualify as cycles in the established sense of the term. Note the high degree of similarity in the upward and downward movements in these four series as well as their conformance with the business cycle reference dates.

Popular interest in business fluctuations has been particularly keen in recent years. During almost all of the 1930s this country—and the rest of the world as well—suffered a prolonged depression. During a large part of this period, many were unemployed. From the fall of 1930 to the spring of 1941 unemployment was less than 5 million in only 6 months (5 of the 6 months being in the latter part of 1937), and during 43 months unemployment exceeded 10 million. During this 11-year period the average unemployment rate was 18% of the labor force. Then in the frantic preparation for World War II and during the war itself, the opposite situation prevailed—a great shortage of labor.

[1] The National Bureau of Economic Research is a nonprofit research organization which has been a leading force in business cycle research in the United States. For an excellent summary of the bureau's work in this area, see *Business Cycle Indicators*, Geoffrey H. Moore, ed., Princeton University Press, 1961.

TABLE 24–1

Business cycle reference dates and duration of expansions and contractions in the United States: 1854 to 1969

Business cycle reference dates	Duration in months			
			Cycle	
	Expansion (trough to peak)	Contrac- tion (trough from pre- vious peak)	Trough from previous trough	Peak from previous peak
Trough to Peak				
December 1854–June 1857 30	—	—	—
December 1858–October 1860 22	18	48	40
June 1861–April 1865 46	8	30	54
December 1867–June 1869 18	32	78	50
December 1870–October 1873 34	18	36	52
March 1879–March 1882 36	65	99	101
May 1885–March 1887 22	38	74	60
April 1888–July 1890 27	13	35	40
May 1891–January 1893 20	10	37	30
June 1894–December 1895 18	17	37	35
June 1897–June 1899 24	18	36	42
December 1900–September 1902 . . .21	18	42	39
August 1904–May 1907 33	23	44	56
June 1908–January 1910 19	13	46	32
January 1912–January 1913 12	24	43	36
December 1914–August 1918 44	23	35	67
March 1919–January 1920 10	7	51	17
July 1921–May 1923 22	18	28	40
July 1924–October 1926 27	14	36	41
November 1927–August 1929 21	13	40	34
March 1933–May 1937 50	43	64	93
June 1938–February 1945 80	13	63	93
October 1945–November 1948 37	8	88	45
October 1949–July 1953 45	11	48	56
August 1954–July 1957 35	13	58	48
April 1958–May 1960 25	9	44	34
February 1961	9	34	
26 cycles, 1857–1960 . . . average 30	19	49	49*
10 cycles, 1919–1961 . . . average 35	15	50	54†
4 cycles, 1945–1961 . . . . average 36	10	46	46‡

* 25 cycles, 1857–1960.
† 9 cycles, 1920–1960.
‡ 3 cycles, 1948–1960.
Note: Since 1961, no cycles have been defined by the Bureau.
Source: *Business Cycle Indicators*, vol. I, "Contributions to the Analysis of Current Business Conditions." Geoffrey H. Moore, ed. Princeton University Press (for the National Bureau of Economic Research), 1961; and *Business Conditions Digest*.

Since the end of World War II the United States has experienced generally prosperous conditions. As can be seen with reference to Exhibit 24–1, however, the general upward movement of broad economic indexes has been broken on four occasions, 1949, 1953, 1958, 1960. While these recessions were relatively mild and short-lived, whenever business growth slackened or employment or prices dropped slightly during the postwar period, fear and talk of depression became very strong. The problems of dislocation, economic waste, and great hardships caused by depressed conditions during the 1930s have left a strong imprint. Probably because of this, tardy and then slow and largely ineffective steps were taken during the early postwar years to combat the prevailing economic malady, inflation.

The word *inflation* denotes a period of rising prices. The unit of account (in the United States, the dollar) loses value, for it can purchase only a diminishing amount of goods and services. When we talk of rising prices we are referring to some index of prices. At no time would the prices of all items be rising at the same rate.

Two often-used price indexes, the consumer price index and the wholesale price index, are shown in Exhibit 24–2. The consumer price index is constructed to measure changes in the living costs of city wage earners and clerical-worker families. The wholesale price index is constructed to measure changes in the prices of a set of basic commodities. As can be seen, both of these indexes rose almost continuously through the entire first decade of the postwar period. Of the four postwar recessions only the 1949 episode is reflected by a decline in the price of goods in both indexes. The consumer price index rose continuously after 1949 except for a very slight decline in the boom year of 1955. The wholesale price index, which is more flexible, declined in the recession year 1953 but not in 1957.

After 1957 these indicators of the general movement in prices tell different stories. The index of wholesale prices moved sideways through 1964, and then began to climb at an increasing rate for the next five years. On the other hand, the consumer price index rose continuously, at a slow rate until 1966 and at rapid rates through 1969.

For purposes of public policy, the sometimes conflicting signals provided by the two indexes present a difficult problem for economic policy. When only the consumer price index was rising, it was an open question as to whether the United States was experiencing inflation or a period of stable prices.

These conflicting signals prompted much controversy and research into just what these price indexes measure. The consensus seems to be that the consumer price index is upward biased, that is, it tends to overstate rises in the cost of living when they occur and to understate declines when they occur. To a large extent this is due to the fact that this index does not take enough account of changes in the quality of products. For instance, if the list price of a basic Ford automobile did not change from 1967 to 1968 this component of the index would be stable. But, if the 1968 model does not need greasing or an oil change for a longer period than the 1967 model, if the tires and other components are built to last longer, or if the guarantee given by the manufacturer or seller covers a

EXHIBIT 24–2

Consumer and wholesale price indexes, 1945–69 *(1957–59 = 100)*

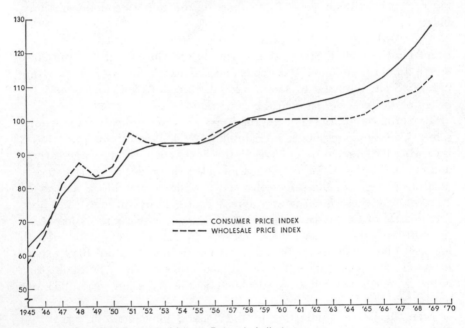

Source: Council of Economic Advisers, *Economic Indicators.*

longer period, or is more inclusive, in effect the consumer cost of owning an auto has been lowered. This type of price reduction is not reflected in the consumer price index. This line of reasoning has in the last several years led to a growing belief that from the end of 1957 through the end of 1964 the general price level correctly measured actually declined.

Thus, the postwar period began with a widespread fear that an impending depression was the important problem facing the nation. Instead of the expected depression the country experienced a long period of inflation and boom interrupted by only minor economic setbacks. Although inflation was really the important problem, it was not until the early

1950s that public policy shifted from constant fear of depression to an attempt to control inflation. In the late 1950s economic forecasters were talking and writing about the soaring 1960s. The main threat of economic instability during the early 1960s was, in the minds of most officials, the threat of inflation. Now by hindsight there is a growing conviction that in the early part of the decade, the concern with inflationary forces was overly strong, mainly because of biased price indexes, and that the deflationary actions of government policies dampened the rate of economic growth. In the latter part of the decade, beginning with the large government deficits of 1967 and 1968 (much of which deficits were financed by the monetary expansions of 1968 and early 1969), rapid price level increases have been experienced. At this writing (late 1970) contractionary monetary policies have succeeded in reducing real output but not inflation; the 1968 surtax legislation had little apparent impact in stemming this inflation.

Relation to economic growth and its desirability

The passage of the employment act committed the federal government to a policy of maintaining high level employment. During the decade of the 1950s a strong concurrence of opinion developed for government to maintain a stable level of prices. In the early 1960s a strong feeling developed that the economic growth of the United States was not as rapid as it could or should be.

The desire for economic growth was of course a part of the rationale for the employment act. Periods of recession are wasteful in terms of unused resources, both human and physical. The goal of a high rate of growth, however, has become a much stronger motive than just a by-product of the attack on economic instability. This feeling emerged most clearly after the Russians' successful launching of the Sputnik and was epitomized by President Kennedy's speeches during his campaign for the presidency calling for a conscious effort to increase the nation's rate of economic growth.

During the latter part of the sixties, as has already been pointed out, large federal deficits financed chiefly by monetary expansion resulted in inflation, so that the concern with price stability once again became a dominant concern of economic policy, and a combination of monetary and fiscal policies was utilized in an attempt to restore stability without undue reduction in employment levels and consequently in growth.

The latter part of the sixties also saw the emergence of a debate over what may be termed "quality of life" issues. All of the above discussions have employed real GNP as a reference point. Thus, countercyclical policy is concerned with preventing fluctuations about the trend in real

GNP; growth-oriented policies are concerned with the trend rate at which real GNP increases. The quality of life debate as presently emerging takes on, in this context, the characterization of a debate over the adequacy of the measure of real GNP. (As mentioned in Chapter 22, the quality of life debate is also concerned with the workings of the price system and the problems of devising other mechanisms for allocation of economic resources in those instances where market failure is found to be manifest.) Proponents of the inadequacy view argue that the GNP figures do not recognize the destruction of resources caused by an industrial society (e.g., air pollution, loss of undeveloped areas, soil erosion, water pollution, and others) and argue that these effects also ought to be included in the measure of economic output. If this were to be the case, the reported rates of growth achieved by the economy could well differ importantly from those signaled by current measures. Some congressmen have observed that if indeed GNP figures were to include these effects, legislation to miminize environmental problems might more easily be enacted.

Fiscal policy

High level employment, stable prices, and a high rate of economic growth are the three traditionally important goals of governmental domestic economic policy which have evolved since the end of World War II. In broad terms, the tools available to implement these goals can be categorized under the headings of monetary and fiscal policy. The use of these tools will now be discussed in an attempt to indicate when their application is appropriate, and also to indicate some of the difficulties which are inherent in their use.

Governmental fiscal policy can be viewed as the policy followed by government in making expenditures and assessing taxes. Since the balance between expenditures and receipts determines whether or not a government has a surplus of revenues or a deficit, fiscal policy determines whether a government can reduce its debt or must add to it. (The distinction made in Chapter 22 between the policy measure of full-employment surplus or deficit and the realized surplus or deficit being discussed here will be recalled.)

What has been said so far could be said equally of the fiscal policies of individuals or businesses. However, an analogy between private finance and public finance is generally misleading. State and local government finance parallels private finance in some respects, though the differences are greater than the similarities. Federal government finance differs greatly from that of the private sector. Our first problem is to identify these differences.

In a private enterprise economy, every individual and every business must limit its outlays to cash on hand, plus current income and borrowing, less debt repayment. When prosperity prevails, these economic units may spend more by drawing down their cash balances or by going into debt. During a recessionary period, the opposite is true. If a business is to survive, expenditures must be kept in line with expected income. When times start looking bad, the prudent businessman starts to cut expenditures and holds cash or repays debts. The same is true for individuals. If all economic units follow this course, the result may be a continued downward spiral of reduced expenditures, reduced employment, reduced income, and reduced expenditures again.

Only the federal government has the resources and strategic position to attempt to halt this process before it has run its natural course. The federal government, because of its monetary powers, does not need to be concerned about debt in the same sense as other debtors must be. National governments, so long as they have sovereign powers to tax and issue money, never become technically insolvent.

In addition, domestically held government debt is not like an individual's debt to a third party; rather, it is like a debt of one of the individual's own bank accounts to that of another of his accounts. Furthermore, the issuance of government debt does not affect the real incomes of future generations in the way that the issuance of private debt affects the future real income of a private sector economic unit. In the case of a society that does not borrow from foreign countries, real resources cannot be transferred from one generation to another through financing arrangements as they can in the case of an individual or a private concern. Also, the service on government debt (interest paid and principal repaid) can always be covered by further taxation or by creating and issuing additional money, if need be.

The basic tenets of the theory behind the use of fiscal policy to combat economic instability are those of compensatory spending. A recession is caused by insufficient demand for goods and services, and some inflations are caused by an excess demand for goods and services. In a recession, the demand at current prices is less than could be produced if all resources, labor, and capital equipment were fully employed. Under these conditions, the federal government should run a full-employment deficit. It should add to the income stream by having expenditures greater than revenue.

Just the opposite is true in a demand-induced inflation. If nothing is done, prices will rise until demand at the higher prices equals the amount of goods and services that can be produced by fully utilizing existing resources. Supply is equated to demand largely by revaluing the same production at higher prices. Under these conditions, the federal government should run a full-employment surplus; its revenue at full-employment levels should be greater than its expenditures. This action may tend to reduce the demand for goods somewhat.

Ideally, fiscal policy attempts to affect demand in such a way that the quantity of goods and services demanded is exactly what can be produced by fully utilizing existing resources; this policy is put into practice by creating changes in government surpluses or deficits. The full-employment surpluses or deficits can be altered either by changing government expenditure plans or by changing tax rates. As we shall see, the two methods each have their own advantages.

Public works and public spending

The simplest instrument of fiscal policy (and one of the earliest to be used) is that of public spending on public works to combat depression. All levels of government—federal, state, and local—spend money for roads, hospitals, school buildings, public buildings, parks, flood-control dams, military installations, and the like. These are public works. It has been contended that government should time its expenditures for public works so as to provide offsets to any shrinkage in private capital expenditures. If times are good and private business concerns are erecting buildings and making other capital expenditures, then government should refrain from similar actions. If times become poor and private business stops making such capital outlays, then government should step in with a program of public works.

The wisdom of such a policy, so far as it is feasible, is not disputed. Conservatives and liberals alike accept its logic. The difficulty is found in the phrase: "so far as the policy is feasible." Should school children be forced to attend school in decrepit buildings while waiting for a recession? Should sick persons be forced to go to inadequate hospitals until unemployment emerges? Can military defense programs be held back while waiting for the price indexes to stop rising? Clearly such extremes to a fiscal policy would be regarded as feasible by few persons indeed.

Nearly all economists now accept the proposition that government spending has important roles to play under all economic conditions; expenditure debates now concern the extent to which spending is appropriate under different economic conditions on the one hand, and the types of projects for which spending is incurred on the other.

Timing remains a problem that must be faced by those who advocate use of expenditure policy as a countercyclical weapon. The typical business cycle has an average duration of about 50 months. Public works usually require a long period between the recognition of need for a project and the time of its actual construction and therefore the creation of employment. It has been argued that it is impossible to plan a project, get an appropriation through Congress, and get work going in time to be of help in a countercyclical program. The time period for these actions is so extended that it is highly probable the employment-increasing effects would come after the need is over and at a time when it is desirable to curtail rather than add to demand.

In view of these criticisms, advocates of public works as a countercyclical measure have recommended that a group of marginal public works be planned with funds appropriated and kept in readiness for quick execution when needed. But there is still question if the major part of the employment-creating power of these projects could be made operative before the need disappeared.

As indicated at the beginning of this section, the difficulty with altering levels of public spending lies in the qualification, so far as the policy is feasible. This consideration applies also to spending at higher levels than are desirable for economic stability during times of high employment. For example, in 1968, the administration's foreign and defense policies called for large budgetary deficits during a time of full employment. The administration was not unaware of the economic difficulties which would be caused by such a policy, but apparently felt that reductions in total spending could not be tolerated either.

Tax policies

The issues of the preceding section are linked to those of appropriate tax policies. First, should expenditures or tax incentives be used for countercyclical policy? The resolution of the question in a deep depression, as the preceding discussion has suggested, is to favor expenditures. Such a policy may be defensible on the grounds that in deep depressions, tax incentives would not be sufficient to stimulate business investment because business confidence is impaired by the prevailing bad conditions. Such is unlikely to be the case in a mild recession; in these circumstances tax incentives might be an appropriate fiscal policy.

Similarly, in time of inflation, higher taxes might be a more effective countercyclical weapon than reduced expenditures. Unfortunately, experience with the recent surtax legislation suggests that such policies are difficult to effect in terms of obtaining the necessary congressional approval, and that once implemented, temporary tax measures have only a small effect on spending. Furthermore, the timing problems that arise in carrying out a change in an expenditure policy arise here as well—it took many months and much urging from the executive branch of government before Congress passed the surtax in 1968.

Built-in stabilizers

The timing problem of increasing and decreasing government expenditures as a countercyclical device has caused a shift toward a reliance on built-in stabilizers. Built-in stabilizers automatically make the shift from a surplus toward a deficit or vice versa and hence bring about a budgetary change which is in the correct countercyclical direction. A number of existing taxes have such built-in stabilization effects, as do some expenditure programs. The most important tax is the income tax; the most important expenditure program is that of unemployment compensation.

To demonstrate how the stabilizers work, consider the program of unemployment compensation. In periods of high level employment few people receive compensation. During such periods payments into the unemployment fund by employed workers and employers increase the reserves in the fund and withdraw purchasing power from the economy. When unemployment rises, withdrawals from the fund are greater than current payments, thus adding to spending. Funds are automatically withdrawn from reserve when it is desirable to inject purchasing power into the income stream, and reserves are automatically increased when it is desirable that purchasing power be reduced.

The progressive structure of the federal income tax also has an important stabilizing effect. As private income increases, the income tax withdraws part of the increase from the private sector. The progressive nature of the tax means that at high-income levels a larger proportion will be withdrawn than at low-income levels. Thus, when incomes are growing in real terms, fiscal dividends can be said to rise because tax collections increase faster than expenditures. The disposition of these funds through tax rebates, revenue sharing programs, or increased federal expenditure thus becomes another public policy issue for a growing economy with a progressive tax structure.

Monetary policy

Monetary policy can be thought of as the policy pursued by the government in controlling the money supply. In the United States, monetary policy is put into effect through the Federal Reserve System. The principal tools used by the Federal Reserve influence the volume of cash reserves available to banks and through these variables the size of the money supply. The way in which banks use reserves was outlined in Chapters 3 to 5, and the way in which the Federal Reserve supplies reserves was described in Chapter 7.

Monetary policy has a variety of complex influences. In the process of supplying reserves to commercial banks, the Federal Reserve influences not only the volume of deposits created but also the ability of the commercial banks to lend or invest. Other financial institutions depend primarily on the voluntary savings that they accumulate. The commercial banking system, however, has the power to create money by virtue of the fact that its demand liabilities serve as a means of payment. Whenever the banking system has excess cash reserves, it can exercise this money creation power if there are demands for its loan funds. Thus the Federal Reserve System, which supplies bank reserves, influences both the market for loan funds and the quantity of deposits held by business and individuals.

Monetary policy also affects interest rates. The volume of reserves made available to banks affects not only their willingness to offer credit but the price at which it is offered. The price prevailing for bank credit has pervasive effects and tends to influence other interest rates. The effect of monetary policy on interest rates generally starts with interest rates on short-term, high-grade obligations, as described in Chapter 8, and later spreads to interest rates on longer term and lower grade debts.

How monetary policy affects economic activity

Monetary policy affects the general level of economic activity in several ways. The quantity of deposit money, as determined by monetary policy, has an effect on the spending decisions of both individuals and businesses. If the quantity of money held by individuals and businesses is smaller than they wish to hold, they will engage in an extensive series of portfolio adjustments the ultimate effect of which is to reduce their expenditures. On the other hand, if the quantity of money supplied is greater than they wish to hold, portfolio adjustments and the price adjustments following therefrom will lead to an increase of expenditures. Whether the increase is in the form of more goods purchased or in the form of the same amount of goods purchased at higher prices depends on whether the economy is at or near full employment when an increase in the money supply is brought about. Decreases in the money supply affect real spending because prices are rigid in a downward direction. The nature of these changes in spending plans has an obvious effect on the general well-being of the community, the prosperity of the country, and the use of economic resources.

Another influence of monetary policy is on the cost and availability of credit. Many types of expenditures, particularly those for capital outlays, depend on both the cost and the availability of credit. If credit is freely available at reasonable rates, capital expenditure plans are stimulated. On the other hand, if credit is not available or is available only at what is thought to be unreasonably high cost, then spending plans tend to be greatly curbed. The net effect of the cost and availability of credit, therefore, also has a direct bearing on the level of business activity.

The effects of interest rates or the cost of credit on business activity are difficult to measure exactly. There is no doubt that high interest rates cause some reduction in investment plans, especially if borrowing is necessary to carry out these plans. In addition, interest rates have an influence, but probably only a minor one, on saving habits. Nevertheless, to whatever extent there is an effect, high interest rates probably promote saving and discourage spending, thereby tending to restrain expansionary tendencies in the economy. Lower rates probably lower saving and encourage spending and thereby tend to stimulate business activity.

Monetary policy works in other ways than through these direct channels of influence. It also has some indirect effects, as, for example, on business expectations. In recent years central banking monetary policy has come to be viewed by the business community as a direct indication of public economic policy. Federal Reserve actions are watched closely by the financial press and are widely considered in the formation of business plans. Therefore, a given type of action by the Federal Reserve is itself likely to induce to some extent the kind of business response that is desired by the Federal Reserve.

Monetary policy inherent in debt management and in fiscal programs

Most of the monetary policy in the United States is exercised by the Federal Reserve in its control of bank reserves, but to some extent the management of the public debt by the Treasury Department is a variety of economic policy, so that there is some governmental division of responsibility in policy formation. When the Treasury pursues a debt-management policy of shortening the average maturity of the outstanding debt, it tends to make the economy more liquid. Such a policy may mildly encourage business activity. Lengthening the average maturity of the debt reduces the liquidity of the economy and, therefore, may tend to have a mildly deterrent effect on the level of business activity. Since these effects are generally thought to be quite moderate, they can easily be taken into account by the Federal Reserve System in its conduct of monetary policy and can be offset if such an action is desirable.

Another type of monetary policy can inhere in fiscal programs involving changes in budgeted surpluses or deficits. Suppose, for example, the Treasury plans to incur a deficit next year of $10 billion. This deficit will increase the money supply by $10 billion if the bonds used to finance it are sold to the Federal Reserve System. However, if the deficit is financed by borrowing from the public, no increases in the money supply will take place. The latter eventuality is the more usual, but the former has occurred—as in 1968, for example.

Need for coordination of the two instruments

It is not appropriate to compare the effectiveness of monetary and fiscal policy as if they were competitors. In practice, they should be considered complementary instruments supporting each other. If the fiscal policy of the government is such as to create surpluses in boom times, this reduces the financing problem and so frees monetary policy for a full-fledged assault on the forces of inflation. Likewise, if fiscal policy creates deficits during periods of reduced business activity, these deficits become a natural vehicle by which monetary policy can stimulate a more rapid increase in the supply of money and of credit. The current view of the two policy instruments which seems quite generally to be accepted by economists is that monetary policy has greater effects than does fiscal policy, and therefore when a choice between instruments is possible, monetary policy may be the more nearly effective tool.

Fiscal and monetary policy in action

The theoretical possibilities in the use of an instrument of public policy, such as fiscal policy or monetary policy, are not always obtained in practice. Many difficulties hinder the achievement of a theoretically optimum performance. Some of these difficulties are inherent in our form of government, some in the nature of the instruments themselves.

In the United States, fiscal policy is formed by the president and Congress combined, as already described in Chapter 22. The budget-making process is time-consuming, likewise the legislative process that passes on both the expenditures and the tax programs submitted. Thus, even with built-in stabilizers changes in fiscal policy tend to be large and cumbersome acts.

Monetary policy has a potential for somewhat greater flexibility. The Federal Reserve can act quickly to change discount rates or to increase or decrease reserves available to banks through open-market operations or changes in reserve requirements. Because monetary policy seems to be geared for quick action, it might be thought somewhat superior to fiscal policy. However, the problem of lagged response to changed monetary conditions must be recognized. That is, an increase in the money supply which is designed to stimulate economic activity may be so long in taking effect that its influence is felt just when activity ought to be restrained. Similarly, monetary restriction seems also to have delayed effects. Moreover, the great federal debt requires frequent trips to the money markets. These frequent periods of treasury financing place a very considerable obstacle in the road of a completely flexible policy by restricting the actions the Federal Reserve System can take at least some of the time. Finally, any given policy instrument generally has different effects which depend on economic conditions when they are being employed (e.g., is GNP increasing or decreasing?), and consequently the effects of a given policy must be carefully assessed in terms of the conditions under which it was effected.

The postwar record

Conscious use of monetary and fiscal policy as stabilization devices is relatively recent; the philosophy of compensatory fiscal policy had not gained much acceptance until just before World War II. During World War II the necessities of war finance overwhelmed other objectives, so that neither monetary or fiscal policy could be used for the primary purpose of stabilization. Only during the period since World War II can a critical review of results be made, thus our experience is relatively brief.

Indicators of the influence of monetary and fiscal policies, during the period from the beginning of 1946 through 1969, are shown in Exhibit 24–3.

The top panel contains two often-cited measures of the impact of monetary policy: one graph shows movements in net free or borrowed reserves of commercial banks, which is widely used as a measure of the ability of commercial banks to make additional loans and extend credit. When free reserves are available to the commercial banking system, banks are believed to be more willing to undertake new lending programs; whereas when the banking system is on balance in debt to the Federal Reserve, banks are believed to take action to restrict new lending commitments. The second graph shown in the top panel is the annual rate of change in the money supply. Many students of monetary affairs believe this measure to be the best indicator of the influence of monetary policy. A rapid increase in the money supply indicates an expansionary policy is being followed, while a slow increase or a decrease suggests a contractionary policy is in effect. Expansionary effects at full employment are inflationary because real output cannot be increased when the economy is operating at capacity.

The middle panel shows the annual cash budget position of the federal government and therefore the net influence of fiscal policy upon the economy. As was explained above, cash surpluses, which indicate the federal government has taken more purchasing power out of the economy in taxes than it returned through expenditures or transfers, result in a net contractionary effect on economic activity; while a cash deficit, which means that more purchasing power is put into the economy than is withdrawn by the federal government, indicates a net expansionary effect.

The bottom panel contains two measures of the desirable direction of monetary and fiscal policy. The first bar graph in each year is the annual percentage change in gross national product in constant 1958 prices. High

EXHIBIT 24–3

Fiscal and monetary policy at work

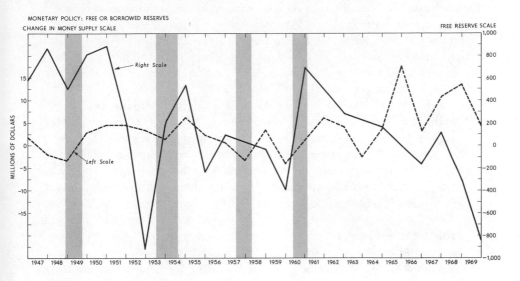

MONETARY POLICY: FREE OR BORROWED RESERVES
CHANGE IN MONEY SUPPLY SCALE

FREE RESERVE SCALE

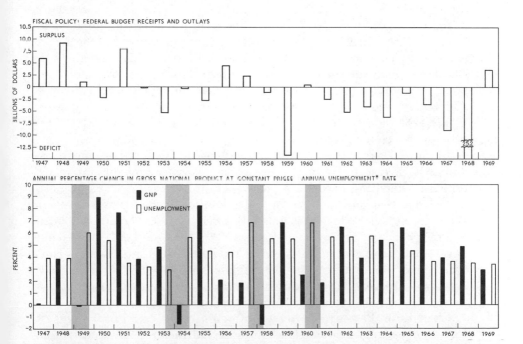

FISCAL POLICY: FEDERAL BUDGET RECEIPTS AND OUTLAYS

ANNUAL PERCENTAGE CHANGE IN GROSS NATIONAL PRODUCT AT CONSTANT PRICES   ANNUAL UNEMPLOYMENT* RATE

* As a percentage of civilian labor force.
    Source: U.S. Consumer Joint Economic Committee, Council of Economic Advisors, *Economic Indicators.*

positive rates of change indicate rapid growth in economic activity; whereas low or negative rates of change indicate slow growth or decline in output. The second bar graph in each year shows annual averages of the proportion of the labor force which was unemployed. In evaluating the data in this chart it should be remembered that until the end of 1957 the United States was with two short exceptions, 1949 and part of 1953–54, experiencing a period of considerable inflation. After 1957, prices were relatively stable until 1965; see Exhibit 24–2.

In the period 1947 to the beginning of 1957, the banking system continually had large amounts of free reserves. This sign of easy monetary conditions was a reflection of the continuation by the Federal Reserve of its wartime policy of cooperation with the Treasury in maintaining low-interest yields on government securities. This action is now widely regarded to have been inappropriate. In effect, during this period monetary policy was not mobilized to combat the inflationary forces in the economy.

During this same 10-year period the federal government ran cash surpluses in every year except 1950. The deficit in 1950 was probably a reflection of both heavy costs of the Korean War late in the year and some late compensatory action because of the 1949 recession. Earlier in this chapter there was a discussion of the growing belief in the early 1960s that the rate of economic growth of the U.S. economy was not high enough during the last half of the 1950s and early 1960s. In fact, this is reflected in the relatively low annual rate of growth in gross national product in the period from 1956 through 1963. But, an important aspect of this belief is the continuous unemployment rate above 5% from 1957 through 1963. The large budgetary deficits of 1967 and 1968, reflecting primarily defense expenditure increases, were eliminated through surtax legislation and budget economies in 1969. Both monetary and fiscal policy were highly expansionary in 1968, and the restrictive fiscal policy of 1969 did little to reduce the inflation stemming from the earlier stimuli.

In the 1950s there seems to be a good conformance of both monetary and fiscal policies to the two cycles which occurred. Probably the major criticism would fall upon fiscal policy because of cash deficits during a prosperous year such as 1955 and the low level of surpluses in other years during a period when inflationary forces were or should have been of great concern. During the 11 years 1958 through 1968, the federal government ran a cash deficit 10 times and had a small surplus once. Thus fiscal policy appears expansive during this period, although on a full-employment basis the budget was in surplus for the earlier part of the period. From 1966 onward the deficit was highly expansionary.

Changes in the net free reserve position of commercial banks suggest that monetary policy was relatively tight and therefore restrictive from the latter part of 1958 to about mid-1960. The downward drift in net free reserves since mid-1960 from very high levels to low levels indicates an increase in demand for bank credit rather than an active policy of monetary tightness. During 1969 and early 1970, monetary policy has been quite contractionary in an attempt to stem the inflation resulting from the earlier expansionary policies.

In conclusion, fiscal and monetary policies, if correctly formulated and carried out, can have desirable effects both in dampening the extremes in changes in business activity and also in increasing the rate of economic growth. In the short period of experience in using monetary and fiscal policies to accomplish these goals, the results have not always been as good as desired. Much more knowledge about the effects and impacts of various policy changes is needed. However, these tools hold great promise and there is good reason to believe our ability to use them wisely will improve through time.

The problem of the balance of payments

The balance of payments problem faced by the United States is discussed at length in Chapter 26. However, because of the particular impact of the recent balance of payment situation on monetary policy it is important that the relationship of these two problem areas be made clear.

The United States sold more goods abroad than it purchased from foreigners throughout the entire postwar period. However, when the dollar cost of gifts, military expenditures, foreign travel of Americans, and investments by American corporations and individuals in overseas facilities is included the United States has since 1950 had an almost continuing string of annual deficits in its balance of payments. Since 1958 these deficits have averaged about $3 billion annually.

The meaning of the deficit is that the United States has used more of other countries' currencies than it has earned. In part this continuing deficit has been paid for with gold. This has brought about a decline in the stock of gold held by the U.S. government from $19.5 billion at the end of 1959 to $11.9 billion at the end of 1969. However, the majority of the deficit was used by foreign citizens, foreign governments, and foreign central banks (like our Federal Reserve) to increase their holdings of dollars and claims on dollars. That is, other countries financed the deficit by lending the United States foreign currencies which it had not earned. These funds are mainly deposited in the Federal Reserve and at commercial banks or are invested in short-term securities in the American money market. At the end of 1969 these holdings of deposits and short-term assets by foreigners amounted to almost $42 billion, having increased from approximately $19 billion at the end of 1959. Thus foreign holdings of dollars and claims on dollars have grown to such proportions that the remaining gold owned by the United States plus all of the readily available short-term foreign assets owned by the U.S. government would be insufficient to redeem even a substantial fraction of these funds.

This latter fact has exercised a considerable influence over policy decisions in recent years. The monetary authorities fear the funds owned by foreigners would be moved out of dollar assets if short-term interest rates in the United States fell to a point where these funds could earn substantially higher income if deposited in banks or invested in short-term securities in other countries. If these dollars were presented for redemption in gold or foreign currency the U.S. government might not be able to redeem them because of a lack of gold and foreign currency holdings.

Because of this consideration the monetary authorities after June of 1960 were faced with a dilemma. To combat a downturn in domestic business, easy money conditions were called for. Easy monetary conditions, however, require a reduction in the structure of interest rates. But, if short-term interest rates were lowered there was a chance that an embarrassing and potentially dangerous flow of dollars into foreign money markets might develop.

This latter situation presents an important problem for the monetary authorities as it constrains the use of monetary policy to combat cyclical instability on the downside. Similarly, to the extent that government budget deficits are regarded by foreigners as indications of an inflation in this country, the purchasing power of the U.S. dollar may be expected to decline, and therefore foreign individuals and central bankers will be less willing to hold U.S. dollars as assets. Thus fiscal policy also must be conducted with the aim of not exacerbating the balance of payments problems; this was an important policy problem of the late 1960s.

Questions and problems

1. (No simple answer can be given to this question but consideration of it is a useful exercise.) Which is worse, depression or inflation?
2. Why can public finance be used to stabilize economic activity, whereas private finance cannot be so used?
3. Characterize the fiscal policy of the past two or three years.
4. Appraise its success in contributing to economic stabilization.
5. Why have public works lost favor as a device of economic stabilization?
6. Characterize monetary policy during the past two or three years.
7. Appraise the value of monetary policy in contributing to economic stabilization during recent years.
8. Appraise the value of fiscal policy in contributing to economic stability during recent years.

9. Appraise the coordination of fiscal and monetary policy during this period.

10. How has the deficit in the U.S. balance of payments influenced monetary policy in the past five years?

Bibliography

United States Monetary Policy, consisting of seven essays by distinguished contemporary economists and published by the American Assembly of Columbia University in 1964, is a general critique of both monetary and fiscal policy. The annual reports of the president's Council of Economic Advisers review current policy and frequently include essays on these general subjects reflecting the special views of the then-presiding chairman. The annual reports of the Board of Governors of the Federal Reserve System review current operations and include essays on special aspects of this subject from time to time. The *Federal Reserve Bulletin,* published monthly by the Board of Governors of the Federal Reserve System, contains many articles of interest. The monthly bulletins of the various Federal Reserve banks include pertinent articles from time to time.

The Committee for Economic Development has published many reviews of fiscal policy; those of particular interest include *Reducing Tax Rates for Production and Growth, Fiscal and Monetary Policy for High Employment,* and *Economic Growth in the United States.* Each year the Bureau of the Budget issues *The Federal Budget in Brief.* Current fiscal policy discussions may be found in the *Economic Report of the President* (annual); extensive data regarding current economic conditions are provided by the U.S. Department of Commerce, *Business Conditions Digest* (monthly).

Both monetary and fiscal policy are the subject of many articles in the learned journals. The library of the Board of Governors of the Federal Reserve System maintains an up-to-date bibliography of such articles as well as of books on these topics.

The Economics of Money and Banking by Lester Chandler (4th ed.; New York: Harper and Row, 1964) and *Macro-economics, Fiscal Policy and Economic Growth* by Norman F. Keiser (New York: John Wiley & Sons, Inc., 1964) describe both monetary and fiscal policy in somewhat more detail than was appropriate for this text. Also of interest are John M. Culbertson's *Macroeconomic Theory and Stabilization Policy* (New York: McGraw-Hill, 1968) and Michael K. Evans' *Macroeconomic Activity: Theory, Forecasting, and Control; an Econometric Approach* (New York: Harper and Row, 1969). Excellent discussions of economic policy may be found in Harry G. Johnson, *Essays in Monetary Economics* (Cambridge, Mass.: Harvard University Press, 1967) and in Milton Friedman, *The Optimum Quantity of Money and Other Essays* (Chicago: Aldine Publishing Co., 1969).

PART VII

INTERNATIONAL FINANCE

The quest for profits often leads to foreign investments and the exchange of goods among nations. The foundation of such opportunities is the economic doctrine of comparative advantage. Production costs, labor skills, climatic conditions, sources of raw material, and the availability of capital all influence the decisions of public and private economic planners. Wartime conditions and special development goals may modify decisions, but geographical regions normally produce and export products that give them the greatest competitive advantage. Relative costs are particularly important because if costs for all possible products are higher in one nation relative to all others, the high-cost nation could still profit if it specialized in production of products with the lowest cost disadvantage.

The determination of what and how to sell are subjects analyzed in foreign trade books. However, trade and investment across national frontiers also create many financial problems. Laws and customs vary, language barriers may exist, credit across national boundaries is often difficult to arrange, long delays between shipment and ultimate collection are common, and foreign governments often intercede in private trade and investment activities. Foreign transactions usually involve two national currencies; for example, dollars are used by American exporters and cruzeiros are used by Brazilian importers.

The complex problems of financing foreign trade and investment, the acquisition of foreign exchange used for settling obligations, the sources of funds, and the various financial institutions involved are discussed in Chapter 25. The monetary theories underlying the balance of payments, international flow of funds, exchange standards, liquidity of nations, and the various institutions that have been formed to facilitate international dealings are covered in Chapter 26.

Financing of foreign trade and investments

Balance of payments—introduction

Before reviewing the techniques and institutions involved in the financing of foreign trade and investment, it is useful to summarize the effects of these activities as reflected in the nation's balance of payments. The balance of payments is a systematic record of economic transactions between the residents of one country and all other nations over a given time that summarizes the many exchanges of merchandise and services, credit operations, and cash payments. All claims by foreigners upon individuals or institutions in the United States appear in our balance as debits, whereas claims of Americans upon foreigners appear as credits.

Because the balance of payments follows the principles of double entry bookkeeping, the statement must balance. If goods are imported, something must be exported to pay for the merchandise purchased. The export may be in the form of other goods, services, gold, securities, or promises to pay; the total offsetting items must bring the statement into balance.

Table 25–1 contains the main components of the balance of payments accounts of the United States for some selected years. Taking 1968 as the example, the first item shows that the United States exported $50,594 million in goods and services whereas imports of goods and services amounted to $48,078 million. Thus the United States had a trade surplus of $2,516 million. American citizens send gifts to relatives and friends abroad and many retired Americans live abroad. These expenditures

TABLE 25–1

U.S. balance of payments for selected years (*in millions of dollars*)

	1946	1950	1960	1968
Exports of goods and services	14,735	13,807	27,325	50,594
Imports of goods and services	−6,991	−12,028	−23,355	−48,078
Balance on goods and services	7,744	1,779	3,970	2,516
Remittances and pensions	−648	−533	−697	−1,159
1) Balance on goods and services, remittances, and pensions	7,096	1,246	3,273	1,357
2) U.S. government grants and capital flows	−5,293	−3,640	−2,768	−3,955
3) U.S. private capital flow (net)	−413	−1,265	−3,581	−5,157
4) Foreign capital flow, net, excluding change in liquid assets	−615	181	364	8,565
5) Errors and unrecorded transactions . .	218	−11	−892	−642
A. Balance on liquidity basis (1 + 2 + 3 + 4 + 5)	993	−3,489	−3,901	168
B. Balance on basis of official reserve transactions	—*	—*	−3,403	1,638

* Not recorded.

Source: 1946, 1950, 1960, *Economic Report of the President*, January 1969; 1968, *Federal Reserve Bulletin*, December 1969, pp. A72–A73.

amounted to $1,159 million. After taking these payments for pensions and gifts into account, the balance is still a positive $1,357 million (item 1). During the year, the government made grants and loans to foreign countries in the amount of $3,955 million (item 2). American citizens and businesses made investments in foreign countries directly through purchasing and building plants and indirectly through purchasing securities or making loans to foreign companies in the amount of $5,157 million. Foreigners invested $8,565 million in the United States; these investments were mainly in the form of purchased securities of American companies, but an increasing amount in recent years is in the form of investment in plants and equipment in the United States by foreign companies. The last item, errors and unrecorded transactions, shows the value of transactions which are not included in the regular accounts. This figure is developed because of the double entry nature of the accounts. The record of claims and payments indicates that $642 million of payments must have been made by Americans and were not recorded.

In Table 25–1, the items 1 through 5 for 1968 sum to a positive $168 million. This implies that to make all the fund flows balance, foreign nationals gave U.S. citizens, the government, and businesses, gold or previously held dollars in this amount. This figure, called the balance on liquidity basis, is shown in item A. Although there are a number of other summary figures which describe the balance of payments position for a period, this one is most often quoted.[1]

Brief history of the balance of payments

Immediately following World War II there was great concern about the large U.S. surplus on international transactions created by heavy exports, which greatly exceeded the amount of dollars paid for imports and the aid extended to foreign nations. During this time there was great concern that foreign nations would never be in a position to trade freely with the United States because of a permanent shortage of dollar reserves. In 1950, however, measured on the liquidity basis, a large deficit of $3.5 billion occurred. This development was accepted as a sign that prosperity was returning to Europe and other areas of the world. The deficit in the U.S. balance of payments suggested European nations had rebuilt their industries to the point where they could compete with the industries of the United States. Moreover, as can be seen in Table 25–1, capital exports increased significantly between 1946 and 1950. The increasing capital investments by American businesses during this period is another indication of prosperity in Europe: prosperous economic conditions are an essential ingredient for American business to make these large investments.

During the period 1952 through 1956, average deficits of $1.4 billion were incurred each year. In 1957 a small surplus resulted from a combination of unique international events, but in 1958 the balance sharply changed and a deficit of $3.4 billion was recorded, beginning a continued series of deficits until the small positive balance in 1968. From 1950 through 1968, the cumulative net deficit amounted to more than $40.3 billion.[2]

Although the United States continues to export considerably more than is imported and the annual deficits are well below 1% of our gross national product, the persistence of the negative balances and the associated outflow of gold and creation of short-term obligations to foreigners has alarmed national leaders and triggered a number of remedial actions described in Chapter 26.

---

[1] A second widely used figure, the balance on basis of official reserve transactions is shown as item B. In this measure only governmental holdings of liquid assets are considered. Thus, if a citizen of a foreign country increases his holdings of dollar balances it is not considered in the official reserve transaction balance. For a good description of the differences in these two measures, see "Balance of Payments in Deficit or Surplus," *Business Review*, Federal Reserve Bank of Philadelphia, November 1969, pp. 26–31.

[2] See *Economic Report of the President,* January 1969, p. 325.

Foreign trade

A key element in our balance of payments position is the size of the surplus of merchandise exports over merchandise imports as shown in Table 25–2.

As can be seen, the surplus has been of substantial magnitude since 1946; there is an indication of a decline in the trade position of the United States in the mid-1960s. The trading results in 1968 produced by far the smallest surplus in the postwar years. The deterioration in the U.S. trade surplus since 1964 is probably a reflection of the prosperous condition of the U.S. economy and the rising level of prices.[3] When domestic prices

TABLE 25–2

Net U.S. foreign trade position

Year	Merchandise		Excess of exports over imports	Export surplus as percent of total mer- chandise exports
	Exports	Imports		
1946	$11,764	$ 5,067	$6,697	56.9
1947–60 average	14,920	10,961	3,959	26.5
1961	20,107	14,519	5,588	27.8
1962	20,779	16,218	4,561	22.0
1963	22,252	17,011	5,241	23.6
1964	25,478	18,647	3,831	15.0
1965	26,447	21,496	4,951	18.7
1966	29,389	25,463	3,926	13.4
1967	30,681	26,821	3,860	12.6
1968	33,598	32,972	626	1.9

Source: *Survey of Current Business*, March 1969.

rise relative to those of other countries the goods and services of the United States become relatively more costly to foreigners; while foreign goods and services become less costly, causing reductions in sales and increases in purchases of goods.

Table 25–2 also indicates the very rapid growth of exports since 1946. In the period between 1946 and 1968, exports increased by almost 300%. However, to keep the relative importance of foreign trade of the United States in perspective, it should be noted that despite the steady increase, exports continue to represent less than 5% of the gross national product. On the other hand, in some industries exports account for a major part of total output.

---

[3] For a detailed description of annual balance of payments developments see the March issues of the *Survey of Current Business*. Quarterly totals are also reviewed in other issues.

The growth of U.S. exports is expected to continue in response to increasing economic activity in many foreign countries. Increased income which accompanies economic growth will lead to increases in the demand for the products of the United States. Although the bulk of our exports go to economically advanced nations, developing areas can also absorb increasing exports as they build up their economies and supplies of foreign exchange needed for payment. In 1968 approximately 70% of American exports consisted of finished manufactured goods; 14%, crude materials and semimanufactured goods; and 15%, foodstuffs. This pattern has remained relatively constant since the late 1950s. During the same period the composition of imports has changed with the proportion of finished manufactured goods increasing from 40 to 63% while the crude materials and semimanufactured products category has declined from 30 to 20%. These patterns reflect the trend to industrialization in many parts of the world and the intrusion of foreign producers into product areas where American technology has traditionally been dominant.

The creation of regional economic blocs to discriminate against exports of nations not included in the group is another threat to American exports that has been only partially met by American companies through establishing foreign production facilities inside the economic unions. International competition and the diversion of trade from manufacturers outside of the formal economic unions will reduce some export opportunities in the future, but experience has proved that American companies have benefited from trading with the advanced economies and it is assumed that these firms will adjust to the new market conditions.

Financing an import

The difficulties of handling international trade transactions prevents the exchange of goods on an open account trade credit basis. A number of leading banks have established international departments to provide the services and financing required by companies involved in foreign trade. Other banks can provide assistance through correspondents. The Federal Reserve Act authorizes national banks to establish foreign branches and to discount acceptances. Banks with international departments may arrange financing, collections, and payments through telegraphic transfers of funds or by using a commercial bill of exchange or acceptance. If the telegraphic transfer is used the bank simply instructs its foreign branch or correspondent to make payments for trade transactions out of its deposits held abroad to absorb receipts and disbursements. This approach is often used by companies in need of only the collection and payments services. In ther cases a sight or time draft may be used as described below.

Exporters are often willing to sell their products on credit if they can be assured of receiving payment. To provide this assurance, importers frequently use a commercial letter of credit—a formal statement by the importer's bank that it will accept drafts drawn upon itself that conform to the conditions prescribed in the letter. In this way the credit of the bank is substituted for that of the relatively unknown importer.

To arrange for this substitution of credit, the importer visits his bank and requests delivery of a commercial letter of credit addressed to himself or the exporter's bank. The importer either agrees to provide funds for payment by the bank prior to the maturity of any obligation, or lending arrangements are created. The exporter then prepares the shipment and receives a bill of lading from the freight carrier. This bill of lading is both a receipt and a document of title. The exporter insures the cargo and secures the various documents required to move the goods out of his country and into the importer's country. The seller then goes to his local bank and draws a draft on the buyer's bank in accordance with the instructions contained in the letter of credit.

The exporter may request his bank to purchase or discount the draft. The exporter's bank is protected by the entire sheaf of documents, including the bill of lading, and credits the deposit account of the exporter either immediately or at the time of collection, depending upon the arrangement. The amount credited depends upon the rate of exchange for the two national currencies at the time of the transaction. The exporter at this point has completed the shipment and received payment from his bank. The exporter's bank then forwards the draft and documents to its correspondent which presents the draft to the importer's bank, the bank that issued the letter of credit. The importer's bank detaches the documents and stamps the word *accepted* across the face of the draft.

If the draft is payable at sight, the accepting bank must immediately remit funds to the correspondent of the exporter's bank. These funds are provided by the importer through a new deposit or by borrowing from his bank. The importer's bank does not release the bill of lading until the buyer has met the obligation or arranged a loan.

If the draft is a time bill with a deferred maturity, the accepting bank would probably release the shipment to the importer under a trust receipt agreement. This arrangement permits the buyer to obtain physical possession, but the title to ownership remains with the financing institution. During the interim period prior to the maturity date, the importer has time to process and sell the goods. The sales receipts could then be used to make payment to the bank under the terms of the original agreement. Title to the goods is held by the bank until the importer's obligation is completely discharged.

If a time draft is used, after acceptance the exporter's bank may hold the document until maturity when payment is made. The bankers' acceptance may also be sold in the open market to another bank, a Federal

Reserve bank, or a specialist acceptance dealer. If the exporter's bank sells the accepted draft, it receives immediate payment of the full amount of the draft less a discount that represents interest income to the acceptance purchaser. If the accepted draft is not sold prior to maturity, the credit to finance the transaction is supplied by the exporter's bank. If the time draft is sold in the open market, the purchaser extends the credit from the time of acquisition until maturity.

Financing exports

A variation of the procedure described above occurs when an exporter agrees to ship goods on the basis of a sight draft drawn directly on the importer without the credit support of a foreign bank. In this situation, an exporter financially unable to wait until acceptance and payment of the sight draft might turn to his local bank to obtain cash or a deposit immediately. This approach requires the exporter to arrange for the shipment including acquisition of the bill of lading and preparation of the draft on the foreign purchaser. The exporter may then turn the documents over to his bank and request that the bank handle the collection. The bank is willing to advance funds to the exporter pending actual collection because of the security offered by possession of the title documents covering the shipment. The bank collects interest in the form of the discount and may also require other service charges and additional collateral in the form of domestic assets.

The exporter's bank then sends the trade draft to its correspondent foreign bank for collection. The title documents are released by that bank to the importer after payment is made. The amount paid in local currency would be determined by the then current rate of exchange.

In addition to handling the advances of credit, currency conversions, and transmittal of documents, commercial banks also make medium-term loans to companies for foreign trade activities. These loans are carefully designed to reflect the risks of foreign transactions and often require the pledging of additional domestic assets as collateral, the making of sizable down payments and periodic installment payments by importers, and Export-Import Bank participation. Loans of 180 days up to five years may be arranged and in isolated cases longer maturities are approved.

Use of drafts to create dollar exchange

Bankers' acceptances may also be used to create dollar exchange in which no immediate shipments are involved. The practice is usually confined to underdeveloped nations whose exports are highly seasonal and who therefore suffer periodic shortages of dollars for the settlement of international trade transactions.

Assume that a bank in Central America sells a local businessman a sight draft on its New York correspondent for the businessman's use in paying one of his dollar obligations. Assume further that the Central American bank does not currently have dollar balances available to cover the draft, but expects to have such balances available in, say, 90 days. The bank in Central America then has its New York correspondent sell a 90-day draft which is in effect a promissory note stating that the Central American bank will make a payment of an equal dollar amount in 90 days. The New York correspondent bank then sells the time draft and uses the proceeds to cover payment of the sight draft. When the time matures, the Central American bank expects to have accumulated sufficient dollar balances from its regular business to cover its second obligation.

Bank drafts may also be used to send funds abroad, to pay foreign debts or purchase securities abroad, for direct investments in operating assets, and for many other types of international transactions which cannot be covered in this brief discussion.

The foreign exchange market

Regardless of the purpose to be served by the movement of funds across international boundaries, the means of payment used are acquired in the foreign exchange market. This is a market in which the moneys of all important nations may be exchanged for one another. Tourists may buy coin or paper currency in small quantities, but most commercial transactions are settled with bills or orders stated in terms of foreign monetary units. They are drafts or checks drawn on tradesmen or on a bank and are commonly called exchange. To be more specific, sterling exchange consists of claims stated in terms of British pounds sterling, the monetary unit of account of Great Britain; and dollar exchange means claims for dollars on businessmen or financial institutions in the United States.

The foreign exchange market has no formal organization such as characterizes the stock exchange or a board of trade. It consists primarily of the foreign departments of large commercial banks but includes also a few small houses and individuals who deal with each other directly or through middlemen. Very few tradesmen enter this market personally in order to acquire or dispose of the instruments used in financing their own operations.

Metropolitan banks with foreign departments facilitate the international movement of goods, securities, and credit through foreign branches or correspondents with whom they maintain deposit balances. If a demand for foreign funds arises in the United States, these banks are able to draw checks or drafts against their foreign balances to meet the demand. If deposits abroad are depleted, thus limiting the supply of exchange available in America, banks in this country may replenish them in several ways. Formerly it was possible to ship gold from a commercial bank in the United States to a branch or correspondent abroad. This practice is now either impossible or so complicated by government restrictions here and abroad that it is used infrequently. A more usual practice is for the American bank to purchase drafts, drawn by local exporters and payable in foreign funds, and forward them to the branch or correspondent for collection; the proceeds are credited to the deposit account of the American bank. It may also be possible for unused funds to be transferred from other foreign centers to the market where reserves are low. Finally, if other means of replenishing the deposit are not available, the American bank may borrow from foreign banking institutions and deposit the proceeds to its foreign account. Thus a large commercial bank with a foreign department is in a position to meet the demands of its domestic customers who are making foreign payments or investments. Similarly, the American bank provides a ready market in which drafts drawn by American exporters on their foreign customers or foreign banks may be sold for cash or deposit credit.

The Export-Import Bank

The Export-Import Bank was formed in 1934 as an agency of the U.S. government at a time when private financing of foreign trade was badly disrupted by the depression. Its goal is to "assist, support, and encourage the overseas trade of United States private enterprise." The Eximbank originally financed a variety of transactions involving short- and long-term maturities including some reconstruction loans following World War II, but it now concentrates on three major programs: direct project loans to foreign companies and governments to enable them to purchase goods from American exporters; providing guarantees for loans to exporters by commercial banks and participation with private lenders in extending exporter credits; and cooperation with private insurance companies to provide guarantees and insurance covering losses from specific commercial and environmental risks associated with selling to foreign buyers on credit. Eximbank operates by drawing on its own capital and borrowing authority with the U.S. Treasury. These two sources combined total approximately $13.5 billion. The agency is supposed to avoid competition with private financial institutions and is prohibited from extending financial assistance if credit is available on reasonable terms from other sources. Short-term credit is not provided and to date the Eximbank has concentrated on financing exports, providing loan guarantees for private lenders, and the medium- and short-term insurance programs.

Project loans to foreign borrowers and U.S. firms for the financing of purchases of American products may have maturities of 8 to 20 years at interest rates of approximately 6%. Such credits are usually guaranteed by the government of the country where the borrower is located or by the buyer's bank. Examples of project loans include: a $13.3 million loan to Venezuela to finance a bridge being constructed by a subsidiary of U.S. Steel Corporation; a $3.5 million loan for construction of an electric power generating plant in Spain handled by Westinghouse Electric Corporation; and, a $3 million loan to three Austrian government owned banks which then advanced the funds to private companies to pay for imports of cotton from the United States.

Loans to American exporters for periods of six months to five years are made by commercial banks on a basis which does not permit recourse against the exporter but does provide the backing of Eximbank. Whenever possible, the Eximbank does not disburse any funds, but only commits itself to guarantee a portion of the financing on a fee basis. If the principal or interest goes into default, the guarantee requires the Eximbank to purchase the obligation from the commercial bank that originally made the exporter loan. Under an alternative approach the Eximbank advances part of the funds and charges interest of 6%. In cases where commercial banks will not provide assistance, the exporter may apply directly to Eximbank.

To be eligible for direct or participation financing by the Export-Import Bank, the following requirements must be met: the foreign country of the buyer must be acceptable to the commercial bank and Eximbank; the export must be a nonmilitary product produced in the United States; a cash down payment of 20% is desirable (10% minimum); terms of sale must be consistent with commercial custom; the exporter must retain at least 15% of the financed portion (total cost less down payment); the commercial bank's share of the financing must be without recourse to the exporter; and loans must be repaid in dollars in equal installments.

A third important function involves participation in a broad guarantee program designed to encourage American exports. Regular commercial credit insurance has been available from private insurers for many years, and since 1954 the Eximbank has offered guarantees providing for reimbursement of exporters suffering losses as a result of war or expropriation. However, it has long been believed that American firms have been hurt in the international markets by the lack of broader coverage. Exporters in Great Britain, West Germany, France, Japan, and several other economically advanced nations have access to comprehensive guarantee and discounting services from partially or wholly owned government agencies. Foreign firms have been able to offer liberal credit terms in the international market because of this support.

To meet this challenge the Foreign Credit Insurance Association (FCIA) was formed in September 1961 to combine the efforts of private insurance companies and the Export-Import Bank. Guaranteed reimbursement of exporters for losses resulting from specific commercial or political risks is provided by FCIA contracts. Commercial risks refer to nonpayment by importers because of insolvency or other business factors. Political risks include war, expropriation, confiscation, currency inconvertibility, civil commotion, or cancellation of import permits. A coinsurance feature limits coverage to 95% of losses from political risks and 85% of commercial losses on short-term credits (coverage of political risks is dropped to 85% as the time period lengthens). Coverage of political risks is handled by the Eximbank and commercial coverage is shared by the private insurers and the Export-Import Bank. Exporters desiring a guarantee may apply to an individual member of the FCIA. If the quotation is acceptable to the exporter, an underwriting agreement is created. The specific rates and details of coverage vary widely according to the time period of the credit extension and various business and political factors. In fiscal year 1968 the FCIA issued or renewed policies covering $716 million of business and political risks.[4]

Foreign investment

From the settlement of the colonies until the end of World War I, the United States was a net importer of capital needed to develop our industrial system. Since the end of World War II, this nation has become an exporter of capital for direct investments in assets, long- and short-term loans, and portfolio purchases of foreign securities. Our government has also made grants to assist in the reconstruction of war-devastated areas, for assisting developing nations to raise their national incomes, and for a variety of economic and military programs designed to strengthen the free world. Private foreign investments by U.S. businesses and citizens totaled $102 billion at the end of 1960. During 1968, foreign investments were increased $8.3 billion as follows: capital outflow of $6.5 billion, reinvested earnings of $1.4 billion, and net price changes and adjustments of $1 billion. The magnitude of net private capital outflow relative to other payments flows for some selected years can be seen in Table 25–1.

Portfolio and short-term investments

When capital markets are not encumbered with regulations, capital moves between nations in response to variations in rates of interest and dividend yields, relative prices of securities, and the financing requirements of international trade. These movements take many different forms including the purchase of stocks and bonds, bank loans of varying ma-

---

[4] *Export-Import Bank of the United States, Annual Report,* fiscal 1968.

turities, financing of foreign trade and other international transactions, and transfers of funds into foreign liquid assets offering higher income. Such movements of capital vary widely and are closely analyzed because of their effects on our balance of payments position.

Portfolio investments. In the early postwar years American investors had little interest in foreign securities. But as foreign companies rebuilt their productive capability and showed substantial rates of earning growth, investor interest was aroused. By the late 1950s, American purchases rose very substantially. In the period 1956–62, such purchases averaged over $750 million per year. At the end of 1964, U.S. holdings of foreign securities had an estimated market value of $14.5 billion—$9.1 billion in the form of bonds and $5.3 billion in corporate stocks. Such purchases contributed to the annual balance of payments deficits experienced in the 1956–64 period. Then the interest equalization tax, which placed a tax on returns from foreign portfolio investments, was passed in September 1964. This tax effectively precluded European companies and those of other advanced nations from selling securities in the United States. Thus, at the end of 1968, bond holdings of U.S. citizens had only increased to $10.6 billion and corporate stocks to $6.5 billion; moreover, a substantial portion of portfolio additions since 1964 is in Canadian companies which are exempted from the equalization tax.

Bank lending. While the outflow of capital from sales of securities in the United States was depressed after 1964 because of the interest equalization tax, the amount of long-term bank lending continued to increase. The growth of long-term loans to European borrowers was particularly rapid, suggesting that some of the loans were being used as substitutes for the sale of securities. In 1964 American banks made long-term loans of $942 million. The pace was even more accelerated in the first two months of 1965 when long-term commitments of $450 million were made to European, Canadian, and certain Latin American borrowers. The unfavorable balance of payments effects of these outflows resulted in the creation of a voluntary program to improve the balance that was presented to Congress in February 1965. Under this plan the interest equalization tax was immediately applied to bank loans with maturities of one to three years. The Federal Reserve Board further requested that U.S. banks voluntarily limit foreign credits so that amounts outstanding as of March 1966 would be no more than 5% greater than the level at the end of 1964. In addition to this pressure from the Federal Reserve to reduce long-term bank loans, the high interest rates in the United States after 1965 have greatly reduced the desirability of U.S. markets for European companies. Thus outstanding bank loans to foreigners declined from $4.3 billion at the end of 1965 to $3.4 billion at the end of 1968.

Short-term investments. In the early years after World War II, interest rates in the U.S. money market were below those available to European companies or companies in other countries such as Japan. When possible, these companies naturally turned to the American market for short-term loans. At the end of 1964, foreign short-term assets reported by banks and others amounted to $10.7 billion. These figures reflect short-term commercial bank loans, the increasing deposits held by domestic banks and nonfinancial corporations abroad to handle commercial transactions, and transfers of liquid assets into short-term foreign securities offering higher returns than are available in this country. With the rise in money-market interest rates after 1965, rates in the United States were not nearly as attractive to European companies and so the demands for loans declined, thus reducing the need for market controls to keep down the outflow of American capital.

Direct investments

Direct investments involve the purchase or establishment of foreign facilities to exploit the growing profit opportunities abroad. They usually involve asset ownership and differ from portfolio investments made to earn income from interest or dividends and possible appreciation in the value of securities purchased. American companies have had interests in foreign petroleum, extractive, and raw materials industries for many years, but most manufacturing and trading companies have traditionally focused on the economic opportunities in the domestic market. Exports were used to fill any foreign demand. This situation has changed greatly during the past decade as many major corporations have become multi-national companies with worldwide operating facilities. Smaller business enterprises have also participated in the move abroad. In fact, several well-known American corporations now derive the bulk of their sales and profits from foreign operations.

Value of investments

In 1950 the book value of U.S. foreign direct investments totaled $11.8 billion, approximately one half of it placed in petroleum, mining and smelting, and public utilities. By the end of 1968, this figure had increased to $64.8 billion, following heavy investments in the late 1950s and through the decade of the 1960s. Industrial firms have also been asked to co-operate in a voluntary program to improve the balance of payments position by repatriating time deposits and other liquid funds and by care-fully analyzing the balance of payments effects of large investments and the sources of funds used. Thus, in recent years, a substantial proportion of the overseas investment of American corporations was financed through the sale of bonds in Europe.

It is interesting to note that the increase in U.S. foreign direct investment is much more rapid than similar foreign investments in this nation. Over a similar time period of 1950 through 1969, foreign direct investments increased from $3.4 billion to $10.8 billion. The 1950 figure represented the residual values of many 19th-century investments that assisted our industrial development. By 1969 the foreign investment total included a number of new joint ventures by prominent American manufacturing firms with European firms displaying outstanding technological abilities. In addition an increasing number of foreign enterprises have entered major investment programs in the United States.

The Euro-bond market

The voluntary restraint program on capital export by American corporations was followed in January 1968 with a mandatory program. This program strongly constrained American corporations from purchasing foreign assets or building plants abroad with funds raised domestically. But the large annual balance of payments deficits incurred by the United States since the 1950s resulted in large holdings of dollar balances by foreigners. Some of these balances are held by foreign monetary authorities (this will be discussed in Chapter 26), but large amounts are held by foreign citizens and businesses. To finance their continued foreign expansion American corporations began to sell debentures and convertible bonds in Europe, thus giving impetus to the development of the Euro-bond market.

Euro-bond issues of American corporations are sold simultaneously in several financial centers in Europe by investment bankers from a number of different countries. The bonds have been denominated in a number of currencies, but a very large fraction are dollar bonds which are purchased by foreigners holding dollar balances.

TABLE 25–3

Euro-bond issues, 1963 through 1968 (*in millions of dollars*)

Country of borrower	1963	1964	1965	1966	1967	1968*
United States	—	—	331	439	527	2,059
Continental Europe	88	408	456	426	886	658
United Kingdom	—	—	25	40	51	134
Japan	20	162	25	—	—	180
Canada	—	—	—	—	—	38
Rest of world	25	5	83	101	305	259
International institutions	5	121	128	101	120	40
Total	137	696	1,046	1,107	1,889	3,368

* Preliminary.
Note: Because of rounding, figures do not necessarily add to totals.
Source: *Monthly Review*, Federal Reserve Bank of New York, August 1969, p. 171.

As can be seen in Table 25–3, American borrowers were not in the Euro-bond market until 1965, and they were not major participants until 1968. But in 1966 American corporations borrowed over $2 billion or approximately 60% of all Euro-bond borrowings.

Thus, the credit restraint program in the United States probably did not directly affect American foreign investments; the main effect was to shift the source of funds from the U.S. capital markets to the capital markets of Europe.

Concluding statement

The financing of foreign trade and investment is attracting increasing attention among businessmen involved in or considering foreign operations and among government officials concerned about the balance of payments, the convertibility of national currencies, and international patterns of competition. The necessity of protecting established foreign markets and interest in participating in the economic development now occurring in many areas has caused many American firms to increase the attention given to exporting and to foreign investment. This brief chapter and the following one on policy matters can only suggest some of the complexities and opportunities in this field of finance.

Questions and problems

1. Explain the economic doctrine of comparative advantage. What special financial problems are created by international trade and investments?

2. Is the balance of payments statement the same thing as a national cash flow statement summarizing holdings of currencies and gold? How is the balance computed?

3. What is the current balance of payments position? What trends are evident? What is the explanation for recent developments?

4. What is the role of commercial banks in international trade transactions? How would you justify the physical expansion of American commercial banks into foreign areas?

5. What is an import letter of credit and how is it used?

6. Why has the United States created a government agency to assist private American firms in international trade transactions? What services are offered?

7. If the United States is now a creditor nation and foreign investments increase our international economic role and create profit flows, why is there so much concern about the outflow of capital for foreign investment?

8. Does the government have any control over the amount of private foreign investment?

9. How would you explain the sudden increase of direct foreign investment in the late 1950s and 1960s?
10. Why have most American companies establishing foreign operations relied upon internal company funds and retained foreign earnings?
11. It has been suggested that private foreign investment should be substituted for government assistance. Is this a feasible approach? Do you agree with the suggestion?
12. What has been the effect by the various measures instituted by the U.S. government to restrict the flow of funds and foreign investments?

Bibliography

No attempt will be made to list the many texts and special interest publications dealing with the subjects of international finance and investments. Reference to any index of publications will provide a long list of sources under a variety of headings, including: international finance, foreign investment, balance of payments, foreign exchange, and the specific financial institutions. An extensive bibliography is also contained in Charles P. Kindleberger, *International Economics* (4th ed.; Homewood, Ill.: Richard D. Irwin, Inc., 1968). A lucid discussion of balance of payments problems and the role of the dollar is contained in Alvin Hansen, *The Dollar and the International Monetary System* (New York: McGraw-Hill, 1965). Other recent publications of particular interest include: John Fayerweather, *Facts and Fallacies of International Business* (New York: Holt, Rinehart, and Winston, 1962); John M. Dyer and Frederick C. Dyer, *Export Financing: Modern U.S. Methods* (Coral Gables, Fl.: University of Miami Press, 1963); Walter S. Salant, et al., *The United States Balance of Payments in 1968* (Washington, D.C.: The Brookings Institution, 1963); Hal B. Lary, *Problems of the United States as World Trader and Banker* (National Bureau of Economic Research, 1963); Raymond F. Mikesell, *The U.S. Balance of Payments and the International Role of the Dollar* (Washington, D.C.: American Enterprise Institute, 1970); and Ramsay A. Moran, *A Company Guide to Sources of Export Financing* (Washington, D.C.: Machinery and Allied Products Institute and Council for Technological Advancement, 1961). The International Finance Section of Princeton University also publishes a number of items on these subjects.

Statistical information may be found in the periodic issues of the *Survey of Current Business, Federal Reserve Bulletin,* International Monetary Fund publications, and United Nations reports. Articles pertinent to these subjects frequently appear in these publications and other sources including: Federal Reserve bank reviews, commercial bank reviews, *International Business, International Executive, Fortune, Harvard Business Review, Business Week,* and many other current periodicals. Information on the various international and national institutions may be found in the annual reports prepared by these agencies.

CHAPTER 26

International monetary policy

The diverse aspects of international exchanges of goods and capital through trade, long-term investments, and short-term flows of funds have already been discussed in Chapter 25. That chapter also explained the method of measuring the economic relationships of one country with the rest of the world—the balance of payments. This chapter examines various factors that influence these relationships.

The economic behavior of a nation with respect to other countries is intimately related to its domestic monetary and fiscal policies. Foreign trade and investment practices that are inconsistent with domestic economic growth will not promote long-run equilibrium of international transactions. At the same time, chronic balance of payments deficits or surpluses disrupt domestic conditions and eventually force adjustments to be made. The various procedures devised by the United States during the 1960s to correct deficits simultaneously with efforts to stimulate domestic economic growth indicate the complexity of creating compatible national and international goals. The extensive use of the dollar in international trade and finance and this nation's position of leadership in the world economy increase the significance of these decisions. Nevertheless, important differences distinguish international from national policies, partly because the powers and objectives of domestic policies are not parallel to those of international relationships.

Presumably there is some power of self-determination within individual nations that enables them to pursue their own monetary goals, even though economic conditions may deteriorate, until other nations apply restrictions. Strong countries may exert indirect pressures on neighboring nations through trade and investment discrimination and directly through consultation and the disciplinary powers of international financial institutions, but the powerful nations normally do not use military force to shape the economic behavior of others (although, unfortunately, examples of such imperialism still do occur). In the absence of any international sovereign force, each nation determines its own policies within the broad limitations of natural market forces.

Another difference is that political considerations may influence international economic relationships more than domestic ones. American economic interests are frequently aimed at strengthening allies or isolating enemies. In the years since the end of World War II, large economic and military aid programs have been created to help develop friendly countries into potential economic competitors under the philosophy that it is better to have strong allies (and economic competitors) than militarily dependent friends. The dominant influence of war—both the threat of future conflicts and the inheritances from past struggles—over international economic affairs once again demonstrates the close relationship between economic and military problems.

This chapter covers first the economic background of international balances of payments. Then, the various standards of foreign exchange are reviewed. Finally, the major international financial institutions that have been created to smooth the completion of international transactions are discussed.

The economic background of international financial relationships

Each nation must balance a variety of national goals. Broad objectives of the United States include: maintenance of an adequate rate of growth; reasonable price stability; full employment; contributions to the military power of the free world; contributions to the economic progress of developing nations; and long-run balance of payments equilibrium based on free convertibility of the dollar and free trade on a multilateral basis. As described in Chapter 25, the payments balance results from a complex of international money flows between nations attributable to trade, investments, services, travel, and various government, military, and economic programs. Most nations strive for approximate balance by accumulating some surpluses to offset deficits in much the same manner as national budgets are balanced over long time periods. History has shown that each individual nation has experienced at least one major balance of payments crisis during the postwar period.

As summarized in Chapter 25, the United States has suffered payments deficits in each year since 1950, with the exceptions of 1957 and 1968. Controversy exists concerning the correct format for recording the balance of payments and the exact size of the payments deficit; however, all measures confirm the fact that the United States has had a chronic deficit. These deficits have caused a large decline in our national stock of

TABLE 26–1

International investment position of the United States, year-end 1958 and 1967 (*millions of dollars*)

	1958	1967
U.S. claims on foreigners		
U.S. government gold stock $20,534		$ 12,065
U.S. government short-term claims 2,139		5,460
U.S. government long-term claims 16,192		23,545
Private short-term investments 3,488		11,845
Private direct investments 27,255		59,267
Private other investments 10,261		22,175
Total $79,869		$134,357
Foreigners' claim on U.S.		
Short-term claims and		
U.S. government obligations $24,006		$ 37,651
Long-term claims 16,652		31,962
Total $40,658		$ 69,613
Net U.S. claims on foreigners $39,211		$ 64,744

Source: Raymond Vernon, *U.S. Controls on Foreign Direct Investments—A Reevaluation*, Financial Executives Research Foundation, Inc., April 1969, p. 11.

gold and substantial increases in short-term obligations held by foreign interests (see Table 26–1). Foreign interests have been willing to accumulate the large dollar claims because of the basic strength of the U.S. economy and the guarantee of the Treasury to exchange an ounce of gold for $35 when presented by a foreign government or central bank. During the decade of the 1960s, as the outflow of gold mounted and dollar claims held by foreigners increased, the willingness of foreigners to continue to accumulate additional dollars has been questioned. Even though the payments deficit represents only a minute proportion of our gross national product, officials have been concerned about the drain on the national gold stock and the strategic impact of the short-term obligations to foreigners. As a practical matter, most nations keep their monetary reserves in the currencies of economically strong nations. The dollar has legal tender status domestically, but its use for settling international transactions depends on the confidence of other nations. Ultimately, the discipline of international finance requires that the objective of long-run payments equilibrium be given equal status with the domestic goals of growth, full employment, and price stability.

The international investment position of the United States is illustrated by the data shown in Table 26–1. As can be seen at the end of 1967, the U.S. government and U.S. citizens held substantially more foreign assets than the value of U.S. assets held by foreigners. Moreover, in the period between 1958 and 1967, the net claims held by the U.S. government and its citizens substantially increased. But, during this same period foreign holdings of short-term claims on U.S. assets increased very substantially, whereas U.S. government holdings of liquid assets and short-term claims on foreign assets declined. Moreover, at the end of 1967, foreign holdings of short-term claims were much larger than the holdings of liquid assets, gold, and short-term claims on foreign assets held by the U.S. government. Thus, the United States in its international payments position is not faced with a problem of wealth: the problem is rather a potential liquidity crisis. If for some reason foreigners should decide to liquidate a large fraction of their claims on U.S. assets, the gold stock and short-term claims on foreign currency held by the government may not be sufficient to meet the demands.

To maintain a stable international payments position, the United States must first maintain the conditions which make it attractive for foreigners to hold dollar claims. This involves maintaining strong expectations of the continued exchange parity between the dollar and other currencies and relatively attractive returns on dollar holdings compared to other strong currencies. Among other things, maintenance of strong expectations requires that continued annual deficits should be converted to a position of long-term payments equilibrium so that the potential liquidity problem does not worsen.

The United States is currently attempting to achieve long-run annual payments equality by: limiting military and economic aid to top priority needs; initiating special promotional programs to attract foreign tourists; encouraging the inflow of foreign investment capital; stimulating exports; a series of fiscal and monetary measures including the imposition of a tax on purchases of foreign securities, efforts to keep short-term interest rates high enough to discourage the outflow of capital, and the sale of medium-term, nonmarketable government bonds by the U.S. Treasury to foreign governments; and a program to limit the outflow of capital involving American banks and business firms. Each of these special programs has attacked a specific problem and beneficial results have been observed, but in the final analysis, payments equilibrium must be based on a strong competitive position relative to other nations.

The problem of balancing payments

The economic difficulties that may beset a country in its relationship with the rest of the world are of many kinds. The various types of difficulties, however, are closely interrelated, so that in the sections that follow a certain amount of overlap of discussion will inevitably be encountered.

Balance between exports and imports

Long-term payments equilibrium depends upon achieving a balance between exports and imports. The United States has had a large trade surplus through the years, but it is interesting to note the increasing competition for export markets (see Table 25–2). The rapid pace of technological development has enabled foreign producers to enter many of our traditional export markets with low-cost products. Many of these foreign competitors now have new facilities, installed during the postwar period. Extremely rigorous international competition has developed in a large number of important industries, including automobiles, steel, electronics, chemicals, office machines, textiles, processed metals, foodstuffs, and aircraft. The intensity of competition for export markets will undoubtedly continue to increase as all nations of the world seek to improve their level of economic development through acceleration of industrialization.

Even if a country pursues reasonably prudent fiscal and monetary policies, it may nevertheless get into trade difficulties that are beyond its control. For example, if a country is dependent on the export of a single commodity that is subject to wide price variations in international markets, it must expect to have sizable fluctuations in its payments position. The export of coffee by Brazil and of wool and meat products by Australia and New Zealand are examples. World demand for these products fluctuates, and changes in growing conditions may influence the supply. Producers in these nations cannot help being exposed to the risks of external business fluctuations. Technological obsolescence is also a great hazard; the displacement of wool by synthetic fibers is one example.

Business fluctuations

The phenomenon of economic instability is international as well as national. Business fluctuations influence the quantity of imports and exports and have an effect on prices. Business fluctuations are also likely to influence the flow of long-term capital into a country. Small countries depending on an inflow of such capital are affected by the nature of economic developments in the countries from which this capital flows.

Economic difficulties frequently seem to originate in the larger countries and then spread to the smaller ones. A leading nation, suffering an initial decline in domestic economic activity, may reduce its demand for the products of other countries before other nations reduce their demand for its products. This sequence helps to reduce the severity of business fluctuations in leading nations, but at the same time it tends to spread difficulties to other areas.

An unusual rate of growth may also disrupt a national balance of payments. Japan, Great Britain, Italy, and other nations have experienced trade deficits in recent years as a result of large increases in imports required to meet record industrial and agricultural production needs. Domestic prosperity also creates demands for consumer product imports. For example, Italy experienced a serious trade deficit in 1963 when its economic boom caused imports to rise 26%, while exports increased only 8%. On the other hand, in the last several years Japan and Germany have experienced very rapid rates of economic growth and have recorded very large balance of payments surpluses.

Price level dislocation

A chronic balance of payments deficit may indicate a higher or more rapidly rising price structure than those of other nations. For example, if one country pursues in isolation a more inflationary monetary or fiscal policy than other countries, this is likely to cause its domestic price level to increase more than prices in other countries, thus unbalancing its trade. Relatively rapid price increases in the United States probably account for the deterioration in the trade surplus which occurred after 1964 (see Table 25–2). Even more important, the pursuit of inflationary domestic economic policies may cause holders of that country's currency—whether its own citizens or other investors—to lose confidence in its future. To protect themselves, the holders may try to transfer their currency into foreign moneys. Such a flight of capital can have a devastating influence on the country's foreign exchange reserve. A reasonable stability of prices relative to those of other countries is an important factor for improving the international competitive position of export industries and domestic industries that face import competition.

Development programs

Many nations have become dissatisfied with the low level of their citizens' incomes and the primitive state of their economic development. Some have initiated economic development programs to stimulate industrialization as the first step in permanently improving the standard of living. While these programs may have important long-run benefits, in the short run they are often accompanied by a considerable degree of inflation and capital imports. When these programs depend on large external borrowings, the balance of payments of the country comes to depend on a continued flow of these funds. A developmental program is especially subject to fluctuations if the external borrowing involves chiefly the import of private capital. Private investors are sensitive to economic and political developments in the countries in which they invest and are likely to reverse their plans whenever they encounter policies not to their liking. Political revolutions and change in the social and economic climate can bring about such abrupt reversals. The very fact of development may cause changes in the social climate, as the large international petroleum companies have found in many of the underdeveloped countries in which they have explored for oil.

War and national defense

War quite obviously has a drastic effect on a nation's balance of payments. War is likely to reduce exports greatly, since the capacity to produce is more urgently needed for domestic use unless the exports are to aid allies. On the other hand, a nation may want as large a volume of imports as it can get and pay for. By the same token, the difficulties of the war period are likely to be reversed in a postwar period in which there may be sharp and drastic changes in international transactions. Neutral nations often export considerably more than they import during wars and, as a result, build large external currency reserves or add to their gold stocks. In the postwar period they are likely to attempt to use these cash reserves to make delayed and much needed expenditures. Thus there is considerable similarity between the deportment of individuals and of nations in war and postwar periods.

War may have another indirect and damaging influence on the balance of payments of a nation. Wars are frequently followed by serious inflation, particularly in devastated and defeated countries, although victorious nations have not escaped the scourge. Domestic inflation due to excessive monetary expansion raises domestic prices. If a country is attempting to maintain fixed exchange rates, then the quantity of foreign goods demanded will increase as the result of domestic price rises. At the same time, that country's exports are likely to fall and its international reserves are then usually depleted by such developments.

Fluctuating long-term capital investment

Long-term investments in foreign countries have been common for many years. The United States has been particularly active in adding to its foreign investments in recent years and has also been the recipient of foreign capital at various times (see Chapter 25 for a discussion of this subject). When the flows of long-term capital movements are reasonably stable and when they are directed to economically desirable long-term investments, the balance of payments of the recipient nation is usually not upset. If a nation, however, comes to depend on the import of long-term capital to balance its payment system, discontinuance of the capital imports for any reason may put its payments system under considerable strain. Shifts in long-term capital investment are often the product more of political than of economic factors. Long-term investors are sensitive to the political stability of a country. If a dictator in whom investors have little confidence comes into power or if there is an abrupt political reversal due to the election of a government not favored by external investors, the inflow of long-term capital can stop quite abruptly.

Since private long-term capital investments have been volatile, some have recommended that such investments be handled by governments. The financial institutions discussed below resulted from such recommendations. While government investment might have the advantage of greater stability, it is less subject to the discipline of economic scrutiny than is private investment. Private investors are quicker to stop investing in a country whose fiscal responsibility they distrust than are governments.

Supporters of foreign investment emphasize the fact that the return flow of earnings and repatriated capital are a positive factor in our payments balance. Nevertheless, the strain created during periods of payments deficits by large foreign investments caused the United States to act to limit the purchases of foreign securities by applying a special tax on such purchases.

Fluctuating short-term flows of capital

Short-term capital flows are largely governed by variations of interest rates and expectations of changes in foreign exchange rates. For example, in 1960 there was a sharp rise in the outflow of short-term capital from the United States to Europe to take advantage of attractive interest rate differentials. The U.S. Treasury and the Federal Reserve System attempted to keep short-term interest rates in the United States high enough to discourage the outflow of capital without hampering domestic economic growth. Thus, the Federal Reserve System raised its discount rate from 3.5% to 4% in November 1964. This action was probably not appropriate from the point of view of domestic economic goals. The United States had a higher level of unemployment than was popularly deemed desirable, and the higher interest rate was expected further to retard employment growth. The discount increase was made in response to Great Britain's decision to increase the Bank of England bank rate to 7%. The raise was expected to increase the amount of short-term capital flowing to Great Britain, thus increasing the U.S. balance of payments deficit. In recent years, flows of short-term capital in response to shifts in short-term interest rate differentials between countries have become increasingly volatile, and on various occasions such shifts have had an important impact on payments balances.

Eurodollar market

The universal acceptability of the dollar has created an interesting development in the last decade known as the Eurodollar market. Eurodollars are short-term, interest-bearing deposits of dollars in London and European banks. These deposits in turn are loaned to foreign borrowers or to overseas divisions of American companies to finance foreign trade, to settle international obligations, and to finance the construction of plants and equipment in foreign countries; or they are purchased by branches of American banks to be used in the domestic lending operations of these banks.

The development of the Eurodollar market has had far-reaching implications for the balance of payments position, the domestic banking system, and U.S. monetary policy. Eurodollars purchased by branches of American banks are not subject to the Regulation Q interest rate maximums of the Federal Reserve System, and until recently reserve requirements were not levied on these deposits. During the period of tight monetary conditions beginning in 1966, when the reserve position of the large money market banks were under severe pressure, European branches of these banks purchased large amounts of Eurodollars to bolster their U.S. operations. Liabilities of U.S. banks to their foreign branches increased from $1.7 billion at the end of January 1966 to over $7 billion at the end of September 1968. During this period Eurodollar yields rose very drastically, which raised the cost of these funds to the banks which purchased them. But, the availability of Eurodollar deposits considerably softened the force of the Federal Reserve's tight-money policy on the large banks which had access to this market. These banks used the funds purchased in the Eurodollar market to make loans to their customers in the United States.

The Eurodollar market has created an international money market of very large proportions. These funds can be easily shifted from dollars to other currencies. Thus, the development of this market is beneficial in terms of allowing a freer flow of capital in the international economy, but it has increased concern about the liquidity problem of the United States. If interest rates in the United States declined at a time when European countries had high rates, a large shift of dollars invested in the Eurodollar market into other currencies could develop. This could be reflected as an increase in the balance of payments deficit of the United

States and could lead to a larger drain on U.S. gold reserves. Thus, the U.S. monetary authority must be concerned about the differentials in interest rates between the United States and other major countries. This situation calls into question the freedom of the Federal Reserve to take actions that would reduce domestic interest rates in some instances when this would result from actions deemed desirable for domestic stability.

Other capital movements

Abnormal circumstances may also cause unusual shifts of funds known as flights of capital. If the citizens of a given country or others that hold the country's currency lose confidence in that currency or in the fiscal responsibility of its government, they may attempt to transfer their funds into the currency of another country. The important role that Switzerland has played as a refuge for nervous money is a demonstration of the magnitude of this business. No other country in the world, including the United States, has such a large concentration of short-term funds in relation to its economic size. These short-term capital movements can have a damaging influence on the payments position of a country, since they may quickly strip a country of its foreign exchange reserves. One of the prime purposes of exchange control is to prohibit short-term capital movements. Experience has shown, however, that exchange control may be evaded in many ways. A country may lose much of its foreign exchange reserves as the result of short-term capital movements, even if it has a fairly strict system of exchange control.

Determination of exchange rates

The term *rate of exchange* as used earlier in this chapter is merely a statement of the cost or price of a unit of money of one country expressed in terms of the money of a second country. Thus a rate of 240 on London in New York means that the value of one pound sterling is $2.40 in U.S. currency. The rates indicate that the relative values of the money units of the two countries, or, regarded collectively, the rates quoted in the United States on all foreign currencies, are a form of index of the external purchasing power of the U.S. dollar.

Although we speak of the rate of exchange as if there were only one price in a market at one time, this is not true. A classification of rates reveals the following:

Buying and selling rates. Rates maintained by the same operator or institution in the foreign exchange market. The difference is called spread and represents the gross profit margin for the operator.

Over-the-counter rates. These are charged persons applying to an institution for a small amount of exchange.

Market rate. Lower than over-the-counter rate and used when a broker or bank sells a large volume to another.

Sight rate. Applies to sale or purchase of instruments payable by the drawee at sight.

Time rate. The price of a draft payable a designated number of days after acceptance by the drawee.

Spot rates. Paid for drafts available for immediate delivery.

Forward rates. Quoted on instruments that are not yet drawn but that will be created and delivered in the future.

An example of how the ratio of exchange between national currencies may vary over time is shown in Table 26–2. The small changes from year

TABLE 26–2

Foreign exchange rates; U.S. dollars and other national currencies (*in cents per unit of foreign currency*)

	Canada (dollar)	France (franc)	Germany (deutsche mark)	Japan (yen)	United Kingdom (pound)
1947	91.999	.8407	—	—	402.86
1948	91.691	.3240	—	—	403.13
1949	92.881	.3017	—	—	368.72
1950	91.474	.2858	23.838	—	280.07
1951	94.939	.2856	23.838	—	279.96
1952	102.149	.2856	23.838	—	279.26
1953	101.650	.2856	—	—	281.27
1954	102.724	.2856	23.838	—	280.87
1955	101.401	.2856	23.765	—	279.13
1956	101.600	.2855	23.786	.2779	279.57
1957	104.291	.2376	23.798	.2779	279.32
1958	103.025	.2374	23.848	.2779	280.98
1959	104.267	.2038	23.926	.27781	280.88
1960	103.122	20.389	23.976	.27785	280.76
1961	98.760	20.384	24.903	.27690	280.22
1962	93.561	20.405	25.013	.27712	280.78
1963	92.699	20.404	25.084	.27663	280.00
1964	92.689	20.404	25.157	.27625	279.21
1965	92.734	20.401	25.036	.27262	279.59
1966	92.811	20.352	25.007	.27598	279.30
1967	92.689	20.323	25.084	.27613	275.04
1968	92.801	20.191	25.048	.27735	239.35
1969	92.855	19.302	25.491	.27903	239.01

Source: *Federal Reserve Bulletin*, various issues.

to year are a reflection of demand-supply variations in the foreign exchange market. The larger changes reflect the periodic devaluations and revaluations which have occurred.

Three methods of establishing the ratio of exchange between the currencies of different nations may be used: a system of unchanging rates of exchange, such as the fixed relationship of currencies to gold under the gold standard; fluctuating exchange rates determined by supply and demand in spot and forward markets, such as Canada's policy of nonintervention in the movement of the Canadian dollar from 1950 to 1962 and again after June 1970; and use of a gold exchange standard that eliminates the official link to gold, but requires central banks to convert currency into gold for the settlement of international transactions and to buy and sell currency in the foreign exchange market to stabilize rates. Countries that belong to the International Monetary Fund and that have agreed not to change the par value of their currencies in relation to gold or the U.S. dollar, except to correct a fundamental disequilibrium, use a variation of the third system.

The gold standard

If two countries are on the same metallic monetary standard, such as gold, they define their monetary unit as a specific quantity of pure gold, maintain a government market for the purchase and sale of gold at fixed prices, and place no restrictions upon imports or exports of gold coin or bullion. Under such circumstances the rate of exchange between the two countries will fluctuate closely about the *mint par* of exchange.

Mint par of exchange. Mint par is the ratio of the pure gold content of the two currency units. For example, in the years before World War I and again in the period 1925–31, when both England and the United States employed a gold standard, the pound sterling contained 113 grains of gold and the dollar contained 23.22 grains. The ratio of 113 to 23.22 is 4.8665. Thus the New York price on London pounds centered about $4.8665.

Specie points. However, an increase in the demand for sterling (growing out of an excess of British exports to the United States or the necessity by Americans to make payments in England) tended to force the rate above $4.8665. The upper extreme to which the price could be driven, under these circumstances, was approximately $4.8865. This specie export point could not be passed because, if the rate went above it, the debt or payment in England could be settled more cheaply by an export of gold from the United States. In other words, as long as the cost of shipping 113 grains of gold was 2 cents, the rate of exchange per pound would not go more than 2 cents above mint par. At the upper gold point, the demand for bills of exchange decreased, and a demand for gold took its place.

Conversely, the lower limit on the pound sterling rate was about 2 cents below mint par, or about $4.8465. American exporters drawing bills on British banks to finance shipment of goods would refuse to sell them to domestic dealers in exchange for less than $4.8465 per pound. Rather than sacrifice on the rate of exchange, exporters would agree to pay for the cost of importing gold that could be sold in the United States at the rate of $4.8665 for 113 grains.

Under the conditions assumed, gold shipments would be made by banks rather than by traders. If sterling bills could be sold at prices above the gold export point, banks would use the funds received to buy gold and ship it abroad and then would sell bills against the resultant balances in London at the high price. But if all banks attempted to take advantage of the opportunity, competition among them would soon bring the price of exchange down to $4.8865. Also, if sterling drafts arising out of the export trade could be purchased at less than $4.8465, banks in America would buy them and send them to England for conversion into gold at the rate of 113 grains for each £1 draft. The rate in New York would then rise to $4.8465 or higher.

What has been said above with respect to the historical rate of exchange between America and England would apply equally well to any two nations on the gold standard. Under the assumed conditions, exchange rates would be relatively stable. This leads to the inference that the purchasing power of gold is everywhere the same and that any disequilibrium of prices between gold standard countries would be adjusted by an automatic flow of gold.

If the demand for gold is substituted for a demand for bills of exchange, the gold flow operates to correct short-run disequilibrium in the balance of payments. The more fundamental correction that is said to follow a gold movement takes place slowly and is in the nature of a long-term adjustment. Supporters of the gold standard note that a loss of gold by a nation will reduce metallic reserves behind currency and bank deposits and cause a contraction in the supply of credit which will tend to increase short-term interest rates. This in turn will be followed by a decrease in the volume of business and finally in the general price level. The opposite will tend to be true in the country or countries receiving the gold. As prices abroad rise relative to those of the domestic market, the movement of foreign trade tends to reverse itself and to restore the former equilibrium. These adjustments are often referred to as the automatic discipline of the gold standard that requires actual gold shipments.

Early in February 1965, France publicly called for a return to the gold standard by all nations to remove the uncertainties and abuses of the present system. Under the system proposed by the French, all payments deficits would be settled by shipping gold. Countries would not be permitted to rely on transfers of dollars, sterling claims, or loans to carry them through periods of deficit. France further announced its intent to redeem large amounts of dollars and called upon other nations to follow its example. Most economists and governments firmly rejected the idea of returning to the gold standard.

The relative stability of foreign exchange rates achieved through fluctuations in the quantity of money, incomes, and prices is considered by many economists and political scientists to be worth less than it costs. The pressure exerted upon an economy by a heavy and long-continued gold drain may result in almost complete business stagnation, with widespread unemployment and impoverishment of many citizens, particularly the working group. Moreover, the deflation in the country losing gold may finally be transmitted through the fixity of exchange relationships to other gold standard nations. This may occur, first, because the people of the depressed nation would be unwilling or unable to import from the gold-receiving nation whose prices were rising and whose exchange rates were fixed at former levels, and, second, because individuals in the gold-receiving country would take advantage of the depressed prices of the other nation by importing its products. Thus, in the nation receiving gold, a reduction in its exports would doubtless be accompanied by a partial reduction in sales in the domestic market. If the velocity of turnover of the expanded money supply also decreased the decline in volume of both domestic and foreign trade could induce a business depression.

The gold exchange standard

The gold standard reached its widest usage prior to World War I. It was revived in many leading countries for a brief period in the 1920s but has since been abandoned or considerably modified in almost all countries of the world, including the United States.

The *gold exchange standard* gives the holder of a nation's money the right to convert it into gold for the purpose of making international payments, but domestic convertibility of currencies into gold is denied. The United States and a few other nations now maintain formal international convertibility of their currencies into gold. In some other countries the same result is accomplished indirectly by allowing the holders of their currency to purchase gold bullion in the free markets of the world.

At the present time neither a U.S. citizen nor a foreigner can convert his dollars into gold, but if the holder of U.S. dollars in a foreign country sells them to his central bank or to his government, these official bodies can use the funds to buy gold from the U.S. Treasury Department. This action would force the United States to deplete its gold reserves or to rely on holdings of foreign currencies to meet demands for foreign exchange. If the foreign interests hold the dollars, the constraints of the formal gold standard in forcing nations to correct payments imbalances are lost. The large increase in the size of dollar obligations to foreign interests created by the series of balance of payments deficits from 1950 through 1968 is often referred to as an example of the inadequacy of the present system. It is claimed that the United States has not been put under strong enough compulsion to correct its continued annual payments deficits.

Convertibility at fixed rates. At the present time, monetary authorities are expected to use foreign exchange reserves and credit facilities to avoid exchange rate fluctuations in excess of the narrow limits permitted by the Articles of Agreement of the International Monetary Fund unless a new par value is adopted. Many observers believe that the maintenance of a fixed parity of one currency with others by adhering to established buying and selling rates is an important factor in stabilizing international economic relations. U.S. officials have repeatedly emphasized the policy of protecting the dollar as a convertible currency at the fixed rate of $35 per ounce of gold. This pledge and the size of the U.S. gold stock give the dollar status as an international currency used by foreign central banks as a reserve equivalent to gold. This procedure also removes much of the discipline of the gold standard by eliminating the spontaneous return to equilibrium created by the immediate settlement of international obligations through the transfer of gold.

The large holdings of dollar claims by foreign interests have created a base of foreign currency reserves for several nations as well as providing a currency that is internationally acceptable for the settlement of obligations (see Table 26–3). In fact, many nations may have a convertible national currency without owning gold reserves if adequate foreign exchange reserves exist to meet all international obligations. Under the present system, international transactions among private interests and governments are usually settled by exchange of a few major national currencies. Many central banks rely on the dollar to settle foreign exchange obligations.

Fluctuating exchange rates. Many leading economists have recommended the adoption of a system of flexible exchange rates as a means of removing the restrictions on trade and investment caused by a shortage of international liquidity. The Canadian dollar was allowed to fluctuate without any official exchange rate being set by the Bank of Canada from 1950 to May 1962 (see Table 26–2). After a period of fixed exchange rates the Canadian government in June 1970 again allowed the value of its dollar to fluctuate. In theory, this policy would remove the problem of maintaining foreign currency reserves and would result in an automatic equality of receipts and disbursements and the adjustment of exchange rates in response to current supply and demand factors. Most policy makers have rejected this theory, at least for the present, and the IMF continues to advocate stable rates of exchange.

A short history of exchange rates

Under conditions prevailing before World War I and during a portion of the interwar period, gold shipments and short-term capital movements satisfactorily performed their function of adjusting short-run imbalances in international exchange. A drastic change occurred in the decade from 1930 to 1940 however. Collapse of the gold standard in the early 1930s, the spread of industrial depression and low prices over the United States, and the heavy investment of foreign funds in long-term securities in the United States brought vast quantities of gold to this country. Widespread political unrest abroad and the fear that gold would be nationalized or impounded by various foreign countries also accelerated the flow of gold into the United States. When the American dollar was devalued (1933–34) and the price of gold increased from $20.67 to $35.00 an ounce, the United States became a veritable haven for gold. The balance of payments of the United States was so favorable in terms of trade and the imports of gold and credit so excessive that it became increasingly difficult for foreigners to acquire dollars abroad. A serious and continuing dollar shortage was created. Even before World War II, many nations found it necessary to curtail imports from the United States and to ration the small amounts of dollar exchange that were available. The breakdown in international trade was followed by a growth of bilateralism, adopted first by Germany and later by several other nations as one phase of the economic mobilization for war. World War II virtually closed the remaining channels of private international trade and concentrated control of commerce and finance in the hands of governments.

The dollar shortage

The problem faced by foreigners in acquiring dollar exchange and gold for use in settling exchange obligations was further accentuated by World War II. This was due not only to the continued concentration of gold in America but also to the inability of foreign producers to compete successfully against the United States for world markets. The technical superiority of the United States as a producer on a low-cost, mass-production basis was not then seriously challenged by any important nation. Moreover, U.S. producers were protected against competition by high tariffs, and American consumers maintained a preference for articles of domestic production. Additional factors contributing to the shortage of dollars abroad in the postwar years were the restrictive trade policies of some nations and the attempts of others to maintain an artifically high value on their currencies.[1] Despite the efforts of various nations, including the

---

[1] Alvin H. Hansen, *Monetary Theory and Fiscal Policy* (New York: McGraw-Hill Book Co., Inc., 1949), pp. 212–13.

United States, and international agencies to promote nondiscriminatory multilateral trade, government exchange regulations and controls in many areas of the world seriously impeded the flow of goods and investments following World War II.

Cure of the dollar shortage

The shortage of dollar holdings abroad created problems for American exporters during the immediate postwar period and shifted much of the burden of financing exports to the U.S. government. In the years 1946 through 1968, government grants and capital outlays totaled more than $87 billion.[2] A large share of these funds was used by foreign nations to purchase American products and materials. In fact, some of the loans and grants included specific stipulations that the funds be spent in the United States. Many developing nations that lack adequate foreign exchange reserves still rely on foreign assistance from the United States and other advanced nations for the financing of imports and domestic investment.

Alleviation of the dollar shortage actually began as soon as foreign nations resumed peacetime economic activity; however, the size and scope of the job of restoring disrupted economies and prewar positions in international trade and investment prevented a rapid return to international equilibrium in the distribution of gold and foreign exchange reserves. An important step toward solution of the dollar gap occurred in the fall of 1949, when Britain devalued the pound sterling from $4.03 to $2.80. Other nations soon pursued a similar course, some reducing the value of their currencies in terms of the U.S. dollar to an even greater extent. The changed relationship of international currency values gradually brought material changes in the balance of payments position of the United States, Britain, and nations of western Europe. The combination of improved economic health in foreign nations, private foreign investments, and the U.S. government program of grants and loans resulted in the distribution of large amounts of dollars to foreign nations so that the dollar gap largely disappeared as early as 1953. The development of chronic balance of payments deficits in the United States in the early 1950s added to the foreign holdings of dollars since virtually all commercial and financial transactions with American residents are settled with dollars.

The dramatic shift in the distribution of reserves among different nations may be seen in Table 26–3. Reserve holdings shifted dramatically between 1946 and 1966. The proportion of total reserves held by the United States declined from almost 54% to less than 21%. In the same period the proportion of total reserves held by other major countries and groups of countries all increased.

---

[2] *Economic Report of the President,* 1969, p. 325.

TABLE 26–3

Total official reserves of gold, gold tranche and reserve position with the IMF and foreign exchange assets, 1948–68 (*dollar items in billions of U.S. dollars*)

| | 1948 | 1954 | 1956 | 1958 | 1960 | 1962 | 1964 | 1968 | Percentage | |
									1948	1968
All countries	$47.9	$53.5	$56.2	$57.7	$60.7	$63.1	$68.9	$76.6	100.0	100.0
United States	25.8	22.9	23.7	22.5	19.4	17.2	16.7	15.7	53.9	20.5
United Kingdom	2.0	3.0	2.3	3.1	3.7	3.3	2.3	2.4	4.2	3.1
Industrial Europe*	4.6	10.2	12.2	15.9	20.1	23.8	28.4	31.6	9.6	41.2
Canada	1.1	2.0	2.0	2.0	2.0	2.5	2.9	3.0	2.3	3.9
Japan	—	.9	1.3	1.1	1.9	2.0	2.0	2.9	—	3.8
Other Europe†	1.6	2.0	2.0	2.0	2.5	3.1	3.9	7.3	3.3	9.5
Australia, New Zealand, S. Africa	2.2	1.8	1.6	1.1	1.4	2.2	2.8	3.1	4.6	4.0
Latin America	2.9	3.2	3.8	3.2	2.9	2.3	2.9	4.0	6.1	5.2
Middle East	2.0	1.3	1.4	1.4	1.4	1.7	2.3	3.2	4.2	4.2
Other Asia	5.1	3.8	3.8	2.8	3.4	3.2	3.3	4.1	10.6	5.4
Other Africa	.3	1.9	2.0	1.8	1.9	1.5	1.3	2.2	.6	2.9

* Includes: Austria, Belgium, Denmark, France, Germany, Italy, Netherlands, Norway, Sweden, and Switzerland.
† Includes: Finland, Greece, Iceland, Ireland, Portugal, Spain, Turkey, and Yugoslavia.
Source: International Monetary Fund, *International Financial Statistics*, March, 1970.

Prior to 1958, Europeans had taken most of the surplus earnings from their foreign trade in the form of short-term dollar holdings in the United States. However, in 1958, because the gold reserve supporting their currency systems was considered inadequate as their international economic position improved, they diverted a growing proportion of their dollar income into improving their gold reserve. The strengthened positions resulting from gold imports was a factor in restoring external convertibility to their currencies in December 1958.[3] At the end of 1968, 34 countries had agreed to comply with Article Eight of the International Monetary Fund Agreement prohibiting the restriction of international currency transactions for balance of payments reasons.[4]

Exchange control continues to be practiced in a very large portion of the world, though in recent years it has been relaxed in many countries. Convertibility has increased considerably, particularly in western Europe, and is a basis of expanded economic relations among these countries and with the rest of the world. In areas where unsound development programs and economic policies have created internal difficulties, however, exchange control continues to be a means of evading or concealing the discipline of world markets.

Institutions for facilitating international financial cooperation

The extreme nationalism of the 1930s was deplored by most nations. Many analysts believe that World War II may be partly blamed on the breakdown of international economic relationships which resulted. Accordingly, during the war a number of plans were developed to restore international economic cooperation. The major institution to accomplish this cooperation, the International Monetary Fund, was created at the Bretton Woods conference held in 1944. Since then many other international organizations have been formed to supplement the work of this agency and to meet other needs (see Chapter 25).

International Monetary Fund (IMF)

When the International Monetary Fund was founded in 1947 its purpose was to restore a sound framework for international monetary relationships. To do so, a pool of gold and various currencies is maintained for the use of member nations requiring temporary sources of funds for the settlement of international obligations. The credit and control operations of the IMF are designed to provide the advantages of the stable rates

---

[3] *External convertibility* means basically that nonresidents holding the currency of a nation adhering to a policy of convertibility may freely exchange these holdings for U.S. dollars or other convertible currencies.

[4] *Annual Report of the International Monetary Fund*, 1969, p. 139.

of a gold standard and, at the same time, the flexibility of rates that may prevail under an inconvertible-paper standard. In recent years, member nations have used short-term drawings from the IMF to finance balance of payments deficits resulting from adverse shifts in trade patterns and capital flows. Drawings for three to five years may be arranged. The goal of the IMF is to provide temporary assistance to members while they correct maladjustments without resorting to drastic policies restricting trade and investment and other serious monetary adjustments. To acquire such assistance a borrower nation must demonstrate its ability and intention to correct the basic cause of payments deficits.

The formal statement of the purposes of the IMF, as contained in the Articles of Agreement, follows:

(i)   To promote international monetary cooperation through a permanent institution which provides the machinery for consultation and collaboration on international monetary problems.

(ii) To facilitate the expansion and balanced growth of international trade, and to contribute thereby to the promotion and maintenance of high levels of employment and real income and to the development of economic policy.

(iii) To promote exchange stability, to maintain orderly exchange arrangements among members, and to avoid competitive exchange depreciation.

(iv) To assist in the establishment of a multilateral system of payments in respect of current transactions between members and in the elimination of foreign exchange restrictions which hamper the growth of world trade.

(v)   To give confidence to members by making the Fund's resources available to them under adequate safeguards, thus providing them with opportunity to correct maladjustments in their balance of payments without resorting to measures destructive of national or international prosperity.

(vi) In accordance with the above, to shorten the duration and lessen the degree of disequilibrium in the international balances of payments of members.

The Bretton Woods agreements established a capital contribution of gold and national currencies from each member nation of the IMF. The quota was based upon the national income and trade position of each country. The gold portion amounted to 25% of the total or 10% of each nation's net holdings of gold and U.S. dollars, whichever was smaller. The total initial fund subscribed was $8 billion, of which $2,750 million was supplied by the United States. As of April 30, 1969, holdings of gold and national currencies had risen to almost $23 billion. The U.S. quota of $5,160 million was still the largest contribution by a large margin. The gold value of each contribution must be maintained, and each nation is expected to make adjustments if the value of its currency held by the IMF declines. The large increase in the assets of the IMF has resulted both from the rapid expansion of its membership to a total of 111 nations as of the end of 1968 and from periodic increases in the size of quotas assessed on members.

Method of operation. The majority of financial transactions between nations continues to be settled through well-established channels. In fact, as long as a nation's balance of payments remains in equilibrium, it does not have any need for IMF credit sources. When a scarcity of foreign currencies develops, a country may turn to the IMF through its central bank or some other authorized fiscal agency. When a nation draws foreign currencies from the IMF, it is in effect borrowing from that institution. The country whose currency is drawn is placed in a creditor position. The borrowing nation thus sells its currency to the IMF. When repayment is made, the borrowing country repurchases its currency, using gold or foreign currencies that are not already in a surplus position with the IMF. Repurchases return currency reserves of borrowing nations to normal quota levels. All drawings are subject to a small transaction charge of one half of 1%, and amounts in excess of the gold tranche quota require the payment of interest based on the size of the drawings and the length of time funds are used.

Limits are placed upon the amount that any nation may borrow. Initial drawings of not more than 25% of a member's quota (equivalent to the gold contribution) are permitted almost automatically. Borrowings beyond this amount must be justified to IMF officials, including proof that corrective action is planned. If the amount borrowed is inadequate, lending limits may be temporarily suspended, or the borrowing nation may obtain permission from the IMF to revalue its currency as a drastic measure to improve its trade position. Devaluation could be initiated by a troubled nation without IMF approval, but such independent action would result in the loss of valuable IMF services, including borrowing rights. If a member country persistently has a deficit (or a surplus, such as West Germany in recent years) in its currency transactions with the IMF, exchange rate adjustment may be recommended to restore equilibrium. The IMF has actively campaigned for elimination of exchange controls and other restrictions on the transfer of national currencies that have been adopted during periods of economic strain. Member nations that utilize such controls must consult annually with the IMF to indicate what efforts are being made to remove such restrictions, and permanent usage of discriminatory controls may result in cancellation of membership.

IMF accomplishments. Following a rather slow beginning, the activities of the IMF accelerated after the Suez Canal crisis in 1956 and have continued to expand as indicated in Table 26–4. This table summarizes the lending and repurchasing activities of the IMF and the amounts of standby arrangements in existence on an annual basis. The experience of Canada may be used to demonstrate the flows of currencies summarized in aggregate form in Table 26–4. In mid-1962, the Canadian government purchased currencies totaling $300 million to shore up its reserves to decrease speculation against the Canadian dollar. Repurchases were made in stages until the final installment of $57.2 million was completed in October 1964. During this time period, Canada's official holdings

TABLE 26–4

Summary of fund transactions, fiscal years ended April 30, 1948–68 (*in millions of U.S. dollars*)

	Total purchases by members	Total repurchases by members
1948..........$	606	—
1949..........	119	—
1950..........	52	24
1951..........	28	19
1952..........	46	37
1953..........	66	185
1954..........	231	145
1955..........	49	276
1956..........	39	272
1957..........	1,114	75
1958..........	666	87
1959..........	264	537
1960..........	166	522
1961..........	577	659
1962..........	2,243	1,260
1963..........	580	807
1964..........	626	380
1965..........	1,897	517
1966..........	2,817	406
1967..........	1,061	340
1968..........	1,348	1,116
Total	14,596	7,664

Source: *Annual Report of the International Monetary Fund,* 1969, Table 49, p. 150.

of gold and U.S. dollars increased from $1.5 billion in May 1962 to $2.6 billion in September 1964.

The IMF has also emphasized the providing of technical training and advisory services for member nations. In some situations, the IMF may even assign staff members to assist national government officials. In these consultations the domestic fiscal and monetary policies of the nations involved are reviewed, as well as their general trade policies. Many times the advice and counsel of the fund may be important in encouraging sounder policies in these countries, something that domestic politicians cannot do without moral support and pressure from the IMF. These consultations have generally been conducted without public notice but often have been important factors in periods of financial crisis and strain. Particular attention is now being directed to the needs of developing nations.

General arrangements to borrow. In December 1961, 10 of the major industrial countries of the IMF completed negotiations to form a special supplementary fund or *lenders' club.* The agreement created a pool of strong currencies totaling the equivalent of U.S. $6 billion that is available to support the IMF if one of the members suffers a major speculative attack on its currency. The United States participates in the arrangement through powers granted by an act of Congress in 1962. Other members include Belgium, Canada, France, West Germany, Italy, Japan, the Netherlands, Sweden, and the United Kingdom. Switzerland is also an associate member. The commitments add strength to the international monetary system in general and the IMF in particular, but each member retains the right to approve the relending of its quota contribution by the IMF. In November 1964, the British currency came under intense speculative pressure created by fears that the government would have to devalue the pound to alleviate the serious balance of payments crisis. Britain's standby credit agreement with the IMF was inadequate to meet the challenge. The first action involved arrangement of a credit equivalent to U.S. $1 billion, composed as follows: an IMF credit equal to U.S. $345 million using available currencies; IMF action to buy currencies, particularly West German marks and French francs, totaling U.S. $250 million using gold reserves; and loans of national currencies equal to U.S. $405 million from 8 members of the group of 10 (the United States and Great Britain were excluded). When conditions continued to deteriorate, the group arranged dramatically for an emergency line of credit equal to U.S. $3 billion to protect the pound from falling below an exchange rate of $2.78. The United States contributed through: $250 million credit from the Export-Import Bank (see Chapter 25) and a $750 million currency swap arranged by the Federal Reserve System. This example demonstrates how quickly and effectively the major nations can act to prevent international monetary chaos.

Direct consultation and cooperation on a bilateral basis has also increased in recent years. Such efforts have been important in preventing speculative raids on specific national currencies. One example of unilateral bargaining is the $2 billion series of swap loans arranged by the Federal Reserve System with several foreign central banks and the Bank for International Settlements. These agreements provide for the exchange of national currencies to prevent the upsetting effects of large outflows of currency. Such swaps are considered to be a short-term expedient rather than a basic solution to balance of payments problems. The actual exchanges do not occur until pressure develops; however, the agreements are arranged in advance to assure an immediate response. The Federal Reserve Bank of New York is responsible for implementation of these agreements in the United States. An example of how this system operates occurred following the assassination of President Kennedy on November 22, 1963. To forestall any panic selling of dollars, the Federal Reserve Bank of New York immediately began offering to sell five major foreign currencies. The sizable reserves of these currencies and the quick action of the Federal Reserve System stabilized the exchange markets and prevented a crisis. The network of reciprocal credit arrangements with foreign central banks has become a vital factor in protecting the strength of the dollar.

The development of a flexible reserve currency

The increased quotas of the IMF, the development of swap agreements between major countries, and the formation of a group of 10 countries in a lenders' club suggest that the existing avenues for creating additional reserves are not believed to have sufficient flexibility. Continued expansion in international trade requires a parallel growth in international reserve assets. It has long been recognized that increments to the stock of gold cannot be relied upon to fulfill this function. Since the mid-1950s, U.S. balance of payments deficits have fortunately supplied substantial additions to the stock of international reserves. But, the actions of the United States in the mid-1960s to eliminate the balance of payments deficit suggest that this source cannot be expected to continue to supply the desired increases in the future.

In 1966 official discussions were begun to explore the feasibility of developing a flexible reserve creation process. In September of 1967, the Board of Governors of the IMF unanimously approved an outline of the features of a special drawing rights (SDRs) facility through which international reserves could be created as needed. The first distribution allocated $9.5 billion of SDRs over a three-year period: $3.5 billion for the first year beginning January 1970 and $3 billion for each of the following two years. Additional SDRs will be created periodically with the amount determined by expected needs.

SDRs are distributed to member nations by the IMF. The amount received by each nation is determined by its IMF quota. Unlike the regular quota, however, the IMF does not use gold or national currencies when SDRs are allocated. The SDRs are entirely book entries. They are shifted between nations on the IMF ledger. The nation receiving a SDR credit transfers an equivalent amount of its currency to the nation that gave up a like amount of SDR balances. Transactions will usually be arranged by the nations involved, but the IMF can designate countries to provide currency for SDRs. Thus, SDRs can be created in any volume which is agreed to by 85% of the weighted voting power of the IMF.

The SDR facility was not designed to allow countries to finance continued or protracted balance of payment deficit positions. As a safeguard against this type of abuse, a reconstitution provision is included. This provision stipulates that a participant nation can use its entire allotment of SDRs, but that its average daily holdings of SDRs over a five-year period must be equal to 30% of its total allotment during that period.

As the SDR facility comes into use some unforeseen shortcomings will, no doubt, be found. The operations and rules will be modified with knowledge gleaned from experience. But there is little doubt that such an arrangement for creating flexibility in the volume of international reserves has long been needed and has strengthened the international system.[5]

Questions and problems

1. Justify the statement that the long-range equilibrium of international transactions is dependent on domestic economic conditions.

2. Using various government publications and other sources, summarize the current status of the U.S. balance of payments position.

3. Is it possible for a nation to achieve an equilibrium of payments without first developing a strong trade position in the international markets?

4. Why is the rate of exchange an index of the external purchasing power of national currencies?

5. Are there any countries now using an unrestricted gold standard? How would you explain the operation of the gold exchange standard used by some nations?

6. Why did the gold standard collapse? What factors prevent the international restoration of the gold standard?

7. Why do nations devalue their national currency? What would the probable results be of any action by the United States to devalue its currency?

8. Explain the components of a typical exchange control system. Are there nations in the world still using such controls?

9. Define the terms *dollar gap* and *dollar glut.*

10. The International Monetary Fund has been referred to as a "first-aid station" for ailing economies. What does this statement mean? What other functions does the IMF perform?

11. What is the Eurodollar market?

---

[5] For an excellent description of the special drawing rights facility, see Martin Barrett, "Activation of the Special Drawing Rights Facility of the IMF," *Monthly Review*, Federal Reserve Bank of New York, February 1970, pp. 40–46.

12. What are special drawing rights?
13. Why were special drawing rights developed?
14. Would you expect the Euro-bond market to continue if the capital constraint regulations were rescinded?

Bibliography

The literature covering the subject of international monetary policy is unusually large and diversified. Probably the best approach to locating material on specific subjects is to review the chapter bibliographies in one of the standard international finance texts. One excellent source is Charles P. Kindleberger, *International Economics* (4th ed.; Homewood, Ill.: Richard D. Irwin, Inc., 1968). Current articles may be found by looking in the *Business Periodical Index* under the following subject headings: finance—international; balance of payments; foreign exchange; Bank for International Settlements; International Monetary Fund; gold, and investments—foreign.

A number of publications include current material on international financial developments. The *Monthly Bulletin* of the Federal Reserve Bank of New York is particularly useful. Other sources include the *Monthly Economic Letter* of the First National City Bank of New York; the *Morgan Guaranty Survey* of the Morgan Guaranty Trust Company; the *Report on Western Europe* published by the Chase Manhattan Bank; *The Economist* (London); the *Financial Times of London;* and the *New York Journal of Commerce.* The annual reports of the various international agencies are also valuable sources of statistics and interpretive articles.

Basic data on the U.S. balance of payments are collected and analyzed by the Office of Business Economics of the Department of Commerce and are published in the *Survey of Current Business.* The Federal Reserve collects data on fund flows between nations. These data are published in the monthly issues of the *Federal Reserve Bulletin.*

PART VIII

CONCLUSION

National development is affected by the uses of the instruments discussed in the last several chapters and by the efficiency of the institutions discussed throughout this book. Finance facilitates saving and investment, transfers of goods and services, reduction of risk, balance of activities among public and private organizations—indeed, the working of our economy. It provides both means for attaining and means for missing the goals we set for ourselves. In this last chapter, we will consider some significant economic goals and ways in which finance affects their attainment.

CHAPTER *27*

Finance and public policy

Finance and economic goals

National goals might seem clear. They can be summed up as the good life. We want to live well and at peace. We want an orderly existence, both nationally and internationally. We want freedom for individual action and for realization of individual goals.

These statements of goals, however, are not operational—they do not tell real people how to act. In practice, more limited and more definite statements must be made, and when they are made they are found to be in conflict. Nevertheless, such statements can be made, and compromises among the conflicts can be found. Here are statements of four goals. Later, we will note how they conflict and how compromises are reached.

Effective income distribution

As a society we hold beliefs about how our national income should be distributed. In general, we believe that an individual should be entitled to have and enjoy whatever level of income he can obtain lawfully for himself. At the same time we demonstrate that we believe that no man should fail to have an income sufficient for a reasonable living. This is shown by social security programs, efforts to eliminate or mitigate poverty, aids to education and training for work, unemployment compensation, pension plans, and the proposed family assistance plan.

Financial institutions in our society—for saving, for insurance, for channeling savings into investment, and for facilitating business activity—

627

all focus on this goal. They allow individuals to use their skills to greatest advantage. They allow them also to adapt their wealth accumulation activities to their personal requirements and capabilities while directing that wealth to productive use. They permit, for example, the accumulation of claims to future income during the years of maximum earning power so that income is available when earning power declines.

Full employment

In the Employment Act of 1946, Congress clearly stated the national interest in maximum employment. Of all the national resources, the opportunity for man to work is most important. Employment at high levels makes possible both the production of as much output as our economy is capable of generating and the incomes required to purchase the output.

The fact that Congress acted is evidence that maximum employment is not obtained accidentally. A traveler in some other lands may still become familiar with the sight of people sitting about their homes or villages with nothing to do or working slowly and wastefully at primitive tasks in their fields or shops. There is clearly a need for more productive output in the places where people do the least work, but the economies of such countries are not capable of supplying employment. The opportunities are not there. Within the United States, regional economies fail of this goal. The traveler here can see people sitting about or, if working, working slowly and wastefully. We employ 54% of the people in this country over 16 years of age, but typically another 3 to 5% is counted as unemployed, the level varying with the level of economic activity. In addition, we have no effective count of the underemployed.

Enough jobs for maximum employment remains a goal. It is made more difficult to attain by another problem of industrial society—business fluctuations. In boom periods, we often find that there is a shortage of labor skills needed to fill available jobs. In recessions, labor skills go unused. Long periods of unemployment, whether they come about because of long recessions (such as that of the early 1930s) or because of a persistent lack of jobs matched to the skills of the unemployed, are destructive of both the will and the skill for work. Human beings adapt; unemployed persons learn to live unemployed, and to drop employment from the list of their personal goals.

Maximum employment implies enough opportunities so that no individual need drop the desire to earn a living from his personal set of goals. It implies too a continuing adaptation of the skills of workers to the demands of the jobs that are available. We have used the monetary and fiscal powers of government to transfer funds to the unemployed. We have taken a few steps with our monetary and fiscal powers of government and with private enterprise to both train and redirect the energies of those unemployed. We are attempting to reduce the extent of the fluctuations in demand for labor skills and to train and redirect the energies of those without jobs.

Economic growth

Growth of the economy at a pace faster than population growth alleviates some of the problems of reaching maximum employment and, hence, some of the problems of reaching satisfactory income distribution. Expanding output requires increased use of available resources. The demands on available resources increase, in fact, somewhat faster than output since some resources must be used to produce the capacity for output. In a period of reasonable growth, recessions become slowdowns and the need for changing skills and for training are evident.

Growth facilitates reaching international goals. From a growing economy we can take funds to support developments in other countries and for the defense program we regard as necessary to maintenance of a peace within which countries can develop. In addition, support for development in other countries may have the effect of facilitating domestic growth through improvements in the markets for domestic output.

Similarly, in a growing economy, it is easier to increase the effort to educate ourselves. With growing incomes, we can allow our young people more time in school and we can develop more ways for training people at work.

Growth at a rate greater than growth in the population comes from increased productivity, i.e., greater output per man-hour. Such productivity increases come from technological improvements in the processes of production. More efficient plant and equipment coupled with higher skills increase the amount of output per labor hour. Technological improvement usually requires more capital intensity, relatively more investment in capital goods per unit of output. A combination of technological advance with saving directed to investment is needed for growth that more than matches the rising level of population. Again, our financial institutions serve to make saving a broadly accepted personal habit and to direct savings to effective productive employment.

Price stability

Growth can be more apparent than real. We measure economic output in terms of its dollar value. If price levels change, the same measure of output changes meaning, for the real change may be quite different from the dollar change. The growth that contributes to well-being is real, not price level, growth.

Price stability, moreover, has a very different kind of significance for individuals. We depend for income at some times in our lives on the returns from investment contracts of one kind or another. Pensions, annuities, and social security payments all are familiar, but so too is individual saving in the form of savings accounts, investment in bonds or stocks, or just cash. Price level changes (of the kinds discussed in Chapter 2) alter the purchasing power both of incomes from these investment contracts and of cash. Over the years, there have been changes within the lifetimes of individuals so great that they were enriched or impoverished through no action of their own. During periods of deflation, such as the long period from 1865 to 1896, those who lent money and later received repayment fixed in dollars were enriched by the price level change. In periods of inflation, such as that from 1896 to 1914, lenders lost purchasing power. In a severe inflation, of the sort experienced during 1941–1951 or 1966–1970, there are sound arguments for the outrage of those who live on fixed dollar incomes.

In yet another sense, price stability affects growth and employment. The commitment of money to investment in business is facilitated if the rules of the game are known. If businessmen are faced with the difficulty of forecasting the price levels at which products of their plant and equipment will be sold as well as the quite formidable problems of forecasting sales when price stability is assumed, they may quite sensibly be reluctant to commit funds to any investment that does not have a rapid payout. Such reluctance inhibits adaptation to technological change and slows growth and reduces the opportunities for employment.

Economic goals and current problems

As our economy continues to grow and to change, new problems appear and as a result new goals for the economy tend to emerge from newly perceived needs for change. Some current problems of this sort are the inadequacy of the nation's housing stock, the plight of cities faced with decaying buildings and declining revenues, the existence of ghettoes populated by the economically disadvantaged, and the existence of rural depressed areas. (Environmental problems, such as air and water pollution, and their relation to our price system were discussed in Chapter 22.) To a large extent, it can be argued that these kinds of problems can be mitigated through a financial system which channels funds into the investments needed to offset the aforementioned conditions. At the same time, it should be recognized that the chief reason these flows do not occur now is that profit margins on investments of the sort required for business to alleviate these social problems are inadequate. Thus, the problem areas may be capable of resolution through governmental actions which provide profit incentives through increasing the returns on these kinds of investments. Naturally, it should also be recognized that the costs of providing the incentives must be borne by the society, and thus questions as to which groups should bear the costs of curing social problems must be faced. To the extent that the price system penalizes groups with low ability to compete effectively for a share of society's income, or to the extent that greater good for society can be achieved by supporting the workings of our economic system, intervention which creates incentives for the private sector to solve these problems may prove justified. The justification is, however, based on notions of fairness and of social value rather than on objective criteria, concerning which reasonable men cannot disagree.

Conflicts between goals

Unfortunately, there are also conflicts between the above-mentioned goals. We cannot perceive, at least with our present state of knowledge, the means for achieving them all simultaneously. The actions that facilitate growth may reduce employment and cause price instability as well as unacceptable income distribution. So, too, actions designed to promote price stability may have adverse effects on growth.

Price stability and employment

Prices are established in a market. They are affected, on the one hand, by those who establish the money supply and by those who hold money with which to buy and, on the other hand, by those who supply goods. Suppliers cannot continue to supply goods unless the prices established in the market cover costs. If the bidding in the market, either because of restrictions on the total money supply or because of restraint on the part of buyers, leads to prices which do not cover production costs of certain goods, suppliers will withdraw. Employment under these circumstances cannot be maintained. A response consistent with offsetting developing underemployment is an increase in the money supply. With more money available, those who demand goods find it easier to pay higher prices. Under these circumstances, full-employment levels may be maintained but under inflationary conditions.

The problem of conflicts between price stability and full employment is made the more difficult by the practice of *administered prices.* In many industries dominated by large companies, prices may be maintained while volume of sales drops. The policy of price maintenance is asserted to be advantageous for the industry over a period of years when the absence of demand is judged to be temporary. However, maintenance of prices may be affected significantly by costs, especially labor costs. Where labor unions have the strength to insist on maintenance of wage rates in the face of falling demands for the labor of union members, the employers, in turn, may feel that keeping prices firm is also important. The result is a tendency for fluctuations in employment to be greatest under precisely the circumstances that lead to the most stable price levels. We have seen some curious price changes in the last several years. During depression, prices have been raised; during booms, prices have been effectively lowered. Both have the effect of exaggerating the demand for labor and the fluctuations in employment.

The conflict between full employment and price stability is of a nature such that full employment (i.e., say, 3% unemployment) and stable prices are not generally capable of being achieved simultaneously in our economy. Essentially, the problem arises because of imperfect markets for both labor and commodities. In particular, institutional arrangements prevent wages and prices from being flexible in a downward direction, so that price increases in any particular market are not offset by price decreases elsewhere. Then, as certain industries bid up wages for the services of members of the labor force in order to attract new employees, unemployment falls but wages rise. Research findings suggest a relation between unemployment rates and price level changes called the Phillips curve; unemployment rates of 3–4% appear to be consistent with annual price level increases of 1–2%.

Employment and growth

Increases in the level of output may result simply from doing more of the same things in the same way and, therefore, result in more employment of the same combination of resources used in the past. The whole concept of profitable investment, however, leads to change. This tendency to change is accelerated by effective maintenance of wage rates. The essence of technological advance is perception of ways to do given jobs with less outlay for resources, particularly labor. We can sometimes find ways to accomplish given ends with different materials or different amounts of the same materials, but in a great many instances the production of goods of equivalent quality cannot be achieved with any reduction in this input. Economy is achieved by reducing the labor time needed to transform a given amount of materials into the desired end product and deliver it to the consumer. What we call growth is an increase in the output of desired goods. To some extent, it can also be a synonym for reduced employment.

Clearly, sufficiently rapid growth will call for continued full employment. It is easy to find examples, however, of technological unemployment, i.e., situations in which output is maintained or expanded while workers are laid off. In many of these instances, in turn, the technological changes that facilitate productive gains make the skills of some workers obsolete. While this phenomenon can be observed most readily in the underdeveloped nations, where the introduction of advanced techniques very clearly creates large numbers of unemployed, it can also be observed in the United States.

Growth and price stability

Obviously, if growth can produce unemployment, it can produce changes in the demands for goods. In the simplest sense, demand for the basic needs may decline while demands for luxuries (for those remaining employed and those obtaining incomes from investments) increase. Shifting demands and accompanying price changes might leave a measure of price level unchanged, but the likelihood is small.

More important, perhaps, is the argument that some price inflation should be accepted as a price for growth. This argument says, in effect, that people can adapt to a slow rate of inflation and that a slow rate of inflation fosters growth. Price level increases make the decisions of managers appear, on the average, better than expected. Thus, they undertake projects more readily, with less reticence, than they would in the absence of this inflation. The rate under consideration is slow, 1 to 2% per year. The savers in our society can adapt to this rate chiefly because they expect about this rate of inflation to continue. In particular, the growth to be expected from a portfolio of stocks exceeds this rate of inflation, and therefore savers can adopt plans that make continued saving reasonable. Those who commit funds to investment, on the other hand, continue to appear wise—their decisions are better than average.

Resolutions

Controlled inflation, direct controls, and more effective uses of monetary and fiscal policy all are suggested as devices for resolving the conflicts.

Controlled inflation

The values of controlled inflation hardly need exposition. The idea is simple. Investment decisions are almost certain to appear more favorable, entrepreneurs almost certainly will act more decisively, a few people will suffer through ignorance but many will adapt as they have before, and the economy will be stronger, more vigorously developmental, more vital.

Some argue that controlled inflation is not an achievable goal. As in the post–World War II period, we can unleash forces that move us to different price levels at rates challenging our ability to hold our economy together. We have seen, in our past, considerable periods of rather slow inflation or deflation without complete breakdown of the economy. These have occurred unplanned. Their existence cannot be denied. Few, however, can show that we have the ability to permit inflation or deflation to persist under controlled conditions. Our experience argues more strongly in reverse. Nevertheless, a suggestion that persists is that we can have maximum employment, effective distribution of income, and growth if we will accept price instability in the form of controlled inflation.

Direct credit controls

Some suggestions for direct control have been made in the past. Indeed, we have experimented with direct controls at different times. Among these have been regulations affecting the terms on which consumer installment credit could be extended and affecting the terms on which mortgages were written. We have seen direct controls applied to inventory credit and to the new issues of capital instruments in Great Britain during their crises. We have applied direct controls to the extension of credit in securities markets.

The arguments for direct credit controls depend mostly on notions about the elasticity of demand for particular forms of credit extension when interest rates change. It is argued that consumers, home buyers, and investors, for example, are indifferent to the cost of credit when they are engaged in carrying out their plans for gaining either consumption or investment advantages from their actions. The basic argument rests on a notion that costs of credit are such a small element in the total costs related to the decisions made in these areas that general controls affecting levels of interest rates cannot alter the frequency or aggregate amount of demand for credit in these areas. There have been challenges to this notion of indifference. The field for argument, however, remains open.

New combinations of policies

Experimentation with new combinations of policies can at times lead to resolution of economic conflicts in a relatively painless manner. One of the boldest moves in recent years involved the personal and corporate income tax reductions inaugurated in 1964, reductions which had a stimulating effect on economic output of about the magnitude predicted by most economists. In addition to achieving full employment, this particular policy created only small changes in the rate of price level increase.

However, not all policy experiments have worked as well; in 1968 an income surtax bill was enacted in the hopes of reducing inflation, but this fiscal measure had a much smaller influence than was anticipated. This latter occurrence was probably due to the fact that the measure was enacted only after considerable delay, that the monetary policy of the time was working counter to fiscal policy, and that the temporary nature of the surtax may have led to its effects being neutralized by expectations. Finally, while it is known that stimulative and restrictive measures do not generally work in a symmetric fashion, this particular fact of economic life may have been given insufficient weight at the time the surtax was passed.

Innovative policies can sometimes achieve relatively painless resolutions of conflicts, but experience suggests that the success of a given policy is frequently due to circumstances which may have changed the next time a similar use of policy is contemplated, thus making policy decisions relatively difficult ones. Economists are currently in general agreement that monetary policy provides a more powerful means of control than does fiscal policy. However, there is also general agreement that monetary and fiscal policy should be coordinated in their application.

Politics

For a number of reasons, the political atmosphere of the United States is involved in the decisions made with respect to the uses of devices to promote effective income distribution, maximum employment, price stability, and growth. We elect representatives to legislative organizations. They reflect what they believe to be the *consensus* among their local constituents. They may err, at times, because personal political biases give rise to peculiar interpretations of that consensus. It is difficult, however, to hold an opinion that consensus is often ignored.

Through our political organizations we make ourselves felt and heard. In the processes of goal setting and of compromise, we depend on these organizations. It is one of the more satisfactory outcomes of our existence that for the most part these organizations seem to have operated to the general advantage of most citizens. It is here that the balancing of actions against goals is made.

It is here also that the basic legislation affecting operations of financial institutions is enacted. In the process of striving to attain goals these institutions are significant. We depend on them to provide the means for investment of individual savings, for direction of accumulated savings into productive uses, and for one of our important forms of income distribution. The appropriate legal bases for organization of financial institutions are among the concerns we should hold and are among the demands we should make on our legislators. Finance, surely, is not the only aspect of our existence that demands attention. Equally surely, it is among those of import.

INDEX

Index

Bank of England, 46, 145
Bank of France, 145
Bank for International Settlements (BIS), 13, 621
Bank building and equipment, purchase of, 51
Bank closing of 1933, 28, 117
Bank drafts; see Acceptances
Bank Holding Company Act of 1956, 120
Bank loans, 52–53, 71, 78–90, 93–95
  applicants for, information required from, 79–80
  classes of, 82–90
  commercial, 86–87
  commercial banks to customers, 52–53
  consumer installment, 88–89
  contraction of, 106–7
  credit analysis, 79–80
  credit cards, 88–89
  deposits created by, 63–64
  discounting of, 53–54
  expansion of
    bank investment account, 105–6
    limitations on, 106
    multiple, 105
    single bank, 100–102
    system of banks, 102–5
  Federal Deposit Insurance Corporation classification of, 82–83
  functions of, 78–79
  guarantee of, 84
  home construction and purchase, 89–90
  industrial, 86–87
  information required for, 79–80
  installment, 84–86
  interest rates on, 90–93
  line of credit, 80–81
  long-term, 93
  minimum balance requirements, 81–82
  participation, 86
  personal, 88–89
  primary function of commercial banks, 172
  prime interest rate on, 93
  real estate, 89–90
  regulation of, 125–27
  relationship with depositing function, 78–79
  relationship to deposits and reserves, 99–107
  repayment of, 53
  restrictions upon, 126–27
  secured, 82–84
  security, 87–88
  short-term, 90–93
  small business financing, 450
  term, 84–86
  use of funds for, 71

Bank Merger Act, 119
Banker's acceptances; see Acceptances
Bankers Trust Company, the, 336
Banking; see Banking system and Commercial banks
Banking Act of 1933, 113, 128–29
Banking system; see also Commercial banks
  branch banking trend, 113–18; see also Branch banking
  capital requirements, 112
  central, 144–46
  chain banking, 121–22
  check payment charges, 112
  clearinghouse associations, 134–39
  consolidations, 118–19
  correspondent banking, 133–34
  deposit insurance, 129–32
  dual system of chartering, 111–12
  examination of, 123–25
  federal chartering application, 111–12
  Federal Reserve System membership, 112
  group banking, 120–21
  holding company
    group banking, 120–21
    one-bank, 122
  interbank relations, 132–39
  investment regulations, 127–29
  lending regulations, 125–27
  mergers, 118–19
  money trusts, 110, 113
  one-bank holding companies, 122
  regulation of, 122–32
  reserve requirements, 112
  size of banks, 112
  structure of, 110–22
    differences in United States, 110–11
  supervision of banks, 122–32
    agencies engaged in, 123
    United States, 122–23
  unit operations, 110, 113
Barrett, Martin, 623 n
Barter, 5, 21
  difficulties with system of, 22
Beacom, Thomas H., 323 n
Belgium, 286, 621
Better business bureaus, 413
Big Board; see New York Stock Exchange
Big-ticket purchases, 466
BLS Wholesale Commodity Price Index, 37
Blue-chip stocks, 296
Blue-sky laws, 296, 410
  fraud, 410
  licensing, 410
  registration, 410
  types, 410
Bond accounts of banks, 127–28

Partnerships—*Cont.*
corporate form compared with, 347–49
dissolution of, 349
evidence of ownership, 348
inception, 347–48
legal entity, 349
liability of owners, 348–49
ownership of assets, 352
transferability of ownership, 349
Pawnshop loans, 474
Peace Corps, 259
Pennsylvania, 115, 245–46, 254, 478
100% financing plan of, 455
Pennsylvania Company for Insurance on
Lives and Granting Annuities, 314
Pension defined, 328
Pension funds; *see also* Retirement plans
accumulation of funds by, 341
assets of, 331
distribution of, 339
capital flow, influence on, 340–41
complete funding of, 336
contributions to, 334–35
conventional group annuities, 330
deposit administration plans, 330
economic effects of, 340–41
economic significance of, 329
funding of, 335–36
growth of, 328–29
individual policy pension trusts, 330
insured, 330
interest rates, 341
investment policies, 337–40
noninsured, 330, 332
old age, survivors, and disability insurance (OASDI), 330, 333–34,
336
partial funding of, 336
payments by, 334–35
persons in labor force, effect on number of, 341
price level changes, protection against,
329
profit-sharing plans, 336
saving through, 328–42
savings, effect on, 340
self-administered, 330, 332, 338
social security, 330, 333–34, 336
tax factor, 329
terms for accumulation and distribution of, 334–37
total book value of assets of, 334
trusteed, 330, 332, 338
types of, 329–34
union-negotiated, 332
variable annuities, 337
vesting of rights in, 336–37
Pension intermediaries, 13
Pension plans; *see* Pension funds

Personal finances, management of, 8–9
Personal loans, 88–89
Philadelphia, 46, 417, 436
Philadelphia National Bank, 119
Pledges
accounts receivable, 378–79
current assets, 380
inventories, 379
Political atmosphere, 635
Pork barrel spending, 523
Port of New York Authority, 549
Preferred stock
call option, 356–57
certificate of, 355
convertible, 356
cumulative, 355–56
direct placement financing with, 387–
88
issuance of, 355
nature of, 357
par and nopar, 357
participation, 356
position of, 357–58
preference of, 355
sinking fund, 357
voting power, 356
Price changes; *see* Purchasing power
Price indexes, 563–64
risks involved, 207–8
Price level risk, 207–8
Price relatives, 36
Price stability, 629–30
economic growth and, 633
employment and, 631–32
Primitive economies, 21
characteristics of, 22
Private placement financing; *see* Direct
placement financing
Productive resources, management of, 8
Profit-sharing plans, 336; *see also* Pension
funds
Property insurance, 278–80
assets, categories of, 280–83
diversification, 281
dual role of, 283
investment policies, 280–83
liquidity factor, 283
maximization of investment income,
283
reinsurance system, 280
underwriting of, 280
Property losses, insurance for; *see* Property insurance
Property taxes, 544–46
Proprietorships, 58–62, 345–47; *see also*
Small business
administrative efficiency, 349
corporate form compared with, 347–
49

Treasury bills—*Cont.*
  investors in, 177–78
  issuance of, 176
  maturity, 176
  nonfinancial corporation investors, 178
  position in money market, 177
  purchase and sale, mechanics of, 176
  yield on, 177
Treasury coin, 30–31
Treasury currency, 29–30, 163
Treasury Department, 12
  cash balance of, 163–64, 534–35
  debt management policy, 164–65, 572
  debt management problems, 535
  influence in tax legislation, 537
  management of public debt, 537
  monetary role of, 163–65, 537
  savings bonds, system of, 12
Treasury-Federal Reserve accord, 186
Treasury gold, 163–64
Treasury notes, 178–79
Trust
  administration of, 311
  corporate bonds, 362
  creation of, 312
  defined, 312–13
  federal management of, 538
  provisions of agreement of, 321–22
  relationship of parties to, 312
  terms used in connection with, 312
Trust agreement, 312, 321–22
  contract distinguished, 312–13
Trust business, 311
  administrator of intestate estate, 318
  ancillary executor, 318
  assets held in, 316–17
  classification of services rendered, 318
  conservator of estate, 319
  defined, 313
  depository under court order, 319
  development of, 314–15
  escrow agent, 320
  executor under will, 318
  extent of, 316–18
  guardian of estate, 319
  history in United States, 314–15
  individuals, services rendered to, 318–20
  insurance trust, 319–20
  investments of, 316–18
  living trust, 319
  national banks' authorization to do, 316
  safekeeping, 320
  services rendered, 318
  supervised agency, 320
  testamentary trust, 318
  trustee under will, 318–19
  volume of, 316–18

Trust companies, 308
  trust departments versus, 315–16
Trust Indenture Act, 387
Trust institutions, 313–14; *see also* Trust business *and related topics*
  charges for services, 325
  summary of discussion of, 325–26
Trustee, 312
  compensation of, 324–25
  corporate, 318
    versus individual, 323–24
  investments of, 322–23
    legal lists, 322–23
    prudent man rule, 322–23
Trusteeship concept, 312–13
Truth-in-lending act, 470

U

Underwriting of property and casualty insurance, 280
Underwriting of securities, 223–24, 399–404
  best-effort distribution, 402, 409
  contract forms, 401–2
  firm contract, 401
  market support, 404
  originating house, 403
  price fluctuations, 404
  risks of, 402
  secondary distributions, 405
  selling group, 403–4
  stabilization of prices, 404
  stand-by agreement, 401–2
  syndication, 403
    secondary distributions, 405
Unemployment, 14, 558, 560
Unemployment insurance account, management of, 538
Uniform Small Loan Law, 478
Unit of account, money as, 22–24
Unit banking system, 110, 113
  interbank relations, 132–39
United States
  balance of payments; *see* Balance of payments
  banking development in, 46–47
  branch banking trend, 113–18
  dual system of bank charter, 111–12
  European investment or operations; *see* Foreign investment *and* Foreign trade
  full employment, government support of, 559–60
  international investment position of, 601–2
  investment companies, development of, 287–88
  long-run annual payments equality, 602

This book has been set in 10 and 9 point Caledonia, leaded 2 points. Part and chapter numbers are in Helvetica italic, part and chapter titles are in Helvetica Medium. The size of the type page is 27 by 46½ picas.